The Catholic Epistles and Apostolic Tradition

The Catholic Epistles and Apostolic Tradition

Karl-Wilhelm Niebuhr
Robert W. Wall
Editors

BAYLOR UNIVERSITY PRESS

© 2009 by Baylor University Press
Waco, Texas 76798

Scripture quotations, where not an author's own translation, are from the New Revised Standard Version Bible, copyright 1989, Division of Christian Education of the National Council of the Churches of Christ in the United States of America. Used by permission. All rights reserved.

Cover Design by Stephanie Milanowski

Library of Congress Cataloging-in-Publication Data

The Catholic Epistles and apostolic tradition / Karl-Wilhelm Niebuhr and Robert W. Wall, editors.
    p. cm.
  Includes bibliographical references (p.   ) and index.
  ISBN 978-1-60258-215-6 (hardback : alk. paper)
  1. Bible. N.T. Catholic Epistles--Criticism, interpretation, etc.--Congresses. I. Niebuhr, Karl-Wilhelm. II. Wall, Robert W.
  BS2777C37 2009
  227'.9068--dc22

                              2009020929

Printed in the United States of America on acid–free paper with a minimum of 30% pcw recycled content.

Dedicated to Professor Dr. Donald J. Verseput
(1952–2004)

CONTENTS

LIST OF CONTRIBUTORS

ERNST BAASLAND, Bishop of Stavanger (Church of Norway)

LUTZ DOERING, Reader in New Testament and Ancient Judaism, Durham University (England)

REINHARD FELDMEIER, Professor of New Testament, University of Göttingen (Germany)

JÖRG FREY, Professor of New Testament, University of Munich (Germany)

SCOTT J. HAFEMANN, Mary French Rockefeller Professor of New Testament, Gordon-Conwell Theological Seminary (Boston, USA)

PATRICK J. HARTIN, Professor of Religious Studies, Gonzaga University (USA)

JOHN S. KLOPPENBORG, Professor of Religion, University of St. Michael's College (Toronto, Canada)

MATTHIAS KONRADT, Professor of New Testament, University of Berne (Switzerland)

KARL-WILHELM NIEBUHR, Professor of New Testament, University of Jena (Germany)

DAVID R. NIENHUIS, Assistant Professor of New Testament Studies, Seattle Pacific University (Seattle, USA)

JOHN PAINTER, Professor of Theology, Charles Sturt University (Canberra, Australia)

ROBERT W. WALL, Paul T. Walls Professor of Scripture and Wesleyan Studies, Seattle Pacific University (Seattle, USA)

Part I

INTRODUCTION

THE SNTS SEMINAR ON THE CATHOLIC EPISTLES (2001–2006)

Robert W. Wall and Karl-Wilhelm Niebuhr

The overarching purpose of this seminar has been to rehabilitate this Society's interest in the Catholic Epistles (CE), which have largely been neglected by both the guild and the church. When they are considered, whether critically or kerygmatically, these letters are typically filtered through a Pauline lens rather than on their own terms or as a discrete canonical collection. In response, the original definition of our seminar's work regards the use of different apostolic traditions reflected by the CE, quite apart from the Pauline canon, as one key to reconstructing the distinctive occasion and purpose of each epistle in turn.

Yet another interest has emerged along the way: consideration of the CE as a discrete collection of writings, with its own distinctive contribution to make and role to perform, when considered in relationship to the other parts of the biblical canon. Against the grain of modern criticism, which typically treats the CE as a collection of disparate, unrelated compositions, one of the seminar's principal findings in this regard—the common result of different interpretive strategies—has been to understand the seven epistles as different parts of a coherent whole; that is, the CE form a discrete, purposeful collection within the New Testament biblical canon, with its own distinctive voice, history of formation, use of common traditions (Christian and not), and strategic role to perform as

1

sacred Scripture. Whilst finding connections within the CE (see the contributions of Feldmeier, Frey, Hafemann, Konradt, Newman, Nienhuis, Painter, and Wall) and with other New Testament writings/traditions (e.g., Gospel/Jesus traditions—Hartin, Kloppenborg, Niebuhr; Acts—Konradt, Wall; Pauline—Newman, Nienhuis, Wall), the seminar papers have typically concluded that the CE, when considered as a whole, speak with a distinctive voice and with an independent theological and moral point to score.

Because the co-chairs of this seminar are scholars of James, our seminar has often developed these findings by critical analysis of what K.-W. Niebuhr has called "a new perspective on James." According to Niebuhr, the newness of this approach to this particular CE (at least for Protestant interpreters) is to resist the post-Reformation tendency to read James over and against historical constructions of Paul's mission or his message found in the Pauline canon, and to privilege certain parts of James by so doing. The result is not only to read James on its own terms and in its own distinctive voice, but to place it within its own socio-religious world, its particular canonical setting within the CE collection, and by doing so to add layers of meaning to it. But then this project has also resulted, perhaps surprisingly so, in a new perspective on the CE collection, introduced by R. W. Wall, who not only has recovered a coherent theological argot from the collection but also interprets the important role this "unifying theology" performs within the New Testament canon.

Different seminar papers on James have developed versions of this new perspective by drawing upon early traditions about a fictive or even historical James—the implied author of James. For example, M. Konradt argues that the predicate of the implied fictive "James" of James is the legendary pastor of Jerusalem—that is, the James of Acts (traditions of whom are also repristinated as the hagiographic "James the Just," mentioned in second- and third-century sectarian writings as a member of the Holy Family, rather than of the apostolate). James is studied from the perspective of a priestly James, then; its use of common traditions and its definition of Christian existence presume a congregational setting apropos for a pastor's address. For this reason, when traditions common to James and 1 Peter are compared, one recognizes that their redaction and intention are consistent with the office of their implied/fictive author, whether pastoral and congregational or missionary and international.

K.-W. Niebuhr has introduced another new perspective on James in particular by avoiding any relationship with the "new perspective on Paul." He argues that the James of James is the brother of the risen Lord, whose perspective toward Christian existence is framed and freighted by his Easter experience, rather than by an adversarial relationship with the

Pauline mission. In this sense, the central question of Christian identity is not the validity of a Pauline gospel or a Gentile mission centered by "faith without works," but rather the struggles of remaining disciples of the risen Jesus in his absence prior to his Parousia.

Wall's new perspective on James moves from a different direction by considering the church's reception of James during the canonical process of the third and especially fourth centuries. The phenomenology of this process is the primary means by which current readers access the continuing role of its product: James is posited as frontispiece of the final redaction of a CE collection; its "readerly priority" in appropriating the collection as a whole witness is indicated by its placement. This canonical perspective of James presumes the existence of a normative portrait of the risen Lord, shaped by the fourfold Gospel canon, and of the Pauline gospel, shaped by the Pauline canon. Sharply put, James is added in order to introduce an emergent CE collection and facilitate a genuinely constructive conversation with Paul and the risen Lord. In Wall's reading, the strategic role of Acts in the formation of the CE collection explains the importance of James: the canonical James, the implied author of James, is the James of Acts, whose relations with other leaders and their missions (especially Paul and Peter) delineate the intracanonical relationship between the Pauline and CE collections of New Testament letters.

Both J. Painter and D. R. Nienhuis speak of the "priority of James" in terms of a Jerusalem or Pillars collection (cf. Gal 2:7) and its relationship to a Pauline collection within an emergent biblical canon; that is, both interpret the interplay of the Pauline and Pillars letter collections within postapostolic Christianity. Significantly, Nienhuis reconstructs a history of the CE collection's formation and argues for the late composition of James to introduce and complete it. In fact, Nienhuis contends that the formation of a second letter canon for the emergent New Testament canon is motivated in part by a growing awareness within the early church of its sometimes misappropriation of the Pauline canon. That is, the Pillars collection, inclusive of James, is intended to bring balance to the church's overuse of Pauline thematics in its preaching and catechesis.

This discussion of a new perspective on James bears upon the ongoing discussion of a text's intended meaning and its continuing performance as Scripture. It is an axiom of modern biblical criticism that the *normative* meaning of a text, otherwise multivalent and capable of different plausible renderings, is delimited by the meaning its author intended; and the *normal* performance of this same text is delimited by the intentions of its original readers/auditors. What these various seminar papers on James have illumined is the contested nature of a text's normative meaning and use, whether this is an authorial property glossed by circumstances posited at the point of a text's origin (Konradt, Niebuhr) or an ecclesial property glossed by the circumstances of the canonical process, subsequent to its composition for the text's future readers (Wall).

Depending on the perspective one takes, the idea of theological (Wall) or ethical (Feldmeier) coherence is also differently assessed. If one understands a biblical writing as an authored book, then its theological coherence and contribution are authorial properties. If, however, one understands James or 1 Peter as a canonical book, and its canonization is part of an integral collection, then its theological contribution and coherence are appraised as part of the whole CE collection first of all, and then as part of an integral collection in relationship with other biblical theologies.

A notable exception to the seminar's general interest in James and the Petrine Epistles, but nonetheless one that maintains the seminar's interest in reading the CE as a whole collection, is J. Painter's probing study of the unity of the Johannine Epistles and their placement within the CE collection. The neglect of the Johannine Epistles in our seminar doubtless reflects the critical *Tendenz* to consider the epistles as part of a Johannine corpus of canonical writings. Painter's study, however, recognizes first of all the phenomenology of the canonical process, during which a collection of three Johannine Epistles was formed and placed within a second corpus of letters for the New Testament canon, rather than with the fourth Gospel and the Apocalypse. These decisions supply a set of hermeneutical prompts, different from the critical norm, for the continuing study of the letters as sacred literature.

Several other papers consider the reworking of apostolic traditions in 2 Peter, whether in relationship with common traditions used in Jude or as tradents of a broader apostolic legacy that adapts its traditions to ever-changing social and cultural settings. What is lacking in this study of 2 Peter, in my opinion, is its relationship to 1 Peter, which is certainly the prompt of the canonical process. I have suggested elsewhere that the composition of 2 Peter was occasioned by recognition of the authority of 1 Peter and the need to complete and more powerfully frame its distinctively Petrine witness to the gospel within an emergent Pillars (or non-Pauline) canon (which may at the time have consisted only of 1 Peter and 1 John). In any case, more study should be given to the precanonical reception of 2 Peter and its relationship with 1 Peter (rather than Jude) as a way forward in a critical assessment of its contribution to the biblical canon.

In fact, if an element of this retrospection is to chart a more viable prospect for this seminar's interests, let me conclude by suggesting that our future interests should concentrate on the second and third centuries, not only on the use of traditions or related theories of composition/

redaction during this time, but upon the earliest reception of individual Catholic Epistles as Scripture (textual and citational evidence) and their subsequent formation into a collection. What will be uncovered by this investigation is another set of clues that will continue to guide our study of them within the Society, for the church's sake.

—*Robert W. Wall*

* * * * *

Thanks to Robert Wall, who acknowledged comprehensively the concerns of our seminar in his retrospective,[1] the characteristic features of every single contribution to our sessions are well summarized. Looking back at a very successful series of meetings, therefore, I will confine myself to highlighting the general tendencies in research of the CE during the last five years. The prospective developments in CE research will clarify to what extent our seminar can be evaluated as a contribution to the field. Provided that the work of the Society of New Testament Studies is to be continued, there will be need for more discussion in order to pinpoint further goals of investigation.

After a long and far-reaching period of marginalization of the CE in exegetical research during the twentieth century, we are confronted with a remarkable change of focus at the beginning of the twenty-first century. It was in 1999 when Robert Wall, Ernst Baasland, Reinhard Feldmeier, and myself met at the SNTS meeting in Pretoria and discussed ideas regarding the possibility of a seminar on the CE for the very first time. Then, any noteworthy activity in CE research did not exist in any of the larger scholarly societies of Bible studies. Comparing the situation today, we have to notice a radical change in the field. Within a short period of time, the CE have been established as a major topic in the three most important international organizations of Bible studies at this time: since 2001, the SNTS has been holding our seminar "Catholic Epistles and Apostolic Traditions"; in 2003, the outstanding and very prestigious Colloquium Biblicum Lovaniense was dedicated to the theme "The Catholic Epistles and the Tradition" (under direction of J. Schlosser); and the 2005 annual meeting of the SBL in Philadelphia incorporated a new unit into its working program, "Methodological Reassessment of the Letters of James, Peter, and Jude" (under direction of J. S. Kloppenborg and R. L. Webb).

Thus, this mere formal evidence marks a turning point in the exegesis of the CE. But the survey has been strengthened by numerous observations that have been made in recent studies on the Epistles. Accordingly, as far as I see, the research centers less and less on the classical questions of *Einleitung* and authorship. The new trend rather recognizes the historical and theological originality of the CE. While before, a specific perspective of Pauline theology was ruling and had to benchmark the theological "quality" of the CE, nowadays a broader access enables us to distinguish the rich variety of theological concepts in the New Testament. As opposed to the schematic understanding of literary and traditio-historical interdependencies and trajectories, now, to a greater extent, the New Testament is becoming a source for self-contained formations of different theological statements, which are to be explored within the specific historical and religious contexts of the sources.[2]

From the outset, the specific focus of our project has been posed by the question of how the CE are intertwined with the apostolic traditions in the time of the New Testament and afterwards, as the title of the seminar reflects. By this title, the new target for researching the CE was formulated precisely. The difference from the classical approach is striking; there, the research concentrated on historical problems, questions of *Einleitung* and of literary interdependencies between the single epistles. Furthermore, certain questions were raised that concerned theology in the narrower sense, or addressed difficulties in the history of theology, such as the relationship between the theology of Paul and the Epistle of James, or the correlation of the First Epistle of Peter with the Pauline tradition. It has been worthwhile to abandon these classical and often stagnant positions, and thus to promote a better understanding of the CE. In my opinion, the most significant result of our work is the adduced evidence that our approach allows for advancing new questions and perspectives.

However, I would like to point out that by raising the problem of the correlation between the CE and the apostolic traditions, we were not striving to pose an antithesis to previous research in general. In fact, our concern was merely to pick up some aspects that, in our opinion, had not yet been taken sufficiently into account. That means our specific approach was not caused by problems that were assigned to the corpus of the epistles from the outside. Rather, we intended to explore precisely what feature had connected the single epistles to each other and determined their specific position within the canon of the New Testament, starting with the very beginnings of the ecclesiastic tradition—that is, their ascription to the leading apostles of the Jerusalem *Urgemeinde*. Therewith, many unsolved questions and problems were brought up necessarily. The newly emerged difficulties have only been addressed and discussed to a small extent during the last five years. Solutions are still outstanding and not about to appear.

At the beginning of the project, we were not aware that the question of the inner connections between the seven CE would turn out to be the center of our exegetical and theological interest. These inner connections can be found by different methods and from varying perspectives. Some contributors have brought to light historical and traditio-historical inter-relations (Konradt); others have discovered historical connections with regard to literature and religion (Frey, Feldmeier, Doering). Another approach is based on the facts of literary form and text transmission in reference to the individual epistles and on this basis tries to analyze the unit of the CE corpus and its inner threads (Painter, Niebuhr).

Robert Wall's expertise, particularly, breaks new ground and chal-lenges New Testament exegesis by turning away from the ruling historical and hermeneutical paradigms of the last two centuries. In a well-directed and reflective manner, he asks about the meaning of the unity of the seven CE. Facing the one-sidedness of exegetical research, which focuses on distinctions and differentiations within the New Testament, he raises the question to what extent the ecclesiastical reception of the canon sets the benchmark for the theological meaning of the New Testament.

In my view, by postulating the theology of the CE as being a signifi-cant part of New Testament theology in general, a project is undertaken that challenges the entire discipline. Such a project bears great poten-tial for attracting attention beyond the exegetical discipline. The con-ventional approach that dominates the exegetical research in Protestant and Catholic departments of theology—at least at German universities—focuses mainly on historical, literary, and religio-historical criticism. But recently, the competence of the exegetical disciplines regarding broader theological questions and common academic matters beyond the tra-ditional fields of theology is more and more in question. This trend confronts the exegetical approach with problems beyond the range of theology as an academic discipline.

Apparently, the book of Acts is of particular importance for under-standing the interrelations between the different CE (Wall, Konradt), though it is symptomatic that in the course of the seminar, the subject of neither a specific Lukan theology nor the relation between the Gospel of Luke and the book of Acts was at stake. On the contrary; from the perspective of the CE, this relation is rather of secondary importance, although historically and literarily not to be dismissed. More important is the function of the book of Acts as a link between the narrative repre-sentations of Jesus and the Apostolic Epistles.

The book of Acts provides a continuity regarding the characters of the whole Jesus story, beginning in Galilee and Jerusalem and extending through his death at the cross and his resurrection, up to the apostolic time of the Jerusalem *Urgemeinde*, and from there to the spread of Christian communities toward the Gentiles. Thus, the fundamental theological connections between the time of the service of Jesus and the time of the Holy Spirit within the post-Eastern communities, as well as the fundamental theological break between both of them, are articulated as one narrative including characters who are part of both periods of the Jesus story. Accordingly, a New Testament theology drafted from the perspective of the New Testament canon would be a narrative theology retelling the basic story of God's saving acts. Such a narrative theology of the New Testament would be shaped and arranged along the plot of salvation history, and therefore would have to incorporate the Old Testament as well in an appropriate way.

After five years of researching the CE, many questions still remain unsolved or, as a result of our research, have occurred only recently. The latter case is particularly represented by looking at the interrelations between the emergence of apostolic authority in early Christian church and theology and the process of canon formation. I suppose that the canon history has so far been interpreted much too closely in relation to the testimonies of the church fathers tracing back to the third and fourth centuries. In accordance with this common trend, little concern has been bestowed on the question of certain procedures—for example, what use was made of the apostolic writings within the religious practice of the communities, or on what institutional basis those writings were transmitted. Here, we still act in a very hypothetical realm of reconstruction. The clarification of both origin and tradition of the early Gospel and Epistle collections, which are documented or at least assumed by several manuscripts, is still unsettled. Also, the ascriptions that occur in the manuscript titles and assign the New Testament texts to specific apostles call for further and comprehensive investigation.

Closely connected to the whole complex mentioned above is the role of personalization within the formation process of credo and doctrine in early Christianity. Were the early Christians actually aware of something like a Pauline, Johannine, Petrine, or Jacobian theology? Did they have basically an understanding of agreement dominating the relations between the theologies of the New Testament period, or rather one of contradiction, tension, and conflict between at least some of them? To what extent was the transmitted knowledge of the impact and meaning of the apostles interlinked with a distinct understanding of specific theological and pastoral intentions? In their polemics against Paul, for example, the so-called New Testament apocrypha point here to a certain aware-ness of such a distinction, at least in the midst of several particular groups. But what about the communities that belonged to the mainstream of the church and handed down to us the scripts of the New Testament?

In regard to the history of tradition, the treatment of early Christian-ity in Antioch turned out to be exceptionally fertile and intensive in effect for the purpose of our project. But also in this respect, several questions remain open. From my point of view, we have already forged ahead when the question of development of Antiochian traditions does not primarily suggest the short period *before* the time when Paul arrived there. This period lasted only for a very short time and left hardly any traces in the sources. Therefore, the time *after* Paul's departure, lasting for decades and including developments of transmission, alteration, and even creation of new traditions, has attracted our notice. We have started to explore this process of transmission, transformation, and regeneration of traditions during a period when Paul's theological input was still effective.

Eventually, one crucial theological question deserves deeper investi-gation: the image of Jesus in the CE. This question cannot be answered merely by reconstructing possible pieces of the tradition of Jesus from the CE. This approach, even regarding the Epistle of James—which in this respect is known to be outstandingly profitable—is very inadequate in terms of theological demands. The pivotal starting point for approaching the image of Jesus in the CE must be the Eastern credo, as is the case even with regard to the Gospels. This is especially true for the two epistles that are ascribed to the physical brothers of Jesus. Those two authors did not know Jesus "according to the flesh," but admitted to him as the resurrected crucified Christ; otherwise their writings would never have passed down in the communities. The central question of New Testa-ment theology is, therefore, which characteristic and irreversible features are contributed by those writings to an image of Jesus appropriate to the entire New Testament? Here lies the core of my own impetus for advanc-ing further research of the CE as a part of the New Testament.

—*Karl-Wilhelm Niebuhr*

Part II

CATHOLIC EPISTLES AS A COLLECTION

CHAPTER 2

A UNIFYING THEOLOGY
OF THE CATHOLIC EPISTLES
A Canonical Approach

Robert W. Wall

Introduction

This paper proposes an interpretive strategy by which the Catholic Epistles (CE) should be read together as a collection whose seven books are integral parts of a coherent theological whole. The perceived theological coherence of the CE is at odds with the modern critical assessment that underscores their literary, rhetorical, and theological diversity, and therefore their independence from each other, no matter what interpretive strategy is employed. Those who chase down the sources of theological beliefs submit theological definitions retrieved from different points of origin, where different authors respond to the spiritual crises of their different recipients, who are shaped within different social and religious worlds. On the exegetical landscape of modern biblical criticism, then, the theological diversity found within the CE corpus has been explained as the by-product of differing moments/places of origin and their respective trajectories/tradition histories.

Those who treat the CE as literary media do not disagree with this conclusion. Their own explanatory constructions, however, explicate the same theological diversity as the by-product of different genres, textual structures, or rhetorical patterns—regardless of who wrote these texts, for whom, when, or where. In this light, then, the critical consensus is that the CE are no real collection at all, but an arbitrary grouping of literary miscellanea gathered together and arranged during the canonical process at a non-Pauline address, without any thought of their theological coherence or canonical function as a per se collection. In fact, the theological incoherence of the CE, and their independence from each other, has become a matter of critical dogma.[1]

The present paper will incline the angle of approach toward the CE collection differently, thereby admitting into evidence new findings from the canonical period, when these seven books were formed into a second collection of letters "to provide a broader and more balanced literary representation of the apostolic witness than the letters of Paul furnished by themselves."[2] In doing so, I intend to challenge the critical consensus regarding the theological incoherence of the CE collection; in fact, my thesis is that when this epistolary collection is rendered by the hermeneutics of the canonical process, both its theological coherence and its canonical role will be more clearly discerned.

At the center of this study are two related observations about the final redaction of the CE collection that are laden with hermeneutical promise. First, when the CE became a collection, the Letter of James became its frontispiece to introduce the deep logic—or what I call the *grammar*— of the collection's unifying theology and its anticipated role within the biblical canon. Second, when the CE became a collection, it did so with Acts, which supplied a narrative context that not only vested the entire collection with religious authority but cued the priority of James within it. At that canonical moment, when the final redaction of this collection evoked a recognition of its theological wholeness, the one (James as its surprising frontispiece) was made explicable by the other (Acts as its narrative context).

A Canonical Approach to the Catholic Epistles as a Collection

The question is reasonably asked whether interpreters should elevate the importance of the canonizing community's intentions when mining these texts for their theological material, especially when the modern bias is to define the theological goods of a biblical writing by those meanings retrieved from original locations or as envisaged by a composition's rhetorical design and literary genre. I think so. In fact, if the angle of one's approach to the theology of the CE is inclined by the relevant properties of the canonical process, then what should be assumed about these books are their theological coherence as a canonical collection and the importance of their collective role whenever the interpreter seeks to render a fully biblical witness to the word of God. In this portion of the paper, let me simply catalogue those findings that are suggestive of a unifying theology and role of the CE collection.

1. I begin with the most basic of observations: the final redaction of the CE collection stabilizes a fluid movement within the bounds of the canonical process. This may be deduced from Eusebius' initial statements about the CE in *Ecclesiastical History*, and what he did and did not observe about received traditions at the outset of the fourth century. He notes, for example, the widespread acceptance and use of 1 Peter and 1 John in the ancient church—at least as early as Polycarp's use of 1 Peter in the early second century (*Hist. eccl.* 3.14)—but observes that other CE are disputed, mainly because of their lack of widespread use by the fathers of the church.[3]

The most important data in consideration of this phenomenon are the variety of canon lists preserved from both the East and the West, and the literature generated by the various theological debates and conciliar gatherings in these regions of the church.[4] Depending upon one's account of the chronology of the canonical process, these data are retrieved from the second through the fourth century. To these data are added the quotations of and allusions to the CE found in early Christian writings—or the stunning lack thereof in some cases—which also span the canonical stage of Scripture's formation.[5] Naturally, the sociology and hermeneutics of the canonical process, by which these data are contextualized and analyzed, could compel a different account of the performance and meaning of these texts than when they were first received by their original readers/auditors. But my principal observation is this: the CE collection did not stabilize until quite late in the canonical process, and the various internal changes that took place along its way to canonization, especially the placement of James as its frontispiece and its initial circulation with Acts as the collection's narrative (biographical) introduction, provide important clues to its theological contribution and continuing role within the biblical canon.[6]

Insofar as the formation of the CE collection occurs within the catholicizing milieu of the canonical process, its final redaction also reflects the general commitments of the canonical process itself. For example, the hermeneutics of the canonical process were not those of conflict but of consolidation, by which common ground rather than irreconcilable differences was sought. The theological perspicuity of every part of the whole was measured by an ecumenical *regula fidei* to ensure the unity of the canonical whole by this common theological referent.[7] While critical exegesis of the seven-letter CE collection articulates the profound theological diversity across the biblical canon—a diversity that aptly reflects what might be found within the church catholic, ancient and modern—the inclusion of each writing within the "catholic" collection of non-Pauline epistles, and this collection's inclusion within the New Testament, assumes a general theological coherence to all other parts of the canonical whole, including the Pauline collection. I suspect this is exactly what Eusebius meant by the rubric *catholic—allgemeingültig* rather than *allgemein*—which would then be apropos of any other collection of biblical literature, not just this one.

2. At the same time, the final redaction of the CE collection was the by-product of an intentional movement. That is, its sevenfold shape does not appear to follow a mechanistic pattern of arrangement—for example, according to length,[8] perceived date of composition,[9] or as a matter largely determined by the print technology of a canonical edition in codex format.[10] In fact, I am aware of no scholar who denies that the production of the New Testament served mostly religious aims, whether epistemic or sacramental. Thus, the different canon lists extant from different regions of the church catholic at the time of the canonical process reflect differing theological judgments made by ecclesial traditions that resulted in different groupings of writings, which were then ranked according to their importance when performing a variety of religious tasks (liturgical, educational, missional, etc.). The arrangement of these different collections, and even of individual writings within them, envisages ecclesial value judgments that reference Scripture's canonical role in forming a community's theological understanding of God, and its practical witness based upon those beliefs.

In this same manner, the emergent New Testament was edited over time into a final canonical edition by particular arrangement of its discrete collections, set in theologically suggestive relationships with each other, rather than by recognition of the importance of individual writings, one at a time. Individual writings did not circulate as such; rather, during the canonical process, individual writings were preserved, edited, reproduced, circulated, read, and then canonized in combination with other individual writings as canonical collections.[11] Indeed, the earliest history of the two epistolary collections would seem to indicate that they were placed side by side within the biblical canon to facilitate a constructive ("self-correcting and mutually informing") conversation between them.[12]

3. In my recent study of the formation of the Pauline canon, I argue that the theological conception of the canonical Paul, articulated initially in a nine- or ten-letter corpus, was brought to its completion and "fixed" by the late addition of a small and marginal collection of three so-called Pastoral Epistles, probably toward the end of the second century. The methodological rubric I use in drafting this idea is the "aesthetic

principle," by which I mean that the final redaction of the Pauline (and any biblical) collection became canonical precisely at the moment the faith community recognized the theological integrity or wholeness of a particular literary shape—in this case, the final grouping of thirteen Pauline letters, inclusive of the Pastoral Epistles. In this sense, the formation of a biblical collection might be studied as a phenomenon of the canonical process, which appears to follow a general pattern by which a fluid body of writings is finally stabilized, completed, and arranged by the addition (or subtraction) of certain writings. Moreover, the recognition of a collection's canonical shape cannot somehow be abstracted from its performance in the formation and practice of Christian faith.[13]

By this same principle, then, the final shape of the CE collection, symbolized perhaps by its sevenfold membership (seven = wholeness), may satisfy an implicit aesthetic criterion by which this particular grouping of seven CE was stabilized, completed, and arranged as canonical upon the community's recognition and religious experience of its theological wholeness. There are at least five properties inherent in the canonical redaction of the CE collection that would seem to envisage a motive to meet such a criterion, however implicit:

A. *James 2:22.* Without proposing a theory of the book's composition as pseudepigraphy, I suggest that the eventual canonization of James accords with a theological judgment made about the canonical function of the CE collection as a whole (see below). Unlike the case for 2 Peter, which was added (and perhaps even composed) to extend the theological conception of 1 Peter, James was added to an emergent collection much later, probably toward the end of the third century, to help delimit its working relationship with a Pauline collection, which was already a fixed property within an otherwise still fluid biblical canon.

The catholic tendencies of the canonical redaction, by which an aesthetic of theological wholeness is pursued, are reflected by what is arguably the controlling text of the book's famous essay on "faith and works," James 2:22.[14] Read canonically, this verse stipulates that "faith alone" (i.e., professed faith without works)—what had become the somewhat troubling hallmark of the Pauline tradition—cannot stand alone, but is rather "brought to completion by the works" (*ek tōn ergōn ē pistis eteleieōthē*)—a phrase that both captures the moral inclination of the entire CE collection and sounds a cautionary note that any reductionistic reading of the Pauline corpus may well degenerate into a *sola fideism*.[15]

B. *Second Peter 3:1–2.* At a relatively early and more fluid stage in the formation of the CE collection, 2 Peter was added to 1 Peter in order to complete a Petrine theological conception.[16] Again without proposing a theory of 2 Peter's composition as pseudepigraphy, whether as 2 Jude (as critical orthodoxy would have it) or as 2 Peter (as the canonical redaction would have it), I contend that 2 Peter was added to the CE collection in light of its relationship to 1 Peter (rather than to Jude). The importance of this composition within Scripture, then, is as a "second letter" written "that you should remember the words spoken in the past" (3:1-2), in order to complete a more robust Petrine witness to better form the theological understanding of subsequent generations of believers.[17]

C. *Coherence of the three John epistles and the church's recognition by the fourth century that the three form a discrete unit.*[18] The intertextuality of the three Johannine letters is clear from even a cursory reading. My point again is that 2 John and 3 John bring to completion the theological conception introduced by 1 John. Painter's recent commentary is helpful in this regard, not only by reading the three epistles together, but then by locating them within the CE collection and resisting the tendency to read them either as three bits of a New Testament Johannine corpus—an exegetical practice as early as Origen—or as a written response to problems created by the Fourth Gospel in a dialectical fashion that decidedly is not prompted by the final form of the New Testament canon itself.

D. *Jude's placement within the Catholic Epistle collection.* Painter's reading strategy agrees with the motive of the canonical redaction that places Jude between the three John letters and the Apocalypse. That is, as a canonical marker, the effect is to indicate that John's letters are to be read together and within the CE collection, and not as members of a New Testament Johannine corpus.

It should be noted that the memorable benediction that concludes Jude (Jude 24-25), which some contend is reason alone for its preservation and canonization, is also a suitable ending to the entire collection, not because of its doxological argot but because of its practical interest in safeguarding those who might "stumble" into false teaching or immoral lifestyle (cf. Jude 4). Significantly, James concludes with a similar exhortation that to rescue believers who "stray from the truth" is to save their "souls from death" (Jas 5:19-20); and, in fact, this orientation to the congregation's internal spiritual welfare will become an organizing thematic of the entire collection. Accordingly, then, Jude's benediction, when reconsidered in the context of the final redaction of the CE, is apropos to the collection's motive and role within the biblical canon.

E. *Jude and James*—books named after brothers of the Lord—form the literary brackets of the entire collection, thereby guaranteeing their religious authority and importance for the future of the church catholic. What must be said, however, is that the authority of this collection is due not only to its connection with the Jerusalem pillars, made famous by the book of Acts, but also to its connection to the Holy Family.[19] The importance of this relationship in the sociology of the canonical process has less to do with the hagiography of persons and more to do with the authoritative traditions linked to their names.

Each of these various properties of a final redaction evinces histori-cal moves that in some sense complete and make more effective (with respect to the church's intentions for its Scripture) an earlier form of the collection. At different moments along the way and in different regions of the church catholic, 2 Peter, 2–3 John, and Jude were added as consti-tutive elements of a more theologically robust whole—a historical phe-nomenon that may reasonably be explained as evidence of the church's recognition of the importance of this second collection of letters within its biblical canon. Such an aesthetic principle is similar to that which measures the integrity of other biblical collections as well; in this sense, religious authority is a property of canonical collections rather than of individual writings. For example, the authority of 2 Peter is recognized in relationship to 1 Peter, or of James in relationship to the CE collection. A roughly parallel case is the fourfold Gospel, which Irenaeus said has an inherent integrity much like the "four corners of the earth," and which, according to most canon lists of antiquity, is placed first within the New Testament to recommend its formative value, with Matthew's gospel typ-ically given priority among the four as the most relevant continuation of Tanak's narrative of God's salvation.[20] That is, the theological integrity of the final redaction of a biblical collection—its placement with the New Testament—or even of an individual composition within the collection "signs" a role apropos to the motives of a biblical canon.

4. The question, when did the sevenfold CE collection become Scripture? appears related to the broad recognition that the Letter of James was necessary to complete the pages of a Peter-John epistolary catalogue.[21] Perhaps the most decisive observation from a canonical per-spective, then, is to discern the motive for this late inclusion of James, which may be properly assessed by its placement as the frontispiece in the collection's final redaction.[22] While the fourfold Gospel and the thirteen-letter Pauline canon were almost certainly fixed by then, and probably Acts had emerged in its two different versions to perform a strategic role within the emergent New Testament canon,[23] the same cannot be said of the CE collection (or either Hebrews or John's Apocalypse).

That a grouping of non-Pauline letters from the two leading apostolic successors of Jesus—especially when read by the first half of Acts, where the story of their triumphant succession from the Lord is narrated—and his two brothers (see above) is formed to add to the biblical canon makes good sense, especially within a community that confesses its identity as a "holy apostolic church" and venerated the memory of the Holy Family.

Moreover, according to Acts, it is Peter who defends Paul's mission—
even using Pauline terms in doing so (Acts 15:6-12)—before the leaders
of the Jerusalem church led by James (cf. Acts 15:13-29; 21:19-26). It
would seem reasonable, then, that the canonical process would delimit an
epistolary collection to reflect their close working relationship, especially
within a community in which the legacy of Paul had evidently triumphed,
and thus within a canonical process for which the relevant question had
become what literature should be read alongside Paul to enable the church
to hear Paul's word more precisely and prevent its distortion. The book
of James became the critical means to that end; but why?

Given the importance of James whose résumé includes founding and
pastoring the Jerusalem church, the brother of Jesus, and an important
leadership role in the missions of both Paul and Peter (cf. Gal 2:1-15; Acts
15:4-29; 21:17-25), the addition of a book in his name to the CE collection
made good sense.[24] This very logic is evinced by Eusebius, who recalls the
narrative of Hegesippus (*Hist. eccl.* 2.23.3–18) regarding the martyrdom
of "James the Just (or 'Righteous One')" as testimony to his courageous
fidelity and Jewish piety, and as the apparent reason why his "disputed"
book should be included in the so-called Catholic collection (*Hist. eccl.*
2.23.25). While the connection between these traditions about the Jewish
piety of James and his "catholic" letter appears to underwrite the authority
of his "disputed" letter, my suspicion is that the canonical portrait of James
found in the book of Acts (rather than those found in other noncanonical
Jewish and gnostic writings) is more decisive for understanding the origins
and ultimate canonization of the Letter of James.[25]

It therefore remains a puzzlement for most scholars, especially given
the evident importance of personal traditions about James reflected in
canonical Acts, that no second- or third-century canon list mentions a
letter from James and no Christian writer quotes from or clearly alludes
to it.[26] While Origen is the first to mention the letter (*Comm. Matt.*
19.61),[27] neither he nor Eusebius seems familiar with its teaching; a generation later, Athanasius is the first to list it as canonical in his famous
Easter letter of 367 CE, a verdict then confirmed by the Councils of Rome
(382) and Carthage (397). Moreover, traditions about the legacy of James
are pivotal to several writings outside the mainstream (Jewish Christian,
gnostic), in which he is depicted as the pious pastor of the Jewish church
and key strategist of the church's universal mission, in particular as the
sometimes opponent of Paul's law-free mission to the nations. These
same writings, however, do not refer to a letter, nor does their portrait of
James explain the thematics found in the Letter of James.[28]

Most explain this silence of an epistolary James by the sociology of
a mainstream church, where the negative response to the anti-Pauline

bashing by the second-century tradents of James, and to their more "conservative" Jewish convictions and practices (and in some cases heretical inclinations), led to the letter's suppression. Only later is this letter from James reclaimed, perhaps in edited form, and put back into circulation as suitable reading for the mainstream apostolic church. Yet the same could be said of the Pauline canon, which was also used by marginal and even heretical movements within the church, but which was already fixed by the end of the second century. The suppression of a letter from James also fails to explain why a similar silence is found in the literature of more marginal Jewish, Christian, and gnostic communities of the second century, for whom the legacy of James was valorized.[29] Again, the present paper offers no alternative theory of the origins and transmission of James in earliest Christianity; my thesis about the performance of James as the frontispiece of a canonical collection of CE does not depend upon a particular theory of its production.[30]

5. If we can assume that the canonical redaction of the CE as an epistolary collection occurred in the fourth century, when a thirteen-letter Pauline canon was already in wide circulation and use, then its primary motive would likely have been to forge a more viable reading of the extant Pauline canon, to which this non-Pauline letter corpus was now added. In this sense, any new reading of the Pauline corpus would have been regulated by the teaching of the CE collection, thereby promising to prevent a distorted reading of the Pauline gospel within the church. Given the history of heretical currents emanating from Pauline traditions in the early church, one should not be surprised that a substantial Pauline criticism, an important hallmark of the James tradition within the early church (e.g., the *Pseudo-Clementines*, *Gospel of the Hebrews*), is largely retained in the Letter of James, especially (but not exclusively) in 1:22–2:26. Moreover, the Jewish roots of these traditions are hardly obscured in the letter.[31] The viability of such an intracanonical conversation between Pauline and Catholic, then, would not rest on the prospect of conceptual harmony, but on a mutual criticism that does not subvert the purchase of the Pauline canon but rather ensures that its use by the church coheres to its own *regula fidei*.[32]

By the same token, the internal calculus of the Catholic collection, consisting early on of letters from Peter and John—which, when viewed through the lens of Acts, merely supplement (rather than correct) the extant Pauline canon—now is transformed by the inclusion of James; the Peter-John grouping is recalibrated as a more functional Pauline criticism. The relationship between the Jerusalem Pillars and Paul, recalled from Galatians 2:1-15 and hinted at elsewhere in his letters and in Acts, is adapted to negotiate the relationship between the two epistolary corpora within the biblical canon. The first element of a unifying theology of the CE is thus conceived in more functional terms. The reception of James cues the church's critical concern about a reductionistic use of Pauline tradition that edits out the church's Jewish legacy, especially an ethos that resists any attempt to divorce a profession of orthodox beliefs from an active obedience to God's law in a pattern of salvation (see below).[33]

6. Trobisch's observation that the book of Acts played a strategic hermeneutical role in the canonical process is certainly correct. But the application of a reading of Acts as an "early catholic" narrative, written to moderate the conflict between Paul and the Jerusalem Pillars articulated in Galatians 2:1-15, to the canon project is mistaken in my view. I remain unconvinced that Acts is early catholic in either its theological or sociological sensibility; my primary concern is that this perspective undermines the special relationship between Acts and the CE collection evinced during the fourth century, when they circulated together and appeared together in the canon lists. Moreover, such a harmonistic reading of Acts fails to recognize the substantial role the James of Acts plays within the narrative world of Acts in moving the plotline of Paul's mission to the nations. In fact, my growing conviction is that the Acts narrative (rather than Galatians 2) best explains the importance of a final redaction of the CE collection that posits the Letter of James as its frontispiece, and therefore central to its theological definition and canonical responsibility, especially if Acts and James arrived together at this same canonical moment.

For this reason, the relevant question for my project is not the historian's, "Is the Letter of James a letter from James?" but rather is, "What does the James of Acts have to do with the Letter of James?" My suspicion is that the portrait of James in Acts not only underwrites the authority of a letter of James, but gives reason why it should function as frontispiece to a second corpus of letters when read as an element of a "self-correcting and mutually informing" conversation within the biblical canon.

The Role of Acts in the Final Redaction of the Catholic Epistles Collection

The Acts of the Apostles narrates a story whose central characters are the same authors (e.g., Peter, Paul, James) and audiences/sources (e.g., Jerusalem, Timothy, Corinth, Ephesus, Rome) referenced or alluded to in the subsequent New Testament letters (see chapter 7).[34] New Testament readers naturally make associations between these common elements, noting as well a common concern for important topics of Christian existence (e.g., sharing goods, purity, suffering, the performance of the word of God, congregational unity). Literary intertexts of this sort suggest a logical relationship as members of the same conceptual universe; from a perspective within the New Testament, Acts supplies the "authorized" narrative behind its most important epistolary texts.

Considered from this angle, then, the critical orthodoxy of reading only the Pauline collection (Knox, Goodspeed, Bruce, Delatte, and many others) by Acts seems misplaced—even though the rehabilitation of Acts (perhaps even in a "new and improved" version) during the second half of the second century, and then a renewed interest in Acts criticism during the second half of the twentieth century, may well have been prompted by the evidently strategic relationship between the Paul of Acts and certain Pauline letters (e.g., Romans, Ephesians, Galatians).[35] During the canonical process, Acts came to supply a narrative introduction for the entire epistolary canon, Pauline and Catholic; in fact, from a canonical perspective, the relationship between Acts and the CE is elevated in importance because they "came into life" together during the canonical process. In any case, the interpreter approaches the New Testament letters with the orienting concerns of Acts in mind and, in light of its story, more wakeful when negotiating between the New Testament's two different epistolary corpora as theological complements.

Given the reemergence of Acts as a text of strategic importance for underwriting the hermeneutics of the canonical process, I consider it highly likely that its narrative portraits of the church's earliest leaders (i.e., Peter and John, Paul, and James)—drawn as they are from early traditions of their teachings and ministries, concurrent to the earliest stage of the canonical process—envisage a particular account of their religious authority,[36] the nature of their ministries (e.g., prophetic, pastoral, missionary), and the subject matter of their kerygmata, which supplied the canonizing community with both an explanatory context and a religious warrant for why these New Testament writings, when considered together, are formative of Christian theological understanding.[37] I especially think Acts provided the impetus for the circulation (and perhaps even composition) of James, which led to the formation of a "pillars" collection.

In particular, the manner by which Acts narrates the personae of Christian leaders and their relations with each other as characters of this authorized story of emergent Christianity frames a particular account of how "intracanonical conversations" between the canonical writings linked to these same leaders might be negotiated. Similarities and dissimilarities in emphasis and theological conception found when comparing the Catholic and Pauline letters may actually correspond to the manner by which Acts narrates the negotiations between the reports from different missions, and of the theological convictions and social conventions required by each (e.g., Acts 2:42-47; 9:15-16; 11:1-18; 12:17; 15:129; 21:17-26). The relations between Peter and Paul, Paul and James, James and Peter or even Peter and John as depicted within the narrative world of Acts are generally collaborative rather than adversarial and frame the interpreter's approach to their biblical writings as essentially complementary (even though certainly not uniform and sometimes in conflict) in both meaning and function. In fact, if the critical consensus for a late first-century date of Acts is accepted, which is roughly contemporaneous with the earliest moment of the canonical process,[38] then it is likely that this collection of portraitures of early Christian leaders provides an important explanatory model for assessing the relationship between (and even within) the two emergent collections of canonical letters: the form and function of these Christian writings and their relationship to each other is another articulation of the early church's "sense" of the more collaborative relationship between their individual people and interpretative traditions, which is reflected then in the Book of Acts. So that, for example, if Peter and John are enjoined as partners in Acts, then we should expect to find their written traditions conjoined in an emergent Christian Bible, and that their intracanonical relation envisages the church's perception of their theological coherence. Likewise, the more difficult although finally collegial relationship between James and Paul as narrated in Acts 15 and (especially) 21 may well envisage their partnership in ecclesial formation in a manner that Protestant interpretation has sometimes subverted.

Because both the narrative world and its central characters are the literary constructions of the storyteller and are shaped by his theological commitments, the interpreter should not expect a more precise connection between, for example, the kerygma of the Peter of Acts and a Petrine theology envisaged by 1–2 Peter. Nevertheless, there is evidence that Luke did indeed draw upon important traditions common to the Petrine letters when composing his narrative of the person and work of Peter. In particular, 1 Peter's interpretation of Jesus as Isaiah's "Servant of God" (1 Pet 2:21-25; cf. 1:10-12), the evident core of Petrine christology, is anticipated by four references to Jesus as "servant" in Acts (and only there in the NT), the first two in speeches by Peter (3:13, 26) and the last two in a prayer by the apostles led by him (4:27, 30).[39] Moreover, the God of the Petrine epistles, who is known primarily through Jesus' resurrection (1 Pet 1:3, 21; 3:21; cf. Acts 2:22-36) and as a "faithful Creator" (1 Pet 4:19; cf. Acts 4:24), agrees generally with Luke's traditions of a Petrine kerygma. Even Peter's claim that the central mark of Gentile conversion is a "purity of heart" (Acts 15:9) is strikingly similar to 1 Peter 1:22. Finally, the most robust eschatology found in Acts, famous for its sparseness of eschatological thought, is placed on Peter's lips (Acts 3:20-23), thereby anticipating the keen stress posited on salvation's apocalypse in 1–2 Peter (cf. 2 Pet 3:1-13).[40] A second example may be the far thinner portrait of John in Acts, who although depicted as Peter's silent partner uses his one speaking role in Acts 4:19-20 to sound a key note of the Johannine epistles: ". . . for we cannot but speak of what we have seen and heard" (cf. 1 John 1:1-3).[41]

When these thematic connections are rooted in the narrative world of Acts—a world in which these characters have enormous religious authority and purchase for the church's future—the epistolary expression and development of these core themes is underwritten as also important for the church's future and formation. Moreover, the certain impression of kerygmatic continuity between the Lord's apostolic successors (Peter/John) and Paul, cultivated by Acts, would seem to commend a more constructive relationship between their writings. Acts performs an interpretive role, not so much to temper the diversity envisaged by the two different collections of letters but to prompt impressions of their rhetorical relationship within the New Testament. According to Acts, the church that claims its continuity with the first apostles tolerates a rich pluralism even as the apostles do within Luke's narrative world, although not without controversy and confusion. What is achieved at the pivotal Jerusalem Council (Acts 15) is confirmation of a kind of theological understanding rather than a more political theological consensus. The divine revelation given to the apostles according to Acts forms a "pluralizing monotheism" (J. A. Sanders) which in turn contextualizes Paul's idiom of two discrete missions and appropriate proclamations, Jewish and Gentile, in Galatians 2:7-10. The variety of theological controversies Paul responds to in his letters, with whatever rhetoric he employs in doing so, is roughly analogous to the "Cornelius problem" in Acts.

Of course, Acts portrays Peter (rather than Paul) as first initiating and then explaining the admission of uncircumcised (i.e., unclean) Gentiles into the church; the Peter of Acts finally defends Paul's mission and its spiritual results in a speech that is remarkably Pauline in theological sensibility (15:7-11)—perhaps reflective of Luke's familiarity with and perceived unity of the Petrine and Pauline traditions used in Pauline/Petrine letters, as many modern interpreters have noted.[42] More remarkably, however, the question of whether or not to "Judaize" repentant Gentiles is settled *before* Paul comes back into the narrative to begin his mission to the nations in Acts 11:1-18. In fact, Peter's second rehearsal of Cornelius' repentance at this "second" Jerusalem Council responds to a different problem altogether, posed by the church's Pharisaic contingent that is concerned (as evidently is James) about a normative halakah for mixed Christian congregations (15:4-5). Peter's response concentrates—presumably agreeing with Paul's initial proclamation (cf. 13:38-39)—on an internal "purity of the heart" (15:9).

James, however, expands this Pharisaic concern for religious purity to include socio-religious *practices* (15:20); in fact, his halakah reflects the more "traditional" worry of Jewish religion regarding syncretism—the "gentilizing" of repentant Israel (15:20; see also 21:17-26)—and in particular the possible attenuation of the church's Jewish legacy in the Diaspora as Paul's mission to the nations takes the word of God farther from Jerusalem, the epicenter of the sacred universe (15:21). It is in response to James' Jewish concerns that the narrative of Paul's mission to the nations is shaped in Acts; and, therefore, he provokes and responds to a different set of theological controversies than does the epistolary Paul who responds to internal opponents who want "to judaize" repentant Gentiles. According to Acts, this issue is settled by Peter at the earlier Jerusalem council (11:1-18), and even though this issue resurfaces in Antioch (15:1-2) those who raise the question again are summarily dismissed by James as "unauthorized" teachers who do not represent the position of the Judean church (so 15:24). In fact, the *entire* narrative of Paul's European mission in Acts (Philippian, Thessalonian-Athenian, Corinthian, Ephesian) is simply not shaped by the same theological controversies that Paul stakes out in his letters as provoked by his Gentile mission.

In general, the Paul of Acts is exemplary of a more Jewish definition of purity (cf. 24:16-21). Thus, he is arrested in Philippi for being a Jew (16:20-21) and earlier circumcises Timothy (16:3; cf. Gal 2:3!), not only to testify to his personal loyalty to the ancestral religion (cf. 21:23-26) but more critically to symbolize the importance of James' concern to preserve it in consecrated form. Consider, for example, the role Timothy performs in Acts in contrast to Titus in Galatians. Timothy is of mixed parentage, Jewish and Gentile, and in prospect of the Diaspora church, Paul circumcises him in order to preserve his mother's Jewish inheritance.[43] He stands as a symbol of Paul's missiological intent in Acts, which is to found Christian congregations in the Diaspora with a mixture of Jewish and Gentile converts but whose faith and practices are deeply rooted in the church's Jewish legacy.

From this canonical perspective, then, it may well be argued that a principal concern of the *second* collection of epistles is to bring balance to a *Tendenz* toward religious syncretism by which the pressures of the surrounding pagan culture may distort if not then subvert the church's substantially Jewish theological and cultural legacy. The repetition of familiar Pauline themes in the CE problematizes them, but acquires a thickened meaning when read in context of the antecedent Acts narrative;

that is, a prior reading of Acts alerts the reader of the CE that an increasingly Gentile (Pauline) church must consider its religious and public purity as God's people according to the redemptive calculus of their Jewish canonical heritage (Scriptures, practices, prophetic exemplars, etc.). As such, a Christian congregation's profession of faith must be embodied in its public and internal practices, in keeping with the ethos of its Jewish legacy.[44] The full experience of God's righteousness is achieved by performance of works pleasing to God and neighbor, and not merely by *sola fide*, no matter how orthodox or sincerely confessed.

A Grammar for a Unifying Theology of the Catholic Epistles Collection: A Proposal

The surprising priority of the Letter of James, indicated by its placement as the frontispiece in the final form of the CE, insinuates its strategic rhetorical purpose upon the entire collection. The typical rhetorical role of a frontispiece within any literary collection is to make introductions; as a theological introduction, James could be read as putting into play a variety of distinctive themes, whose linguistic and conceptual similarity with other CE may reasonably be explained as the sharing of common traditions, albeit from different regions and for different ends (see, e.g., Konradt).[45] These thematic agreements could then be pressed into service as the rubrics for a "unifying theology of the CE" (see, e.g., Schlosser). Such a unity, however, strikes me as somewhat artificial, since the mere sum of their linguistic or conceptual similarity does not necessarily envisage a coherent understanding of Christian faith. A more robust unifying theology requires a grammar that supplies a kind of logic by which the collection's thematic agreements cohere together to form a distinctive, decisive whole greater than the sum of its theological bits. The principal rhetorical role of the Letter of James is to provide such a grammar.

First stated in general terms, the subject of this grammar, articulated succinctly by James 2:22, is that a congregation's profession of faith in God (2:19a) is "made complete" by its obedience to God's "perfect law of liberty" (1:25; 2:12). Such acts of obedience are the criteria of friendship with God (2:24; cf. 2:8) and ensure the believer's eternal life with God (1:12; cf. 2:5). The collection's thematic agreements, then, cohere together as the predicates of this subject matter in stipulating a non-Pauline (rather than anti-Pauline) pattern of salvation that centers a congregation of believers (rather than a "world" of sinners) upon the performance of those works consistent with God's law (1:22-27; 4:4-17). By embodying devotion to God by observance of Torah's commands, the theological grammar introduced by James is the complement of (rather than the counterpoint to) Paul's more missional subject matter that sinners are initiated into life with God by their public profession of faith ("with their lips") that "Jesus is Lord" (Rom 10:9). The effective result of their interplay within the biblical canon, Pauline and non-Pauline, aims at a more robust expression of God's gospel that lies at the heart of the canonical process.

The shift of rubrics from Catholic to non-Pauline in the above summary is intended to underscore the potential of my earlier observation that when the final redaction of the CE collection occurred, the canonical Paul (i.e., the Paul of Acts and the Pauline epistolary corpus) was already in place. It is reasonable to presume, then, that the formation of the CE collection had the Pauline collection in view all along—to "make complete" a Pauline understanding of the faith (par. Jas 2:22). Understood from this new perspective, the formation of the CE into a collection reflects the catholicizing hermeneutics of the canonical process, by which the completion of a non-Pauline collection glosses the Pauline to complete the epistolary whole—a whole that instructs biblical readers regarding a pattern of salvation that concerns both the sinner's initiation into life with God and the believer's ongoing friendship with God. In fact, when considered holistically, it should be apparent to the reader that either epistolary grammar, Pauline or Catholic, when appropriated to the exclusion of the other will ultimately subvert the formation of Christian faith and life, which is the principal purpose of the biblical canon.

Moreover, the emergent role of the book of Acts to mediate these two epistolary corpora within the biblical canon must be regarded as an important factor of this new perspective as well. Quite apart from the importance of traditions about the historical James as a Christian leader, the brother of Jesus, and as exemplar of Jewish piety, it is the canonical James of Acts that makes the strategic importance of the epistolary James explicable. Sharply put, James' speech found in Acts 15:12-21 (22-29) and its narrative recapitulation in 21:21-25 underwrite the theological grammar of the epistolary James.

While my recent commentary on Acts provides an exposition of these texts within their historical, theological, and narrative settings, in defense of the thesis of this paper, let me simply say that James expresses a profoundly "Jewish" anxiety over Paul's mission to the nations: that the church's social identity, which is marked out by traditional Jewish purity practices, might be threatened by the church's mission to pagans. James' agenda is both pastoral ("table fellowship" between repentant Jews and Gentiles) and articulates an ethical interest in the church's mission with virtually no apparent interest in the publicly professed beliefs of Pauline orthodoxy. While he tacitly agrees with Peter's Paulinism that the purity of unclean (uncircumcised) Gentiles (e.g., Cornelius) originates from the inward affections of "hearts made pure by faith" (15:9, 19; cf. Jas 1:13-15), his midrash on the quoted prophecy from LXX Amos 9 (15:16-18) glosses this inward form of purity: those Gentiles who turn to the God of Israel by faith must nonetheless mind the Diaspora synagogue's teaching of Moses, specifically as it delineates the cleansing that is necessary for fellowship with Jews (15:19-21). Even though James agrees with Peter (who speaks for the Pauline tradition) that the pagan is initiated into life with God through faith (15:13-14, 19), he also seems aware that Peter's witness proffers an incomplete response to the important question earlier raised by faithful Pharisees regarding the halakah of a mixed Christian congregation in the Diaspora (15:5). The subtext of their question, which had become relevant to Luke's church, concerns whether the Jewish legacy should continue to define the church's religious identity in terms of those public purity practices in keeping with God's Torah, according to which fellowship with God and within a mixed congregation is possible (15:20, 29; cf. Jas 1:22-27; 2:8-13).[46] In fact, the James of Acts extends a Pauline understanding of the inward "purity (circumcision) of the heart" vocalized by Peter (15:8-11) to include social practices (including circumcision in Acts 16:1-3); this concern of James then controls the plotline of Paul's European mission in Acts 16–20.

Before moving to an initial draft of my proposal, let me express two caveats pertaining to the larger project of constructing a unifying theology of the CE. First, while many critics have noted the anti-Pauline note sounded by James, the Pauline cast of 1 Peter, and the non-Pauline (or Johannine) perspective of the Johannine letters, this approach to the CE as a discrete biblical collection, read by the theological grammar of James, regulates (and transforms) how their intracanonical relationships with the Pauline corpus (and every other biblical collection) are assessed.

Second, as a convention of the early Catholic Church, the canonical process gathered together diverse writings into collections whose roles and subject matter are consistent with the theological agreements and purpose of the *regula fidei*; the hermeneutics of the canonical process were of coherence, not dissonance. In this sense, the biblical theologian should presume that a unifying theology of the CE collection, and its ongoing performance in constructing a fully biblical theology, is rendered coherent by the rule's own grammar of theological agreements.

Of course, the same can be assumed of every other canonical collection, since the whole of Scripture is a literary analogue of this Rule. On this basis, for example, I submit that the internal structure and deep logic of a unifying theology of all Scripture must reflect precisely the church's *regula fidei*. Moreover, it is precisely because the theological grammar would be the same when rendering every part of the whole canon that the biblical theologian is able to assess more adequately the distinctive contribution each makes to the whole, and what the whole would lack if constructed in absence of every part—whether a rendering of the theological subject matter of the New Testament in absence of the Old Testament, or of the Gospel in absence of the Letters, or of the Pauline Letters in absence of the CE. But this is a much more ambitious project for another Colloquium Biblicum Lovaniense.

To conclude the present study, then, let me briefly discuss the following sequence of themes as the constitutive predicates of a unifying theology of the CE collection, which are introduced and logically rendered by the Letter of James as the framework for a distinctive articulation of the Christian faith.

1. Human suffering tests the faith community's love for God.

2. In response to the suffering of God's people, God discloses a "word of truth" to map the only way of salvation.

3. In obedience to this word, the community must practice "pure and undefiled" behavior as the public mark of friendship with God.

4. Theological orthodoxy by itself is inconclusive of friendship with God and is made effective only when embodied in loving works.

5. Finally, the reward for steadfast obedience to God's word is eternal life with God.

1. *Human suffering tests the faith community's love for God.* According to James, the principal threat to Christian existence is the suffering provoked by "various trials" (1:2), which are not caused by God (1:13-16) and evidently are inherent in a chaotic, demonic "world" (1:27b; 3:6, 15-16). The theological crisis addressed by James is not sociological—it is neither the congregation's poverty nor its sense of political powerlessness (2:2-4; 5:1-6) as a dislocated people (1:1). Rather, the principal threat addressed concerns a testing of faith in/love for God that has been occasioned by their difficult social circumstances (1:3-8, 12).

While the prospect of doubt (1:6-8; 3:9-10; 4:8), theological deception (1:13-16), broken relationships (2:2-3; 3:9-16; 4:1-2), and even spiritual disaffection (5:19-20) is occasioned by social conflicts of one kind or another, its principal source is inward and deeply spiritual: a human soul inclined toward doubting God's generosity (1:13-18) and even toward "friendship with the world" rather than with God (4:4-5; cf. 2:21-24; 3:5-

6, 9-12; 4:6-10, 11-12, 13-17; 5:1-6). That is, the problem of suffering is its potential to erode a community's love for God. The most evident mark of a community's spiritual failure, according to James, is the interpersonal strife within the faith community (2:14-17; 3:6; 4:1-3) and the attenuation of "loving neighbors," which is the essential ethos of God's people in contretemps to the world order (1:26-27; 2:1-13). While James casts the problem of theodicy in terms of human suffering, the relevant issue addressed is not so much a faithful God's relation to suffering (1:13-18) but rather the community's own faithful response to God in the face of their "various trials." James introduces a highly nuanced conception of *Leidenstheolog*[47] then, in that a definition of Christian existence is not concentrated by an experience of suffering but by the spiritual test it occasions. Further, while the community's suffering is provoked by popular opposition (2:6-7) and expressed as verbal slander (3:7-8), James finally casts spiritual testing in more cosmic terms, since creation itself is being contested by "the devil" (3:6, 9-12; 4:4-5), who is in the midst of it all (4:7-10).

Petrine letters. Even without using James to decipher 1 Peter's theological conception, the reader will find the thematic of suffering believers featured in this CE; in fact, the vocabulary of 1 Peter employs more "suffering" words than any other New Testament letter. Their suffering is the consequence of living as "strangers and aliens," both socially and religiously, within pagan society (2:11-12).[48] As in James, suffering appears to be more that of verbal slander, economic poverty, and political powerlessness than of physical abuse. Unwarranted suffering, which typifies the ideal reader of 1 Peter, is the ironic result of "good behavior" (i.e., obedience to God), probably because such behavior is considered odd by the moral standards of an ignorant society (3:13-17; 4:1-6).

When compared to James, 1 Peter pays more attention to the community's relationship with hostile outsiders than to the effects of suffering on relations within the community itself; yet, as in James, 1 Peter interprets suffering as a spiritual test (1:6) that prompts God's judgment of the community's continued identity as God's elect (1:2; 2:4-10), and as proof of its salvation (1:7-9), which is predicated on its obedience to God's word in the face of hostile opposition (1:17; 4:12-19).

Christ plays an important role as God's "suffering Servant" in 1 Peter's conception of human suffering. This christological justification is lacking in James, and 1 Peter's gloss thereby adds significantly to how the collection as a whole addresses the theological crisis occasioned by human suffering. The suffering of an obedient Christ is both the medium of God's salvation (1:18-19; 2:22-24; 3:18; 4:13) and exemplary of the congregation's identity in the world (2:21; 3:17-18); in this regard, Christian existence implies a sharing in Christ's suffering in both soteriological and moral senses.

The implied audience of 2 Peter, which does not speak of suffering, appears to be more a stable household, and surely lives in a different symbolic universe than the audience addressed by 1 Peter. The theological crisis of 2 Peter concerns an internal challenge to apostolic traditions that otherwise define the community's orthodoxy. Second Peter insists that what is taught, whether or not it is right, determines how life is lived, whether or not it is righteous (2:18-21). When 1 Peter and 2 Peter are studied together as integral parts of the collection's Petrine witness, the biblical reader is reminded that the spiritual failure most often provoked by suffering is to compromise or attenuate the community's core beliefs as a strategy for avoiding the very hostility generative of suffering. Typically, orthodoxy is the first casualty of hardship (see Jas 1:13-16).

Johannine letters. While the Johannine letters agree that the surety of the congregation's devotion to God will be tested, whether or not every professing believer is truly a child of God, the language of suffering is notably absent. Nonetheless, Painter is correct when pointing out that "the purpose of 1 John is to address the confusion and heal the trauma caused by [the departure of schismatics who were, until recently, members of the Johannine community]."[49] The community's solidarity remains the central aim of these letters and is threatened not so much by external pressures exerted by outsiders (religious or secular) but by "Christian" opponents—"anti-christs" (2:18-22; 2 John 6-7)—whose conception of gospel truth is at odds with apostolic traditions about Jesus, the "word of life" (1:1-4). The result is the corollary of the Petrine witness: hardship is the first casualty of heterodoxy.

More critically, this intramural conflict has evidently had a pervasively negative (divisive) effect upon the community's life together, and has occasioned a spiritual test—what Robert Law long ago called "the tests of life."[50] But while the spiritual test concerns false teaching, its principal effect is moral. That is, the spiritual test concerns how to live a life of loving others; in fact, there is no gap whatsoever between knowing God's word, disclosed in the life of Jesus (2:6), and obeying God's command to love one another (2:7). In this fundamental sense, then, to respond rightly to a God who is love is to love one another (4:7-21), and to love one another is to abide in God and so in eternal life (2:28–3:18).

2. *In response to the suffering of God's people, God discloses a "word of truth" to map the only way of salvation.* Unlike proverbial wisdom, which is learned by human experience, this "word" is revealed by a good and generous God (1:18), especially through Torah (1:22-25; 2:8-10; 4:11-12) and Jesus tradition (i.e., "the faith of the Lord Jesus Christ, the glorious

One," 2:1), then implanted and "humbly" received within the faith community—presumably through the instruction of "wise and understanding" teachers (3:1, 13)—with an aim to save believers from deception and death (1:21; cf. 1:13-16).

For James, however, this redemptive word is clearly practical, not dogmatic. Unlike in the Pauline tradition, truth claims are less about what to believe or in whom to trust than about how to live life together in a milieu fraught with suffering, powerlessness, false teaching, and other external and internal threats to the congregation's solidarity. For this reason, the mark of friendship with God rather than with the world (4:4-10) is to control an inward "passion for material things," because "worldly desires" provoke intramural strife (3:6-8, 9-12; 4:1-3) and promote disregard and even the murder of the righteous poor (2:2-4; 5:1-6)—the very ones whom God has elected as heirs of the coming kingdom (2:5). In this sense, then, a rejection of the "word of truth," which trains the community how to respond to suffering with wisdom, only increases the community's suffering and otherwise leads it toward gehenna (3:6). Simply put, the wisdom that God discloses refocuses the community's attention from selfishness and worldliness toward caring for others, especially for brothers and sisters who are poor and powerless.

Petrine letters. This same connection between the divine word and the community's love for each other is also a critical feature of the moral vision of 1 Peter, which is evidently challenged by the community's social status as "aliens and strangers" and the suffering its status occasions. As with James 1:27, the community's response to its trials is purity before God, which is validated by obedience to God's truth and evinced by friendship within the household of faith (1:22; cf. 2:15; 3:17; 4:2, 19). The structure of the Petrine response to human suffering, then, is roughly the same as that introduced by James.

The divine word for 1 Peter, however, is not disclosed as practical wisdom but as proclaimed gospel (1:22-25); it is kerygmatic, not sapiential. In the Petrine version of the formula, Jesus is not merely the exemplar of the life-saving word, but its medium. The initial articulation of this divine word, then, is prophetic (Isaiah; cf. 1:24-25a; 2:22-25) and concerns Jesus' suffering (1:10-12), which is then "preached to you" (1:12, 25) for the salvation of souls (1:9). According to this missionary redaction of the formula, God's *logos* (1:23) becomes the Lord's *rhēma* (1:25). Not only is the convert's "rebirth" into purity/holiness of life the result of accepting this christological truth, it also becomes the nourishment of the convert's theological and sociological formation (2:2; cf. "oracles of God," 4:11).

This same move from prophetic *logos* to apostolic *rhēma* must be what 2 Peter has in mind in 3:2's exhortation to "remember the *rhēmata*" when commenting on 1 Peter (cf. 3:1). Yet apostolic proclamation has been reified into a tradition that confirms the "prophetic word" (Isaiah) about Petrine Christology (1:19), and now performs the role of the community's norm by which teaching and lifestyle are judged as either "true" or "false" (cf. 2:1-2), righteous or profane (2:17-22). And if 2 Peter is viewed in some sense as a later redaction of 1 Peter's theological argot, then what seems critical to note, if only in passing, is its apocalyptic gloss: whatever or whoever does not meet this apostolic norm is "stored up for the day of judgment and destruction of the ungodly" (3:7) and thereby excluded from existence in the "new heavens and a new earth in which righteousness dwells" (2 Pet 3:13). In this sense, 2 Peter transforms the motive for the convert's new life of holiness, into which s/he is initiated by the word of God, and within which is realized a community of loving relationships (1 Pet 1:22-25); no longer is it the generative powers of the divine word, but the imminence of God's coming cosmic triumph.

Johannine letters. Similarly, the Johannine Epistles articulate the importance of the "word [*logos*] of life" (1:1), which is also funded by memories from Jesus' life (1:2) and is coextensive with the apostolic proclamation/traditions of the gospel (1:3-4). This word is the truth and exposes what is therefore false; moreover, it is this christological word the community must obey as God's commandment (2:3-7).

As with the other CE, this word of truth disclosed in Christ's life issues a moral directive that is centered on God's command to "love one another" (i.e., other believers) and, according to these epistles, to love others self-sacrificially, in contrast to the world, whose affections are centered selfishly on "the things in the world" (2:15-17; cf. 3:11-18; 2 John 5-7). In fact, the subject matter of this divine word qua commandment is the manner of Jesus' lifestyle (2:6; cf. Jas 2:1; 1 Pet 2:21) in relationship to others (3:16), which was observed by the apostles (1:1-3) and now provides the epistemic basis of what they write down (1:4) for those who are confused by the trauma of the community's recent schism (2:18-27). Simply put, to live as Jesus lived is to obey God, and to obey God's "new commandment," personified by Jesus, is to supply the hard evidence of the believer's purity (3:3; cf. 4:10)—and so of abiding fellowship with God as a member of God's eternal family (3:4-10).

Jude. Once again, Jude defines the terms of "our common salvation" by apostolic traditions (vv. 3, 17, 20), but washes them with Israel's story, which is prompted by constant reference to well-known Old Testament and Jewish "types" of events and persons (vv. 5-16). The resulting conception, then, is Jewish in its sensibility, so that doctrinal error is morally constructed even as eternal life with God is conditioned on one's moral effort (vv. 21-23). Likewise, those who perform "ungodly deeds" will be judged (vv. 14-16) and punished (v. 7), especially those "ungodly persons who pervert the grace of our God by licentious behavior" (v. 4; cf. 8-11). In fact, Jude contends that such behavior constitutes a denial of Jesus (v. 4) and is devoid of the Holy Spirit (v. 19).

While the problem of suffering no longer pertains to the present situation of the implied readers, since they are probably members of established (and middle-class) congregations, their suffering remains prospective of the future situation of those who have departed from the moral rigors of the apostolic tradition for the shameful behavior of those who deny the Lord Jesus (vv. 4, 11-13, 14-16): Jude predicts they will undergo "a punishment of eternal fire" (v. 7). Yet this threat is stated with some irony, since Jude's theology of suffering is due to the severe judgment of "the only God" against "all ungodly for their deeds of ungodliness" and is not precipitated against believers by outsiders (as in 1 Peter) or because of their difficult circumstances (as in James).

While the particular circumstances of Jude are different from those envisaged in James, the structure of the author's recommended response to their eschatological situation is roughly the same: believers are to rescue those communicants who have failed spiritually from "the fire" (v. 23a; cf. Jas 5:19-20) while maintaining their own purity (v. 23b; Jas 1:26-27) by engaging in the religious practices of the "most holy faith" (vv. 20-21; cf. Jas 1:12, 27). To love God is to obey God (v. 22; cf. 1 John 4:16), and to obey God is to have mercy for others (v. 23; cf. Jas 1:22–2:26). What seems increasingly clear from the CE collection, then, is not only a firm resistance against any divorce of right belief from moral behavior, but also an equally firm conviction of the eternal consequence of a Christian faith that is not imbued with right conduct. Sharply put, the faith community's participation in God's coming triumph is conditioned upon its ongoing obedience to God, as God's word is defined by the congregation's authoritative traditions (biblical, Jesus, apostolic).

3. *In obedience to this word, the community must practice "pure and undefiled" behavior as the public mark of friendship with God.* Rather than a code of right conduct, the most important element of the moral universe introduced by James consists primarily of purity practices—again, congregational practices that serve both ethical and eschatological ends. While the interior life of the individual believer is surely an important feature of this same moral universe, the "word of truth" for "religion" that stands "pure and undefiled" before a holy God stipulates that the congregation must resist the moral pollutants of the surrounding "world" (or anti-God) order (1:26) and care for the needy neighbor in accordance with God's "perfect law of liberty" (1:27; 2:1-13). There is a sense in which the rest of the composition articulates more fully what practices a "pure and undefiled" congregation

performs as acceptable to God (cf. 2:24). I note four purity practices in particular with references to other CE, noting only in passing that the centrality of these same purity practices for the church's social identity is confirmed by the book of Acts:

a. The legacy of the Jewish piety personified by legendary James is articulated in the letter as a piety of poverty/powerlessness, of which the Lord Jesus himself is exemplary (2:1), which may occasion suffering that tests the community's devotion to God. In fact, according to James, the hallmark of religious purity is to protect and care for the poor (1:27; 2:2-7), in keeping with the Torah's stipulation (2:8; cf. 1:25). This practice of a community of goods reflects an asceticism—a world-denying ethos—that has replaced the world's preoccupation with material goods with a heartfelt devotion to God (4:1-5:6; 1 John 2:15-17).

b. The concern of a community of goods for a radical social purity extends also to speech (Jas 3:17) as a principal element of good human relations, which identifies a collective interest in healthy speech patterns as a fundamental moral property of Christian existence (1 Pet 3:13-17; 2 Pet 2:3; 1 John 3:18; 3 John 10).

c. The literary *inclusio* of James (1:1 and 5:19-20) delineates a kind of spiritual Diaspora that frames another practice of the community's ethos: a commitment to rescue wayward believers from theological and moral error, not only to preserve doctrinal purity, but also to ensure their end-time salvation (cf. 2 Pet 2; Jude 17-25).

d. The thematic of hospitality in James, not only to strangers as in 3 John but also to marginal members of one's own congregation (1:27; 2:14-17), is central to the CE discourse on Christian community (cf. Jas 2:14-17; 1 Pet 1:22; 4:9-11; 1 John 3:17-20a; 2 John 9-11; 3 John 5-8). What is critical about the development of this theme is that hospitality is never proffered indiscriminate of spiritual status; thus, for example, according to 2 John 9-11 and 3 John 5-8, hospitality is rendered (or not) only to those who have been purified (see 1 John 3:3) by the "doctrine" of the "word of life" (2 John 9-11; cf. 1 John 1:1-4). In this way, then, hospitality toward other believers is an effective means for maintaining a congregation's solidarity against its external threats, but it is also a concrete demonstration of separation from the world.

4. *Theological orthodoxy by itself is inconclusive of friendship with God and is made effective only when embodied in loving works.* This conviction is perhaps the most central to this collection's theological grammar, especially when viewed in canonical context as bringing balance to the church's historic appropriation of the canonical Paul; it is nicely stated by James 2:22-24 in the form of a traditional midrash on Abraham's enduring legacy for Israel's faith: "[Abraham's] faith was completed by [his] works" (2:22), and on this

basis he "was called the friend of God" (2:23). On the basis of this biblical example, James concludes that "a person is justified by works and not by *sola fide*" (2:24). James does not argue that works replace faith; nor is James vague about the more liturgical and formalistic expression of faith that is being criticized, a faith that is incanted as magically productive of divine approval (see 2:14). Faith in one God is presumed by the Jewish author of this letter. Rather, James intends to define a more traditional (or Jewish) variety of Christian faith that articulates an effective pattern of salvation in ethical terms, so that the means of divine approval is not reduced to the facile act of publicly professing orthodox beliefs (Rom 10:9); James demonizes this practice (2:19). His emphasis is clearly posited on the moral act of doing those works prescribed by God's "word of truth" (i.e., purity practices; see above) as the complement of professed faith by which a congregation's devotion to God is both confirmed and recognized. Nonetheless, the moral rigors stipulated by Christian faith, which embodies a manner of life that is contretemps to the world order, are not an afterthought for James but rather the hard evidence demanded for God's final approval (2:12-13): works that confirm faith save, even as faith without works does not. If the trajectory of Pauline tradition into the canonical period evinced the kind of fideism that James opposes, as I think is likely, then the high purchase of this conviction for regulating the performance of the Catholic collection as Scripture must not be underestimated.

Petrine letters. The literary (paraenetic) shape of 1 Peter, which generally prescribes the conduct of a holy people formed by divine mercy rather than by profane society, helps to underwrite Christianity as an ethical religion. The hortatory mood of the Petrine tradition, which equates right conduct with God's will (3:13-17), is justified by two statements that extend and clarify the theological grammar of James. The first is that a community that has been "reborn" to obey God does so in a manner predicated by God's own holiness (1:13-16); that is, God's holiness begets a holy people and stipulates their holy conduct—a purity formula that summarizes the protasis of a prophetic history of Israel (cf. 1:10-12). But 1 Peter's emphasis is on the apodosis of this very history, whereby the prophets anticipated the impartial judgment of Israel's conduct by their holy God. In view is not God's paternal authority over God's people, but God's holy character that renders impartial judgments "according to each one's deeds" (1:17). The spiritual test occasioned by suffering can be failed; it is the eschatological accounting of "one's deeds," whether one measures up to God's standards, that becomes the believer's central motive for "doing right, if it be God's will, than doing wrong" (3:17).

The second statement is christological: namely, that "Christ suffered for you, leaving you an example that you should follow in his steps"

(2:21). Of course, that Messiah Jesus serves God's redemptive purposes as a moral exemplar is a point that James also makes (2:1), but more allusively than does the robust Christology of the Petrine Epistles. Christ's example stipulates not only the manner of obeying God as suffering servant but also the redemptive consequence of those works, both presently (2:12; cf. 3:18-21) and in the future (2 Pet 3:10-11).[51]

Johannine letters. The theological crisis that has generated the succession of "antichrists" from the faith community is the separation of loving works from traditional beliefs about Christ. The "world" of these epistles is ecclesial, divided along the lines of right and wrong beliefs; what the false teachers—the antichrists—believe about Christ and Christian life constitutes the world from which a purified people must separate. Confession of traditional beliefs about Christ, which can be known only through the "anointing" of abiding in him (2:20, 27), is only one necessary piece of evidence that a people are now participating in new life with God; the mere profession of faith is insufficient (cf. 3:18) and requires the assurance that only the "deed" of loving one another provides (3:17-24). Confirmation that a people truly abides in the truth that belongs to God is right conduct: "the person who does right is righteous . . . whoever does not do right is not of God, nor is the one who does not love other believers" (3:7). That is, to maintain fellowship with God requires the more holistic evidence of right beliefs and right behaviors, since one without the other is contrary to the truth and will subvert, therefore, the congregation's assurance of God's eternal love.

5. *Finally, the reward for steadfast obedience to God's word is eternal life with God*. According to James, the believer who perseveres through trial and tribulation with love for God and neighbor intact will be blessed by God with the "crown of [eternal] life" (1:12). The horizon of the "salvation of the soul," which is the destiny of those who obey the divine word (1:21, 22-25), is set in the future when the Lord will come (5:7-9) to restore and complete human existence (1:3-4). At that concluding moment of salvation's history, God promises to grant to those who obey God's word, especially its principal command to love the poor and powerless neighbor (2:8-13), whatever they lack (1:3-4, 9-11). Conversely, those who fail God and disobey God's "law of liberty" will be shown no mercy (2:13) and will be judged and then destroyed (5:4-6), for only God has authority to judge the foolish and bless those who purify themselves and pursue God's will (4:7-12; 5:5-11).

Petrine letters. Following the lead of James, 1 Peter posits that the "salvation of the souls" will be fully disclosed at the future "revelation of Jesus Christ" (1:7, 13; cf. 4:13; 5:4). While the hope of this future salvation is one outcome of faith (1:9) and is made possible by the "precious blood of Christ" (1:19), the authenticity of a faith that saves is validated by the believer who "does right" according to God's will (3:17). The moral force of this contingency is made more urgent because "you may suffer many trials," which will occasion a testing of faith (1:6b-7a). The absence of holy works, which denotes spiritual failure, will therefore not secure a favorable verdict from the Holy Father, whose impartial judgment is not of the orthodoxy of a sinner's faith but of the holiness of a believer's works (1:13-17).

Significantly, the beginning point for 2 Peter's conception of the future is not the resurrection of Jesus but his transfiguration (1:16-17). The precise reason for this shift from 1 Peter's emphasis on the resurrection is not clear to me, although perhaps its tacit appeal to the Petrine tradition (Peter as eyewitness to Jesus' messianic authority) is intended to justify a discredited account of future (the delayed Parousia) promoted by the apostolic tradition (cf. 3:1-4). In this sense, Christ's transfigured "majesty" is the prolepsis of "the power and the parousia of the Lord Jesus Christ" (cf. 1 Pet 5:1), and those false teachers who disbelieve that God is capable of either creation's destruction or its new beginning (3:3-4) or a judgment of believers' moral actions will themselves be discredited.[52]

Johannine letters. When compared to the Fourth Gospel, the final form of the Johannine letters emphasizes the faith community's future reward at the Parousia of Jesus (1 John 2:28), which will be made "complete" even as it is "won" by God's children who abide in "the doctrine of Christ" (2 John 8-9). The particular distinction of this future reward is to see God as God is (1 John 3:2), which is a status of intimacy and revelatory insight allowed only the Son to this point (cf. John 1:18). For this, then, the true believer "hopes" (1 John 3:3a); however, it is a real possibility only for the believer who "makes himself pure just as Christ is pure" (3:3b)—a purity whose character agrees with the moral competence of Jesus (cf. 2:6). A future that can realistically envisage godlikeness (3:2) as its reward is logically heralded by a present lifestyle that embodies the morality of Christ.

Such is the "eschatologic" of the Johannine letters, which underscores the moral competence of those who abide in doctrinal truth: God's nature abides in the believer so that the one reborn of God does not commit sin (1 John 3:4-10), for "everyone who does right is born of God" (2:29), and on this basis "we may have confidence and not shrink from God in shame at [Jesus'] coming" (2:28). Not only will this event disclose the legitimacy of a cruciform community's response to God in following the lead of God's Suffering Servant, but the Lord's future return purposes to disclose God's final triumph over hostile forces that continue to provoke the suffering (and martyrdom?) of God's holy children.

Jude. The doxology of Jude supplies an apt *peroratio* of the entire CE collection, concluding by iterating its central subject matter a final time in eschatological garb: the future prospect of a believer's eternal life with God is motivated by the implicit demand to live presently "without [moral] blemish" and preserved "from falling [into sin and death]," not only by "building yourselves up in your most holy faith . . . [and] keeping yourselves in the love of God" (20-21), but also by the actions of a congregation whose vocation it is to save those immature believers "by snatching them out of the fire" (22-23).

PART III

JAMES

CHAPTER 3

JAMES IN THE MINDS
OF THE RECIPIENTS
A Letter from Jerusalem

Karl-Wilhelm Niebuhr

What did the addressees of the Epistle of James imagine when they received and read this letter from Jerusalem? This rather speculative question could be better based, according to my view, on features of the transmitted text than the question most often discussed in research into historical identification of the author of the letter. Starting with a definition of the letter genre and a reconstruction of the communication from which it originated, I will attempt to draw some contours of the portrait of the implied author of the Epistle of James. I will relate particular features of the text to a view of the origins of the early Jesus movement that seems to be accepted in most parts of current New Testament research, being based itself on observations of the transmitted texts, rather than depending on a systematic reconstruction of the history of early Christianity.

Aside from the personal traits of James in the epistle, I will also draw some lines of a theology of the brother of the Lord that could arise with the recipients of his letter. Unlike the paraenesis of the Epistle of James, which was always in the focus of New Testament research, for a long time the theological contexts of those paraenetic sections were neglected, with the exception of the argumentation in 2:14-16, which mostly was treated from a Pauline point of view. But in this respect, a change can be observed in recent research, which I have delineated recently under a somewhat provocative heading.[1] Some of the considerations brought forward in this article, and in an earlier one,[2] I will try to carry on here.

The Epistle of James in Recent Research

Recent research on the Epistle of James has been characterized by removal of the "Pauline spectacles."[3] The interdiction to look for a coherent argumentation[4] or for the context of the distinct statements of the letter,[5] which was in effect since the famous commentary by Martin Dibelius,[6] has been superseded during the last decades. Today, most exegetes no longer even keep in mind the interdiction of looking for theology in the letter.[7] But removing the Pauline spectacles means more than just realizing some specific theological arguments or even a distinct theology of the letter within the New Testament canon.[8] There is almost a new perspective from which the letter and its author are perceived. And with the new view on James, as is the case with the "new perspective on Paul,"[9] different perspectives and the shifting of lights lead to a new and more exact overall picture, with foreground and background, with sharp contrasts and some more faint structures, with colors and gray areas.[10]

If one did not read the letter from a Pauline perspective, one would hardly get the idea that the argumentation in 2:14-26 is the theological core of the epistle, belonging to the early Christian debate regarding the specific Pauline argument on justification by faith.[11] Rather, one would choose the beginning at the starting point for understanding the text: the text opening, where the author introduces himself to his addressees as "James, slave of God and of the Lord Jesus Christ," saluting them as "the twelve tribes in the dispersion" and approaching them with a paraenetic address regarding their faith, in which they are supposed to persevere (1:1-4). The letter form, particularly the prescript, is characteristically different from, and probably not influenced directly by, the Pauline form.[12] What can be seen about the addressees from the Letter of James is almost without any consonance with what we know about the communities that received the Pauline Letters—and this is quite a lot! In particular, there is not the slightest hint of problems or arguments with regard to Torah observance by Jews and non-Jews in Christian communities. Still, there exists the danger of mirror-reading and introducing Pauline problems into the situation of the addressees of the Letter of James, or even missing the problems there and drawing conclusions from their absence.

The Epistle of James as a Jacobian Letter

Thus, by removing the Pauline spectacles and reading the Epistle of James as what it wants to be, the questions arise of what it means and what are the implications of its authorship by the Lord's brother, which is claimed by the letter for its interpretation (another James is out of the question). The historical solution and verification of the problem of authorship in this respect is a secondary one. Whatever answer one chooses to give, the question of the meaning and the implications of authorship by the Lord's brother arises in any case, and remains independent, to a great extent, of any decision on a historical level.

The perspective of the recipients of the letter will be a guiding principle for my own interpretation of the Epistle of James. As an exegete, I try to identify with the part of the reader or the audience of the letter, rather than with its fictional or real author. However, the part of the reader/audience covers a broader spectrum, beginning with the implied reader of the text, and then continuing with the historical first readers/audience, who can be reconstructed from text-internal and text-external evidence as the twelve tribes in the Dispersion, including those who took responsibility for keeping, spreading, and collecting the letter together with other epistles and, eventually, for its canonization; the readers/audience during the various periods of its reception history and history of interpretation; and the readers/audience of the epistle today in worship, in theological discussions, in church life and church projects, or in their perception of it within the life of the present society.

Therefore, the text-internal relations of the statements of the letter have to be clarified and explained first. The second step, even before reconstructing and interpreting the historical connections, according to my view, should be to indicate and to interpret canon-internal links between statements of the text. This includes cross-references within different writings of the New Testament with regard to the Letter of James—in particular, its relationship to Jesus and to other leading personalities of early Christianity, like Peter in Jerusalem or Paul—and references to writings of the Old Testament. In this regard, one has to take into account that for the author and the addressees of the letter, even the Old Testament writings were not considered either as canon in the later Christian sense or as historical sources in the modern historical-critical sense of biblical exegesis, but were part of the authoritative tradition of Israel in the form of its early Jewish reception, and were used in this way. Therefore, the reference to this early Jewish level of reception history of the Scriptures of Israel proves to be decisive for the question of whether and in what way the Old Testament could be significant for the interpretation of the Letter of James.

Following a method of interpretation that tries to shed light on the process of text reception, one has to address the question of the authorship of the Epistle of James by first asking about the perceived intention of the author in the minds of the recipients. Christian readers/audiences who received a letter from "James, the slave of God and the Lord Jesus Christ," directed to "the twelve tribes in the dispersion" (1:1), would have been unable to perceive anything other than the voice of the brother of their Lord in all words that followed.

There is an abundance of hints to the recipients throughout the letter that underline this direction of interpretation. Not least because of this, it proves to be a "real" letter, even if a formal letter ending is missing. The communication process that can be reconstructed by perceiving the hints to the recipients supports the definition of the genre, which is suggested already by the text opening. By this, some text-internal cornerstones are fixed, and have to be taken into account for any historical reconstruction of authorship, whether assuming a pseudepigraphic author or the historical identification of the implied author with James, the brother of the Lord.

Starting from these text-internal hints to the reception process, the author appears as James, the Lord's brother, according to the letter prescript. This does not only arise from a combination with the prescript of the Epistle of Jude, where the letter-writer introduces himself as "Jude, slave of Jesus Christ, the brother of James" (Jude 1). Rather, it would be inconceivable for the recipients of the letter, within the bounds of early Christianity as we know it, to assume anybody other than the Lord's brother to be the author. Such another James would have to be invented. From the perspective of the letter recipients, all the remaining bearers of this name in the New Testament are out of the question.

James is writing to the twelve tribes in the Dispersion. This implies that the author is writing from Jerusalem after Easter, during the lifetime of James, the Lord's brother (i.e., between 30 and 62 CE).[13] He is addressing members of Israel, the people of God.[14] The recipients are addressed by a letter whose Christian content appears as the unifying basis of the author and the addressees. Such a group we usually call Jewish Christians. There are no perceptible references to contact with non-Jews in the letter; nor are there hints of any discussion on matters such as circumcision, Sabbath observance, or food laws of the Torah. Paul is referred to as little as Peter, John, Barnabas, Mark, or any other personalities whom we know from the New Testament writings, and there are even fewer hints to the specific problems in the Pauline churches that are dealt with so thoroughly in his letters. The letter genre of James is close to Jewish Diaspora letters and differs characteristically from that of the Pauline Letters, as well as from the genre of 1 Peter.[15] The intention of the Letter of James is primarily paraenetic.[16]

Giving priority to the study of those text-internal features should not lead one to overlook or disregard historical questions in the broadest sense. In regard to the Epistle of James, according to my view, those historical questions would best be raised via a text-pragmatically oriented approach and methodology. Studies on the author and the addressees, the traditio-historical contexts, the language, the rhetorical and stylistic means, or the theological peculiarity and aim should be directed toward the question of to what extent they can contribute to explaining the communication process between the author and his audience. The aim of this approach is less oriented in explaining what the author would have meant with his statements than in asking how his statements could have reached the addressees and affected their thoughts and actions. Even references from Hellenistic-Roman, early Jewish, or early Christian literature are relevant only so far as they can help to better explain the communication process between author and addressees.

Traditio-historical links to other early Christian writings and layers of tradition cannot be dismissed completely, of course. They can be commented on only from case to case. Perhaps this may lead to better arguments for an answer to the question of the historical author, as many modern exegetes assume or claim. However, one should not dismiss in this connection the creative power of James, the brother of Jesus, from the outset. This has already proved to be unreliable with regard to the often discussed problem of so-called pre-Pauline traditions. There was, at any rate, a period of almost thirty years at least between the call of James (cf. 1 Cor 15:7) and his martyrdom, during which such traditions originating from Jerusalem could spread. There is plenty of evidence that the Lord's brother not only played a leading role in Jerusalem but also maintained a lively and enduring communication with all important early Christian authorities known to us (Gal 1:18-19; 2:9-12; 1 Cor 16:1; 2 Cor 8–9; Rom 15:14-33; Acts 12:17; 15; 21:18). Comparable constellations in other places of early Christianity, for instance Antioch, are much less testified.

By way of such analysis and interpretation of the communication process, one can also better deal with the problem of the historical place and theological space of the Epistle of James in early Christianity. Regarding this letter in particular, it seems to be necessary time and time again to ask what is specifically Christian in its statements, and in what sense and what characteristic way this New Testament writing refers to the Christ event and gains recognition of it for the church, in its own time as well as in all the generations since. The hermeneutical principle, according to which all theological concepts of the New Testament have to be based on the Christ event and measured by this standard, applies to the Epistle of James just as much as, for instance, to Paul or to the Gospel of John. Measured by this standard, they all stay on an equal level.

The Theological Aim of the Letter

The judgment of the theological value of the Epistle of James should take as its starting point that which it has to say, not that which is missing from it in comparison, for instance, with Paul.[17] Following the structure of the letter, the text opening in 1:2-11/12 is of highest significance, next to the prescript and the letter ending. Here, the letter-writer aims to encourage the addressees in an enduring and active faith in view of its testing (cf. the opening admonition in 1:2-4 with πίστις as its center).

Two topics that are connected to this basic intention and are mentioned already in the letter opening are expounded in more detail, one after the other. 1:5-8 articulates the tension between faith and doubts, in which such an enduring and active faith has to be fulfilled and proved. This topic will be taken up again and developed further in 1:12/13–3:12. 1:9-11 expresses the evaluation of wealth and poverty in the face of the judgment of God as a concrete matter of the life of the community. This will be picked up by the exposition in 3:13–5:6. The letter ending (5:7-20) underlines the paraenetic intention of encouragement to an enduring and active faith.

The section in the beginning of the first exposition, 1:12/13-25, is of fundamental importance theologically. One may ask whether and in what sense this basic theological statement is leading for both of the following expositions of the aim of the letter. For the first, this is the case without any question. There, the idea of faith, which was articulated already in the letter opening (1:3, 6; cf. also 2:1, 5, 14-26; 5:15), is explained more specifically as fulfilling the "word of truth" that was received with the "rebirth" (1:18, 21b). This faith is a gift "from above" (1:17) and holds a soteriological function. It leads to perfection, but only at the last judgment (1:12). It proves to be alive in prayer, endurance, trusting in God, holding out when tested, and most of all in "doing the word" (1:22)—in other words, in a way of life that is entirely, in hearing and doing, devoted to following the perfect law of freedom (1:25). The soteriological aim of the idea of faith in the Epistle of James is underlined in the beginning as well as the end of the letter (1:2-4; 5:19-20), and therefore is of fundamental importance for its interpretation.

The particular nature and aim of the Epistle of James in regard to its addressees cannot be derived from a reconstruction of the conditions of its origin, but may be recognized by specific features of the text. This text has been proven to be a coherent unit in recent research, in opposition to the view of Dibelius, which was dominant for a long period of time. This judgment is accepted as a consensus in most recent studies and does not need further justification here. The theological importance and hermeneutical potential of the letter can best be developed by hearing it and taking it seriously as a message from James, the Lord's brother, to the people of God living in the Dispersion. This insight is accompanied by the recognition that the theological nature and aim of the letter can be derived neither from its relation to Paul and his letters nor from a historical origin hypothetically reconstructed and attributed to any "Christianity of the second or third generation" (which in former times used to be called early Catholicism, horribile dictu). Instead, it should be accepted as a theological position of its own value, derived from the characteristic connection of faith with life. In this context, the letter opening 1:12/13-25, and not the subsection 2:14-26, is of decisive importance. This basic statement of the theology of the letter, seen in connection with the prescript, leaves no doubt that the connection of faith and work to which the author is admonishing his addressees has received its fundamental stimulus from Jesus and is based in the Christ event.

James and His "Big Brother"

The understanding of faith in the Epistle of James is non-Pauline in the best sense of the word, as long as it is compared with Paul's statements on faith in connection with justification. Nevertheless, the idea of faith in James is determinately a Christian idea as long as it has its basis in the Christ event, finds its shape in the orientation to the word of God, and arrives at its end with the eschatological return of the resurrected Christ. This idea of faith also founds the basis for the argumentation in 2:14-26 regarding the question of faith and works, which looks like a digression in its context. I myself, as several other recent commentators, do not find in this passage any reference to the Pauline doctrine of justification by faith as we know it from his letters. This does not exclude any relationship between James and Paul himself, particularly since one has to take into account their personal encounters with each other (cf. Gal 1:19; 2:6-9), all the more so as even Jesus comes into play with reference to the issue of the connection between faith and works.

The relationship between James and Jesus is not concerned primarily, or at least not only, with historical or traditio-historical reconstruction, but should be viewed from a reception-historical perspective first. There is no question that the addressees of the Epistle of James knew about Jesus and that he constituted the core of their faith. We do not know exactly what they knew about him, but it would be unwise to leave aside completely the relationship between James and Jesus when we try to understand the reception of the letter. For the Epistle of James, as for all New Testament writings, the Easter event functions as the starting point of understanding. Only after Easter can James appear as "slave of the Lord Jesus Christ" in the minds of the readers of his letter, whether they knew or not what Paul was writing about him in 1 Corinthians 15:7 or the author of Acts in Act 1:14, let alone what we can read today in Mark 3:20-21 and 31-35 or 6:3-4. In asking about any substantial relationship between the Epistle of James and Jesus, either thematically or traditio-historically, one always has to take into account the Easter perspective of the letter and its author, even though the testimony of the Easter event does not play any important part in it explicitly. Only from the conditions of the communication process between the author and the addressees does there follow cogently the transformation of all traditions and all knowledge about Jesus, with the belief in the resurrection of Christ as the precondition for understanding the Letter of James.

On this basis, far more sensible conclusions can be drawn regarding the relationship between James and Jesus as meaningful for the exegesis than those reached only by attempts to reconstruct traditio-historical links between the Letter of James and the synoptic Jesus tradition. Therefore, according to my view, the question of whether the understanding and the specific function of the Torah with regard to faith in James is connected in some way to the understanding of the Torah with Jesus could be one of the central issues of the exegesis of the letter. Comparing their views to early Jewish Torah paraenesis, with its sapiential coloring and its social orientation, could shed more light on both of them, and could even perhaps uncover a hidden missing link.[18]

The idea of faith in the Epistle of James can be related more productively to the idea of faith with Jesus, especially if removed from a specifically Pauline understanding of faith, as long as the transformations by the Easter event are taken into account. The same holds true for the importance of Israel as part of the system of convictions of Jesus as well as of the Epistle of James. In both of them, the people of God play an implicit rather than an explicit part; but, at the same time, belong to the fundamental elements of each one's semantic universe.

Finally, the eschatology of the Epistle of James could also be studied and interpreted from the perspective of a transformation of Jesus' preaching of the last days. All these theological issues to be raised in the exegesis of the Epistle of James do not exclude, of course, but rather include traditio-historical and historical analyses. However, what matters is the configuration of questions and methods in the process of exegesis. What matters is to show and to explain how the letter can be seen as a piece of evidence for Jesus, stemming from one of his closest relatives.

The Epistle of James in Its Canonical Context

Not only the first readers of the Epistle of James are to be understood as its readers, in the sense of an interpretation that is focused on the reception process and its theological value. The only access we have to those first readers is via the text of the letter. That they did not remain the only readers is proved by the history of its transmission and influence. For all later generations of readers, as far as we know anything about them, the connection was decisive, not only with Jesus himself, but also with further references to him that we can find in the New Testament.

As part of the New Testament canon, the Epistle of James belongs to the collection of Catholic Epistles (CE) and is connected by the book of Acts to the four gospels, as well as to the collection of the Pauline Epistles.[19] These two letter collections, framed by the collection of four gospels (*tetraeuangelion*) together with the book of Acts in the beginning and by the book of Revelation at the end, result in a *heilsgeschichtliche* structure of the whole canon. The period of Jesus as the fundamental period for the church is followed by the period of the apostles, which is based in the Easter belief and leads to the future return of the resurrected Christ. The Epistle of James corresponds as a microstructure to this macrostructure of the canon; the readers of the canon may notice from the name of its author an implicit hint at the Jesus period, although this connection is not expressed explicitly in the letter. The aims of the letter corpus presuppose the Easter belief of the churches and their Christian life, which is based in this belief. The letter articulates the voice of one of the most authoritative apostles, whom the readers of the canon are familiar with by what they know about him from the book of Acts in particular, but also, for instance, from the Pauline Letters and the Gospels. The eschatological viewpoint of the canon, with its prospect to the coming of Jesus (cf. Rev 22:20), can be rediscovered by its readers even in the Epistle of James (cf. 5:7-8).

Reading the New Testament in its canonical shape reveals a certain continuity of personalities between the different parts of the canon and the different periods of salvation history represented by them. Through the identification by name of the authors of the CE, which have been an obvious identification since the Epistles' collection as part of the canon at the latest, all information about the authors from the Gospels and Acts appears as guidelines for reading their letters.

One of Acts' decisive guidelines that arises for the readers of the canon is the apostles' community with each other. The model of the community between the apostles is drawn in Acts 15 by means of an example. Here, Peter and James appear as spokesmen of the Jerusalem church when they meet Paul and Barnabas as emissaries from the church of Antioch. Both pairs of spokesmen are portrayed as being in agreement with each other, as well as against differing positions. The fundamental agreement of the apostles, in spite of varying attitudes about and strategies of mission, building up churches, or expressing belief, is the precondition for introducing and arranging their writings into the canon, as well as for their reception.

Even the relationship between Peter, Paul, and James, as it appears in the Letter to the Galatians, has to be taken into account if one reads the Epistle of James from a canonical perspective. The events that are reported in Galatians 2:1-10 cannot be understood by the readers of the canon without reference to what they know from Acts 15. This means that they will inevitably identify the "false apostles" who invaded the consultations in Jerusalem (Gal 2:4) with the Pharisaic opponents from Acts 15:5. And with regard to the "people from James," according to Galatians 2:12, they will wonder, as we still do today, whether the same James whom they know from his letter would have really supported or even launched their position in Antioch. In particular, they would ask the question that, according to my view, came neither to the mind of the author of the Letter of James nor to those of its first readers, namely: how does what James is writing regarding faith and works relate to what Paul is saying with the same words? They probably would have found an answer similar to that of the church fathers, following the guidelines of the canon and its model of the fundamental agreement and community between the apostles, according to whom Paul is dealing with the "works of the Law" in connection with the justification by faith, whereas James is referring to works by which the faith received with baptism has to be fulfilled in the life of the Christians.

Reception History of the Epistle of James

If the Epistle of James is read as a letter from James, the Lord's brother, this should be reflected to some extent in its history of reception. This may be difficult to prove in the face of the rather sparse sources. There are no references at all to the letter's effects on its first readers, who, according to my view, would be Jewish Christian communities before 70 CE without contact with any Gentile Christian groups. The first addressees disappeared very soon, at least what concerns their traces in the sources. Regarding the evidence from the church fathers, the lack of any sensitivity to the contradictions between James and Paul is striking from a modern point of view. Does this cohere with some unreadiness, in a milieu influenced by the Pauline strand of Christianity, to accept the idea that the great apostle (i.e., Paul) could have had something against a brother of Jesus, particularly since the book of Acts offered the right way to read the letters of both of them? During the Middle Ages, there were stronger concerns regarding a physical son of Mary than there were about the authority of a relative of Jesus as letter-writer. A potential solution could be that James, the son of Alphaeus, in this way became a member of the Holy Family.[20]

Although there is some early evidence of doubts regarding the authorship of the Lord's brother, this did not hinder the acceptance of the letter as part of the canon or its importance as such. The opposite assumption, that the rather late attestation and use of the Epistle of James in the church was related to some uncertainty regarding its authorship, cannot be testified, as far as I can see, from the ancient sources. Even its supposed anti-Pauline orientation obviously did not jeopardize its canonization and was not at all perceived as such, according to the sources, not even by Augustine. Rather, the reasons for some concerns about the canonization of the Epistle of James were related, according to my view, to a somewhat one-sided preference for all material coming from Paul, Peter, or John, or what looked like this at least. In this context, it would be hard to find some interest for a nonpolemic, "purely" Jewish Christian letter. The milieu in which it once originated had lost any importance in the period of, and for the forces that were responsible for, the canonization process.

The theologically substantiated criticism of the Epistle of James expressed by Martin Luther led him at the same time to a degradation of its canonical value, together with the Epistle of Jude, the Epistle to the Hebrews, and the book of Revelation. This shows what high importance Luther attributed to the canon for the reception history. Nevertheless, this "private" canon of Luther had no chance of being accepted in the long run, and the reason for this was not so much the opposite decision regarding the canon of the Holy Scripture by the Council of Trent, but rather the uninterrupted use of these New Testament writings in worship, even in the churches of the Reformation, and their never-reduced importance with regard to their authoritative meaning. The canon took the victory.

In recent research, the Epistle of James seems to be of no importance for the Jesus quest. Investigations are usually made only in Galilee. Why not in Jerusalem too? The brother of Jesus, perhaps, could also provide some information. He would do it his way, certainly, and he would do it from a certain distance, only indirectly, only to be deduced later from what he wanted to say to the addressees of his letter in the Dispersion. Nevertheless, his reference to his "big brother" cannot be overlooked, even though he does not call him that.

James Today

Some aspects that are pointed to in the Epistle of James look to be of relevance to the present situation, so much that it could be rather dangerous to apply them unconsidered. With others, the present relevance seems to be hidden, but waiting to be uncovered. How to make audible the particular voice of James from the New Testament today seems to be an open question for the exegete. The same holds true for the question of where readers can be found for this letter and how they would understand it. This James may hardly look like a holder of theological principles as raised in some controversial ecumenical debates of today. Even Paul, who frequently appears as his counterpart in those debates, no longer resembles the Paul with whom exegetes think they have become more familiar with from a new perspective. A new perspective on James may find it even harder to gain acceptance in those debates than did the new perspective on Paul. However, I entertain the hope that the ecumenical potential of the New Testament (and Old Testament) canon may be detected and introduced into the talks and debates between churches.

What about the ideal reader of the Epistle of James in today's churches? Its strong concern for personal relationships and responsibilities in a community without any fixed forms or institutions for ministry could be attractive to Christian congregations today. Trustfulness in dealing with words, in particular, is of high value even today, as is the idea of wholeness. On the other hand, the strict boundary delineating the non-Christian environment gives offense to many modern Christians. And *wisdom* calls into mind quite different ideas for many people today, even in Christian circles, than a collection of devote admonitions and solid commandments. At any rate, the Epistle of James does not look very esoteric.

But in one sense the letter is very clear: with regard to poverty and richness. Whichever way one interprets the figure of the rich in the assembly (cf. 2:2-3) or the addressees of the prophetic condemnation (cf. 5:1-6), one has to take seriously the orientation of all statements of the letter toward a social ethos based on the Bible that entrusts the needy to the special care and mercy not only of God, but also of the congregation (cf. 1:9-11; 2:5-6, 15-16). From this orientation, one may not be able to derive a social program for perfect justice in society. However, this does not tone down the demand for a social compensation, but underpins it with special regard for the next neighbor.

Chapter 4

JAMES AND THE JESUS TRADITION
Some Theological Reflections and Implications

Patrick J. Hartin

Through a conscious use of the art of rhetoric, the Letter of James aims at persuading its hearers/readers to embrace and remain true to a way of life that provides an identity that is distinct from the wider society. The ethical instructions provide a framework enabling the individual and the community to live in harmonious relationship with one another and with God. This paper examines the roots of this ethical instruction within the traditions and thought of Jesus. It will be argued that the thought of this letter is in harmony with Jesus' own reassessment of Judaism. Through this letter, the reader comes into close contact with Jesus' message, his central vision,[1] and the heritage of Judaism. In particular, significant theological implications will emerge from this twofold relationship demonstrated in James,[2] namely from its relationship to Jesus' vision and his traditions on the one hand, and its roots within the world of Judaism and Jesus' reassessment of Judaism on the other hand.

James' Use of the Jesus Tradition

Scholarship on the Letter of James continues to remain divided on many issues, especially those related to date, authorship, or origin. Some scholars view the letter as an early writing from James, the brother of the Lord, or at least attributed to him by a scribe who communicates James' message and teaching to his readers. Others argue that James is a late writing coming from the end of the first or beginning of the second century.[3] One's position on these matters is important because it affects, among other things, the interpretation of the evidence regarding James' relationship to the Jesus tradition. As Richard Bauckham has argued in another context, the first stage in a method for establishing dependence of one text on another must be to establish the place and dates of origin.[4] My understanding of the Letter of James is that it is an early writing, probably coming from a scribe handing down James' teaching and vision in the late 60s, and written to Christian Jews outside Palestine.[5]

While many scholars agree that James reflects Jesus' traditions in varying degrees, the question still remains, can we identify those traditions more precisely?[6] Despite criticism to the contrary, I still remain convinced that James is using traditions of Jesus' sayings as they are reflected in the Q source and the community of Matthew. My conviction is based upon the following observations:[7]

- Studies that have been undertaken in recent times on the ancient art of rhetoric show that ancient writers tended to use their sources as a way of performing their source anew, much in the manner in which James is seen to handle his sources.[8]

- There is a lack of agreement on what actually constitutes an allusion or a parallel. No one is arguing that James is quoting a Jesus saying verbatim. The claim is that James does have a saying in mind, and the hearer/reader would be reminded of this saying. I endorse the perspective of Peter Davids, who defines an allusion as "a paraphrastic use of phrases or ideas from a logion, with the probable intent of reminding the reader of it."[9] This means that James offers a paraphrase of a saying of Jesus within the tradition. Robert Alter gives further insight into the concept of allusion when he defines it as "the evocation in one text of an antecedent . . . text."[10]

- James' use of the Jesus tradition is analogous to his usage of his sacred writings, or more appropriately, the Septuagint. While James does quote the Septuagint directly on a few occasions,[11] he more often makes allusions to scriptural phrases and sayings by reformulating them and adapting them to his own world and argument.

- The closest correspondence between James and the Jesus tradition is that of the taking of oaths in James 5:12 and Matthew 5:33-37, which is identified as belonging to Matthew's special tradition.[12]

An examination of the allusions that have been identified between James and the synoptic tradition shows that these allusions are found throughout the letter and are not simply confined to one part.[13] Some years ago, Davids gave attention to the use of the Jesus tradition in the letter, and contended that "each major paragraph in the epistle contains one or more allusion, and further analysis would demonstrate that in every paragraph the allusion(s) support the main point.[14] This was an important observation. An examination of two passages will illustrate this rhetorical use that James makes of the Jesus tradition and its implications.

Antithesis between the Rich and the Lowly (Jas 1:9-11)

This passage contrasts the lowly and the rich. Each is given reason to boast: the lowly rejoice in the conviction of being raised up, while the rich rejoice in humiliation. The poor are exhorted to rejoice in the reversal of their situation now within the Christian community, where they are raised up to experience equality with others and a special relationship with God. The rich, on the other hand, rejoice because in this new community they are honored, not because of their wealth or status, but because they are simply part of this community.[15]

This contrast of exaltation/humiliation is reminiscent of the Jesus saying, "For all who exalt themselves will be humbled, and those who humble themselves will be exalted" (Q 14:11 [Luke 14:11/Matt 23:12]; Luke 18:14). Noteworthy here is James' rhetorical use of this saying. In these verses (1:9-11), James introduces for the first time what will become a central focus in his letter, namely the attitude toward poverty and riches (Jas 2:1-13; 5:1-6). James sets forth his basic premise that a reversal of fortunes occurs within the community of those who embrace Jesus' message. To illustrate this, James reaches back into the Jesus tradition and applies this Jesus saying to his hearers/readers. James composes it in his own way. He draws out the contrast between the lowly and the rich and shows how for each, the reversal of situations within the community can be a reason for rejoicing.

To strengthen his argument, James makes rhetorical usage of another allusion, this time to Scriptures:

The grass withers, the flower fades,
when the breath of the LORD blows upon it;
surely the people are grass.
The grass withers, the flower fades:
but the word of our God will stand forever. (Isa 40:7-8)

James does not quote this Isaian text directly here, but the imagery of grass withering in the heat of the day is reminiscent of the images of Isaiah 40:7-8. James' allusion to this Isaian text is instructive. One notes the freedom that he has used in accommodating it to his new context.[16] This provides a good illustration of the same freedom that James uses, I believe, in applying the sayings of Jesus as well to a new context and argument.

Studies on the ancient art of rhetoric in application to the New Testament help to shed light on James' method of using both the Septuagint as well as the sayings of Jesus. In a recent monograph, Wesley Hiram Wachob investigates the *progymnasmata* and the ancient rhetorical handbooks whereby students were taught the art of rhetorical argumentation and applies this to the Letter of James. His analysis argues that "the artful activation of an antecedent text was a common ploy in rendering a given proposal more readily acceptable to an audience."[17] He shows that the argument is built upon a previous text that is activated in its own way. The writer does not simply quote this previous text, but has the freedom to weave it into his own text in whatever way suits his purpose.

In an important study, Vernon Robbins shows that ancient writers and in particular the Synoptic Gospels "continually recast the material by adding to it, subtracting from it, rearranging it, and rewording it."[18] The rhetorical purpose of the text was aimed at getting the hearer/reader to think and to act in a particular way. The aim was not simply to copy the existing text or source. Instead, it was to actualize the text or the source in such a way that it became a new performance in the hands of the writer, by which he made it conform to his new rhetorical function. Robbins expresses this in a very succinct way when he says:

> In previous research, verbal similarities among written versions of stories and sayings regularly have been discussed in terms of "dependence" on written or oral sources. This terminology emerges from a presupposition that written performance of the material was guided by copying an oral or written antecedent. This language and this perception impose goals and procedures on the writers which are inaccurate, since, even if the writer recently had heard or was looking at a version of the story, the version existed in the eye, ear, and mind of the writer as a "recitation" that should be performed anew rather than a verbal text that should be copied verbatim.[19]

This entails looking at the relationship between ancient texts in a different way. The approach of source criticism views the writer as copying the text or source. This was not necessarily always the case. Writers saw their task as performing their source in new ways in order to persuade their hearers/readers to act or think in a particular way.

This approach, referred to as recitation composition[20] gives insight into what the writer of the Letter of James endeavored to do. In this particular context, his task was to persuade his readers/hearers about the countercultural reversal of roles within the community of Jesus' followers. He used the sources to speak to this context, but he recited them in his own way, using his own voice. We see how clearly he did this with the Isaian text, which becomes an example for the way in which he dealt with the sayings of Jesus.

Wiard Popkes endeavors to explain the freedom James demonstrates with his use of his sources by arguing that James did not have access to the original text, but instead was using "second-hand material."[21] While such an explanation is possible, it fails to fully appreciate the rhetorical culture of these documents, as I have indicated above. One needs to make a shift from viewing the world of New Testament documents as part of a scribal culture to seeing it as part of a rhetorical culture.[22] The primary goal of a scribal culture would be to copy the sources. If, however, the documents emerged from what is termed a rhetorical culture, then the concern would be different. They would not aim at transmitting the source verbatim, but at performing the source in new ways, with a freedom to speak to the new exigencies of the readers/hearers to whom they are addressed.

Partiality and Distinctions between Rich and Poor (Jas 2:1-13)

This passage is a well-ordered unity that unfolds systematically. The opening command expresses its main concern: do not discriminate, because it runs counter to the faith of "our glorious Lord Jesus Christ" (2:1). As a hypothetical example of discrimination,[23] James identifies distinctions made between rich and poor. The basic thought on which the example hinges is contained in 2:5: "Has not God chosen the poor in the world to be rich in faith and to be heirs of the kingdom that he has promised to those who love him?" Would not a hearer/reader of this text be reminded of the Jesus saying, "Blessed are the poor in spirit, for theirs is the kingdom of heaven" (Matt 5:3) / "Blessed are you who are poor, for yours is the kingdom of God" (Luke 6:20)? There are a number of features common to James and this Q beatitude, the basis for the beatitude in both Matthew and Luke. They both identify the poor, and in both the promise of the kingdom is made to those who are poor. James takes this Jesus saying and develops it more fully, creating a clear antithesis between the poor and the rich, the world and the kingdom:

Poor in the eyes of the *world*
rich in faith and heirs of the *kingdom*. (emphasis mine)

James makes the Q beatitude his own by composing it in his own way as he adapts it to his own argument and message.

When James promises that the poor will "become heirs of the kingdom" (Jas 2:5), he uses the term κληρονόμους. This is noteworthy in that in Matthew's third beatitude, which parallels this opening beatitude, the verb κληρονομήσουσιν is used: μακάριοι οἱ πραεῖς, ὅτι αὐτοὶ κληρονομήσουσιν τὴν γῆν (Matt 5:5). I would suggest that when James is making his argument, he is using both beatitudes from the Matthean tradition. His argument is being influenced by the language of the beatitudes, especially as found in the Matthean tradition.

To give further weight to his teaching, James alludes to Leviticus 19:18c: "You shall love your neighbor as yourself." In using the text from Leviticus, James limits himself to the third clause of the verse, for that is what interests him in his argument. Again, the rhetorical culture influences James here. He does not copy the text of Leviticus verbatim. Instead, using the approach of recitation composition, he composes a new text with a persuasive force for his community. As Wachob comments when examining James' use of Leviticus, "Technically speaking, then, James 2:8 is an 'abbreviation' . . . of Leviticus 19:18; and the Jamesian performance of the love-commandment is properly a rhetorical 'recitation' . . . of an ancient authority."[24]

In continuing his argument, James draws on the teaching of Jesus as it appears in Matthew's tradition of the Sermon on the Mount. He stresses the obligation to keep the whole law, which is reminiscent of Matthew 5:17-19:

> Therefore, whoever breaks one of the least of these commandments, and teaches others to do the same, will be called least in the kingdom of heaven; but whoever does them and teaches them will be called great in the kingdom of heaven.

James' line of reasoning continues with illustrations similar to those appearing in Matthew's tradition of the Sermon. Just as Matthew 5:21-30 refers to the illustrations of adultery and murder as examples of how the believer is to uphold the whole law, so James uses the same two examples to emphasize the need to keep the law in its entirety. Finally, the section concludes with a saying reminiscent of Jesus' teaching on the quality of mercy: "For judgment will be without mercy to anyone who has shown no mercy: mercy triumphs over judgment" (Jas 2:13). Matthew's Sermon on the Mount has another beatitude that stresses the quality of mercy: "Blessed are the merciful, for they will receive mercy" (Matt 5:7).

This passage shows well James' rhetorical usage of, on the one hand, the sayings of Jesus as seen in Matthew's tradition of the Sermon, and on the other hand the saying found in Leviticus 19:18c.[25] Understood within this context of a rhetorical culture, James' intent was to perform these sayings with a freedom that enabled him to express them in new ways. He aimed at persuading his hearers how to act so that their community could maintain an identity distinct from the world around them. The biblical Torah continued to function for James' community, and James' intent was to show how it provided the boundary markers for his hearers/readers. Wachob's monograph (*The Voice of Jesus in the Social Rhetoric of James*) provides an insightful examination of this passage (Jas 2:11-13). His argument takes seriously the rhetorical culture out of which the letter emerged, and shows James' "artful performance" of Jesus' sayings with the rhetorical function of showing his community how to appropriate Jesus' fulfillment of the Torah.[26]

James used Jesus' sayings rhetorically to persuade his hearers/readers to put their faith into action in relevant social situations. The hearers/readers would surely have been reminded of Jesus' voice behind this advice, just as they would be reminded of the voice of the Scripture allusions on which James also built. However, James made that voice his own; these are the sayings and advice of "James, a servant of God and the Lord Jesus Christ" to his community.

James and the Heritage of Judaism

The Letter of James is rooted in the heritage of Judaism. Both Jesus and James continued to define themselves in relation to their Jewish heritage. I shall examine two aspects here in order to draw out the implications, since they illustrate the closeness of James' ethical vision to that of Jesus. While attention could be given to many other aspects, I shall confine myself to the aspects of purity and the restoration of the twelve tribes.

Purity and Perfection in the Letter of James

Martin Dibelius' commentary on James in 1921 and his understanding of the letter held sway over scholarship on James to a large extent for well over half a century.[27] The essence of his approach viewed James as a "book of popular slogans,"[28] which he designated as *paraenesis*. "By paraenesis we mean a text which strings together admonitions of general ethical content."[29] Consequently, no unifying theme was seen to hold the letter together. Instead, according to Dibelius, the letter consisted of a number of individual passages that were simply strung together by means of catchwords.[30] Scholars tended to embrace this approach almost uncritically.

In the past two decades, this approach has been seriously challenged, and many scholars have attempted to identify various themes that tend to give the writing a unity. The theme of wholeness or perfection is one such theme that a number of scholars have indicated, as John H. Elliott has noted.[31] What is even more noteworthy is that this identification has been reached independently.[32]

The use of the Greek adjective τέλειος (perfect) and its cognates occurs some seven times throughout this short writing.[33] Proportionately, its use is more frequent than in any other New Testament writing. I have examined the background of this word τέλειος in the Hebrew Scriptures and more especially in the Septuagint in *A Spirituality of Perfection*.[34] In the Septuagint, this adjective τέλειος (as well as the adjective ἄμωμος) is frequently used to translate the Hebrew word *tamim*.[35] The origin of the use of this concept is clearly that of the cult and the sacrificial worship of Israel. In the context of the cult, τέλειος referred to an animal suitable for sacrifice. Cultic laws defined that only "unblemished" (τέλειος) animals could be offered in sacrifice. For example: "Your lamb shall be without blemish [τέλειος], a year-old male" (Exod 12:5). Only what was whole or complete could be offered to God. Here appears the essence of the concept of perfection: a being that conforms to its original makeup, its wholeness or completeness.

This concept was analogously applied to other dimensions of life as well. For example, "Noah was a righteous man, blameless [τέλειος] in his generation" (Gen 6:9). The conceptual meaning of τέλειος, as it emerges from the different contexts in the Septuagint, gives expression to three essential dimensions:

1. The idea of wholeness or completeness, whereby a being remains true to its original constitution.

2. The giving of oneself to God wholeheartedly and unconditionally, which includes a relationship between God and God's people. Above all, it rejects idolatry or the worship of other gods. It is akin to the adjective *saddiq*. If the person were grounded in this relationship, she or he would be seen as whole, perfect. Perfection includes a community relationship, not just an individual dimension.

3. The wholehearted dedication to the Lord that is demonstrated above all in obedience to God's will. This in turn includes a life led in obedience to the Torah, the laws of the Lord. The Hebrew phrase "walking with God" (Gen 5:22, 24; 6:9; Mic 6:8; Mal 2:6) calls for moral obedience, in which faith and works are intrinsically united.[36]

This threefold understanding of the conceptual meaning of τέλειος helps to appreciate James' usage of this adjective τέλειος throughout his letter.

On the individual and community levels, believers are called to endure in the midst of the testing of their faith (1:2-4). Faith becomes whole or complete through endurance in times of trials. The second use of the term τέλειος in this verse, "so that you may be mature [τέλειος] and complete, lacking in nothing" (1:4), refers directly to believers who remain true to their faith in the midst of these trials. They are that "perfect work," as Martin Dibelius expresses it.[37] They are perfect and complete, as unblemished offerings in the Israelite cult are offered to the Lord. They are people whose faith is undivided and who conform to their original constitution as God intended. The cultic dimension continues in 1:18. In a cosmic context, believers hold a special place in God's plan of creation; they are "the first fruits of God's creatures" (1:18). This cultic image is a reminder of Israel's offering of the first fruits of their fields, flocks, and animals to God. Against this background, the hearers/readers as the "twelve tribes in the Dispersion" (1:1) are the first of God's creatures to begin the reconstitution of God's people.[38]

For James, the concept of τέλειος means embracing one's identity as an individual and as a member of a community with access to God. Perfection is a search for wholeness as an individual and as a community in relationship to the one God, who guides them through the Torah. James' community is one that shares common bonds and common values. The values of the individual are the values of the community. The advice that James offers in the course of his instructions in the letter has as its rhetorical aim the socialization of a community of believers. They take their values from their own community, not from the wider society.

In expressing his understanding of perfection as wholeness and integrity, James relies upon the fundamental notions of purity and holiness within his society, notions that he owes to his Jewish heritage. The social-scientific study of Christian origins has brought increased understanding and awareness, particularly in recent times, of the role that cultic, moral, and social purity rules played in Second Temple Judaism and the world of early Christianity.[39]

These purity rules provided a framework whereby life (whether personal or community) was structured in order to promote right relationships between the individual, the community, and God. Bruce Malina defines purity rules succinctly when he writes:

> If purity rules are to facilitate access to God, and if the God to whom one wants access has human welfare as the main priority in the divine will for the chosen people, it follows that proper interpretation of purity rules must derive from giving primary consideration to relationships with one's fellows. This is what

righteousness is about. For righteousness means proper inter-personal relationships with all those in one's society, between God and covenanted human beings and between human beings and their fellow beings.[40]

Purity rules are designed to indicate how to have and maintain access to God. They set the individual and the community off from the wider society. In effect, they identify those who have access to God, who act in a particular way, as the holy ones—those who belong to the sphere of the sacred. Those who do not act in this way are the outsiders, who belong to the world of the profane.

James describes the Torah as the "perfect law" (1:25). Here the concepts of purity and perfection come together. The law spells out the boundaries that the believing community is to observe in order to main-tain access to God and to keep their wholeness. "To be holy, according to James, is to be whole—with respect to personal integrity, communal solidarity, and religious commitment."[41]

James builds his advice around the contrasts of two ways of life: one led in friendship with God, the other in friendship with the world (4:4). These two ways of life are further demarcated by the contrast between a way of life that is informed by the values of wholeness, purity, and har-mony, and one that is incomplete, divided, and polluted. This contrast emerges most clearly in the distinction that James paints between the two types of wisdom: from above and from below (3:13-18). The very first quality that James identifies regarding the wisdom from above is that it is "pure" (3:17). This pure wisdom has come down from above (3:17), as opposed to the wisdom from the earth, which is "devilish" (3:15). This provides the backdrop for the search for wholeness and purity, which comes from having access to God and being in a wholehearted relation-ship with God. When one is separated from this source of wholeness and holiness, one is divided like a wave of the sea that is tossed about in the wind (1:6).

Fidelity to the way of life that remains true to the whole law embraces a threefold bond: the personal, the communal, and the divine. Wholeness and holiness on all levels are experienced when the individual is in right relations with the community and with God: "Draw near to God, and he will draw near to you. Cleanse your hands, you sinners, and purify your hearts, you double-minded" (4:8). James' definition of religion in 1:27 captures very beautifully the essence of the purity laws. Keeping oneself undefiled from the world implies showing that one has kept oneself away from the alien values of society, while at the same time remaining true to the values that belong to the community of "the twelve tribes in the

Dispersion." These values are captured above all in a concern for the poor, as exemplified by the roles of widows and orphans.

The rhetorical function of the instructional advice in the Letter of James is to define the boundaries of the community.[42] Purity rules function within the Letter of James in exactly the same way that they functioned within the world of Second Temple Judaism. The distinguishing feature, however, is that for the Letter of James, the temple no longer occupies prominence as the area of sacred space. A focus on the purity rules of a ritual and dietary nature is replaced with a focus upon the moral laws of maintaining a relationship with and access to God.

This shift of emphasis is also clearly seen in Jesus' vision that emerges from the Gospels. Jesus' vision of purity focuses on moral concerns related to people, rather than to places and things such as the temple.[43] His reversal on the role of the Sabbath immortalizes this approach: "The Sabbath is made for humankind, and not humankind for the Sabbath" (Mark 2:27). Here Jesus replaces concern for purity rules regarding the Sabbath with a concern for the welfare of human beings. His vision embraces an Israel that has been restored and is in conformity with God's will. He replaces the temple with table fellowship.[44]

James' concern, as with Jesus, rests on the eschatological Israel ("the twelve tribes in the Dispersion," 1:1). James' hearers/readers are Jews who believe in Jesus. But this belief "does not lead them away from Judaism."[45] James is fully in line with the preaching of Jesus. Central to Jesus' preaching is the law of love. James embraces this same understanding when he identifies the law, the Torah, as "the royal law, according to the scripture, 'You shall love your neighbor as yourself'" (2:8). James sees the law as fulfilled in the law of love, in the way Jesus interpreted this law. As with Jesus, James' focus is on moral instruction rather than ritual or dietary concerns. This demonstrates how close James remains to the way of seeing things as Jesus did.

Restoration of the Twelve Tribes

A further area where the Letter of James remains rooted in Jesus' vision occurs in Jesus' vision of the restoration of the twelve-tribe kingdom.

James 1:1 is one of the most variously interpreted verses of the whole letter.[46] I have argued elsewhere that this expression should be read against the background of Israel's hope for a restored twelve-tribe kingdom.[47] When the nation was destroyed, first by the Assyrians in 721 BCE and then by the Babylonians in 587 BCE, the hope emerged that God would at some stage in the future reconstitute the twelve-tribe kingdom.[48] This hope was based on God's fidelity to promises made in the past. Since God had promised Abraham that the land given to him and his descendants would last in perpetuity, the hope grew that God would reconstitute this twelve-tribe kingdom. This hope was further strengthened by Nathan's promise to King David: "Your house and your kingdom shall be made sure forever before me; your throne shall be established forever" (2 Sam 7:16). The prophets in particular gave strength and impetus to this hope: "Thus says the Lord God: I will take the people of Israel from the nations among which they have gone, and will gather them from every quarter, and bring them to their own land. I will make them one nation in the land" (Ezek 37:21-22).[49]

The events surrounding Rome's occupation of Palestine from 63 BCE onward increased the people's longing for a restoration of their nation. This can be seen in a number of writings emanating from this time.[50]

The traditions behind the Gospel of Matthew give expression to this restoration hope and present Jesus as conducting a ministry whose chief aim was to reconstitute this twelve-tribe kingdom. Matthew 10:6 is most revealing in this context. When sending out the Twelve, Jesus instructs them, "Go nowhere among the Gentiles, and enter no town of the Samaritans, but go rather to the lost sheep of the house of Israel."[51] The Gospel of Matthew shows that while it endorses a mission and outreach to the Gentiles, the traditions on which the Gospel depends show Jesus' mission as being confined to the people of Israel, and one that envisages the restoration of the twelve-tribe kingdom. Jesus' task is envisaged as gathering together the lost tribes of Israel ("I was sent only to the lost sheep of the house of Israel," Matt 15:24). That is not only Jesus' task; he also extends that task to his disciples, and they share in the same outreach and vision (Matt 10:6).

The fulfillment of this outreach and ingathering is reserved for the end of time. The twelve apostles are given the responsibility of judging the twelve tribes: "And I confer on you, just as my Father has conferred on me, a kingdom, so that you may eat and drink at my table in my kingdom, and you will sit on thrones judging the twelve tribes of Israel" (Q 22:29-30 [Luke 22:29-30/Matt 19:28-29]). The ministry of the twelve disciples is seen to continue to the end of time, when they will share in the role of Jesus, whereby they will bring in those who belong to the twelve-tribe kingdom.

Against this background, we are to read this address of the Letter of James. James stands immersed in this enduring vision of the people of Israel, who hoped for the restoration of God's twelve-tribe kingdom. In a similar vein to Jesus, who (in the traditions behind Matthew's gospel) saw his ministry as directed to the restoration of God's twelve-tribe kingdom of Israel, James addresses his hearers/readers as the fulfillment of this centuries-long hope. As the "first fruits of God's creatures" (Jas 1:18), they constitute the beginnings of this twelve-tribe kingdom. The theological implications of this vision are important. God is at work bringing to birth this restoration (Jas 1:18). For James, the purity rules that derive from the Torah remain essential for this restored twelve-tribe kingdom. They are the defining form that gives direction to the life members are to lead. The community associated with Jesus during his ministry as well as now at the time of James is the beginning of that restored twelve-tribe kingdom. In this symbol of the twelve-tribe kingdom, James shows again his indebtedness, but more especially his closeness, to Jesus' vision. The parting of the ways between Judaism and Christianity had not yet taken place. Theologically, James' vision still lies at the heart of the world of Judaism, and sees no incompatibility between being a follower of Jesus and an adherent of the traditions of Israel. As McKnight says, "But, the two presentations of James are a witness to the kind of Christian Judaism that continued the vision of Jesus into the next generation as this form of faith in Jesus led to a parting yet within the way of Judaism."[52]

Theological Implications: In the Spirit of Jesus

The above examination has demonstrated the closeness that exists between James' letter and Jesus' vision. James used that vision rhetorically in order to build up the community that received this letter. James breathed the same Jewish atmosphere that Jesus did. James also appropriated and directed his understanding of the Jewish tradition in the same way in which Jesus did. Jesus' sayings provided direction for the way James appropriated this Jewish tradition. This has a number of theological implications.

The Original Movement Started by Jesus and Continued by James Was a Jewish Restoration Movement

In both Jesus' preaching and James' letter, God is at work reconstituting the people of Israel as the twelve-tribe kingdom. James' rhetorical concern in his teaching, as it was for Jesus, was that the whole Torah be followed, since it is the expression of God's will for God's people. No attention is given to the ritual aspects of the Torah; the focus rests predominantly on the laws that define the relationship of the members of the community with one another and with God.

The earliest picture of Jesus that emerges from the traditions shows someone whose mission extended to his own people, a mission that was confined within the world of first-century CE Judaism. James, in his turn, shows that he too was within the world of first-century CE Judaism; the parting of the ways between Judaism and Christianity had not yet taken place. As such, it reflects the earliest stage of the development of early Christianity. The Letter of James remains in the context of this earliest paradigm of the Jesus movement. James gives no attention to the issue of the relationship of Gentiles to the Jesus movement. Since James does not address this relationship, it presents no issue or problem for him. James' hearers/readers are Christian Jews whom he identifies as "the twelve tribes in the Dispersion" (1:1). Seen against this background, Paul's world appears to be vastly different from that of the Letter of James, since Paul's communities were predominantly Gentile Christian. This called for a new paradigm to emerge.

James' letter is a writing that truly bridges the world of Judaism and the world of Christianity. It brings awareness of the common heritage that Christians and Jews share. Above all, it shows how the visions of Jesus and James continue to be in conformity with the thought and vision of Judaism, and are not to be seen as distinctly different from it.[53]

Fidelity to Jesus' Central Vision: Concern for the Poor

Jesus' message is, above all, countercultural. It reaches back into the prophetic message of God's concern for the poor. The plight of the poor was not simply an economic issue. Their economic situation largely stemmed from their lack of honor, or social status. This resulted in a lack of power.[54] Three groups in the Old Testament world were identified as the poor: the widows, the orphans, and the strangers (Exod 22:22; Deut 24:17). Their poverty stemmed largely from their lack of social status. Since no one was there to champion their cause, God became their champion (Pss 22:26; 35:10).

In the traditions of Israel, the prophets gave voice to the need to extend justice to the poor. They drew attention especially to the evils of their society, such as the rich amassing fortunes at the expense of the poor: "Ah, you who join house to house, who add field to field, until there is room for no one but you, and you are left to live alone in the midst of the land!" (Isa 5:8).

As do the prophets and the whole Israelite tradition, James' letter presents God as the vindicator of the poor (Jas 5:1-6). As a champion of the poor, James condemns every situation in which the poor are unjustly treated (Jas 2:6-7). He has this tradition in mind when he defines religion as "care for orphans and widows in their distress" (Jas 1:27). Concern for the poor, in James' mind, embraces all who are rejected or marginalized by society in any way. Since all are created in the "likeness of God" (Jas 3:9), all are equal in God's eyes. No one can claim a special status that demands superiority over others. The Christian community must demonstrate an equality that stems inherently from its relationship with God. This theological vision gives impetus to the countercultural nature of James' community; its values are permeated by the values of equality and concern for the well-being of all. In the ultimate analysis, James envisages within his community a reversal of status, where the rich are brought low and the poor raised up, achieving an equality in faith (Jas 1:9-11).

In this short letter, James shows fidelity in continuing Jesus' central vision and message: an option for the poor and avoidance of every form of discrimination. The wholeness of the individual and of the community is illustrated through the attention given to achieving this equality in all actions. It is a message that continues to issue a challenge to every believer at every age and place.[55]

The Letter of James Continues Other Aspects of Jesus' Ministry

Jesus' ministry is characterized as well by actions of healing, forgiveness, outreach to sinners, and a desire to draw all into his kingdom. These features are also characteristic of James' letter[56] The letter's conclusion reflects these themes, which are so central to Jesus' ministry:

> Are any among you suffering? They should pray. Are any cheerful? They should sing songs of praise. Are any among you sick? They should call for the elders of the church and have them pray over them, anointing them with oil in the name of the Lord. The prayer of faith will save the sick, and the Lord will raise them up; and anyone who has committed sins will be forgiven. . . . My brothers and sisters, if anyone among you wanders from the truth and is brought back by another, you should know that whoever brings back a sinner from wandering will save the sinner's soul from death and will cover a multitude of sins. (Jas 5:13-20)

The way James introduces and addresses this call to pray, to anoint, and to forgive sins shows that these rituals are central to the community to which he writes. Since James does not explain any of these customs, he is clearly not introducing them to his hearers/readers for the first time. Instead, he is reminding his hearers/readers of the importance of these aspects that are central to their way of life. One sees in these customs and rituals a reflection of Jesus' own ministry. One of the central features of Jesus' ministry was his concern for the poor, suffering, and marginalized. He reached out to them at every opportunity and healed them (Mark 3:9-10).[57]

In addition to the similarities already mentioned between James and the Sermon on the Mount, the concept of prayer also features prominently in James' letter. Behind his consideration on prayer, the simple yet categorical statement of Jesus coming from the Q tradition is reflected: "Ask and it will be given you; search, and you will find; knock, and the door will be opened for you" (Q 11:9 [Luke 11:9/Matt 7:7]). James seems to grapple with this very categorical promise of Jesus. In reality, one knows that not everything that one prays for, one receives. For this reason, James gives expression to the way this saying of Jesus should be understood. Prayer should be made in faith without doubting (Jas 1:5-8; 5:15). Prayer is also to be made in the name of the Lord (Jas 5:14). For James, prayer is not just an individual experience; it is also fundamentally communitarian (Jas 5:14). Faced with sickness, the community rallies behind the sick person in prayer (Jas 5:15). Prayer is also meant to be fervent and confident: "The prayer of the righteous is powerful and effective" (Jas 5:16). From his Jewish tradition, James offers the example of the prophet Elijah, whose life of prayer is to be imitated (Jas 5:17-18).

Prayer acts as another social marker identifying the members of the community. It unites the believing community together in their relationship with God and the community. The qualities that mark Christian prayer for what it is—persistence, fervor, constancy—are qualities that the Gospels attribute to the teachings of Jesus.[58] Prayer gives the individual and the community power to maintain their identity and wholeness.

Conclusion

The Letter of James provides a distinct ethic for its readers to follow, an ethic that is at home both in the world of Judaism and in the vision of Jesus. In its solidarity with the poor, its rejection of all forms of discrimination, and its call for friendship with God as opposed to friendship with the world, James advances a vision that is challenging and refreshing.

The aim of this study has been to illustrate that the Letter of James lies very close to the central thought and vision of Jesus. James' rhetoric uses the Jesus tradition to communicate his own voice. Situated in the context of the rhetorical culture of the world of early Christianity and Second Temple Judaism, the Letter of James effectively composes the Jesus tradition in James' own key to define the way of life for the community of his hearers/readers.

Not only does James show an awareness of Jesus' sayings as found in the traditions behind the Gospels, but the letter's thought and paraenetic advice have been shown to closely reflect Jesus' central vision. Most importantly, James continues the thrust of Jesus' mission, in that both he and Jesus continue to define themselves in relation to their Jewish heritage. Through concepts such as purity, perfection, and the restoration of the twelve-tribe kingdom, James shows that he is the true heir to Jesus' message of fidelity to their Jewish heritage.

CHAPTER 5

THE RECEPTION OF THE JESUS
TRADITION IN JAMES

John S. Kloppenborg

Since almost the beginning of the critical study of the Letter of James, the relationship of James to the Jesus tradition has puzzled scholars. Three features of the letter give rise to this puzzle. First, James never expressly attributes any of his sayings to Jesus; nor does he call on Jesus as an authority—this despite the fact that six times the author cites texts from the Tanak (in Septuagintal form), using an introductory quotation formula.[1] Not only is Jesus not called on as an authority, but the name *Jesus* appears only twice in the letter (1:1; 2:1), and in its second occurrence appears in an extremely awkward formulation.[2] Thus Christoph Burchard raises the possibility that whatever traditions James employed were not even associated with the name of Jesus.[3] Second, in addition to the citations of the Tanak, there are four sayings that are marked with formulae such as οὐκ οἴδατε ὅτι or εἰδότες ὅτι, formulae that often signal the presence of material that is supposed to be common knowledge and which conceivably might include the Jesus tradition. But none of the sayings thus marked display strong verbal parallels with sayings of Jesus reported by the Synoptics, John, or the *Gospel of Thomas*, and only one appears to be a candidate for a saying of Jesus (4:4).[4] In fact, although scholars have sometimes perceived many Jacobian parallels with the Jesus tradition, none of James' sayings, with the exception of the prohibition of oaths (5:12), display very extensive verbal parallels with the sayings attributed to Jesus by other documents. And third, despite this, there are many thematic affinities and some points of verbal contact with sayings of Jesus, in particular those occurring in the Sermon on the Mount/Sermon on the Plain. Just how many points of contact there are is a matter of considerable dispute, with estimates ranging from just four (McNeile)[5] to more than forty (Mayor, Spitta, Schlatter, Davids),[6] and interpreters averaging eighteen parallels.[7]

This statistic is remarkable when compared with Paul's reminiscences of the Jesus tradition.[8] Even if we accept the average of eighteen points of contact, James' 108 verses have a far higher relative incidence of contact with the Jesus tradition than does the much larger corpus of authentic Pauline letters, which has two explicit citations (1 Cor 7:10-11; 9:14) and barely two dozen allusions.[9]

James and the Jesus Tradition: Six Models

A survey of the past century of literature on James shows that these three features of James have been explained by means of six basic models.

1. First, a small number of scholars have argued that James in fact contains no Jesus tradition, and that the two references to Jesus Christ are secondary interpolations. Massebieau and Spitta, for example, believed James to be originally a non-Christian Jewish document that was lightly Christianized through the addition of references to *Jesus Christ* in 1:1 and 2:1. Massebieau admitted some superficial similarities between James and the Sermon on the Mount, but underscored the differences in tone:

> Les paroles qui rappelent son [Jesus'] enseignement ne portent plus sa marque, sont d'une généralité pure, ne se distinguent pas par un ton d'authorité spécial des préceptes avoisinants, ne contiennent pas ses parties les plus saintement originales et l'écrit qui semble, à première vue, pénétré des discours de Jésus-Christ, les contredict ici et là directement.[10]

Spitta also conceded numerous apparent candidates, listing fifty-five possible parallels between James and the Synoptics. But he argued that in each case one could find Jewish texts that better accounted for the form and content of James' sayings.[11] For example, apropos of James 5:12, the Jacobian text cited most frequently as a reminiscence of a Jesus saying,[12] Spitta urged that it was likely that James and Jesus had a common source for their prohibitions of oath-taking (even though he could cite no such source), just as the similarities between 4 Maccabees 7:19 and Matthew 22:32/Mark 12:26-27 (the belief that the patriarchs were alive) should not be explained by Mark's dependence on 4 Maccabees, but by reliance on common tradition.[13] Spitta observed that the reference to God's promise of the kingdom to the πτωχοί in James 2:5, frequently linked with Q 6:20b, not only differs substantially from the formulation of the Synoptic sayings but also simply reflects beliefs common in "late Judaism."[14] Hence, there is no strong reason to see the presence of Jesus tradition in 2:5.

This approach found a more recent champion in Arnold Meyer, who argued that James is a Jewish composition, similar to the *Testaments of the Twelve Patriarchs* and modeled on Jacob's address to his sons in Genesis 49.[15] The alleged contacts with the Synoptic Gospels, Meyer averred, are just as easily explained on the basis of borrowings from the moralizing traditions of contemporary Judaism.

> Es liegt also kein Grund vor, Jac von den Evangelien abhängen zu lassen und zeitlich später zu setzen. Ja, die Selbständigkeit von Jac 5,12 3,12 4,3 läßt uns annehmen, daß Jac entweder vor unsern Evangelien oder so entfernt von ihnen schrieb oder so selbstständig nach Tradition und Anschauung vor, daß keine Kenntnis ihres Wortlautes ihn beinflußte.[16]

The attempts of Massebieau, Spitta, and Meyer to read James as a Jewish document have not fared well and have little following today.[17] As Dibelius pointed out, James 1:18 (εἰς τὸ εἶναι ἡμᾶς ἀπαρχήν τινα τῶν αὐτοῦ κτισμάτων) can only refer to "some small group of the reborn in whose footsteps all creatures soon should follow"—presumably Jesus' followers. The reference to the rich blaspheming "the good name that is called over you" (τὸ καλὸν ὄνομα τὸ ἐπικληθὲν ἐφ᾽ ὑμᾶς) in 2:7 would make no sense as a general address to Jews, but would make sense if it were directed at a small group—presumably members of the Jesus movement—that stood over against the rich. And the famous distinction between faith and works in 2:14-26 presupposes a specifically Christian debate, since "Paul's struggle over this matter would make no sense if Jewish circles prior to him had established the antithesis."[18]

2. While Dibelius' approach did not oblige him to dispense with 1:1 and 2:1 as interpolations or to deny all contacts with the Jesus tradition, he did minimize such contacts. To be sure, Dibelius acknowledged that James 5:12 was a conscious or unconscious use of a saying of Jesus,[19] and that James 4:3 was "a correction to Matt 7:7 rather than an echo of it."[20] But it was the common use of paraenetic genres that accounted for the commonalities between James and the tradition of Jesus' sayings. Moreover, James' adoption of the genre of paraenesis explained the curious fact that James does not ascribe any of its sayings to Jesus.

For this relationship [of James to the Jesus tradition] is not due primarily to characteristics shared exclusively by the Letter of James and the sayings of Jesus, but rather it corresponds to the fact that they belong to a common literary genre: our text and the collections of sayings on the Gospels both belong to the genre of paraenesis.[21]

Formally, James and the Jesus tradition include paraenetic sayings, often connected by catchwords. From the point of view of style, both use brief, pointed imperatives with a small canon of tropes and metaphors (and so naturally often use the same tropes and metaphors). And James shares with the Jesus tradition "the atmosphere of an ethical rigorism," "piety of the poor," and hostility to the rich, which, Dibelius observes, "occasionally falls into the level of the sub-Christian."[22] Thus the similarities between James and the Jesus tradition do not necessarily point to James' dependence on the Jesus tradition, but rather to "similarities in intuition" and common use of contemporary Jewish moralizing traditions.

3. In sharp contrast to Massebieau, Spitta, Meyer, and Dibelius, a few have insisted that despite inexact verbal parallels and the lack of direct attribution to Jesus, James was literarily dependent on one of the Synoptics, usually Matthew. This view, of course, also necessitates a late dating of the letter. As early as 1874, Brückner thought that the simplest way to account for the similarities between James and the Jesus tradition was simple dependence on Matthew.[23] But the case was put most trenchantly by Massey Shepherd, who divided James into eight didactic discourses, each of which, he argued, was built around a central macarism or gnomic saying that had striking parallels with Matthew.[24]

Thus, Shepherd urges, Matthean texts "relate to every single section of the Epistle, and to almost every major theme."[25] But since Shepherd recognizes that James' replication of the Matthean texts was not exact, he concludes that James knew Matthew's gospel not directly, but only via its use in public liturgical reading. More recently, Gryglewicz has contended that James reflects characteristic Matthean expressions, and thus likely depended on the written text of Matthew.[26]

While ingenious, these arguments do not withstand scrutiny. Dean Deppe points out three key problems with Shepherd's argument. First, none of the central gnomic sayings identified by Shepherd are in fact allusions to a Matthean saying of Jesus. Of the eight gnomic sayings listed by Shepherd, only James 2:5 (οὐχ ὁ θεὸς ἐξελέξατο τοὺς πτωχοὺς τῷ κόσμῳ πλουσίους ἐν πίστει καὶ κληρονόμους τῆς βασιλείας ἧς ἐπηγγείλατο τοῖς ἀγαπῶσιν αὐτόν;) offers a close parallel to a saying attributed to Jesus by the Synoptics. But James 2:5 is in fact closer to Luke 6:20b than to its Matthean counterpart. James 5:11 (πολύσπλαγχνός ἐστιν ὁ κύριος καὶ οἰκτίρμων) might also be treated as an echo of Matthew 5:48/Luke 6:36, but in this case too, James is closer to Luke's formulation than to Matthew's. Moreover, Deppe points out that James' exhortations concerning those who weep (4:9) and the rich (5:1) have closer parallels in Luke 6:24-26 than with anything in Matthew. Second, Shepherd's claim that the materials surrounding the central gnome are Matthean in character cannot be sustained. It is not at all obvious, Deppe observes, that James 1:2-18 is a commentary on Matthew 6:13 or 7:7, or that Matthew 7:21-24 lies behind James 1:19-27, or that James 3:1-12 is an illustration of Matthew 12:36.[27] The material in Shepherd's seventh section concerning merchants (4:13-17) has no obvious parallels with the Matthean Jesus tradition at all,[28] and there is no Jesus saying at the core of 2:14-26. Third, maxims such as James 3:12 (συκῆ ἐλαίας ποιῆσαι ἢ ἄμπελος σῦκα;) are better understood as reflections of general Mediterranean wisdom than as specific allusions to sayings of Jesus.[29]

Even more to the point are the observations that the agreements between James and Matthew have to do for the most part with (1) wording that Matthew shares with Luke (and hence is that of Q) or (2) phrases that, in all likelihood, Matthew has taken over unaltered from Q. Moreover, (3) none of Matthew's redactional vocabulary appears in James' version of the parallel sayings.

To illustrate each point: (1) James 1:5 has αἰτείτω . . . καὶ δοθήσεται αὐτῷ, the latter phrase agreeing with both Matthew 7:7 and Luke 11:9 (and hence Q 11:9). Hence, it is impossible to distinguish between dependence on Matthew, on Luke, or on Q. All that one can say is that James' use of the pair αἰτεῖν–διδόναι puts him closer to the Synoptics than to Thomas' ζητεῖν–εὑρίσκειν.[30] And the adducing of the example of the prophets as a model of suffering in James 5:10 does not bring us closer to Matthew 5:11-12 than to Luke 6:22-23, since both (and hence Q) refer to the example of the prophets.[31] (2) If James 1:17, πᾶσα δόσις ἀγαθὴ καὶ πᾶν δώρημα τέλειον ἄνωθέν ἐστιν, καταβαῖνον ἀπὸ τοῦ πατρὸς τῶν φώτων, is an allusion to Matthew 7:11, it is significant that Matthew's δόματα ἀγαθά (cf. James' δόσις ἀγαθή) is likely closer to the wording of Q than Luke's πνεῦμα ἅγιον. Moreover, James' πατὴρ τοῦ φώτων is no closer to Matthew's ὁ πατὴρ ὑμῶν ὁ ἐν τοῖς οὐρανοῖς than to Luke's (Q's) ὁ πατὴρ ἐξ οὐρανοῦ.[32] Thus on the first point, James agrees with Q, and on the second disagrees with both Matthew and Q, and so there is no way to know whether James is alluding to (and adapting) Matthew or Q, if indeed James 1:17 is an allusion. (3) Finally, James 2:5 does not display knowledge of Matthew's redactional τῷ πνεύματι (Matt 5:3) or

Matthew's antithetical framing of the prohibition of oaths (Matt 5:33-36).[33] Nothing in James points to knowledge of Matthean redaction.[34]

4. There remain a number of scholars who hold that the letter is not pseudepigraphic, a view that leads to a different approach to the three puzzling features listed above. Among these, it is common to explain the contacts with the Jesus tradition as a matter of James' own memories. The lack of attribution of the sayings and of exact correspondence to known Jesus sayings is made a function of the author's peculiar psychology, having completely internalized his brother's thought and made it his own. The density of parallels is, of course, a function of James' close association with Jesus.

Thus Mayor accounts for both the presence of Jesus tradition in James and its lack of direct attribution with the supposition that Jesus' ideas and style of thought had been so thoroughly appropriated by James that he could simply reproduce Jesus' ideas at will.[35] According to Zahn, the striking similarities are due neither to direct imitation of Jesus' sayings nor to "conscious dependence" on them; instead, James was acquainted with Jesus' sayings in part from direct association with Jesus and in part from oral tradition in the church, and so he internalized them both fully.[36]

Many slight variations of this view exist, now mainly associated with evangelical scholars.[37] Obviously, this thesis makes no sense apart from the logically prior thesis of Jacobian authorship, and defenders normally factor in the accounts indicating that Jesus' immediate family was not sympathetic to his activities (Mark 3:20-21; John 7:5), so that James is made to assimilate Jesus' teachings in spite of his earlier hostility or indifference.

5. The most commonly espoused view—that James' material derives from oral Jesus tradition—was formulated in reaction to the thesis that James depended on the written gospels.[38] The tacit or express assumption operative in this explanation is that oral transmission can best account for the second feature of James mentioned above—the lack of exact correspondence with Jesus' sayings preserved in gospel literature—since sayings transmitted orally are given to a kind of natural diversification in wording, structure, and application. Kittel's version of this explanation also holds that the earliest phase of oral transmission was anonymous, thus accounting for James' failure to credit Jesus with any of his materials.

Although the oral tradition hypothesis accounts for certain features of James' use of the Jesus tradition, what it leaves unexplained are the particulars of that usage. Several proponents of this thesis observe, rightly, that James' repertoire of traditions does not extend much beyond Q[39] or the Sermon on the Mount/Plain.[40] There are few if any real contacts with Mark, and no allusions to sectors of the Jesus tradition that relate wonders, controversy stories, or the death and resurrection of Jesus. Even the overlap with the Q Sermon is limited. James lacks many of the main elements of the sermon: admonitions to love of enemies, non-retaliation, and unstinting lending (Q 6:27-30); the Golden Rule (Q 6:31); the measure-for-measure proverb (Q 6:38); and the metaphors of blindness (6:39), obstructed vision (6:41-42), and housebuilding (6:47-49).[41] Other elements of Q are also missing: there is no hint of the repentance preaching of John the Baptist (3:7-9, 16-17) or its recapitulation by Jesus (10:13-15; 11:31-32), no polemic against "this generation" (Q 7:31-35; 11:29-32, 49-51), no attacks on the Pharisees and scribes, no Son of Man sayings. Some of these absences are, no doubt, a function of James' editorial purpose, which is generally hortatory rather than apologetic. A defense against the Beelzebul accusation (Q 11:14-23) would hardly be expected. Other lacunae are perhaps a matter of the audience of James; attacks on Pharisees and scribes (Q 11:39-52) would likely be pointless if the letter was meant to be read outside of Jewish Palestine. Nevertheless, the somewhat vague appeal to James' dependence on oral tradition in fact leaves unanswered important questions about the particular nature and shape of the oral tradition to which James allegedly had access.[42]

6. A final approach responds to this latter issue and argues that the particular constellation of allusions in James points to dependence on Q or on a document very much like it. Streeter was the first to think that James "had read Q in the recension known to Luke,"[43] since James' critique of wealth found closer analogies in Luke than in Matthew.[44]

Patrick Hartin has put the case for James' dependence on Q (or Matthew's version of Q) most cogently.[45] Hartin examined twenty-six possible parallels between James and the Synoptics, twenty-one of which appear in the Sermon on the Mount. He found that James betrays a knowledge, first, of the Q macarisms (and woes)[46]—Jas 2:5 (Matt 5:3; Q 6:20); 2:15-16 (Q 6:21); 1:2; 5:10 (Q 6:22-23); 5:1 (Q/Luke 6:24); 4:9 (Q/Luke 6:25)—and second, of elaborations of the Q macarisms in the Matthean community, elaborations that he takes to be pre-Matthean: 2:13 (Matt 5:7; cf. Q 6:36); 4:8 (Matt 5:8); 3:18 (Matt 5:9). At the same time, James does not show any acquaintance with the specific elements of Matthean redaction of the macarisms.[47] Next, Hartin argues that the (pre-)Matthean elaboration of Q 6:27-33, containing antitheses on the topics of murder and adultery (Matt 5:21-30), can be seen reflected in James 2:11 and in the vocative "adulteresses!" in 4:4. Q's admonition not to judge (Q 6:37) underlies James 4:11; 5:6; 5:9.[48] Somewhat closer connections are seen in 3:12 (Q 6:44), in the trope of trees not producing atypical fruit, and in 1:22 (Q 6:47-49), which contrasts mere hearing with "doing the word." Thus, although James lacks the Golden Rule (6:31) and the sayings on disciples and masters (6:39-40) and impeded vision (6:41-42), "the vast majority of the sayings contained in the Q sermon find a correspondence in the Epistle of James."[49]

By itself, this finding could admit of at least two explanations: either James and Q 6:20-49 drew on common (oral) tradition, or that James knew the Q Sermon. In order to make the latter possibility the more likely, Hartin argues that further knowledge of Q is betrayed by James 1:5-8; 2:10 (Q 16:17); 4:3 (Q 11:9-13); 4:4 (Q 16:13); 4:10 (Q 14:11); 5:2-3 (Q 12:33-34); and 5:19-20 (Q 17:3). Of course, 5:12 is the clearest point of contact with M tradition (Matt 5:33-37) and indicates that James also knew tradition within the Matthean orbit (though Hartin does not think that James here knew Matthew). But given the contacts between James and Q, not only in Q's Sermon (and its pre-Matthean expansion), but also in the Q sections dealing with prayer (Q 11:2-4, 9-13), anxieties (12:22-31, 33-34), discipleship (Q 17:1-6), and a block of miscellaneous sayings (13:23–16:18),[50] Hartin concludes:

> Only two possible explanations can be given of these similarities. Either both James and Q are dependent upon a common tradition, which is reflected in these examples; or James is dependent directly on the Q tradition. The argument of this investigation supports the direct dependence of James on Q. The main reason for opting for this second possibility arises from the closeness of the language used. While no one example is capable of proving the point conclusively, all these examples taken together provide an argument from convergence. If one were to opt for the first possibility whereby James and Q are independent of each other, yet dependent upon a common tradition, one would in fact have to postulate a common tradition very similar to Q.[51]

Hartin's appeal to the principle of parsimony in explanations can be strengthened further with the observation that James 1:2 (12) and 5:10 adduce the example of the suffering (κακοπαθεία) of the prophets, a theme that is likely redactional in Q generally and a redactional addition to the persecution macarism (Q 6:22-23). This macarism is remarkable for the fact that we have five occurrences of versions of the macarism (Q 6:22-23; *Gos. Thom.* 68, 69a; 1 Pet 3:14; 4:13-14), and only one, Q 6:22-23, contains a reference to the persecution of the prophets (see below, in italics). The phrase οὕτως γὰρ διώξωσιν τοὺς προφήτας τοὺς πρὸ ὑμῶν is indeed superfluous, since the motive clause for χαίρετε is already supplied by ὅτι ὁ μισθὸς ὑμῶν πολὺς ἐν τῷ οὐρανῷ.[52] Its presence in Q 6:22-

23 is likely due to the redactional activities of the compilers of Q, who wished to underscore the connection of the Q group with the prophets, understood through the lens of Deuteronomistic theology.[53]

1:2 πᾶσαν χαρὰν ἡγήσασθε, ἀδελφοί μου, ὅταν πειρασμοῖς περιπέσητε ποικίλοις,	Q 6:22 μακάριοί ἐστε ὅταν ὀνειδίσωσιν ὑμᾶς καὶ διώξωσιν καὶ εἴπωσιν πᾶν πονηρὸν καθ' ὑμῶν ἕνεκεν τοῦ υἱοῦ τοῦ ἀνθρώπου· 23 χαίρετε καὶ ἀγαλλιᾶσθε, ὅτι ὁ μισθὸς ὑμῶν πολὺς ἐν τῷ οὐρανῷ·
5:10 ὑπόδειγμα λάβετε, ἀδελφοί, τῆς κακοπαθείας καὶ τῆς μακροθυμίας τοὺς προφήτας, οἳ ἐλάλησαν ἐν τῷ ὀνόματι κυρίου	οὕτως γὰρ διώξωσιν τοὺς προφήτας πρὸ ὑμῶν.

Not all of Hartin's parallels are equally persuasive. It seems rather a stretch of the imagination to see an appeal to Matthew 5:8 in καθαρίσατε χεῖρας, ἁμαρτωλοί, καὶ ἁγνίσατε καρδίας (Jas 4:8) or to see Matthew 5:21-30, on murder and adultery, as informing James 2:11 (ὁ γὰρ εἰπών, μὴ μοιχεύσῃς, εἶπεν καί, μὴ φονεύσῃς), especially when in the latter instance James is likely simply quoting the Tanak (Exod 20:13-14; Deut 5:17-18). The vocative μοιχαλίδες in 4:4 is hardly a clear allusion to Matthew's discussion of adultery in 5:27-30 or to the phrase γενεὰ πονηρὰ καὶ μοιχαλίς in Matthew 12:39. As noted above, the trope of the impossibility of trees producing atypical fruit is not unique to Q, and in fact a closer parallel exists in Seneca.[54] The notion of "doing the word" in 1:22 is only vaguely related to Q's parable of the two builders (Q 6:47-49), and James 2:10, that violation of one law amounts to violation of the entire law, is more closely related to Stoic maxims than to Q's affirmation of the perdurance of the Torah.[55] The connection between James 3:18 (καρπὸς δὲ δικαιοσύνης ἐν εἰρήνῃ σπείρεται τοῖς ποιοῦσιν εἰρήνην) and Matthew's seventh macarism is not at all strong, for James uses an agricultural metaphor and a Septuagintalism (καρπός δικαιοσύνης), both missing in Matthew. The only connection between the two texts is the notion of making peace.

Other allusions that Hartin sees are rather subtle in nature: he sees in 2:15-16 (ὑπάγετε ἐν εἰρήνῃ, θερμαίνεσθε καὶ χορτάζεσθε) an ironic allusion to Q 6:21a (μακάριοι οἱ πεινῶντες, ὅτι χορτασθήσεσθε). But this suggestion is cogent only on the prior assumption that James knew the Q macarisms. Similarly, only on the prior assumption that the Q^{Mt} macarisms are intertextually present in James is it possible to see an allusion to

Matthew 5:7 (μακάριοι οἱ ἐλεήμονες, ὅτι αὐτοὶ ἐλεηθήσονται) in James 2:13 (ἡ γὰρ κρίσις ἀνέλεος τῷ μὴ ποιήσαντι ἔλεος· κυ ιυκαυχᾶται ἔλεος κρίσεως). But as Deppe has shown, the sentiment expressed by James is also widely attested in contemporary Judaism.[56]

While not all of Hartin's parallels are equally persuasive, there remains a sufficient number of likely contacts in James (1:2, 5, 12; 2:5; 4:2c-3, 4, 9, 10, 11; 5:1, 2-3, 9, 10; and perhaps 5:19-20), drawn from various parts of Q, to sustain his thesis.[57] The fact that James reflects Q's (redactional) penchant for correlating its experiences with those of the prophets (6:23c; 11:49-51; 13:34-35) makes best sense if James was aware not merely of Q tradition but also of the document itself—to be sure, in a somewhat elaborated, pre-Matthean form.[58]

James' Recitation of Jesus Tradition in Q

If it is a reasonable conclusion that James is indebted to the Jesus tradition as available in Q in a pre-Matthean recension, this still does not help us to understand the remaining two puzzles: why James fails to attribute any of his sayings to Jesus, and why the level of verbal correspondence is relatively low.

Commentators have generally not been very helpful in dealing with these puzzles, being mainly satisfied to establish the thesis that James knew and used the Jesus tradition (or, in the case of Massebieau and Spitta, that he did not). As far as I am aware, only two models have been advanced to account for James' actual use of the Jesus tradition, the first psychological and the second based on inferences about scribal practice.[59]

The view that the epistle is genuine and that its author was the brother of Jesus is often attended, implicitly or expressly, by the supposition, essentially psychological in nature, that James' verbal art is explicable through familial osmosis. Zahn explains the lack of verbal convergence with the elaborate speculation that although James had never been under Jesus' direct tutelage, nonetheless,

> there were not a few of these sayings which he had heard from Jesus' own lips, though often with doubt and disapproval. After he became a believer, what he learned from others and what he had heard himself fused together in his thought, and the impression of the personality of Jesus, under the influence of which he had been ever since his childhood, made the tradition so vital that it developed in him a Christian character which in the early Church made him seem all but superior to the apostles themselves.[60]

Mayor's account is not essentially different. He imagines the process of Jesus' words "sinking into the heart of the hearer [James], who reproduces them in his own manner."[61] These approaches are of course wedded to the hypothesis of Jacobian authorship, with all of its attendant problems. More importantly, they lack scientific rigor, for they operate in default of any general model for understanding conformity and divergence in linguistic and conceptual patterns in ancient Mediterranean families, and they lack reliable data about the particulars of Jesus' family. No attention is given to formulating models for understanding how, in Mediterranean families, clans, villages, and regions, conceptual and linguistic patterns were replicated, extended, modified, or rejected. Instead, the suggestions of Zahn and Mayor rest on anachronistic and essentially whimsical assumptions drawn from nineteenth-century European families. Moreover, since we know nothing about the psychological dynamics within Jesus' family; its age distribution, size, and intergenerational aspects; the size of Jesus' clan; or the psychosocial dynamics of first-century Nazareth, any conclusions about whether James' linguistic and conceptual patterns might have conformed to those of Jesus are utterly gratuitous.

Richard Bauckham has recently proposed a much more controlled and serious model.[62] Bauckham also holds that James, the brother of Jesus, is the authority behind the letter, and seeks a model for understanding the relationship between Jesus and his brother James. This he finds in Sirach, who composed a wisdom book in his own name (rather than attributing his work pseudonymously to some distinguished predecessor such as Solomon). Of course, Sirach did not compose his book ex nihilo, but employed various texts from the Tanak. But in doing so, Sirach emulated rather than quoted those predecessor texts. Sirach's procedure is elevated to the level of self-conscious practice in Sirach 39:1-3, 6:

> 1 On the other hand he who devotes himself to the study of the law of the Most High will seek out the wisdom of all the ancients, and will be concerned with prophecies; 2 he will preserve the discourse of notable men and penetrate the subtleties of parables; 3 he will seek out the hidden meanings of proverbs and be at home with the obscurities of parables. . . .
> 6 If the great Lord is willing, he will be filled with the spirit of understanding; he will pour forth words of wisdom and give thanks to the Lord in prayer. (RSV)

Sirach here describes an intellectual process that is not simply a matter of replication or quotation of traditional sayings, but what I have elsewhere called *sapiential research*—the effort of weighing, probing, and evaluating traditional sayings—that leads to assimilation of the ethos of wisdom and then its emulation and reproduction by the speaker.[63] Thus I am in essential agreement with Bauckham, who argues that James does not quote Jesus' sayings, but instead reformulates them:

> He does not repeat [the wisdom of Jesus]; he is inspired by it. He creates his own wise sayings, inspired by several sayings, sometimes encapsulating the themes of many sayings, sometimes based on points of contact between Jesus' sayings and other Jewish wisdom. The creativity and artistry of these sayings are missed when they are treated as allusions to sayings of Jesus.[64]

The combination of references to predecessor texts and the creative reformulation of those texts can be seen vividly in Bauckham's examples of Sirach's transformation of earlier texts. Compare, for example, Deuteronomy 6:5 and Sirach 7:29-30:[65]

Deut 6:5: καὶ ἀγαπήσεις κύριον τὸν θεόν σου ἐξ ὅλης τῆς καρδίας σου καὶ ἐξ ὅλης τῆς ψυχῆς σου καὶ ἐξ ὅλης τῆς δυνάμεώς σου.

Sir 7:29-30: ἐν ὅλῃ ψυχῇ σου εὐλαβοῦ τὸν κύριον καὶ τοὺς ἱερεῖς αὐτοῦ θαύμαζε. 30 ἐν ὅλῃ δυνάμει ἀγάπησον τὸν ποιήσαντά σε καὶ τοὺς λειτουργοὺς αὐτοῦ μὴ ἐγκαταλίπῃς.

You shall love the Lord your God with all your heart and with all your soul and with all your power.

With all your soul fear the Lord and revere his priests. And with all your power love your maker and do not neglect his ministers.

The verbal agreement of Sirach with Deuteronomy 6:5 is in fact quite low; Sirach preserves the phrases ἐξ ὅλης τῆς ψυχῆς σου (ἐν ὅλῃ ψυχῇ σου) and ἐξ ὅλης τῆς δυνάμεώς σου (ἐν ὅλῃ δυνάμει), but introduces two new verbs (εὐλαβάνειν, θαυμάζειν), substitutes τὸν ποιήσαντά σε for the Septuagint's κύριον τὸν θεόν σου, and introduces the connection between loving God and respect for the priesthood. With this, the admonition from the Torah is redirected to the concrete situation of second-century BCE Judah and its priestly aristocracy.

Equipped with the analogy of scribal procedure as seen in Sirach, Bauckham argues that

> James is not *quoting* or alluding to the saying[s] of Jesus, but, in the manner of a wisdom sage, he is *re-expressing* the insight he

has learned from Jesus' teaching. . . . Just as Ben Sira, even when he repeats the thought of Proverbs, deliberately refrains from repeating the words, so James creates an aphorism of his own, indebted to but no mere reproduction of the words of Jesus.[66]

This model of verbal transmission and transformation is considerably superior to the whimsical, psychological model of Zahn and Mayor, since it is grounded not in pious fancy but in a model that was self-consciously undertaken and explicitly described by Sirach. Moreover, since we have access to Sirach's sources, we are in a position to deduce some of the actual techniques of verbal transformation that he used. In other words, Bauckham proposes an empirically grounded model, and one that can be tested. It is a model with explanatory force.

Though Bauckham himself adheres to the notion of Jacobian author-ship, it should be observed that his model for understanding the relation-ship between Jesus and James does not logically require any assumptions about authorship. It would work just as well in accounting for the shape of James' text if James were dependent on oral tradition or an early written collection of Jesus' sayings. Both sources could equally serve as examples for emulation, just as Deuteronomy and Proverbs did for Sirach. And although Sirach writes in his own name, the same process of emulation of older sayings might just as easily be found in a pseudepigraphon.

An instance of the latter is found in Pseudo-Phocylides, attributed to a sixth century BCE Greek gnomic poet but composed between 50 BCE and 100 CE by a hellenized Jew.[67] It is clear that the author had portions of the Torah in view when he composed his poem, fusing its moral teaching with more typically Greek sentiments. The first section (3–8), for example, is a summary of the Decalogue, paraphrasing the prohibitions of adultery, murder, theft, covetousness, and false witness, and concluding with the injunction to "Honour God first, and thereafter your parents" (8), equally at home in the Decalogue and in Greek ethics. Although the author's purpose is not entirely clear—was it for protreptic purposes, directed at fellow Jews, or apologetics, demonstrating to Gentiles the basic agree-ments between the Torah and Greek moral teaching?—the author's technique involves adapting the Torah to a verse presentation in dactylic hexameters and reducing the Torah's formulations to terse imperatives. Take Pseudo-Phocylides' paraphrase of Leviticus 19:15:

μὴ ῥίψῃς πενίην ἀδίκως, μὴ κρῖνε πρόσωπον (10)

οὐ ποιήσετε ἄδικον ἐν κρίσει, οὐ λήψῃ πρόσωπον πτωχοῦ οὐδὲ θαυμάσεις πρόσωπον δυνάστου, ἐν δικαιοσύνῃ κρινεῖς τὸν πλησίον σου. (Lev 19:15)

Cast the poor not down	You shall commit no injustice in
unjustly, judge not partially.	judgment, nor show partiality to the
	poor or defer to the great, but in
	righteousness shall you judge your
	neighbor.

Like Bauckham's example of Sirach 7:29-30, Pseudo-Phocylides paraphrases the predecessor text in a manner appropriate to his audience and literary intention. Rather than attributing the resulting paraphrase to Moses or representing it as his own (as did Sirach), the author attributes the teaching to an ancient Greek teacher. Nonetheless, it seems likely that a Jewish audience, at least, would recognize that Pseudo-Phocylides was engaging in a paraphrase of the Torah. The key point is that, like the audience of Sirach and Pseudo-Phocylides, the audience of James is likely to have recognized that the author was engaging in paraphrase of received wisdom, and would not have been surprised that there was no attempt at either verbatim repetition or attribution to the actual source of the wisdom.

The model of verbal transmission and transformation that Bauckham proposes in order to account for the features of James' work is in fact much more widely attested than merely in the world of Jewish scribes.[68] The basis of literate education in the Hellenistic and Roman eras was the copying, emulation, and imitation of predecessor texts, especially gnomologia, chria collections, Aesop's fables, and Homeric verses.[69] While the most elementary forms of education involved the simple copying of exemplars, the initial stages of rhetorical education, as evidenced in the *Progymnasmata*, trained students to manipulate these materials in various ways through restating (or paraphrasing), supplying a rationale, and offering arguments from the contrary, analogies, examples, and other proofs. *Recitation* or *restatement* (ἀπαγγελεία), according to Aelius Theon, allowed for the reporting (or interpreting) of a saying or chria "very clearly in the same words or in others as well" (αὐτοῖς ὀνόμασιν ἢ ἑτέροις σαφέστατα ἑρμηνεῦσαι).[70] The existence of large numbers of school notebooks, many reproducing gnomes and others containing rhetorical exercises, permits us to judge the scope of verbal transformation that was actually allowed in these exercises.[71]

In practice, there was considerable variation in various recitations of a gnome or chria, as examination of school exercises shows. Sometimes the saying component of a chria was reproduced mainly unaltered, but the introduction modified and reframed it to suit the rhetorical situation. Students learned to inflect chriae in all three grammatical numbers (singular, dual, plural) and five cases (including the vocative), and to state the chriae actively and passively. Thus Isocrates' famous chria, ᾽Ισοκράτης ὁ ῥήτωρ τὸν εὐφυέα τῶν μαθητῶν θεῶν παῖδα ἔλεγεν εἶναι (Isocrates the orator said that the student with natural ability was a child of the god), could be transformed into ᾽Ισοκράτους τοῦ ῥήτορος τοὺς εὐφυεῖς τῶν μαθητῶν θεῶν παῖδας λέγοντος εἶναι τὸ ῥηθὲν μνήμης ἔτυχε (the saying has become memorable that Isocrates . . .). A Diogenes chria could be put into the dative (Διογένει τῷ Κυνικῷ φιλοσόφῳ ἰδόν τι μειράκιον πλούσιον ἀπαίδευτον ἔδοξεν εἰπεῖν οὗτός ἐστι ῥύπος περιηργυρω-μένος, "to Diogenes the Cynic philosopher, seeing a rich youth who was uneducated, it seemed right to say, 'He is dirt plated with silver'"), and so on.[72] It was also common to practice copying chriae but standardize the opening frame, as can be seen in a comparison of a chria recorded by Diogenes Laertius with a school rhetorical exercise:

Πρὸς τοὺς ἑρπύσαντας ἐπὶ τὴν τράπεζαν μῦς, ἰδού, φησί, καὶ Διογένης παρασίτους τρέφει.	᾽Ιδὼν μυῖαν ἐπάνω τῆς τράπεζαν αὐτοῦ εἶπεν· Καὶ Διογένης παρασίτους τρέφει.
When mice (*mys*) crept onto the table, he addressed them, "See, even Diogenes keeps parasites." (DL 6.40)	Seeing a fly (*myia*) on his table he said, "Even Diogenes keeps parasites." (P. Bouriant 1.141–68)[73]

From a formal point of view, both versions are what Theon calls εἶδος ἀποφαντικὸν κατὰ περίστασιν, a declarative chria that relates to a certain circumstance.[74] But the chria in the papyrus exercise book, like the other four chriae in this papyrus collection, has been standardized as a particular type of circumstantial chria with the form ἰδών + substantive + εἶπεν, followed by the pithy statement. In other exercise books, the student has copied a string of chriae in responsive form εἶδος ἀποκριτικὸν κατὰ πύσμα), characterized by ἐρωτηθεὶς διὰ τί + ἔφη, followed by the saying.[75] Preliminary rhetorical training thus involved learning how to manipulate sayings to suit the grammatical construction in which they were to be quoted and to present them in various forms—as unmotivated pronouncements, as responses to particular circumstances, as answers to questions, and so forth.

Advanced exercises involved more substantial paraphrasing—shortening, lengthening, and substituting other vocabulary—and even introducing another conceptual framework.[76] Parsons discusses an elaborate third-century CE prose paraphrase of the first twenty-one lines of the *Iliad*.[77] The student modified the texts in various ways, substituting Attic vocabulary for archaic words, omitting Homeric epithets (e.g., "[Apollo] who smites afar," *Il.* 1.14, 21), and altering descriptions (changing "and made themselves to be a spoil for dogs and all manner of birds" [*Il.* 1.4–5] to "they abrogated the rule of burial for some" [*Il.* 1.9–10]). Morgan observes that the periphrast introduced the thoroughly unhomeric word *hypothesis* (three times) to refer to his effort to give a rational explanation of the events that in Homer form a rather more tangled account.[78] Chryses' speech is recast in Athenian courtroom style, and events are reordered to emphasize strict causality. Morgan observes philosophical influence here and argues,

> it might indicate the extent to which the language and simplified concepts of philosophy seem to have been part of the ordinary frame of the educated mind, as seems to have been the case in the theory behind the teaching of grammar.[79]

Hermogenes gives the example of the paraphrase of a gnome in his discussion of elaboration (ἐργασία).[80] The elaboration exercise begins with a gnome, which is then paraphrased:

Gnome	*Paraphrase*
οὐ χρὴ παννύχιον εὕδειν βουληφόρον ἄνδρα.	δι᾽ ὅλης νυκτὸς οὐ προσήκει ἄνδρα ἐν βουλαῖς ἐξεταζόμενον καθεύδειν.
A man who is a counselor should not sleep throughout the night.	It is not fitting for a man, proven in councils, to sleep through the entire night.[81]

The gnome, here taken from *Iliad* 2.2.24, 61 and containing two uncommon words,[82] is rendered in good literary Attic by the paraphrase. The paraphrase is so extensive that only one word from the original, ἄνδρα, remains. Also worth noting is the fact that the Homeric source is not identified in either the initial citation of the gnome or in the paraphrase; yet it is likely that Theon's audience would have recognized the source, since this Homeric verse was widely quoted in the first and second century CE in a chria concerning Alexander and Diogenes of Sinope.[83]

Chriae could be transformed significantly, as can be seen with a chria recorded once by Athenaeus and a second time by Diogenes Laertius:[84]

Ἀρίστιππος ῥαινόμενος μὲν ὑπὸ τῶν τοῦ Διονυσίου θεραπόντων, σκωπτόμενος δ᾽ ἐπὶ τῷ ἀνέχεσθαι ὑπ᾽ Ἀντιφῶντος, "εἰ δ᾽ ἁλιευόμενος ἐτύγχανον, ἔφη, καταλιπὼν τὴν ἐργασίαν ἂν ἀπῆλθον;" (*Deipn.* 12.554D)

Διονυσίου δὲ προσπτύσαντος αὐτῷ ἠνέσχετο. μεμψαμένου δέ τινος, "εἶτα οἱ μὲν ἁλιεῖς," εἶπεν, "ὑπομενοῦσι ῥαίνεσθαι τῇ θαλάττῃ ἵνα κωβιὸν θηράσωσιν· ἐγὼ δὲ μὴ ἀνάσχωμαι κράματι ῥανθῆναι ἵνα βλέννον λάβω;" (DL 2.67)

Aristippus, being soaked by the attendants of Dionysius [the tyrant], and then being teased by Antiphon for tolerating it, said: "If I happened to be fishing just then, would I have left my work and departed?"

When Dionysius [the tyrant] spat upon [Aristippus], he put up with it. And when someone censured him, he said "Well, fishermen endure getting soaked by the sea so that they may catch gudgeon. Shouldn't I then put up with being soaked with spit so that I may get a *blennos*?"

While one cannot determine that one of these versions is a paraphrase of the other, the chria in Diogenes Laertius displays the wordplay typical of other Diogenes chriae: βλέννος means both "slime" and "a fish related to the κωβιόν [gudgeon]" (Aristotle, *Hist. an.* 591a28), and is related to βλέννα, "mucous discharge" (LSJ 318).

Paraphrase, according to Quintilian and Theon, is not merely an explication of the original. "Its duty," says Quintilian, "is rather to rival and vie [*aemulatio*] with the original in the expression of the same thoughts" (*Inst.* 10.5.5). Theon illustrates paraphrase with three quotations from Thucydides, Theopompus, and Demosthenes:

φθόνος γὰρ τοῖς ζῶσι πρὸς τὸ ἀντίπαλον, τὸ δὲ μὴ ἐμποδὼν ἀνανταγωνίστῳ εὐνοίᾳ τετίμηται.	ἐπίσταμαι γάρ, ὅτι τοὺς μὲν ζῶντας πολλοὶ μετὰ δυσμενείας ἐξετάζουσι, τοῖς δὲ τετελευτηκόσι διὰ τὸ πλῆθος τῶν ἐτῶν ἐπανιᾶσι τοὺς φθόνους.	τίς γὰρ οὐκ οἶδε τῶν πάντων, ὅτι τοῖς μὲν ζῶσιν ἅπασιν ὕπεστί τις ἢ πλείων ἢ ἐλάττων φθόνος, τοὺς τεθνεῶτας δὲ οὐ δὲ τῶν ἐχθρῶν τις μισεῖ;
There is envy in rivalry with the living, but one who no longer stands in the way has been honored with unchallenged good will. (Thucydides, 2.45)	For I know that many look upon the living with ill-will, but they abandon their envy of the dead through the number of years. (Theopompus, fr. 395 Jacoby)	Who among all of us does not know that some envy, greater or smaller, exists for all the living, but not even one of their enemies hates the dead? (Demosthenes, *Cor.* 315)

Here, despite the fact that the three express a common view that no one is envious of the dead, there is almost no agreement in their wording. Moreover, there is no attempt to credit the maxim to some other author;

in Thucydides, it appears on the lips of Pericles during his funeral speech, while Demosthenes employs it as a piece of self-evident wisdom in his own speech on the crown (no context is available for the Theopompus fragment).

The rhetorical practice of paraphrase thus provides us with a model for understanding both the lack of verbatim agreement between a predecessor text and its re-performance, and the fact that the product of paraphrase might be represented as the work of the paraphrast rather than as a citation of some earlier text. In this sense, the predecessor text is not a source, but rather a resource for rhetorical performance. The differences between the predecessor text and the paraphrase are due not to the vagaries of oral transmission, but to deliberate and studied techniques of verbal and conceptual transformation. What we might call plagiarism and intellectual theft is what rhetoricians called *aemulatio*—the restating of predecessors' ideas in one's own words. It is relatively clear that Theon expected that his student audience would recognize the ultimate source of his paraphrases, especially when it was Homer being paraphrased. Whether all audiences could be expected to recognize the predecessor texts is not clear, but it seems reasonable to assume that the rhetorician could count on some of his or her audience recognizing the predecessor text and thus appreciating the excellence of the formulation and its aptness in application, which was indeed the very goal of *aemulatio* for Theon and Quintilian.

Since there are other indications in the Letter of James that the author understands and uses rhetorical figures and forms,[85] and given the generally good quality of the author's Greek,[86] it is not unreasonable to suppose that the author likewise understood the principles of paraphrase and *aemulatio* in his reproduction of the early Jesus tradition. It is unnecessary for my case to assume that the author of James was the beneficiary of a formal rhetorical training, though that is not impossible. The level of rhetorical training illustrated by the *Progymnasmata* is indeed not terribly advanced, and it is conceivable either that the author had some exposure to such exercises, or that as a literate person he was able to recognize and imitate rhetorical practices.

Testing the Model

James' use of paraphrase and *aemulatio* may now be illustrated by reference to one of his sayings. For reasons of space, I shall consider only three instances, two that are regularly identified as allusions to the Jesus tradition (1:5; 2:5) and one, 1:2 (12), that is less commonly attributed to the Jesus tradition. In each case, it is necessary to show how the practice of *aemulatio*, the techniques of paraphrase, and the rhetorical exigencies of these three pericopae can account for details of the transformation that James has effected on the Jesus tradition.

James 1:2, 12 and Q 6:22-23

The exhortation to rejoice in the midst of trials (πειρασμοί) in 1:2 is followed immediately by a sorites that asserts that such trials are the means of testing (τὸ δοκίμιον), producing endurance, which in turn leads to maturity and completeness (1:4). It is this logical chain that provides the rationale for the initial exhortation of verse 2.[87]

Some have doubted that there is any connection between James 1:2 and Q 6:22-23. The actual verbal contacts are slight (χαρά–χαίρω and ὅταν); James does not frame the saying as a macarism or intimate that πειρασμοί occur because of one's association with Jesus; and for James 1:2-4, the final state is less an eschatological reward or compensation for persecution than it is the natural result of the refining that comes from endurance.[88] The second and final points can be mitigated, however, by the observation that the recapitulation of the theme in 1:12 is framed as a macarism that speaks of "receiving the crown of life," evidently a notion of eschatological reward.[89]

The notion that the faithful are tested and proven through hardship and suffering is of course common, not only in the Tanak and Second Temple Judaism, but also in Greco-Roman thought.[90] What is less common is the admonition to rejoice in the midst of suffering. Though the motif is attested in Judith (with εὐχαριστήσωμεν rather than χαίρετε), 4 Maccabees (with μακάριόν ἐστιν), and *2 Baruch*[91]—the latter two belonging to the first century CE—it is particularly common in the literature of the Jesus movement.[92] Nauck disputes the suggestion that the motif in 1 Peter 1:6; 4:13-14 and James 1:2 shows any dependence on the Jesus tradition, arguing instead that "in all probability it depended on earlier [Jewish] traditions."[93] In the case of 1 Peter 4:13-14, however, the strong verbal contacts with Q (χαίρετε / χαίρετε, εἰ ὀνειδίζεσθε / ὅταν ὀνειδίσωσαν, ἐν ὀνόματι Χριστοῦ / ἕνεκεν τοῦ υἱοῦ τοῦ ἀνθρώπου, μακάριοι / μακάριοι) make it likely that 1 Peter is adapting the Jesus tradition.[94] In the case of James, the case is somewhat weaker, but not significantly so, since James 1:2, 12 shares with Q 6:22-23 the form of a macarism (in 1:12), the admonition to rejoice in adversity (χαίρετε / χαρὰν ἡγήσασθε), and the notion of eschatological reward (in 1:12). It is difficult to see how deriving James 1:2 from Jewish tradition is a more efficient explanation, especially when 4 Maccabees, one of the two main exemplars of that tradition, is not significantly earlier than James, and the other, *2 Baruch*, is contemporaneous at best.[95]

If one proceeds on the assumption that James 1:2-4, 12-15 is a paraphrase and elaboration of Q 6:22-23, one can observe how James has reframed and adapted the saying for his own uses. First, the author compresses and generalizes Q's three actions (ὀνειδίσωσιν, διώξωσιν, εἴπωσιν πᾶν πονηρόν) into a single alliterative phrase, πειρασμοῖς περιπέσητε ποικίλοις.⁹⁶ A similar generalizing paraphrase can be seen in Aphthonius' transformation of a gnome from Theognis:

χρὴ πενίην φεύγοντα καὶ ἐς μεγακήτεα πόντον ῥιπτεῖν καὶ πετρῶν, Κύρνε, κατηλιβάτων.	ὁ πενίᾳ συζῶν ἀγαπάτω πεσεῖν, ὡς ἄμεινον τοῦ βίου προαπελθεῖν ἢ τὸν ἥλιον αἰσχύνης κτήσασθαι μάρτυρα.
One fleeing poverty, Cyrnus, must throw himself into the yawning sea and down steep crags. (Theognis 175)	Let the one living in poverty be content to fall, since it is better to cut life short than to make the sun a witness to shame.⁹⁷

The paraphrase here illustrates the overriding virtue of *aemulatio*—vying with the original for beauty of expression. Aphthonius comments that it is easy to see its beauty (ὡς καλῶς). The paraphrase not only reduces the florid language of Theognis, an example of one of the *modi* of paraphrase that Quintilian recommends, to remove effusive language (*effusa substringere*, 10.5.4) and to express the original in nonfigurative language (*hoc oratio recta, illud figura declinata commendat*, 10.5.8); it also introduces the process of elaboration by supplying a rationale for the admonition, a process that is continued in the rest of Aphthonius' elaboration exercise.

James' paraphrase generalizes by referring to trials (πειρασμοί) rather than to more specific instances of abuse. Commentators regularly dispute whether the trials of verse 2 should be interpreted as instances of either persecution or the more ordinary pressures of life.⁹⁸ The former is clearly the sense of Q 6:22-23 and the texts from 4 Maccabees and *2 Baruch*.⁹⁹ But as will become clear from James 1:14-15, James will eventually argue that trials are caused by ἐπιθυμίαι, that is, that whatever the occasion of trial, the key issue is not persecution or more quotidian testing but the danger of corrosion of the self that these both occasion. The paraphrase, then, not only invokes the persecution beatitude and the admonition to rejoice in the midst of suffering because this is a badge of blessedness, but also generalizes the admonition so that it can compass other sorts of adversities.

James' next step is to supply a *causa* in the form of a sorites (using the figure of a κλῖμαξ, *gradatio*), which connects testing with endurance and endurance with maturity and completeness (1:3-4).¹⁰⁰ In doing this, it is important to note the reframing that is taking place. The immediate grounds for rejoicing are not that one will be rewarded by God, but that such testing will produce (or disclose) maturity and perfection of character. There is, no doubt, an overriding assumption that such character will also be rewarded by God (1:12), and James' elaboration of ἐν μηδενὶ λειπόμενοι (1:4) in reference to the acquisition of wisdom (1:5-8) makes it clear that God's benefactions are always in view. It is important, nevertheless, to note how the paraphrase and elaboration concentrate on detailing the intervening steps between suffering and its reward.

The final step of the elaboration appears in 1:12-15 with a second paraphrase of the beatitude, this time framing it in the μακάριος + ὁ ἀνήρ form typical of Wisdom Psalms, Proverbs, and Sirach.[101] Key elements of 1:2-4 are resumed—ὑπομένει, πειρασμόν, δόκιμος γενόμενος—and it is here that the motif of reward in Q 6:23 appears, τὸν στέφανον τῆς ζωῆς, ὃν ἐπηγγείλατο τοῖς ἀγαπῶσιν αὐτόν. The choice of στέφανος (crown, wreath) over μισθός (wages) is an expression of aptum—the "virtue of the parts in fitting themselves harmoniously together into the whole."[102] For James 1:12 invokes vocabulary of civic honors (being approved, respected) and athletic achievement (endurance), which are typically rewarded with crowns rather than wages.

The second paraphrase of Q 6:22-23 leads to an argument from the contrary, again framed as a sorites, contending that the cause of trials is desires (ἐπιθυμίαι), not God, and that these desires, if left unchecked, produce sin, which in turn produces death. James' formulation of verse 15 is a verbal counterpart to verses 3-4, with ἀποτελεσθεῖσα answering ἔργον τέλειον ἐχέτω:

3 τὸ δοκίμιον ὑμῶν τῆς πίστεως κατεργάζεται ὑπομονήν·
4 ἡ δὲ ὑπομονὴ ἔργον τέλειον ἐχέτω, ἵνα ἦτε τέλειοι καὶ ὁλόκληροι.

εἶτα ἡ ἐπιθυμία συλλαβοῦσα τίκτει ἁμαρτίαν,
ἡ δὲ ἁμαρτία ἀποτελεσθεῖσα ἀποκύει θάνατον.

If the initial premise is granted, that James 1:2 has Q 6:22-23 in view, James' paraphrastic and elaborative techniques are fully intelligible against the background of the practices of aemulatio and elaboration outlined in Quintilian and the Progymnasmata of Theon, Hermogenes, and Aphthonius. Bauckham is indeed correct that this is not a matter of James "quoting" the Jesus tradition; rather, it is a matter of James using the Jesus tradition as resource and engaging in the emulation and elaboration of a protreptic maxim. James' procedure can be illustrated as of paraphrase and the supplying of a rationale:

Gnome	Gnome paraphrased	Rationale
Q 6:22 μακάριοί ἐστε ὅταν μισήσωσιν ὑμᾶς καὶ ὅταν ὀνειδίσωσιν καὶ ἐκβάλωσιν τὸ ὄνομα ὑμῶν ὡς πονηρὸν ἕνεκεν τοῦ υἱοῦ τοῦ ἀνθρώπου· 23 χαίρετε καὶ ἀγαλλιᾶσθε, ὅτι ὁ μισθὸς ὑμῶν πολὺς ἐν τῷ οὐρανῷ·	2 πᾶσαν χαρὰν ἡγήσασθε, ἀδελφοί μου, ὅταν πειρασμοῖς περιπέσητε ποικίλοις, 12 μακάριος ἀνὴρ ὃς ὑπομένει πειρασμόν, ὅτι δόκιμος γενόμενος λήμψεται τὸν στέφανον τῆς ζωῆς, ὃν ἐπηγγείλατο τοῖς ἀγαπῶσιν αὐτόν.	3 γινώσκοντες ὅτι τὸ δοκίμιον ὑμῶν τῆς πίστεως κατεργάζεται ὑπομονήν· 4 ἡ δὲ ὑπομονὴ ἔργον τέλειον ἐχέτω, ἵνα ἦτε τέλειοι καὶ ὁλόκληροι, ἐν μηδενὶ λειπόμενοι *Argument e contrario* 13 μηδεὶς πειραζόμενος λεγέτω ὅτι ἀπὸ θεοῦ πειράζομαι· ὁ γὰρ θεὸς ἀπείραστός ἐστιν κακῶν, πειράζει δὲ αὐτὸς οὐδένα. 14 ἕκαστος δὲ πειράζεται ὑπὸ τῆς ἰδίας ἐπιθυμίας ἐξελκόμενος καὶ δελεαζόμενος· 15 εἶτα ἡ ἐπιθυμία συλλαβοῦσα τίκτει ἁμαρτίαν, ἡ δὲ ἁμαρτία ἀποτελεσθεῖσα ἀποκύει θάνατον.

In each of the paraphrases, James picks up significant vocabulary or ideas from the resource text (Q 6:22-23), paraphrases it, and then begins the process of elaboration, first by supplying a rationale (vv. 3-4) and then, in the second elaboration, supplying an argument from the contrary to demonstrate that the failure to resist trials leads to the precise opposite (death) of the reward of such resistance (the crown of life).

James 1:5 and Q 11:9-10

The case for James' use of the Q aphorism, "ask and it will be given you, seek and you will find," is much clearer than for 1:2, 12. This saying is widely attested in the Jesus tradition, appearing in Q 11:9-10; James 1:5; *POxy* 4 654.6-9 (*Gos. Thom.* 2); *Gospel of Thomas* 92, 94; *Gospel of the Hebrews* 4a-b; *Dialogue of the Savior* 9-12, 20d; John 14:13-14; 15:7, 16b;

16:23-24, 26—twelve occurrences, counting *POxy* 4 654.6-9/*Gospel of Thomas* 2 and Q (Matt 7:7-8/Luke 11:9-10) as single occurrences. In surveying all of the performances, it is noteworthy that most have to do with the seeking of wisdom or life. This application of the saying is appropriate, of course, given the association in Wisdom literature between the verbs ζητεῖν and εὑρίσκειν and wisdom or life.[103]

The saying has been transformed in the Sayings Gospel Q and related to the practice of prayer. This is obvious both from the fact that it is prefaced by the Lord's Prayer (Q 11:2-4) and that it is followed by an illustration, Q 11:11-13 (unattested in any of the other occurrences of the admonition), which picks up key vocabulary from the prayer (πατήρ, ἄρτος, διδόναι). As Ronald Piper observes, Q's interest in the admonition is not in seeking/finding or knocking/opening, but only in asking and receiving.[104] Thus, Piper argues, an admonition that did not originally have specifically to do with prayer has been given a setting where αἰτεῖν clearly now means "to pray."

Of the twelve occurrences of the admonition, only Q, James 1:5, and three occurrences in John include the verb αἰτεῖν and apply it to prayer. The application of the admonition to the practice of prayer appears to derive from Q's particular framing of the saying and represents a secondary elaboration. From this, one can conclude that the version in James is related to a specific development in the history of the Q saying.[105] It cannot be shown that James depends on the final form of Q, since the unit in Q 11:2-4, 9-13 is not usually thought to derive from Q's final redaction.[106] Nevertheless, Q's application of the seek/find saying to prayer is clearly the result of redactional arrangement in Q at some stage.

James' paraphrase of the admonition not only borrows Q's application but also preserves the extraordinary confidence reflected in Q 11:9-10, αἰτείτω / αἰτεῖτε . . . καὶ δοθήσεται. At the same time, James is fully aware of the likely "original" context of the injunction as an admonition to seek (pray) for σοφία.[107] The variation in syntax is required by the conditional introduction employed by James (εἰ δέ τις ὑμῶν λείπεται σοφίας), and required in turn by the final flourish of verse 4, ὁλόκληροι, ἐν μηδενὶ λειπόμενοι.[108]

James' paraphrase is what Quintilian calls paraphrase through expansion (10.5.8). The original admonition is systematically expanded, first by elaborating on the nature of God, who is the object of αἰτεῖν and who is implied in the passive δοθήσεται. The insistence on the unstinting generosity of God (παρὰ τοῦ διδόντος θεοῦ πᾶσιν ἁπλῶς καὶ μὴ ὀνειδίζοντος) not only accounts for the categorical nature of δοθήσεται αὐτῷ but also shows an awareness of Q's *qal wehomer* argument concerning the super-beneficent character of God (Q 11:11-13). As I have suggested elsewhere, this elaboration also anticipates the argument of James 2:1-13 against the practice of patronage. James 1:5 employs the tropes of simple and non-reproachful giving, which are in fact the precise opposite of satirists' description of patronage, which required the client to endure reproaches and insults and to engage in demeaning demonstrations of gratitude that underscored the subservient status of the client.[109] God's beneficence is thus the polar opposite of demeaning patronage. The very next admonition in James (1:9-11) in fact touches on status differentials, warning the wealthy of the transient nature of their wealth.

The second part of the elaboration focuses on the subject of the verb αἰτείτω and, like 1:2-4, 12-15, concentrates on the inner disposition of the petitioner. James first insists that asking should be done ἐν πίστει, μηδὲν διακρινόμενος, but the bulk of the elaboration (vv. 6b-8) is an argument from the contrary: ὁ γὰρ διακρινόμενος ἔοικεν κλύδωνι θαλάσσης ἀνεμιζομένῳ καὶ ῥιπιζομένῳ· 7 μὴ γὰρ οἰέσθω ὁ ἄνθρωπος ἐκεῖνος ὅτι λήμψεταί τι παρὰ τοῦ κυρίου. 8 ἀνὴρ δίψυχος, ἀκατάστατος ἐν πάσαις ταῖς ὁδοῖς αὐτοῦ. The introduction of the theme of "doublemindedness" is another instance of aptum, since the word itself is one of James' favorites (1:8; 4:8) and may even be a new coinage.[110] The effect of this argument from the contrary is to qualify Q 11:10 (πᾶς γὰρ ὁ αἰτῶν λαμβάνει, καὶ ὁ ζητῶν εὑρίσκει), which might suggest that prayer automatically results in one receiving the thing requested.

A second qualification of Q 11:9-10 appears in the second paraphrase of the admonition, found later in 4:2-3. James' substitution of λαμβάνειν for the passive of διδόναι has the effect of shifting attention from God's non-giving to human non-reception, and focuses on the conditions that obviate the possibility of reception: conflict and pursuit of pleasures. Like the elaboration in 1:6b-8, James' interest lies with inner dispositions.

The texts of James 1:5-8 and 4:2-3 thus both betray dependence on Q's particular transformation of the older seek/find admonition into an admonition on prayer, buttressed by the image of a super-generous God, and illustrate the way that, through paraphrasis, aemulatio, and elaboration, James appropriated the saying and redirected it to his own usage as an exhortation to seek wisdom with the appropriate disposition. The practices of paraphrase and aemulatio account for both the continuities with Q 11:9-10 and the significant differences in wording, syntax, and application. James' procedure can again be illustrated by the chart on p. 96.

The first paraphrase (Jas 1:5) expands the original gnome and then elaborates on the key word αἰτείτω, qualifying Q's unbridled optimism and explaining the grounds for non-reception. The second paraphrase restates the gnome but now in its opposite form, again explaining that non-reception can be traced to evil intentions, a penchant of James.

James 2:5 and Q 6:20b

Along with James 1:5, James 2:5 is one of the verses most frequently cited as evidence that James knew the Jesus tradition.[111] It is clear from the grammatical structure of 2:5 that James is appealing to something that is taken as common knowledge for his addressees. Moreover, as Deppe points out, βασιλεία is not typical Jacobian vocabulary, and hence it does not seem far-fetched to see an intertextual reference to Q 6:20b.[112] There are, of course, dissenters. Spitta argued that James merely reflects the same view of the poor that can be found in pre-Christian Jewish literature.[113] Meyer argued similarly, citing Psalms 37:11, 22-23; 1 Samuel 2:8; and *Psalms of Solomon* 5:12 and 15:2 as expressive of the same sympathetic views of the poor that James conveys.[114] What is lacking in these alleged parallels, however, is not discourse about God's care of the poor, but any sense that the poor are definitively privileged with respect to the βασιλεία.[115] In fact, it is only in the Jesus tradition and James 2:5 that we find *kingdom* and πτωχοί together.[116] I will indicate below that there are other reasons to suppose that James was aware of Q 6:20b, but for now it is sufficient to conclude that James' invocation of a belief that the poor are especially privileged in the kingdom is a good indication of a material link with Q 6:20b.

Wachob is the only author to date to appeal to the rhetorical practice of recitation (ἀπαγγελεία) with respect to James' citation of Leviticus 19:15-18 and the Jesus tradition in James 2:1-13.[117] According to Wachob, James' recitation involves an alteration in the *stasis*—in rhetorical theory, the fundamental issue that underlies a particular case.[118] In Q (and *Gos. Thom.* 54), the *stasis* is that of fact and the macarism is predominantly epideictic, predicated on the premise that those addressed by the macarism already belong to the kingdom.[119] Matthew's formulation, μακάριοι οἱ πτωχοὶ ἐν πνεύματι, ὅτι αὐτῶν ἐστιν ἡ βασιλεία τῶν οὐρανῶν, is like James', deliberative and related to surrounding assertions concerning the importance of keeping the Torah (Matt 5:17-20; Jas 1:25).[120] The macarisms of the Sermon on the Mount describe a set of qualities directly pertinent to the overarching value of "doing the Torah," and as such they have deliberative force: "one ought to be poor in spirit, i.e., humble." Likewise, for James, the *stasis* is that of quality, and James' interests are deliberative:

> Hence, the construction of James 2:5 makes it very clear that whatever God's reasons for choosing the poor the promise of the kingdom cannot be interpreted as a reward for their earthly poverty. For like the "in spirit" qualification of "the poor" in Q^Matt

Gnome	Gnome paraphrased through expansion	Elaboration
Q 11:9-10 λέγω ὑμῖν, αἰτεῖτε	5 εἰ δέ τις ὑμῶν λείπεται σοφίας, αἰτείτω παρὰ τοῦ διδόντος θεοῦ πᾶσιν ἁπλῶς καὶ μὴ ὀνειδίζοντος,	
καὶ δοθήσεται ὑμῖν, ζητεῖτε καὶ εὑρήσετε· κρούετε, καὶ ἀνοιγή-σεται ὑμῖν. 10 πᾶς γὰρ ὁ αἰτῶν λαμβά-νει, καὶ ὁ ζητῶν εὑρίσκει, καὶ τῷ κρούοντι ἀνοιγή-σεται. τίς ἐστιν ἐξ ὑμῶν ἄνθρωπος, ὃν αἰτήσει ὁ υἱὸς αὐτοῦ ἄρτον, μὴ λίθον ἐπιδώσει αὐτῷ. ἢ καὶ ἰχθὺν αἰτήσει, μὴ ὄφιν ἐπιδώσει αὐτῷ; εἰ οὖν ὑμεῖς πονηροὶ ὄντες οἴδατε δόματα ἀγαθὰ διδόναι τοῖς τέκνοις ὑμῶν, πόσῳ μᾶλλον ὁ πατὴρ ἐξ οὐρανοῦ δώσει ἀγαθὰ τοῖς αἰτοῦσιν αὐτόν.	καὶ δοθήσεται αὐτῷ.	6 αἰτείτω δὲ ἐν πίστει, μηδὲν διακρινόμενος, ὁ γὰρ διακρινόμενος ἔοικεν κλύδωνι θαλάσσης ἀνεμιζο-μένῳ καὶ ῥιπιζομένῳ· 7 μὴ γὰρ οἰέσθω ὁ ἄνθρωπος ἐκεῖνος ὅτι λήμψεταί τι παρὰ τοῦ κυρίου, 8 ἀνὴρ δίψυχος, ἀκατάστατος ἐν πάσαις ταῖς ὁδοῖς αὐτοῦ.

Gnome	Gnome reversed	Rationale
Q 11,9-10 λέγω ὑμῖν, αἰτεῖτε καὶ δοθήσεται ὑμῖν, ... 10 πᾶς γὰρ ὁ αἰτῶν λαμβάνει. ...	οὐκ ἔχετε διὰ τὸ μὴ αἰτεῖσθαι ὑμᾶς· αἰτεῖτε καὶ οὐ λαμ-βάνετε,	διότι κακῶς αἰτεῖσθε, ἵνα ἐν ταῖς ἡδοναῖς ὑμῶν δαπανήσητε.

5:3, James 2:5 positively qualifies "the poor" whom God has chosen as the "rich in faith." And, also like "the poor in spirit" (Q^Matt 5:3), "the poor" who are "rich in faith" (James 2:5) refer to an achieved status; moreover, in James 2:5 "rich in faith" is synonymous with "loving God" and both are functionally equivalent to fulfilling the law of God.[121]

Although Wachob discusses the general transformation of an epideictic to a deliberative saying, he does not treat the details of James' paraphrase.[122] James' individual choices in the paraphrase of Q 6:20b can be understood by seeing the rhetorical exigence at work. Wachob has shown that James 2:1-13 exhibits the form of the elaborated argument described in Pseudo-Cicero's *Rhetorica ad Herennium* 2.18.28.[123] The elaboration consists of five main parts: a statement of the theme (*res*) or proposition to be argued (*propositio*); a brief explanation that sets forth the basis for the proposition (*ratio*); the proofs (*confirmatio*); an embellishment (*exornatio*) consisting of similes, examples, amplifications, or previous judgments; and finally a résumé (*conplexio*).[124]

On this view, James 2:5 is not the *propositio* or *ratio* but the beginning of the *confirmatio*. The proof comes in two main sections, verses 5-7 and verses 8-11, with the first part consisting of three rhetorical questions (vv. 5-6a, 6b, 7),[125] each anticipating an affirmative response. James' overall purpose is to show that acts of partiality (προσωπολημψία) both are against self-interest (vv. 5-7) and amount to a violation of the Torah (vv. 8-11). The specific strategy in both parts involves demonstrating that values that the addressees claim to embrace are in fact violated by their acts. Thus, both parts of the proof begin with an appeal to a principle to which the addressees would evidently assent:

οὐχ ὁ θεὸς ἐξελέξατο τοὺς πτωχοὺς τῷ κόσμῳ πλουσίους ἐν πίστει καὶ κληρονόμους τῆς βασιλείας ἧς ἐπηγγείλατο τοῖς ἀγαπῶσιν αὐτόν;	8 εἰ μέντοι νόμον τελεῖτε βασιλικὸν κατὰ τὴν γραφήν, Ἀγαπήσεις τὸν πλησίον σου ὡς σεαυτόν, καλῶς ποιεῖτε·

The argument then continues with a contrasting statement, which shows that the addressees do not in fact live up to what is implied in the principle:

6 ὑμεῖς δὲ ἠτιμάσατε τὸν   9 εἰ δὲ προσωπολημπτεῖτε, ἁμαρ-
πτωχόν.   τίαν ἐργάζεσθε, ἐλεγχόμενοι ὑπὸ
                                τοῦ νόμου ὡς παραβάται.

The purpose in both constructions is to demonstrate a collision between shared principles and the behavior that James believes to be in evidence. In both cases, it is not sufficient to indicate that the addressees assent mentally to the principle. They must also believe that they live in accordance with the principle—hence the commendation, καλῶς ποιεῖτε, in the second main argument. In the first argument, it is insufficient merely to state what for James' addressees is a truism, that the poor are blessed because they have the kingdom. James' elaboration of Q's bare οἱ πτωχοί as οἱ πτωχοὶ τῷ κόσμῳ makes it clear that these poor are aligned with one of the main binary oppositions of the letter, between the (actual) rich and (actual) poor. These poor are not Matthew's "poor in spirit," as James 2:2 shows (πτωχὸς ἐν ῥυπαρᾷ ἐσθῆτι). They carry the emblems of their status on their bodies. Nevertheless, James evidently expects the addressees to incline to these poor and against the rich. The second aspect of the elaboration involves three claims that James presents as though they should not be controversial: that the poor are chosen to be "rich in faith" (a key value for James; cf. 1:3, 6; 2:1, 5, 14, 17, 18, 22-24, 26; 5:15); that they will "inherit the kingdom"; and that the kingdom is for "those who love God," a phrase James has already used in respect to those rewarded with the "crown of life" (1:12). These three elaborative elements are intended to appeal to the addressees' beliefs about themselves. James' expansion of Q 6:20b is a function of his need to cement the identification of the addressees with the poor of Q 6:20b.

It is only once this has been accomplished that the contrasting minor premise, ὑμεῖς δὲ ἠτιμάσατε τὸν πτωχόν, can have its full force. The argument in 2:5-6a involves the topos of *the honorable*, since 2:5 associates the poor with the honor of the divine King. But the combination of the major (2:5) and minor (2:6a) premises shows that acts of the addressees run counter to God's honoring of the "poor in the world." And insofar as the addressees identify with those poor, their acts are acts against self-interest. That is, the rhetorical appeal in this argument is to pathos.

The rhetorical exigence of demonstrating that acts of the addressees (or more properly, acts that the author believes to be his addressees') are incompatible with shared principles thus accounts for the details of James' elaborative paraphrase of Q 6:20b. James has paraphrased the Jesus saying in such a way that his addressees would recognize the ultimate source, but also so that it will serve the particulars of his argument.

Gnome	Gnome paraphrased by expansion	Argument from the contrary
μακάριοι οἱ πτωχοί, ὅτι ὑμετέρα ἐστὶν ἡ βασιλεία τοῦ θεοῦ	5 ἀκούσατε, ἀδελφοί μου ἀγαπητοί. οὐχ ὁ θεὸς ἐξελέξατο τοὺς πτωχοὺς τῷ κόσμῳ πλουσίους ἐν πίστει καὶ κληρονόμους τῆς βασιλείας ἧς ἐπηγγείλατο τοῖς ἀγαπῶσιν αὐτόν;	6a ὑμεῖς δὲ ἠτιμάσατε τὸν πτωχόν.

It should also be noted that the context of James 2:5 betrays knowledge of the larger Q context at two points. The topic of the rich dragging the poor ("you") into court is implied in both Q 6:29—the scenario of a lawsuit to recover a surety after default—and Q 12:58-59. It is worth noting that both Q texts are framed from the point of view of the victim of the courts, the poor debtor from whom sureties or payments are extracted.[126] James preserves the same perspective by identifying the addressees (ὑμᾶς) with those dragged into court and by stating what is left unstated in Q: that it is the rich (οἱ πλούσιοι) who are their legal adversaries.

James 2:7 echoes a second element from the Q context when it alleges that the rich "blaspheme the honourable name called over you." A likely reconstruction of Q 6:22 uses the phrase ἐκβαλῶσιν τὸ ὄνομα ὑμῶν ὡς πονηρόν,[127] a Semitism (רע שם הוציא) that means "to defame" or "to slander" (Deut 22:14, 19). James' adaptations of Q 6:22 are twofold: first, to identify the subject of Q's third person plural verbs as οἱ πλούσιοι (v. 6a), and then to rephrase Q's idiom as τὸ καλὸν ὄνομα τὸ ἐπικληθὲν ἐφ᾽ ὑμῶν, perhaps a reference to baptismal identification of the subject with the Jesus movement.[128] This turns Q's general reference to slander into a particular accusation of disparaging members of the Jesus movement for their very identification with Jesus. The paraphrase preserves, however, Q's focus on the topic of the honorable, and the argument again amounts to an appeal to pathos. If the name called over the addressees is honorable, associating them with the divine King and with Jesus (?), it is an act against self-interest to associate with the rich, who slander that name.

As with James 1:5, James 2:5 not only appeals to Q 6:20b as a maxim known by the addressees but also betrays knowledge of the wider literary context of Q 6:20-29 (and 12:58-59). James' paraphrase is controlled by the rhetorical exigence of 2:1-13 to construct an argument against partiality. This requires the reframing of the (indicative) macarism as a rhetorical question, parallel to the two other questions in 2:6b-7, and amplification of the saying so as to underscore the fact that the addressees identify themselves with the poor of the macarism.

Conclusion

This analysis could be extended to all of the sayings of Jesus reflected in James, and with similar results. In his paraphrases, James reveals dependence on both individual Q sayings (and in the case of 5:12, on a version of Matt 5:33-37) and the ways that the Sayings Gospel frames and deploys those sayings, a sure indication that James is not merely dependent on the oral tradition from which Q also was compiled. At the same time, James, composing in an environment similar to Sirach's scribal culture and employing the rhetorical techniques of recitation and paraphrase, transformed the Jesus sayings grammatically and in application and, typical of the practice of *aemulatio*, represented the product as his own. The practice of *aemulatio* presupposes, on the one hand, that the audience will normally be able to identify the intertext that the author is paraphrasing, and thus will see how the author aligns himself or herself with the ethos of the original speaker; and on the other, that the audience will appreciate the artistry of paraphrase and application of the old maxim to a new rhetorical situation.

CHAPTER 6

THE HISTORICAL CONTEXT
OF THE LETTER OF JAMES IN LIGHT
OF ITS TRADITIO-HISTORICAL
RELATIONS WITH FIRST PETER

Matthias Konradt

If James is "authentic," then it was written in Jerusalem before 62 CE, the year of the death of the Lord's brother. If it is not,[1] as the exegetical majority—in my opinion correctly—assumes, then the question of the historical location of James is open, and difficult to answer. "Lokalkolorit fehlt."[2] The traditio-historical relations of James to other writings of its time present a possible point of access to this question. This would most especially apply if it were possible to differentiate between varying strains within a certain piece of tradition, and to then assign the formulation of the tradition found in James to one of them. Since oral tradition is dependent upon (groups of) tradents, one might continue from here with the inquiry into whether the traditio-historical findings can be set in relationship with known data about the history of early Christianity.

A side aspect of the historical localization is the question of the pseudepigraphic background of the letter: why did the author choose to portray his arguments and admonitions as a writing of James, the brother of the Lord? Did he profess to a form of Christianity that honored James as the ecclesiastical authority? Is there a relationship between the traditional material taken up in James and the leader of the congregation in Jerusalem on a material level? Or can other reasons be cited for ascribing the epistle to James?

The discussion of the traditio-historical background of James generally concentrates on the (positive) relations to the Jesus tradition on the
one hand,[3] and the (negative) relations to the Pauline tradition on the
other.[4] Affinities with the Apostolic Fathers, especially with *Shepherd of
Hermas*, also occasionally receive attention.[5] Although scholars have long
taken note of the close resemblances to 1 Peter,[6] which is also pseudepigraphic,[7] the discussion only moves between two alternatives—whether
literary dependence exists,[8] or whether common traditional material was
processed[9]—and finds an end with the resolution of this question. With
the triumph of *Formgeschichte*, the latter option has prevailed—justly, in
my opinion—as the view of the majority. In some cases, however, the
resemblances are so close that the traditio-historical correlation must be
pursued more exactly, instead of generally pointing to the wide ocean of
the occurrence of individual motifs elsewhere. To put it another way, the
question must be posed whether a starting point for the historical localization of James (and of 1 Peter) can be found here.

That the close relationship between James and 1 Peter, which shall be
demonstrated in the remarks to follow, has not been given more attention
to date may also be due to the fact that from a theological standpoint, the
assessments allotted to both writings have been diametrically opposed. As
is well known, Martin Luther compared everything with Paul theologically. While 1 Peter met with a positive estimation, James was degraded
to a "strawy epistle."[10] In modern exegesis, the postulate of the theological
proximity of 1 Peter to Paul has been flanked traditio-historically by the
hypothesis that 1 Peter is deeply rooted in the Pauline tradition.[11] Most
recently, however, James has experienced a theological upgrading over
against Luther's judgment, and perception of James has broadened over
against a narrowed viewpoint through the receptional filter of Pauline
statements on justification. This has gone to the extent that the consensus
of an antithetical reference to Paul—or more precisely, to a Paulinism
that distorts Paul himself—in James 2:14-26 has been put in question in
some recent publications.[12] Simultaneously, with respect to 1 Peter, its
"Paulinism" has been assessed more reservedly or even denied altogether
by some scholars.[13] A new round of discussion has been opened, to which
the following remarks intend to make a contribution. The emphasis shall
thereby be laid upon James.

My hypothesis is that the close resemblances between James and 1
Peter offer a starting point for historically localizing James on the map
of early Christianity. For that purpose, I will attempt to set the traditio-
historical findings in relationship with historical data on early Christianity, especially with data on James' and Peter's activities and impact. At the
same time, linking both perspectives builds a foundation for being able to

make considerations on the background of the pseudepigraphic ascription of James.

The Common Traditions of the Epistles of James and First Peter and Their Respective Redactional Tendencies

James 1:2-3; 1 Peter 1:6-7

Recent research on James widely recognizes that the letter contains a prologue in which the themes treated in the corpus are introduced summarily. The delimitation of the prologue is controversial;[14] in my opinion, a caesura must be set after 1:12. Within the programmatic introductory verses, 1:2-4 stands out as a thematically fundamental opening section, in which the writer names the ground coordinates of his ethical concern with a few strokes of his pen. In 1:2-4, he formulates the topic of steadfastness of faith in the face of temptation (1:2-3) by taking up traditional material, as Romans 5:3-5 and 1 Peter 1:6-7 demonstrate.

It is striking that only one of the parallel texts consistently converges with James, so that Romans 5:3-5 and 1 Peter 1:6-7 do not display any closer relationship to one another. While James 1:2-3 and Romans 5:3-5 are similar in structure, literal agreeement can only be pointed to in κατεργάζεται ὑπονονήν[15] and, more indirectly, in δοκίμιον/δοκιμή. By contrast, striking common ground between James and 1 Peter can be found in vocabulary, but not in structure. The resemblances to Romans 5:3-5 are confined to the ὅτι-clause in James 1:3, the content of which is portrayed in the sentence's introduction with γινώσκοντες as a reminder of what the addressees already know. If one additionally considers that τὸ δοκίμιον ὑμῶν τῆς πίστεως also occurs in 1 Peter 1:7, the conclusion suggests itself that the ὅτι-clause in James is a citation. In verse 2, πειρασμοὶ ποικίλοι stems from the tradition; otherwise, the verse seems to have been formulated relatively freely,[16] as far as its language is concerned. Paul does not have to have been familiar with the tradition in the exact form in which the author of James took it up. It could just as well be a side strain, but in the end, this question cannot be clarified. To put it another way: θλῖψις instead of τὸ δοκίμιον ὑμῶν τῆς πίστεως could be—but does not have to be—Pauline redaction. At any rate, no traces of the πειρασμοὶ ποικίλοι remain in Romans 5:3-5.

One is on firmer ground when the commonalities between James and 1 Peter are taken into account. Even if the common usage of πειρασμοὶ ποικίλοι might be viewed as purely accidental,[17] the expression τὸ δοκίμιον ὑμῶν τῆς πίστεως, which occurs only here in ancient literature, stands out so prominently—with respect not only to the word δοκίμιον,

seldom enough in and of itself, but also to the identical word order—that
a closer connection between the two texts can hardly be denied. This
common ground cannot be sufficiently explained by referring to the
traditionality of the motivic connection or the semantic field "tempta-
tion/trials-steadfastness-perseverance/patience-joy."[18] Rather, both texts
represent a specific elaboration of this motivic connection in early Christianity. The author of 1 Peter treated the piece of tradition more freely
than the author of James. The former only adopted the two striking main
words and the motif of joy in this strain of the tradition, while the latter
took up the tradition in citation form in 1:3, as has been shown.

The differing reception of tradition displays itself not only in a formal
respect, but also in content. The expression πειρασμοὶ ποικίλοι is seman-
tically open, allowing for a wider spectrum of application when taken for
itself.[19] If one looks at the respective contextual references to the tradition
adopted in James and 1 Peter, differences occur. In 1 Peter 1:6, the focus
is on the theme of suffering, central to 1 Peter as a whole,[20] and more specifically on the oppression of the Gentile Christian congregation by the
surrounding pagan society that was affronted by the Christians' rejection
of their previous life context—entailing the termination of communal ties
and common interests—and reacted to this with harassment, invectives,
and calumny. With the aid of the familiar motif of the refinement of gold
or silver by fire, suffering is interpreted here as a trial,[21] thereby spanning
a theological horizon of understanding for the addressees' situation.

This is different in James. Although the theme of suffering plays a
part at the end of the letter (5:6, 10-11), it is not the main topic of the
writing. Rather, the reference to πειρασμοὶ ποικίλοι in the fundamental
section of the summarizing exposition is explicated in the corpus (1:13–
5:6) with regard to the problem of endangerment of the Christians' ethical identity through their own desire, which belongs on the side of the
cosmos hostile to God, and attempts to entice the Christians with the
ungodly, "worldly" way of life with which they are confronted constantly
in their everyday life. Concretely, the theme of riches appears here as the
central problematic field.[22]

Diverging tendencies with regard to the motif of joy accompany
these differing adoptions of tradition. PsJames urges his addressees to be
joyous because of the πειρασμοί, since they offer opportunities to train
the immune system against the world and thereby foster steadfastness
(ὑπομονή). By contrast, in 1 Peter 1:6, joy is future joy[23] while the present
is characterized by affliction (λυπηθέντες) because of the current situation
of suffering.

To sum up: in James 1:2-3 and 1 Peter 1:6-7, two fundamentally
different adaptations of one common tradition, which was probably

originally part of baptismal instruction,[24] display themselves, each exactly corresponding to the varying overall intent of the two letters.

James 4:6-10; 1 Peter 5:5c-9

An analogous case to James 1:2-3 and 1 Peter 1:6-7 occurs in James 4:6-10 and 1 Peter 5:5c-9. In both texts, the double admonition to subject oneself to God and resist the devil follows a citation from Proverbs (3:34), and both present the same text variant differing from the Septuagint: ὁ θεός instead of κύριος.[25] Furthermore, humiliation before God is bound to the promise of exaltation in both, taking the participation in eschatological salvation into perspective.[26] In comparing James 4:10 and 1 Peter 5:6 with the related synoptic wisdom saying (Matt [18:4]; 23:12b; Luke 14:11; 18:14b),[27] the common deviations are also conspicuous. The imperative, which is not used reflexively (ἑαυτόν) but takes God as the object, replaces the participle ὁ ταπεινῶν. The active form ὑψώσει, with ὑμᾶς as an object,[28] takes the place of the *passivum divinum* ὑψωθήσεται. James 4:6-10 and 1 Peter 5:5c-9 apparently also originate from a common piece of tradition.

Simultaneously, both go their own ways in the elaboration of the tradition. In the Petrine adaption, the tradition is interpreted again with regard to the theme of suffering through affliction (1 Pet 5:9). The admonition to ταπεινοῦν is elaborated with the image of God's strong hand (5:6).[29] In line with the interpretation of suffering as a trial by God, affliction is to be accepted. The direct succession of the admonitions to subject oneself to God and resist the devil, which James 4:6 attests to in its probable original form,[30] is interrupted in 1 Peter 5 by various interpolations that underline the orientation of the piece of tradition toward the theme of suffering.[31]

Again, the case is otherwise in James. In the preceding passage, PsJames incriminates friendship with the world, which shows itself in a striving for material goods (4:1-3)[32] as incompatible with a relationship to God (4:4).[33] The tradition adopted in 4:6-10 is embedded in this context. Redactional elements underline this orientation. PsJames doubles the admonition to subjugate oneself to God by varying the call for humiliation (v. 10) taken from tradition, which he shifts to the very end, with the phrase ὑποτάγητε . . . τῷ θεῷ (v. 7; cf. LXX Ps 36:7). In light of verse 4, this doubling makes good sense; considering the addressees' friendship with the world, calling them back to God is the matter at hand. Verse 8a emphasizes this intention further. The imperatives in verse 7 appear in this context as admonitions to repent. Concretely, resistance against the devil means the renunciation of the behavior criticized previously.[34]

Finally, urgent admonitions to penitence in verse 9 are added on to the summons to purify hands and heart (v. 8b-c). Again, the following is clear: the authors of James and 1 Peter have also here interpreted and elaborated common traditional material differently, taking the respective congregational problems they have in sight—the theme of suffering in 1 Peter and the deplorable ethical conditions in James—into account.

James 1:18-21; 1 Peter 1:22–2:2

While the two previous examples give an indication of the different elaborations of common traditional material in James and 1 Peter, James 1:18-21 and 1 Peter 1:22–2:2 also display the close traditio-historical relationship of both writings over against other early Christian strains of tradition. To begin with, the interpretation of conversion as (re) birth is common to both text passages.[35] Terminologically, a difference displays itself: while PsJames, who was perhaps inspired by 1:15, uses ἀποκυεῖν, 1 Peter 1:23 speaks of an ἀναγεννᾶσθαι, as in 1:3. The concept of birth can also be verified, with variable terminology as well, for other circles of tradition.[36] However, the word is introduced as the effective medium for conversion only in James 1:18 and 1 Peter 1:23.[37] Furthermore, the word is defined in James 1:18 more specifically as λόγος ἀληθείας, which fits well with the context of conversion theology,[38] and ἀλήθεια is also mentioned in the Petrine context (1:22). The expression "word of truth" occurs at various points in the corpus Paulinum with reference to missionary proclamation,[39] but never in the framework of the interpretation of conversion as birth.

The significance of these findings is vividly highlighted by the resemblances between James 1:21 and 1 Peter 2:1-2. PsJames and Peter apply a bipartite paraenetic scheme here, in which the Christian's reaction—initially occurring in conversion and constantly expected of him—to God's soteriological action is formulated concisely by referring to the break with the old life, indicated by the verb ἀποτίθεσθαι, in the negative part, and to the new existence in a positive demand. Several parallels to this scheme can be found in early Christian tradition.[40] In Pauline and deuteropauline references, the idea that the old life is cast aside like a garment corresponds to the description of the new life as an ἐνδύεσθαι: of the weapons of light (Rom 13:12; cf. 1 Thess 5:8), of Christ (Rom 13:14; cf. the indicative in Gal 3:27), and of the new man (Col 3:10; Eph 4:24).[41] Hebrews 12:1 offers an elaboration sui generis in which the positive part, with its admonition "let us run with perseverance the race that is set before us," is clearly determined by the overall theme of the letter.

James 1:21b and 1 Peter 2:2 do not resemble the Pauline and deuteropauline references in the choice of either the verb or the object,[42]
but display a close relationship to each other.[43] In addition, the bipartite
scheme follows the interpretation of conversion as birth in the sense of
a paraenetic conclusion only in James and 1 Peter. As mentioned, birth
is only brought into connection with the word (which discloses truth) in
these two passages. Precisely, the word is taken up in the positive section of the paraenetic scheme in both texts, and again, this is not paralleled anywhere else.[44] What James 1:21b expresses in the familiar phrase
"receive the Word,"[45] 1 Peter 2:2 portrays in an image by continuing
with the metaphor of the preceding soteriological statement: like[46] new-
born infants, the addressees should demand the milk (i.e., word)[47] necessary for the preservation and growth of new life. To summarize: by
referring to the word, the birth statement and the paraenetic scheme in
James and in 1 Peter not only present a special elaboration contrasting
with parallel texts, when taken for themselves, but also are linked with
one another only in these two writings, forming a coherent interrelationship; the admonition to seize the new life—since Christians have turned
their backs upon their previous existence (Jas 1:21b; 1 Pet 2:1)[48]—and to
constantly nurture it through the very acceptance of the word draws the
consequence from God's soteriological initiative, which opened up a new
life for Christians precisely through the word.

Furthermore, the close association between the two text sequences
is additionally underlined by the fact that both refer to the attainment
of eschatological salvation as a (motivating) goal (Jas 1:21: σῶσαι; 1 Pet
2:2: εἰς σωτηρίαν). One further aspect is that the word is conceived of as
a force or effective power in both texts. In James 1:21b, this is expressed
by τὸν δυνάμενον.[49] In 1 Peter, this is the foundation of the argumenta-
tive connection between 1:22b and 1:23, but is apparently also implied
in giving the word the attribute *vital*. And not least, the similar metaphoric language must be pointed out. While 1 Peter 1:23 speaks of σπορὰ
ἄφθαρτος, λόγος is qualified in James 1:21b by ἔμφυτος. In light of the
other resemblances, it is certainly a probable estimation that the authors
met with this metaphorical concept in the tradition, even if not in their
respective formulations. Furthermore, it must be considered that the citation from Isaiah, with which 1 Peter 1:24-25 highlights his characterization of the word as "enduring," is taken up by James in 1:10-11.[50] Finally,
if the negative first part of the bipartite scheme is taken into account,
James 1:21a and 1 Peter 2:1 agree with one another in the attributive
usage of πᾶς with the object.[51]

In overviewing these findings, the conclusion must be made that
James 1:18-21 and 1 Peter 1:22–2:2 display many significant resemblances

to one another, as well as differences from individually related statements, so that they can be classified under one single strain of tradition. The individual elements of the tradition are documented elsewhere only in deviating forms and never occur together otherwise in one textual sequence. In view of the central position often attached to the Pauline tradition when judging 1 Peter traditio-historically, it must be emphasized most especially that James 1:18-21 and 1 Peter 1:22–2:2 prove that the letters ascribed to the two prominent figures of the Jerusalem congregation belong together traditio-historically, over against the Pauline-deuteropauline tradition. As the Pauline-deuteropauline parallels to James 1:21 and 1 Peter 2:1-2—and to λόγος ἀληθείας—allow us to perceive, however, there is also one common fundament of tradition. But the greater agreements between James and 1 Peter point to an independent elaboration or continued development as a common traditional background of the two catholic letters.

Simultaneously, one must again conclude that the authors of James and 1 Peter tread different paths in elaborating the traditional material handed down. In James 1:13-25, 1:18 forms the axis of the theologically fundamental development of the program set out in 1:2-4,[52] and consequently, it constitutes the basic soteriological assertion of James.[53] According to 1:18b, the aim of God's soteriological action is the selection of the Christians as his very own possessions.[54] PsJames thereby takes the positive counterpart to the dissociation from the world, which is entailed by conversion, into perspective. PsJames has inserted 1:19-20 between the birth statement and the paraenetic scheme. The filth of the old manner of existence (v. 21a), which has been cast aside, is illustrated by the warning against wrath that leads to imprudent speech, which damages the community—a main point in the ethical statements of James (1:26; 3:1-11)[55]—while the reason given in 1:20 builds a contrast to τὸν δυνάμενον σῶσαι . . . (1:21b). When PsJames qualifies the word by the term ἔμφυτος in 1:21b—most likely on the basis of the tradition handed down—he envisages it as a force (1:14b) implanted into the Christian that opposes desire, underlining the rejection of any attempt to exculpate oneself from defeats by the manifold temptations at God's expense, as laid out in 1:13, 17-18. With 1:22-25, PsJames develops and clarifies the admonition from 1:21b. In correspondence with the general ethical direction of the letter, PsJames thereby focuses on the imperative side of the word, on the νόμος. In summary, one must hold to the following conclusion: in the face of ethical shortcomings, PsJames takes up the tradition, with its reference to the event of conversion, in order to impress the ground coordinates of Christian existence upon the addressees as a basis for his further remarks.

Again, the adaption of tradition is different in 1 Peter. In 1:22a, the author initially looks at the human side of the event of conversion. By saying that the addressees have purified themselves[56] by[57] obedience to the truth—whereby nothing is meant other than God's word or revelation (1:23)[58]—Peter is already influenced by the tradition elaborated in 1 Peter 1:23–2:2, as is evidenced by the phrase λόγος ἀληθείας in James 1:18.[59] Unhypocritical brotherly love is the aim of this purification. It is now essential that the addressees proceed upon the path they have begun to tread. In the admonition in 1:22b, which builds the (pragmatic) center of the text passage, ἀνυπόκριτον is taken up by ἐκ καθαρᾶς καρδίας.[60] In 1:22b, the emphasis lies on the adverb ἐκτενῶς (cf. 4:8), which must be understood in the sense of *permanent*, as the following verses in 1:23-25 indicate.[61] The matter at hand is not the criticism and correction of the addressees' conduct, as in James, but rather—in keeping with the theme of suffering—encouragement and admonition to steadfast continuation of what has been begun, to remaining in the truth. In short, PsJames corrects while Peter strengthens and encourages to carry on.

The tradition that 1 Peter has in common with James is taken up and developed with this intention in mind; more specifically, it serves to substantiate ἐκτενῶς. Thereby, the addressees' knowledge of the tradition seems to be presumed. In 1 Peter 1:22–2:2 Peter offers a new application. The emphasis lies no longer on the interpretation of conversion itself as a new, divine procreation, but on the attributes given to the seed or the word. In correspondence with ἐκτενῶς, the accent falls upon μένοντος through its end position and the attached Isaian citation (μένει, v. 25a).[62] As with the attributes given to the word, the citation from Isaiah must also be understood as redactional interpolation[63] whereby James 1:10 displays that it belonged to the common theological repertoire of the letters' authors. In 1 Peter, therefore, the tradition is tailored to provide an indicative foundation for 1:22b, or more exactly, for the perpetuance and steadfastness of love. The call for permanent brotherly love results consequently from the fact that the effective word, to which Christians owe their conversion, is not transitory, but remains eternally. It does not merely give one single impulse, but works permanently, continuously providing the necessary vital elements for the new life.

The formulation of the positive section of the bipartite scheme can also be understood well in the framework of the usage of the traditional material, as it is determined by the admonition in 1:22b. In the phrase about the desire of newborns for the "milk of the Word,"[64] the processual moment comes to fruition more emphatically than in the traditional phrase δέχεσθαι τὸν λόγον, stressing that the word constantly supports Christians on the path they begin to tread with conversion.[65]

The fact that 1 Peter aims ethically at brotherly love can also be incorporated into the theme of affliction. Traditionally, the admonition to practice brotherly love is bound to the aspect of strengthening internal cohesion,[66] which is especially significant in the context of existence as a minority with a tense relationship to its surroundings.[67] It is fitting that 4:8 not only especially emphasizes steadfast brotherly love, but that 4:8b also concretely refers to the forgiveness of sins with a citation from Proverbs 10:12 (MT). This citation from Proverbs is also taken up by PsJames (5:20). In addition, the agreement with the Hebrew text over against the Septuagint version points to a common early Christian tradition as a fundament.[68] The two writings differ in their adaptations here as well, since PsJames interpolates the words into a call that concisely summarizes the overall intention of his letter, namely the call to rescue Christians who have erred from the truth.[69]

Interim Results: The Epistle of James and the First Epistle of Peter as Two Different Witnesses of the Same Branch of Tradition

In reviewing the findings on James 1:18-21 and 1 Peter 1:22–2:2, one must conclude the following: the resemblances are so close, and deviate so significantly from related statements in their elaboration, that it is impossible to explain them sufficiently by means of a general reference to the wide ocean of paraenetic traditions. The common ground between James 1:2-3 and 1 Peter 1:6-7 as well as between James 4:6-10 and 1 Peter 5:5c-9 points in the same direction. Especially on the basis of the last example, with its intertwining of agreements and deviations, one can demonstrate that the resemblances can hardly be explained through a direct literary dependence, since neither of the two versions can be conclusively derived from the other. Rather, a common fundamental structure becomes apparent in both sections, which both have elaborated differently on the basis of their diverging intentions. To formulate it conversely: the indicated differences can be comprehended as redactional elaborations. In conclusion, the traditional material linking James and 1 Peter to one another makes up an independent branch in the development of early Christian tradition.

If this assumption is correct, then other resemblances, which mean little when taken for themselves, gain more significance. The similarities between James 5:20 and 1 Peter 4:8 have already been pointed out.[70] In the prescripts of the two letters, and only here, the addressees are localized in the Diaspora (Jas 1:1; 1 Pet 1:1). 1 Peter 2:11 speaks of desires of the flesh: αἵτινες στρατεύονται κατὰ τῆς ψυχῆς; James 4:1 designates the activity of the ἡδοναί in the body's limbs as στρατεύεσθαι. In the New Testament, this verb is only used in these two passages, to describe the internal struggle of human beings. Both writings make remarks on speech ethics (1 Pet 3:9-12; Jas 1:26; 3:1-11), and the incrimination of καταλαλιά in 1 Peter 2:1 finds its Jacobian counterpart in James 4:11.[71] Early Christian use of the term ἀναστροφή is quite prevalent,[72] but only James 3:13 and 1 Peter 2:12 speak of καλὴ ἀναστροφή.[73] The "purification of the soul" from 1 Peter 1:22 has an equivalent in PsJames' call ἁγνίσατε καρδίας (4:8). Aside from 1 John 3:3,[74] a comparable usage of ἁγνίζειν in a figurative sense is found nowhere else in the New Testament. In James 1:25, the verb παρακύπτειν refers to the law, while 1 Peter 1:12 relates it to the proclamation of the gospel; in the rest of the New Testament, it is only used in the context of the empty tomb (Luke 24:12; John 20:5-11). This list could be continued with one smaller resemblance or another.[75] In summary, the conclusion that James and 1 Peter represent one and the same branch of tradition cannot be denied. Furthermore, it can be determined that the traditional material common to James and 1 Peter—as has become apparent with relation to James 1:18-21 and 1 Peter 1:22–2:3, and which also offers a plausible explanation for James 1:2-3, 1 Peter 1:6-7, and Romans 5:3-5—testifies to a strain of tradition differentiated from the Pauline sphere of tradition. Nevertheless, both are bound to one another at the root.

In the following section, an attempt will be made to contextualize these findings historically. On the one hand, the inquiry must be made whether it is possible to localize the traditio-historical branching-off between James and 1 Peter on the one side and the Pauline tradition on the other, and to progress from there to a hypothesis on the position of James in the history of early Christianity by including other traditio-historical data in the analysis. On the other hand, one must also try to determine the character and background of the author ascription on this basis. For both, the role of James and his influence in early Christianity must be considered in outline and extract form. The apostolic convent and, most of all, the so-called Antiochian incident, which I will concentrate on next, are of predominant importance.

Attempt at a Historical Contextualization of the Traditio-Historical Findings

Next to Peter, James was the most prominent figure in the Jerusalem congregation.[76] The question of whether the Lord's brother took over the leadership of the congregation in Jerusalem from Peter in the wake of Peter's persecution and flight under Agrippa I,[77] as is generally assumed,[78] or whether the two had cooperated beforehand in guiding the congregation (cf. Acts 12:17)[79] remains unresolved in this context.[80] It is recognizable that Peter and James played different yet complementary roles, insofar as James (from the very beginning?) apparently performed a function more strongly, even if not exclusively,[81] oriented internally to the congregation[82] than that of the roaming missionary Peter.[83]

According to Paul's portrayal of the apostolic convent (48 CE), James, Peter, and John the Zebedee were looked upon as στῦλοι (Gal 2:9). If this metaphor reflects an understanding of the church as an eschatological building of God, then the church as a whole, and hardly only the congregation in Jerusalem with its Jewish or Palestinian background, is apprehended as such. According to its own understanding, this triad represented the upholding pillars of the church.[84] As the starting point for the spreading of the gospel, Jerusalem is the mother congregation of early Christianity, possessing singular, supraregional significance and authority. The fact that James increasingly emerged as the central leading personality in the Jerusalem congregation forms the historic core of Jewish Christian and other ecclesiastical traditions[85] about his predominant position in early Christianity.[86]

It is not beyond doubt that the sequence of the designation of the three pillars in Galatians 2:9 reflects an internal hierarchy.[87] At any rate, one can view the frontal position of the Lord's brother in correspondence with his portrayal in Acts 15, according to which James is the very one who pronounces the decisive vote, even if Luke is presumably responsible for the amalgamation of different historical contexts by interpolating the apostolic decree into the framework of the apostolic convent in Jerusalem. According to the concurring testimony between Galatians 2:1-10 and Acts 15, it must certainly be concluded that not only Peter but also James voted for the Gentile mission of Paul and the Antiochians, which did away with circumcision, over against the vote of another Jewish Christian group, whom Luke classified as Christian Pharisees (Acts 15:5) and Paul polemically denigrated as "false brothers" (Gal 2:4).

In the context examined here, the incident at Antioch (Gal 2:11-14) after the apostolic convent is of great significance.[88] In Antioch, Jewish and Gentile Christians practiced meal fellowship, perhaps as a consequence of a Pauline interpretation of the convent's resolutions. If one considers that the Lord's Supper was linked to a satiation meal (cf. 1 Cor 11:17-34), which was also affected, then it becomes clear that the conflict involved one of the essential elements of Christian communal life. In Antioch, either Jewish meal taboos played no role at all, or—what I consider more probable—they were at least not sufficiently observed in the eyes of James' followers.[89] To put it another way, the conclusion that pork was served is not compelling.[90] The assumption suffices that James' followers criticized that the origins and preparation of the food were not adequately regarded when meals took place in the homes of Gentile Christians.[91] Whether all Jewish Christians in Antioch took part in meals with Gentile Christians or whether some of them had reservations against this is beyond our knowledge.[92] If it is correct that there were several house churches in Antioch, then the possibility exists that purely Jewish Christian circles were also able to hold their ground.[93]

Like Barnabas, however, Peter adapted to the mixed meal practices in Antioch when he came to the Syrian metropolis[94] but changed his stance after the arrival of James' followers.[95] Paul's accusation that Peter's "fear of the circumcised" was the impetus for his withdrawal is part of the polemical situation in Galatians.[96] Rather, James' followers may well have cited good reasons which theologically convinced Peter, Barnabas, and the rest of the Jewish Christians.[97] Hereby, two interlinking aspects probably played a decisive role: First, Antiochian practices showed either no consideration or no sufficient amount of consideration for the Jewish identity of Jewish brothers in faith, in the judgment of James' followers, so that the unity of the ecclesia was being realized at the expense of the Jewish side. With respect to the food laws, Peter may have taken a liberal or lax stance, which (some?) other Jewish Christians (in Antioch) might have been able to share, and contemporary Judaism might have paved the way for this sporadically.[98] But apparently, there were also other positions in Jewish Christianity on the food halakah. The Antiochian practice made participation in meal fellowship impossible for representatives of other viewpoints, thereby standing in the way of a supraregional unity of believers in Christ,[99] and must have been a hindrance to the Jewish mission.

The followers of James would scarcely have pleaded a cause merely for the reservations of other Jewish Christians against Antiochian practices (like the Christian Pharisees in Acts 15, for example), but would have represented their own standpoint as well. If inferences can be drawn about the Lord's brother from their intervention, then the conflict in Antioch makes recognizable a difference between James and Peter in their halakic practices, which most likely corresponds to an ecclesiastical difference insofar as James perceived the Christian congregation (more) consequently from the perspective of Israel's history as the chosen nation, and thus in the framework of the opposition between Israel and the other nations. He had accepted the Gentile mission without circumcision; however, the realization of the communion of Jewish and Gentile Christians (who had not become Jews) at the expense of the Jewish side could not receive his placet. This does not allow the inverse conclusion that James or his followers would have especially emphasized the food laws in opposition to Jesus' interpretation of the law.[100] Quite apparently, he was not a rigorist at all. Nevertheless, his conscientious orientation and adherence to the Torah (in the interpretation of Jesus),[101] which soon incurred his epithet "the Just,"[102] must be marked as his essential characteristic.

The second aspect that would have essentially incurred the criticism of James' followers is connected with the ecclesiological position of the Lord's brother that has just been alluded to. The food laws are not to be obeyed only for their own sake, but point to something greater than themselves; they have an important function in marking the boundary between God's people and the Gentiles.[103] If the stipulations of the apostolic decree (Acts 15:20-29; 21:25) originally belong in the context of the resolution of the problem in Antioch,[104] as is often assumed—correctly, in my opinion—then this aspect finds its confirmation precisely here. The communion of Jewish and Gentile Christians ought not lead to watering down the line of demarcation between the people of God and paganism, and thus become a gate of access for paganism. This explains the prominent placement of εἰδωλόθυτα and the demand that πορνεία[105] be avoided in the apostolic decree, which goes beyond the food halakah.[106]

One need not interpret Peter's withdrawal from Antioch as a change of his halakic position. It suffices to assume that he discerned factors in the arguments of James' followers that ought to have taken precedence and had not been taken into consideration in the Antiochian practice. Thereby, the aim of his withdrawal (and of the Jacobian followers' intervention) was not the future division of Jewish and Gentile Christians, but rather a new founding of the communion of Jews on a basis that would bear the Jewish identity of Jewish Christians in mind and observe the boundary between God's people and the pagan world.[107]

If the problematic situation in Antioch was solved by the apostolic decree, then Paul was the defeated one.[108] This assumption is supported indirectly by Galatians; if Paul had prevailed in Antioch, then he hardly would have let this go unmentioned in the face of the analogous crisis in Galatia. In this case, his silence is eloquent. Paul has left Antioch.

Henceforth, the congregation in Syrian Antioch moved along the same lines as Jerusalem. The demands to refrain from idolatry, the consumption of blood and strangled animals, and fornication constituted the minimal requirements for Gentile Christians, which oriented themselves to the regulations for *gerim* in the land of Israel (cf. Lev 17-18),[109] as need not be reiterated. According to this compromise, Gentile Christians remained accepted as Gentiles, Jewish Christians could preserve their Jewish identity,[110] and the "cleanliness" of God's people was safeguarded.[111] Doubtlessly, this resolution of the problem, which was apparently not yet present in the framework of the apostolic convent,[112] is a moderate one. Indeed: "die Entscheidung war offenbar zugleich theologisch und

geschichtlich so situationsentsprechend einleuchtend, daß sie sich öku-
menisch durchsetzte. Die Bestimmungen des Dekrets stehen alsbald in
der ganzen Kirche in Geltung."[113]

In our context, these findings are of great significance in two respects.

1. As an important center of early Christianity, the Antioch church
stood in close contact with the mother congregation in Jerusalem. An
agreement with Jerusalem was sought in the question of the Gentile mission without circumcision, and the position of Jerusalem also prevailed in
view of meal fellowship of Jews and Gentiles.

2. In the tradition handed down in Acts 15, the resolution of the
conflict is connected with James, the brother of the Lord. Historically,
we can leave open the question of whether the stipulations were decreed
by Jerusalem or whether a common solution was reached with the Antioch church, as I would presume. Either way, James can be viewed as the
leading figure of this solution;[114] there is no reason for presuming that the
reminiscence Luke presents is historically unreliable on this point. At any
rate, the orientation to the Torah fits well with the brother of the Lord.
If this assertion is correct, then James proved himself to be a leading
personality and a "man of consensus"[115] by the apostolic convent as well
as by the incident at Antioch, for the apostolic decree is a document that
makes concessions, a true compromise clearly displaying James' interest
in the unity of the church.[116] Simultaneously, the incident at Antioch and,
especially, its solution document James' influence, which radiated beyond
Jerusalem and Judea into the Antiochian area, influencing not only the
Jewish Christians there. Instead, the fact that the congregation apparently was not split in two by this conflict lets us recognize that the Gentile
Christian faction also showed understanding for the Jerusalem position
linked to James,[117] that his intention could be supported by them, that his
word was held in seemingly high estimation, and consequently that he
was valued as a significant authority.[118]

In an additional step, an attempt can be made to set the traditio-
historical findings outlined in the first part of this article in relationship
with the remarks made in the second part on the Lord's brother and
his sphere of influence. My assertion is that the traditio-historical findings, as they have been ascertained here and subsequently are to be con-
toured, can be plausibly explained by the development that took place
in this important center of early Christianity because of the incident at
Antioch. The branching off between James and 1 Peter on the one hand
and the Pauline and deuteropauline tradition on the other corresponds
to the parting of the ways initiated by the conflict in Antioch. In concrete
terms, the twofold paraenetic scheme found in James 1:21 and 1 Peter
2:1-2 and at various points in the Pauline tradition belongs to a common

Antiochian fundament of tradition that experienced different elabora-tions. The fusing of pieces of tradition that were originally independent of one another, as in James 1:18-21 (par. 1 Pet 1:22–2:2), is an indication of this later development. Antiochian Christianity and its environment after the incident at Antioch, which recognized Peter and also James as influential authorities, were the tradents of this continuation of tradi-tion. The pseudepigraphic ascriptions of these two letters to James and Peter document exactly this. At the same time, the question must be asked whether the resemblances of 1 Peter to Pauline and deuteropauline epistles can be understood, at least to a sufficient extent, on the basis of a dependence upon Antiochian tradition.[119] Mutatis mutandis, the same is true for resemblances between James and Paul.[120]

One other piece of evidence supports this approach. It has been pos-tulated repeatedly that James is deeply rooted in the Jesus tradition. In my opinion, more reserved judgment should be practiced in many cases, for the relationship is often an indirect one.[121] However, the hypothesis of influence from the Jesus tradition is only modified by this.[122] Thereby, it is not only the prohibition of oaths in James 5:12, which probably presents an older form of reception than the antithesis form of Matthew 5:33-37,[123] that points to a special proximity to Matthew.[124] If 1 Peter is the closest relation of James in the matter of resemblances of pieces of tradition, then this designation is due to Matthew with respect to theo-logical affinity.[125] Localizing James in the context of the scope of tradi-tion that left its mark on Matthew would offer a plausible explanation for these resemblances.

This fits in well with the very striking affinities that can also be reg-istered between 1 Peter and Matthew, as in 1 Peter 3:14 with Matthew 5:10 and 1 Peter 2:12 with Matthew 5:16. If the passages in Matthew 5:10 and 16 that agree with 1 Peter are Matthean redactions,[126] then 1 Peter could be the earliest testimony to the usage of Matthew.[127] On the other hand, since the First Evangelist presents himself so clearly as a spokes-man of his congregation, it is equally possible that the Matthean passages are rooted in the congregation's tradition, so that the resemblances could be sufficiently explained by a common fundament of tradition. One way or another, an interesting interwoven pattern of relationships results for James, 1 Peter, and Matthew.[128]

Furthermore, it must be taken into consideration that Matthew not only delineates Peter's central position among the Twelve much more vividly than does Mark,[129] but also mitigates the negative Markan per-ception of the family of Jesus and thereby of his brother.[130] Finally, the wheel comes full circle when one recalls that, according to a large con-sensus, Matthew is to be located in Syria.[131] As a testifying document of

Syrian Christianity from the approximate beginning of the decade 80–90 CE, Matthew matches excellently with the development in the Antioch church as it occurred in the resolution of the so-called incident at Antioch. At this time, Antioch stood in close connection with the mother congregation in Jerusalem, which possessed two prominent leading personalities in James and Peter.

For James, it must be concluded that the traditio-historical development, as it comes to light in the structure of relationships between James, 1 Peter, and Pauline-deuteropauline writings, points to Antioch as the point of intersection for this tradition, and this traditio-historical development can be related to the development of the Antioch church after the incident at Antioch. The proximity of James to Matthew fits with the Syrian area, and an environment is documented here that makes the ascription of the letter to James understandable and plausible. In short, on the basis of the traditio-historical relationships, I consider the thesis that James originated in the Syrian area to be the best option.[132] Since PsJames has no knowledge of Matthew, James can hardly be dated later than 85 CE,[133] given the rapid spread of the first Gospel.[134]

The Epistle of James as a Letter of the Brother of the Lord

The previous remarks illustrate a historical context in which the pseudepigraphic ascription is understandable and James' relationship to other early Christian writings—more specifically, to 1 Peter and Matthew—can be explained. However, the question of why the actual author chose to place his letter under the authority of the brother of the Lord, and not of Peter, for example, still has to be answered. What was the motivation for his choice?

Occasionally and in various forms, the hypothesis of a dual-stage genesis of James has been held. According to it, a close connection exists on a material level between the letter and the brother of the Lord. It is postulated that material that can be traced to the leader of the Jerusalem congregation was taken up and/or adapted in James. Recently, for example, Davids postulated "that the Epistle of James is either a product of James himself or, more likely, a Diaspora letter preserving his sayings for the church at large shortly after his martyrdom."[135] According to Martin, pupils of James settled in Antioch as a result of the Roman-Jewish War, and in this manner brought instructional material of the Lord's brother into the Syrian metropolis, which was then collocated and adapted "to meet the pastoral needs of some community in the Syrian province."[136] As grounds for this localization, Martin points to James' proximity to Matthew and to the *Didache*. The close resemblances with 1 Peter are not the focus here.

However, no clear indications can substantiate a broad material relationship to the instructional material of the Lord's brother, as Davids, Martin, and others postulate. In the present context, this cannot be discussed for every individual text segment of the letter. Three aspects ought to suffice:

1. As has been indicated, influences from the Jesus tradition are perceptible in various passages of James. It is plausible that these influences were cultivated in the surroundings of the mother congregation in Jerusalem, but they do not have to have been initially brought to Syrian Antioch by followers of James in the second half of the decade 60–70 CE.

2. The material that is common with 1 Peter can only be proven to be traditional material from Antioch's field of radiation with some plausibility; but it cannot be specifically traced to the Lord's brother (or to Peter). Nevertheless, this material is positioned in the crucial passages of James 1:2-3; it makes up the headpiece of the foundational section of the summarizing exposition (1:2-12). πειρασμοὶ ποικίλοι and τὸ δοκίμιον ὑμῶν τῆς πίστεως allow us to recognize with certainty that this tradition was formulated in the Greek language from the outset.[137] The birth statement and the twofold paraenetic scheme in 1:18-21 are the central elements of the theologically fundamental passage in 1:13-25.[138] The list could be continued. But even the two examples referred to make it clear that traditional material has been taken up in central parts of James that cannot be directly traced to the brother of the Lord.

3. In James 2:14-26, PsJames attempts to correct a misunderstanding about the idea of "saving faith" or, more precisely, about the aspect of daily ethical practice included in faith. Speaking of saving faith seems to have been part of the missionary preaching in early Christianity. The misunderstanding that PsJames recognized on the part of his addressees can be explained better against the background of a pagan horizon of understanding of πίστις and veneration of God than in a Jewish Christian context.[139] Yet 2:19 does not present an obstruction to this. On the contrary, in a Gentile Christian context, the monotheistic confession can be accurately designated as the characteristic of the new religious orientation. As such, it makes very good sense in the ductus of argumentation.[140] In short, 2:14-26 can also hardly be traced to the brother of the Lord.

Next to this, dual-stage theories must be questioned from another angle. Dibelius' literary assessment of James as a "freischwebende ethische Hausapotheke"[141] finds an aftermath by Davids, especially when he conceives of the letter as a "collection of traditions"[142] and "a series of sayings and sermons."[143] Such an estimation of the literary shape of James is virtually a prerequisite for theories postulating a dual-stage genesis for it, according to which James' pupils attempted to secure the legacy of their master after his death.

In my opinion, the coherence of James must be estimated to be considerably higher. It possesses a well-considered and coherent outline; its cause, intention, and themes are primarily determined by the ecclesiastical situation upon which the actual author comments.[144] The intention of the letter is not the securement of the legacy of the Lord's brother for the entire church, but rather the elimination of problems as the actual (circle of) author(s) perceived them in the ecclesiastical surroundings: predominantly, the dangers of faith without works, worship that is in vain because the active dimension of Christian faith remains underemphasized, and the strife to gain wealth and social prestige, which damages the community. For these reasons, PsJames employs the authority of the brother of the Lord.

But why precisely his authority? The (minimal) prerequisite for such an ascription, as has already been displayed, is an ecclesiastical milieu in which James was positively evaluated and esteemed as an authority. In the Syrian area, which is the first address to consider when looking for an explanation of relationships with 1 Peter and Matthew, this prerequisite is fulfilled, as is proven above all by the outcome of the incident at Antioch, and is also indicated by the restraint of the negative perception of the family of Jesus in the Gospel of Matthew over against its Markan model. If a substantial number of Palestinian Jewish Christians found refuge in Syria after 70 CE, then this is even more accurate. One possibility is certainly that (Jewish Christian) circles also existed that were not absorbed by resident congregations, but constituted a specifically Jacobian Christianity that honored James as the authority of the early Church per se.[145] However, the postulation of such a context of origin as an explanation for the pseudepigraphic ascription is not absolutely convincing by any means, and is quite improbable for James if one reckons on a significant number of Gentile Christians among the addressees.[146] In short, it suffices to assume that James originated in an ecclesiastical environment in Antioch's field of influence that honored the mother congregation in Jerusalem and thus regarded its head leader James as a significant personality in early Christianity—which might have been intensified by a stream of Jewish Christians from Jerusalem and Judea, but which cannot be categorized as specifically Jacobian Christianity, despite this.

In my opinion, the fact that James was chosen (and not Peter, for example) is fundamentally based on the judgment that the authority of the brother of the Lord bore the most weight for a writing that was strongly motivated ethically. Already in logion 12 of the *Gospel of Thomas*, which most likely stems from Syria, James is given the epithet "the Just." This does not mean that the motive for the pseudepigraphic ascription can be solely reduced to an orientation to the fame of James.[147] Rather, such an authorization would suggest itself even more if the author could have held the opinion that he was writing in the spirit of the Jerusalemite apostle, or to put it another way, if there were correspondences between his intention and what he knew of James' position. Such an affinity should also be considered with regard to the plausibility of the pseudepigraphic ascription in the circle of addressees. This does not lead to the search for "authentic" material in James after all. The matter of concern is rather an image of James that plays a role in the background by the contextual usage and elaboration of the traditional material common with 1 Peter, a kind of knowledge of what James advocated and which viewpoints he represented. If James was written no later than fifteen or twenty years after the death of its fictive author, one can reckon on lines of continuity between James as a historical figure and the perception of him that stood sponsor for the letter. Conversely, the hypothesis that the pseudepigraphic ascription is not merely oriented to the fame of the brother of the Lord, but that James can be read as a reflection of the actual author's perception of James, stands and falls with the provability of such lines of continuity. In my opinion, this hypothesis bears enough validity to stand firm.

For a first example, I recur to the redaction and continuation of the piece of tradition handed down in James 1:18-21, as it was displayed in part one. As indicated, there is no evidence that this tradition is specifically Jacobian in any way whatsoever. But its elaboration in the interpolation of 1:19-20 and the explication of 1:21b in 1:22-25 fit well with what was probably known as the theological standpoint of the Lord's brother. In 1:25, PsJames designates the ἔμφυτος λόγος from its imperative angle as νόμος. The unqualified positive treatment of the law, which is a feature of the entire letter, not only links James to Matthew but also harmonizes with the fact that faithfulness to the Torah was obviously an essential characteristic of the Lord's brother, which also comes to light in the Lukan perception of James in Acts 15:13-21 (see above all 15:21).[148] Simultaneously, considering the widely documented connection of the motifs *law* and *liberty* in the traditions of Hellenistic Judaism and popular philosophy, the expression "law of liberty" points to a context strongly influenced by Hellenism, as does a series of other textual indications.[149] Even though Hellenistic influences on Palestinian Judaism are not to be denied,[150] a Hellenistic background fits better with a kind of Christianity that was nurtured in Hellenistic Diaspora Judaism.[151] What we can discern about the content of the law of liberty[152] matches this without a hitch. In short, although the understanding of the law in James is hardly identical to that of the Lord's brother, and although we must proceed on the assumption that a transformation took place that makes reference to a different ecclesiastical milieu, surely a thematical continuity exists: living according to the law appears as an essential structural element of Christian faith. For PsJames and for the Lord's brother, Christian existence without ποιεῖν νόμον is a contradiction in itself. To summarize: this piece of tradition cannot be traced back to James, but its elaboration in James reflects one of his theological concerns.

Thematical continuity, in the sense of a transformation of theological viewpoints of the Lord's brother, can also be shown to be probable in another passage. PsJames perceives a primary ethical danger to his "brothers and sisters" in the strife for wealth and social prestige, which is accompanied by behavior damaging to the community (4:1-4).[153] In order to lead them back to the "truth" (5:19), he breaks out in sharp criticism of the rich and drastically illustrates their terrible fate (1:10-11; 2:6-7 4:13–5:6). He does not expect Christians to renounce their property entirely, but rather to show mercy to the poor, beginning with respectful treatment (2:1-5) and continuing with concrete support (1:27; 2:15-16). Partiality that expresses itself in an orientation to a worldly status and system of values violates the command to love one's neighbor.[154]

(Most of) the Judean Christians appear to have lived in economically moderate circumstances (see Gal 2:10; Rom 15:26).[155] With respect to the idea of "community of property" in the mother congregation, as summarized in Acts 2:42-47 and 4:32-35, the difficulties of drawing precise historical conclusions from Luke's portrayal cannot be discussed in detail here.[156] It seems certain to me that Luke is not merely fantasizing, but that his portrayal is based on a tradition handed down to him.[157] The fact that the mother congregation had a valid ethos on property, which was oriented to social equity and renounced "hanging on to one's possessions" as a consequence of the criticism of wealth in Jesus' preaching,[158] lies at the historically incontestable core of his account.[159] Furthermore, James might possibly have represented the interests of the poor outside of the congregation as well. According to the account of Josephus, the driving force behind the trial against James was the high priest Ananus, who originated from the Sadducean circles (*A.J.* 20.200) that recruited their members from the upper class.[160] It could well be that the stoning of James for supposed breaches of the law was actually motivated (at least in part) by the fact that he had criticized unjust social conditions in Jerusalem.[161] Due to the slight basis of data we have, certainty is unattainable here. Nevertheless, it is plausible to assume that the mother congregation in Jerusalem, and most especially its leader, James "the Just," convincingly embodied the rejection of Mammon, and that this could well belong to the conception of the Lord's brother held in the Syrian area.

If this picture is correct, then PsJames could therefore justly call upon the authority of the Lord's brother in his concern to depict wealth as the central factor of endangerment for Christian existence.[162] In this context, the Hellenistic coloring of PsJames' treatment of this topic can be recognized in his thematization of the ἡδοναί, in the body's members who go to battle, and in his derivation of the "wars and fightings" from the ἐπιθυμεῖν for material goods in James 4:1-2.[163] The admonition to repent in 4:6/7-10 is again formulated with the reception and elaboration of a piece of tradition common with 1 Peter, which PsJames reshapes paraenetically, and which most likely goes back to a Jesus logion. Again, no instructional material that can be specifically traced to the Lord's brother was interpolated into the epistle, but a facet from the portrait of him as head of the mother congregation, which is rooted in James himself, might be mirrored in the central position of wealth as an ethical endangerment. James is the model ταπεινός, who submits himself to the will of the Lord and has nothing to do with the worldly strife of the arrogant rich. Again, we can conclude that, as with the significant position of the theme of rich and poor in general, the contextual application and redaction of the piece of tradition handed down in 4:6-10 harmonizes well with the author ascription.

The same is true for 1:2-3. Once again, there are no indications that this piece of tradition can be traced to the brother of the Lord in any manner whatsoever. If 1 Peter 1:6-7 and the more remote Pauline parallels in Romans 5:3-5 are taken into account, an explanation offers itself on the basis of the traditio-historical model developed on the grounds of James 1:18-21 and 1 Peter 1:22–2:2. James 1:2-3 and 1 Peter 1:6-7 are continuations of a tradition widely spread in the Antiochian area, which was elaborated differently in another shape in Romans 5:3-5. However, the thematic integration that occurs with the piece of tradition in James can easily be brought into connection with a perception of James that can be ascribed to the author of the epistle with historical plausibility.

Finally, a third aspect must be pointed out. As the tradition of the circle of the Twelve and the self-designation ἐκκλησία τοῦ θεοῦ,[164] which goes back to the beginnings in Jerusalem, display, the Jerusalem congregation understood itself as "das von Gott gesammelte und erwählte Aufgebot . . ., dazu bestimmt, Kristallisationspunkt des nun von ihm zu sammelnden endzeitlichen Israel zu werden."[165] As has been seen, James did not reject the inclusion of the Gentiles (Gal 2:1-10; Acts 15), and with respect to the problem of meal fellowship between Jewish and Gentile

Christians that broke out in Antioch, he was apparently decisively involved in finding a moderate solution oriented to the Torah. At the same time, the incident at Antioch and its resolution document that James was an advocate of Jewish identity and a theologian who consequently placed the Christian congregation in the context of Israel's history of election.

Turning to 1 Peter, which is at least predominantly addressed to Gentile Christians, one can observe that it applies honorific designations for Israel to the Christian congregation (2:9), apparently without taking Israel itself into account.[166] PsJames also displays a Christian self-understanding in continuity with Israel. As the greater exegetical majority correctly presumes, the *adscriptio*'s "twelve tribes in the diaspora" designates Christendom.[167] In the same manner, the expression ἀπαρχή in James 1:18b is to be interpreted as a transference of a self-understanding of Israel to the church (cf. Philo, *Spec.* 4:180). "Our father Abraham" (2:21) is now the father of the Christians,[168] among whom—as I have already indicated—hardly Jewish Christians alone are numbered.[169]

The unusual verbalization of Christian self-understanding in continuity with Israel in speaking of the "twelve tribes" in James 1:1 results from the fact that "der Absender Jakobus heißt";[170] that is, it is inspired by an allusion to the patriarch Jacob.[171] This is hardly a statement that can be systemized in such a way that the brother of the Lord would be declared to be the progenitor of a new Israel, but it is rather a loose scribal association. Again, this is more likely to be credited to someone other than the actual sender named. As mentioned above, the addition of ταῖς ἐν τῇ διασπορᾷ as a location links James 1:1 to the prescript of 1 Peter, which speaks to the addressees as ἐκλεκτοὶ παρεπιδημοί διασπορᾶς. The Christians' foreign existence in the world is one main ecclesiological motif in 1 Peter,[172] which is verbalized along with παρεπίδημος (1:1; 2:11) in πά ροικος/παροικία (1:17; 2:11), but also resonates in Diaspora. Similarly, ἐν τῇ διασπορᾷ in James 1:1 does not primarily refer to a dispersal of the Christian congregation, but states "daß sie in der Welt getrennt von der Welt leben müssen (s. 1,27)."[173] Thus, an essential feature of the ecclesiological program resounds in ἐν τῇ διασπορᾷ also in James (cf. 1:18b; 4:4). This usage of διασπορά, which is exclusively employed in the New Testament in James 1:1 and 1 Peter 1:1 to refer to the Christian congregation,[174] must apparently be assigned to the reservoir of tradition connecting these two writings. Diasporal existence and a self-understanding in continuity with Israel are cornerstones of the common fundament of tradition for James and 1 Peter.

In my opinion, a significant realignment over against the theological position of the brother of the Lord must be registered again at this point. The church is no longer the core of the eschatological Israel that has to be gathered (in this, the church is a part that is related to the whole); it has simply become Israel, apparently without taking non-Christian Israel into its field of vision anymore.[175] From my viewpoint, this is another argument against the authenticity of the letter.[176] Simultaneously, however, the ecclesiological position of PsJames can be understood as a transformation and perpetuation of the Israel-related self-understanding of the Jerusalem congregation in a social context, in which the close relation to non-Christian Israel no longer had predominant significance.

One other line can be drawn here. As has been portrayed above, the apostolic decree (Acts 15:20-29) points to the intention that the boundary between the nation of God and other nations ought not become blurred. James also endeavors to draw a clear border, namely between the Christian congregation and the world. Christians are to "keep [themselves] unstained by the world" (Jas 1:27).[177] Here as well, reading these admonitions of James as a transformation of a theological intent of the brother of the Lord is easily possible.

In conclusion, the prerequisite for the pseudepigraphic ascription is an environment in which James, the Lord's brother, was recognized and esteemed as an authority of the Jerusalem congregation. If one considers the traditio-historical findings as well as our knowledge of the field of influence of the Lord's brother and sets these two factors in relationship to one another, (mixed) Syrian Christianity with Antioch at its center presents itself as a context for the origin of James. James' impact as an ethical model, which takes shape in his epithet "the Just," builds the foundation for the author ascription and makes him suitable as a fitting authority for a letter like James, a writing possessing the character of ethical correction.[178]

Nevertheless, the pseudepigraphic background is scarcely exhausted with this. The relationship is close, but it cannot be proven that specific instructional material of the brother of the Lord was adopted into the letter. However, the actual author takes stances that find support in the historical James, making the hypothesis plausible that not only the fame of the Jerusalemite authority but also a specific perception of James, containing theological standpoints of the Lord's brother, stand sponsor for the author ascription.

Most of all, (1) living according to the law as a central structural element of Christian existence, (2) the theme of rich and poor, and (3) cum grano salis, the self-definition of the Christian congregation in continuity with Israel reflect standpoints that can be comprehended as perpetuations of theological positions of the Lord's brother, insofar as they can be reconstructed in view of the source situation. All these points make the author ascription plausible for the circle of the addressees.

Simultaneously, differences can be registered that are to be classified, from a historical perspective, as transformations of the theological positions of the Lord's brother. These reveal an early Christian environment nurtured on the soil of Hellenistic Judaism in the Diaspora as the letter's context of origin. If at least Gentiles also belong to the kind of Christianity PsJames has in perspective, this does not speak against the connection presented here between the author ascription and the Lord's brother by any means. James did not close his mind to the inclusion of the Gentiles. In the Syrian Christianity that constitutes the context of origin for James, this also belongs to the perception of James and is, as an element of this picture, historically plausible.

To put it concisely, PsJames writes with the conviction that he is representing positions of the brother of the Lord. In this sense, James can in fact be read as a theological legacy of James, the brother of the Lord— a legacy, to be sure, that only mirrors standpoints and presents them in transformed shapes, one which merely reflects a perception of James but does not cite traditions from James.

CHAPTER 7

ACTS AND JAMES

Robert W. Wall

This paper argues for two related claims, both cued by consideration of the canonical process as a phenomenon guided by hermeneutical factors rather than purely sociological forces.[1] The first claim, made in the first two sections of the paper, is a constructive claim about the theological unity of the Catholic Epistles (CE). For this reason, my argument is more programmatic than exegetical in focus and is suggestive of future work in relating the theological conceptions of the Catholic and Pauline corpora, in my view, as constitutive of an internal apparatus of checks and balances, perhaps to correct an epistolary theology that remains more Pauline in perspective. For the sake of argument, I have drawn the Pauline theological conception sharply and in an overly Protestant fashion, and would admit on exegetical evidence that there is more thematic continuity between the Pauline and CE corpora than I have allowed. But my programmatic point is to introduce into conversation an interpretive calculus that arranges and relates these themes together as elements of a coherent whole that are at once different and complementary.

Especially in the appendix (see p. 142), I attempt to illustrate this constructive project. What seems important to clarify is that here, I make a more implicit claim for a criterion by which to account for the theological unity of the CE and then relate it to a Pauline perspective: the church's rule of faith. That is, unlike the various quests for a unifying center of Pauline theology, whose source is the historical Paul or Pauline tradents and which therefore defend the integrity of a particular tradition (Pauline) or founder (Paul), the theological unity of the CE lies outside the individual writings and in the church's grammar of theological agreements—Creator, Christ, community, consummation.[2] Further, I would argue (I think) that this same external source—the church's rule of faith—is a more useful device for scoring the intracanonical conversation between the theological conceptions envisaged by both Pauline and CE corpora. Rather than seeking some thematic consistency between them through selective and creative exegesis, I commend a different approach that is rooted in a particular idea of canon: that its various parts are roughly analogous to the church's rule of faith.

A second claim more narrowly concentrates upon the relationship between Acts and the CE, which were found together from the earliest stage of the canonical process. More specifically, I am interested in the evident privileging of James within the CE, and what Acts might be able to tell us about the priority of James in the New Testament canon. I doubt this interest will be fully satisfied by historical investigation,[3] but the question of James' importance is rather more adequately inflected by theological or religious construction. For example, Bede is one of the church's earliest interpreters of the CE as a whole collection; he suggests it is because of James' stature within Christianity's "mother" church in Jerusalem. My strategy is to read this problem from context of Acts, where James performs a pivotal role at the narrative's central moment at the so-called Jerusalem Council (Acts 15:4-21; cf. 15:22-30; 21:21-26). His verdict and commentary on Scripture actually proffer the essential hermeneutic by which the entire narrative is understood and, within the New Testament canon, by which the two epistolary corpora are related together toward the end of theological understanding.

Introduction

Acts was combined with the CE from the earliest stage of the canonical process. In fact, we know of no period in the reception of these compositions within the ancient church when they were not read together, and their working relationship continues to be an established interest of biblical criticism to this day—typically spurred on for reasons born of common sense more than of criticism, and in presumption of authorial rather than ecclesial intent. That is, the Acts of the Apostles narrates a story whose central characters are the same authors (e.g., Peter, Paul, James) and audiences/sources (e.g., Jerusalem, Timothy, Corinth, Ephesus, Rome) referenced or alluded to in the subsequent New Testament letters.[4] New

Testament readers naturally make associations between these common elements, noting as well a common concern for important topics of Christian existence (e.g., sharing goods, purity, suffering, the performance of the word of God, congregational unity).[5] Literary intertexts of this sort suggest a logical relationship as members of the same conceptual universe; from a perspective within the New Testament, Acts supplies the "authorized" narrative behind its most important epistolary texts.

Therefore, the critical tendency of reading Acts exclusively with the Pauline collection (Knox, Goodspeed, Bruce, Delatte, and many others) seems misplaced—even though the rehabilitation of Acts (perhaps even in a "new and improved" version) for a later stage of the canonical process, and then a renewed interest in Acts criticism during the second half of the twentieth century, may well have been prompted by the strategic relationship between Acts and certain Pauline letters (e.g., Romans, Ephesians, Galatians) in service of both literary/rhetorical and historical interests.[6] Within its canonical setting, however, Acts supplies a narrative introduction for the entire epistolary canon, Pauline and Catholic; in fact, if the canonical process yields hermeneutical prompts, then the relationship between Acts and CE within the New Testament should be elevated in importance. In any case, the interpreter approaches the New Testament letters with the orienting concerns of Acts in mind and, in light of its story, more wakeful when negotiating between the New Testament's two different epistolary corpora as theological complements.

In this same regard, the more modest prospectus of the present paper considers the relationship between Acts and the Letter of James in particular as a representative member of the CE. If, according to the "canon logic" of the New Testament, a prior reading of the book of Acts is presumed, then its portraits of the church's earliest leaders (Peter, John, Paul, James)—drawn as they are from early traditions of their teachings and ministries, concurrent to the earliest stage of the canonical process—envisage a particular account of their religious authority,[7] the nature of their ministries (e.g., prophetic, pastoral, missionary), and the subject matter of their kerygmata, which supplies interpreters with both an explanatory context and religious warrant for why these New Testament writings, when considered as a whole, are formative of Christian theological understanding.[8]

The Role of Acts within the New Testament

Among the most important roles Acts performs for readers[9] (if not also scholars) of the New Testament is to proffer biographical introductions to the implied authors of the New Testament letters that follow. In canonical context, such biographies serve a theological (rather than historical) purpose by orienting readers to their authority (religious and moral), thereby underwriting them as trustworthy interpreters of God's word and actions, and their writings as trustworthy interpretations of God's gospel for the future church. While the historical reliability of Luke's portraits of Peter, Paul, James, and other leaders of earliest Christianity remains contested, if not doubtful, their perceived moral authority and theological reliability within Luke's narrative world guarantees the importance of their letters for Scripture's implied audience—faithful readers of the church who seek theological understanding. In any case, the salient issue that shapes Acts' narrative of Christianity's expansion into pagan territory, which is narrated with great optimism, is its use not as a historical resource but as a theological source that contributes to the church's ongoing understanding of its vocation and identity in the "real" world.

In this regard, Acts provides a distinctive and formative angle of vision into both Pauline and Catholic epistolary collections that follow. In particular, the manner by which Acts narrates the personae of Christian leaders and their relations with each other as characters of this authorized story of emergent Christianity frames a particular account of how intracanonical conversations between the canonical writings linked to these same leaders might be negotiated. Similarities and dissimilarities in emphasis and theological conception found when comparing the Catholic and Pauline Letters may actually correspond to the manner by which Acts narrates the negotiations between the reports from different missions, and the theological convictions and social conventions required by each (e.g., Acts 2:42-47; 9:15-16; 11:1-18; 12:17; 15:129; 21:17-26). The relations between James and Paul, or Peter and James, or even Peter and John, as depicted within the narrative world of Acts, are generally collaborative rather than adversarial, and frame the interpreter's approach to their biblical writings as essentially complementary (even though certainly not uniform and sometimes in conflict) in both meaning and function. In fact, if the critical consensus for a late first-century date of Acts is accepted, which is roughly contemporaneous with the earliest, precanonical stage in the formation of the New Testament,[10] then it is likely that its collection of portraitures of early Christian leaders provides an important explanatory model for assessing the relationship between (and even within) the two emergent collections of canonical letters. The form and function of these Christian writings and their relationship to one another is another articulation of the early church's sense of the more collaborative relationship between their individual people and interpretative traditions, which is reflected then in the Book of Acts. So that, for example, if Peter and John are enjoined as partners in Acts, then we should expect to find their written traditions conjoined in an emergent Christian Bible, and their intracanonical relations envisaging the church's perception of their theological coherence. Likewise, the more difficult, although finally collegial, relationship between James and Paul as narrated in Acts 15 and (especially) 21 may well envisage their partnership in ecclesial formation in a manner that Protestant interpretation has sometimes subverted.

Because both the narrative world and its central characters are the literary constructions of the storyteller and are shaped by his theological commitments, the interpreter should not expect a more precise connection between, for example, the kerygma of the Peter of Acts and a Petrine theology envisaged by 1–2 Peter. Nevertheless, there is evidence that Luke did indeed draw upon important traditions common to the Petrine letters when composing his narrative of the person and work of Peter. In particular, 1 Peter's interpretation of Jesus as Isaiah's "Servant of God" (1 Pet 2:21-25; cf. 1:10-12), the evident core of Petrine Christology, is anticipated by four references to Jesus as "servant" in Acts (and only there in the New Testament), the first two in speeches by Peter (Acts 3:13, 26) and the last two in a prayer by the apostles led by him (4:27, 30).[11] Moreover, the God of the Petrine Epistles, who is known primarily through Jesus' resurrection (1 Pet 1:3, 21; 3:21; cf. Acts 2:22-36) and as a "faithful Creator" (1 Pet 4:19; cf. Acts 4:24), agrees generally with Luke's traditions of a Petrine kerygma. Even Peter's claim that the central mark of Gentile conversion is a "purity of heart" (Acts 15:9) is strikingly similar to 1 Peter 1:22. Finally, the most robust eschatology found in Acts, famous for its sparseness of eschatological thought, is placed on Peter's lips (Acts 3:20-23), thereby anticipating the keen stress posited on salvation's apocalypse in 1–2 Peter (cf. 2 Pet 3:1-13).[12] A second example may be the far thinner portrait of John in Acts, who, although depicted as Peter's silent partner, uses his one speaking role in Acts 4:19-20 to sound a key note of the Johannine Epistles: "for we cannot but speak of what we have seen and heard" (cf. 1 John 1:1-3).[13]

When these thematic connections are rooted in the narrative world of Acts—a world in which these characters have enormous religious authority and purchase for the church's future—the epistolary expression and development of these core themes is underwritten as also important for the church's future and formation. Moreover, the certain impression of kerymatic continuity between the Lord's apostolic successors (Peter/John) and Paul, cultivated by Acts, would seem to commend a more constructive relationship between their writings. Acts performs an interpretive role, not so much to temper the diversity envisaged by the two different collections of letters, but to prompt impressions of their rhetorical relationship within the New Testament. According to Acts, the church that claims its continuity with the first apostles tolerates a rich pluralism even as the apostles do within Luke's narrative world, although not without controversy and confusion. What is achieved at the pivotal Jerusalem Council (Acts 15) is confirmation of a kind of theological understanding, rather than a more political theological consensus. The divine revelation given to the apostles according to Acts forms a "pluralizing monotheism" (J. A. Sanders), which in turn contextualizes Paul's idiom of two discrete missions and appropriate proclamations, Jewish and Gentile, in Galatians 2:7-10. The variety of theological controversies Paul responds to in his letters, with whatever rhetoric he employs in doing so, is roughly analogous to the "Cornelius problem" in Acts.

Of course, Acts portrays Peter (rather than Paul) first initiating and then explaining the admission of uncircumcised (unclean) Gentiles into the church, and the Peter of Acts finally defends Paul's mission and its spiritual results in a speech that is remarkably Pauline in theological sensibility (15:7-11)—perhaps reflective of Luke's familiarity with, and the perceived unity of, the Petrine and Pauline traditions used in Pauline/Petrine letters, as many modern interpreters have noted.[14] More remarkably, however, the question of whether or not to "Judaize" repentant Gentiles is settled *before* Paul comes back into the narrative to begin his mission to the nations in Acts 11:1-18. In fact, Peter's second rehearsal of Cornelius' repentance at this second Jerusalem Council responds to a different problem altogether, posed by the church's Pharisaic contingent, which is concerned (as evidently is James) about a normative halakah for mixed Christian congregations (15:4-5). Peter's response, presumably agreeing with Paul's initial proclamation (cf. 13:38-39), concentrates on an internal "purity of the heart" (15:9).

James, however, expands this Pharisaic concern for spiritual purity to include socio-religious practices (15:20); in fact, his halakah reflects the more traditional worry of Jewish religion regarding syncretism—the "gentilizing" of repentant Israel (15:20; see also 21:17-26)—and in particular the possible attenuation of the church's Jewish legacy in the Diaspora (15:21). It is in response to James' Jewish concerns that the narrative of Paul's mission to the nations is shaped in Acts; therefore, he provokes and responds to a different set of theological controversies than does the epistolary Paul who responds to internal opponents who want to Judaize repentant Gentiles. According to Acts, this issue was settled by Peter at the earlier Jerusalem council (11:1-18), and even though it resurfaces in Antioch (15:1-2), those who raise the question again are summarily dismissed by James as "unauthorized" teachers who do not represent the position of the Judean church (so 15:24). In fact, the entire narrative of Paul's European mission in Acts (Philippian, Thessalonian-Athenian, Corinthian,

Ephesian) is simply not shaped by the same theological controversies that Paul stakes out in his letters as provoked by his Gentile mission.

In general, the Paul of Acts is exemplary of a more Jewish definition of purity (cf. 24:16-21). Thus, he is arrested in Philippi for being a Jew (16:20-21) and earlier circumcises Timothy (16:3; cf. Gal 2:3), not only to testify to his personal loyalty to the ancestral religion (cf. 21:23-26), but more critically to symbolize the importance of James' concern to preserve it in consecrated form. Consider, for example, the role Timothy performs in Acts in contrast to Titus in Galatians. Timothy is of mixed parentage, Jewish and Gentile, and in prospect of the Diaspora church, Paul circumcises him in order to preserve his mother's Jewish inheritance.[15] He stands as a symbol of Paul's missiological intent in Acts, which is to found Christian congregations in the Diaspora with a mixture of Jewish and Gentile converts whose faith and practices are deeply rooted in the church's Jewish legacy.

From this canonical perspective, then, it may well be argued that a principal concern of the second collection of epistles is to bring balance to a *Tendenz* toward religious syncretism by which the pressures of the surrounding pagan culture may distort, if not then subvert, the church's substantially Jewish theological and cultural legacy. The repetition of familiar Pauline themes in the CE (e.g., James, 1 Peter, Jude), even though perhaps idealized for rhetorical purposes, acquires a thickened meaning when read in context of the antecedent Acts narrative: that is, a prior reading of Acts alerts the reader of CE that an increasingly Gentile (Pauline) church must consider their religious and public purity as God's people according to the redemptive calculus of their Jewish canonical heritage (Scriptures, practices, prophetic exemplars, etc.). As such, their public profession of faith must be embodied in the community's public practices.[16] The full experience of God's righteousness is by performance of works and not by *sola fide*.[17]

Reading the Catholic Epistles as a Collection

Let me begin this section of the paper by iterating an observation made earlier about the canonical process that carries, in my view, substantial hermeneutical importance: the CE was always received and read within the ancient church as a collection of individual letters.[18] The perceived coherence of these different compositions implied by this historic phenomenon is at odds with the critical assessment of the CE, which underscores their literary, rhetorical, and theological diversity, and therefore their independence from each other (or attachment with other New Testament writings or traditions). In fact, the presumption of modern biblical criticism, often stated, is that the disunity found between the individual compositions within the CE makes it impossible to speak of a unifying theology in the same way the interpreter often presumes (perhaps too glibly) the theological coherence of the Pauline corpus, of the Johannine writings, of the Synoptic Gospels, and so on. Each CE is typically analyzed in turn—sometimes with note of the different authors' use of common traditions (e.g., James and 1 Peter, 2 Peter and Jude) and/or the distinctive contribution each makes to a New Testament theology—but rarely if ever together as a complement of writings that constitute a discrete thought/symbolic world.

Even though the ancient church nowhere explains this particular element of the canonical process, nor should we expect it to have, I am aware of no scholar who denies that the production of the New Testament served largely theological aims, whether epistemic or sacramental. In fact, different canon lists extant from different regions of the church catholic reflect differing judgments by church leaders/traditions that resulted in different arrangements of writings, which were routinely ranked not according to their length but according to their aesthetics when performing a variety of religious tasks (cf. 2 Tim 3:14-17). For example, Marcion's canon list, which combines a version of Luke's gospel with an extant collection of Pauline letters to seven congregations, envisages a particular post-Pauline understanding of the gospel. In some canon lists of the East, John's gospel is placed/ranked before Synoptic in tacit support of a Logos Christology, just as in most other canon lists Matthew is placed first for its liturgical and catechetical utility, and so forth. The arrangement of collections, and even of individual writings within collections, envisages ecclesial value judgments that reference Scripture's canonical role in forming a community's understanding about God. For this reason, it is rather easier for me to understand the final form of the New Testament as a theological construction rather than the result of an arbitrary decision about each part's relative length, or a technical decision about their reproduction in uncials, or the like.

The emergent New Testament is given final form by its discrete collections, set in "proper" relationship with each other, rather than by its individual writings. Individual writings did not circulate as such; the atomism that considers individual writings in isolation from their canonical collection is a modern critical convention. During the canonical process, individual writings were preserved, edited, reproduced, circulated, read and then canonized in combination with other individual writings as canonical collections.[19] In fact, in the early history of the CE, they were known only as a collection, called *Apostolos*, rather than from histories of the individual writings. The inference drawn is that their performance and religious authority within the faith community is valued more as an inspired collection than as a collection of inspired individual writings, read independently from the others and with differing valences within different communities. That is, the earliest history of these writings would seem to indicate that these compositions were read as integral parts of respective epistolary collections, Pauline or Catholic.

The number of writings in a collection typically symbolizes the church's recognition of their completeness. Thus, for example, Irenaeus can speak of the four Gospels as encompassing a self-contained whole similar to the four corners of the earth. The earliest collection of Pauline writings consisted of letters written to seven churches, since seven symbolizes completeness and is the "perfect" number. With similar significance, then, the collection of seven CE circulated as a self-contained and catholic witness to God's word. The canonical process evinces an aesthetic value such that the church's recognition of the divine inspiration of the CE is of a collection, rather than of per se individual writings.

Clearly, the CE are arranged and titled differently than the Pauline collection. Even if the Pauline Letters were ultimately arranged into a sequence from longest to shortest, or more deliberately by combining one subcollection of letters to seven congregations (Romans to Thessalonians) with another to a triad of individuals (Timothy to Philemon), the CE are rather arranged and titled by reflection upon Paul's index of the three pillars of the Jewish church in Galatians 2:9. Although such a recognition may be a mere convenience, the church seems intent on relating the two collections, Pauline and Pillars, together in some fashion that would then facilitate the New Testament's performance as witness to God's word. Moreover, the titles of the CE, which reference the names of early Christian leaders rather than of Christian congregations, may well envisage people traditions that posit religious authority as witnesses to Jesus or as interpreters of the *regula fidei* the church received from him. Finally, the Bede, who also appeals to Paul's catalogue of pillars in Galatians 2:9 as a ranking of due respect, writes in his preface that "the Letter of James is placed first among these for the reason that he received the government of the church of Jerusalem, from where the source and beginning of the preaching of the Gospel took place and spread throughout the entire world."[20] While agreeing with the Bede's interpretive instinct, my own reckoning of the priority of James is quite different (below).

Reading James within the Context of the New Testament

The above observations, proffered provisionally as a rough draft, construct a rhetorical context for consideration of the more focused question of whether Acts cultivates a particular approach to a reading of the Letter of James as Scripture, and if so, what of Acts the interpreter should keep

in mind when reading James in a faith setting. The functional priority
of James within the CE, raised already by the Bede in the preface to his
commentary on the CE, may well be a canonical reflection of the important role performed by James at the second (15:4-21) and third (21:18-
25) Jerusalem Synods narrated in Acts. Perhaps Paul already recognized
the importance of James for the church's future in his somewhat ironical
ranking of the reputed pillars of the Jewish church,[21] in which James is
placed before Peter and John (Gal 2:9).[22] In any case, this privileging of
James in the New Testament canon—at least according to Acts—is not
based upon the principle of apostolic succession or even upon his per
se religious authority, which by either criterion would have privileged
the Petrine or Johannine Epistles. Even the familial relationship between
James and Jesus, which later church leaders appealed to in explaining
the canonicity of the letters from James and Jude, is given no currency
whatsoever in the New Testament itself. From a canonical perspective, however, the importance of the Letter of James is clarified by the
James of Acts, who articulates the central theological crisis facing emergent Christianity at the end of the first century: namely, the loss of the
church's Jewish legacy as the church's mission moves farther away from
Jerusalem, the epicenter of God's sacred universe, toward pagan Rome,
and becomes increasingly "uncircumcised" in constituency. The sheer
distance between the church's spiritual resources, including the apostolic
memories of Jesus preserved within the Jewish church, and the missiological frontier in places such as Philippi, where the "house of prayer"
exists outside of city limits; or other Roman cities, where the synagogue is
evidently a marginal institution within Acts' narrative world (e.g., Athens,
Ephesus); or Malta, where there is no Jewish presence, depicts the lack of
Jewish presence and threatens to paganize the church. James reflects Jewish theology in its call for Torah observance and concern for social purity;
that is, a Pauline concern for the purity of the believer's repentant heart
(Acts 15:9) must then be embodied in the social practices of the entire
faith community (Acts 15:20; Jas 1:27).

1. *The portrait of James in Acts.* The images (traditions) of various
leaders within earliest Christianity found in Acts underwrite the religious
authority of the implied authors of those letters that follow in the New
Testament canon, and so also of their particular accounts of God's word.[23]
In this regard, James is portrayed as the respected leader of the Jerusalem
church. Unlike Peter, Paul, and other leaders whose religious authority is
predicated by their missionary vocation as prophets like Jesus, the religious
authority of James is tied to his pastoral vocation and tasks (midrashist,
strategist, power broker, letter writer, pastor) within the church. These
more ecclesial contours of his authority, placed within the repentant Jewish

community, are reflected by the Letter of James, whose tone and interests are more Jewish and pastoral—that is, its instruction is concerned with the relational and religious well-being of a particular congregation of believers in accordance with the Jewish Scriptures. Thus M. Konradt argues that the different applications of common traditions in James and 1 Peter may be explained by the different profiles of James and Peter found in Acts: whereas Peter is a missionary and more interested in the reception of the gospel truth (and the faith community) by pagan outsiders, James is a pastor and more interested in the internal adherence to the gospel imperatives by faithful insiders.[24]

Konradt's important traditional critical conclusion is slightly adjusted when viewed from a canonical angle: these precious stories of James (and other leaders) in Acts contextualize a reading of their epistles that conforms to these different vocations/conceptions of authority introduced by Acts. Within this canonical context, framed by their prior reading of Acts, the implied readers of the New Testament (i.e., the faith community) are predisposed to approach the Letter of James as Scripture that proffers priestly advice about how they should resist their impure affections that may subvert their lives together, and rather pursue a way of divine wisdom. These same New Testament readers approach the Petrine Epistles as proffering instruction about how purified believers should live courageously in contretemps to the surrounding pagan (and hostile) society, and so forth.

The second and more important element of this intracanonical relationship between Acts and James is thematic. The theological interest of the James of Acts in purity suggests that his principal concern is not with the "Judaizing" of Gentile believers (as found earlier in the Pauline Letters) but with the "gentilizing" of the church's Jewish legacy, which he evidently thinks threatened by the church's (Paul's) mission to the nations. Indeed, rather than oppose the church's mission or seek to subvert God's redemptive purpose, the repentant Pharisees who raise the salient issue of table fellowship between believers (15:5) for deliberation (15:6) do so without contending that such purity practices are required for salvation (cf. 15:1). While Peter contends in Pauline voice that "purity of the heart" is sufficient, clearly this does not satisfy James.

The theological shaping of James' verdict (15:13-21, 22-29) within this narrative world no doubt reflects the situation of the narrator's own religious location toward the end of the first century/beginning of the second century (and so from the very earliest period of the canonical process). The salient issues at stake concern the right interpretation (and transmission) of Israel's Scriptures and the purity of the church's practices ("resurrection practices"), whether they are contaminated by "the pollutions of idols, unchastity, from what is strangled and from blood" (Acts 15.20; cf. 15:29; 21:25)—that is, by the insinuation of pagan religious practices upon the Diaspora synagogues where Moses is taught (Acts 15:21) and Messiah is proclaimed. In his response to James/Jerusalem, the Paul of Acts takes considerable care to identify himself publicly as an observant Jew and to maintain a Jewish way of faith in the congregations he founds in the Diaspora; there is in Acts no parting of the ways, Jewish and Christian. Ironically, he is like James and other Jewish believers in Palestine, "zealous for the law" (Acts 21:20) as a mark of covenant loyalty to Israel's God.

2. *Acts, Paul, and the pillars of the Jewish church*. Besides the portrait of James in Acts, the only other relevant New Testament text that shapes the reader's impressions of the implied author of the Letter of James is Galatians 2:11-18, where Paul describes different responses to James—a so-called pillar of the Jewish church (2:9). On the one hand, he speaks of certain missional agreements made with James (2:7-10), but then in famously polemical terms implies that he has certain theological disagreements with those "who came from James" to subvert his ministry in Antioch (2:12). In the context of his letter, Paul seems to identify the James tradition with a definition of the "Israel of God" (6:16; cf. 2:15) that posits the "works of the law" over the "faith of Jesus Christ" alone (2:16; cf. 6:12-16). In this case, Torah observance forms a Jewish identity that bears public witness to its covenant with God. While the Reformation may have been incorrect in defining "works of the law" as the "good works of self-achievement," to use Bultmann's famous phrase, or in understanding that in Galatians, Paul describes two mutually exclusive kinds of justification, one by faith in Christ alone and the other by good works, surely the Reformation was right to suppose that the plain meaning of Paul's polemic is against the centrality of Torah observance as an identifying mark of Christian community. On this issue, the biblical Paul apparently disagrees with the biblical James.

Given my earlier comments, this conclusion must be qualified: whatever were the circumstances that provoked the famous conflict between the church's Jewish and Gentile missions reported by Paul in Galatians, and however this conflict is then skewed by the rhetorical design of Paul's letter to the Galatians, it envisages a different controversy from that found within the narrative world of Acts. Perhaps this difference is a simple matter of time; when Paul wrote Galatians, there evidently still was optimism surrounding the church's mission to the Jews (Gal 2:7; cf. Acts 21:21-26). This is no longer the case when Acts is written and the Paul of Acts begins his mission. Now the controversy pertains to Paul's mission to the Jews, whether their religious legacy and social identity will be attenuated (see above). In any case, Paul's ironical reference to his personal relations with the church's pillars—"James, Cephas and John" (an index that the ancient church may have used to arrange the CE as Scripture)—may well suggest something about the literary relations between the two collections of New Testament letters, and in particular between Paul and James.

Within a canonical setting and following Acts, then, the cautionary note sounded by James in Acts 15:20-21 (cf. 21:25) regarding the possible attenuation of the Jewish practices (halakah) and social identity of the church has its roots in the Jewish-Gentile tensions of the Antiochene church, and perhaps also in widely circulated reports (Jewish Christian traditions) concerning the Pauline mission to the nations (cf. 21:20-21).[25] The face of these tensions in the Jerusalem church (cf. 15:4-5) seems to have been more abstract and perhaps reflects an anti-Gentile bias that is native to observant Jews, as reflected in several of their Second Temple writings. James, a Palestinian Jew, may be worried that Paul, a Diaspora Jew with more liberal attitudes toward all things "Gentile," may be unwilling to maintain a more scrupulous separation from "the pollutions of idols" and other defiling activities pertaining to pagan moral and religious conventions (15:20, 29; 21:25). From his perspective, Paul may have been more inclined to accommodate some negotiable aspects of pagan culture into the practices of his congregations (cf. 1 Cor 9:19-23), which some leaders of Judean Christianity evidently feared might result in the disappearance of the church's distinctive Jewish identity.[26]

3. *"Test case": Acts and James 2:14-26.* In my commentary on James, I argued that among its various roles within Scripture, James sounds a cautionary note that the church must become more "Jewish" in order to become more fully "Christian."[27] The same can be said of Acts. The traditional Jewish concerns registered by the James of Acts, for repentant Gentiles to embody their "purity of heart" in religious practices separated from cultural idols and pagan practices, have profound currency in shaping a theology that resists the facile separation of orthodoxy from orthopraxy.[28] Moreover, the role of James as an inspired midrashist for his community exemplifies the importance of Israel's Scriptures in resolving the variety of intramural squabbles the emergent church must deal with to maintain its vocation and identity. Perhaps Luke is responding to a nascent Marcionism within his own church, fostered in large part by the failure of the church's mission to Israel and its successes among Gentiles, and deepened by the pervasive anti-Semitism of Roman culture. Against a resulting tendency away from Scripture as a medium for God's Spirit and from those religious practices that maintain the church's public identity within a pervasively pagan world, the James of Acts interprets the relevant meaning of Scripture for his congregation in practical terms and then writes that his findings "seemed good to the Holy Spirit" (15:28; cf.

15:19). When James is read with Acts, these same concerns of the James of Acts frame and freight the contribution the Letter of James makes within the New Testament canon.

As an example of the performance of this interpretive strategy, what follows briefly considers the influence Acts may have—as the canonical narrative behind the text—upon an interpreter of James 2:14-26. It hardly needs noting that the recent history of this text within Protestantism has lifted it from its immediate rhetorical context to perform a role as principal foil to a particular reading of Pauline theology that accords with the terms of the Magisterial Reformation (see appendix). Within James, however, this passage is merely illustrative of the principle that God blesses those who are doers of the "royal law" of neighborly love (1:12, 25-27; 2:8-13).

Significantly, the density of purity language used in drafting this congregational principle in James (1:21, 27; 2:9-11), especially when coupled with quotations from and loud echoes of Leviticus and other Jewish writings that touch on halakic requirements,[29] resonates with the concern for social purity expressed by the James of Acts (15:20, 29; 21:25). In fact, the regulatory norms of corporate life given in the book of James are cast in "insider-outsider" terms (e.g., 1:27; 2:2-3) in a way that continues the subtext of James' halakic midrash in Acts 15:20, and is supported by clear allusion to the Levitical injunctions regulating Israel's social relations with its unclean neighbors (Lev 17–18).[30] What seems also clear is that religious practices (i.e., abstaining from pagan conventions [15:20] and embracing a Jewish pattern of worship [15:21]) are not viewed by James as a condition of salvation but rather as its social, public expression (cf. 15:19). Consistent, then, with the pattern of conversion found in Acts, being cleansed from sin (cf. 2:38; 3:19) in prospect of eternal life (cf. 13:46) is the experience of those who repent, whether Jew or Gentile; and the community's religious practices (cf. 2:42) mark out its common life as "graced" by God's presence (cf. 2:47; 4:33) as mediated through God's Spirit (cf. 2:38). Purity/social practices and a repentant response to the "word of God" about Jesus are not causally related but represent deliberate and distinct properties of the community's religious life together.

Likewise, according to the epistolary James, the community's faithful reception of the "word of truth" and "putting away of all filth" (1:21) are discrete, deliberate choices of the repentant "soul" that form a whole witness to the righteousness of God (2:22). In this symbolic world, then, "pure and undefiled religion," uncontaminated by the anti-God world order, is characterized by religious acts (1:27; *thrēskeia* = *thrēskeuein*)—caring for the poor and powerless in obedience to God's law (1:27; cf. Acts 2:43-44; 4:32-35; 6:1-8)—while mere professions of faith are judged "vain" (1:26; 2:14-17, 18-20). There is no bifurcation of "heart" religion from the performance of public service, nor is one the logical cause of the other; each is the mutual complement or concrete evidence of the other (2:22, 26). While James has unmistakable eschatological commitments and concerns, so that divine judgment—whether the community has the faith of Jesus (2:1)—is rendered upon evidence (or lack) of obedience to God's law (2:8-13), his pastoral intent is equally unmistakable: there are impoverished believers who presently lack justice (2:2-7) and material goods (2:15; cf. 1:27), whose very existence depends upon the faith community's obedience to God. That is, the social and spiritual well-being of the eschatological community depends upon the performance of those public practices that mark out its faith as the "faith of the Lord Jesus Christ, the Glorious One" (2:1).

While the intertextuality of Acts 15:13-21 and James 2:14-26 is illuminating in several ways, now especially in light of the *Wirkungsgeschichte* of James since Luther, let me draw attention to one conclusion of particular importance. The James of Acts does not underwrite the church's Jewish legacy, whether to abstain from idols (15:20, 29; cf. 21:25) or to maintain Mosaic definitions of purity (21:21-26; cf. 15:21), as a substitute for repentance—which remains in Acts the defining mark of Christian conversion (15:14, 19; cf. 2:38). For him, as for all the other Christian leaders who populate Luke's narrative world, "there is salvation in no one else, for there is no other name ["Jesus Christ of Nazareth whom God raised from the dead," 4:10] under heaven given among humankind by which we must ["the *dei* of divine necessity"] be saved" (4:12). For this reason, he says that those who promote a different gospel in Antioch (cf. 15:1) are "without portfolio" (15:24)—they have no authority to do so. Rather, the preservation of this Jewish legacy protects the integrity of Christian mission, Christian fellowship, and the Christian gospel. I rather think this is precisely the relationship the epistolary James also asserts between faith and works in 2:14-26. The performance of works has not displaced the profession of faith as heaven's currency, nor is the "obedience of faith" viewed as the progenitor of the "obedience of works." The profession of an orthodox faith is presumed by James (2:14): he addresses believers, not sinners; communicants, not outsiders. Brought to sharper focus by Acts, James 2:14-26 advocates a variety of Christian existence that is characterized by the interpenetration of faith and works. When the performance of Moses is replaced by mere professions of orthodox faith (1:25-27; 2:2-3; 2:18-20), faith itself remains incomplete (2:22), and in any case is not the faith of the Lord Jesus Christ (2:1). Even though faith is central, "faith alone" without a complement of purity practices is ultimately ineffectual for building Christian community or preserving Christian witness. If the book of James introduces the CE to orient its readers to this collection's principal contribution to a fully biblical witness, then I would argue it is this concern for the practices of the faith community that should concentrate a theological reading of the CE as a whole.

Appendix
A Theology of the Catholic Epistles

The fact that the CE always circulated as a collection within the church cultivates the impression, among others, that its individual members, noteworthy because of their theological and literary diversity, form a literary and theological whole. In making this claim, one should not imagine that this perceived coherence can be reduced to a theological uniformity; however, the complementary nature of this collection's diverse membership does in fact evince a grammar of theological agreements that guarantees its own distinctive (and nonnegotiable) contribution to Scripture's witness to God. Moreover, the logic of beginning the collection with James is made clear, not only by Paul's implied ranking of the pillars of the Jewish church found in Galatians 2:9, but also by the plotline of Acts—not by the priority given to the traditions about the person James, but by the importance the narrator gives to the worry of James that the church's (Paul's) mission to the nations will threaten the profoundly and pervasively Jewish legacy of the church, without which the church simply cannot be the location of God's presence and truth in the world.[31]

In light of this canonical prompt, the theological grammar of CE, consisting of a "logical" sequence of themes (Creator, Christ, Community, Christian Life, Consummation), is introduced by the Letter of James and thereby retains an essentially Jewish cast: believers must remain ever faithful to the Creator's will (1:5-8; 4:11-12), exemplified by the life and teachings of Christ (2:1), and so resist the moral and religious contaminants of the surrounding social order (1:21, 27) in order to enter into the blessings of the coming age (1:12, 25). What emerges in the CE, then, is an overarching pattern of salvation different from but complementary to that found in the Pauline collection. It is unlike the Pauline collection, whose missiological pattern of salvation concentrates on what Gentile sinners must do ("obedience of faith") in order to be baptized into Christ, where the resources of a transformed self, and so the believer's relationship with God and neighbor, are found, and where a destiny of eternal life is guaranteed by God. According to Paul's redemptive calculus, then, sin is a universal problem that cannot be settled by human effort, no matter how noble, but by God alone. This faithful Creator, the only God, who has promised to deliver creation from corruption, has now sent a Messiah, Jesus of Nazareth, into the world in order to fulfill God's promise and save all things from death. It is God alone who has accepted Jesus' faithfulness to God, even to death on a cross, as a sacrifice for the sins of the world. The sinner can participate in the redemptive results of Jesus' sacrifice for sin by converting to him—by public profession that he is Lord and by confession of faith that God raised him from the dead in confirmation of his lordship.

If the Pauline collection concentrates on what God has done in and through Christ Jesus for all those who remain "in Adam" and are in need of salvation, and then on what the sinner must believe/entrust to God in response to be initiated into life with Christ, the Catholic collection concentrates on what the believer must do in order to maintain that life. This is a profoundly and pervasively Jewish calculus, which demands that the faith community demonstrate its allegiance to God by obedience to the commandments (Jas 1:25; 1 Pet 2:20; 3:16-17; 2 Pet 2:21; 1 John 2:3; Jude 3). If Pauline exhortation recalls the (pagan) sinner's prior life without Christ, and so by contrast the radical (and typical) changes that take place under the aegis of the Spirit in the believer's existence with Christ, then the CE bid the believer to make moral/religious choices, which presuppose but are independent of choices made for Christ, that guarantee their future with God.[32]

Set within this intracanonical conversation between two very different collections of New Testament letters, what follows is a programmatic (and provisional) first draft of a unifying theology of the second collection. Time and space allowances restrict this illustration to the first element of my theological rubric, which regards "the Creator."

Creator

1. The God of James is the only true God (2:19). God is the Creator, who has made every person in God's own likeness (3:9; cf. 1:17-18). God is therefore personal, to whom the believer turns when lacking in wisdom needed to pass daily spiritual tests (1:5). God is the heavenly Father (1:17, 27; 3:9), from whom the wise humbly receive (1:21) good and perfect gifts (1:17) that are generously provided by God, in every case (1:17) and without discrimination (1:5). Therefore, this generous God sends forth the "word of truth" to reveal the Creator's perfect plan of salvation in order to guide the redeemed humanity into the age to come (1:18), which is a restored creation, made complete, perfect, and lacking in nothing (1:4).

In particular, God has chosen those of this broken and corrupted world who are its last, least, lost, and lame to be enriched by their love for

God (2:5): as Scripture teaches, "God gives grace to the humble" (4:6b). Thus, not only are the sick healed and the sinners forgiven by the Lord in the present age (5:14-16); their worship of God (5:13) will be vindicated and their fortunes reversed at God's coming triumph, while those who oppress them will be destroyed (5:5-6; cf. 1:9-11). Indeed, God promises future blessing, "the crown of life," to all those who love God (1:12; 2:5; cf. 1:25).

To love God is to obey God's perfect law, and eternal life is granted to those who do God's will (4:15; cf. 1:12, 25; 2:8-13). In that God is not only Savior but also Judge (4:11-12; 5:9), with the authority to save and destroy humanity (4:12), all are obliged to obey God's rule. A concrete record of God's will is transmitted by the gift of the biblical Torah, which is the rule of faith for the faith community (1:17-27; 2:8-13). God will bless those who obey God's law (1:25; 2:13) and will destroy those who live foolishly and disobey the law of God. As Scripture also teaches, "God resists the arrogant" (4:6a). The apocalypse of God's triumph over God's enemies (the deceived, the slanderous teacher, the arrogant rich, the impatient complainer, the sinner and apostate) is imminent (5:7-8), at which moment creation will be purified and restored (1:4; cf. 5:17-18), the reign of God will be secured on earth (2:5), and blessing will be dispensed therein to all those who evince by their wise responses to their spiritual tests a robust love for God (1:12; 2:5)—such as the patriarch Abraham, who is called a "friend of God" (2:23), and the prostitute Rahab, who demonstrates her faith in God by what she does on behalf of God's people (2:25).

2. First Peter relates the revelation of God to the resurrection of Jesus (1:3, 21; 3:21). God is the "faithful Creator" (4:19), who supplies parental care (1:2-3) to a community of "resident aliens" (1:1; 2:11) who presently suffer as Christians (1:6; 2:20; 3:14; 4:16) but whose obedience to God results in the salvation of their souls (1:9; 4:17-19) in the coming age.

God's redemptive purpose, already presaged by biblical prophecy (1:10-12), requires the suffering of God's Messiah (1:11; cf. 2:22-24) and then of those who follow after him (1:7; 2:21; cf. 1:1-2). Indeed, God's resurrection and glorification of the messianic Servant (3:18-22), whose faithfulness resulted in his suffering (3:22-24), testifies to the vindication that awaits those who suffer as a result of their own faithfulness to their faithful Creator (4:12-19).

A holy God has called an elect people out of a profane world (1:1; 2:10), purifying (1:18-19) and protecting (2:25) them through the Messiah for their eternal salvation (5:10). In response, the faith community reveres God (1:17) and worships God (4:11). Yet nonbeliever (4:1-6) as well as believer (4:16; 5:5-6) stand under the just judgment of this holy

God, whose final verdict is based on the hard evidence of a manner of life lived (1:17). Thus, those who obey God's will are judged righteous (3:13-17); their rejection and suffering at the hands of evil outsiders (2:11-12; 4:3-4) provide the evidence that warrants God's blessing in the age to come (3:9). Since God is Creator of all things, God's judgment extends to all, and the faith community need not seek vengeance against its enemies (3:8-12). Likewise, God's good intention extends to every human relationship, so that for the Lord's sake, believers "submit to every human institution" (2:13–3:7) and love each other (1:22).

3. The question addressed by a canonical approach is how the theological conception of 2 Peter interplays with 1 Peter in forming a Petrine complement to the CE whole.[33] Even as the Christian confession of God as Creator is central to 1 Peter's moral vision (1 Pet 4:19), so it is central to 2 Peter's apocalyptic vision (2 Pet 3:5). Even as the heavens and earth are brought forth by the word of God, so it is by that same powerful word that both apostles and prophets spoke from God (1:19-21; 3:2; cf. 3:15-16) to map the promise of creation's salvation from the "defilements of the world" (2:20). Ultimately, by this word, the punishment of God will be executed upon the present godless order (3:7). Thus, while 1 Peter concentrates on the inauguration of this salvation in the suffering and resurrection of Jesus, 2 Peter emphasizes its consummation at the coming triumph of the Lord's Parousia and so rounds out a Petrine conception of salvation's history.

Significantly, 2 Peter defends the delay of creation's purging and renewal by appealing to God's patience (3:9, 15). The topos of divine patience is already employed by 1 Peter (3:20), but there to interpret the cleansing waters of Christian baptism by which believers participate in Christ's passion and its redemptive results (3:18-22): the believer's sin is purged and life renewed as the primary evidence that God has triumphed over evil and death. Thus, 1 Peter has the risen Jesus journey to hades to proclaim there God's victory over the powers and principalities of the evil one (3:19). Second Peter expands the space and extends the time of this same theological point. That is, God's plan of salvation is mapped for a different time zone, where the coming of a single "day of God" (3:12) is the historic consummation of "a thousand years"—a seemingly endless dispensation—of divine patience (3:8; cf. Ps 90:4; Rev 20:3).

Of course, the question remains for 2 Peter: what is it about this old order that now exists under God's curse and will ultimately pass away at the Parousia that so distresses its Creator? God's displeasure is concentrated by 2 Peter upon those false teachers (2:1) who work against the redemptive purposes of the Creator in the same manner as the false prophets of the Jewish Scriptures (1:19–2:22), and who therefore embody all that is wrong with the present state of God's creation.[34] The issues are both theological and moral. These are teachers who deny (2:1) and distort (3:16) the central beliefs of the apostolic tradition, which is grounded in their witness to God's revelation through Christ (1:16-18), which has subsequently been codified as the community's rule of faith (3:2). They also subvert the community's moral rule by leading impure lives (2:2, 7-14; cf. 2:18-19). Rather than being motivated by pious devotion to God, they exploit the loyalty of the community for monetary gain (2:3), in clear violation of 1 Peter's exhortation to the community's teachers to be content in the humble circumstances of one's life (5:1-5; cf. Jas 4:1-10).

The decisiveness of this final moment of "real time," the just execution of God's righteousness, circumscribes God's patience in 2 Peter in a way that feels different than in 1 Peter. Scripture's witness holds God's mercy and justice in critical yet uneasy balance, and so it is with its Petrine witness that God is both patient and demanding. In 1 Peter, God's revelation in the sufferings of the messianic Servant is one of "great mercy" (1:3), by which a marginal community of resident aliens, who themselves suffer for righteousness' sake, hope for their eternal inheritance in the coming age. In 2 Peter, God's revelation in the Parousia of the majestic Lord is the apocalypse of justice; the coming age has now arrived as "the day of judgment and destruction of the godless" (3:7), especially for those whose teaching undermines the faithful. To confess allegiance to a holy God, who governs creation as Father and Judge, is both life-generating and life-threatening.

4. The theological conception of 1 John is elevated by the existential claim that believers "have fellowship [*koinonia*] with God" (1:5) and the even more stunning logic that as God's "children," believers are reborn by God, and God's "nature" abides in them (3:9) even as they "abide" in God (2:28; 3:2). Yet this redemptive calculus remains essentially Jewish, since this intimate relationship between a knowable and experienced God and the community that abides in God is conditioned upon obedience to God's commandments (2:3; 3:24; 4:12-17). Thus, God promises eternal life to those who abide in God by performing the commandments—specifically, the command to love one another (2:24-25).

As already insisted upon by 2 Peter, the community's rule of faith that regulates what is known and experienced of God is informed by apostolic tradition, even as this tradition—and thus the community's relations with God—is potentially subverted by false teachers ("antichrists"): the "message we have heard from Jesus and proclaim to you" (1:5a; cf. 3:11), the truth of which is confirmed in believers by a mysterious religious experience of "anointing" (2:20, 27).

The subject matter of this faith tradition, now written down in 1 John, is first apprehended historically by apostolic witness of Jesus (1:1-4; cf. Acts 4:20). Its principal claim is that God is "light" (1:5), in whom there can be no "darkness" (deductive). The theological topos that God is light infers that through Jesus, the essence of God is disclosed within history and made known to humans—even though God is not fully known until the coming age, when believers become like God (3:2; cf. 1:7; 3:9). That is, through the expiatory death of Jesus (2:2), God is disclosed as faithful and forgiving (1:9; 2:12); and by forgiving, the repentant God purifies the believer from all sin to have fellowship with God and one another (1:7; 3:3). Through the incarnation of the Son, God is disclosed as love (4:7-10), so that the principal disposition of this fellowship is love-like-God (4:11-21). What becomes abundantly clear from 1 John, again, is that the Jewish calculus of this apostolic tradition is ultimately cast in ethical terms. Thus, the confession of core beliefs about who God is—that God is light, that God is love—is finally cashed out in the terms of ethical practice (cf. Jas 2:14-26; 1 Pet 4:12-19).

5. Again, the question addressed by a canonical approach to the CE is how the theological conception of 2–3 John interplays with 1 John in forming a Johannine complement to the CE whole, since the Johannine letters are bits of this second collection of New Testament letters. Put another way, what would the Johannine witness lack without these two neglected Johannine Epistles?[35]

This question seems especially important given the interpretive tendency to read only 1 John as constitutive of this Johannine witness. The canonical question is not satisfied by noting evident linguistic links between the three letters, or even the similarity of polemical rhetoric, as though each is responding to the same intramural conflict (cf. Black, 372–74). Again, the canonical presumption, which still must be demonstrated, is that the church has added 2 John and 3 John to 1 John as complements to its essential Johannine theological conception, and that, as a result, its witness to the gospel is expanded and enhanced in spiritual effect.

From this perspective, a variety of historical questions are made irrelevant. For example, the sequence in which these letters were written is of little consequence, since the privileged order by which they are read is not a historical matter but rather a canonical one: the interpreter begins with 1 John and then proceeds to consider 2 John, and finally 3 John. Nor is it necessary to consider the Johannine Epistles as the precipitate of a "Johannine network" (Black, 369–70). Moreover, the literary dissimilarity between these writings—while 1 John is non-letter in form and more hortatory in function, 2 and 3 John are "real" letters (Black, 370–71)—may well reflect their different roles and supply important clues as to their intracanonical relationship. However, this too is a determination made on the basis of a close reading of their inspired content.

Second John confirms the internal threat posed by unnamed false teachers who teach against "the coming of Jesus Christ in the flesh" (7; cf. 1 John 2:18-19, 23; 3:7; 4:2)—that is, against the incarnation of the Son of God as Jesus from Nazareth, through whom the truth and grace of God is made personally known. The nominative *deceiver* is here repeated and added to the pejorative *antichrist* to underwrite their threat.

Critically, the familiar idiom of *abiding*, which is used in 1 John to underwrite the intimacy of God's familial/personal relations with the faith community (Father/Son abides in believers and believers in them), is in 2 John the "doctrine [*didache*] of Christ" (9-10) that measures whether one "has God" (cf. 1 John 2:23). The impression given is that the apostolic tradition has now been fashioned into a curriculum or rule of faith (rather than a proclaimed gospel or written exhortation; 1 John 1:1-4) by which "any [teacher/tradent] who comes to you and does not bring this doctrine of Christ is not received" into Christian fellowship ("house," 10). Again, as elsewhere in the New Testament, hospitality symbolizes the reception of the word—in this case, the lack of hospitality symbolizes the rejection of heresy (11). Such christological dogma is a church order, and perhaps is suggestive of an institutionalized community by which the anticipated visitation of the church elder (12; cf. 3 John 10a, 13-14) purposes to inspect the congregational life to make certain the deceiver has been shown the door.

The other contribution made by 2 John is to add to the Johannine conception of a future consummation of God's salvation. Both writings understand that one's status before God is conditioned upon obedience to God's commandment (4-5; cf. 1 John 2:7-11), in part measured by rejection of the antichrist. The tone of 1 John glosses the consummation of God's salvation (at the Parousia of Jesus, 2:28) as a "day of judgment" (2:17a; 2:28; 3:19-21; 4:17-18) when the disobedient believer is "shamed" or "condemned." Second John says that while the believer may "lose" (*apollymi*; cf. John 6:27, 39-40; 10:10, 28; 12:25; 17:12, where what is "lost" is faith in Jesus and the lifestyle that reflects that faith, "commandment of God," makes belief and life integral; cf. 1 John 3:23), it goes on to claim that this may also be a time "to win a full reward" (8). This text glosses 1 John 3:2, which specifies that this future "reward" (*mithos*) is to see/know God like it is—a symbol of increased intimacy with the Holy Trinity in the coming age (see Rev 21:3; 22:3-5). Clearly this text indicates a "theology of merit" that implies that eternal life has a future, when the experience of living with God is made "full," and that this is the consequence of abiding in the "doctrine of Christ."

6. Third John confirms the teaching of 1 John that truth is a lifestyle: the believer "walks" the truth (3-4, 8b). Moreover, to walk the truth is to mimic good rather than evil (11a), and to demonstrate that one is "of God" (11b; 1 John 2:29; 3:10). Critically, however, 3 John understands this walk in terms of congregational practices. The critical New Testament word for church (*ekklesia*) is used three times (6, 9, 10)—the only time it is used in the Johannine letters. The repetition of *church* cues the interpreter to 3 John's role in constructing a fuller portrait of the community's practices (or "works," 5). Regarding these practices, consider the following: (1) hospitality (5-8, 10b) or "love" (6a) toward strangers (5b; cf. 10b), who apparently are itinerant teachers in "God's service" (6b) and dependent upon the financial support of the church (7-8a); (2) recognition of elder rule (9-10b), which with Paul is executed by pastoral "house calls" (10a, 13-14; cf. 2 John 12); and (3) public testimony to the truth (6c; 12; cf. 1 John 1:2; 4:14), which is embodied in the practice of loving hospitality, an important narrative thematic of Acts.

7. The polemical cast of *Jude* places the apostolic tradition (3) supported by various prophetic antitypes gleaned from the Jewish Scriptures (5-16) against false teachers (4; cf. "these men," 8, 10, 12, 16, 19), whose theological error has been embodied in destructive, immoral behavior. For this reason, a rule of faith reading of Jude is more antithetical—this erroneous teaching over and against apostolic tradition.

The antithesis of "the faith that was once for all delivered to the saints" (3b, "once for all," 5a)—that is, the faith community's apostolic tradition (17-18, 20)—is the false teaching of those "ungodly persons who pervert the grace of our God into licentiousness and deny our only Master and Lord Jesus Christ" (4). In what sense is God's grace as Savior (1, 24-25) perverted by the false teachers, presumably leading them to tolerate "loose morals" (*aselgeia*)? And what are these false teachers claiming about Jesus that "denies" him to be Lord/Master (14, 17, 21, 25) and Christ/Messiah (1, 17, 21, 25)?

While it is difficult to cut through the polemical, often enigmatic rhetoric to retrieve with precision what the false teachers actually taught about God's grace and Jesus' lordship, the practical implications are much clearer: their teaching is embodied in moral (8, 23b) and social practices (12) that are subversive to the purity of the faith community. In a word, their theology of grace and their Christology warrant a kind of antinomian (lawless) spirituality, similar in form (but not in "theo-logic") to what Paul challenges in 1 Corinthians 6:12ff. (cf. 6:9-11) and 10:23ff., and in Romans 5:12–8:2.

According to Paul, our trust in what God's grace has already accomplished through the death of Christ makes sin irrational activity for the believer; the believer who exists as a new creature "in Christ" is assured of eternal life (Rom 5) and sins no more (Rom 6). The deep logic of this Pauline gospel, underwritten by Paul's radical conception of God's grace and of Jesus' lordship over God's enemies of sin and death, marginalizes the importance or even the reality of sin in the believer's life, and leads quite naturally to the antinomian heresy. The Pauline *Tendenz*, currently reflected in certain Protestant traditions in particular, is that God's grace has so thoroughly triumphed over human sin because of Christ's work that "licentious" behavior is tolerated without fear of future judgment. If this contemporary Paulinism is something like the ancient teaching in Jude's line of sight, then Jude's canonical function is to supply another check to balance this dangerous tendency of the Pauline witness within the faith community that tolerates morally and socially subversive behavior with impunity.

Against this teaching, then, Jude conceives of God as the "only God" (25), whose authority is singular and eternal. God is named as the community's "Father" (1) and "Savior" (25), whose covenant "love" (21) is conditioned upon the community rejecting the "scoffers" (17-19), remaining allied to "your most holy [and apostolic] faith," and worshipping "in the Holy Spirit" (20). By these holy practices, God the Father "keeps" (1, 24) the community for the future day of salvation, when they will be presented to God as a people "without blemish" (24). In fact, these redemptive activities of God (24-25a) are the natural outworking of God's character (25b).

Toward a Unifying Idea of God in the Catholic Epistles

It is time to try to put Humpty-Dumpty back together again. Rather than compiling a catalogue of those various attributes or dispositions that characterize the God of the CE according to the above summary or arranging them as complements of an integral whole, it is more true to the temper of the canonical approach to describe what distinctive contribution the CE makes as an integral whole to a fully New Testament idea of God. That is, what peculiar contour of New Testament theology would the interpreter lack, were the New Testament lacking the CE?

In attempting to answer this question, I would simply recall an observation previously made about the CE construal of God's redemptive purpose: sharply put, that salvation is cast in terms of what believers are required to do in order to maintain their relationship with God in final prospect of divine blessings in the coming age (what we Methodists sometimes refer to as God's final justification). For this reason, there is a much keener emphasis posited in the CE than in Paul's writings on God's performance as "lawgiver and Judge" (Jas 4:12)—a belief that defines the nature of God's continuing relations with the faith community (rather than with outsiders).

While this idea of God the Judge does not displace the centrality of repentance for initiating the community's life with God, in agreement with Acts, it nonetheless shapes a different ethos than does the Pauline witness. "True religion" is an ethical religion, measured by its conduct toward others rather than by the orthodoxy of its faith commitments about God alone (J. A. Sanders). While readers are consistently reminded in the CE not to depart from received (apostolic, orthodox) traditions that aim at the revealed truth about God (e.g., Jas 1:13-21; 2 Pet 2; 1 John 1–2; Jude), the community is repeatedly told that mere confessions of truth are in themselves never sufficient measures of a saving relationship with God; what is known and believed about God must always be embodied in community practices for faith "to be made complete." That is, the spiritual test of whether the believer is properly related to God is whether that believer obeys God's will/word/law (e.g., Jas 1:22-25; 1 Pet 4:17-19; 2 Pet 2:17-22; 1 John 2:3-6; Jude 4).

This studied and consistent emphasis upon the active performance of faith in God cultivates a particular ethos that is reflected by/in this literature. First, since God is Lawgiver, a positive definition of Christian faith is cast in ethical terms. Much of the CE consists of paraenetic literature because Christianity is an ethical religion; a believer's existence is regulated by moral rules as much as by orthodox beliefs. True religion is obedient to God's command to love others, especially those who are most vulnerable to the vicissitudes and vulgarities of a corrupt, corrupting world: the poor (James 2), the stranger (1 Peter), the itinerant teacher (3 John), the wayward or immature believer (James, 2 Peter, Jude), and so forth. What seems also true of this literature is that the primary (although certainly not exclusive) focus of this moral code is to regulate life within the faith community, rather than between it and the surrounding social order. Love for God is embodied most especially in love for the congregation's own sisters and brothers. For this reason, unlike the Pauline Letters, whose teaching shapes a more missional and universal ethos, the ethos of the CE is more introspective and sectarian. The community is made fully conscious of their status as contretemps to the surrounding social world, and their corresponding need to love and support one another as friends as the distinguishing mark of their purity (1 Pet 1:22). In this sense, to obey the law/commandments God has given to regulate the community's holy practices is to prepare for God's coming judgment (Jas 2:12-13; 1 Pet 1:13-17; 2 Pet 3:11-13; 1 John 2:12-21; 2 John 6-9; Jude 20-21).

Second, since God is creation's Judge, the ultimate measure of the quality of repentance is cast in apocalyptic terms. That is, even believers, who confess an orthodox faith in God, will finally be judged by God on the basis of whether they have obeyed God's law (hence the logical relationship between God's roles as both Lawgiver and Judge—e.g., Jas 2:12-13; 2 Pet 2:21). Yet God's role as Judge is inextricably tied to God's role as Savior, so that God's end-time judgment of all people is a function of God's redemptive purpose. For this reason, the various activities of God as Savior (specifically of believers rather than of sinners) are expressed in terms of God's rescue of those believers—in collaboration with a faithful community—whose salvation is imperiled by spiritual failure or theological disaffection (Jas 5:19-20; 1 Pet 5:10; Jude 22-24). In any case, for this reason the symbolic world in which the CE operate is organized by God's future, and by the prospect of God's impending judgment of believers according to what manner of life each has lived. Christian existence has this more provisional cast, then, that makes obedience to God's rule more urgent but the assurance of God's salvation less certain—hence 1 John's apt reminder that the believer's assurance of God's salvation on the day of judgment is not so much a matter of belonging to a confessing community, but rather belonging to a community that actively loves each other by word and deed (4:12-21; cf. Jas 3:9-12).

Of course, the danger of this ethos—if cultivated in isolation of the Pauline witness—is a tendency toward a graceless legalism, in which "true religion" is defined in terms of human achievement, and purity is presumed when a social protocol is observed or a moral code is rigorously obeyed in fearful conviction that God is Lawgiver and Judge of the believer, without holding on with equal firmness to the more generous conviction that God is Savior and friend of the sinner. Such is the self-correcting interplay of Pauline and Catholic witnesses within the New Testament whole.

CHAPTER 8

THE PRIORITY OF JAMES

*

Robert W. Wall

Introduction

The present study is the fourth in a series of papers arguing that the
placement of James as frontispiece of the Catholic Epistles (CE) collection envisages its canonical function: to introduce a set of thematics
that organize a "unifying theology of the CE collection," which in turn
facilitates an intracanonical conversation that complements the Pauline
collection, either to complete its theological conception or to correct its
myopic misuse.[1]

While parallel thematics as well as plausible historical constructions
may help to underwrite the canonical function of James, my initial observations, made at the Durham meeting, were largely rhetorical, predicated
by the placement of James in the final literary form of the CE collection
and by the portrait of James in Acts that defines and justifies the ongoing importance of the canonical James.[2] In the second of these seminar
papers, I argued that this initial impression of the "priority of James"
is confirmed by appraising the phenomenon during which the different
CE were formed into a discrete collection of the biblical canon. Rather
than being studied in context of a literary location regulated by rhetorical rules, the purpose of James within the final redaction of the New
Testament canon is now illumined by the motives of its reception and

placement in completing the sevenfold CE collection.[3] Accordingly, this process of formation was governed by an aesthetic principle that recognized and valued theological coherence and a sense of completeness, two salient properties of the biblical canon. The canonical function of James is now understood as facilitating these canonical properties.

The social location of the canonical process insinuates ecclesial and catholic properties of the various phenomena of the canonical process, including the formation of the Pauline and CE collections, the composition of certain letters within them (e.g., 2 Peter, James), and the intracanonical relationship between the two epistolary corpora of the emergent biblical canon. In this sense, then, the performance of the CE collection (and of James within it) and the distinctive theological contribution it forges confirm the church's intent that this second epistolary collection complement (a catholic *Tendenz*) the extant Pauline collection, to produce a more faithful and fruitful understanding of God's gospel in service of the church.[4]

Central to my proposal of the priority of James is the observation, laden with hermeneutical promise, that with the addition of James, the CE collection was made complete and received into the biblical canon with the book of Acts.[5] The most plausible explanation for this phenomenon is that Acts supplies the theological motive for shaping the final redaction of the CE collection with James as its frontispiece. As I put it while introducing the thesis of last year's paper, "when the CE became a collection, it did so with Acts, which supplied a narrative context that not only vested the entire collection with religious authority but cued the priority of James within it. At that 'canonical moment' when the final redaction of this collection evoked a recognition of its theological wholeness, the one (James as its surprising frontispiece) was made explicable by the other (Acts as its narrative context)."[6] On this ground, a reading strategy is devised by which the theological conception of the entire collection may be constructed, an outline of which concludes my paper.

The Reception of Acts as Scripture

The purpose of this year's seminar paper is more modest: to supply a footnote regarding the earliest reception of Acts as Scripture, especially by Irenaeus in book three of *Adversus haereses*. If the working relationship between Acts and the CE during the canonical process was decisive for explaining the surprising role James comes to perform within the final redaction of the second letter collection, then it strikes me as necessary to consider the prior moment that Acts was first used as Scripture.[7] That canonical moment defines, if only vaguely, the prospective role that Acts performed in the formation and reception of the CE collection as Scripture.

Whilst I welcome recent studies on the reception of Acts,[8] the methodological interests that determine these treatments typically fail to define *reception* in a way that includes the phenomenology (and hermeneutics) of the canonical process. Rather, the reception of Acts is defined in terms of literary dependence and reduced to theories of composition set within ancient social worlds, with careful attention given to the possible redactional uses of Acts by others or their use of common sources, all of which are concentrated by dates dependent upon still other dates that are uncertain for lack of clear evidence.[9] For this reason, I consider this approach to settling the critical problem unprofitable—at least with regard to my present proposal, which concerns the theological motive for using (and therefore receiving) Acts as Scripture. The salient question is not when but *why* the church first uses Acts to help forge its self-understanding as the church.

Irenaeus' Use of Acts as Scripture in *Adversus haereses*

The central character in the narrative of the church's reception of Acts as Scripture is surely Irenaeus, who uses Acts in his polemics against so-called heresies to formulate a normative account of Christian origins (or apostolic succession) to ground his definition of the church's rule of faith by which all truly apostolic traditions cohere.[10] His initial use of Acts as Scripture, more than any other single episode in its early *Wirkungsgeschichte*, defined its subsequent role within the biblical canon; in fact, "the canonical status of Acts is the result of [his] late second-century apologetic for a certain form of Christianity."[11]

Irenaeus gives no indication that he knew of James (which probably was not yet in circulation, if even composed) or a collection of CE (which belongs to a later stage of the canonical process). Given his interest in an emergent biblical canon to lend support to an apostolic definition of the faith, then, we should expect his relative lack of interest in the James of Acts (or in my proposal): there is not yet a James to unify with his Pauline canon. Moreover, whilst he pays considerable attention to the traditions of the Jerusalem pillars in his commentary on Acts, he is an apologist for his own day, mostly interested in giving credibility to the theological unity between the three gospels from the Jerusalem apostles (rather than their letters)[12] and the one marginal (late?) gospel linked by tradition to Paul (Luke's gospel). The unity of a fourfold Gospel tradition is not only against those who use Luke for heretical ends but against any who privilege a single gospel over its fourfold articulation; this myopia tends toward unprofitable ends. The central feature of his apologia is a call for the unity of a diverse fourfold whole.

In any case, Irenaeus (followed then by Tertullian and still other Fathers)[13] clarifies the role Acts should perform within a biblical canon, and in doing so anticipates the deep logic that will prompt the church, generations later, to attach Acts to a Pillars collection of letters with James as its frontispiece:[14] Acts plots a narrative of apostolic succession from a common christological fount to defend the theological unity and religious authority of a fourfold "Gospels of the apostles."

The rhetorical design of Adversus haereses. The design of Irenaeus' commentary on Acts in book three of *Adversus haereses* envisages two relevant properties. First, his commentary on the plotline of Acts is shaped by the passing exigencies of his social world and is polemical against the perceived heresies of particular people or groups, such as Marcion, Valentinus, the Ebionites, and other second-century gnostic movements within the church. While his reading of Acts provides us with an excellent example of patristic exegesis, his commentary hardly has normative value for the church's future. In fact, we might judge that his reading of Acts is deficient and that other readings of Acts, especially related to James' role at the so-called Jerusalem Council (Acts 15:13-29; cf. 21:21-26), should be substituted for his. But then, secondly, Irenaeus' commentary is also typological of a way of thinking about the church's different apostolic traditions (esp. Pauline and Jerusalem pillars) in a manner that unifies them by agreement with the Rule of Faith, by common succession from the same christological fount, and in service of a common missionary purpose by virtue of a common spiritual authority derived from God. This typological appropriation of Acts had continuing purchase during the entire canonical process and has come even to us as a means to clarify the theological motive of its different phenomena, however implicit, including the formation of the CE collection and the priority of James within it.

This extended footnote concerns only Irenaeus' typological use of Acts, and includes the following observations which, while not new to me, reflect a more recent assessment of the earliest reception of Acts as Scripture during the second century, when the idea of a New Testament had just been introduced and the formation of a distinctively Christian canon was just under way. What is new to this proposal, in my judgment, is the observation that Irenaeus' commentary on Acts anticipates the relationship between Acts and the final redaction of the CE collection, and the priority of James within it. This footnote contains elements of the social world of the late second century and the phenomenology of a canonical process within it. So why, then, did the church come to recognize the book of Acts as Scripture?

The unity of Luke-Acts. While the consensus since Cadbury has been that Luke and Acts should be read as a circumscribed and continuous narrative that comes to us within the biblical canon, packaged with its own particular social world and coherent in regard to a unified theological conception, the presumption of this consensus subverts the critical investigation into the motive of the church's reception of Acts as Scripture as a phenomenon of the canonical process. In fact, there is no evidence that a unified reading of Luke-Acts was ever the original intention of the church. Whilst Irenaeus certainly believed Luke and Acts were written by a single author, his evident interest is not to prove their unity as a continuous narrative or as a narrative shaped by a distinctive theological conception; this is a modern interest. Rather, Irenaeus' interest is the unity of the four Gospels of the apostles, inclusive of Luke's gospel, which must be received as a unified analogue of the rule of faith.

Quite independent of any theory of composition of Luke-Acts, which I think is finally indeterminate, the evidence at hand would indicate that the catholic reception of Acts as Scripture followed an independent path into the New Testament canon, for different reasons and with a different role to perform than Luke's gospel.[15] Those few canon lists, mostly in the East, whose gospel canon begins with John's gospel, concludes with Luke, and is placed adjacent to Acts, have absolutely nothing to do with a critically constructed Luke-Acts, but rather with the theological priority of John's gospel in narrating the story of Jesus as incarnate Logos. That Luke and Acts stand together in this early listing of canonical writings is incidental to the inherent logic of an emergent New Testament canon, according to which a fourfold Gospel prepares a reader for Acts, which in turn prepares a reader for the multiple-letter canon, which logically concludes with the "end times" envisaged by the Apocalypse. To make the case for an intentional Luke-Acts and to review the reception of Acts on this basis as a phenomenon of the canonical process is an anachronism of contemporary scholarship.[16]

Irenaeus' reading of Acts as typological of the unity between epistolary corpora. When read as typological of a book's continuing authority, Irenaeus' use of Acts stipulates two interrelated criteria and proffers a reading strategy that ensures the book's religious profit margin, which shaped the hermeneutics of the canonical process.[17] In particular, it is Irenaeus' typological use of Acts (rather than his exegesis) that illumines the motive for placing Acts with the CE collection during the canonical process: to regulate the CE collection formation and underwrite its inclusion in the New Testament canon.

The first criterion is that the substance of a book/person/tradition's teaching must cohere to the church's Rule of Faith. The second criterion, related logically to the first by Irenaeus, is that a book/person/tradition to which an appeal is made must be linked to an apostle, since the Rule of Faith comes to the Catholic Church from Jesus through his apostolic successors. For example, Luke's gospel has authority despite its marginal status and use by heretic groups because of his connection with Paul. Acts upholds the religious importance of Paul for the future of the church, not only because of his Damascus Road visitation from the risen Jesus, but also because of his unity in purpose and proclamation with the apostolic successors to Jesus. That is, Luke is Paul's successor, who is successor to the apostles, who are successors to Jesus—a succession authorized by God and imbued with the Spirit's presence. What is interesting here is that *apostolicity* is defined differently than in Acts 1:21-22, since spiritual authority is granted even to those early Christian leaders outside the Apostolate, such as James and Paul—clearly a contested point even into the third century. In any case, the succession of a Christian leader to the risen Christ underwrites the continuity of both purpose and unity of proclamation of the tradition he founded. Orthodoxy and apostolicity— so far, so good.

But herein lies the great deceit (or conceit) of heresy-making: heresies are clothed in ecclesial respectability, if not a presumptive theological superiority, by appeal to a particular apostle. Using his definition of Christian unity constructed by his reading of Acts, Irenaeus points out that the content and performance of any book linked to a particular apostolic tradition will be necessarily distorted because of its inherent theological myopia. The issue at stake is not so much whether a teacher appeals to an authorized apostolic tradition—to the memory of early Christian leaders or to their collected writings. All heretics did. The problem, as Irenaeus understands it, is that no one tradition must be used to the exclusion of all others. I would submit that this ushers in a definition of canonicity predicated on notions of apostolic succession and Christian unity that assume all apostolic traditions work together in forming a completed whole greater than the sum of its particular parts. Stated in negative terms, the use of a single tradition is more easily distorted for lack of balance and incomplete revelation. Thus, the problem with Marcion's use of a "mutilated" version of Luke's gospel (even though it may have only been an earlier recension than the one used in Irenaeus' church) is not so much what he has edited out, but that he does not use it as part of a fourfold Gospel whole—the number four symbolizing holism to make this very point. Likewise, the problem with Marcion's appropriation of an incomplete Pauline canon is not so much that it is incomplete (without Pastorals, Philemon), but that in drawing upon only Luke and Paul, he rejects the full Gospel of the apostles. It is the particularity of an appeal to use for universal (or canonical) ends to which Irenaeus finally objects.

Whilst we should leave open the real possibility that such theological myopia is not intentional (the result of a conscious editing of tradition) but rather a reflection of an inchoate canon, Irenaeus also claims that the appeal to a single tradition is often set in adversarial relation with others, thus subverting Christian unity. By quick survey of *Adversus haereses*, Marcionists appealed to Paul against the Jerusalem pillars, the Montanists to John rather than to Matthew, various gnostic/libertine groups to Paul and John, the so-called Ebionites and other Jewish groups to Saint James the Just (i.e., to the memory of his renowned piety but not yet to James, which is never cited in the pseudo-writings of these Jacobian groups) against Paul, and so forth.[18] This observation in turn infers a interpretive practice that resists the myopia that attaches itself to one particular apostolic tradition to the exclusion of other authorized apostolic traditions. The roots of heresy are not found in the attenuation of the per se apostolic tradition in teaching and worship; rather, it is the privileging of one tradition above all others. The use of a pluriform collection (e.g., fourfold Gospel), all parts of which cohere to the Rule of Faith and are linked to apostolic tradition, protects the church against theological myopia and thus heresy.

In summary, what is forged by the nature of Irenaeus' polemics is a positive *typos* of theological unity, according to which every single biblical tradition coheres in general to a common Rule of Faith. No matter to what religious tradition an appeal is made, if that tradition is apostolic, then what is expected is essential coherence with the received teachings of Jesus. But also forged is a negative definition of unity, so that a departure from the truth is not only the per se rejection of the Rule of Faith; it is also the result of considering only a single apostolic tradition to the exclusion of the full complement of apostolic traditions. In this sense, then, ecclesial unity is defined by a plurality that forges, in J. A. Sanders' phrase, a "self-correcting, mutually-informing apparatus." Thus, the unity of the apostolic traditions is another way of speaking of their completeness, of the complementarity of their different strands (not of the harmonizing *Tendenz* of patristic hermeneutics that F. Bovon claims). The value of Acts is that it allowed Irenaeus to speak of the incompleteness of any single apostolic tradition that is used without benefit of all the others that draw from a common Christological source and bear witness to a single rule of faith.

Irenaeus and the Priority of James

Even though Irenaeus did not know of a Pillars collection, the deep logic of his appropriation of Acts as Scripture illumines the use of Acts during its formation into a collection: what is true of Gospels of the apostles is also true of letters of the apostles. Set against the use of particular apostolic letters against others, the formation of the CE collection under the auspices of Acts presumes the theological unity of the per se collection, even though from different apostolic traditions; further, it is in their wholeness or completeness that their religious profit margin is fully realized. Moreover, the Pauline and CE corpora are complementary parts of an epistolary whole. The myopic appeal to Paul to the exclusion of the CE results in heresy—that is, in something other than a robust articulation and incarnation of the Rule of Faith.

Of course, Irenaeus' use of Acts to defend an early shape of the biblical canon must be updated to apply to the "final" edition of the New Testament. In particular, I argue that the portrait of James in Acts aims New Testament readers to the priority of James within the CE collection. Yet my understanding of its priority—what explains the canonical function of James—is largely inferred from the canonical function of Acts. For this we have Irenaeus to thank.

CHAPTER 9

JAMES AS THE FIRST CATHOLIC EPISTLE

John Painter

The Catholic Epistles (CE) are often treated as what is left after the really important stuff: the Gospels, Acts, and the Epistles of Paul. What is left over includes the seven CE. From our earliest knowledge of them, that is their number and that is what they were called collectively. They are often referred to as General Epistles, taking "Catholic" to mean that they are not specifically addressed. But that is not true of 3 John. What is left over also includes Hebrews and Revelation. Some modern treatments confirm that this is a ragbag collection by treating one or both of these within the General Epistles, for example, Gerhard Krodel's (editor) Proclamation Commentary on *The General Letters: Hebrews, James, 1–2 Peter, Jude, 1–2–3 John.*[1]

There are two aberrations here: the inclusion of Hebrews in the collection, and the placing of Jude before the Johannine Epistles. The location of James as first of the CE, is first noted by Eusebius (ca. 320 CE).[2] He mentions by number the seven CE, but does not specify the order of the remaining six epistles, of which he names only Jude. The first evidence of the complete order of the CE is in the thirty-ninth Paschal Letter of Athanasius in 367 CE. He lists the Epistles in the order known to us, which may be the order known to Eusebius. Krodel's editorial arrangement suggests that there is nothing special about what is in this collection or the order in which the books appear.

It is unlikely to be a coincidence that the first and final books in the collection are attributed to brothers of the Lord. The principle of ordering the Pauline Epistles appears to be from longer to shorter. This is not true of the CE. James (1,749 words) is slightly longer than 1 Peter (1,678 words), but 1 John (2,137 words) is longer than either of them, and Jude is longer than either 2 or 3 John. It seems that 1, 2, and 3 John and 1 and 2 Peter are treated as subcollections, and 1 and 2 Peter together are longer than 1, 2, and 3 John. Each of these subcollections is ordered from the longer to the shorter. But why is James placed before them? It is likely that the order of the first six epistles was determined by the reference to James, Cephas (Peter), and John, the pillar apostles named in Galatians 2:9. The intent seems to have been to have a collection bounded by writings attributed to brothers of the Lord. The first was attributed to the first of the three pillar apostles, leader of the Jerusalem Church in succession to Jesus and known as James the Righteous. The status of the pillar apostles reinforces the authority of the collection as the Jerusalem Epistles alongside the Pauline Epistles.

Contrary to the order of the English Bible, in almost all Greek manuscripts of the New Testament, the catecheses of Cyril of Jerusalem (348 CE), and the fifty-ninth canon of the Council of Laodicea (360 CE), the CE follow Acts and come before the Epistles of Paul. This is the order of the earliest full canonical list of the twenty-seven books of the New Testament (Athanasius' thirty-ninth Paschal Letter of 367 CE). A collection issuing from the Jerusalem pillars is placed alongside and before the Letters of Paul, suggesting that Paul's letters should be understood on the basis of the Jerusalem corpus. Tensions between James and Paul are evident within the New Testament, especially in Galatians 2 and Acts. James 1:22-25 and especially 2:14-26 are intelligible in this context. The early priority of the CE is recognition of the status of their four authors, and especially of the preeminence of James.

Canonically, James is the first of the CE, though not necessarily the first of the seven to be written. Reference to them as CE reflects their struggle to emerge from the contested writings (thus Clement) and to be accepted by the Catholic Church. That four of the seven do not have specific local addressees may have suggested the description of General Epistles, addressed to the church at large. But this understanding is problematic. From a canonical perspective, all Scriptures speak to the church at large without ignoring their original context.

Two of the longer epistles in the collection are addressed to the Diaspora (James and 1 Peter). The longest of the Epistles is not addressed to any readers (1 John), but its connection to 2 and 3 John implies a readership within a circle of house churches (in Asia Minor?). Though 2 and 3 John appear to be addressed to individuals, 2 John may use the metaphor of sisters to signify related individual house churches in a region. Second Peter is addressed to believers more generally, as is Jude. Only 3 John is clearly addressed to a specific individual (Gaius).

James and the Diaspora

But what of James and 1 Peter? Is their use of Diaspora part of a metaphor for believers generally living as aliens in the world, making them General Epistles? James is addressed to "the twelve tribes of the diaspora." This expression is not found elsewhere in the early Christian or contemporary Jewish literature, though aspects of the address are found in the Septuagint and early Christian literature. Reference to the "twelve tribes" is rare in the Septuagint, but see Matthew 19:28/Luke 22:30; Acts 26:7; and Revelation 7:4-9; 21:12. In the New Testament, Diaspora is found only in James 1:1; 1 Peter 1:1; and John 7:35, and the verb (*diaspeirō*) in Acts 8:1, 4; 11:19. The unprecedented expression "the twelve tribes of the diaspora" has been understood broadly in three ways:

1. *All believers, Jews and Gentiles.* This symbolic interpretation is adopted by Martin Dibelius and may represent the view of the church in recognizing James as apostolic and canonical, the first of the CE. But there is no early evidence of the symbolic use of the twelve tribes of the Diaspora as an image of the church.
2. *All Jews of the Diaspora.* If the letter were to be dated later than 135 CE, there is a case for understanding this as a reference to all Jews. That is because the Jewish experience of Diaspora became more or less universal after 135 CE, not because the reference to Diaspora can be disregarded. If the letter is dated before 135 CE, the case is strong for recognizing Jews in the Diaspora as distinct from those in Judea and Galilee.
3. *All believing Jews of the Diaspora.* The prima facie case for this position is not strong because the address makes no such limitation. Nevertheless, effective circulation might well have been largely limited to Diaspora Jews who believed in Jesus.[3]

The epistle, like the mission of the historical James, was oriented to the Jewish people. Yet the case is strong for seeing James as effectively addressed to believing Jews of the Diaspora. In terms of reception history, it is possible that the symbolic interpretation aided the inclusion of James (and 1 Peter) in the canon. Nevertheless, there is a need to read

James on its own terms and as the first Catholic Epistle addressed to believers generally.

Dangers and Opportunities in a Bioptic Reading of James

The Epistle to the Hebrews (11:10-16) uses the wandering of Abraham and his descendants in search of the promised land as a paradigm for those who "looked for a city, whose builder and maker is God." Thus they lived "as strangers and *exiles* [παρεπίδημοί] on earth."[4] First Peter firmly relates the language of exile to the Diaspora experience (1:1; 2:11), but the language of exile is absent from James. The treatment of Diaspora as a metaphor for the believer's life in the world is charged with the potential to devalue life in the world. The danger of despising life in the world as of no value, and longing only for the life of heaven, has often been realized. But James lends no support for this view. His understanding of God stands firmly within the central Jewish affirmation of the goodness of God's creation.

Reading James as addressed to the universal church obscures the Jewish character of James. The stress on obedience and action, which is so forceful, is undone because it is not taken as evidence of the call to Torah observance. If James gives priority to the ethical demands of the Law, that does not mean he disregards its ritual embodiment.

At the same time, James is to be read by the universal church as canonical Scripture. Hermeneutically, the task requires that the reader should not do violence to the text in reading it in its new context. Diaspora is not a metaphor for life in the world away from heaven. Rather, Diaspora is life away from the land, with its social and cultural roots. This experience relates directly to modern life in the Western world, where people rarely grow up and live their lives in one geographical location. Lives are more often lived scattered like seed to the four winds, away from extended families and generational friends. The fragmentation of life is common even if we remain in our own country. Our large cities have diverse population groups, bringing together people from many places and different cultures, so that the experience of Diaspora is common and complex. It is from this perspective that the epistles to the Diaspora can be read with fresh insight and profit.

Date and Authorship

James' canonical status was tied to its recognition as an epistle of the brother of the Lord. This position is defended by modern commentators (J. B. Mayor, J. B. Adamson, R. Bauckham, L. T. Johnson) who argue that it emanates from the Jerusalem church before the death of James in

62 CE. Dating on this basis varies from the 40s through the 50s. Other scholars treat James as pseudonymous, coming from the late first or early second century. An extreme form of this view argues that James is a Jewish document into which the name of Jesus has been inserted in 1:1 and 2:1. Other views of pseudonymity are differentiated by the supposed place of composition—Palestine (J. H. Ropes), Alexandria (S. G. F. Brandon), Rome (S. Laws), or somewhere in the Diaspora where a Hellenistic Christian community had developed out of a liberated Diaspora Judaism (M. Dibelius). Dibelius argues that the epistle was perhaps based on earlier Palestinian tradition. In time, it came to be understood as addressed by James to the church in every place.

Other scholars, building on insights from Dibelius, recognize a synthesis of Jewish and Greek characteristics in the epistle. There is evidence of a Palestinian socio-economic context (the problem of poverty and wealth) and significant contact with the teaching of Jesus in the Sermon on the Mount (Matt 5–7). Yet the epistle also has an orientation to the Diaspora (1:1) and a somewhat more polished use of Greek than might be expected from James and his Jewish mission in Jerusalem (see the section "Literary Analysis" below). This suggests a two-stage hypothesis in which a Jewish believer developed the epistle in the Diaspora some time after the destruction of Jerusalem. At the time of the war, refugees from the Jerusalem church may have fled to Antioch, bringing with them tradition from James containing his understanding of the teaching of Jesus. Some time later, an editor made use of the tradition in this epistle, now directed to the twelve tribes of the Diaspora (P. Davids; R. P. Martin; J. Painter).[5]

Also against the direct authorship by James is the late appearance of the letter, first quoted by Irenaeus (ca. 180 CE), and its rough and disputed path to canonical status. Eusebius notes that Clement of Alexandria listed it and all the CE as disputed books. For Eusebius (ca. 320 CE), of these books, only 1 John and 1 Peter were no longer disputed. Not until 367 CE (in the thirty-ninth Paschal Festal Letter of Athanasius) did the CE, including James, appear as undisputed in the canonical list of books.[6] Had James been the outstanding figure that I, and others, have set out to reveal, this tardy road to acceptance is hard to explain. There are two divergent routes of explanation.

The first is to assert that James was not the outstanding figure that I have depicted. The case proceeds by arguing that various references in the New Testament generally identified with the brother of the Lord may refer to different people, and that the second-century (and later) focus on James is legendary.[7] While there are likely to be legendary elements, such developments build on historical evidence of the leadership of James, which is confirmed by multiple independent sources. Thus I do not think that this argument can be sustained. Paul's references to James as the first of the three pillar apostles (especially Gal 2:9) are enough to show his status in the early church. Though much of the second-century evidence is preserved by Eusebius, it is not possible to dismiss it as his creation. That diverse evidence portrays James as one of the leading (if not the leading) figures of the early church. Even Jerome, who is at pains to distance James from Jesus by explaining the universal designation of James as "the brother of the Lord" as referring to a near relative, a cousin, makes no attempt to belittle the importance of James. In his *Lives of Illustrious Men*, James is treated second, following only Peter, and Jerome's account of James is twice as long as his account of Peter.[8] There is no route to an explanation of the difficult path of James to canonical status here. James was an outstanding leader in the early church, and he was recognized as such by those who made the path of the epistle into the canon tortuous.

Slow reception of James is intelligible if it appeared some time after the death of James. Evidence from the epistle suggests that it was written after the death of James, utilizing tradition from James and directing it to a Diaspora readership. Because it appeared later, at a time when the Jerusalem church was no longer preeminent and Gentile Christianity had become dominant, an epistle directed to the Jewish Diaspora had little appeal to the church at large. Only when the Diaspora address came to be interpreted symbolically of Christians spread throughout the Empire was the way opened for the reception of James. The latter part of the second century reveals the proliferation of pseudepigraphic works, many of them in the name of an apostle or a member of the family of Jesus. James probably antedates these, but appeared near enough to that time to be caught up with the disputed books, needing to be saved from oblivion and received as Scripture.

James and Jesus

Studies have shown a relationship between James and the teaching of Jesus through traditions unique to Matthew (M) and shared with Luke in the form found in Matthew (Q^{Mt}), especially in the Sermon on the Mount. In the delineation of M, it is necessary to distinguish it from the final redaction of Matthew, which modifies the Jacobian tradition in a Petrine direction (see Matt 16:17-19). The teaching about the benevolence of God in creation (Matt 5:45; 6:26-32; and Jas 1:17) is linked to the demand for greater righteousness in law observance (Matt 5:17-48; and Jas 1:25; 2:8-12; 4:11). Both Matthew and James show a concentration on the inner moral demand of the law, but neither repudiates the ritual and purity requirements of the Torah. The unique connection between the prohibition of oaths in James 5:12 and Matthew 5:33-37 provides a basis for recognizing more links between the teaching of Jesus in Matthew and the ethical teaching of James. Almost one hundred years ago, G. Currie Martin observed that, where James addresses his readers as "brothers" (or "my brothers" or "my beloved brothers"), this form of address accompanies words closely paralleled by sayings of Jesus in Matthew.[9] He also draws attention to parallels with possible agrapha in the Letters of Paul. Important to his argument is the evidence from *1–2 Clement* and the Epistles of Ignatius, where the address "brethren" seems to be a signpost to indicate quotations from Scripture or the words of Jesus.

James' presentation of God and religion is nearer to that of Matthew than to the other Gospels.[10] James Adamson has interpreted this point of contact in terms of an understanding of the true fulfillment of the law. He draws attention to vocabulary and content links between James and Matthew:

	James	*Matthew*
"perfect"	1:4	5:48; 19:21
"righteousness"	1:20; 3:18	3:15; 5:6, 10, 20; 6:1, 33; 21:32
beatitudes on the poor	2:5	5:3
the merciful	2:13-14	5:7
ambitious teachers	3:1	23:8
the peacemakers	3:18	5:9
anxiety for tomorrow	4:13-14	6:34
"church"	5:7	16:18; 18:17
"parousia"	5:7	24:3, 27, 37, 39
"oaths"	5:12	5:33-37

Adamson insists that such correspondences need to be carefully evaluated for differences within broad similarities. James is hostile to riches, while Matthew is more conciliatory. Matthew is hostile to Judaism, while James promotes a form of Christianity that is uncritical of and firmly grafted on Judaism.[11] There is evidence of tensions between tradition used in Matthew and the final redaction of Matthew. From this evidence, it appears to be right to conclude that James and Matthew independently use something like the same tradition, but in different situations.

Martin Dibelius argues that parallels with the Gospels show only James' familiarity with the Jesus tradition, rather than any knowledge of the Gospels themselves.[12] James is to be compared with the collections of the Jesus tradition known as Q and M. J. H. Ropes argues that "James was in religious ideas nearer to the men who collected the sayings of Jesus than to the authors of the Gospels."[13] While James has drawn on the Jewish wisdom tradition, including the tradition of the righteous sufferer, the Jesus tradition, especially as drawn together in what is now Matthew's Sermon on the Mount (Matt 5–7), has made a manifest impact on James, so that it may be that James draws on the wisdom tradition through the wisdom of Jesus.

R. P. Martin also sees a relationship between James and the tradition found in Matthew, drawing attention to twenty-three allusions, while P. J. Hartin concentrates on James' relation to Q.[14]

	James	*Matthew*	*Source and Luke*
1. Joy in trial	1:2	5:11-12	**Q** (Luke 6:22-23)
2. Call to perfection	1:4	5:48	**M**
3. Asking and being given	1:5, 17; 4:2-3	7:7, 11	**Q** (Luke 11:9, 13:9-10)
4. Faith and doubting	1:6		**Mark 11:23**
5. Enduring and being saved	1:12	24:13	**Mark 13:13** (Luke 21:19)
6. Against anger	1:20	5:22	**M**
7. Doers of the word	1:22-23	7:24, 26	**Q** (Luke 6:46-47, 49)
8. Blessing of the poor	2:5	5:3, 5; (11:5)	**Q** (Luke 6:20; [7:22])
9. Warning against the rich	2:6-7	19:23-24	**Q** (Luke 19:24)
10. Law of love	2:8	22:39-40	**Mark 12:38-44** (Luke 10:27)
11. To work sin (lawlessness)	2:9	7:23	**Q** (Luke 13:27)
12. Royal law of love of neighbor	2:10-12	22:36-40	**Q** (Luke 10:25-28)
13. Obligation to keep whole law	2:10	5:17-19	**M Q** (Luke 16:17)

	James	*Matthew*	*Source and Luke*
14. Do not kill . . .	2:11	5:21-30	**M**
15. The merciless will be judged	2:13	5:7; 6:14-15; 7:1	**M Q** (Luke 6:36)
16. Against lip service	2:14-16	7:21-23	**M**
17. Help to the poor	2:15-16	25:34-35	**M**
18. Fruit of good works	3:12	7:16-18	**Q** (Luke 6:43-44)
19. In praise of meekness	3:13; contrast 4:6, 16	5:3, 5	**M**
20. Meek . . . peacemaking	3:17-18	5:5, 9	**M**
21. Against divided loyalty	4:4	6:24	**Q** (Luke 16:13)
		12:39	**Q** (Luke 11:29)
22. Pure in heart	4:8	5:8	**M**
23. Mourn and weep	4:9		**L** (Luke 6:25)
24. Humility and exaltation	4:10	18:4; 23:12	**Q?** (Luke 14:11; 18:14)
25. Against slander	4:11	5:22; 7:1-2	**M Q** (Luke 6:37-38)
26. Weep	5:1		**L** (Luke 6:24-25)
27. Against hoarding	5:2-3	6:19-21	**Q** (Luke 12:33-34)
28. Do not condemn	5:6	(7:1)	**Q** (Luke 6:37)
29. Eschatological imminence	5:9	24:33	**Mark 13:29** (Luke 21:31)
30. Example of the prophets	5:10	5:11-12	**Q** (Luke 6:23)
31. Prohibition of oaths	5:12	5:33-37	**M**

	James	*Matthew*	*Source and Luke*
32. Elijah as example	5:17		**L** (Luke 4:25)
33. Relation to sinful brother	5:19-20	18:15	**Q?** (Luke 17:3)

The parallels are more than interesting, and some are closer than others. Nothing compels acceptance that James knew and used Matthew. Rather, the allusions to common words, themes, and motifs show that Matthew and James are independently working out of a common pool of tradition that can be identified as wisdom tradition and Jesus tradition, perhaps Q and M. Patrick Hartin thinks it is likely that James had some contact with Q[Mt].[15] Importantly, when dealing with Q, Hartin quotes J. P. Meier, who asserts that "M was the living sea of oral tradition in which Mark and Q floated and were steeped."[16] Hartin continues,

> M would exert an influence upon Mark and Q before Matthew began the writing of his Gospel. I have argued consistently that the Q source, once accepted into the Matthean community, underwent a development through the incorporation of other Q sayings as well as the insertion of the M material. This was evident in the development of the Sermon on the Mount and, in particular, in the growth of the Beatitudes. Ultimately a written form of Q, which we term Q[Mt], emerged within the Matthean community and was used by Matthew in the construction of his Gospel.[17]

Hartin thinks Q[Mt] influenced James, Q floating on and saturated by the living sea of M. While Hartin thinks of M as the living sea of oral tradition in the Matthean community, I am more inclined to accept a modified form of Streeter's position. The core of M is tradition emanating from James, which may well have attained written form after the death of James. Whether written or oral, this body of tradition, more than any other, shaped the ideological position of Matthew. This means that the orientation of Matthew is determined to a large extent by M, even when Q material is being used. Q brought to Matthew an openness to mission to the Gentiles, which was accepted on terms appropriate to the ideology of M. Thus:

> for a Gentile convert to become a member of the Q community probably meant, in effect, a Christian Jew, following the Jewish law and customs like the rest of the community. It is precisely

this kind of Gentile mission that Paul was adamantly opposed to but one which the Q community could hardly have conceived in any other way.[18]

What Havener has expressed in terms of the Q community, I take to be true of Q[Mt]. In all probability, both Q and M emanated from the Jerusalem church. M may well emanate from James, while it is likely that Q is a Petrine tradition. If, in Matthew, Q was modified by M, the final redaction of Matthew is oriented to the mission to the nations on the terms of the circumcision mission (28:19-20 indicates a law observant mission, "teaching them to observe"), of which Peter was the figurehead (Gal 2:7-8). What distinguishes the Epistle of James from Matthew is its orientation to Jewish believers in the Diaspora. The epistle, like James of Jerusalem, remained oriented to the Jewish people, the one in Jerusalem while the other was directed to the Diaspora.

Genre

James' opening form of address is consistent with a Hellenistic letter: "From A to B, greetings." At this point the clear indications of genre are exhausted. James is not a brief Hellenistic letter like 2 or 3 John. Apart from the address and greeting, James is more like 1 John. But James lacks any indication of a specific situation, whereas 1 John deals with the trauma caused by a recent schism. Nevertheless, the perspective adopted is consistent with an underlying Jewish theology in which elements of theodicy are never far from the matter under discussion. James lacks any form of closing salutation even as vague as the admonition of 1 John 5:21.

Since the work of Adolf Deissmann, it has become a commonplace to distinguish between the popular Greco-Roman letter (such as 2 and 3 John) and a literary epistle. More recently, two developments have blurred this clear-cut distinction. First, in practice, defined literary genres are not clear-cut, and individual writings imperfectly fit the ideal of a genre and often overlap a number of genres. Second, a writing belonging to a particular literary genre may well make use of a number of rhetorical styles or strategies, such as paraenesis and diatribe. Rhetoric is associated primarily with oral communication but also has an impact on the written word. A letter may overlap the form of an epistle or a discourse.

James may be a circular letter (an encyclical) to Jewish believers in the Diaspora, utilizing epistle and discourse forms. Other circular letters may be seen in 1 John and 1 Peter. But whereas 1 John seems to have been sent to a circle of local communities in a specific region, James is addressed generally to Jews of the Diaspora. Acts 15:22-29 depicts the sending of a letter to the Gentile believers in Antioch, Syria, and Cilicia.

Although the letter in Acts was sent by the apostles and elders with the whole church (15:22-23), the substance of the letter was the decision of James reported in 15:19-20. In a sense, then, this can be seen as a letter from James, even if it came on the authority of the whole Jerusalem church. That letter to Gentile believers can be seen as comparable to the Epistle of James addressed to the Jewish believers of the Diaspora. A variation of this view is to see James as a posthumous gathering of the tradition of James, sent as a letter from him to scattered Jewish believers following the Jewish War, some time after 70 CE.

Literary Analysis

The epistle is written in a way suggestive of paraenesis and diatribe and makes use of rhetorical devices and the characteristic Greek greeting *chairein*. It can be analyzed in terms of a series of sayings loosely strung together using such literary devices as catchwords (*Stichworte*). This favorite device is found in 1:4-5, 12-13, 15-18, 26-27; 2:12-13; 3:11-14, 17-18; and 5:9, 12, 16-20. These catchwords depend on being written in Greek and are used so frequently that any notion that the epistle might have been composed originally in a language other than Greek is untenable. The author uses the Greek Bible, which is consistent with the other evidence indicating that the author was a native Greek speaker. Most likely the author of James was a Jew of the Diaspora for whom Greek was his mother tongue.

Dibelius defines paraenesis as text that strings together admonitions of general ethical content. Such sayings normally address themselves to a specific (though perhaps fictional) audience. They do not disclose an actual epistolary situation. Contrary to Dibelius, it need not follow that there is no significant thematic continuity and development in James. The nature of the Greek of James and the relationship of the themes to the work of the Greek moralists make it unlikely that James of Jerusalem was the direct author of this epistle. Those who defend the tradition of direct authorship of the letter by the brother of the Lord in pre-62 CE Jerusalem often assert that those who reject this position do so because "they have not caught up with" the recognition of the hellenization of both Palestinian and Diaspora Judaism. This argument fails to take account of the difference between pre- and post-70 CE Jerusalem. Pre-70 CE Jerusalem was concerned with ritual in a way that was not uniformly true of Diaspora Judaism. Even if hellenization was universal in the Roman Empire, it was not uniform, not the same in every place. The Jerusalem temple made it a different place, even if the architecture was Hellenistic; so did the use of Hebrew/Aramaic. It is not that a Galilean Jew could not have written such an epistle. Rather, it is the nature of the Jewishness of James that makes it unlikely that he was the direct author. All of the evidence suggests that James remained located in Jerusalem, preoccupied with the mission to the Jewish people in Jerusalem. The primary language of that mission was Hebrew/Aramaic. This hardly fits the language, style, and rhetoric of James.

From the point of view of language, James stands out from the rest of the New Testament. There is a large number of words that are found only in James in the New Testament. I noted forty-eight words not found elsewhere in the New Testament, and my list is probably not exhaustive. Of the forty-eight, no less than nine are unattested in the Septuagint or pre-Christian Greek writings, and two are not found in the Hebrew books translated in the Septuagint or in the pre-Christian Greek corpus. Another five are not found in the Septuagint, and one is not found in the pre-Christian Greek writings. A further five are not found in the Septuagint translation of Hebrew books. Thus twenty-two of the forty-eight words are more unusual than absence from the New Testament alone implies. I counted another seventy words rarely used in the rest of the New Testament. One of these is unattested in the Septuagint or pre-Christian Greek writings and is used only by James and Paul in the New Testament. For more details, see the appendix, "The Distinctive Vocabulary of James," below.

The Structure of James

Following the address and greeting (1:1), the remainder of chapter 1 contains a number of aphorisms. All are taken up, somewhat randomly, and developed in the following chapters, which come to a suitable conclusion in 5:19-20. The theme of enduring testing (1:2-4) is taken up in 5:7-11; the prayer of faith (1:5-7) is taken up in 5:13-18; the reversal of the fortunes of rich and poor (1:9-10) is taken up in 2:1-7; 4:13–5:6; sinful desire or lust (*epithymia*) set over against God's good and perfect gift to those who ask of him (1:12-18) is taken up in 3:13–4:10; speech ethics (1:19-20, 26) are developed in 3:1-12; and the need for faith to be actualized in works (1:22-27) is developed in 2:14-26 in a way that reflects the Pauline controversy about justification by faith apart from works. The conclusion recognizes that, in the kind of world the epistle implies, it is possible to stray from the path of the truth. The author alerts the readers, addressed as "my brothers," that if one of them "returns a brother from the error of his way, he will save him from death and cover a multitude of sins" (5:19-20). While precise meaning is unclear, the general sense provides a suitable ending to James. The loose structure outlined here is fairly clear. Attempts to find a tighter structure have not been widely persuasive.

The struggle to establish a clear and coherent structure has led to the common view that James lacks a coherent message. The charactcrization of its contents as paraenesis may suggest a miscellany of subjects and sayings. Certain texts in James impress me as windows into the underlying message, powerfully revealing the source of the ethical passion of James in its implied understanding of God.

True Religion in Relation to God as Father

References to religion (*thrēskeia*) and the religious (*thrēskos*) are rare in the New Testament. Outside James 1:26-27, only *thrēskeia* is used, and then only in Acts 26:5 and Colossians 1:16. James is concerned to identify the pure religion that is acceptable to God, the Father.

> If any think they are religious, and do not bridle their tongues, but deceive their hearts, their religion is worthless. Religion that is pure and undefiled before God, the Father, is this: to care for orphans and widows in their distress, and to keep oneself unstained by the world. (Jas 1:26-27)

Religion is normally understood in terms of cultic obligations, but James has a burning ethical and prophetic interpretation of pure religion. It is not surprising that James first excludes those who do not control their tongues (1:19-20, 26; 3:1-12) but deceive their hearts. This ethical treatment of the tongue is rooted in the Wisdom literature (in LXX Prov 10:8, 14, 19, 31; 11:12-13; 12:13, 18; 13:3; 14:3; 15:2, and many other references in Prov, Eccl, Wis; Sir). Israel's Wisdom literature shares the theme widely with wisdom tradition of the ancient Near East.[19] James has in mind idle talk, including the talk of those who talk but do not act or act otherwise. The religion of such persons is vain, useless. James then turns to religion that is pure and spotless before God, the Father. This language reflects the Jewish concern for purity. Nevertheless, the primary concern is not with ritual purity. Just as hands and heart form an outer and inner pair in 4:7-8, so here also do tongue and heart. The ethics of action are rooted in an undivided heart fixed on God the Father, and ethical speech is rooted in a pure heart. Pure religion involves ethical action in visiting the orphans and widows in their affliction. James fixes his attention on orphans and widows, the weakest and most vulnerable people in Israelite society, being without traditional protectors, husbands and parents. As elsewhere, James affirms that God is on the side of the poor. Those who obey the law (the word), who are not only hearers of it, are contrasted with those who gaze into a natural mirror and immediately forget what they saw and thus do nothing. But the mirror for those who do the law is the law of liberty. They carefully pay attention to what they see and take action, and are thus blessed in their doing (see the emphasis on action in 1:22-25; 2:14-26).

There is also a concern for purity. Pure religion involves keeping unstained from the world. The world is that social and spiritual reality constituted by enmity with God (4:4) and the fulfillment of sinful desire (*epithymia*).[20] The language of ritual purity is integrated with ethical concern. James, like the prophets of old and Jews such as Philo of Alexandria, gave priority to ethical action without ignoring the ritual embodiment of Israel's religion.

Such religion is lived in relation to (or in the sight of) God the Father. This description of God is not a reference to the first person of the Trinity but a reference to the character of God, in whose presence pure and spotless religion is possible. It is not the stern and judging God but the loving and benevolent Father. This is established early in the epistle (1:5-7) and comes from the heart of Jesus tradition. "If any of you is lacking wisdom, ask God, who gives to all generously and ungrudgingly, and it will be given to you. But ask in faith . . ."

Asking in faith is contrasted with the instability and vacillation of the double-minded person (*dipsychos*).[21] But for those who ask in faith, God is described as the one who gives generously, ungrudgingly.[22] What God gives is wisdom, the wisdom from on high (3:13-17). From this perspective, we may characterize God as "the one who gives generously." This is the essence of the goodness or benevolence of God, who is characterized as Father (1:17, 27; 3:9). God is again portrayed as the giver in 1:16-18: "Do not be deceived my beloved brothers. Every generous act of giving with every perfect gift, is from above, coming down from the Father of lights, with whom there is no variation or shadow due to change."

While, in Jewish thought, God is the lord of all creation, God's sovereign control of the heavenly lights is a special and fundamental mark of God's power (*T. Ab.* 7:6 and see CD 5.17-18; 1QS 3.20). James extends the teaching about creation to include God's action in the ongoing life of the world. God is the generous giver of every perfect gift. James stresses the constant goodness of God, in contrast with the fleeting, changing light of the sun in its journey across the sky.

We may ask what is the source of the understanding of God in James and whether it is consistent and coherent. The broad basis for recognizing a link between James and Jesus now needs to be deepened by focusing on the teaching of Jesus on the goodness and benevolence of God. For a start, there is Q (Matt 7:7-11 and Luke 11:9-13), which in its Matthean form (Q[Mt]) affirms that God, like a father responding to the requests of a child, gives good things to those who ask him (see Jas 1:5; 16-17). The overlapping themes of asking, giving to all, and good gifts/things point to the roots of James' teaching in the teaching of Jesus. The root of ethical action in the benevolence of God is seen also in the Q passage (Matt 5:43-48). The love command is rooted in the call to "be sons of your heavenly Father, who causes the sun to shine on the evil and the good, and the rain to fall on the righteous and unrighteous." The call to "be perfect as your heavenly Father is perfect" depends on the recognition of the benevolence of God. This too is the ground of Jesus' exhortation, "Do not be anxious for your life . . . for your heavenly Father knows you have need of all these things" (Q, Matt 6:25-34; 10:29-31).[23]

Recently, Sean Freyne has again drawn attention to the significance of Galilee for Jesus.[24] In so doing, he treats the ecology of Galilee and notes that "Jesus is reported to have combined Israel's distinctive understanding of God, based on the *Shema'* (Deut 6:4), with the Genesis idea of the good God: . . . (Mark 10:17)." He asks if awareness of the goodness of God made Jesus more sensitive to the natural world, and how humans should behave toward each other and the gifts of the earth. The foundational God story declares the goodness of all that God has created (Gen 1:4, 12, 18, 21, 25, 31). Freyne's treatment suggests the impact of Galilee on Jesus' theology of creation and God's continuing care for all creatures. From the gift-laden creation, James speaks of the gracious, giving, and faithful God. If Genesis affirms the goodness of God's creation, the Psalmist affirms the goodness of the creator. "Oh give thanks to the Lord for he is good, for his great love is without end" (Ps 136; and Pss 106:1; 107:1; 118:1-4, 29). In each case (in Gen and the Pss), the Hebrew word for *good* is טוֹב. Jesus affirmed the exclusive goodness of God, implying the derived goodness of all else (Mark 10:17-18). In line with this, the key to James' understanding of God is found in 1:16-18. James, like Jesus, extends the teaching about creation to God's action in the ongoing life of the world. God is the generous giver of every good and perfect gift. There is a good case for accepting that Galilee influenced Jesus, who developed and mediated a theology of creation that drew attention to God's gracious goodness and presence in daily life.

James and Paul

Because of strong positive views of God's grace in creation, James exhibits an optimistic view of the human potential to live a life pleasing to God. In James, we find no equivalent of Paul's desperate cry, "Wretched man that I am! Who will rescue me from this body of death?" (Rom 7:24). James appeals to the gracious God, who gives generously to all who ask in faith (1:5-6). With the gift of wisdom from God, nothing is lacking. With knowledge of the way of truth, there is the ability to walk in it. James provides the readers with a sample of the godly wisdom from above.

The teaching about faith and works in James 2:14-26 resonates discordantly with the theme in Paul, especially in Romans 3–4. James' use of Genesis 15:6 (in 2:23) presupposes its use by Paul (in Rom 4:3, 9, 22; Gal 3:6). Paul exploits the wording of Genesis, which says that Abraham believed God and it was reckoned to him for righteousness. He argues that a person is justified by faith apart from works of the law (Rom 3:28; 4:6). James makes use of the same text to argue that a person is justified by works as well as faith, not by faith only (2:24), thus denying the efficacy of faith apart from works (2:18, 26). Though Paul recognizes the necessity of faith working through love, he rejects the notion that a person is justified by any work. The argument of James is directed against the language of Paul without addressing Paul's view. Though James affirms the graciousness of God in creation (1:17), it does not feature the distinctive nature of grace in justification found in Paul. We may also say that James features the gracious Creator and grace in creation in a way that is not featured by Paul.[25] But because every generous act of giving and every perfect gift is from above, James no less than Paul excludes the grounds for human boasting before God (Jas 4:16; 1 Cor 4:7).

Theodicy, Testing, and Temptation

For James, evil is encountered in testings or temptations. The complexity of the subject is reflected in the multivalence of *peirasmos*, which can convey the sense of testing and temptation. James appears to refer to one and then the other. But it is an oversimplification to suggest that 1:2-8 deal with the testing effect of hostile external circumstances, while 1:12-15 focus on the inner ground of temptation in sinful desire (*epithymia*). Whether in the allure that appeals to *epithymia* or the testing circumstances confronting the faithful, James rejects the notion that God tempts or tests the faithful (1:13). Nor is there any suggestion that the devil is the agent of testing or temptation. Temptation takes its power from *epithymia*. From *epithymia* come all the woes that are heaped on mankind (4:1-6). The solution to this self-infliction is: "Submit yourselves therefore to God. Resist the devil, and he will flee from you. Draw near to God, and he will draw near to you. Cleanse your hands, you sinners, and purify your hearts, you *dipsychoi*" (4:7-8). Here, the *dipsychoi* are identified with sinners in two parallel clauses, as James deals first with hands (sinners) and then heart (*dipsychoi*). The implication is that actual sins committed by hands arise from hearts, and hands once cleansed will soon be defiled again if hearts are not purified. Here, though not in 1:8, the Hebraic root of the use of the Greek *dipsychoi* is made clear by the associated reference to the heart, "purify your hearts you *dipsychoi*" (4:8). Sinful desire destabilizes the *dipsychoi*, defiling the heart and creating the world at enmity with

God. Friendship with the world so constituted is enmity to God (4:4). While sinful desire may seem to be rewarded with riches, James warns of a coming reversal (1:9-10; 2:1-7; 4:13–5:6). The rich are warned to weep and wail because of the miseries coming upon them. Departure from the truth to the way of error leads to death (5:19-20).

It is a mistake to see James as a mere moralist. His call to moral action arises from his understanding of God, who is without partiality and gives to all generously. The impartiality of pure religion is grounded in the impartiality of God (2:1 and see Rom 2:11). That love for the neighbor has a cutting edge in relation to the rich and on behalf of the poor (Jas 2:5) may be a word the Western world does not wish to hear.[26]

Appendix
The Distinctive Vocabulary of James

The lists in this appendix are constructed on the basis of my intuition about words that are rarely used in the New Testament, if not found only in James. My selection of words has been tested, and is offered without any claim that the words identified constitute exhaustive lists of each category. In each list, words are given in the order in which they first appear in James.

Forty-Eight Words Found Only in James in the New Testament

Nine of these are not used in the LXX or the pre-Christian Greek corpus

δίψυχος	Jas 1:8; 4:8
ἀπείραστος	Jas 1:13
ἀποσκίασμα	Jas 1:17
θρησκός	Jas 1:26
χαλιναγωγέω	Jas 1:26; 3:2
χρυσοδακτύλιος	Jas 2:2
προσωπολημπτέω	Jas 2:9
ἀνελέος	Jas 2:13
πολύσπλαγχνος	Jas 5:11

Five are not used in the LXX

ῥυπαρία	Jas 1:21
αὐχέω	Jas 3:5
ἐνάλιος	Jas 3:7
βρύω	Jas 3:11
κατήφεια	Jas 4:9

Five are not used in the LXX books translated from Hebrew Scripture

ἀποκυέω	Jas 1:15, 18
ἔμφυτος	Jas 1:21
ἐπιλησμονή	Jas 1:25
εὐπειθής	Jas 3:17
μετατρέπω	Jas 4:9

One is not used in the pre-Christian Greek corpus
σητόβρωτος

Two are not used in the LXX books translated from Hebrew Scripture
or the pre-Christian Greek corpus

δαιμονιώδης	Jas 3:15
κατιόομαι	Jas 5:3

Twenty-six are found only in James in the New Testament

ἔοικα	Jas 1:6, 23
ἀκατάστατος	Jas 1:8; 3:8
ἐξέλκομαι	Jas 1:14
παραλλαγη	Jas 1:17
τροπή	Jas 1:17
ἐφήμερος	Jas 2:15
ἐπιτήδειος	Jas 2:16
φρίσσω	Jas 2:19
μετάγω	Jas 3:3, 4
ὕλη	Jas 3:5
φλογίζω	Jas 3:6 (x2)
τροχός	Jas 3:6
θανατηφόρος	Jas 3:8
ὁμοίωσις	Jas 3:9
χρή	Jas 3:10
πικρός	Jas 3:11, 14
ἁλυκός	Jas 3:12
ἐπιστήμων	Jas 3:13
ἀδιάκριτος	Jas 3:17
ἄγε	Jas 4:13; 5:1
ὀλολύζω	Jas 5:1
σήπω	Jas 5:2
ἀμάω	Jas 5:4
βοή	Jas 5:4
τρυφάω	Jas 5:5
κακοπαθίας	Jas 5:10

Another seventy words are used by James and rarely elsewhere in the New Testament. Of these, two groups of words have a special interest: (1) words shared only by James and Paul in the New Testament, and (2) words shared by James and other works that manifest a more polished use of Greek, like Luke-Acts, Hebrews, and 1 Peter.

Sixteen words used only by James and Paul in the New Testament

ὁλόκληρος	Jas 1:4	1 Thess 5:23
ἀκροατής	Jas 1:22, 23, 25	Rom 2:13
παραλογίζομαι	Jas 1:22	Col 2:4
ἔσοπτρον	Jas 1:23	1 Cor 13:12 (not in LXX Heb)
ἀπατάω	Jas 1:26	Eph 5:6; 1 Tim 2:14
κριτήριον	Jas 2:6	1 Cor 6:2, 4
παραβάτης	Jas 2:9, 11	Rom 2:25, 27; Gal 2:18 (not in LXX Heb)
κατακαυχαόμαι	Jas 2:13; 3:14	Rom 11:18 (x2)
ὄφελος	Jas 2:14, 16	1 Cor 15:32
συνεργέω	Jas 2:22	Rom 8:28; 1 Cor 16:16; 2 Cor 6:1 (not in LXX Heb)
ἡλίκος	Jas 3:5 (x2)	Gal 6:11; Col 2:1
ἰός	Jas 3:8; 5:3	Rom 3:13
σπαταλάω	Jas 5:5	1 Tim 5:6
κακοπαθέω	Jas 5:13	2 Tim 4:5, 9
ψάλλω	Jas 5:13	Rom 15:9; 1 Cor 14:15 (x2); Eph 5:19

*One word in James and Paul not used in the LXX
or the pre-Christian Greek corpus*

Προσωπολημψία	Jas 2:1	Rom 2:11; Eph 6:9; Col 3:25

This word is related to two others not found in the Septuagint or the pre-Christian Greek corpus.

Προσωπολημπτέω	Jas 2:9
Προσωπολήμπτης	Acts 10:34

Two of these words are used by James, one distinctively and the other shared by Paul. The third word is known only in Acts. Each of these uses relates to the character of God, with ethical implications for humans. In this usage, James and Paul appear in relation to Acts, where Hellenistic influence is strongly present in literary and other ways.

Words Shared Only by James, Luke-Acts, Hebrews, and First Peter

This association of relationships is intended to place James in a context in which Greek literary conventions and practices are more clearly evident than in the New Testament generally. That Paul should appear in this group is also true, but distinctively Pauline vocabulary found only in James and Paul in the New Testament supports the conclusion that James was working, to some extent, in the shadow of Paul, and *vice versa.*

ἀμίαντος	Jas 1:27	Heb 7:26; 1 Pet 1:4
ἐσθής	Jas 2:2 (x2), 3	Luke 23:11; 24:4; Acts 1:10; 10:30; 12:21 (not in LXX Heb)
καταδυναστεύω	Jas 2:6	Acts 10:38
ὑποδέχομαι	Jas 2:25	Luke 10:38; 19:6; Acts 17:7
πηδάλιον	Jas 3:4	Acts 27:40
ὁρμή	Jas 3:4	Acts 14:5
ἀνάπτω	Jas 3:5	Luke 12:49
ὀπή	Jas 3:11	Heb 11:38
εἰρηνικός	Jas 3:17	Heb 12:11
ἀτμίς	Jas 4:14	Acts 2:19 (Joel 3:3)
ἀλαζονεία	Jas 4:16	1 John 2:16 and cf. ἀλαζών in Rom 1:30; 2 Tim 3:2
οἰκτίρμων	Jas 5:11	Luke 6:36 (x2)
εὐθυμέω	Jas 5:13	Acts 27:22, 25
κάμνω	Jas 5:15	Heb 12:3
ὁμοιοπαθής	Jas 5:17	Acts 14:15 (not in LXX Heb)

Two expressions found only in James

τὸ καλὸν ὄνομα	Jas 2:7	Though καλόν and ὄνομα are common New Testament words, this formulation "the good name" is not found elsewhere in the New Testament.
ἀδελφὸς ἢ ἀδελφὴ	Jas 2:15	The masculine form may be used to cover both brothers and sisters in James 5:19.

CHAPTER 10

THE LETTER OF JAMES AS A
CANON-CONSCIOUS PSEUDEPIGRAPH

David R. Nienhuis

As is well known, many if not most twentieth-century biblical scholars have denied the authenticity of the Letter of James. Until recently, the dominant viewpoint has considered the letter to be an eclectic and discontinuous string of general ethical exhortations, held together in many places by catchword associations, with an epistolary prescript attached. It was understood to have no overarching theological perspective, addressing no particular social context. Over the last thirty years, of course, this position has been partially dethroned. Karl-Wilhelm Niebuhr has recently noted that the deposing of this view is due at least in part to the removal of the "Pauline spectacles" that have dominated readings of the letter since the Reformation.[1] James did not look like an actual letter and appeared to lack a robust theological perspective simply because it had long been read under the normative shadow of the Pauline Letters. The removal of this constricting lens has allowed interpreters to read James on its own terms, according to the way in which the letter presents itself, and as a result, a number of fresh perspectives have been generated that have taught us a great deal more about the text. Perhaps most notably, these new insights have enabled an increasing number of contemporary scholars to turn against the widespread modern opinion that the Letter of James is pseudepigraphic. Now it is more common to find interpreters who will argue that there is little reason to conclude that James, the Lord's brother, could not have written the letter himself.[2]

Though we must be grateful for the work of those who have enabled a clearer understanding of the letter, a few concerns must be raised in response to certain aspects of this new perspective on James. First, the removal of the Pauline spectacles in the name of reading James on its own terms has in some cases led interpreters to quickly marginalize the possibility (and therefore the effects) of Pauline influence on the letter at all.[3] If reading a text on its own terms means anything, it means reading it against the historical, literary, and theological terms appropriate to the presumed date and provenance of that text; and given the uncertainty surrounding the letter's historical origin, as well as the quantity and quality of semantic and conceptual parallels it shares with those of Paul and other proto-New Testament letters (especially 1 Peter, but also 1 John), the notion that James should somehow be read in isolation from Paul needs to be challenged. Those who pursue a reading of James on its own terms by bracketing out Pauline influence sometimes seem to be less interested in James' actual terms and more concerned to reverse the overly Paulinist readings of the letter that have dominated since the Reformation.

Second, many recent champions of James' authenticity have failed to contend adequately with the troublesome issues surrounding the letter's historical reception. The question has been asked many times: if the letter was indeed written in the mid-first century by James of Jerusalem, the brother of the Lord, why is it that we can find no solid evidence for its existence until Origen championed it in the first half of the third century? This problem becomes increasingly troublesome when one considers the stature of James in the early centuries, for the picture that materializes is that of an apostolic leader whose influence on the developing traditions of Christianity cannot be underestimated.[4] How could an authentic letter penned by him in the mid-first century have been lost or ignored for 150 years in the Eastern church, and even longer in the West? Advocates of an early date for the letter end up offering a wide variety of rationalizations for its late arrival, and while any of them might be argued to be possible, few if any seem truly plausible given the high stature of this figure in the second century.

Finally, and perhaps most significantly for my own line of research, most James scholars consider the issues surrounding the origins and canonical reception of the letter in isolation from the historical development of the Catholic Epistles (CE) collection it heads.[5] But what happens when we consider the origin of James in light of the phenomenology of ancient canonical collection building? I would suggest that many of the puzzling features of the letter are cleared up when it is read as a canon-conscious pseudepigraph. As I have argued more extensively elsewhere,[6] it is my opinion that the Letter of James was not written by the famous mid-first-century James, but by a second-century pseudepigrapher who penned the letter in the hopes that it might provide a distinctive shape to the emerging collection of apostolic letters held as authoritative in proto-Catholic circles. The writer of James created a sort of bridge text that included careful intertextual linkages to the authoritative apostolic literature of his day in order to forge together a collection of letters under the organizing rubric of the Jerusalem pillars—James, Peter, and John (as identified by Paul in Gal 2:9). This James-headed collection was crafted to provide a canonical counterbalance to the Pauline collection, correcting the most pressing Paulinist misreadings that emerged over the course of the second century.

In this essay, I will address these three concerns in turn. Issues surrounding the first two (Pauline influence and canonical reception) will not be new to my readers, but I will be using my comments in relation to these to build the case for the third. That is to say, after arguing that attempts to make sense of James apart from Paul are untenable, and reviewing key issues surrounding the reception history of the letter, I will offer an alternative account of James as a second-century, canon-conscious pseudepigraph.

James without Paul?

The origins of the Letter of James are murky, as current assessments of its provenance attest. Its earliest tradents, however, appear to have read it against a Pauline backdrop, and indeed all readers of the letter since have unavoidably read it in this way, for it has been delivered to the faithful wrapped in a package that includes the Letters of Paul, and it contains a striking amount of verbal parallels to the words of Paul. It is precisely because of this packaging and these parallels that the letter has so often been read myopically since the Protestant Reformation, with its particular preference for an orthodoxy focused strictly around the Pauline justification formula. The so-called Pauline spectacles of that era reduced the meaningful content of the letter down to the faith and works discussion of 2:14-26, and as we have noted, the recent removal of this restrictive lens has enabled us to see so much more of what the Letter of James has to offer its readers. But is it not equally reductionistic to call these spectacles simply Pauline in the first place? Just as recent work has shown that James cannot be reduced to the content of 2:14-26 without distortion, so also Pauline scholarship has come a long way from reading Paul through the lens of the Magisterial Reformation. The so-called Pauline spectacles that disfigure the Letter of James are in fact those of Protestant orthodoxy, and only those of the literary Paul by derivation. Readers who attempt to liberate the letter from its Protestant fetters by reading it in isolation from Pauline influence make a serious misstep, for we have very good reason to believe that the letter was actually composed with the intent that it be read with Paul in view.

Much attention has been paid to the parallels between the Letter of James and those of Paul, with the majority of it focused on the undeniable connections between their relative discussions of faith and works in Christian justification. Space does not permit a thorough review of the evidence here, but the key points of correspondence are already well known:

1. Romans 3:28, Galatians 2:16, and James 2:24 are the only verses in all of Christian Scripture where πίστις and ἔργον are paired with the verb δικαιόω.
2. The rejection of ἐκ πίστεως μόνον in James 2:24 is only sensible against a Pauline backdrop, for nowhere in Jewish thought before Paul do we find anyone arguing for a clear distinction between πίστις and ἔργα in discussions of justification.
3. We find an argument appealing to the same figure (Abraham) and the same Scripture (Genesis 15:6) to make apparently competing arguments about the same subject (faith and works in justification).
4. These competing arguments are made using not just the same vocabulary but also a similar structure:
   a. Gal 2:16: εἰδότες δὲ ὅτι οὐ δικαιοῦται ἄνθρωπος ἐξ ἔργων νόμου ἐὰν μὴ διὰ πίστεως. . .
   b. Jas 2:24: ὁρᾶτε ὅτι ἐξ ἔργων δικαιοῦται ἄνθρωπος καὶ οὐκ ἐκ πίστεως μόνον.

In case one is tempted to claim that the parallels between Paul and James are reducible to mere "isolated expressions,[7] consider further the precise degree of larger formal agreement between James 1–2 and Romans 2–4.[8]

1. Preparatory echoes and parallels:
   a) Partiality forbidden: Rom 2:11   Jas 2:1
   b) On being doers of the law/word
      and not hearers: Rom 2:13   Jas 1:22-25
   c) Condemnation of partial
      law-keeping: Rom 2:21-23   Jas 2:8-11
2. Acknowledgment that some have misunderstood the Pauline message:
   "Why not do evil that good may come of it?"   Rom 3:8

3. Precise sequential agreement between Jas 2:14-24 and Rom 3:27–4:22:

    a) Issue posed in terms of faith
       and works: Rom 3:27-28   Jas 2:14-18
    b) Significance of claiming
       "God is one":   Rom 3:29-30   Jas 2:19
    c) Appeal to father Abraham as
       authoritative test case: Rom 4:1-2   Jas 2:20-22
    d) Citation of proof text, Gen 15:6:   Rom 4:3   Jas 2:20-22
    e) Conflicting interpretations
       of the proof text: Rom 4:4-21   Jas 2:23
    f) Conclusion of the argument: Rom 4:22   Jas 2:24

It is extremely difficult to account for how two texts could so closely parallel one another without positing some kind of formal relationship between the two. Indeed, we should not allow the Protestant spectacles to so focus our attention on the faith and works parallels that our sight is drawn away from the many other significant agreements that exist between James and the Pauline Letters, some of the most striking of which are displayed in the table below.

Jas	Rom	1 Cor	2 Cor	Gal	Link
1:2-4	5:3-4				"Boast" / "be joyful" (καυχώμεθα΄ χαρὰν ἡγή-σασθε)
1:6; 2:4	4:20; 14:23				Condemnation of doubting (διακρίνω) as part of larger discussion of the faith of Abraham
1:8; 3:8, 16		14:33	6:5; 12:20		Personal and communal instability described using the ἀκατάστατος/ ἀκαταστασία found only here in the NT apart from Lk 21:9
1:13-25	7:7-12			4:21-31	Descriptions of what law observance brings using thematically related yet opposing terms "slavery" and "freedom"

Jas	*Rom*	*1 Cor*	*2 Cor*	*Gal*	*Link*
1:16		6:9; 15:33		6:7	"Do not be deceived" (μη πλανᾶσθη) followed by a correction
1:22	2:13				Exhortation to be not "hearers" (ἀκροαταί) but "doers" (ποιηταί) of the "word" / "law"
1:26		3:18; 8:2; 11:16; 14:37		6:3	"If anyone thinks himself to be" (εἴ τις δοκεῖ … εἶναι), found only in these NT texts
2:1, 8-11	2:1, 11				Partiality (προσωπολημψία) forbidden in conjunction with a condemnation of partial law observance
2:8-11	13:8-10			5:3,14	Description of fulfilling the law with quotation of Lev 19:18; Jas and Gal refer to keeping "the whole law" (ὅλον τὸν νόμου)
4:4	8:7-8				Association with "world" / "flesh" is "hostility with God" (ἔκθρα τοῦ θεοῦ / εἰς θεόν)
4:12	14:4				"Who are you to judge" (σὺ τίς εἶ ὁ κρίνων) your neighbor / the servant of another?
5:3	2:5				"Storing up" (θησαυρίζω) "for the last days / day of wrath" (ἐσχάταις ἡμέραις / ἡμέρα ὀργῆς)

The combined weight of these more prominent parallels leaves us with the strong sense that the author of James was not simply aware of Pauline ideas "in the air" at the time,[9] but was in contact with a collection of Pauline letters and wrote to readers who knew those writings as religiously authoritative. But on what grounds do we conclude that James is the one in the dependent position? Could it not be that the parallels reflect the relative simultaneity of their discussions, or even that Paul is the one responding to the earlier Letter of James, as Joseph B. Mayor argued so long ago?[10]

A fairly standard set of claims has long been marshaled in support of postdating James in relation to Paul, the two most potent of which are (1) the fact that the letter joins in the pressing debate on faith and works in justification without appealing in any way to circumcision and the Gentile mission, which was the ground upon which this topic was discussed in mid-first-century Christian circles, and (2) the letter's startlingly late emergence as authoritative scripture, which is the focus of my own work on the subject.[11] One should add to this list Margaret Mitchell's recent study,[12] which argues that the letter is a document of later Paulinism, on the basis that it shares a number of affinities with the canonical and noncanonical Paulinist texts produced between ca. 70 and 120 CE. These include (1) invocation of Paul by name, allusion, or textual echo as authoritative teacher; (2) free incorporation of other materials, both traditional and original, with Pauline teaching; (3) lack of reference to real disputes over circumcision; (4) lack or diminished mention of Paul's characteristic theme of the cross/crucifixion; (5) de-emphasis on the christological title Son of God; (6) insistence on traditional forms of ethical behavior; (7) emphasis on church offices (ἐπίσκοποι, πρεσβύτεροι) and on the concordant running of the house/church; and (8) an attempt to insist upon the "right interpretation" of Paul.[13]

My own work agrees with that of Mitchell (and others who have argued similarly):[14] the author of James was writing from within a tradition that embraced Paul as an authoritative teacher of the faith and was concerned, in part, to shape subsequent interpretation of Pauline thought. If we are right about this, then reading James on its own terms requires that we read it in direct relation to the Letters of Paul. But what would have motivated the production of such a text under the particular authority of James of Jerusalem, and why did it take so long for the letter to emerge as authoritative scripture? We will attend to the latter question as a means of addressing the former.

Key Issues in the Reception History of the Letter of James

Virtually every commentator on the letter feels obliged to offer some remarks on its surprising absence from the extant writings of church fathers from the late first through the mid-third centuries. A review of these ancient authorities makes it quite clear that 1 Peter, 1 John, and Jude among the proto-CE enjoyed widespread acceptance in Eastern and Western churches alike.[15] As for James, it is widely accepted that the letter was not clearly cited or referred to by any church father prior to Origen in the third century; nevertheless, some scholars claim to hear "echoes" of the letter in early to mid-second century texts, and others do not. We do not have the space here to review the candidate texts in detail, so let us simply take a moment to consider the relationship between James and the *Shepherd of Hermas* (ca. 130), a text often appealed to (occasionally along with *1 Clem.*) in an attempt to secure a first-century terminus ad quem for our letter.

In fact, there is little agreement on these matters. Those who support the authenticity of James also tend to argue in favor of *Hermas'* dependence on the letter,[16] but others admit the evidence is inconclusive,[17] and still others have argued against any literary dependence between them at all.[18] In reality, there are far too many uncertainties to appeal to *Hermas* with any confidence as a terminus ad quem. The evidence suggests that the two texts are related in some way,[19] but even if such parallels were to be firmly established, one could not say for sure which text was in the dependent position. For that matter, James and *Hermas* could each be dependent on yet another source,[20] both texts could simply be passing on some of the same paraenetic material,[21] and the case could even be made that the author of James used *Hermas* as a source.[22] Ultimately, if we accept the notion that the Roman writer Hermas was appealing to the Letter of James, we are then forced into the implausible conclusion that the letter was a quotable authority by the early second century in Rome, but was not mentioned again for over 200 years in the Western church until it was picked up and used by Hilary of Poitiers in the mid-fourth century. At best, we can say that while the Letter of James is not clearly cited in the early to mid-second century, it shares a number of similarities in word and thought with texts from that period, including especially those texts of later Paulinism identified by Mitchell.

As we turn to a brief examination of the patristic witness leading up to Origen, we should acknowledge that thorough analyses of external evidence for the letter must go beyond merely providing a list of possible echoes and allusions. A more complete picture of the canonizing process can be had if one also considers the changing state of the nascent Catholic Christian canon in the period, as well as the developing configurations of apostolic authority among Catholic leaders. Irenaeus of Lyon (writing his *Adversus haereses*, ca. 180), who shows no knowledge whatsoever of the Letter of James,[23] was deeply concerned to demonstrate the harmony of the apostolic kerygma against those who would champion a single apostle (generally Paul) over the others, and to protect the continuity of God's covenants with Israel and the Christian church against those who sought to extract Christianity from its roots in Judaism. Against them Irenaeus brought forth the witness of the Acts of the Apostles (*Haer.* 3.12), which enabled a properly "catholic" understanding of Paul as an apostle who worked in complete harmony with the members of the apostolic mission to Jews in Jerusalem. Irenaeus' reading of this text focused almost exclusively on the role of Peter as leader of the Twelve. As for James, Irenaeus had nothing to contribute beyond what he had read in Acts 15 and Galatians 1–2. Along the way, he never mentions a text written by James, which is rather significant given his pressing concern to ground Christian faith in a publicly accessible lineage of churches, leaders, and the Scriptures they preserved; indeed, when he does list apostles in relation to the available Scriptures of his day, he only names Peter, John, Matthew, and Paul (3.21.3). His key insistence is that Peter and the other members of the Jerusalem apostolate were witnesses of "every action and of every doctrine" of the Lord and therefore could not be excluded, as Marcion had insisted (3.12.15), but he makes this claim without giving James any substantive role.

We find a development in this line of argument when we turn to Irenaeus' theological heir, Tertullian of Carthage (ca. 160–223), and his masterwork, *Adversus Marcionem.* Like Irenaeus, he also appeals to the Acts of the Apostles in support of a proper understanding of Paul, and mocks Marcion for his inability to provide any background information for *his* Paul.[24] Of crucial importance is the way in which Tertullian moves beyond Irenaeus's spotlight on Peter to focus quite narrowly on Paul's relationship with James, Peter, and John in particular, the pillars of the Jerusalem church as identified in Galatians 2:9. Indeed, he consistently links the three together as a unit of authority, even insisting that all three apostles were censured by Paul in Antioch, and not simply Peter alone.[25] Tertullian's rhetoric against the Marcionites derisively demotes Paul beneath these three, whom he calls "the originals" or "primitive authors" (*auctores,* 4.2.5).[26] "Even if Marcion had introduced his gospel under the name of Paul in person," Tertullian insists, "that single document would not be adequate for our faith if destitute of the support of his predecessors" (4.2.4).[27]

Tertullian wanted his readers to know that Paul lacked authority on his own, that he needed the Jerusalem pillars in order to legitimate his own apostolic credentials, and that any apparent difference among them was based on their amicable division of apostolic labor, not disagreements about doctrine.[28] One can easily see how Tertullian's vision of two harmonious yet different early Christian missions, which "preached the same gospel to different people,"[29] might eventually become the model for a dual collection of letters, one representing the Gentile mission (Pauline Letters) and the other representing the Jerusalem mission to Jews (Pillars/

CE). But Tertullian nowhere seeks to ground this "apostolic logic" in a corresponding letter collection, and this is presumably the case because he did not possess a letter from James. Indeed, nowhere in his many extant works can we find any hint at all that he knew of the letter.

A consideration of Origen's immediate forebear Clement of Alexandria (fl. ca. 190–215) will show that this tendency to view James, Peter, and John as a unity of apostolic authority was not limited to the Western fathers. Clement's extant writings suggest that he too had no knowledge of a letter by James, which is especially striking given his persistent moral concern, as well as his tendency to quote any theological authority that serves his purposes regardless of its orthodoxy. Nevertheless, fragments from his *Hypotyposeis* indicate he was well aware of significant traditions about James in relation to Peter and John. "After the resurrection," says Clement, "the Lord gave the tradition of knowledge to James the Just and John and Peter, and these gave it to the other apostles and the other apostles to the seventy, of whom Barnabas was also one."[30] Here we find additional evidence for the existence of an elevation of the Jerusalem pillars in the later second century. Given his awareness of a tradition that James was one of three primary apostolic recipients of divine gnosis, it makes it even more difficult to understand how he could avoid making use of the letter (or even mentioning its existence) if he were aware of it, especially given the deep ethical concern that permeates his writings. Clement was able to highlight these three because of their unique contact with the Lord, but like Tertullian, Clement was also apparently unable to establish their authority in a corresponding apostolic letter collection— and it makes best sense to assume that neither was able to do so because they both lacked a letter of James.

This absence of James into the early third century is rendered even more puzzling when one recognizes the intense interest in James and the explosion of James-oriented material composed and disseminated throughout the second century. The *Protevangelium of James*, the Pseudo-Clementine *Recognitions*, the *Memoirs* of Hegesippus, the various gospel traditions associated with Jewish Christianity, accounts of James' martyrdom, and several Nag Hammadi texts (*Ap. Jas.*, *1–2 Apoc. Jas.*, as well as the *Gos. Thom.*) all bear witness to the widespread increase in veneration of James among Jewish and gnostic Christians in this period. So-called Jewish Christians appear to have always viewed James as the highest apostolic authority, generally emphasizing his power over Peter and Paul (and sometimes presenting him in opposition to Paul).[31] So-called gnostic Christians took these Jewish traditions and extended them to cast James as a gnostic revealer figure whose spiritual knowledge and authority placed him in a rank far higher than any of the other apostles.[32]

It is most striking that even in these later James-oriented texts, we find no evidence anywhere that the authors had any awareness of the canonical Letter of James. If the letter dated from the mid-first century, would we not expect to find these texts appealing to (or combating) it in some way, as we so often do with other later pseudo-apostolic texts?

While these "alternative" Christian traditions were busy championing the Lord's brother in their own way, how might second-century proto-Catholic Christians have viewed James? Their image must have left them feeling rather ambivalent. Assuming for the moment that they did not possess our canonical letter, they would have been aware of his authority in Jerusalem from his depiction as head of the church in Acts 15 and 21, as well as Paul's identification of him as one of the pillars there and, of course, his relation to the Lord (Gal 2). He was also known to have received a resurrection appearance of the Lord Jesus (1 Cor 15). Some would likely have had contact with the James traditions of non-Catholic Christianity, so they would have known of the high honor accorded him in those circles. Yet he is also sorely underrepresented in the Gospel and Pauline texts accepted by proto-Catholics of the day, and what one finds there is easily construed in unflattering ways: James appears not to have been a committed disciple of the earthly Jesus (e.g., Mark 3:21, 31-35; John 7:5);[33] the Judaizers who demand Gentile circumcision in Galatians are explicitly said to have come "from James" (2:12); in Acts he is mentioned almost as an afterthought in Peter's miraculous escape from prison (12:17), and his main appearances in chapters 15 and 21 show him to be primarily concerned about the right performance of the Jewish law by Paul and the targets of his Gentile mission.

It is my hypothesis that this figure held both problem and promise for second-century proto-Catholics. He was a problem in that he was an irrevocably well-known figure from the apostolic age who was championed by rival traditions and poorly represented in apostolic texts accepted by proto-Catholics. But his figure also held great promise in an age when Pauline writings were being used to support antinomianism and anti-Judaism, for the traditional picture of James (derived from both canonical and noncanonical texts) was of an apostle of Jesus whose authority predated that of Paul (Acts, Gal, and elsewhere), whose "Jewishness" was unquestioned, whose Torah-observant piety was unrivalled (Hegesippus), who had himself received a direct appearance from the risen Lord (1 Cor 15), and who was martyred for his faithful witness to Christ (Hegesippus et al.). A letter from this figure could redeem the figure of James from the clutches of his many non-Catholic supporters, and also help reclaim Paul from his heretical friends by presenting a distinctively Christian Torah piety that would "clarify" the relation of faith and works in justification and underscore the essential relation of Israel and the church. Further, it could establish on literary grounds the Paul-Pillars distinction well known to second-century Catholics, providing the final link that would gather an otherwise rather disparate collection of non-Pauline letters into a coherent, robust collection from the ancient apostolic mission to Jews in Jerusalem.

It is out of this state of affairs that the Letter of James "arrived" in the third century, and the way it was used by its earliest tradents suggests that it was championed for these very purposes. The first of these, Origen (especially in his commentary on Romans), celebrates the letter as the "answer" to those who were haunted by the teachings of Marcion, those who struggled to reconcile the Pauline justification formula with the ethical injunctions of the gospels, those who were troubled by the stories suggesting Paul was divided from his colleagues in Jerusalem, and those who wondered about the authority of the Jewish Scriptures after hearing on Pauline authority that the law was "abolished" in Christ (Eph 2:15).[34] Indeed, one is at pains to find any ancient church writer express any anxiety at all over the apparent tension between James and Paul on justification. In this light, any problem between the two is revealed to be an issue arising out of the Protestant Reformation, for nearly everywhere James was used in the ancient church, it was warmly embraced as a remedy to the "perplexing problem in the writings of the Apostle Paul" that led certain readers into heresy.[35]

Though Origen knew and used James, he nowhere witnesses to the existence of a discrete seven-letter collection called "Catholic." By the end of the third century, however, Eusebius wrote under the assumption that his readers knew of a set of seven non-Pauline letters, titled Catholic Epistles, that had James as its lead letter.[36] Evidence from the period after Eusebius makes it clear that "the seven Catholic Epistles" (standardized in the order James-Peter-John-Jude) were considered an authoritative canonical quantity in the Eastern church, though it would be the middle of the fourth century before James and the distinctively Eastern Catholic Epistle collection made its way into the Western church through the work of Hilary, Rufinus, Jerome, and Augustine.[37]

However one accounts for James' reception history, it is evident that within a generation after Origen, the letter went from relative obscurity to being the lead letter in a new, second apostolic letter collection. With the addition of James, a kind of fit appears to have been made that enabled the collection to gain widespread purchase in the churches. It is as though this fit happened by design. But is there anything in the letter itself that would support such an unusual hypothesis?

The Letter of James as a Canon-Conscious Pseudepigraph

My composition hypothesis for the Letter of James follows closely on several recent studies on 2 Peter, a text that is almost universally considered to be pseudepigraphic and is generally dated somewhere in the late first to mid-second century.[38] Several scholars have promoted the notion that the letter is not simply pseudepigraphic, but a pseudepigraph written for the purpose of providing a distinctive shape to a nascent collection of authoritative Christian writings—a "canon-conscious pseudepigraph." The pseudepigrapher was quite literally striving to create Scripture by carefully linking his letter intertextually with the authoritative scriptural writings of his day, with the ultimate goal of restructuring the emerging collection.[39] Second Peter parallels the opening salutation and closing doxology of 1 Peter[40] and identifies itself as "the second letter" written from the author (3:1), making it all but unavoidable that readers identify the sender as the Apostle Peter. The author incorporated a good deal of the already authoritative Letter of Jude into his text (2 Pet 2:1-18), and in his reference to "all the letters" of "our beloved brother Paul" (which have the same status as "the other scriptures," 3:15-17), the author clearly shows his concern to harmonize Peter and Paul against those who would drive a wedge between them. Throughout the letter, we find an underscoring of the authority of the Jewish Scriptures: there are references to God's "precious and very great promises" (1:4), readers are told to be attentive to the prophetic message that derives from the Holy Spirit (1:19-21), and a list of Old Testament examples underscores the claim that the Old Testament offers reliable accounts of how God acted in the past and will act in the future (2:1-22).

In all this, 2 Peter can be seen to function as a kind of bridge text written to span a gap between existing authoritative writings, reauthorizing them, linking them, and commenting on them in such a way as to forge together a collection firmly established on the dual apostolic authority of Peter and Paul. David Trobisch calls 2 Peter an "editorial note" composed by those responsible for the final redaction of the New Testament. He and others argue that the text betrays the familiar second-century "catholicizing" or "harmonizing" interests we have already seen in Irenaeus, Tertullian, and others: against the teachings of Paul's "heretical friends," who championed him in isolation from the rest of the apostles and extracted him from his Jewish context, 2 Peter emphasizes the reconciliation of Paul and the Jerusalem apostolic leaders as represented by Peter; likewise, against those who sought to divorce the new Christian movement from its roots in Judaism, 2 Peter endorses the full authority of the Jewish Scriptures for Christian faith.

When we allow ourselves to assume a late date for James, we find that it can be read in much the same way as 2 Peter. There is little to identify the author beyond the unadorned "James" in 1:1, since second-century readers would have been unlikely to have identified the sender as anyone other than the one who had become the most famous James of the early church, James the brother of Jesus. Readers of the letter have long noticed that the voice of Jesus hovers palpably over the text. The constantly recurring echoes of Jesus' words (which most closely parallel Matthew's Sermon on the Mount, though others point to Luke, Q, and elsewhere)[41] increase the author's clout by imparting the sense that he is intimate with the ethical admonitions of the Lord, in relation to whom he is identified as a "servant" (1:1). As in 2 Peter, so also in James the Jewish Scriptures are unambiguously advocated as authoritative Scripture for Christian readers and auditors. There are constant echoes and quotations from Torah (e.g., 2:8-11), Prophets (e.g., 1:9-11), and Writings (e.g., 1:19-21), and a number of Old Testament heroes are presented as models of Christian piety: Abraham (2:21-24), Rahab (2:25), Job (5:11), Elijah (5:17), and the prophets (5:10) are all mentioned. Likewise, in contrast to Paul's familiar characterization of the law as that which brings "slavery" (Rom 7–8 and Gal 2, set in contrast with the gospel of the Spirit, which sets believers "free from the law of sin and death," Rom 8:2), in James the law itself is identified as the "word" that brings "liberty" to those who are "doers" of its commands (1:22-25)—commands which are indeed altered because of Christ, but in no way "abolished" (Eph 2:15) as a guide for God's people (Jas 1:22-25; 2:8-11).

Just as 2 Peter appears to intentionally link itself with 1 Peter, Jude, and the Letters of Paul, so also James includes a number of significant verbal links—not only with Paul (as we have already seen), but also with other proto-New Testament apostolic letters held as authoritative in the second century. Most strikingly, James' opening chapter bears remarkable resemblance to the opening chapter of 1 Peter. There are at least eight significant parallels between the two, the first five of which occur in sequence within the first twenty-five verses (see table on p. 197).

A number of different explanations have been proffered for the correspondence between these two texts, the most common of which is that they are pulling independently from the common stock of early Christian tradition. One increasingly hears complaints that this explanation is less than satisfactory,[42] however, since such persistently strong intertextual connections seem more suggestive of some sort of formal relationship between the two.

According to my reckoning, the primary concern of the second-century author of James was to have James and Peter speak with one voice;

James	1 Peter	Link
1:1	1:1	Letter recipients are in the in the διασπορά
1:2-4	1:6-9	Same phrases "Rejoice" / "be joyful in various trials" (ποικίλοις πειρασμοῖς) because such events involve "the testing/genuineness of your faith" (τὸ δοκίμιον ὑμῶν τῆς πίστεως)
1:10-11	1:23-24	Extended allusion to / quotation of Isa 40:6-8
1:18	1:23	Both describe a "birth" (ἀποκεύω / ἀναγεννάω) by a "word" (λόγος)
1:21-25	1:23-25	The "word" (λόγος) subsequently identified as the gospel / law
3:13; 4:1	2:11-12	Jas: "By his good conduct let him show his works" (δειξάτω ἐκ τῆς καλῆς ἀναστροφῆς τὰ ἔργα αὐτου) Peter: "Maintain good conduct" (ἀναστροφήν . . . καλήν) so that "they may see your good works" (ἐποπτεύοντες ἐκ τῶν καλῶν ἔργον)
4:6-10	5:5-9	Shared quotation of Prov 3:34 in a call to submit (ὑποτάσσω), followed by calls to resist the devil (ἀντίστητε τῷ διαβόλῳ), ending with call to humble self (ταπεινώθητε) before God / the Lord that he may exalt (ὑψόω) you
5:20	4:8	Shared allusion to Prov 10:12 (καλύψει / καλύπτει πλῆθος ἁμαρτιῶν)

the main goal was to convey a sense of coherence in the message of the Jerusalem pillars, not to provide correction, as he needed to do for Paulinists wandering into heresy. But the author was not merely echoing 1 Peter, for in its parallels James subtly reshapes our reception of that letter. Numerous points could be made on this score,[43] but for the purpose of this essay I limit myself to two.

First, both texts are addressed to readers in the Diaspora. First Peter clearly uses the term figuratively, as a means of describing the social location of believers whose faith is being tested through their status as exiles and aliens in a foreign land. Peter is presented as an alien himself, residing in "Babylon" (5:13). Despite his status as chief of the apostles, Peter is here presented as a fellow sufferer following Christ in exile. The Letter of James, by contrast, is addressed "to the twelve tribes in the diaspora"

(1:1). There is no reason to assume that the term is being used figuratively here; the letter is addressed to believers who are dispersed from their homeland, and it is written by one who is not caught up in that dispersion, who writes from a center and has the authority to address the whole of believing Israel on essential matters of faith. When the two addresses are read in conjunction, a clear line of demarcation between the two figures is established: Peter may have ended up being associated with Paul in Antioch, Corinth, and Rome, but James and Peter shared an earlier connection to the earthly Jesus and the earliest mission in Jerusalem; likewise, Peter may have eventually become the first bishop of Rome, but James was the first bishop of the first church in Jerusalem, and both Peter and Paul were under his authority. In short, the address in the Letter of James is designed to remind readers that the Christian church did not emerge out of the Gentile mission, that indeed the "Jewishness" of Christianity is not merely figurative but historic. Apostolic authority cannot be grounded solely along a Peter/Paul axis, as 2 Peter attempts, for such a configuration fails to adequately press the genuine, historic connection between Christianity and Israel.

Following this logic, one notes how the parallel passages in James consistently assert the actual Jewish underpinnings of Christianity against 1 Peter's tendency to absorb historic, ethnic Israel in the figurative landscape of his Gentile readership. First Peter uses Diaspora figuratively, but James uses it quite literally. First Peter describes its Gentile readership in terms previously associated with the people of Israel, but the implied readership of James is ethnic Israel itself; 1 Peter looks to the prophets as witnesses to the coming Christ (1:10-12), who is the primary example of the faithful life (2:20-25; 4:1), but James looks to the prophets themselves as examples of piety (5:10), along with other Old Testament heroes and heroines (2:20-26; 5:11, 17); in 1 Peter, the "word" is the Christian gospel preached (1:23-25), but in James it is the Torah of Israel (1:22-25). When we keep in mind the second-century crisis over Christianity's relation to Israel, along with the early authority of 1 Peter and the later emergence of James, it becomes far less likely that the remarkable parallels between these two texts are the result of incidental appeals to the very same features of the larger stock of early Christian tradition. They reflect design and purpose.

There are also less frequent but equally significant links with 1 John, most notably in each letter's emphasis on the vital connection between speech and deed, the impossibility of devotion to both God and the world, and in the formally similar closing comments on prayer and restoration of the sinner.

James	1 John	Link
1:13; 2:14; 4:13	2:4-9; 3:18	Both emphasize the contrast between faithless saying and faithful doing
2:14-17	3:16-18	Both describe a hypothetical encounter with a poor sibling (ἀδελφός) to illustrate the superiority of works (ἔργα) over words
4:4	2:15-16	Friendship/love with/of the world (φιλία τοῦ κόσμου / ἀγαπᾷ τὸν κόσμον) is incompatible with devotion to God
5:13-20	5:14-17	Prayer for another is effective for restoring the sinner and delivering from death

Again, the chief concern here was coherence; James must be heard to speak in the same voice as his co-pillars Peter and John. But here, too, we find that the parallels have a shaping effect on the larger collection. First Peter and 1 John both underscore the importance of the conduct of the believer in the world, but between the two, 1 John intensifies the issue by repeatedly making it the ultimate determinant of one's relation to God (e.g., 1:6-10; 2:3-6, 9-11, 15-17; 3:6, 14-18; 4:7-12, 19-21). Likewise, both texts exhort readers to be distinct from nonbelievers, but while 1 Peter aligns with Paul in its maintenance of an essential openness to the world for evangelistic purposes (2:9, 12; 3:1-2), 1 John is much more sectarian in its insistence that "the love of the Father is not in those who love the world" (2:15) since "the whole world lies under the power of the evil one" (5:19). James endorses the ethical dualism of 1 John in its insistence on the soteriological significance of righteous deeds (2:1-26) and the corrupting dangers of friendship with the world (1:26-27; 4:4). Their combined witness in tandem with 1 Peter intensifies the latter's ethical emphasis to produce a strident exhortation from the pillars of Jerusalem, calling for believers to separate themselves from the seductive practices of their surrounding pagan cultures. The result is a Pillars collection with a more sectarian, conduct-based ecclesiology to balance out the more evangelistic ecclesiology of the Pauline collection.[44]

Along with these significant intertextual links, we can close by pointing to other important formal elements of the larger CE collection that would not exist were it not for the presence of James in its midst. The prescript to the Letter of Jude, which identifies the author as "a servant of Jesus Christ and a brother of James" (Jude 1), reminds readers that these servant-brothers also happen to be brothers of the Lord (Matt 13:55; Mark 6·3), and creates a kind of *inclusio* for the collection as a whole that suggests it is delivered to readers in the embrace of Jesus' family in Jerusalem. Further, 1 Peter, 1 John, and Jude (which were, again, the earliest non-Pauline letters to achieve canonical authority) would have little to nothing in common with one another (literarily or thematically) were it not for the linking presence of James in their midst. Without James, the church had a disorganized assortment of apostolic epistles, including a large collection of Pauline letters with meaningful links to Letters of Peter (which were linked with the Letter of Jude), along with a Johannine collection that had more to do with the Gospel and Revelation than any of its epistolary kin, and a receding list of other authoritative letters like *1 Clement*, *Barnabas*, and those of Ignatius and Polycarp. Add James to the mix and the apostolic letter collection is tightly reorganized under the far more meaningful rubric of the ancient two-sided Christian mission to Jews and Gentiles. The creation of a letter from James of Jerusalem, then, didn't simply serve the corrective, harmonizing interests of second-century proto-Catholics. It also promoted a certain "aesthetic quality"[45] that quickly facilitated the final closing of the canon of apostolic letters, as the history of its canonical development in the East and then in the West bears witness.

PART IV

PETRINE EPISTLES

CHAPTER 11

SALVATION AND ANTHROPOLOGY
IN FIRST PETER

Reinhard Feldmeier

The following article exposes that 1 Peter absorbed more concepts of the religious koine of the time than is commonly accepted. Thus, the eschatological aspect of his message of salvation became more plausible in the context of the Hellenistic world. This will be provocatively typified in reference to the perception of the soul and the concept of rebirth together with the intertwined dualistic tendencies. At the same time, the demonstrated correspondences should indicate the kinds of transformations that these concepts underwent due to accommodation of the Christian context. As a result of this process, these concepts enriched the language of early Christian theology (and probably beyond it).

Salvation of the Soul

The prevalent notion of *soul salvation* (σωτηρία ψυχῶν) occurs in ancient literature for the first time in 1 Peter (1:9). This is remarkable, but just as noteworthy is the little interest this fact has received. On the contrary, already the equivalence of the Greek σωτηρία ψυχῶν and the English *soul salvation* (German: *Seelenheil*) is up for discussion. The exegesis of 1 Peter has been gravely influenced by the common rejection of any concept of the soul, owing to the critique of metaphysics within the realm

of theology. This influence has misled most of the commentaries of
1 Peter, despite all opposing evidence. The interrelation between 1 Peter
and the Greek concept of the soul has been rejected (and therefore also
the assumption that σωτηρία ψυχῶν points to the salvation of the soul).
Hereby, in 1 Peter, the alleged meaning of ψυχή has not been derived
from the epistle itself; rather, this interpretation is influenced by a tradition historical deduction that claims that the soul in 1 Peter is the equivalent of life, or the personal pronoun. Gerhard Dautzenberg's inquiry
into the concept of σωτηρία ψυχῶν exemplifies this method. Up to the
most recent commentaries, Dautzenberg has been cited with agreement.[1]
Dautzenberg came to the conclusion that there is no concept of soul in
1 Peter 1:9 and the underlying Jewish tradition.[2] On closer examination,
it can be shown that his entire argument is not coherent in itself. From
the outset, he poses a narrow view of the Jewish and Christian tradition,
wherein for him, Jewish chiefly means the (Hebrew and Aramaic written)
Qumran documents, and not the writings of Greek-speaking Judaism—
for example, the works of the Jewish philosopher of religion, Philo, who
developed a specific teaching of the soul.[3] Thus, Dautzenberg's argument
is based on a *petitio principii* that predetermines the result of the inquiry
due to the arbitrary limitation of the compared material. Dautzenberg
confirms this tendency with another false conclusion, which he bases on a
misleading either-or assumption. He claims there is an unbridgeable gap
between the Greek dualistic concept of the soul and the biblical understanding of ψυχή: either ψυχή has to be denoted as life/existence according to the Jewish and Christian tradition, or it is the upraised part of the
human that, according to the dualistic philosophical concept, is opposed
to the body. Since the latter concept is not applied in 1 Peter, the meaning "life" or "existence" must be intended. Yet it is not that simple. Of
course one cannot expect the entire Platonic concept of the soul in 1
Peter; this would be incompatible with the central role of eschatology in
the epistle. But from here, it does not necessarily follow that the notion
of the soul may be merely "a Semitism standing for a reflexive pronoun."[4]
Further inaccuracies are added to these false conclusions. Dautzenberg
does not ask where the expression σωτηρία ψυχῶν might come from, or
if there are other phrases equal or similar to it. Misleading in this regard
is Dautzenberg's claim (which is configured as a supplementary justification) that 1 Peter is not interested in the distinction between the internal
and external human being (Dautzenberg, "Σωτρηία ψυχῶν (1 Pet 1:9),"
274). In Paul, the notion of the inner human being occurs only twice (1
Cor 5:12; 2 Cor 4:16; cf. Eph 3:16), although the expression mentioned
in 1 Peter 3:4 comes very close to the Pauline distinction between the
internal and external human. Here is spoken of "the hidden ἄνθρωπος of

the heart" who owns the "imperishable . . . of the meek and quiet spirit," which is explicitly opposed to outward trappings.

In contrast, an impartial view of the passages of 1 Peter that speak of the ψυχή shows a completely different picture. In 1:9, σωτηρία ψυχῶν alludes to other texts of the New Testament, such as Mark 8:35. But aside from the question of whether the word *soul* in Mark points to more than mere life, it can be said with the utmost probability that against the background of the ancient concept of the soul (which was a current idea within Diaspora Judaism as well), for every Greek reader or listener, this certain expression might have evoked the idea of soul salvation—all the more so as the salvation message of rebirth is linked with the everlasting heritage (1:3-4), which is opposed by the mortality of all flesh (1:23-24). A closer look at the type of early Jewish literature that is factored out by Dautzenberg confirms this assumption, although this literature comes much closer to 1 Peter than Qumran, especially that of Philo of Alexandria.[5] In fact, the Jewish philosopher does not make use of the succinct expression σωτηρία ψυχῶν, but he does refer to the salvation of the soul in various places; thus he interprets Exodus 15:1 (the annihilation of the Egyptians by God) in such a way that God besteads the soul in its struggle against the "unreasoning impulses of passion" in order "to bestow on it full salvation" (σωτηρία, *Ebr.* 111). Philo's interpretation of Abraham's exodus in Genesis 12:1-3 starts with the noteworthy statement that "God begins the carrying out of His will to cleanse [καθῆραι] man's soul by giving it a starting-point for full salvation [σωτηρία] in its removal out of three localities, namely, body, sense-perception, and speech" (*Migr.* 2). These two facts of evidence are enlightening, not only for mentioning the salvation of the soul, but also for explaining it in a way that refers directly to the next two verses in which 1 Peter speaks explicitly of the soul: verse 1:22 claims that the "souls" are to be purified in obedience to the truth, and Philo's repeated reference to the struggle of the soul against passion and lack of restraint (cf. beside *Ebr.* 111 also *QG* 4:74; *Opif.* 79.81) is in accordance with 1 Peter 2:11. Here, the struggle of the soul against fleshly desires is at stake. The salvation of the soul, the purification of the soul, the struggle between fleshly desires and soul—from my point of view, these well-defined equivalences between Philo and 1 Peter demonstrate without a doubt that 1 Peter is influenced by the Diaspora synagogue and states a concept of the soul as the higher self of the human being. This is in line with the other mentions of the notion of ψυχή in 1 Peter.[6]

Thus, the notion of ψυχή in 1 Peter seems to describe the anthropological correlative of God's relation to the world, that is, the soul as both the passive recipient of acts of salvation and rescue (1:9; 2:25; 4:19) and the self that has to be actively purified (1:22), subordinated to God (4:19), and kept from fleshly desires (2:11). The First Letter of Peter denotes this concept with ψυχή, and thus ties in with the Greek-speaking addressees' horizon of association. In Platonism as well as in the Diaspora synagogue, the concept of ψυχή signifies the human being insofar as he or she relates to God. Moreover, the notion of the soul can clarify the concept of salvation, which is central to 1 Peter. Thus salvation points to an everlasting life that transcends the vain *conditio humana*, although hereby—and this is obvious—immortality becomes eschatologically related to God's life-giving act of salvation in Christ, which already dominates the believer's life in terms of a living hope. In other words, here immortality is not determined by the essential participation of the soul in the divine, as stated by the contemporary Middle Platonism.[7] Nevertheless, in 1 Peter are to be found some hints at a dualistic anthropology. Although not explicitly opposed to the body or the flesh, the soul functions as the addressee of the divine salvation and participates as such in the glory and immortality of God (see below), while the flesh distinctly represents the sphere of impermanence (1:24), suffering (4:1), and death (3:18; 4:6). Especially noteworthy in this context is the principle statement that in 2:11 introduces the second main part. Here it is expressed that the fleshly desires wage a war—not as Paul would have expressed it (cf. Gal 5:16-17, against the (divine) spirit, but against the (human) soul (2:11). This clearly hellenized anthropology corresponds to the soteriology in 1 Peter, which resumes the motif of rebirth.

The Concept of Rebirth in the Context of the Religious Koine in Later Antiquity

Insofar as we can make a judgment on the spare basis of source material, it can be said that the metaphor of rebirth (in the sense of a religiously determined metamorphosis of the human being) has occurred only since the first century CE. In a relatively short time period, the metaphor was dispread in a noteworthy manner: in pagan mysteries, rebirth described the effects of initiation; in Hellenistic Jewish texts, it was the metamorphosis of a human being in communion with God and in early Christendom the appropriation of the salvation that has been brought to the world through Jesus Christ—not to mention popularity of the metaphor in gnostic and hermetic texts (cf. *Corpus Hermeticum* 13).

In terms of tradition history, Philo, *QE* 2:46 is probably the earliest and most interesting parallel to 1 Peter in the Jewish sphere. Here, the Jewish philosopher of religion interprets Exodus 24:16b allegorically: the tradition that Moses was summoned to God on the seventh day points to the "second birth" through God himself, which is contrasted to the first birth by "corruptible parents." This second birth causes the release of the soul, which receives the "ever-virginal nature of the Hebdomad." In hellenized Diaspora Judaism, the further application of this metaphoric field is testified by Pseudo-Philo, *De Jona*, where the prophet in the stomach of the fish, who turned back to God (25-26 [95.99]), and the converted inhabitants of the city Nineveh (46 [184]) are called the reborn.[8] Related to this metaphoric field is the conversion novel *Joseph and Aseneth*, which originates from Egypt; here, in connection with her conversion to Judaism, the daughter of the Egyptian priest uses the verbs ἀναζωοποιεῖν (8:11; 15:5; 27:10), ἀνακαινίζειν (8:11; 15:5.7), and ἀναπλάσσειν (8:11; 15:5) as expressions of the divine acting within her.

The pagan testimonies date a little later. They stem from the surroundings of the mystery cults. Among them, the most prominent document is the eleventh book of *Metamorphoses* (*The Golden Ass*) of Apuleius. The redemption of a certain Lucius from his donkey stature through Isis prefigures rebirth through inauguration into the mysteries. By means of the inauguration, the protagonist is delivered from his blind fate and subordinated under the protection of a "seeing deity."[9] As *numen invictum* (11.7.1) and *omnipotens dea* (11.16.3), this deity—in a kind of patronage relationship—guarantees its follower benefits in this life and in the realm of the dead. This deed of salvation is commentated on by a priest, who breaks out in a beatitude at the end (11.16.4: *felix hercules et ter beatus . . .*) and denotes the rescued as "quasi reborn" (*renatus quodam modo*). Once again, the mystics are called by the priest as "quasi reborn to a new life" (11.21.7), and accordingly Lucius celebrates his inauguration as his new birthday (11.24.4–5). The prevalence of the metaphoric field of rebirth in connection with inauguration into the mysteries is also witnessed by an inscription in the Mithraeum of Santa Prisca in Rome. Here, the day of initiation is called the new birthday. Similarly, some of the taurobolium inscriptions refer to the birthdays of the mystics.[10] That the terminology of rebirth is a specific feature of mystery cults is also shown by Sallustius in the fourth century.[11]

In the New Testament beyond 1 Peter, this concept can be found particularly in Jesus' nighttime talk with Nicodemus in John 3; here (esp. in John 3:5), and also in Titus 3:5, the concept is used to interpret the baptism (cf. further in John 1:13). In opposition to these texts in which rebirth and baptism are related to each other, James 1:18 emphasizes, as does 1 Peter, the potency of the divine word without any reference to baptism.

Seemingly, the concepts that are marked with the metaphor of rebirth are so disparate that they can hardly be assigned to one uniform concept.[12] Even more hypothetical are all attempts to give a proof for direct dependencies between all the differing testimonies.[13] In this respect, most contemporary interpretations are right to reject the direct derivation of the concept of rebirth in 1 Peter from those parallel occurrences. Less convincing is their further treatment of the theme: either interpreters are content with the identification of rebirth and baptism in 1 Peter (on the basis of John 3:5 and Titus 3:5)[14] that allows the subsumption of the statements of rebirth under the statements of baptism in the New Testament,[15] thereby losing the meaning of the drastic metaphor for the new beginning of the whole existence; or they highlight the parallels in the history of religions in order to demonstrate the dissimilarity of the concept of rebirth in 1 Peter in an apologetic manner and then replace the term *rebirth* with another theological term, as for instance re-creation[16]— if they do not accentuate the uselessness of comparing 1 Peter with its parallels in the history of religions in the first place.[17] These approaches to the central statement of rebirth in 1 Peter are surely not appropriate to an adequate perception of its meaning.

The analysis of historical testimonies should not only be committed to the (often very hypothetical) attempt to state dependencies. In the same way, the other method, which strives to highlight the (without a doubt extant) particularity of the Christian statement on rebirth, has to be questioned. The elementary question, why the concept of rebirth came into fashion at a certain point in history, is much more significant to pose. What kind of mental climate and what (possibly social and economic) conditions led to a mentality in which a new perception of salvation, the rebirth as metamorphosis into another existence, could emerge? To express it in a more distinctive way: the question of to what extent the rebirth in 1 Peter should be connected to the whole context of baptism is worthy of consideration. But the fact that 1 Peter does not mention baptism when rebirth is at stake, and vice versa, leads to the methodical assumption that one should interpret each concept in its own terms. In either case, presupposing a Christian teaching of a (sacramental) baptism, we should not understand rebirth as a more or less trivial synonym for baptism. The same can be stated for possible relations to further theological terminology, such as *new creation*. However, the relationship of 1 Peter to the various parallels in the New Testament and in Jewish and pagan sources has to be pinpointed;[18] at any rate, it has to be acknowledged that the pastoral letter written in the name of the pillar apostle describes Christian existence with a metaphor that definitely does not derive from biblical tradition, but from the religious koine of the time. This is even more noteworthy since the very same metaphor plays a key role in the definition of Christian existence: in 1:3, God is called ἀναγεννήσας, the Father, the Creator of the new being;[19] in 1:23, the believers are born anew "of imperishable sperm . . . by the living word of God"; and in

2:2, "as newly born nursing infants," they grow up to salvation because of the λόγικον γάλα, "the milk of the word." Procreation, birth, breast-feeding—this evolvement of the metaphor of rebirth in 1 Peter embraces maternal and paternal aspects of rebirth. Hereby it is stressed that this new being is determined by God in an entirely elementary, and comprehensive sense. At the same time, the reborn become related to this God in a new manner (see below).

As already mentioned above, the meaning of the term *rebirth*, which shapes the whole chapter 1:3–2:3, reflects the endeavor of 1 Peter to clarify the eschatological Christian existence in a new context. In its eschatology, the script does not speak any more of the kingdom of God or the new creation, but instead personalizes the Christian message of salvation: the break-in of the *eschaton* is signified by the metaphor of the new birth. Therefore, the crucial point of this eschatology is the redemption from the inane life (1:18-19) and from impermanence (1:23-25), that is, the overcoming of the circumstances conditioned by the first birth. A closer look shows that 1 Peter also profiles its speech of the σωτηρία in the same way. Indeed, the prelude of the eulogy in 1 Peter 1:3-4 uses an already Christian terminology—especially the well-known terminology of the Pauline Letters—but shifts its stress to turn the whole complex in a new direction. God is introduced here as somebody who "has procreated us anew." This new existence consists in the fact that the addressees are set in a straight relationship with this God; creatures become children, and that means they participate essentially (almost genetically) in this God. This is affirmed by the more accurate determination of the new procreation "unto a living hope." The accentuation of hope as the center or even the basis of the Christian existence combines 1 Peter with other texts of the New Testament that transfer Christianity into the Hellenistic world.[20] On the other hand, the repeatedly applied attribute *living* is rather unusual: besides hope, it also designates the divine Logos in 1:23 and Christ in 2:4—the living stone. The significance of all three so predicated items is their close connection to the believer's new life: the living hope is the goal of rebirth, and therefore the "hope that is in you" (3:15); the living word is the word that has created the new being with imperishable sperm (1:23) and, as the word of God, "was proclaimed to you as gospel" (1:25); the living stone is the stone that the believers connect to as living stones themselves, in order to build up one common "spiritual house" (2:4-5). The attribute living is used as synecdoche that is related both to the saving good and to its addressee. The latter participates in the imperishable vitality of God through the word, the hope, and the living stone of Christ, and is therefore newly sired. The following verse (1:4) explains this in a distinctive way. Here, the matter of inheritance stems from the Jewish tradition of the Old Testament,[21] but refers to the child-parent relationship, which in 1 Peter is based on the concept of rebirth.[22] In addition, here the "foreigner" is promised a new homeland.[23] This inheritance is specified more precisely with the three attributes *imperishable*, *undefiled*, and *unfading*. Such a sequence of negative attributes, primarily formed with α privativum, is characteristic of the negative theology of antique metaphysics.[24] In Hellenistic Diaspora Judaism, such attributes were used to describe the transcendence of the biblical God.[25] This is valid for imperishability,[26] and also for immaculacy.[27] All three attributes together determine the divine in terms of a negative theology. The divine is characterized by its independence from that what is regarded as the essence of this world, namely the maelstrom of transitoriness that appears in destruction, contamination, and aging, and destroys all beauty and goodness.[28] First Peter takes over this theological pattern—again, probably through intermediation of the Diaspora synagogue[29]—but with a new feature: if the heritage "in heaven," distributed by God among those who were newly sired, is designed as imperishable, undefiled, and unfading, then the divine attributes do not only denote the divine as such in unalterable contradiction to the human, but also connote the salvation. Likewise, this phenomenon has its forerunners in the tradition of the Diaspora synagogue.[30] Even more forcefully than in the sources of Hellenistic Judaism that are familiar to us, in 1 Peter these metaphysical attributes, which define the divine sphere by negation of the earthly human reality, become inclusive soteriological attributes. The participation in the imperishable fullness of divine life through the new divine procreation is conceded to the chosen.[31] In this respect, the formulation of 2 Peter 1:4, which alone in the New Testament speaks about participation in God's divine nature, describes quite adequately what rebirth in 1 Peter is about.

The second mention of rebirth in 1:23-25 confirms this interpretation. Here, the procreation from the perishable sperm is in antithetic contradiction to the new procreation through the imperishable sperm (v. 23). The saying of the divine σπορά strengthens even the bold metaphor of procreation in 1:3. In our context, only one meaning applies to it: as much as the perishable existence emerges from the perishable sperm—as the flesh that faded away and perished like grass—the very sperm that has been equated with the living and enduring divine word (v. 24) generates an everlasting life. This sperm itself becomes identified with the gospel, which was "proclaimed to you" in verse 25. Insofar as the new is not present yet but is based on the word of the promise, it already establishes the relationship to God's imperishable life. As "living hope" (1:3) and as "hope that is in you" (3:15), the new is represented in the middle of the perishable world of the flesh.

A glance at the reflections on the soul in the text above sheds new light on the quotations of the book Isaiah in 1 Peter 1:24-25. While in the context of the Old Testament, the flesh that perishes like grass simply denotes the human faint against the power of God, here in 1 Peter the flesh designates the sphere of transitoriness and death (cf. 3:18; 4:6) in contrast to God's immortality and vitality.

The Overcoming of Impermanence

The core of the statement on rebirth is the conviction that the conditions of this inane, perishable, and dark world do not limit this life, since God's life-giving act in Christ (1:3; 3:18; et al.) opened up a new horizon in the middle of the perishable world. In the beginning, the explanation goes in one single direction and follows the goal of showing that the resurrection happens in order to lead to "an imperishable, undefiled, and unfading inheritance that is kept in heaven for you." In the main part, the over-coming of transitoriness by rebirth is emphasized by harsh contrasts, not merely by the almost stereotypical contrast of 1 Peter that opposes the contemporary suffering to the coming glory (1:6-7, 11; 4:13-14; 5:1.10), but primarily by the contrast of perishability and imperishability. This contrast has already been comprehensively explained with regard to the rebirth from the imperishable sperm in 1:23-25. A variety of other texts and the antithetical expressions in the letter confirm this.[32] In this regard, I see in the hymnal passage of 1 Peter 1:18-21, with its price of the redemption through the blood of Christ, one of the most pregnant examples. The interpretation of the passage focuses mostly on the question of whether the analysis of the death of Jesus is primarily ruled by ideas of atonement or redemption of slaves that dominate the field. The new and striking emphasis that the author places on the reception of the traditional motifs has been much less of interest. First, the redemption results in liberation "from your vain way of life that was handed down to you by your ancestors" (1:18), which, as a contrast to the *mos maiorum*, is hardly to be overbid in pungency. Second, it is explicitly stressed that this redemption did not take place "with corruptible things." Third, in antith-esis to it, the lamb whose blood brings redemption is qualified with two α privativum attributes; thus the superiority over the earthly condition is emphasized, strengthened by the specification that, fourth, the entire redemption is determined in the divine resolution "before the found-ing of the world," which precedes the whole creation and may therefore transgress it (1:20).

In conclusion, by stressing participation in the divine imperishability (in contrast to the vain and perishable present), 1 Peter represents the common tendency of later antiquity to transcend the passing world; to emphasize the remaining of the word of God in contrast to the flesh, which perishes like grass, is therefore not superfluous for 1 Peter.[33] The attribution *imperishability* and its synonymous applications underscore the contrast of the divine salvation against the inanity and perishability of the existing world. These concepts seek to comprehend in a new context what the act of God at the resurrection of Jesus Christ has to do with the Christian self-conception. From this follows that the process of hellenization is more extended and more central to the soteriology of 1 Peter than is commonly realized.

The Integration into the People of God Tradition

Admittedly, the soteriology of 1 Peter is not only influenced by the Hellenistic concept of rebirth as overcoming the inanity and the moribund being. Backed by Jewish traditions of the Old Testament, the explanations of the first main part in 1:3–2:3, 1:1-2, and 2:4-10 highlight the integration of the reborn into the people of God. This is indicated by the addressees, who are spoken to as the "chosen foreigners of the dispersion." The somewhat unusual address *foreigners* can be understood from the perspective of the Christians: in the ancient society, they were stigmatized and criminalized as strangers and outsiders. However, this form of address is intended not only to describe but also to interpret the situation. With specific recourse to a small Jewish tradition of the Old Testament,[34] here the outsider is aligned with those who were called by God and therefore became foreigners, such as the patriarchs (cf. Gen 17:8; 23:4; 28:4; 35:27; 36:7; 37:1), individual pious believers (cf. Ps 39:13; 119:19-54), and the entire congregation (1 Chr 29:15; cf. Lev 25:23). In early Judaism, mainly in the scriptures of Philo of Alexandria, this tradition was widely accepted as a self-label by the Jews.[35] This connection to the people of God tradition is reinforced twice, once via the motif of election that yields the reason for selection and a second time via the διασπορά, the *terminus technicus* for the dispersion of the people of God among the nations. The extension of the address in verse 2 through the allusion to Exodus 24:7-8 refers to the covenant at Mount Sinai and therefore to the constitution of the people of God. In the following passages, the theme does not entirely disappear. Thus the people of God are alluded to in the metaphor of the heritage (1:4); through the reference to the prophetic presages (1:10-12; cf. 1:24-25); and in the request for sanctification in correspondence to God, where Leviticus 11:44-45 is quoted in the résumé of the chapter that contains the segregating dietary laws of Judaism. The theme of the people of God noticeably recedes in 1:3–2:3. Yet in the concluding chapter of the first main part (2:4-10), it comes to the fore again: in 2:4-5, with the allusions to the community as God's spiritual house and his priesthood; with the mention of the foundation of the site on Mount Zion in 2:6-8; and above all in 2:9-10, in which the notion λαός is mentioned three times beside the "chosen race" and the "royal priesthood." The notion λαός is used as synonym for Israel almost continuously in the Septuagint. The term ἔθνος ἅγιον also relates 1 Peter to the Septuagint, through the hint to the theophany of God at Mount Sinai in the context of the covenant, where it is used as the equivalent of λαός (Exod 19:6; cf. 23:22). Thus, the people of God theme plays an important role in the introduction and conclusion of the first part of the letter. The theme frames the section of 1:3–2:3 that contains the statements regarding the rebirth. This interlocking of both motifs makes it clear that 1 Peter relates them consciously to each other and understands them as complements. On the one hand, the concepts of rebirth and salvation of the soul accentuate the celestial, quasi-vertical dimension of the soteriology that overcomes the misery of the *conditio humana*; this dimension is illustrated by means of contemporary religious concepts ruling at the time. On the other hand, the recourse to the people of God theme underlines that the stigmatized and criminalized foreigners are members of a community. Newly born "unto a living hope," they are "living stones" in the "spiritual house" of God (2:5). Moreover, this community is rooted in the traditions of the old covenant, related to the prophetic presages and thereby located within the history of salvation. And finally, the "chosen foreigners" are brought together as an identifiable group and thus receive a place in the society, as it is shown in the second main part of the letter. This frame fends off the individualistic, ahistoric, and escapist misunderstanding of A salvation, whose (liberating) transcendence through rebirth and salvation of the soul was emphatically underlined.

CHAPTER 12

FIRST PETER AS EARLY CHRISTIAN DIASPORA LETTER

Lutz Doering

Introduction

Among interpreters of 1 Peter who are more interested in its epistolary character than in daring source-critical operations, the text-pragmatic affinity of 1 Peter with Jewish letters to the Diaspora has occasionally been noticed. The first proposals of this kind came from Erik Peterson and especially Carl Andresen. A number of other scholars have joined this view (e.g., K. Berger, J. R. Michaels, F. Schnider and W. Stenger, M. Tsuji), some of them with slight modifications, others (e.g., L. Thurén, D. Verseput) with certain reservations.[1] On the other hand, the existence of a genre or text type *Diaspora letter* has occasionally been questioned. Thus, Peter Davids, in an earlier contribution, claimed with respect to the typical examples invoked for the genre that they "bear only one similarity to each other—they are all letters."[2] Still others dismiss the classification of 1 Peter (and James) as Diaspora letters due to the lack of Jerusalem's central position in these texts.[3] And finally, on a more general note and in contrast to the widely acknowledged impact of Hellenistic epistolography, Georg Strecker skeptically predicted "that recourse to early Jewish letter-writing will contribute little to our comprehension of early Christian letters."[4]

Are these skeptical views justified? There are good reasons to doubt this. To begin with Strecker's general objection, it typically underestimates the significance of the text-pragmatic use of authoritative letters to Jewish communities or groups of Jews (and, earlier, Judeans). As such, they are much more similar to "official" Greco-Roman letters than to the private letter tradition, without of course belonging to the Hellenistic or Roman administration; one might perhaps label their use *quasi-official*. And it is precisely in this feature that they are particularly close to early Christian letters. Against the tendency to underestimate the impact of Jewish epistolography in New Testament scholarship, Irene Taatz has argued in her dissertation, submitted to the University of Halle,[5] that Paul's use of letters further develops Jewish models of community leadership. However, apart from a few inaccuracies in the presentation of Jewish sources in her work, two main issues have been criticized in Taatz' contribution. First, regarding Paul himself, she has likely overshot the mark, because she has not sufficiently allowed for the impact of common Hellenistic (thus, not specifically Jewish) epistolography in Paul.[6] Apart from quasi-official Jewish letter writing, Paul is clearly also influenced by the Hellenistic letter of friendship and the philosophical letter. Second, and strangely enough, Taatz has virtually neglected precisely those letters in the New Testament that are even closer to Jewish letters to the Diaspora, when judged by their formal elements, their communicative setting, their contents, and/or their pragmatic purpose, than the Pauline Letters—namely, the Catholic Epistles (CE), particularly James and 1 Peter, as well as the letter in Acts 15:23-29 containing the apostolic decree.

In what follows, I shall therefore provide an updated discussion of the evidence for early Jewish Diaspora letters, with some qualification in the description of the genre or text type. Next, I shall examine the evidence for early Christian Diaspora letters. I shall briefly argue why and how these letters should be distinguished from Jewish Diaspora letters. I shall then look at other specimens of this letter type apart from 1 Peter. Finally, I shall discuss the individual features of 1 Peter that warrant its classification as an early Christian Diaspora letter, concluding with a few considerations on how this letter type ties in with the image of the Apostle Peter as the explicit (not, in my view, the real) author of the letter.[7]

Early Jewish Diaspora Letters

What, then, is the evidence for Jewish Diaspora letters? We commence with a distinction between two types of letters. The first type is closely related to the Prophet Jeremiah and partly also to his companion Baruch, and is predominantly paraenetic in nature. I have discussed these letters in detail elsewhere,[8] and shall therefore present them in a more basic fashion here. The second type is subject to the authority of leading representatives of Palestinian Jewry and deals mainly with issues of administration, calendar, and halakah.

Letters in the Jeremiah-Baruch Tradition

(1.1) The Prophet Jeremiah's letter in Jeremiah 29 (LXX 36):1-23 purports to be sent "from Jerusalem to the remaining elders among the exiles (אֶל־יֶתֶר זִקְנֵי הַגּוֹלָה), and to the priests, the prophets, and all the people, whom Nebuchadnezzar had taken into exile from Jerusalem to Babylon" (v. 1). It is introduced as divine speech transmitted by the prophet (v. 4) and consists of four thematic lines: (1) verses 5-7, an encouragement to settle down in Babylon because the exile will be more than a short stay abroad; (2) verses 10-14, a promise to the exiles that their exile will end "when Babylon's seventy years are completed" (v. 10); (3) verses 8-9, 15, 21-23, an argument about "false" prophets; and (4) verses 16-19 (20), an announcement of disaster for those left in Jerusalem. Apart from this passage, which is apparently so late as to be absent from the *Vorlage* of LXX Jeremiah, and apart from the issue of "false" prophets, which links the chapter with Jeremiah 27–28, the letter is concerned with perspectives for the addressees' lives in exile, for whom the letter writer takes responsibility as divine mouthpiece. In LXX Jeremiah 36:1, it is prefixed by the additional headline ἐπιστολὴν εἰς Βαβυλῶνα τῇ ἀποικίᾳ, "A letter to Babylon, to the exile." The letter caused further correspondence: at first, letters to Jerusalem from a certain Shemaiah of Nehelam, dismissing Jeremiah's letter; then, upon divine commission, Jeremiah's reply to the *Golah* (vv. 24-32). The whole chapter has become crucial for the topos of Jeremiah as letter-writer that has found its realization in further texts.

The oldest text of this sort is (1.2) the Epistle of Jeremiah in the Septuagint (*Epistula Jeremiae*; in the Vulgate, Bar 6), according to the *inscriptio*, "a copy of a letter Jeremiah sent to those about to be led captive [ἀχθησομένους αἰχμαλώτους] to Babylon." However, except for the use of the second-person plural for addressing the recipients, the text has no further epistolary features. Striking is the future tense of ἀχθησομένους, which suggests that this letter wants to be taken as sent to the later exiles before their deportation (it is thus not a copy of the letter in Jer 29 [LXX 36]:1-23).[9] Verse 2 takes up the duration of the exile (cf. Jer 29 [LXX 36]:10), but modifies it to "up to seven generations" and qualifies it as "many years and long time" (ἔτη πλείονα καὶ χρόνον μακρόν; cf. Jer 29 [LXX 36]:28). For this time of the exile, which seems to extend to the very present of the author and his first readers (on which see below),[10] this text provides instruction for demeanor with respect to Babylonian idols, reacting to passages such as Jeremiah 16:13 or Jeremiah 51 and drawing particularly on Jeremiah 10 (cf. the repetitive refrain μὴ φοβηθῆτε αὐτούς, "do not fear them," which resembles Jer 10:5).[11] It is likely that the Epistle of Jeremiah thus reacts to challenges caused by the strengthening of Babylonian cults in the eras of Alexander the Great and the Seleucids.[12] Thus this text, for which often a Semitic, probably Hebrew, *Vorlage* is claimed,[13] seems to have been composed for the Babylonian Diaspora sometime between the late fourth and the second century BCE.[14] However, since it was, in literary terms, probably devised as an appendix to the book of Jeremiah, reception in Eretz Israel is equally suggested.[15]

We can compare the Epistle of Jeremiah with (1.3) the thematically similar letter in *Targum Jonathan*'s elaboration on Jeremiah 10:11.[16] In its introduction, this passage, even more closely than the Epistle of Jeremiah, refers to Jeremiah 29:1: "This is a copy of the letter that Jeremiah the prophet sent to the remnant of the elders of the exile who were in Babylon." Nevertheless, the letter in the Targum is not necessarily to be identified with the letter in Jeremiah 29.[17] In terms of content, it prepares the addressees for answering to the nations that force them to worship idols; the letter thereby provides orientation for a belief in God the Creator vis-à-vis the challenge of idolatry, presented as the situation in Babylon. Of course, it is difficult to date such a targumic passage.[18] It is even more difficult in the present case because one scholar has claimed that the letter is a later addition to the targumic text, although without decisive reasons to my mind.[19] But even if he is correct, the letter could well be an ancient tradition, secondarily domiciled at its present place, elaborating on and rewriting the biblical topos of Jeremiah as letter writer with a particular situation in mind.

This topos is probably also adopted in (1.4) a text from Qumran, *4QApocryphon of Jeremiah C*. This text, published by Devorah Dimant in *Discoveries in the Judaean Desert* 30 (2001), is still in an initial stage of scholarly evaluation, also regarding the issues discussed in the present article.[20] According to Dimant, the composition dates from the second century BCE. One of the fragments, 4Q389 (4QapocrJer C[d]) fragment 1, reports some action by Jeremiah "from the land of Egypt" (מארץ מצרים, line 5) and then continues (lines 5-7): "[. . . And it was] | [in the thi]rty-sixth year of the exile of Israel, they read [these] things (or: words) [before] | a[ll the Children of I]srael upon the river Sur in the presence (or: while standing) [. . .]."[21] Important in this section is the word קראו, "they read," a reading unrecognized before Dimant's edition but supported by an infrared photograph requested by the present writer of the Israel Antiquities Authority in 2003.[22] "These things (or: words)" most likely refers to Jeremiah's writing "from the land of Egypt" to the Babylonian *Golah*, to whom it was read at the river Sur. This public reading can be compared with the setting of Baruch 1:1-5 (below, 1.5), to which the passage is closely related in terms of structure and phraseology. The evidence of this text is significant for our investigation because it implies, in the tradition of Jeremianic letter writing, authoritative communication from a place other than Jerusalem—more precisely, from the (Egyptian) Diaspora to the (Babylonian) exiles, a communicative situation that is arguably similar to the one in 1 Peter (below, 4.3).

(1.5) The book of Baruch (LXX), as already mentioned, has close traditio-historical and structural links with the Jeremiah Apocryphon from Qumran. Thus, a date in the second century BCE, as suggested by Jonathan Goldstein, Odil Hannes Steck, and (within a theory of literary growth) also by Otto Kaiser,[23] seems likely to me. Most scholars assume a Hebrew *Vorlage* of the Greek, at least for Baruch 1:1–3:8.[24] As the introduction claims (1:1-15a), the book is a piece of writing that was composed by Baruch in Babylon (v. 1) and read (v. 3) by him to Jeconiah and the people at the river Sur, now also attested in 4Q389. Then, thus the claim, this book was sent, together with the temple vessels and money for sacrifices, from Babylon to Jerusalem, apparently by the people (v. 7, "they"; v. 14, "we sent"). Whether the book was designed for dispatch from the outset must remain open. On the one hand, the shift from "Baruch" at the beginning to "they" and "we" (i.e., the people) would support a merely secondary dispatch; on the other hand, Baruch 1:1 shows a clear intertextual reference to the biblical Letter of Jeremiah (cf. καὶ οὗτοι οἱ λόγοι τοῦ βιβλίου οὓς ἔγραψεν Βαρουχ with Jer 29 [LXX 36]:1). Thus, even if Baruch is not strictly or not only a letter, it is nevertheless modeled on Jeremiah's communication between Jerusalem and Babylon. However, in contrast to the biblical letter, apart from the replacement of the author by Jeremiah's companion Baruch,[25] the inverted direction of communication (from Babylon to Jerusalem) is to be noted: the authoritative writer has swapped places and is now to be found among the exiles themselves.

The existence of Diaspora letters in a later period is documented by (1.6) the epistolarily extremely important Letter of Baruch (*2 Bar.* 78–87),[26] for which a date sometime between 95 and 130 CE is discussed.[27] The letter is arguably an original element of the whole composition of *2 Baruch*.[28] However, manuscript evidence shows that chapters 78–86 were copied (and read) early on as an independent letter.[29] The present Syriac version has been translated from the Greek; it is often assumed that the Greek ancestor in turn goes back to a Semitic original, but this is not sure.[30] According to the introduction (*2 Bar.* 78:1), Baruch ben Neriah, who in this composition remains in Judea while Jeremiah accompanies the exiles to Babylon and supports them there (cf. 10:2, 5; 33:2), sent the letter (according to 77:19-26, by means of an eagle) to the nine and a half tribes beyond the river Euphrates, thus to the Assyrian exiles. According to 77:(12), 17-19 and 85:6, Baruch also writes to the Babylonian exiles, but this letter is not spelled out in *2 Baruch*. Since its content is "the same" (*henên hâlên*, 85:6 {+ no Syriac}) as the first one's, we can assume that the letter that is textually reproduced is given *pars pro toto* for Baruch's communication with the exiles. Nevertheless, the differentiation among the areas of addressees should be noted and compared with other evidence to be considered below (2.6 [Gamaliel letters] and 4.1 [1 Peter]). Notably, the recipients are addressed as "brothers" (78:2, 3, [5]; 79:1; 80:1; etc.), which underscores cohesion within the people resident both in exile and in the homeland, and is a remarkable feature of the second type of Diaspora letters (below, 2.1–2; 2.6; cf. 4.2). In contrast to Jeremiah 29, this letter is not stylized as divine speech (cf. 78:2, "Thus speaks *Baruch*"). However, the addressor is writing with the authority of a recipient of revelation and from Eretz Israel, so that the letter is aptly suited to "'function' as a Diaspora letter with claims of religious authority."[31] In doing so, it merges the temporal horizons of the Babylonian exile and the post-70 CE addressees, which can be demonstrated from the use of tenses and temporal markers.[32]

In (1.7) *Paraleipomena Jeremiou* (*4 Bar.*),[33] we find one letter from Jerusalem to Babylon (Baruch to Jeremiah) and another one from Babylon back to Jerusalem (Jeremiah to Baruch). Designed for their present literary co-text, both letters nevertheless (or, conversely, because of that) attest, at the beginning of the second century CE,[34] the firm place of letters between the land of Israel and Babylon (or, in second-century terms, the Diaspora) within the Jeremiah-Baruch tradition. As in *2 Baruch*, "70 CE" is read through the traditional lenses of "587 BCE." However, the purported temporal setting of the letters in *Paraleipomena Jeremiou* is different from that of other letters in the Jeremiah-Baruch circle, because they are exchanged closer to the end of the exile. Many assume a Semitic *Vorlage* for this composition, but Berndt Schaller demurs and assumes a Greek text originating in the land of Israel.[35] Neither of these letters is a real private letter:[36] Baruch's letter (*4 Bar.* 6:17-23) conveys God's word to Jeremiah (cf. 6:22) and is later read by Jeremiah to the people (7:20-22); it is sent, together with the Ethiopian Abimelech's figs, symbolizing both the imminent end of the exile and the resurrection, via an eagle that authorizes it in front of the people in Babylon (7:1-19). Jeremiah's letter to Baruch (*4 Bar.* 7:23-29),[37] despite its personal tone in the address, "My beloved son" (Υἱέ μου ἀγαπητέ), voices Jeremiah's broader concern for the return of the people, who under pressure from Nebuchadnezzar have begun to call on foreign gods (7:25-26; cf., for the threat posed by this issue, Jer 16:13 and Ep Jer [above, 1.2]). As remedy,

Baruch, together with Abimelech, is asked to pray that the people listen to Jeremiah's words (7:28), which is a condition of return according to Baruch's letter as well (6:22). Thus this letter, too, aims at strengthening mutual responsibility within the people of God in Babylon and at home, as well as at safeguarding their identity. The letter is intriguing for the analysis of 1 Peter—but hardly appreciated in this respect so far—because it is evidence for an authoritative letter from Babylon (cf. 1 Pet 5:13; below, 4.3), not to another place in the Diaspora, but (like LXX Bar) to Jerusalem. Another aspect that may shed light on one aspect of 1 Peter is the extent to which the letter writer is portrayed as witness of the people's suffering in Babylon.

Letters of Judean or Jewish-Palestinian Community Leaders

Let us now take a look at the second group of letters, issued (actually or fictitiously) by Judean or Jewish community leaders resident in, or at least connected to, Eretz Israel and dealing with administrative, calendrical, and halakic problems.

The oldest one of these is (2.1) the so-called Passover Papyrus from Elephantine (AP 21 = TAD A4.1).[38] The Aramaic letter dates from 419 BCE; the internal address reads: "[To my brothers, J]edaniah and his colleagues, the Jewish ga[rrison], your brother Hanan[i]ah" (line 1; cf. the external address line 10). Addressor and addressee are Jews. As we know from other letters, Jedaniah was at the time leader of the Jewish colony at Elephantine, while Hananiah was an approximately equally ranked functionary from Yehud (or perhaps Babylonia) who intervened with the Persian satrap of Egypt, Arsham, on behalf of the Jews there.[39] The letter body is bipartite: the mutilated report of an edict of Darius is followed, in lines 4-9, by fragmentarily preserved instructions on counting fourteen days (in Nisan), keeping the Passover, observing the Massot week, the requirement of being pure, and the prohibition of work as well as of leaven. Thus, apparently in the context of Persian administration, calendrical-halakic information is communicated by a Jew coming from outside Egypt, with probable links to Yehud, to the military colony at Elephantine in the interest of strengthening cultic unity.[40]

A similar interest can also be noted in (2.2) the so-called first introductory letter of 2 Maccabees (1:1-10a). Following E. Bickermann, this letter is widely considered authentic and its given date (v. 9: 188 of the [Babylonian] Seleucid era [henceforth Sel.], ca. 124 BCE) thought to be reliable.[41] It is addressed "to the brothers, the Jews in Egypt"; addressors are "the brothers, the Jews in Jerusalem and those in the Land of Judea" (v. 1). The letter features an interesting prescript, with an apparently deliberate mixture of Greek and oriental elements, which suggests that it was conceived in Hebrew or rather Aramaic and subsequently translated into Greek;[42] this is corroborated by the use of the structuring expression καὶ νῦν (vv. 6, 9; cf. Hebrew [ה]תע[ו], Aramaic ןעכ[ו], ת[נ]עכ[ו]).[43] In verses 2-5 we find, in a similar position to the well-being wish in some Aramaic (and many Greek) letters,[44] an elaborate wish asking (in Greek in the optative) that God may remember his covenant with the patriarchs, do good to the addressees, grant them a heart ready for keeping his commandments, and not forsake them "in the time of evil" (ἐν καιρῷ πονηρῷ, v. 5). The phrase καὶ νῦν in verse 6 arguably opens the body of the letter, turning the assurance of the Judeans' prayers into the first issue in the body.[45] In verses 7-8 follows what appears to be a quotation from an earlier letter (dated to 169 Sel., ca. 143 BCE, the reign of Demetrius II). According to one interpretation, this letter refers to the turmoil during the reign of Antiochus IV Epiphanes,[46] "in the distress and (its) full measure [ἐν τῇ θλίψει καὶ ἐν τῇ ἀκμῇ] that came upon us in these years, since Jason and those with him had split from the holy land and the kingdom" (v. 7), a turmoil that was ended when God heard the prayers (this connects with vv. 5, 6) and temple service with sacrifices, lamps, and loaves was resumed (v. 8). Set off within the body, again by καὶ νῦν, verse 9 then requests that the addressees celebrate the festival of "Tabernacles" (σκηνοπηγία), here (as well as in the second letter, 2 Macc 1:18; below, 2.3) a peculiar designation for Hanukkah because of its equal length of eight days (cf. 10:6). In light of this, verses 7-8 provide an etiology of Hanukkah, and it is possible (though not clear) that the earlier letter had already contained a request to celebrate the festival. At any rate, the addressors of the letter of 124 BCE present themselves as responsible and competent to advise the Egyptian Jews on the celebration of the festival commemorating the rededication of the Jerusalem temple.[47]

Another specimen is (2.3) the second introductory letter (2 Macc 1:10b–2:18). It is addressed by "the [people] of Jerusalem and of Judea and the *gerusia* and Judas [sc. the Maccabee]" and directed "to Aristobulus, teacher of the king Ptolemy, of the family of the anointed priests, and to the Jews in Egypt" (v. 10b). The references to "the *gerusia* and Judas" contribute to the quasi-official tone.[48] The letter has a remarkable proem (1:11-17), with two phrases used similarly in New Testament proems, εὐχαριστεῖν (v. 11) and εὐλογητὸς ἡμῶν ὁ θεός (v. 17), forming an inclusion around an idiosyncratic account of the death of Antiochus IV.[49] In the letter body we find once again a request to celebrate the "festival of Tabernacles," namely the "purification of the Temple" (1:18), which is taken up, with a redundant introduction and a conventional "phrase of polite request"[50] (καλῶς οὖν ποιήσετε), in 2:16. In between is a lengthy section with legends about Nehemiah and Jeremiah concerning altar fire and temple vessels (1:18b–2:15). Praise of God mentioning his acts of saving and an expression of hope that he will gather the people "from (everywhere) under the heaven into his holy place" because "he has purified the place" concludes the letter (2:17-18). There is considerable debate about the dating, authenticity, and unity of this letter. Its references to Antiochus' death and temple purification suggest a date of 164 BCE, but the view that the letter is a uniform composition dating from this period[51] is unconvincing. Rather, 1:18b–2:15, with its legendary material, gives the impression of a long interpolation. Depending on how one assesses the account of Antiochus' death, one will therefore assume either a brief authentic letter of 164 BCE that was later interpolated or the creation of a fictitious letter in order to accommodate the material in 1:18a–2:15.[52] Since 2:18 mentions that God has already "purified the place," the purification the addressees of the letter are urged to attend most likely refers to the celebration of commemorative Hanukkah, not the historical incident of temple purification by the Maccabees.[53] Whether this letter had a Hebrew or rather Aramaic *Vorlage* remains uncertain.[54]

Both introductory letters of 2 Maccabees are, in terms of their contents, festal letters and serve the purpose of strengthening the cohesion between communities in Eretz Israel and the Diaspora while underlining the leading role of Jerusalem.[55] They have come to us, though, as an integral part of 2 Maccabees.

This brings us to the phenomenon of (2.4) Jewish festal books claimed to be dispatched in epistolary form. It is possible, on account of the prefixed letters and 2 Maccabees 10:1-8, to view the whole of 2 Maccabees as a festal book promulgating the festival of Hanukkah. To be sure, it is highly debated how the epitome of Jason's work (see 2:23, ending with the decree to celebrate Nicanor's day, not Hanukkah), the letters, and perhaps 2 Maccabees 10:1-8 were joined together. However, the emphasis on Hanukkah in the final form (as a festival to be celebrated) should not be missed.[56] On account of the letters, 2 Maccabees might be perceived as an extended letter, a notion already evidenced in early reception of the book, such as the subscription in Codex Alexandrinus (Ιουδα τοῦ μακκαιου [sic] πράξεων ἐπιστολή). Alternatively, 2 Maccabees may be viewed as a collection of letters, with the main part of the book as an extended historical enclosure.[57] While this cannot be pursued further here, suffice it to note for our purposes that 2 Maccabees can be read as a book with epistolary features sent from Judea to the (Egyptian) Diaspora.

This can be compared with the book of Esther, which in its "canonical" form (MT) serves to promulgate the festival of Purim (Esth 9:20-32), notably by means of letters sent out to all Jews in the Persian Empire (v. 20, 26, 29; cf. also v. 30 [here letters only in MT]). By the second century BCE, the Mordecai-Esther tradition had reached Egypt, where both the name Mordecai and the festival "Mordecai's day" (2 Macc 15:36) were known, perhaps via a Greek version different from the later Septuagint translation.[58] Some time during the Hellenistic period, the book of Esther was adopted and adapted, and the festival of Purim propagated, by certain circles in Eretz Israel as well,[59] whereas the absence of a copy of Esther among the Dead Sea Scrolls—but not of material related to, and perhaps also knowledge of, the book—suggests resistance to embrace the new festival in the communiti(es) responsible for the Scrolls.[60] What is more, the Septuagint version of Esther shows that this Palestinian reshaping of the book was subsequently translated and communicated to the Egyptian Jews. Thus, the colophon of LXX Esther (Addition F 11) labels the whole book a "Purim letter" (ἐπιστολὴν τῶν Φρουραι), translated by a certain Lysimachus, a member of the Jerusalem community (τῶν ἐν Ἱερουσαλημ), and brought to Egypt "in the fourth year of the reign of Ptolemy and Cleopatra" by three named individuals. There is some debate about the exact date of this transmission,[61] and it is unclear whether the letter comes with any (quasi-)official endorsement (contrast the introductory letters to 2 Macc), but the colophon testifies to a perception of the book of Esther (LXX) as a Purim letter from Jerusalem Jews. The overall evidence thus suggests a staggered process of promulgation of the festival of Purim (and the book of Esther) in writing: within the Persian Diaspora, to Judea and Jerusalem, from Jerusalem eventually to Egypt (where the Mordecai-Esther tradition was already known). Although only the Greek book sent from Jerusalem to Egypt is explicitly labeled a letter, the earlier stages of the process show nevertheless that such writing could come also from places within the Diaspora (as above, 1.5, 1.6, 1.7 [Jeremiah to Baruch]).

Rabbinic literature has also preserved a few Diaspora letters. Apart from the mention of letters of recommendation to the Diaspora, known from the Yerushalmi and already from the New Testament[62] one specimen is (2.5) the brief letter "From Jerusalem the Great to Alexandria the Small."[63] According to the versions in the Talmud Yerushalmi, it deals with the return of the *nāśî'*, Yehudah ben Tabbai, who had fled to Alexandria. Even if not authentic, "the letter can be taken as evidence that epistolary contacts of an official nature, i.e., regarding issues of community organization and cult, existed between Jerusalem and communities in the Diaspora,"[64] since it would then have been composed imitating extant style.

Particularly important for our topic are (2.6) the three letters of Rabban Gamaliel.[65] According to the scenic introduction, these letters were dictated by Gamaliel[66] "on the stairs at the Temple Mount." The addressees are "our brothers, the inhabitants of Upper and Lower Galilee" (letter no. 1), "our brothers, the inhabitants of the Upper and Lower South" (letter no. 2), and "our brothers, the inhabitants of the Diaspora in Babylon and the inhabitants of the Diaspora of Media[67] and all the remaining Diaspora of Israel" (letter no. 3). The address is followed in each case by a salutation, reminiscent of certain circular letters in the biblical tradition, that proffers a close parallel to the one in 1 Peter and will be further discussed below. In the bodies of the letters, instructions on issues of tithing (no. 1: olives; no. 2: sheaves) or intercalation (no. 3) are given. However one imagines the historical situation and decides on the authenticity of these letters, they clearly evidence the existence of authoritative letters of halakic and calendric contents, partly to remote areas of Eretz Israel (nos. 1 and 2), partly to the Diaspora proper (no. 3). This, however, urges a slight shift in the description of the genre: what we call Diaspora letters may at times be directed to the more remote areas of the homeland. This applies also to two letters attributed to Rabban Simeon ben Gamaliel and R. Johanan ben Zakkai, whose independence from the Gamaliel letters is debated in scholarship. Both are directed to remote areas within Eretz Israel.[68]

Jewish Diaspora Letters as Genre/Letter Type

Thus, do Diaspora letters constitute a discrete genre or, according to a helpful terminological suggestion, a *letter type* (German *Briefsorte*)?[69] I propose an affirmative answer, provided the modifications and refinements in the description of the genre discussed above are taken into account: Jewish Diaspora letters are letters that involve attribution (factual or fictitious) to an authoritative addressor and communication with Judeans or Jews resident outside the Land of Israel or on its fringes. Since they are directed to communities or areas in which Jews dwell, they have, text-pragmatically speaking, more in common with official than with private letters and may thus be labeled quasi-official. Some of them are circular letters, addressing more than one community or area (not normally in a "universal" manner but retaining the specificity of regional or topographic names). Exceptionally, we find address to a single person, but then with concern for a wider group of Judeans or Jews (see 1.7). Contents focus on instruction and exhortation, with an emphasis either on exhortation and Torah paraenesis (in the subtype of the "prophetic letters") or on administrative-legal issues (in the "community letters"). Jerusalem plays a leading role in many of these letters, particularly in the community letters, but both here and in some of the prophetic letters, we are able to perceive occasional authoritative written communication also from outside Eretz Israel. The main concern of these letters, then, is the cohesion and unity of the people of God, rather than the role of

Jerusalem. Group cohesion is also served by various rhetorical elements, like reference to a common salvific metanarrative, mutual concern (not least in prayer), or the "brothers" address. This letter type is not characterized by a consistent and distinct letter form; however, as we shall see below in this chapter, the salutation of circular letters in the biblical tradition, used in the Gamaliel letters, enjoys some popularity. In sum, more indeed can be said than—to quote Peter Davids' earlier statement again—"they are all letters."

First Peter in the Context of Other Early Christian Diaspora Letters

Let us now turn to Christian specimens of the letter type, which we will consider in their own right. This is suggested by the assumed semantic shift in the notion of Diaspora within the Christian milieu, which needs to be merely mentioned here and will be discussed in greater detail below. Whether one should speak, however, of the early Christian Diaspora letter as a letter type of its own or as an adoption and adaptation of the (Jewish) Diaspora letter type is a matter of nuance. My discussion below will identify three, perhaps four, Christian Diaspora letters, which might be taken as sufficient evidence for a letter type of their own. Further, some of them have influenced the phraseology of other CE and Christian community letters, without these being Diaspora letters sensu stricto. On the other hand, the specimens discussed below arguably develop Jewish models and adapt them to suit a new readership. Moreover, it should be evident from recent debate that "Jewish" and "Christian" do not denote firm entities and clear-cut oppositions in the second half of the first century, with which we are dealing here. It is therefore best, in my view, to use "Christian" as a low-key modifier here: these letters are adaptations of the (originally Jewish) Diaspora letter type for Christian readers by Christian authors; it is probable that these authors have their origin in Judaism, and this is possible also for some of the addressees.

Specimens Apart from 1 Peter

Apart from 1 Peter, classification as Christian Diaspora letters is discussed for two further letters in the New Testament, James and the letter in Acts 15:23-29 with the apostolic decree. Outside the New Testament, the strongest influence of the Diaspora letter traditions can be perceived in *1 Clement*.[70]

(3.1) The Letter of James, in recent publications, is increasingly considered a Diaspora letter.[71] The *superscriptio* or *intitulatio* (Ἰάκωβος θεοῦ καὶ κυρίου Ἰησοῦ Χριστοῦ δοῦλος, Jas 1:1) merges the labeling of extraordinary figures in the Old Testament and early Judaism—for example, Moses, David, and (this may have been primarily in view here) prophets—as "servant of God" et cetera[72] with the title of the early Christian missionary officeholder, "servant of Jesus Christ" et cetera,[73] and by the name of the addressor at least indirectly refers to the Jerusalem authority of the brother of the Lord.[74] The address (ταῖς δώδεκα φυλαῖς ταῖς ἐν τῇ διασπορᾷ, Jas 1:1) applies both the Diaspora situation and the twelve-tribe structure of Israel to the Christian addressees.[75] Equally, the paraenetic letter content, with the topics of temptation and trial, fits Diaspora letters well,[76] particularly those of the Jeremiah-Baruch tradition (above, 2.1). Karl-Wilhelm Niebuhr has pointed in detail to correspondence between these texts (and the introductory letters to 2 Macc) regarding Torah paraenesis, as well as their statements on God, the people of God, and expectations for the future.[77] With respect to the two types of Jewish Diaspora letters, James may therefore be described as a *mixed type*, merging prophetic authorization (but moving beyond the previous limitation to Jeremiah and Baruch) and the authority of a community leader, with greater affinity to the former type in terms of contents.

(3.2) The letter in Acts 15:23-29 containing the apostolic decree shows features of form and content that suggest its classification as an early Christian Diaspora letter.[78] To be sure, it is debated whether the letter in its present form is basically traditional or comes from the Lukan redactor. Some scholars justifiably argue a midway position, that is, that the apostolic decree was traditionally extant in the form of a letter, but Luke elaborated on it redactionally. They arrive at this solution by way of an analysis that finds both traditional and redactional traits, and through general considerations regarding the communication form of the apostolic decree. I deem such a solution most convincing.[79]

The letter in Acts 15:23-29, as well as its hypothetical *Vorlage*, is a circular letter. According to verses 22-23a (cf. 27, 30-33), Judas Barsabbas and Silas were sent (alongside the returning Paul and Barnabas) to deliver it. Occasionally, an affinity in style with Hellenistic decrees or Roman magistrates' letters has been noted.[80] Nevertheless, the prescript quite specifically develops further form-elements familiar from Jewish Diaspora letters: "The apostles and the elders, brothers, to the brothers who are of Gentile origin in Antioch and Syria and Cilicia, greetings" (v. 23b). The featuring of the title "brothers" in both the *intitulatio* and the *adscriptio* recalls the prescripts of the Passover Papyrus (above, 2.1; here: singular) and the first introductory letter of 2 Maccabees (2.2).[81] The address can be understood from the Jerusalem perspective as "Diaspora." However, in contrast to James and 1 Peter, the term is missing. I suggest that the address must be understood in a *partitive* way: apart from those "of Gentile origin," there are also brothers of Jewish origin in the addressed territories. Moreover, I note that the address geographically comprises parts of what counts as Diaspora in Jewish perspective. Not merely formally but also in terms of theme and content, the letter is close to Jewish Diaspora letters of the administrative-halakic type. It serves to implement a modus vivendi in mixed Gentile and Jewish Christian communities on the basis of a specific number of required "abstentions" (cf. Acts 15:20, 29; 21:25).[82] Thus, both the assumed epistolary form of the historical apostolic decree and its presentation in Acts 15 testify to the impact of the tradition of Diaspora letters on early Christian letter production.

(3.3) *First Clement* is a letter from the Roman community to the Christian community in Corinth, prompted by the conflict over the removal of presbyters from office in the latter community (cf. *1 Clem.* 44:4-6). A link with the Diaspora letter tradition can be seen, first, in the qualification of both the addressor and the recipient communities as παροικοῦσα, "sojourning, being exiled" (*1 Clem.* inscr.). Thus, *1 Clement* claims to be a letter from one community in exile to the other. Second, the *inscriptio* (prescript) of *1 Clement* features a salutation,[83] close to the one in 1 Peter, which picks up elements of encyclical letters in the biblical tradition also present in the Gamaliel letters (discussed below, 4.4). Apart from these reading instructions at the very beginning of the composition,[84] the exhortative, instructive, and warning character of the letter (which combines concern for brotherly unity [cf. particularly 62:1-3][85] with authoritative self-confidence in intervening in the conflict), its transmission by three messengers as witnesses (63:3; 65:1), and its reception as a publicly recited letter, perhaps circa 170 CE,[86] have been named as indicative of the tradition of Jewish letters.[87] However, scholars seem to be hesitant to label *1 Clement* a Diaspora letter right away; most authors are content with stating "some influence" (or the like) of this letter type.[88] The reasons for this are not fully clear; relevant factors may be the considerable length of the text and its peculiar setting as a letter from one community to the other. In this respect, it should also be noted that the issue is overshadowed by the debate whether *1 Clement* should be seen as a catholic letter, which was one of Erik Peterson's conclusions from the influence of Diaspora letters—that is, that the letter was not only to Corinth but also to the whole Diaspora.[89] However, as our discussion of Diaspora letters has shown so far, the issue of wider receivability by secondary readers must be separated from the immediate address, which often shows awareness of geographic distinctions. We conclude that *1 Clement* is *perhaps* a Christian Diaspora letter, noting its unusual length in comparison with the New Testament specimens (but bearing in mind that early Jewish Diaspora letters vary in length, with longer specimens such as *2 Bar.* 78–87, or 2 Maccabees and Esther, which can be perceived as letters).

(3.4) Further letters are influenced by the tradition of Diaspora letters. (1) The Letter of Jude has connections to the Letter of James in the way the explicit author is stylized (Ἰησοῦ Χριστοῦ δοῦλος) and in his presentation as "brother of James" (Jude 1), as well as to salutations of encyclical letters by virtue of the greeting ἔλεος ὑμῖν καὶ εἰρήνη καὶ ἀγάπη πληθυνθείη (Jude 2). However, its address is more general than that of any Diaspora letter discussed so far (τοῖς ἐν θεῷ πατρὶ ἠγαπημένοις καὶ Ἰησοῦ Χριστῷ τετηρημένοις κλητοῖς). (2) Second Peter is intertextually dependent both on Jude, with which it stands in a literary relationship (the opposite theory of Jude being dependent on 2 Peter is less likely), and on 1 Peter, to which it apparently refers (2 Pet 3:1). Reminiscent of (some) Diaspora letters is, again, the encyclical salutation formula (2 Pet 1:3). However, the address (though not necessarily the situation the letter addresses) is again a general one (τοῖς ἰσότιμον ἡμῖν λαχοῦσιν πίστιν, 2 Pet 1:1) and proffers no Diaspora reference. (3) It is possible to see an afterlife of Diaspora letters in several second-century community writings, such as the Letter of Polycarp, which arguably makes intertextual use of 1 Peter and probably knows *1 Clement*, and the *Martyrdom of Polycarp*, whose epistolary form should not be overlooked.[90] Both texts feature an encyclical salutation formula in the *inscriptio*. The Letter of Polycarp qualifies the addressee community as παροικοῦσα; *Martyrdom of Polycarp* does so with respect to both the addressor community and the one addressee community mentioned by name, but it then widens the address to "all communities of the holy and Catholic church everywhere sojourning in exile [παροικοῦσα]."[91] Another example is the prescript of the letter from the communities of Lyon and Vienne to those of Asia and Phrygia, handed down by Eusebius (*Mart. Lugd.*, post-177 CE; Eusebius, *Hist. eccl.* 5.1.3). Here, the labeling of the addressors as παροικοῦντες δοῦλοι and the addressees as brothers is particularly striking. A transformation occurs in the synodical letters at the end of the second century, when they become the "mouthpiece of inter-community gatherings" in which the communities are represented by their bishops; Andresen sees the impact of the early Jewish letter tradition peter out here.[92]

First Peter: An Early Christian Diaspora Letter

It is now time to come to 1 Peter proper and argue for its classification as an early Christian Diaspora letter.

(4.1) Initial evidence for viewing 1 Peter as a Diaspora letter is its explicit Diaspora address: ἐκλεκτοῖς παρεπιδήμοις διασπορᾶς Πόντου,

Γαλατίας, Καππαδοκίας, Ἀσίας καὶ Βιθυνίας (1 Pet 1:1). To begin with, what is remarkable in this address is the differentiation in the geographical data, which corresponds to what we are able to see in some Jewish Diaspora letters (particularly in *2 Bar.* 78–86 [1.6] and in the Gamaliel letters [2.6]). Though broad, this is not a catholic address (although concern for the "brotherhood in all the world" is present elsewhere: 1 Pet 5:9). Issues of the extension of these areas and the implied dispatch of the letter cannot be discussed in the confines of the present article. I only wish to recall here that I, with the scholarly majority, consider 1 Peter a pseudonymous letter; this shifts the emphasis to the kind of letter 1 Peter purports to be, and how it fits with the image of the Apostle Peter, adopted as its explicit author.[93]

It needs be clarified, however, what is meant by *Diaspora* here. The following options are being discussed in current scholarship: (1) Diaspora may refer exclusively to the Jewish Diaspora, so that the letter would be addressed to Christians in (the area of) the Jewish Diaspora of Asia Minor.[94] (2) Alternatively, Diaspora in 1 Peter may refer to a Christian Diaspora analogous to the Jewish Diaspora by virtue of its situation, in which the Christian addressees live—like the Jews, but for other reasons—in a concrete dispersion.[95] (3) Finally, some scholars think of Diaspora as an explicitly metaphoric statement, either (a) in the sense that Christians "must live in this world, but separate from this world,"[96] or (b) with the nuance that they are anyway strangers since they are remote from their heavenly home.[97]

As to the last nuance, though tempting in view of a number of early Christian references, it needs to be said that it is not explicitly present in 1 Peter (and not in James either). What is "kept in heaven" for the addressees (1 Pet 1:4) is not citizenship or a home but an imperishable future inheritance that is "vouchsafed by God."[98] Over against James, in which the recipients are addressed as the twelve tribes (of Israel) in the Diaspora (Jas 1:1), it is important to note the specific relation between Diaspora, election, and life as strangers in 1 Peter: the addressees are "the elect strangers of the Diaspora" in the areas mentioned (ἐκλεκτοῖς παρεπιδήμοις διασπορᾶς, 1 Pet 1:1); they are urged "as exiles and strangers" (ὡς παροίκους καὶ παρεπιδήμους, 2:11) to abstain from fleshly desires, and exhorted "to live in [reverent] fear the time of your exile" (ἐν φόβῳ τὸν τῆς παροικίας ὑμῶν χρόνον ἀναστράφητε, 1:17). As Reinhard Feldmeier has shown, 1 Peter draws here particularly on a sparse early Jewish tradition that values life as strangers as counterpart to divine election,[99] but the implications of election in the wider Jewish discourse on Diaspora existence need to be borne in mind as well (see below). However, the (predominantly though not exclusively) Gentile addressees of 1 Peter are members of the elect people (cf. 2:9-10) by virtue not of their birth but of their rebirth (1:3, 23; 2:1-3). Thus, a purely geographic understanding of the concept of Diaspora in 1 Peter misses part of the intension of Diaspora within its semantic field. Similarly, Diaspora in 1 Peter does not refer to a people who have been physically and histori-cally dispersed from their homeland, but rather to addressees who have entered into a Diaspora existence by their rebirth. Even if we therefore prefer to call this a metaphoric use of Diaspora,[100] we shall not overlook that this concept is closely modeled on the analogy with Jewish Diaspora experience.[101]

In this respect, two basic notions of Jewish identity in the Diaspora are the complementary concepts of election and otherness. In the vertical dimension, the story of election serves to create identity as the people of God; to this corresponds, in the horizontal dimension, the maintenance of boundaries and the perception of difference vis-à-vis the non-Jewish population. These two sides of the same coin figure not only in a good number of the Diaspora letters discussed above[102] but in other Jewish discourses on Diaspora life as well.[103] First Peter takes these notions on board, but sharpens them by making election the intrinsic reason for Diaspora and reconceiving otherness in terms of an existence as strang-ers, which figures positively only in a small string of Jewish tradition. The author has thus creatively reinterpreted the Diaspora metaphor to reflect the stance of the community chosen by rebirth and called to a life as strangers.

Troy Martin has further suggested that the tripartite expression "elect strangers of the Diaspora" (1 Pet 1:1) allows the structuring of the body middle of 1 Peter along three metaphor clusters: "the elect household of God" (according to Martin: 1 Pet 1:14–2:10), "aliens in this world" (2:11–3:12), and "sufferers of the Dispersion" (3:13–5:11).[104] However, the parallel introduction ἀγαπητοί in 2:11 and 4:12, together with some rise in the "temperature" of suffering from 4:12 on[105] and continuing ref-erences to future glory (cf. 4:13; 5:1, 4), warrants a different delimitation of parts two and three of the letter body, which disturbs the neat dis-tribution of "strangers" and "suffering in the Diaspora." Without being able to argue this in detail in the present context,[106] I suggest that a more convincing proposal for structuring the letter body will take 1:13–2:10 as a first, foundational part dealing with rebirth, new conduct, and election; 2:11–4:11 as a second part (probation as strangers); and 4:12–5:11 as a third part (partakers in suffering and glory). Thus, parts two and three, in my view, develop with different accents the implications of divine elec-tion and rebirth, as outlined in the foundational first part, for a Diaspora situation of experienced socio-religious nonidentity.[107]

(4.2) The paraenetic character of 1 Peter,[108] text-pragmatically geared toward this situation, corresponds to one of the functions we are able to discern for Jewish Diaspora letters. The idea of the elect people of God (1 Pet 2:9-10; here referring to Gentiles by birth), the call to holiness (1:14-16), instruction for conduct "among the Gentiles" (2:12), the exhortation to make their defense to the Gentiles (3:15-17), as well as the references to communion with the "brotherhood in all the world" (5:9; cf. the exhortation to mutual [fraternal] love, 1:22; 3:8; 4:8; Silvanus as "brother," 5:12) and the cohesion of the "living stones" in the building of the "spiritual house" (2:5) take on functions we are able to see, muta-tis mutandis and with varying emphases, in early Jewish Diaspora letters too.[109] Here it becomes patent that 1 Peter is indebted to motivations of paraenesis, drawing on a *heilsgeschichtliche* metanarrative and a communal context that are prefigured in the Jewish, but absent from the Greco-Roman, paraenetic tradition.[110] The theme of suffering is less prominent in Jewish Diaspora letters, although it is addressed in some of the Jewish specimens.[111] This is not to say that paraenesis in 1 Peter otherwise "looks like" paraenesis in Jewish Diaspora letters; one major difference between these and 1 Peter is that many of the former combine exhortation and law to form what may be called Torah paraenesis,[112] while in 1 Peter exhor-tation is characteristically blended with christological and soteriological statements. Nevertheless, the correspondence in the respective relations between election, Diaspora situation, and paraenesis is remarkable.

Compared with Jewish Diaspora letters, there are no statements in 1 Peter that explicitly color the Diaspora situation as punishment and express hope for a return of the dispersed. However, these two motifs are not present in all Jewish Diaspora letters either. Qualification of the Diaspora as punishment is mainly to be found in some letters of the Jere-miah-Baruch type, in which the exile becomes transparent for the present situation of dispersion.[113] There are hints of this transparency in 1 Peter (see below), and we must therefore ask why this letter does not follow the lead of the Jewish specimens in their qualification of the Diaspora. The reason is apparently the different notion of Diaspora in Christian letters (see above); there, it is not a physical, historical dispersion that would lend itself to explanation in terms of punishment. This difference notwithstanding, one could even argue that the references to suffering for only "a little while," to the "imperishable heritance . . . kept in heaven," and to future glory (1 Pet 1:3-5, 8-9; 4:13; 5:10) remotely correspond to the hope for an ingathering of the dispersed in (some) Jewish Diaspora letters.[114]

(4.3) A further link with the Diaspora letter tradition in 1 Peter is the mention of Babylon as the alleged place of composition (5:13: ἀσπάζεται ὑμᾶς ἡ ἐν Βαβυλῶνι συνεκλεκτή). This mention in the letter closing—more likely referring to a church than to a female individual—suggests a correspondence with Diaspora in the letter opening,[115] forming an *inclusio* around the entire letter. This correspondence is easily missed when Babylon is too quickly taken as a code name hinting at Rome as the place of the letter's origin. Numerous scholars have opted for this solution (most of them concluding from this a post-70 CE origin of 1 Peter, *pace* C.-P. Thiede),[116] some of them with the further reaching thesis that this is evidence for 1 Peter's factual composition in Rome, perhaps in a Petrine circle or "school."[117] Often a pertinent article by Claus-Hunno Hunzinger is invoked to prove the point.[118] However, careful reading of this article and the sources suggests a much more nuanced picture. First, early evidence for this identification of Rome is sparser and less unambiguous than sometimes claimed by those relying on Hunzinger. While two passages in the *Sibylline Oracles* (5:143 [on Nero's alleged flight], 159)[119] use "Babylon" in reference to Rome without invoking broader Babylon traditions, and thus may be indeed using a code name, the situation is different in the book of Revelation (14:8; 16:19; 17:5 [cf. 9]; 18:2, 10, 21), which provides an angled portrait of Babylon as "whore" in light of various prophetic traditions and thus does not merely use a code word.[120] Further, texts such as *2 Baruch* or *4 Ezra*, when speaking of Babylon, *may* contain a reference to Rome, but their narrative situation is consistently that of the Babylonian exile, as Hunzinger carefully notes.[121] What we find again is that, in these texts, the contemporary era of dispersion and Roman domination is seen through the lens of the Babylonian exile. This needs to be taken into account in the interpretation of 1 Peter. If Rome were indeed meant here, it would more likely be a qualification of Rome as ultimately held responsible for persecution and dispersion[122] rather than an oblique reference by code name, since mere suppression of the name of Rome would not be warranted by the letter's contents. Second, Hunzinger himself suggests that the letter originated in the East,[123] where the respective label for Rome is first attested. While I tend to see in the Babylon reference an allusion to Rome as the purported location of the addressor and as part of the Peter image in 1 Peter, it needs to be emphasized that the way this allusion is made fits the imagery of exile and Diaspora.[124]

Along these lines, 1 Peter can therefore be understood as a letter from the Diaspora (qualified in terms of the Babylonian exile) to the Diaspora. This is a communicative situation that has to be assumed, mutatis mutandis, for the piece of writing in 4QapocrJer C[d] (1.4), too, but it is also alluded to in an early Christian setting by παροικοῦσα, mentioned twice in the *inscriptio* of *1 Clement* (3.3). Since we have seen that Diaspora letters could have been written and/or dispatched from places other than

Jerusalem or Judea (see 1.4–5, 1.7 [Jeremiah to Baruch], and 2.4 [Esth as letter]), the arguments that have been launched so far against a classification of 1 Peter[125] as (early Christian) Diaspora letter can no longer be considered to hold water.

(4.4) Another element common with—to be sure, only some—Diaspora letters is the salutation in 1 Peter 1:2: χάρις ὑμῖν καὶ εἰρήνη πληθυνθείη, "grace to you and peace may abound." The fact that, despite the following verb, the combination χάρις ὑμῖν καὶ εἰρήνη remains firm suggests, in my view, that 1 Peter has taken up and supplemented the well-known Pauline salutation (in its short form, represented by 1 Thess 1:1). Probably the phrase "grace to you and peace" had already gained some sort of apostolic aura.[126] This is corroborated by the way this phrase is supplemented (and thereby significantly modified) by πληθυνθείη, which is clearly taken from epistolary peace greetings in the Greek versions of Daniel (Theodotion and additions in the Septuagint). There, however, the word order is εἰρήνη ὑμῖν πληθυνθείη, which suggests that it was indeed εἰρήνη in the Pauline formula that triggered the supplementation, and that this formula, at the same time, was too firm to be split up. The Greek references, however, are themselves translations of greetings in Aramaic royal encyclicals in the Masoretic Text of Daniel.[127] Both the Greek and Aramaic salutations are unattested outside the biblical Jewish tradition, although they have presumably been loosely modeled on certain Imperial Aramaic greeting formulae.[128] It is likely that their biblical feel was noticed by ancient recipients, at least by those who had some contact with Jewish communities,[129] which has, in my view, to be assumed for the intended audience of 1 Peter on account of the massive use of Old Testament traditions in this letter. With respect to early Christian letter conventions, recourse to this encyclical salutation contributes a non-Pauline accent, which, at such a sensitive location as the prescript of an ancient letter, likely functions as a reading instruction: the saluting apostolic authority of this letter, while sharing some common ground with Pauline tradition, links up with encyclical letter writing in the biblical Jewish tradition.

Interestingly, the same salutation in Aramaic can be found in the three Gamaliel letters as well (שלמכון יסגא). Although such a salutation is not a necessary element of Diaspora letters, it is nevertheless a conventional greeting option for these letters, apparently because it is already biblically connected with circular letters. As already mentioned above, the Letter of Jude and *1 Clement*, the two earliest Christian specimens for comparison with 1 Peter, feature a similar salutation. As is well known, it is debated whether these two texts are independent from 1 Peter. If they are, they may be viewed as witnesses in their own right for a similar use of this conventional greeting—in *1 Clement*, with explicit reference to the situation of παροικία; in Jude, with reference to the (Jerusalem) authority of the brother of the Lord, James. If they are not, they would at least follow 1 Peter in using this greeting formula, supplying their own modifications.[130]

(4.5) Finally, another implication of the Diaspora reference should be noted. The fact that both 1 Peter and James feature this term in their letter openings points to traditional contacts between the two. This can be pursued on various levels, such as (further) material traditions 1 Peter shares with James.[131] Here we shall limit ourselves to the respective author constructions. Apparently it was apposite for apostolic figures associated with the Jewish Christian church in Jerusalem, such as James and Peter, to communicate with their respective addressees in the form of Diaspora correspondence (cf. to some extent also Jude, presented as the "brother of James"). The key to this responsibility for the Diaspora is probably the traditional image of these apostles. This also comes to bear on a comparison of these texts with Paul and his letters. While Paul apparently adopts the quasi-official claim and the community address from Jewish epistolography (as per Taatz), but merges it with conventions and topoi of Greco-Roman letter writing, the main representatives of Palestinian Jewish Christianity are more specifically associated with the tradition of Jewish Diaspora letters, many of which are either encyclical or addressed to a specific region. Further, it is in this respect remarkable that Peter and particularly James are the key figures involved in the realization of the third Diaspora letter in the New Testament, the letter with the apostolic decree (Acts 15:23-29): in Acts 15:14, James virtually skips over the summary on "signs and wonders," to which Barnabas and Paul are cut down (15:12), and instead resumes what "Symeon"—that is, Peter—has related earlier and comes up with the proposal of a written decree. Most likely, we see here a reflection of the responsibilities attached to (the images of) James and Peter. In other words, it seems to be no coincidence that the two figures taking the floor as authors of New Testament Diaspora letters are also crucially involved in the third letter of this type in the New Testament. However we are to imagine these links (common tradition, or dependence of at least 1 Peter on Acts?), the respective author constructions seem to map apostolic tradition apart from Paul and lend it a specific epistolary voice, perhaps in response to an early collection of Pauline letters.

But not only this: the different apostolic images of James and Peter also render plausible why, if we compare the Letter of James with 1 Peter, the author fictions were developed in their present form. Here, regarding the image of the Apostle Peter—who, according to early Christian tradition, was initially the leading figure of the Jewish Christian community of

Jerusalem and Judea; then, after a period of imprisonment under Agrippa I, left Jerusalem for "another place" (Acts 12:17), probably taking up a more itinerant lifestyle (cf. 1 Cor 9:5); at some point began to accept Gentiles into the church (cf. Acts 10:1–11:18) and was involved in the mission to the Gentiles (cf. 1 Cor 1:12); and finally suffered and was crucified (cf. John 21:18-19) in Rome (cf. *1 Clem.* 5:3-4; Ign. *Rom.* 4:3; *Ascen. Isa.* 4:2-3)[132]—a Diaspora letter to suffering Christians of largely Gentile provenance, purportedly written not from Jerusalem but from "Babylon," may be considered nothing less than what is to be expected.

PART V

JOHANNINE EPISTLES

CHAPTER 13

THE JOHANNINE EPISTLES AS CATHOLIC
EPISTLES

John Painter

In the last fifty years, the Catholic Epistles (CE) have received little attention as a corpus within the New Testament canon alongside the Gospels
and Paul.[1] One reason for this is the renewed focus on the Johannine
literature in this period taking 1, 2, and 3 John into a different context.
This tends to support the notion that the CE are the "leftovers." There
are three other notable leftovers—Acts, Hebrews, and Revelation—that
belong to no corpus. There is no ancient evidence of a tendency to include
Acts, Hebrews, and Revelation within the Catholic corpus.[2] Not being
part of another collection was insufficient reason for inclusion amongst
the CE. Thus we need to identify positive reasons for the inclusion of the
seven writings that make up the CE. At first sight, they do not seem to
have much in common. In this paper, the integrity of the CE is viewed
from the perspective of the Johannine Epistles.[3]

Before examining the place of the Johannine Epistles within the
canon, something needs to be said about the surviving literary evidence
of their path to canonical status. Like the CE generally, evidence of the
use of the Johannine Epistles is late and, in the case of 2 and 3 John,
their status was disputed. Eventually the Johannine association ensured
their acceptance. It has not always been recognized just how important
2 and 3 John are for our understanding of the Johannine Epistles and

their place within the CE. Judith Lieu has helped to redress that imbalance, but work remains to be done to nuance our understanding of the relationship of the Johannine Epistles to each other, the context in which they were shaped, and the contribution they made to the development of Christian life and thought.

Tradition

Perhaps the earliest evidence for recognizing the Johannine literature is to be found in the titles of the books. The titles of the Gospels may be from the early second century, though evidence cannot be traced beyond the last quarter of the second century. The title, "According to John," does not explicitly lift the veil of anonymity by identifying which John is meant. Probably the apostle, son of Zebedee and brother of James, is intended. There are minor variations in the title of 1 John in the Greek manuscripts, all of which bear a title. The great codices of Vaticanus (B), Sinaiticus (ℵ), and Alexandrinus (A) have the title *The First Epistle of John*. Other manuscripts add the descriptions *apostle* and *evangelist*. These are clearly secondary clarifications to identify the John named in the title. Second and Third John are named *The Second* and *Third Epistles of John*, respectively.

Just how the name of John came to be associated with these books is unclear. Nothing within the books provides a clue. In the Johannine literature, only the text of Revelation (1:1, 4, 9) lifts the veil on its author, naming him John. Because tradition, at least from the time of Irenaeus, linked the Gospel, the three Epistles, and Revelation, this might be enough to suggest the name of John as the author of all five books. But Revelation does not identify this John; nor does the title of the Gospel or many forms of the title of the Epistles, though, as mentioned above, some add *apostle* and *evangelist*.

Irenaeus provides important information concerning John and the book of Revelation. Reference is generally to the Apocalypse of John (*Haer.* 1.26.3) or what John says in the Apocalypse (*Haer.* 4.17.6; 4.21.3; 5.28.2; 5.34.2), but on four occasions this John of the Apocalypse is described as "the Lord's disciple" (*Haer.* 4.20.11; 4.30.4; 5.26.1; 5.35.2), a description he regularly uses of the author of the Gospel and Epistle of John, which seems to include 2 John also.

The use of the titles thus needs to be illuminated by other literary testimonies. Before Irenaeus, who wrote in the last quarter of the second century, we have no certain reference to the Epistles, only possible allusions. These are set out chronologically, beginning with *1 Clement* (circa 96 CE), attributed to Clement, an early bishop of Rome. Allusions are noted in descending order of probability: 49:1 (cf. 1 John 5:1-3); 49:5;

50:3 (cf. 1 John 2:5; 4:12, 17-18); 27:1; 60:1 (cf. 1 John 1:9). In the final group of texts, reference to God who is faithful and righteous is so common in the Old Testament that it is not possible to identify an allusion to 1 John on this basis.

The Epistles of Ignatius, bishop of Antioch, are dated circa 110–115 CE. He was familiar with and wrote to the churches of Asia Minor, the traditional area associated with John. That he mentions Paul but not John is puzzling if the Johannine tradition is associated with this region. Allusions may be another matter, but we are again in an area where lack of certainty has led to widely divergent views. Some allusions may be seen in Ignatius, *To the Ephesians* 11:1 (cf. 1 John 2:18); 15:3 (cf. 1 John 3:2).

Many of the following works cannot be placed with any degree of probability with regard to time and place of authorship. The evidence of the *Didache* is marred by uncertainty as to its date and provenance. Some scholars hazard a guess at a very early date. Links between it, the Gospel of Matthew, and Ignatius have encouraged some scholars to locate it in Antioch. A date around 120 CE (after Ignatius) seems marginally more probable than alternatives. Some allusion might be seen in *Didache* 10:5-6 (cf. 1 John 2:17). The reference there, "to perfect it in your love," may draw on the negative "not perfected in love" of 1 John 4:18; *Didache* 11:7 (cf. 1 John 4:1); *Didache* 16:4 (2 John 7). The case for such allusions must be regarded as very tentative.

The *Epistle of Barnabas* may be from the mid-second century CE. The crucial Johannine christological confession finds parallels in 5:9-11; 12:10 (cf. 1 John 4:2; 2 John 7); 14:5 (cf. 1 John 3:4, 7, 8). But this might arise from contact with tradition rather than the text of 1 or 2 John.

The *Second Epistle of Clement*, though disingenuously attributed to Clement of Rome, must date from the mid-second century CE. In 6:9, there is a reference, "Who shall be our advocate [παράκλητος]," that might allude to 1 John 2:1. Given that in the New Testament, παράκλητος is used only by the Gospel and 1 John, there seems to be a prima facie case. But there is a problem in that 1 John appeals to the advocate for the situation "if we sin," whereas *2 Clement* implies that the advocate is effective only for those having "pious and righteous works." This difference undermines confidence in a possible allusion.

From the middle of the second century, phrases and themes similar to those in 1 John become more common in works like the *Shepherd of Hermas*. In *Hermas, Mandate* 3:1, "in him there is no lie" perhaps echoes 1 John 2:27. *Hermas, Mandate* 12:3:5 may echo the assertion that "his commandments are not burdensome" in 1 John 5:3. In *Hermas, Similitude* 9:24:4, reference to receiving the Spirit might reflect 1 John 4:13. The proposed allusions are not particularly persuasive.

The writings of Justin also contain parallel phrases. That reference to Christ's blood in *Apologia i* 32.7 might echo 1 John 1:7 is supported by *Apologia i* 32.8, which refers to the seed of God, the word, dwelling in the believer (cf. 1 John 2:14; 3:9). *Dialogus cum Tryphone* 123.9 might express ideas found in 1 John 2:3; 3:1, 22; 5:3, where we find the association of keeping the commandments with being called children of God.

The *Epistle of Diognetus* 10:2–3 is close to 1 John 4:9, 19 in regarding the idea of the sending of the Son as an expression of the love of God to which human love is the response. Reference to the Word as the one who was from the beginning (*Diogn.* 11:4) echoes 1 John 1:1; 2:13-14.

Polycarp's *Epistle to the Philippians* (not later than 140 CE) contains a number of passages almost certainly dependent on both 1 and 2 John. It speaks of false brethren (6:3) and says that "everyone who does not confess Jesus Christ to have come [perfect infinitive] in the flesh is Antichrist," then goes on to say that they belong to the devil (7:1). The comparison is with 1 John 4:2-3, which uses the perfect participle, and perhaps 2 John 7, which uses the present participle. Both texts also refer to the antichrist. First John 3:8, 10 also speak of children of the devil. Polycarp also speaks of the Word that is from the beginning (7:2), which echoes the common theme of 1 John 1:1; 2:7, 24; 3:11. That Polycarp knew at least 1 John is supported by the evidence of Eusebius concerning Papias, the bishop of Hierapolis and contemporary of Polycarp. Papias made use of the testimonies of the First Epistle of John (*Hist. eccl.* 3.36.1–2; 3.39.17).

The most important witness to the Johannine Epistles in the second century is Irenaeus, a native of Asia Minor, who became bishop of Lyons and wrote circa 180 CE. See the evidence of Irenaeus (*Haer.*), which is often repeated by Eusebius (*Hist. eccl.*). *Adversus haereses* 3.1.1 corresponds with *Historia ecclesiastica* 5.8.4; *Haer.* 2.22.5 with *Hist. eccl.* 3.23.3; *Haer.* 3.3.4 with *Hist. eccl.* 4.14.3–8 and 3.23.4; the letter to Florinus with *Hist. eccl.* 5.20.4–8. See also *Adversus haereses* 1.8.5; 1.9.1–3; 2.2.5; 2.22.3; 3.31.3 (cf. *Hist. eccl.* 5.25.1–7); 3.8.3; 3.11.1–4, 7, 9; 3.15.2, 5, 8; 3.16.5, 8; 3.22.2; 4.2.3; 4.6.1; 4.10.1; 5.18.2; 5.33.3; and *Epideixis tou apostolikou k rygmatos* 43.94. From these references, it is clear that Irenaeus identified John, the disciple of the Lord, with the Beloved Disciple as author of the Gospel and Epistles, published in Ephesus in the reign of Trajan. He claimed to have this information from the elders of Asia Minor, of whom he names Polycarp of Smyrna and Papias of Hierapolis (see Ep. ad Flor., *Hist. eccl.* 5.20.4–8; Ep. ad Victor of Rome; *Haer.* 2.22.5; 3.1.1, 4; 5.33.3–4). Irenaeus had grown up around Ephesus, where he had come to know Polycarp and Papias.

Nevertheless, Irenaeus' use of the Johannine Epistles is sparse and reveals some puzzles. In *Adversus haereses* 1.16.3, he quotes from 2 John

11 as from John, the disciple of the Lord. He also quotes from 1 John 2:8-19, 21-22 in 3.16.5 and 1 John 4:1-2; 5:1; 2 John 7-8 in 3.16.8. Thus it is clear that Irenaeus knew both 1 and 2 John, but the form of the quotation in 3.16.8 refers back to the epistle already quoted (in 3.16.5) and, having quoted 2 John 7-8, continues with a reference to "this epistle" before quoting 1 John 4:1-2; 5.1. Thus it seems that the form in which Irenaeus knew 1 and 2 John did not distinguish the two epistles. The reason for this may be that 2 John was originally the covering letter for 1 John, and it was in that combined form that 1 and 2 John were known to Irenaeus in Asia Minor. See also 1.9.5, which may allude to the "spirit of error" of 1 John 4:6; and 5.1.1, which may allude to 1 John 1:1-4, "hearing with our own ears . . . we have communion with him."

To this point, there is evidence of allusion to and quotation of 1 John. In addition, Irenaeus quotes from 2 John 7-8, but seems to attribute this quotation to the same epistle as the other quotations. If the earlier uncertain allusions to 2 John 7 can be accepted, they too support a knowledge of 1 and 2 John. We have no way of knowing whether they were known at the time as two separate epistles or in some combined or attached form such as was known to Irenaeus. We have no evidence of the use of 3 John by the end of the second century.

The Muratorian Fragment (so-called canon) is known from an eighth-century Latin fragment. Because of the barbarous Latin, it is thought to be the translation of a Greek original, perhaps dating from the late second century. Traditionally it is located in Rome. While evidence of a Greek original does not preclude this, as Greek was common in Rome until well into the third century, it does not make the Roman case secure. Thus A. C. Sundberg ("Canon Muratori: A Fourth Century List" [1973], 1–41) argues for an Eastern origin in the fourth century. Whatever its origins, it is not clear that it is an official list. Thus it is misleading to refer to it as a canon. The text deals with the conditions that gave rise to the writing of the Gospel of John and makes reference to Johannine Epistles. The latter is unclear. The most probable rendering of the rather obscure text finds in it the acceptance of two Johannine Epistles in the Catholic Church. This is probably a reference to 1 and 2 John. As 1 John 1:1-3 had been quoted already in defense of the Gospel, it was certainly known, and other evidence supports the recognition of 2 John as the second epistle in view. A less likely alternative is that the earlier reference to 1 John in relation to the Gospel implied its place there with reference to 2 and 3 John, the two (other) Johannine Epistles, following. But, although there is evidence placing the Johannine Epistles after the Gospel and before Acts in later Western manuscripts (such as Codex Bezae Cantabrigiensis), the Epistles are not separated. Consequently, the Muratorian Fragment also supports the use of 1 and 2 John, further raising a question about the history of 3 John.

From the end of the second century, there is evidence of widespread and frequent use of 1 John in both West and East. Tertullian cites 1 John almost fifty times; Clement of Alexandria frequently cites 1 John (*Strom.* 3.5.44; 3.6.45 cite 1 John 2:4, 18-19; and *Quis div.* 37.6 cites 1 John 3:15), naming it "the greater Epistle" (*Strom.* 2.15.56), implying that he knew at least one other Johannine epistle, which is confirmed by his commentary on 2 John in his *Hypotyposeis*. Although this work is lost, there is a Latin translation of part of this work entitled *Adumbrationes*, attributed to Cassiodorus (ca. 540 CE). By the middle of the third century, there is evidence of the use of 3 John also. Eusebius attests Origen's use of both 2 and 3 John (*Hist. eccl.* 6.25.10). Dionysius of Alexandria knew that John wrote the Gospel and Epistles, but rejected the Johannine authorship of Revelation (*Hist. eccl.* 7.25.7–8, 11). The seventh Council of Carthage recognized 2 John as well as 3 John; the thirty-ninth Festal Letter of Athanasius (367 CE) lists the CE in order, including 1, 2, and 3 John; and the Synod of Hippo (393 CE) and the Council of Carthage (397) acknowledged the three Epistles as Johannine. Didymus the Blind (d. 398 CE) wrote a commentary on the three Epistles. Thus, by the end of the fourth century, acceptance of the three Epistles was more or less complete in the East and the West.

Only in the third century does evidence of the use of 3 John appear, and doubts about the authorship and authority of 2 and 3 John continue throughout the third and much of the fourth centuries. R. E. Brown notes that 1 John was associated with the Gospel and, like it, was attributed to the authorship of the Apostle John. But 2 and 3 John name their author as the Elder. Eusebius' reading of Papias distinguishes the Elder from the apostle (*Hist. eccl.* 3.39.4). Thus, not only because they were short letters and seemingly insignificant in comparison with 1 John, but also because, at least according to some authorities, they lacked apostolic authorship, their road to acceptance was more difficult than it was for 1 John.[4] Although 2 John is first evidenced in connection with 1 John, it became disconnected, perhaps because 1 John also existed independently and the assumed author of 1 John was the apostle, while the declared author of 2 John was the Elder.

The Canon

The question of the canon is relevant to the Johannine Epistles in a number of ways. How and why did the Johannine Epistles find their way into the canon? Where did they find their home within the canon? What problems are evident in the ordering of the canon?

Place in the canon. The Johannine Epistles are included amongst the Catholic or General Epistles in the great fourth- and fifth-century codices containing the New Testament: Sinaiticus (א) and Vaticanus (B) from the fourth century, Alexandrinus (A) and Ephraemi Rescriptus (C) from the fifth century. Sixty-seven sheets, which contained the CE between the Gospels and Acts, are missing from the great Western codex Bezae (D). Nevertheless, this implies the presence of the Johannine Epistles in the CE of D. Removal of the CE from D means that, apart from a Latin fragment of 3 John 11-15, the important witness of the Western text provides no evidence of the text of the Johannine Epistles.[5] Nevertheless, the Johannine Epistles are well attested in surviving manuscripts.

The naming of the collection as the CE can be traced back as far as Eusebius (*Hist. eccl.* 2.23.23–25), who says that James is the first of the seven CE. Obviously, this is a reference to the order of the collection rather than the order of writing. He also names Jude, but without indicating its place in the seven. Naturally, he names James at the close of the story of James and his martyrdom. James' Epistle is said to be the first of the seven. Why, of the other six, is Jude singled out? Very likely because he, as well as James, is also known as a brother of Jesus. Perhaps he is also named because, with James, Jude forms an *inclusio* marking the boundaries (first and last) of the CE. In the thirty-ninth (Easter) Festal Letter of Athanasius (367 CE), the order of the CE is set out as James, 1 and 2 Peter, 1, 2, and 3 John, Jude. This might have been the order presupposed by Eusebius, though we have no clear indication that it was because he does not name the other CE.

The earliest known use of the term *catholic* is in relation to a single epistle. Clement of Alexandria refers to the letter issuing from the Council of Jerusalem to Gentile believers (Acts 15:22-29) as a "Catholic Epistle" from "all the apostles" (*Strom.* 4.15). As we know, this is Clement's evaluation and is not to be found in the text of Acts. When Eusebius gives Clement's summary account of the canonical writings (*Hist. eccl.* 6.14.1), including disputed works, he explains what is meant by disputed works: "I refer to Jude and the other Catholic Epistles, and Barnabas and the so called Apocalypse of Peter." Clearly this is the language of Eusebius. It seems that Clement named each of the writings and Eusebius, having named Jude, bundles the rest under the title "the rest of the Catholic Epistles." It seems that the title had, by his time, become traditional for the seven.

Clement's reference to a catholic epistle denotes an encyclical letter sent out to Gentile believers, wherever they may be; it was universal in the sense that it was addressed to all Gentile believers. But it was limited in scope, being addressed only to Gentile believers. Eusebius also refers to a certain Apollonius who, circa 200 CE, refuted a Montanist teacher by the name of Themiso. What we know of Apollonius is largely found in Eusebius (*Hist. eccl.* 5.18). One accusation against Themiso is that "in imitation of the apostle, he wrote a certain Catholic Epistle" (5.18.5). There is no suggestion that Themiso referred to his writing as a catholic epistle. Rather, he sent his epistle out to a general readership. Apollonius is affronted by the implications of this action. It implied that Themiso was able "to instruct those whose faith was better than his own." What makes this a catholic epistle is not the title, which it probably did not have, but its address to a general audience. Thus it is Apollonius who names it as a catholic epistle. He also implies that "the apostle" wrote a catholic epistle, because what Themiso did was in imitation of the apostle. To whom did Apollonius refer as the apostle? Perhaps Paul? If so, which epistle is the catholic epistle of Paul? Or, given that 1 John is referred to as the catholic epistle, could it be John, or Peter? Whoever this was, nothing suggests that the epistle concerned was self-styled as a catholic epistle. Rather, it was identified by its general or encyclical address. Concerning which apostle and epistle Apollonius had in mind, we can only guess, and without grounds for thinking we might guess aright. What is important is that we have another indication that a catholic epistle was an encyclical letter.

Use of the term *catholic epistle* to denote an encyclical letter may be confirmed by Origen, who used the term to refer to 1 John (*Comm. Jo.* 1.22.137; 2.23.149) and elsewhere to 1 Peter (*Comm. Jo.* 6.35.175; cf. Eusebius, *Hist. eccl.* 6.25.5). In the case of 1 Peter, the encyclical nature is clear. It is addressed to "the exiles of the dispersion in Pontus, Galatia, Cappodocia, Asia, and Bithynia." To be sure, the proposed circulation is limited to exiles (παρεπιδήμοις), temporary dwellers in the διασπορά. The geographical limitation is not so much the διασπορά, which excludes only Judea. It is the reference to specific regions within the διασπορά (Pontus, Galatia, Cappodocia, Asia, and Bithynia). Given the attribution of this epistle to Peter, the address to Jewish (believers) in the διασπορά should also be taken seriously.

While Eusebius identified James as the first of the CE, there is no earlier reference to James as a catholic epistle. As Eusebius noted, "few of the ancients quote it." Nevertheless, James admirably fits the understanding of catholic in terms of an encyclical. It is addressed "to the twelve tribes in the dispersion." Both 1 Peter and James combine Jewish terms to reinforce the address to Jewish readers. Common to both is the reference to the diaspora. That this is a technical term for the Jewish διασπορά is reinforced by reference to the παρεπιδήμοις in 1 Peter (1:1 and cf. 2:11) and the twelve tribes in James (1:1). The latter in particular, in conjunction with reference to the διασπορά, should not be allegorized in the context of James. It is not to be understood as a metaphor for the new people of God. The reference is limited to a Jewish audience that is likely to self-select as a Jewish believing audience. First Peter is specifically addressed to believing Jews in the διασπορά, and is restricted in scope to Pontus, Galatia, Cappodocia, Asia, and Bithynia. Thus 1 Peter and James qualify as encyclical letters. Second Peter is addressed "to those who have received a faith as precious as ours," and Jude is addressed "to those who are called, who are beloved by God the Father and kept by Jesus Christ." These forms of address have no geographical or ethnic limitations. They are addressed to believers anywhere and everywhere they may be found. They, too, qualify as encyclicals.

Canonical orders. The uniform placement of the Gospels first in the canonical collections of the New Testament suggests that the fourfold Gospel was the first collection of early Christian writings to receive recognition. According to Origen, the canonical order of the Gospels is based on the order of writing (see *Hist. eccl.* 6.25.4–6).[6] Although the Pauline Epistles are the earliest Christian writings, there is good reason to think that the Gospels formed the earliest public collection. We would expect the Pauline corpus to follow the Gospels unless Acts had already attained recognition in its own right, as it did with the canonical order of Gospels, Acts. In the Western canon, Acts is followed by the Pauline corpus. Running contrary to this position is the Western witness of Codex Bezae (D), where the CE follow the Gospels, before Acts and the Pauline corpus.[7] While the placement before Acts is unique, the placement prior to the Pauline corpus is consistent with the witness of the Eastern canon.

The Eastern alternative is represented by Vaticanus (fourth century), the catecheses of Cyril of Jerusalem delivered around 348 CE, the fifty-ninth canon of the Council of Laodicea (360 CE), and Athanasius' Easter Letter of 367 CE, which place the seven CE after Acts and before the Letters of Paul. Certainly the collection of the Pauline corpus antedated the collection of the CE. Placing them before the Pauline corpus reflects a value judgment about the superior apostolic status of the authors of these works, the first three of whom are the pillar apostles mentioned by Paul in Galatians 2:9 (James, Cephas, and John). In this group of apostolic letters, James and Jude are attributed to brothers of Jesus. The other two authors are identified as the two leading disciples of Jesus (according to the Synoptics), who, with James, constituted the three pillar apostles of the Jerusalem church, the mother church of the early Christian movement.

The evidence shows that the Johannine Epistles were accepted and grouped with the CE by the beginning of the fourth century.[8] Both the Pauline corpus and the CE are treated as the work of apostolic authors.

Clearly, the placing of the CE was a matter of some importance and of some difference of opinion. Here, as elsewhere, East and West were divided in their views.

In the CE collection, epistles attributed to James and Jude, the brothers of Jesus, form an *inclusio* around the collection. The order of James, Peter, John corresponds to the order of the pillar apostles according to Galatians 2:9. These three represent the mission and gospel of the circumcision, in contrast to Paul's mission to the nations. While Jude is not mentioned in Galatians, he too, as a member of the family of Jesus, belonged to the Jerusalem mission. The contest for priority between the Pauline and Catholic collections may well have been ideological. But by the fourth century, both collections, and the missions that spawned them, had been domesticated to become undifferentiated expressions of the Great Church, the Catholic Church. In particular, this led to a reading of James and 1 Peter that lacked the distinctively Jewish perspective of the original letters.[9] In the emerging Catholic Church, the differentiation between Jew and Gentile had been assimilated in a movement that increasingly became a part of the Roman Empire. In the meantime, a new differentiation with its own tensions was emerging between East and West. This, too, was a manifestation of the reality of the Roman Empire.

Paul's letters are collected in descending order of length. Following the Pauline corpus, the order of the works is only partly explicable. Hebrews is the longest of the remaining works apart from Revelation, which is appropriately the last book of the New Testament (see the conclusion, 22:16-21). Both fall outside the collections of the Pauline corpus and the CE. Hebrews may follow the Pauline corpus because of its length. That it is not regarded as Pauline is clear. It falls outside the descending order of length of the books in the Pauline corpus. Nevertheless, it might have been placed next because some thought Hebrews to be Pauline in some sense (as Clement and Origen did).[10]

In the CE, James (1,749 words) is slightly longer than 1 Peter (1,678 words), and 1 John (2,137 words) is longer than either of them. James as a single work might have been placed first, but this does not explain why 1 and 2 Peter come before 1, 2, and 3 John. More likely, the order of James, Cephas, and John, named in that order as pillar apostles in Galatians 2:9, influenced the order of the collection of the CE. Although 2 and 3 John are the shortest works (245 and 219 words respectively) in the New Testament, their place was secured ahead of the short epistle of Jude by their connection to 1 John. Thus, within the General Epistles, the collection of Johannine Epistles was recognized (as was the connection of 1 and 2 Peter). In each case, the collection was ordered from the longer to shorter works. Jude, the shortest of the works standing alone, is the last of the CE, and separates the Johannine letters from Revelation.[11] The collection of the CE was more important than the connection between the Johannine Epistles and Revelation, even though tradition as early as Irenaeus acknowledged their connection. The separation might also express the conviction that Revelation was by another hand. The collection of the Gospels was more important than the connection between the Gospel and Epistles of John.

The principle of the order of the Johannine Epistles in the New Testament appears to be based on length, placing the longest first and the shortest last. Thus the canonical order may imply nothing about the order of writing, though it makes good sense as the chronological order. The titles of the epistles clearly indicate that they are associated with the Gospel of John. This is borne out by the additions to the title of 1 John and the discussion of them by Irenaeus. Though divided by the canonical collections, the Johannine literature has again become a focus of modern studies.[12]

The Johannine Epistles as Encyclical Letters

But is 1 John an encyclical letter? If not, what is the meaning of Origen's specific reference to it as "the Catholic Epistle" (*Comm. Jo.* 1.22.137; 2.23.149)? Dionysius of Alexandria, the pupil of Origen, also refers to "the Catholic Epistle of John" (*Hist. eccl.* 7.25.7, 10). He distinguishes this from "the reputed second or third epistle of John" (*Hist. eccl.* 7.25.10–11), neither of which is referred to as a catholic epistle before the fourth century. This seems to be grounded in Origen's distinction when referring to the writings of John: "He has left us also an epistle of very few lines; perhaps also a second and third; but not all consider them genuine; and together they do not contain a hundred lines" (*Hist. eccl.* 6.25.10). The disputed status of 2 and 3 John is noted. Could that be the reason why the designation *catholic epistle* is withheld from them but used without reservation of 1 John? Eusebius may give some support for this understanding of *catholic* when he notes that Origen appealed to the universal acceptance of 1 Peter, which he calls a catholic epistle, but not the disputed 2 Peter (*Hist. eccl.* 6.25.5, 8). There may be something in this. But it is more likely that the specific address of 3 John ("to the beloved Gaius") and 2 John ("to the Elect Lady and her children") made reference to them as encyclical letters seem inappropriate. That they were disputed has a bearing on their canonical status.[13]

What, then, are we to make of 2 and 3 John? Do they, with 1 John, fall outside the classification of an encyclical letter? The position that I support is that 2 John is an encyclical letter. The address "to the Elect Lady and her children" is a metaphor designed to cover a number of house churches in the circle of churches within the radius of the Elder's influence. In this context, *Elect Lady* symbolizes and personifies any one of these particular churches addressed. The members of the church are addressed as her children. The concluding salutation, addressed directly in the second person, confirms this reading. "The children of *your* elect sister greet [ἀσπάζεται] *you* [the Elect Lady]" (emphasis added). But there is no greeting from the sister. There is no separate parting greeting for the children of the Elect Lady. There is no greeting from the Elder, unless he is one of the children of "your elect sister." The reason for this symbolic form of address is that it works for an encyclical letter. Second John can serve as a letter to any one of the churches in the Elder's circle of influence.

But is 2 John of sufficient weight to justify an encyclical letter? It is if it is seen to be a letter accompanying and introducing 1 John. Support for this conclusion is to be found in the evidence that 2 John was first known attached to 1 John. Irenaeus quotes it as if it were part of 1 John. First John certainly needed some personal introduction if it were to be sent beyond the author's local community.[14] But if 1 John were designed to be used both in the author's community and amongst the house churches within the circle of his influence, that could account for its lack of opening address. It has something of a personal closing in the exhortation of 5:21, "Little children, guard/keep yourselves from idols." But, with 2 John as an introductory letter addressed to the Johannine circle of churches, the problem of lack of personal address at the beginning of 1 John is overcome. Second John briefly introduces the two major issues handled in 1 John. As in 1 John, the interrelationship of the two issues is made clear, as is the relationship of the two issues to the false teachers (deceivers) who have gone out, separating from fellowship with the Elder. The two issues concern the refusal to confess Jesus Christ come in the flesh and the rejection of the obligation to love one another. As in 1 John, the crisis within the Johannine circle of churches is viewed as an eschatological phenomenon, with the opponents being named the deceiver and the antichrist. Second John also extends the scope of 1 John, taking up a closely related issue not dealt with in 1 John. It exhorts the readers to have nothing to do with those who do not agree with the teaching of the Elder. Such people are to be given no hospitality, not even a cordial greeting.[15]

If 1 and 2 John can be seen as encyclicals sent within a limited region around the Elder, there seems to be no case for treating 3 John in this way. It is addressed to one reader, Gaius. Nevertheless, it seems to be part of the correspondence generated by the issues dealt with in 1 and 2 John. Probably in response to the circulation of 1 and 2 John, Diotrephes rejected 1 and 2 John (see 3 John 9) and refused to give hospitality to messengers/missionaries emanating from the Elder. What is more, he forbade those under his influence to do so and excommunicated any who failed to comply with his decision. His actions can be seen as a response to the policy of the Elder outlined in 2 John 10-11. It is also intelligible as a refusal to give hospitality to all traveling missionaries, the assertion of local authority over itinerant authority (see the issue dealt with in the *Didache*). Thus 3 John is clearly relevant to the issues dealt with by the encyclical letters, 1 and 2 John. While it was not itself an encyclical, as it was addressed to Gaius, it was drawn into the CE by association. The Johannine Epistles were addressed to a circle of house churches, perhaps around Ephesus, though this is little more than a hazardous guess. Third John was addressed to one person, Gaius, who was a leader in one of the churches in this circle. The issues of 3 John clearly illuminate our understanding of 1 and 2 John.

But is their being encyclical letters all that binds the seven CE together as a collection? Our suspicion is that these works are bundled together in this way for want of a more suitable collection, and the number of seven epistles might have symbolic significance. At the same time, we have seen that this small collection was not a catchall for writings that found no natural place in the major collections.

Relationship of the Epistles to Each Other

Detailed argument concerning the relationship of the epistles to each other calls for a full exegesis of the Johannine Epistles. Only an outline can be given in this paper. It argues that 2 John stands in a close relationship to each of the other Johannine Epistles, but 3 John is more independent of the language and subject matter of 1 John. The common letter form, authorial address, and subject matter provide a basis for a common stock of language in 2 and 3 John. Both deal with the issue of the practice of hospitality in the mission. Strecker thinks the literary evidence points to their independence of 1 John and argues that they are earlier than 1 John.[16] The theory of independence is possible because the Elder does not identify himself as the author of 1 John. Nevertheless, Strecker underrates the connections with 1 John, especially those between 1 and 2 John. He also fails to take account of how much the differences arise from the letter form of 2 and 3 John, which is not shared by 1 John. Here it is argued that it is likely that the three epistles were written by the Elder about the same time, perhaps in canonical order.[17] First and Second John may have been sent out to a circle of churches at the same time, with 3 John following a little later. Third John responds to a crisis in one of the regions to which 1 and 2 John were sent. The crisis took the form of the reaction of Diotrephes, who refused to receive what the Elder had written (the combination of 1 and 2 John), and refused hospitality to the messengers and supporters (the brothers of verse 10) of the Elder. He was in a position to enforce his view by excommunicating any in his region who defied his authority by offering hospitality to supporters of the Elder. The Elder's policy of the refusing hospitality to those not in accord with his teaching (2 John 10-11) was met by Diotrephes, who refused hospitality to the supporters of the Elder (3 John 9-10).

Within the limits of the two short letters, 2 and 3 John share significant vocabulary and forms of expression with 1 John. This statement needs to be elaborated. First John stands closer to 2 John than to 3 John, and 2 John is closer to 3 John than to 1 John. Thus, 2 John is the link connecting 1 and 3 John. Unlike 1 John, however, 2 and 3 John clearly comply with the features of the Greco-Roman personal letter, in length, form of address, opening greetings, and farewell. The author of each of the two short letters identifies himself as the Elder, which sets them apart from 1 John. Because 1 John is no letter in the ordinary sense, the letter form and some clear identification of the sender are hardly to be expected.

Self-identification of the author as the Elder is meaningful only if the author was well known to the readers by this designation. Otherwise, we would expect an identification such as "John the Elder." That the author does not add his name implies that he was known. This we must assume unless the letter form of 2 and 3 John is a cloak for some more general publication. Given the independent insignificance of these letters, such a theory seems unlikely. Their relative insignificance is attested by the flimsy evidence of their use in the first two centuries. This was not because of controversy concerning them, but rather because there was not much interest in their contents. Nevertheless, the author's identification of himself as the Elder implies a sense of his own authority as a leader.

Second and Third John are specifically addressed, apparently to individual readers. Third John is addressed to "Gaius the beloved, whom I love in truth." There is no reason to think that Gaius is anything but an individual believer known to the Elder. He is perhaps one of his protégés, included amongst those referred to as "my children" (3 John 4). Given that the Elder writes to him, it is implied that they live some distance apart. Gaius seems to occupy a position of leadership alongside Diotrephes and Demetrios. They may be leaders in the same community or in neighboring communities. Perhaps it is more likely that Demetrios was one of the "brothers" (3 John 3, 5, 10), an itinerant missionary associated with the Elder who was likely to arrive in the locality of Gaius and Diotrephes at any time. While Diotrephes opposed the Elder, Demetrios was a supporter of the Elder. This is indicated by the Elder's fulsome support of Demetrios

(3 John 12). The Elder asserts a threefold testimony, for Demetrios, "by all, by the truth itself, and we also bear witness, and you know our witness is true." If this reading is correct, the drift of 3 John may be to ensure that Demetrios, when he arrives, will receive an appropriate welcome.

Because of the opposition of Diotrephes, Gaius will need to make a strong stand. The Elder reminds Gaius of the hospitality he has shown in the past (3 John 5-7). Reference to past action leads to the exhortation, "Therefore we ought to support such people, so that we may be co-workers with the truth" (3 John 8). Then comes the case of Demetrios. He is most likely one of the brothers who will soon arrive in the locality where Diotrephes and Gaius exercise authority. With the words of 3 John 8 still ringing out, the Elder provides testimonial support for Demetrios (3 John 12).[18]

The major issue in 3 John is the offering of hospitality to those in fellowship with the Elder. This was provided by Gaius but refused by Diotrephes, who would not receive what the Elder wrote to the church (3 John 9). Diotrephes also spread false charges against the Elder and those associated with him (ἡμᾶς seems to include τοὺς ἀδελθοὺς, 3 John 10). This group is referred to as "fellow workers" (συνεργοὶ) in 3 John 8, reminiscent of the Pauline use of this term to describe his close associates.[19] The expression in 3 John is both similar and different. Where Paul speaks of his fellow workers, the Elder describes himself and his associates as "fellow workers with the truth" (συνεργοὶ τῇ ἀληθείᾳ). Paul remains the dominant figure in his partnerships, but the Johannine reference characteristically gives priority to the truth. Diotrephes refused hospitality to supporters of the Elder, forbade others from providing this, and excommunicated them (ἐκ τῆς ἐκκλησίας ἐκβάλλει) if they did not comply with his wishes.[20]

What was it the Elder wrote to the church (3 John 9)? Most likely this is a reference to 1 John.[21] If this is right, 1 John was written prior to 3 John, and the conflict with Diotrephes could well be an expression of the schism reflected in 1 John 2:18-27; 4:1-6. That need not mean that Diotrephes was one of those who separated from the community of the writer of 1 John. He might have been a sympathizer, as the Elder was, or at least not implacably opposed to them.

What are we to understand by "the church" (ἐκκλησία) in 3 John 3, 6, 9, 10? This term is not used in the other Johannine letters, nor in the Gospel.[22] Reference to something (τι) written to the church (τῇ ἐκκλησίᾳ) suggests that it was not addressed simply to a local church. More likely, it refers to a group of house churches scattered throughout a region and in fairly close communication with each other. The use of ἐκκλησία in 3 John lies somewhere between the Pauline use in 1 and 2 Corinthians and the reference to the universal church found in Ephesians 1:22; 3:10; 5:23-25, 27, 29, 32. Perhaps in Ephesians, ἐκκλησία is a theological concept rather than an empirical church, local or otherwise. Ephesians is not addressed to the church in Ephesus but to the saints in Ephesus. First John was written for a circle of house churches in a region in which the Elder exercised authority. The schism mentioned in 2:19 might have occurred in one local community, perhaps the author's own. It obviously had repercussions throughout the whole network of believing communities, which the Elder collectively designates the ἐκκλησία. Diotrephes refused to receive 1 John and rejected messengers from the Elder, maintaining a harsh discipline to see that his policy was maintained.

Second John is addressed to ἐκλεκτῇ κυρίᾳ καὶ τοῖς τέκνοις αὐτῆς. Two interpretations seem to cover the probabilities: either the elect lady is the head of a house church or the expression is itself an analogy for a local house church, with the reference to her children indicating the individual members of that local church. The latter view seems to be confirmed by the closing greetings from "the children of your elect sister," which is apparently a reference to the members of the author's community. This confirms the probability that the Johannine Epistles were addressed to a network of local churches in some region. As in 3 John (5-8, 10, 12), the issue of hospitality is at the heart of 2 John 10-11. Both letters provide evidence of the mobility of missionaries within the network of Johannine churches. Together, they show that there was a mutual rejection of missionaries by the Elder and his opponent Diotrephes. If 2 John accompanied 1 John and was rejected by Diotrephes, his rejection of messengers from the Elder might have been a response to the Elder's attempt to prevent hospitality being shown to those who did not agree with his teaching (2 John 10-11).

If 2 John is an introduction to 1 John, 2 John 7 should be looked at in relation to 1 John 2:18-24; 4:1-6. Reference to many deceivers (πλάνοι) who have gone out into the world is reminiscent of 1 John 2:18, which mentions that many antichrists have appeared. They deny that Jesus is the Christ, which the author says is a denial of the Father and the Son (1 John 2:22-23). This finds further elaboration in 4:1-6, where the antichrist is recognized by the refusal to confess Jesus Christ is come in the flesh (ἐν σαρκὶ ἐληλυθότα). Second John 7 deals with these details in a way that clarifies the close connection between 1 John 2:18-27 and 4:1-6. The three passages are linked by the identification of the antichrist. In a variety of ways, these three passages make clear that the expectation of a single eschatological figure, the antichrist, has been modified by the appearance of a multiplicity of figures.[23] Thus 1 John 4:1-6 and 2 John 7 confront the issue of the secessionists, introduced in 2:18-25. In 2 John

7, the many deceivers are recognized by their failure to confess Jesus Christ coming in the flesh (ἐρχόμενον ἐν σαρκί). The context of each passage (1 John 4:1-6 and 2 John 7) concerns confession or failure to confess Jesus Christ in the flesh.

The denial that Jesus is the Christ (1 John 2:22) is the equivalent of the refusal to confess Jesus Christ having come (coming) in the flesh (4:2 and 2 John 7).[24] There is no explicit reference to deceivers in the description of those who refuse to confess that Jesus is the Christ (2:18-25). The many deceivers (πολλοὶ πλάνοι) are identified with the deceiver (ὁ πλάνος) and the antichrist in 2 John 7. But when 1 John 2:26 says, "I wrote these things to you concerning those who would deceive you [τῶν πλανώτων]," it refers back to identification of the antichrist with the appearance of many antichrists in 2:18-25. The fluidity with which these letters express agreement suggests the freedom of a common author rather than the stereotyping of a copyist. This freedom is seen in the way each letter expands the expectation of a singular deceiver/antichrist into the plural, many deceivers/antichrists. They do this because of the contemporary crisis being faced, a crisis involving many deceivers (1 John 2:26 and 2 John 7), many false prophets (1 John 4:1). Given the lack of any known precedent for use of the term *antichrist*, this overlapping use of the term and the freedom with which this common understanding emerges are impressive evidence of the close connection between the two letters.[25]

In the common christological confession, the main difference in language is between the tenses of ἐληλυθότα (1 John 4:2) and ἐρχόμενον (2 John 7). The present participle of 2 John 7 has been taken as a reference to the future coming in the Parousia.[26] If that is the case, the issue of 2 John 7 is quite different from that of 1 John 4:2, which refers to the incarnation (cf. John 1:14). It is more likely, however, that 2 John 7 also refers to what we have come to call the incarnation. In 1 and 2 John, it is Jesus Christ who has come (or comes) in the flesh. We should not expect exact agreement of language in each case, as if a precise formula with the authority of some church council were in view. Rather, the language is more fluid and becomes the basis of a more uniform formulation in a later century. The language of 2 John 7 probably presupposes 1 John 4:2. If that is correct, those letters belong together. Given that 2 John 7 summarizes a central issue for 1 John, overlaps discussion of the new commandment (abiding in the Father and the Son), and uses the language of the confession of faith (ὁμολογεῖν), all in the space of thirteen verses, a good case can be made for recognizing 2 John as an accompanying letter introducing and commending 1 John to a specific community or circle of communities.

First John was written to deal with the crisis precipitated by a schism (2:19). The aftermath threatened to disturb and fragment the believers in a network of house churches in a region where the Elder had exercised some authority. In 3 John, though Gaius is addressed as a supporter, it is clear that the Elder is anxious and concerned that he might waver from his resolve. The reason is that Diotrephes rejects the authority of the Elder and refuses hospitality to his supporters, excommunicating from his house church anyone who resists his wishes. Given that he could do this, Diotrephes must have exercised considerable authority in the community with which Gaius had some connection. But the Elder was not without support, and not only from Gaius; it seems that there were others, who were part of the community where Diotrephes exercised authority, who wished to offer hospitality to those who came to them from the Elder. In contrast to the actions of Diotrephes, the Elder was content to use strong exhortation. It is a moot point whether this "softer" course of action is an indication of an inability to enforce excommunication rather than the deliberate choice of persuasion. Yet the opponents of 1 John 2:19 were not excluded. They separated themselves from the community of the Elder; "they went out from us."

Third John was written to bolster the support of those, like Gaius, who were inclined to acknowledge the Elder's authority, in spite of the authoritarian action of Diotrephes. Though the Elder writes of Diotrephes in threatening terms, the best he can do is warn what will happen "*if* I come" (3 John 10; emphasis added). What he foreshadows is not particularly forceful: "I will call attention to what he is doing in spreading false charges against us [the Elder and the brothers]." He then draws attention to Diotrephes' policy of excommunication, the effect of which was to neutralize support for the Elder. The Elder feared the influence that Diotrephes might have on Gaius, with consequences for Demetrios.

Diotrephes may have been sympathetic to secessionists and unwilling to reject them as antichrists and deceivers. Alternatively, Diotrephes may have resented the intrusion of the Elder's authority into the churches in the surrounding area, including his own. However we read this, it seems clear that the disturbance caused by the schism was far from over in this network of the churches. The Elder was concerned to neutralize the influence of the secessionists. One of the consequences of the schism was the widespread trauma, anxiety, and uncertainty of those who remained. It was for this reason that 1 John was written and sent out under the cover of 2 John to each of the churches in the network. Third John was later sent to one of these churches to deal with the specific secondary crisis caused by the enforced policy of Diotrephes.

Johannine Characteristics Common to the Catholic Epistles

Despite their distinctive character, the Johannine Epistles share a number of perspectives common to the CE. These epistles belong to the period following the first blush of growth of the early Christian movement, a period described in terms of the emergence of early Catholicism, with its concern for continuity through routinization and institutionalization. Three issues emerged in the struggle to establish an ongoing movement: stable leadership, correct belief, and sacramental initiation and life establishment. The literature of this period is concerned with establishing the church in the face of heresy. The struggle with the secessionists is not adequately described as a power struggle. The Elder portrays his opponents as themselves deceived and deceiving others (1 John 1:8; 2:26). The error of their way struck at the heart of the faith as understood by the Elder. It affected fundamental belief in God and had consequences for the way believers lived in the world and in relation to others. Failure to love the brothers had as its corollary love of the world and the things of the world.[27] Consequently, the Johannine Epistles reveal a clash of values between the Elder and his supporters on one side and the opponents on the other.

The situation was destabilized by traveling prophets (*Did.*, 2–3 John). Had the opponents simply gone out from the community of the Elder, the problem would have been over and done with. First John 2:19 speaks of their departure, but the epistle bristles with the sense of their presence on every page. If they went out, they did not go far, and the reader senses their appeal to those who remained, luring them to follow. The community of the Elder stood out against the values of the surrounding society. The opponents embraced those values, which the Elder was aware were a lure to his readers. Hence he exhorts them, "Do not love the world or the things of the world" (1 John 2:15-17). He concludes his appeal to his readers, "Little children, guard yourselves against idols" (1 John 5:21). There is a tendency among some scholars to read this verse metaphorically. To do so shows an inability to grasp the serious problem that idolatry posed for believers in the Greco-Roman world.[28] Indeed, idolatry symbolizes the values of the Greco-Roman world that the Elder calls on his readers to withstand. It seems likely that his opponents saw no reason not to embrace these values enthusiastically. The Elder's call to withstand idolatry was at the same time the call to withstand his opponents.

The struggle with the opponents brings to light the problem of sin in the Johannine community. The opponents dealt with the problem by denial (1 John 1:8, 10). The Elder calls on his readers to confess their sins (1 John 1:9) and seeks to establish a means by which those who sinned can be restored to their place in the community (1 John 2:1-2; 5:16-17). Thus he deals with the problem of sin within the community through a disci pline of reestablishing the sinner within the community.[29] The struggle with the opponents is portrayed as a struggle with serious error. It involves the sin that leads to death, for which the Elder says he requests no prayer. Yet he does seek to establish a means by which the wayward brother might be restored. In this, the Elder exercises leadership in a network of communities and seeks to strengthen the role of local leaders who are sympathetic to his position. In these communities there were settled leaders, but here were also itinerant prophets and teachers. In the network of communities, the danger threatened to come from itinerants moving in with what the Elder considered to be false teaching. These itinerants came from other settled communities that had separated from the communities loyal to the Elder. Thus, there is no simple evaluation of good, settled leaders over against false itinerant prophets and teachers. The Elder also sought to establish support for itinerant teachers from his own group.

In contrast to James and 1 Peter, there is no suggestion of a specifically Jewish readership of the Johannine Epistles. There is no quotation from the Jewish Scriptures in any of the Epistles. The only clear allusion is the reference to Cain. This probably is not drawn directly from Jewish Scripture. Rather, the tradition of Cain was transmitted widely outside Scripture. The absence of scriptural reference is incompatible with a writing addressed to Jewish readers, especially one attempting to persuade such readers to adopt the writer's point of view. The names of those addressed or mentioned in these writings also confirm a non-Jewish readership. Γάϊος (3 John 1), Διοτρέφης (3 John 9), and Δημήτριος (3 John 12) are all Greco-Roman names and do not suggest a Jewish readership. The final exhortation, "Little children, guard yourselves from idols," is consistent with a letter addressed to those living in the context of the Greco-Roman world, unshielded by the buffer of a surrounding Jewish society.

Relationship to the Gospel of John

The relationship of the Epistles to the Gospel of John is complex. Some kind of relationship is obvious, but it is necessary to work through evidence of similarities and differences if that observation is to be made more precise. Certainly the Johannine Epistles (especially 1 John) and Gospel are closer to each other with respect to language, style, and theology than either of them is to any other early Christian writing in the New Testament. Because some form of relationship is so obvious, scholars have concentrated on differences, with a view to discussing the tradition of common authorship.

Common authorship? For the first half of the twentieth century, the preoccupation was with the question of whether a common author wrote the Gospel and 1 John. In many ways, the assembly of evidence and argument against common authorship reached a watershed in the 1937 paper by C. H. Dodd, *The First Epistle of John and the Fourth Gospel*.[30] The conclusions of his paper appear in more summary form in his 1946 commentary on *The Johannine Epistles*.[31] In these studies, Dodd builds solidly on the work of A. E. Brooke.[32] But Dodd did not have it all his own way. The publication of his commentary provoked a series of responses defending the unity of authorship, the first by W. F. Howard, "The Common Authorship of the Johannine Gospel and Epistles,"[33] and then W. G. Wilson's "An Examination of the Linguistic Evidence Adduced against the Unity of Authorship of the First Epistle of John and the Fourth Gospel."[34] Somewhat later, the response was continued by A. P. Salom in "Some Aspects of the Grammatical Style of 1 John."[35]

Dodd argues that differences between the two writings indicate different authors. About forty words in the Epistle are not used in the Gospel, while groups of important words in the Gospel are not used in the Epistle. Then there is the matter of substantial differences in thought; Dodd argues that 1 John is closer to primitive Christianity and more naïvely open to Gnosticism than is the Gospel.[36] It is sufficient to say here that the relationship to emerging Gnosticism is more apparent in 1 John because the author is specifically confronting the position of his opponents. The language of the opponents makes an impact on the language of the letter, as the author is responding to the position of the opponents. But the author of 1 John is critical of emerging Gnosticism.

Those elements of primitive Christianity that, according to Dodd, separate 1 John from the Gospel concern eschatology, the Spirit, and the death of Jesus. While the imminent future emphasis is more prominent in 1 John, it is not absent from the Gospel (see 5:21-30; 6:39, 40, 44, 54; 12:48; 14:3; 17:24). Attempts to reinterpret the Evangelist's eschatology wholly in realized terms are only possible by excluding such passages. At the same time, a recognition of fulfillment in the present is not absent from 1 John (2:8; 5:20). That is not to say that the nuances in the tension between these two emphases are equally worked out in the two writings. There are differences between the Gospel and 1 John on the teaching concerning the Spirit and the death of Jesus. The Gospel nowhere uses the expression Paraclete of Jesus, or describes him as the ἱλασμός περὶ τῶν ἁματιῶν ἡμῶν (1 John 2:2). On the other hand, 1 John does not speak of the Spirit as the Paraclete or develop the role of the Spirit along the lines found in the Farewell Discourses in the Gospel. Instead, the Spirit inspires the true confession of faith in the confrontation with false prophets understood as antichrists. John 15:26-27 implies a prophetic witness inspired by the Spirit in the context of persecution. This suggests an inspired confession not unlike that of 1 John 4:2, but set in a different historical context. While these differences are not so sharp that they rule out common authorship, they point to quite different situations.

The linguistic evidence adduced to argue for separate authorship is neutralized to a degree by noting that 1 John is only about one-sixth the length of the Gospel, and the two are very different kinds of books. Size, genre, and subject matter have a marked bearing on the language used. The Gospel is predominantly narrative, concerning the mission of Jesus. This is quite different from the discursive nature of 1 John, which has more in common with the language of the discourses of the Gospel, especially the Farewell Discourses, than the narrative sections. Linguistically, the Gospel and 1 John are no more different from each other than the variations we find amongst the Pauline Letters.

The evidence, linguistic and theological, concerning the relationship of 1 John to the Gospel is somewhat inconclusive. As early as we can trace evidence about the order of the Gospels, the Gospel of John was regarded to be the fourth. Evidence within the Gospel itself suggests that it is the product of a lengthy process of composition, and in that process, more than one hand can be discerned (see John 20:30-31 and 21:24-25). From this perspective, the possibility of a Johannine school emerges. Jesus gathered disciples around him, founding what can be understood as a school, though perhaps not as tightly organized as was argued by Birger Gerhardsson.[37]

Johannine school. Examples of schools that studied and handed on teaching traditions are to be found in the philosophical schools and, in the Jewish context, in the "house of Hillel." There is evidence, too, that Philo of Alexandria formed a school that might have influenced the formation of the catechetical school, best known under the leadership of Clement and then Origen in Alexandria. No exact parallel with any of these schools is claimed for the Johannine school, only that there were ample precedents for such a development.[38]

While it is important to distinguish the Johannine school from the community or communities it sought to influence, it should not be distanced from those communities. The school developed its teaching in order to teach the Johannine community. The evidence of the Gospel suggests that, in its development, this process was sometimes more open, so that mission to the world outside was prominently in view. At other times, both the school and the community were suffering trauma and focused on community relations. This may be true of the times after the struggle with the synagogue and after the secession of 1 John 2:19.

Through the struggle with the synagogue, there is evidence that the Johannine community became increasingly isolated from the broader Jewish community.

The survival of the school was threatened by the death of the founder. It might not have survived long after the deaths of the leaders who directly followed him. The school seems to have depended on the vitality and inspiration of the founder. Those who followed him may have been lesser figures. This is suggested by the rich and creative use of symbolism in the Gospel, where a relatively limited vocabulary is used with mastery and to good effect. Of the Epistles, 1 John stands closest to the Gospel. By comparison, its syntax is so unclear that problems confront the reader in almost every verse. In spite of this, the author of 1 John has his moments. "This is the message that we have heard from him and report to you, 'God is light and in him there is not darkness at all'" (1:5). "This is the message that you heard from the beginning, 'Let us love one another'" (3:11). "By this we know love, he gave his life for us and we ought to give our lives for the brethren" (3:16). "Beloved, let us love one another, because love is of God, and every one who loves is born of God and knows God" (4:7). See the whole passage 4:7-12, as well as "God is love, and the one abiding in love abides in God and God abides in him." The love for the brethren is not allowed to remain in the ether. Rather, it is tied to Christian charity in the deepest sense (see 3:17-18). Where the Gospel stands out is in the clarity of its message, in contrast to the often conflicting and unclear statements of 1 John.

While the evidence does not exclude the possibility of a common author, it does not make common authorship probable. The evidence of 1 John and the Gospel leads us to a view of common authorship only in the light of tradition, which we can trace back only as far as the late second century. The gap between that evidence and the origin of the Johannine Gospel and Epistles is too great to inspire confidence in the reliability of the evidence.

The position argued in this commentary is that the evidence makes it unlikely that the Evangelist wrote 1 John. It is true that 1 John is closer to certain parts of the Gospel than to others, especially to the Farewell Discourses. If the Gospel is the culmination of a lengthy process of composition, 1 John may well be closer to some later stage of its development. This may suggest multiple hands in the writing of the Gospel, though there is good reason for thinking that a single inspired vision guided the hands that produced it.

Literary and thematic evidence. The author of 1 John lacks the fundamental literary skills manifest in the Gospel. Commentators note textual problems and the lack of clear meaning in verse after verse of 1 John. By comparison, the meaning of the text of the Gospel is largely free from problems. The first four verses of 1 John constitute a single sentence and provide the unsuspecting reader with fair warning of the difficulties to be faced in untangling the meaning of what follows. Thus, while there are so many connections with the language and thought world of the Gospel, the author of 1 John rarely rises to its literary heights. Care must be taken here in speaking of the Evangelist's literary skills. Certainly he writes clear and correct Greek. But the artistry of the Gospel does not inhere in the command of an impressive vocabulary and a sophisticated use of syntactical constructions. Rather, it is in the impressive use of a limited vocabulary to tell a dramatic story, full of surprises and layered with levels of meaning. The discourses, too, provide an interpretation of the story that illuminates the various layers of meaning. Through this, there emerges what we recognize as the Johannine interpretation of the gospel. This can be seen as making explicit what is, at best, implicit and undeveloped in the gospel tradition. Alongside this achievement, the author of 1 John appears to be somewhat inept. Nevertheless, it is argued that he was working with the tradition of the Gospel of John and interpreting it against the position of his opponents. Perhaps the difficulties of this task led the author to be less than fully coherent from time to time.

Whether or not the Gospel and Epistles have a common author, it is important to note the main lines of contact between 1 John and the Gospel. The main common vocabulary has been set out, with a view to showing how the language of the Gospel and Epistles compares to the rest of the New Testament.[39] There is a good case for recognizing characteristic Johannine language. The force of the evidence is strongest when we take into account the way the Gospel and 1 John use this language. This has been well set out by A. E. Brooke, who shows that the similarities and differences are best weighed when the use of common words is seen in phrases.[40] His work makes free use of the 1881 and 1882 studies by H. J. Holtzmann, whose comparisons, based on the Greek words and phrases, should be consulted by anyone seriously concerned to understand the relationship between these two works and to gain a firm grasp of the nature of the Johannine tradition. Simply listing the parallel texts side by side provides a preliminary analysis, making some observations fairly obvious. Some of the more notable parallels are set out below. Attention is drawn to the use of common and significant words in similar phrases. Specific examples are also related to broader Johannine syntax and style. As far as possible, translation agreement in the comparisons reflects a common use of vocabulary and syntax.[41]

Though Holtzmann argues that the evidence indicates different authors, Brooke (ix) quotes Holtzmann (134) with approval: "In the whole of the first Epistle there is hardly a single thought that is not found in the Gospel." While there are differences between the Gospel and the Epistle, Brooke thinks that none of these preclude common authorship. He argues that an author "who had steeped himself in the thought of the Fourth Gospel might produce the First Epistle." Perhaps John 21 is the work of the same imitator. Nevertheless, Brooke thinks that the tradition of common authorship "remains the most probable explanation known to us" (xviii). In agreement with Holtzmann, I consider 1 John to be the work of another author. I do not doubt that this author was steeped in the thought of the Fourth Gospel. The adaptation of the tradition to meet the crisis caused by the secessionists is a creative achievement, though not of the same order as that we find in the symbolic transformation found in the Gospel. The adaptation of the tradition to deal with a specific crisis in the Johannine circle of churches calls attention to the relationship between 1 John and the Gospel. I accept Brooke's conclusion that the Epistle is a later composition than the Gospel, written to clarify the situation caused by the opponents. This accounts for the limitations of the Epistle when compared with the Gospel, and for the change in viewpoint in 1 John. It does not adequately explain the tangled Greek of 1 John and its consequent lack of clarity. This, more than differences of thought between the Gospel and 1 John, poses a problem for the view of common authorship. Given that the author was steeped in the Gospel, it is not surprising that there are striking similarities.[42]

Evidence of priority. What does this comparison of the prologues reveal? A copyist is likely to follow a text rather mechanically. Yet a more creative use of a source need not provide evidence of a common author. Authors frequently use sources creatively. Brown argues that 1 John's use of the Gospel's prologue manifests the author's literary ineptness by comparison with the evangelist. Nevertheless, Brown also argues that this reinterpretation attempted to clarify the meaning of the Gospel in opposition to the interpretation of the secessionists. But in doing so, Brown fails to show how 1 John clarifies the Gospel.

Alternatively, it has been argued that the prologue of 1 John is a primitive first attempt at what we see more fully developed in the Gospel. Holtzmann considers this order to make sense if common authorship can be demonstrated, but he argues for different authors and the priority of the Gospel. Although A. E. Brooke accepts common authorship, he argues for the priority of the Gospel. Here Holtzmann is persuasive. If common authorship is accepted, the priority of 1 John must follow. There is surely no going back to the confusion of 1 John after the prologue of John. But the priority of 1 John makes no sense of the evidence that 1 John is wholly derivative and dependent on the Gospel, whereas the Gospel is freestanding in relation to 1 John, even though 1 John may clarify aspects of the Gospel.

Strecker suggests that the authors of the Gospel and 1 John independently drew on a common tradition, which he describes as "the independent language and world of ideas of the Johannine school."[43] This view becomes more credible in the form espoused by R. E. Brown, that 1 John was dependent on the Gospel but not necessarily in its final form. My own view is that the Johannine school is not to be understood as a group that brought together the bits and pieces of the Gospel. Rather, the Johannine tradition bears the mark of the powerful vision of one teacher who shaped the school with an inspired interpretation of the Jesus tradition. On this view, any earlier form of this tradition is an earlier form of the Gospel. While Strecker's view cannot be ruled out, it is made less likely by the recognition that 1 John also shares the form of closure found in the Gospel. The language of the concluding statements of purpose (John 20:30-31; 1 John 5:13) is similar in each writing, but with some differences. What is particularly impressive is that, in each case, the closure comes before the end. So conclusion-like is John 20:30-31 that many scholars think it was the original conclusion to the Gospel, perhaps taken over by the Evangelist from a source he used. I am inclined to think that it is a Johannine composition, strongly manifesting distinctive Johannine characteristics. If 20:30-31 was once the conclusion, it seems that chapter 21 was added by other members of the Johannine school (see 21:21-24, especially 21:24), making use of Johannine tradition. Similarly, the conclusion-like 1 John 5:13 is followed by a second ending in 5:14-21. Our first task is to look at 20:30-31 in relation to 1 John 5:13:

> Jesus performed many other signs in the presence of his disciples, which are not written in this book; but *these things* [ταῦτα] are written that you may *believe* that Jesus is the Christ *the son of God* and that believing *in* his *name* you may *have life*. (John 20:30-31; emphasis added)

> I wrote *these things* [ταῦτα] to you that you may know that you *have* eternal *life*, who *believe in* the *name of the son of God*. (1 John 5:13; emphasis added)

The comparison of 1 John 5:13 is mainly with John 20:31. There are striking points of contact and agreement, though the stated purpose of 1 John is certainly not exactly the same as that indicated in John 20:31. It can be said to build on that purpose in a way reminiscent of 20:31. Both refer to the purpose of writing, using a common verb (different tenses of γράφω) and concerning a common subject. For both, what is written is referred to as ταῦτα, though its antecedent is the Gospel, encompassing a collection of signs, on the one hand and the Epistle on the other. For both, the purpose is stated using ἵνα, with the following verb in the subjunctive mood. The content, with some variation, is in terms of believing and having eternal life. It is difficult to resist the conclusion that the one was based on the other.

If literary dependence is suspected, this evidence implies the use of the Gospel by the author of 1 John. The placing of 1 John 5:13 prior to the end of the Epistle seems to presuppose the comparable conclusion of the Gospel prior to its actual end. Because chapter 21 appears to have been added by a hand or hands other than those of the Evangelist, this implies that 1 John presupposes the final form of the Gospel, including chapter 21.

The dependence of 1 John on the Gospel is also implied by a comparison of the stated purposes. The Gospel was written so that its readers may come to believe and thus have eternal life. The Evangelist simply asserts that those who believe have eternal life. The objective is to lead the readers to believe, and the strategies of the Gospel are designed to achieve this end. Whether the Evangelist used a present or an aorist subjunctive (πιστεύ[σ]ητε) in 20:31, he wrote to promote belief, because such belief opened the way to eternal life. It need not be shown in detail that this belief assumes the christological content proclaimed by the Gospel, because the point to be made here is simply that the purpose of the Gospel is to lead readers to believe. But 1 John is written to those who already believe, and the purpose of the letter is to assure them that they have eternal life. It is to provide assuring knowledge (5:13).

To this point, differences in content have been ignored in order to draw out the strong connections between the two passages. Some of the differences are consequences of the genre of the Gospel and the kind of writing that 1 John is. While the Evangelist was aware that the Gospel was a book (20:30), both authors refer to their writings as "these things" (ταῦτα) (John 20:31; 1 John 5:13). In each writing, something different is in view; the signs (σημεῖα) narrated in the Gospel are in view in the Evangelist's use of ταῦτα, while the author of 1 John refers more straightforwardly to what he has written. The language of the Gospel, using the passive (γεγραμμένα . . . γέγραπται), is suggestive of a reference to Scripture. The author of 1 John unpretentiously says, "I wrote [ἔγραψα] these things to you."

The Evangelist wrote, "that you may believe that Jesus is the Christ . . . that believing in his name you may have life." First John 5:13 assumes that truth but needs to concentrate on another problem. The assurance of eternal life had been shaken amongst the Johannine believers, or some of them at least. First John is written to assure: "that you may *know* that you have eternal life, who believe in the name of the Son of God" (emphasis added). This difference of purpose is explicable as a consequence of the confusion and uncertainty produced by the schism involving the departure of a significant group from what had been the believing community (1 John 2:18-19).

That the community left behind was destabilized by the schism was at least the perception of the author of 1 John. First John is preoccupied with the task of reestablishing confidence and community. His strategy is twofold: to make his readers aware (that you may *know*) (1) that the opponents were in error and (2) that those who believe have eternal life. To this end, it is crucial that the object and content of belief be "correct." Both the Gospel and 1 John focus on the correct content, using ὅτι clauses to clarify the content of belief and knowing. The use of ὅτι is concentrated in the Gospel (271 times) and the Johannine Epistles (78 times). Elsewhere, it is used 141 times in Matthew, 101 times in Mark, 173 times in Luke, 120 times in Acts, 282 times in Paul (including the deuteropaulines), and 62 times in Revelation. Thus there is a far greater concentration in the Johannine Gospel and Epistles than in any other part of the New Testament. Even here, however, there are differences in the midst of a profound common perspective. In the Gospel, believing and knowing seem to be interchangeable to a large degree, so that those who believe have eternal life (3:16), as do those who know (17:3). The order of believing and knowing (8:31-32) can be reversed to knowing and believing (4:53).[44] In 1 John 5:13, knowing is the self-conscious awareness of believing—and awareness of eternal life as its consequence. It is a more reflective response to the reality of believing than is to be found in the Gospel. To know or believe is one thing; to reflect—that is, to know that you know or believe—is another. From this perspective, the position of 1 John is logically dependent on that of the Gospel.

Believing in the name (εἰς τὸ ὄνομα) is an important expression (1 John 5:13, and see John 1:12; 2:23; 3:18). In this one phrase, we have two important Johannine characteristics: the use of πιστεύειν followed by εἰς, and the use of this expression with the name (ὄνομα) as the object of believing.[45] Eternal life as a consequence of believing and knowing is characteristically Johannine. This theme separates John from the Synoptics, where kingdom of God (heaven) terminology dominates, while eternal life is rarely mentioned. In John, kingdom of God language is rare, while eternal life is a common theme, as in 1 John. Knowing is central to both the Gospel and Epistles, but the noun γνῶσις (knowledge) is not found at all in the Johannine Gospel or Epistles. The similarities between the openings and closings of the Gospel and 1 John strongly suggest some kind of relationship between these two writings and draw attention to distinctive Johannine characteristics in terms of both dominant Johannine vocabulary and idioms. The Epistles are the fruit of some relationship to the developing tradition of the Gospel in oral or written form, perhaps at an early stage of its development. On the other hand, the similarities between the two endings seem to imply that the Gospel was known complete with chapter 21. Thus 1 John 5:14-21 follows the conclusion in 5:13 just as John 21 follows the conclusion of John 20:30-31.

The finished Gospel is generally dated around 85–90 CE. The overall evidence of the Gospel confirms that chapter 21 was appended to an earlier version that concluded at 20:30-31. The evident conclusion in 20:30-31 implies that chapter 21 is an addition. 21:21-24 reveals that a hand or hands other than the primary author's added the whole of chapter 21, and perhaps other material as well in the body of the Gospel. The purpose of the addition of chapter 21 is complex. First, it is a response to the death of the Evangelist (Beloved Disciple), and seeks to provide a rationale for it. Second, it narrates the restoration and recommissioning of Peter to a position of legitimate leadership alongside the Beloved Disciple. Third, it modifies the Gospel's Jerusalem orientation by adding the return to Galilee, where Jesus meets with apparently disillusioned disciples and regathers and recommissions them via the recommissioning of Peter.

If 1 John presupposes the Gospel replete with chapter 21, the relationship of the Gospel to the Epistles must be explained via someone other than the primary evangelist. The hands responsible for the completion of the Gospel are effectively what is meant by the Johannine school. It comprised the disciples of the Evangelist, teachers who recognized his authority and sought to establish his understanding of the tradition. Although a uniform interpretation of the tradition did not emerge, a high degree of coherence was achieved.

If scholars in the first half of the twentieth century were concerned with the question of the common authorship of the Gospel and 1 John, scholars today generally reject common authorship. The debate now concerns whether the Gospel had a single author and the Epistles a common author. It is now a question of the relationship of the Epistles to each other and to the Gospel.

It is generally recognized that a breach between Johannine believers and the synagogue had already taken place by the time the Gospel was published, though some critics think that the failure to establish the enforcement of *birkath ha-minim* as a datable event invalidates this hypothesis. Some of those who accept that the evidence in John establishes a breach, at least within the Johannine community, think of it as long past and minimize its impact on the shaping of the tradition in the Johannine Gospel.[46] What is not always taken into account is the evidence of the shaping of the tradition in the Gospel at various earlier stages of its history. The trauma of the breach with the synagogue left its mark in the Johannine tradition. If the Gospel was published around 90 CE, the tradition was in the process of being shaped between 30 and 90 CE. The trauma belongs to a stage of that development. First John was written after that period, when the Gospel was complete. While the publication of the Gospel was the consequence of a lengthy transmission of tradition, the Epistles were written in a relatively short space of time in response to a significant new crisis, which produced a schism that traumatized the Johannine circle of churches.

Marks of the Johannine School

Of the Gospels, only John has a closely related group of epistles written to a network of house churches. That network can be thought of as the Johannine community in its broadest sense. Within the network, some of the churches were likely to have been more in accord with the Johannine point of view than others. We may take the church of Diotrephes (3 John 9-10) as an example of a more distant relationship. But even in that church, there were those sympathetic to the Elder and his cause. The church of Gaius, to whom 3 John is written, was more closely a Johannine church. Second John is probably addressed to a group of churches. Thus, the broad Johannine community provides a spectrum of responses to the Johannine vision. The Epistles are instruments used to realize the Johannine vision more effectively within that broad community.

The existence of the Epistles alongside the Gospel of John suggests the activity of a Johannine school. Third John provides evidence of a group closely associated with the Elder in his work of disseminating the Johannine vision. First, there is Gaius (v. 1), whom the Elder implies is one of his children—that is, one of his protégés (v. 4). Then there are the brothers (3 John 3, 5, 10) who traverse the network of churches bearing letters from the Elder. Demetrios (3 John 12) is also a member of this team, which the Elder describes as "fellow workers with the truth" (3 John 8). While this description relates the worker to the truth, it is clear that they share in this work together and with the Elder. To this we can add those who produced the Johannine writings. John 21:24 reveals a group, led by the Beloved Disciple who bore witness and wrote and the group that added chapter 21, attesting the veracity of what was witnessed and written. This certainly reveals a nucleus of the Johannine school. If the Johannine Epistles were written by another author or authors, the web of the Johannine school was spread even further.

What are we to make of the Johannine school? First, we can say that it was a tightly knit group (but not without differences) that was responsible for the shaping and dissemination of the Johannine vision. Its achievement was the creation of the Johannine community. Yet the members of the group stand in the shadows. Even those we can name, like Gaius and Demetrios, remain unknown to us because these names do not identify known persons. Second and 3 John name their author as the Elder, and 1 John provides no explicit indication of authorship. The Gospel identifies no author, although 21:24 refers to the Beloved Disciple in an active role. Because the Beloved Disciple is not identified, this takes us little further.

Even if the Beloved Disciple is identified with John, John 21:24 seems to rule out the straightforward authorship of the Gospel and Epistles by this John. Nor does anything in John 1–20 or 1 John imply that John was the author of either work. Other identifications are possible on the basis of the evidence. On the other hand, it is possible that Irenaeus may be right in associating the Johannine writings with the Apostle John, but few scholars today think that this can be done in a straightforward fashion. Scholars today tend to think in terms of a Johannine school in which John the apostle may or may not have played a defining role. The evidence of a school producing and disseminating the Johannine writings is strong; it is found in the common language and perspective of these writings, alongside significant differences. The hypothesis of a Johannine school provides a reasonable basis for understanding this balance of agreement and difference. The plural attestation of John 21:24, "we know that his witness is true," adds weight to the perception of a school shaped by a singular influence as the source of the Johannine writings.

R. Alan Culpepper defines an ancient school in relation to the following characteristics: (1) the school gathers around a founding figure, (2) the founder is a teacher and exemplar of wisdom or goodness, (3) members of the school are disciples (pupils) of the teacher and loyal to his teaching, (4) teaching and learning are the focal activities of the school, (5) common meals commemorate the role of the founder, (6) there is an emphasis on φιλία and κοινωνία, (7) rules define the lives of members, (8) the school is distanced from wider society, and (9) institutional structures (routinization) provide a basis for the perpetuation of the school.[47] The relevance of this profile to the Johannine school is readily apparent, though it needs to be lightly nuanced to fit the particularities of the Johannine situation. Other evidence of the perpetuation of the school tradition can be seen in the catechetical school of Alexandria, which probably had its roots in a school tradition going back to Philo.[48]

The Johannine Epistles confirm the actuality of both the Johannine school and a broader Johannine community made up of a network of Johannine house churches. While these were in a single region, they were spread widely enough to require special journeys to visit the different churches. For this reason, the Elder was in closer and more intimate contact with some of the churches than others. He probably felt that those situated remotely from him were more exposed to the dangers of false teachers than his own community. On the other hand, 1 John might indicate that the schism that tore apart the Johannine community began in the author's own community (1 John 2:18-19). Even if this is true, it is clear that the waves generated by the schism threatened the whole network of churches. The threat called the Johannine school into action, though not, of course, into existence. This group was responsible at least for the final editing and publication of the Gospel as we know it (John 21:24), and for the Johannine Epistles.[49]

Style and Language of the Letters

The letters display a semitizing Greek. Language is always influenced by the culture of the author. It can also be shaped by the author's intention to use language appropriate to the envisaged readers. Culturally versatile authors have the facility to do this. Does the semitizing Greek of the Johannine Epistles reflect the author's cultural context, or was it carefully chosen for the readers? Because the characteristics of this Greek are found in the Gospel and Epistles, a good case can be made for arguing that the Semitic character of the language tells us more about the author of the Epistles than about their intended readers.

A number of clues suggest that the Epistles are directed to a dominantly Gentile readership. As distinct from the Gospel, arguments in the Epistles are not supported by appeals to the Scriptures. The point is not that Gentile believers did not use the Jewish Scriptures. The force of the argument comes from the opposite direction. It is inconceivable that a Jewish believer (the author) would not appeal to the Scriptures when seeking to persuade other Jewish believers of the truth. It is no real help to assert that "Old Testament language and thought permeate our text."[50] Edwards here appeals to the work of J. Lieu, "What Was from the Beginning."[51] Just what constitutes Old Testament language and thought is difficult to establish where the evidence falls short of quotation or specific allusion. Even if an author has used Old Testament language, it is not like an appeal to the authority of the Scriptures to deal with issues. Nothing in the letters confirms that the readers would have recognized Old Testament language and thought.

The letter is characterized by a stylistic duality. "The change in style in the text of 1 John is in itself well observed and susceptible of a positive explanation, in part from the dual purpose of the document. For it is both a didactic and a polemical work directed against the heretics (e.g. . . . , 1:6-10), and at the same time a homiletical and parenetic work addressed to the community (e.g., 2:1-2)."[52] Although the polemical passages are directed against the opponents, they are addressed to the community with a view to dissuading them from following the secessionists into schism. The paraenetic material also deals with the issue, but as a form of encouragement in the face of the trauma caused by the schism. The trauma can be understood in terms of emotional pain resulting in confusion and uncertainty. A major aim of 1 John was to rebuild certainty and the joy of a confident faith, all of which had been undermined by the schism. The duality is recognized in the swing from passages of a polemical tone to those of pastoral concern. "The double nature of the material is not the result of the author commenting on a source, but is the consequence of the author's double purpose for writing. He wrote to oppose the heretics and to encourage the believers." "Though the heretics had withdrawn, the community was in turmoil and continued to be threatened by the false teaching." "1 John was written to bring the assurance of faith to those who had been troubled by the heretical teachers." "Thus the confession of true faith and active love for the brethren have become the tests which expose the heretics and provide the believers with the assurance of faith."[53]

While one strategy was to deal with the position of the opponents in a polemical way, exposing the error, 1 John was not written to the opponents. It was written to the traumatized and disturbed community whose assurance of faith had been undermined. The aim of the letter was to restore that assurance and to place it on a solid basis. To this end, we find the many assurances, "By this you know . . ." (ἐν τούτῳ γινώσκετε) and the like. These are supported by the strong pastoral concerns of 1 John.

The Rhetoric of First John

The struggle to define the genre of 1 John has produced no clear results, and the attempts to outline its structure have fared no better. One reason for this can be seen by reference to the character of 1 John in terms of the rhetoric of the time. Hans-Joseph Klauck argues that 1 John is an example of deliberative rhetoric, which is strong in exhortation and dissuasion, seeking to influence decision and action.[54] Certainly 1 John does this. Alternatively, Duane Watson makes a case for recognizing the marks of epideictic rhetoric in 1 John. Also known as demonstrative rhetoric, it is designed to advance knowledge by setting out accepted views that establish and maintain group unity. Two things seem to support this case. First, from the beginning, the author is attempting to nurture the bonds of community and to reassert the values that bound the community together prior to the schism. Seen as a response to schism, 1 John readily fits the category of epideictic rhetoric. In particular, Watson draws attention to the multifarious uses of amplification in 1 John. He argues that 1 John uses a full range of the methods of amplification to demonstrate his position.[55] But this need not mean that other forms of rhetoric are excluded from 1 John. Second, there is ample evidence of exhortation and attempts to dissuade the readers from following the schismatics out of the community. The author utilizes skills of rhetoric to reinforce the art of persuasion that he brings to bear on his readers. The stakes are high. The urgency of the task lifts the level of communication. The author reveals his concern in his exhortations and recalls the readers to commitment to the common Johannine tradition as the foundation of their *koinønia*, their community (1:5-10).

Attempts to identify the genre of 2 and 3 John have been more successful.[56] They clearly fit the profile of a popular Hellenistic letter. It may also be helpful to identify types of letters. Perhaps 2 John is a letter of introduction and commendation, introducing and commending the teaching of 1 John. Third John can also be seen as a letter of commendation for Demetrios and the brothers, fellow workers in the truth with the Elder. In each case, the single type description is an oversimplification, even for such short letters. This reminds us that genres or types are heuristic models or ideal types that are seldom a perfect fit with the phenomena they are intended to illuminate. Real letters often overlap types and make use of multiple kinds of rhetoric. This is true not only in the case of 1 John, which does not fit any sharply defined genre, but also for 2 and 3 John. There is no problem in identifying them as popular letters. Sharper definition of the types of letter is less satisfactory, as is the attempt to find a single form of rhetoric for each of the Epistles.

Polemic and the Purpose of First John

Since the influential work of Robert Law, which characterized 1 John as "vigorously polemical in its whole tone and aim,"[57] commentaries have tended to follow this line of interpretation. Recently, however, Law's observation that, although controversial allusions are limited to two passages (2:18-19; 4:1-6), "there is no New Testament writing which is more vigorously polemical in its whole tone and aim" has been challenged. A tendency has emerged to restrict reference to the opponents to these specific texts. Other texts, which Law and other commentators read with reference to the polemical situation, are now treated as evidence of the author's rhetorical style.[58] It is also argued that 1 John is not to be read as polemical text. Rather, its concern is pastoral. Here there is a misunderstanding of what has been argued in significant treatments of 1 John in relation to its polemical purpose. The confusion is apparent in such statements as "Its purpose is not first of all to engage in polemic with outsiders or with their views"[59] and Edwards' assertion that "it is more likely the author of 1 John is directing his thoughts to his own community rather than outsiders or particular adversaries. . . . but 1 John is probably less polemical than often assumed (3 John contains no theological polemic)."[60]

Agreed, the Johannine Epistles are not directed to outsiders or to the opponents, but to the continuing Johannine community and the situation subsequent to the schism referred to in 1 John 2:18-19. First John is addressed to those who have been confused and made unsure by the departure of the schismatics who were, until recently, members of the Johannine community. The purpose of 1 John is to address the confusion and heal the trauma caused by the schism. A concise statement of purpose is given:

> I wrote these things to you [plural] that you may know you have eternal life, you who believe in the name of the Son of God. (1 John 5:13)

The Gospel also provides a statement of purpose that is formally comparable:

> These things are written that you may believe that Jesus is the Christ the Son of God, and that believing in his name you may have life. (John 20:31)

The Gospel was not written as a tract to convert unbelievers. It is directed toward believers, to lead them into Johannine belief and consequent eternal life. Such belief has a specific content: "that Jesus is the Christ, the Son of God." This confessional formula presupposes the meaning unfolded in the Gospel. First John was also written to believers, but 5:13 makes no reference to modifying their belief. The Gospel assumes that those who (truly) believe have eternal life. First John does not question that. The problem is that believers have become uncertain whether they have eternal life. The aim of 1 John is to reassure believers that they do. The pastoral concern of 1 John is to provide assurance. What made it urgent was the crisis caused by the opponents, who had undermined the stability of the Johannine community. Explicit references to the schism are few, but make clear the serious nature of the event. In the Johannine community, which believed itself to be a manifestation of the unity of the divine love, a schism threatened disaster. As Law notes, awareness of the destructive consequences pervade the letter, which is as a whole a response to them.

The textual duality of 1 John provides an effective response to a schism that has left those who remain in a state of shock. First John sets out to minimize the shock. The aim of the tests (cf. 4:1-6) is to reassure those who remain that they are in the truth, in the one who is true, and that they have eternal life. To do this, it is necessary to show that the opponents are in error, that they do not know God, and that their position is destructive and deceptive, opposed to Christ; they are deceivers, false prophets, antichrists, and of the devil. The description *antichrists* puts the opponents in an eschatological frame, affirming the coming of the last day (1 John 2:18-19).

The effects of this schism had a pervasive impact on 1 John. Both the specific evidence of the schism and the evidence of the author seeking to reassure his reader attest to its impact. Robert Law describes the pastoral purpose of 1 John as "The Tests of Life." Clearly, Law saw this not as an inquisitional form of testing but as a reassuring series of tests. Law rightly notes that these tests are aimed at assuring the readers that they have life. But they can only do this by showing that the opponents are in error. Assurance of the believers and polemic against the views of the opponents are thus two strands running though 1 John. The result is a positive and coherent message, even if there are numerous unclear and difficult passages.

A Profile of the Opposition

My article "The Opponents in 1 John" (1986) grows out of my Ph.D. research and finds expression in *John: Witness and Theologian* (1975), 115–25. The paper carries on a dialogue with Brown's then-recent commentary. His treatment of the opponents is marked by caution.[61] Brown was aware that Pheme Perkins was critical of the focus on the adversaries.[62] She argues that the apparent polemic in 1 John is a function of the author's rhetoric, and warns against identifying it with the historical situation. Brown considers some of the language of 1 John to be far too pointed and extreme to be reduced to rhetoric.[63] Nevertheless, with growing interest in Hellenistic rhetoric, the position briefly advocated by Perkins has gained momentum and is taken further by Judith Lieu, who appeals to support from Perkins' position.[64] But this rhetoric is expressed in a polemical situation; it is designed to persuade the readers, the Johannine believers spread throughout the circle of Johannine churches, that the position of the opponents is to be rejected. It aims to reassure those who believe the Johannine Gospel that they have eternal life. Such assurance is the basis for the recovery of a stable Johannine community.

Scholars widely acknowledge evidence of the opponents in the text and find evidence of their activity in 2:18-25 (26); 4:1-6. Some scholars restrict what we know of the opponents to these texts or parts of these two texts. This decision is based on three kinds of evidence or argument.

First, the opponents are not explicitly mentioned until 2:18-19.[65] The argument is that the reference is held back to the middle of 1 John, and thus can be taken to mean that the schism was not the critical event that I have depicted. Yet when the schism is mentioned, it is in apocalyptic terms, signaling the last hour. Further, it is held back only if reference to the event is restricted to the two self-contained passages mentioned. Lieu, who adopts this approach, recognizes the schism as a recent event.[66] That being the case, can it be as peripheral to 1 John as this interpretation suggests?

The second line of argument is that other passages of polemical tone can be attributed to the writer's rhetorical style without reference to any polemical situation. Lieu refers to the work of Pheme Perkins, who "emphasizes the rhetorical nature of the language and warns against taking it too literally as a reflection of the actual historical situation."[67] Both Lieu and Edwards refer to the same pages in Perkins' commentary on the *Johannine Epistles* (xxi–xxiii), as Brown had noted.[68] This is a fragile basis for rejecting an obvious reading of the evidence. Is it likely that polemical language is merely rhetorical when we know that a schism had occurred recently, and those involved in it are called false prophets and antichrists and, in 2 John, deceivers? In the mind of the author(s) of 1 and 2 John, this would hardly look like a storm in a teacup. In discussing the schism, Lieu perceptively says of 2:26; 3:7, "This implies some continuing relationship or dialogue, and it is not clear whether the separation is as absolute as the author would like."[69]

This situation makes unlikely the containment of the polemic to the two christological passages (2:18-22; 4:1-3). The community that remained was open to the influence of the opponents. They were in danger, and the author attempted to set up defenses and tests that would expose the false teaching and reveal the truth—tests of life.

The third line of argument is that the christological error should be separated from the moral dilemma dealt with in 1 John, which is nowhere associated with the opponents.[70] If this is the case, why is 1 John at pains to root the command to love one another in the revelation, which is summed up christologically (3:16-18, 23; 4:7-12, 19-21)? Indeed, for 1 John, the giving of the Son as the foundation of the love command involves his coming in the flesh:

By this we know love, he gave his life for us; and we ought
[ὀφείλομεν] to give our lives for the brothers. (3:16)

What follows confirms that this giving of life is a manifestation of love,
and 3:16-17 applies this in very practical terms. In 4:7-12, the ground
of love recalls God, who is love. This love is revealed in his sending of
his Son into the world, "that we might live through him" (4:10-11). The
obligation (ὀφείλομεν) to love one another is grounded in this. Recognition that the opponents do not love one another (their brothers) is not
based on a theological deduction. It arises from an analysis of the polemical material.

Developed from the work of Robert Law and A. E. Brooke, Rudolf
Schnackenburg's literary analysis led me to recognize seven slogan-like
assertions.[71] These assertions encapsulate the "truth claims" of the opponents. They are grouped in sayings introduced by quotation formulae: a
threefold "If we say . . ." (1:6, 8, 10), a threefold "he who says . . ." (2:4,
6, 9), and a final "if anyone says . . ." (4:20). Given their content, these
assertions form an important strand of evidence. Two of the sayings are
opposed outright. The others are subjected to tests to show what vali-
dates or falsifies the claim. Given the recent schism, it seems unlikely that
the author was making up problems that were of no present danger to the
community. One objection to the attribution of these claims to the opponents is that the first three sayings are not attributed to them, but are
introduced by "if we say."[72] Judith Lieu's recognition that the separation
of the opponents is not as clear as the author would like makes precisely
the right point.[73] As long as these assertions could be contained amongst
the opponents, now outside the community, no more damage would be
done. The danger lay in the continuing influence of the opponents within
the community, causing the wound of schism to continue to bleed.

The claims begin to provide a coherent pattern of the position of the
opponents. This coherence is something of a confirmation that the claims
are not simply a random selection of rhetorical statements, ungrounded
in the life of the community. In dealing with them, the author builds
his own coherent response. The shape of that response was chosen by
our author to deal with the claims of the opponents on his own terms. If
the response is the expression of our author's coherent theology, it was
nevertheless crucial that he respond fully and adequately to the claims of
the opponents in their christological position, and to the seven assertions
recorded in 1 John.

Six of the seven assertions are concentrated in 1:6–2:11(17?). Thus
the first section after the prologue is a concentrated response to the
claims of the opponents. The first three assertions are introduced with

"If we say." This formulation makes us aware that the opponents were, until recently, members of the community. It also alerts us to the threat that they continued to pose within the community. These three warnings concentrate on the ethical area. Two of them concern the claim to be sinless (1:8, 10). Clearly these are considered to be false claims. The first claim concerns communion with God. While the claim is expressed in the terms of the opponents, our author does not repudiate it in principle. Rather, he provides a statement about God that enables him to falsify the claim to have communion with God. Because God is light, in whom there is no darkness at all, it is self-evident that those who walk in the darkness do not have communion with God. What is not yet clear is that the light symbolizes the love of God and the darkness is the realm of hatred of the brother (2:8-11; 4:7-12, 16b). For the opponents, the claim to be sinless is not an ethical claim. It has nothing to do with the love of the brother. Their claim relates to communion with God, without reference to or consequence for social relationships.

The second group of three assertions is introduced by the formula "The person who says" (2:4, 6, 9). The claim to know God is false when it disregards his commandments. Keeping the commandments is related to the fulfillment of the love of God. Again, the ethical test disproves the claim made by the opponents. Already there is a clue to suggest that God's commandments can be encapsulated in the command to love the brother, which is grounded in the event that reveals God's love (see 3:23). The claim to abide in him is tested by walking as he walked, another formulation of the ethical test. Thus the claim to be in the light is proven false by hating the brother, behavior that exposes a person who is in the darkness. The person who loves his brother is in the light (2:9-11).

From this point, 1 John deals with two major issues, the true confession of faith and the necessity of love for the brother in the authentic response of faith. If the treatment of the sixth claim ends with the test of loving the brother, the seventh claim, "I love God" (4:20), is shown to be false by the failure to love the brother. Much of chapters 3 and 4 concerns the theme of love. The Father is the source of love, and love is defined in terms of God's love for us. The failure to love the brother disproves the opponents' claim to love God.

The other major area in which 1 John confronts the opponents is their denial of what our author considers to be the true christological confession (2:18-23; 4:1-6). Here, 1 John does not tell us what the opponents affirmed, only that they denied what our author affirmed. They denied that Jesus Christ had come in the flesh. This was a denial of the incarnation, a denial that the divine Son is to be identified with the human Jesus, that Jesus is the Christ, that Jesus is the Son of God. This denial struck at the heart of our author's theology. The separation of the human Jesus from the divine Son or Christ meant that the life and work of Jesus could not be seen as the revelation of the divine life and love. Crucial for 1 John was the extrapolation of the love of Jesus in giving his life for us, for the world, so that it was not merely the human love of Jesus but the love of the Father in and through Jesus. The christological difference between 1 John and the opponents meant that ultimately they had different views of God. They also were opposed on the understanding of love, ethics, and relationship to God.

While there is much other data in 1 John concerning the opponents, the seven assertions focus attention on the ethical failure of the opponents to understand God's love as the basis for the love command. Their denial of the author's christological confession shows that their faulty Christology was the basis for their defective understanding of God and their failure to acknowledge the obligation to love the brother.

In one of the explicit references to the opponents, the author calls them false prophets (4:1-6). Here he distinguishes between the spirits that inspire true and false confessions of faith, describing them as the spirit of truth (spirit of God) and the spirit of error or deception (τὸ πνεῦμα τῆς πλάνης). Elsewhere (2 John 7), the Elder speaks of the opponents, saying that many deceivers (πολλοὶ πλάνοι) have gone out into the world. In 1 John 4:1, it is many false prophets who have gone out into the world. In each case, what marks the false prophets and the deceivers is their refusal to make the true confession of faith. What they denied is as important for the profile of the opponents as the claims that they made. The confession is worded slightly differently in each place, but the parallel is unmistakable. Thus the spirit of error is encountered in deceivers. When, following 2:18-25, the author of 1 John writes (2:26), "I wrote these things to you concerning those who would deceive you [περὶ τῶν πλανώντων ἡμᾶς]," this is patently a reference to the opponents. Verse 27 is the author's response to those who would deceive his readers, and it resumes verse 20, where the author affirms of his readers, "And you have the anointing from the holy one and you all know."

Verses 20 and 27 are difficult to understand. They seem to be a response to the opponents' appeal to the Spirit as the inspiration of their utterances. Against this, 1 John asserts its own teaching on the Spirit. But there is also a tendency to turn attention to the word. The opponents might have developed their claims to have Spirit-inspired teaching on the basis of the tradition of the Spirit Paraclete in the Farewell Discourses of the Gospel. The author of 1 John was uncomfortable with the direction taken in their use of this tradition. To deal with this, he identifies the spirit of truth with the confession of Jesus Christ come in the flesh, while identifying the rejection of this confession with the spirit of error (4:6).

Then there is a whole series of antithetical statements, in which the author sets his position over against what, in his view, is not true. It is unlikely that the author opposed purely theoretical positions just because he had a liking for antithetical statements. It is probable that the statements were used to oppose actual rather than purely hypothetical problems. All of the problems with which 1 John deals are intelligible in relation to the known crisis. Consequently, there is a good case for recognizing that 1 John confronts one set of opponents.

It would be a mistake to think that this single group of opponents held a unified and tightly logical position. It is also probable that there were tensions within the continuing Johannine community. It was the function of the Epistles to attempt to hold those tensions together and direct them along the line of the author. Thus the recognition of one group of opponents need not mean that there are no loose ends in our understanding of their position. As it is, we have only what we learn from their implacable opponent, the author of 1 John, and the Elder, if he is to be distinguished from him.

Recognition that 1 John is a response to the threat of the opponents does not mean that 1 John is intelligible entirely in the light of the threat of the opponents. The author's response to this crisis is called forth from his own coherent and powerful understanding of the gospel. It is distinctively Johannine, and if the author is not the evangelist, he has drawn deeply on the Johannine gospel tradition. Even if 1 John is preoccupied with the life and faith of the community, that life and faith is grounded in Jesus Christ come in the flesh as the basis of faith and of the obligation to love one another. As the ground of faith, the Son who gave his life for us reveals the God who is love. There is in this complex an authentic grasp of what is essential to the gospel, which is ultimately the gospel of God, revealed in his Son, Jesus Christ.

The Theology of First John and the Johannine Epistles

The theology of the Johannine Epistles poses problems. Inevitably, the theology of 1 John overwhelms the theologies of the smaller letters. On its own, each of the smaller letters provides only fragments of theology. On my reading, those fragments fit into and fill out the theology of 1 John.

In one sense, the opponents set the agenda for 1 John, and the author (Elder) responds to the issues and problems that they raise. At the same time, it is clear that the Elder has not allowed the perspective of the opponents to determine his theology. It is true that in dealing with the opponents, he adopts their language at times.[74] But in so doing, he deftly modifies its meaning. It seems likely, too, that the Elder's theological perspective determines the way he handles the issues raised by the opponents. If he responds to the questions and issues they raise, he does so in his own way, and it is likely that his perspective determines the order and manner of his response. He insists that the understanding of God and the way human life is to be lived in the world are revealed in the Father's sending of the Son and the Son's giving of his life for the life of the world.

God. Following the prologue (1 John 1:1-4), the reader might be forgiven for expecting that 1 John is about to launch into an exposition of Christology. In the prologue, the author speaks of what we have seen, heard, and handled concerning the word of life, the eternal life that was with the Father and was revealed to us. "This is the message we proclaim to you" (1:5) could easily be a summary of the Gospel prologue that announces the incarnation of the Word in whom was life, leading to the confession "and we beheld his glory."[75] Yet what follows in 1 John 1:5 lays the foundation for the Epistle's theology, its God talk. The role of Jesus here is that of authoritative teacher or theologian. "And this is the message [ἀγγελία] that we have heard from him [Jesus] and we proclaim to you, 'God is light and there is no darkness at all in him.'" First John places the initial focus on the message of Jesus concerning God. The prologue affirms the revelation of the message of life (τοῦ λόγου τῆς ζωῆς, 1 John 1:1) and roots that message in the revelation "to us" of the life that was with the Father (1:2; cf. John 1:4). This is consistent with John 1:14, and also resonates with John 1:18: "No one has ever seen God, the only begotten [μονογενὴς] God/Son [textual variant] who is in the bosom of the Father, he has made him [the Father] known." Although Christology is prominent, the point of John's Christology lies somewhere else. It is to make God known. In the Gospel, this is reinforced by the dominant imagery of God as the Father who sent Jesus, and Jesus as the sent one whose mission is determined by the sender.[76]

In 1 John, Jesus is also the one sent by God (4:9, 10), sent by the Father (4:14). These references fall in a section of 1 John that deals with the grounding of the obligation to love one another in God who is love (4:7-21).[77] This obligation is also expressed in terms of the love of the brothers.[78] The grounding of the obligation in God depends on the affirmation that God is love (4:8, 16). Awareness of the character of God is recognized in a specific revelation of God's love "for us" (4:9). God "sent his only begotten son into the world that we may live through him." Here, the phrase "that we may live through him" has the meaning of eternal life (5:13). This corresponds to the use of the verb (ζῆν) in the Gospel (5:25; 6:51, 57; 11:25, 26; 14:19), where *life* (ζωή) is shorthand for eternal life (John 1:1; 3:15, 16, 36; 4:14; 5:24, 29, 39-40; 10:10; 20:31. See especially 5:24, 29, 39-40). The Son came "that they may have life" (10:10). "God loved the world like this, he gave [ἔδωκεν] his only begotten Son so that everyone who believes in him may have eternal life" (3:16). All of this is the substance that 1 John builds into a more specific statement about God. The giving of life in the sending of the Son is understood to reveal the very character of God, so that twice in this passage the affirmation is made that "God is love" (1 John 4:8, 16). The second affirmation is prefixed by the testimony that provides its foundation (4:14), "And we have seen and bear witness that the Father has sent the Son as the savior of the world."

Reference to Jesus as "the savior of the world" resonates with John 4:42 and confirms the development of a central theme of the Gospel in 1 John. In 1 John, the theme is given extensive treatment in relation to the Johannine understanding of God. Here, the emphasis on the love of God for the world as the motive power expressed in the sending of the Son is more systematically developed than in John. The scope and purpose are clear in the phrase "savior of the world." The scope of the mission is the world; the purpose is to save. The context of 1 John 4:7-21 confirms that God's love has the world in view (compare John 3:16; 17:21, 23, 26). The Son is sent to give life, to save, and those who believe and receive life from God find themselves under obligation to love one another as God loves them.

The statement that God is love recalls the initial announcement of the message (1:5), "God is light." In 1 John, more clearly than in the Gospel, the message that God is light affirms the moral content of the revelation. Certainly the notion of revelation is fundamental to John's use of the symbolism of light. To affirm that God is light is to assert that it is of the very nature of God to reveal; that is what light does. But the formulation "God *is* light" (emphasis added) makes God himself the subject of the revelation, which has content. The content is the action of God, revealing the character of God. That action is motivated by love and is itself the fundamental loving action of God. The giving or sending of the Son reveals the heart of God in love for the world, and expresses it in dealing with the sin of the world (2:1-2; 4:10). The language of expiation used in these texts alerts us to the place where that action is to be seen. In the death of Jesus, God's Son deals with our sins, "and not ours only but also the sins of the whole world."

Reference to sin draws attention to the darkness exposed by the light. The light is understood to be God's love for the world, expressed in the sending of the Son to be the savior of the world. That light determines the lives of believers who abide in it and walk in it. But sin remains a force, and people continue to walk in the darkness, which is constituted by the rejection of the light and means to walk in hatred, in the rejection of love. Thus, if the revelation is motivated by the love of God, the love of God is also the content of the revelation, because God is love. The message that God is light affirms this in the context where the darkness of hatred rules. "God is light, and in him is no darkness whatsoever." Like the Gospel, 1 John provides no solution to the origin of the darkness. At the same time, the prevailing presence and influence of the darkness are recognized as antithetical to the being and purpose of God.

Christology. Christology is the point at which the revelation of God encounters the world of darkness. The concentration of the christological focus in 1 John is the historical intersection of the divine and the human in Jesus. This intersection is asserted in the confessions "Jesus is the Christ" (2:22; 5:1), "Jesus [Christ] is the Son of God" (4:15; 5:5), and "Jesus Christ has (is) come in the flesh" (4:2; 5:6; 2 John 7). In the first of these confessions, "Christ" has the same meaning as "Son of God" in the second and refers to the divine Son sent by the Father/God. At the same time, "Jesus" signifies the historical human person. The affirmation that Jesus is the Christ/Son of God also finds expression in the use of the double name Jesus Christ (1:3; 2:1; 3:23; 4:2, [15]; 5:6, 20; 2 John 3, 7). The use of the double name is rare in the Gospel, being found only in John 1:17; 17:3. Both of these references fall in passages often thought to belong to later strata of the Gospel. In the Gospel, Christ elsewhere retains its Jewish sense of *messiah* and is not construed as a personal name (see John 1:20, 25, 41; 3:28; 4:25, 29; 7:26, 27, 31, 41, 42; 9:22; 10:24; 11:27; 12:34; 20:31). This makes the exceptional use in John 1:17; 17:3 the more marked and suggests connections with the use of the double name in 1 and 2 John.

In 1 and 2 John, both references to coming in the flesh (1 John 4:2; 2 John 7) are unequivocally affirmed/denied of Jesus Christ. To affirm that Jesus has come in the flesh would not have served the author's purpose, because *Jesus* signified the human flesh and blood person. To say that the human flesh and blood person has come in the flesh is a tautology. But to affirm that Jesus Christ has come in the flesh identifies the human and the divine in the one flesh and blood person. In 1 John, this confession is controversial, and there are those who refuse to make it. Their refusal marks them as those who are inspired by the spirit of the antichrist. They are opponents of the author of 1 John.

The development of the use of the double name in the Johannine writings may have been motivated by the crisis caused by the opponents. The schism they initiated had a christological basis (4:1-6). Thus the use of the double name has a different meaning than in Paul and the rest of the New Testament. The difference is signaled in 1 John 4:2 and 2 John 7 and, once seen in these texts, is evident elsewhere in these writings. In the early church, christological developments were often a response to perceived false teaching. This is the case in the Johannine Epistles.

The coexistence of human and divine in the flesh-and-blood person, Jesus Christ, is crucial for the Christology of the letters and has clear implications for the understanding of God. To deny that Jesus is the Christ is to deny the Father and the Son, because the person who denies the Son does not have the Father, and the person who confesses the Son has the Father also (2:22-23). As in the Gospel, Christology is the way in which 1 John speaks of God where existing understandings are being modified. This is especially true in relation to understanding the world in terms of God's purpose to overcome darkness with the light of his presence (2:8, 17; 3:8, 14). Because the whole world lies in the power of the evil one (5:19), God sent his Son to be the savior of the world (4:14). The power of the evil one is the power of darkness, which has blinded the eyes of those who do not believe (2:11 and see 2 Cor 4:4). The means of deliverance are found in the coming of the Son of God to bring knowledge of the one who is true, "and we are in the one who is true, in his Son Jesus Christ. This is the true God and eternal life" (5:20). Here, 1 John echoes John 17:3: "This is the eternal life, to know you the only true God and Jesus Christ whom you sent." In John, the distinction between the Father and the Son (Jesus Christ) is maintained more clearly than in 1 John, although the unity of action is affirmed (John 5:17; 10:30). But it is less than clear whether 1 John 5:20 refers to the Father as the one who is true, or to the Son, or to both Father and Son. This may be a consequence of the more tangled Greek of 1 John, which could itself be a consequence of imprecise thought. It could be argued that such imprecision is a theological advance, due to the unity of presence and action of the Father in the Son.

Christology also has implications for understanding the way God encounters the world of darkness. In a world where death reigns, it is the work of the Son to give life (4:9; 5:13), and it soon becomes clear that this involves dealing with the problem of sin (1:7; 2:2; 3:5; 4:10, 14). Relevant to this subject are the references to Jesus Christ the righteous as the "*expiation* for our sins" and "the sins of the whole world" (2:2; emphasis added)—"the *blood* of Jesus his son *cleanses* us from all sin" (1:7; emphasis added)—and the definition of what love is: "in this is love, not that we loved God but that he loved us and sent his Son as an *expiation* for our sins" (4:10; emphasis added). The term translated as expiation is ἱλασμός. In relation to sin(s), it has the sense of expiation, the appropriate means of dealing with sin(s). Used in relation to God, the term means propitiation. In the Johannine literature, this language is invariably used in relation to sin(s). This is generally true in the New Testament, including Paul. In 1 John, the reference to blood and expiation suggests that God's way of dealing with sin is bound up with the death of Jesus. His death deals with the problem of sin(s) by providing expiation and cleansing. As Jesus Christ the righteous, he is also the advocate whom sinners have with the Father. But that advocacy presupposes both the expiation of sins and the cleansing of the sinner.

Two other related aspects have a bearing on Christology. First, there is the reference to "the message we have heard from him" (1:5). This is a reference to the message of the sent one, Jesus Christ. The message is that God is light. It is unclear whether what follows is part of the message or the elaboration of it by the author of 1 John. The message concerns God. This is consistent with the preaching of Jesus in the Synoptics, where Jesus' proclamation finds its focus on "the kingdom of God." Here in 1 John, the message that God is light is opposed to the darkness, so that the rule of God is opposed to the powers of the world. The power of the light is manifest in the sending of the Son, whose mission is motivated by the love of God and reveals God's love and actualizes it in the world. As a result of his coming, the true light already shines (2:8-10). Also coming from Jesus Christ is the commandment. Just as 1:5 says, "This is the message that we have from him," so now it is said, "And this is the message that we have heard from the beginning, that we love one another" (3:11). Almost certainly, the reference to the commandment that we love one another is to the commandment given by Jesus (John 13:34). There it is spoken of as "a new commandment." In 1 John, there is reference to it as an old commandment (2:7-8; 2 John 5, 6). What was once new has become the old foundational commandment. Thus the message concerns God and the love commandment, expressed in reciprocal terms. Following the idiom of 1:5; 3:11 says, "This is the commandment that we have from him" (4:21 and cf. 3:23). Here, the commandment is addressed to those who claim to love God, telling them it is necessary to love their brothers as well. The message that God is light and the command to love one another form the message of Jesus Christ in 1 and 2 John.

First John also presupposes the Parousia of the Son of God. This is to take place at the end, bringing judgment. Those who believe in him may have confidence on the day of judgment (2:28; 4:17). The christological emphasis of 1 John is weighted to the past: "Jesus Christ has come in the flesh" (4:2), "the Son of God has come" (5:20), "the darkness is passing away and the true light is already shining" (2:8). Nevertheless, the presence of the power of darkness remains, and sin continues to be a problem (5:16-17). First John remains oriented to the coming of Jesus and the day of judgment for a final resolution of the struggle with evil.

Believing, confessing, and knowing. Much of the theology of the Epistles is concerned with the response to God sending his Son. In the Gospel, the world is divided by belief and unbelief. It is true that the Gospel is concerned about authentic belief, which is indicated by the verb *to believe*, followed by a construction indicating the content of such belief (πιστεύειν ὅτι). Belief that does not yet attain this authenticity is nevertheless on the way, and it stands over against unbelief. In 1 John, the problem is not unbelief but false belief. This is not belief on the way to authenticity, but a rejection or denial of such belief. Consequently, the whole weight of the treatment of belief falls on the correct content.

The focus on believing is complex in the Gospel, where the verb is used ninety-eight times, seventy-six of which are in chapters 1–12. In these chapters, Jesus challenges the world to believe, and the struggle between belief and unbelief is fought out. In chapters 13–21, the verb is used twenty-two times. When length of chapters is taken into account, this is proportionately closer to the nine uses in 1 John than to the concentration in John 1–12. Only in 1 John is the noun *faith* (πίστις) used (5:4). In 5:4-5, "our faith" is identified with believing that (πιστεύειν ὅτι) Jesus is the Son of God. Thus in 1 John, "our faith," correct belief, becomes the dividing line for the world. This finds expression in terms of those making or refusing to make (deny, 2:22, 23) the true christological confession (2:23; 4:2, 3, 15; 2 John 7). In 1 John, the struggle with the false teachers determines the perspective, rather that the outright unbelief of the world. Nevertheless, the world is redefined, to a degree, in terms of the false teachers (2:15-17; 3:1, 13, 17; 4:1, 3, 4; 5:4, 5, 19; 2 John 7). The identification of the false teachers with the world is especially clear in 4:1, 3, 4, 5; 5:19; 2 John 7.

The true confession of belief, our faith, is the means and evidence of victory over the world, over the power of darkness and the evil one. The whole world lies in the power of the evil one, who obstructs the true confession of faith. But "the Son of God has come and has given us a mind [διάνοιαν] that we should know the one who is true" (5:20). Knowing the one who is true breaks the tyranny of falsehood, so that it is both the means and expression, or evidence, of the victory over the world. Thus the true faith is itself the victory.

The true faith is also the means and expression of eternal life: "This is the true God and eternal life" (5:20). First John was written so that those who believe in the name of the Son of God may know that they have eternal life (5:13). Both 5:13 and 5:20 are framed to emphasize the importance of knowing that those who believe have eternal life. But believing is only one aspect of the evidence of eternal life. Belief is balanced by its twin; evidence is loving one another (3:23). The authentic confession of faith is inseparably tied to the realization of the love command. Believing rightly and loving one another are two aspects of the one reality grounded in the one who is true.

In the Gospel, the two verbs meaning *to know* are used fifty-six times (γινώσκειν) and eighty-five times (εἰδέναι). The same two verbs are used twenty-five times and fifteen times, respectively, in 1 John. The choice of verb seems to be determined grammatically rather than because the verbs convey different shades of knowing. But there is something of a difference between their uses in the Gospel and in 1 John. In the Gospel, the theologically significant uses signify the cognitive content of belief. In 1 John, there is an emphasis on knowing the consequences of believing (see 5:13). Another characteristic use in 1 John concerns the formula for testing the authenticity of claims, "By this you know," each instance of which uses the verb γινώσκειν.

Mutuality. The stress on mutuality in the Johannine writings can be seen first in the use of the reciprocal pronoun ἀλλήλων. Meaning "one another," this word is used one hundred times in the New Testament, of which three uses are found in Matthew, five in Mark, and eleven in Luke. A greater concentration is found in the Gospel of John (fifteen times). First John uses the term six times and 2 John once. More important than the number of uses is the concentration of the command to love one another in John 13:34 (twice), 35; 15:12, 17; 1 John 3:11, 23; 4:7, 11, 12; 2 John 5. The formulation to "love *one another*" (emphasis added) is exclusive to the Gospel and Epistles of John in the New Testament. We should add to these references John 13:14, "you *ought* [ὀφείλετε] to wash one another's feet" (emphasis added). In John, Jesus' washing of the disciples' feet is both the motivation for the action of the disciples and the model for what loving one another should mean. The mutuality of love is expressed in the love command, but the love command is itself grounded in Jesus' loving action. First John treats the theme more fundamentally by grounding the obligation to love one another in God: "Beloved, if God loved us like this, we *ought* also to love one another" (4:11; emphasis added). The grounding action of God is the sending of his Son as the expiation of our sins (4:10; cf. 1 John 2:6; 3:16; 3 John 8). The obligation is grounded in God's loving action in Jesus, and is expressed in the love command (ἐντολή); see John 13:34 and note the importance of commandment(s) in John 10:18; 12:49, 50; 14:15, 21, 31; 15:10 (three times); 1 John 2:3, 4, 7 (three times), 8; 3:22, 23 (twice), 24; 4:21; 5:2, 3; 2 John 4, 5, 6 (twice).

Because the mutuality of love is grounded in God's loving action in his Son Jesus Christ, those who bear the message of that love assert that acceptance of the message is the means by which the love of God becomes effective, creating community (κοινωνία) (1 John 1:3, 6, 7). Community with God does not bypass community with believers, and that community is expressed in love for one another. The obligation to love one another is thus grounded in the gospel. Because of this, the commandment can be expressed in terms of "that we believe in the name of his son Jesus Christ and love one another" (3:23). Although the word church is not used in the Gospel or 1 and 2 John, the believers are described in terms of the community of mutual love, which is grounded in God's love.

That community is also an expression of a mutual abiding (μένειν) with God. The verb *to abide* is used 117 times in the New Testament: three times in Matthew, twice in Mark, seven times in Luke, forty times in John, twenty-three times in 1 John, and three times in 2 John. In these Johannine writings, we find over half the uses in the New Testament, as well as the distinctive sense of the abiding of God's word, seed (σπέρμα), anointing (χρῖσμα), or spirit with the believer and the reciprocal abiding of the believer in the light, in God, in the truth; see 1 John 2:6, 10, 14, 17, 24, 27, 28; 3:6, 9, 14, 15, 24; 4:12, 13, 15, 16; 2 John 2, 6. The reciprocity of abiding is explicit in 3:16: the believer abides in God and God in the believer. The concentration of this theme in 1 John is pronounced. Not only is the verb used twenty-three times in five short chapters, but almost all uses there fit into this theme.

Because the theme of mutual abiding suggests an emphasis on interiority rather than externals, E. Malatesta argues that 1 John is to be interpreted in terms of the new covenant of Jeremiah 31:31-34. In arguing this, he contends with a complex of evidence that seems to run contrary to his thesis. First, the term *covenant* (διαθήκη) is nowhere used in the Gospel or Epistles of John. Indeed, the term is rarely used in the New Testament: only thirty-three times, of which seventeen are in Hebrews. There, the theme of the new covenant is clearly important. The word is used four times in the Synoptics (one each in Matt and Mark and twice in Luke), twice in Acts, once in Revelation, and nine times in Paul (twice in Rom, once in 1 Cor, twice in 2 Cor, three times in Gal, once in Eph). There are points at which God's covenant with Israel is important for Paul, but this is not consistently expressed in his letters. It emerges when the subject of Israel's place in God's purpose is raised. But the Epistles of John show no explicit interest in the covenant, old or new, nor in the continuing place of Israel in the purposes of God.

Malatesta also confuses John's focus on mutual abiding with the interiority of the law in the new covenant: "I will write my law on their hearts." Not only is there no reference to the covenant, but there is no allusion to these words. Rather, the evidence of mutual abiding can be found in the confession of the true faith and in mutual love in the community. Covenant deals with the ground rules governing the relation ship of God with his people. It is, however, a case of category confusion to read covenant into any discussion of relationship with God. Had it been the point of 1 John to deal with relationship with God in terms of covenant, this could easily have been done. If the readers of the Epistles were not predominantly Jewish, this might have made little sense. Even in the Gospel, which reflects the struggle of Jewish believers with the synagogue and unbelieving Jews, there is no sign of the author's direct use of covenant. Associated themes are developed instead.

Sin. Teaching about sin in 1 John is complex. Because Christology is the point at which the revelation of God encounters the world of darkness, we may expect that Christology encounters the problem of sin head on (3:5, 9). This is apparent in the first references to sin in 1:7-10. Here, paradoxically, walking in the light is accompanied by cleansing from all sin. In this first discussion of sin, walking in the light, at first glance, might seem to exclude the possibility of sin This clearly is not the case. Only those who walk in the light have the promise of reciprocal community (κοινωνία μετ᾽ ἀλλήλων) and cleansing from all sin through the blood of Jesus, God's Son, because to walk in darkness is to hate the brother (2:9). Thus, to walk in the light is to enter the reciprocal love for one another and experience cleansing from sin. Cleansing is one metaphor alongside the description of forgiveness. Acknowledgment and confession of sins are presupposed as a basis of forgiveness and cleansing from all sin. If it can be said that the blood of Jesus as God's Son cleanses us from all sin, it can also be said that God is faithful and just to forgive us our sins and to cleanse us from all unrighteousness. Fundamental to 1 John is the view that what Jesus is and does is grounded in God and what God does. While this is implicit in the Gospel, 1 John makes it emphatically explicit in a number of places.

First John 2:1-2 begins with the exhortation, "Do not sin." Yet the author presumes the possibility of sin and outlines the way that sin is to be dealt with. Just as God was described as faithful and righteous, so now our advocate with the Father is named "Jesus Christ the righteous." An isolated reading of 2:1-2 could be taken to mean that the Father can only reluctantly be persuaded to forgive and cleanse us. But God seems to be in view in 1:9, and 4:10-11 is quite explicit in making God and his love for us the ground for the sending of the Son as the expiation for our sins. Further, 2:2 makes it quite clear that the Son was sent to deal with the sins of the whole world.

First John 3:4-10 begins by identifying sin with lawlessness. It follows by saying that the Son of God was revealed to take away sins, to destroy the works of the devil. The children of God and the children of the devil are contrasted; the one does righteousness and the other sins. Doing righteousness is identified with loving the brother, implying that sin is hating the brother. In this contrast between the children of God and the children of the devil, several claims are made about not sinning: "Everyone abiding in him does not sin" (3:6). "Everyone born of God does not commit sin, because his seed [σπέρμα] abides in him and he is not able to sin because he is born of God" (3:9). "Every one who believes that Jesus is the Christ is born of God" (5:1). "Every one born of God conquers the world; and this is the victory that has conquered the world, our faith. Who is the one who conquers the world if not the one who believes Jesus is the Son of God?" (5:4-5).

At a glance, 3:4-10 is in serious conflict with 1:7–2:2. The author has modified his view of sin in the life of the children of God, in the context of the contrast between the children of God and the children of the devil. One way to handle this is to limit the scope of sin in 3:4-10 to the refusal to confess Jesus is the Christ, the Son of God, come in the flesh, and the failure to love one another as obligated by the revelation of the love of God. The refusal to make this confession and the failure to love one another is the sin unto death mentioned in 5:16-17. This is the sin committed by the false teachers and their supporters. The coming of the Son of God has delivered them from the power of the evil one (5:18-20). But there are sins that are not mortal; believers may commit such sins, and prayerful intervention is sought on their behalf so that they may receive life. The false teachers and their followers have committed mortal sin and revealed that they "are not of us" (2:18-19). Their separation from the community, their refusal to love their brothers, and their rejection of the confession of faith bear the mark of mortal sin and identify them as children of the devil. This evaluation of the opponents is harsh, and finds expression in terms like *children of the devil, deceivers, false prophets,* and *antichrists.*[79]

The world (κόσμος). Of the 185 uses of *world* in the New Testament, seventy-eight occur in John, twenty-three in 1 John, and one in 2 John. Only in 1 Corinthians, where world is used twenty-one times, does any book come near the number of uses in 1 John, and then in a composition much longer than 1 John. Like the Gospel of John, but more emphatically so, in 1 John the whole world lies in the power of the evil one (5:19). For this reason, the mission of the Son of God is to destroy the works of the devil, to take away sins (3:5, 10). Jesus Christ the righteous is God's way of dealing with the sins of the world (2:2); he was sent to be the savior of the world (4:14). Nevertheless, the world remains in the power of the evil one, and the false teachers belong to it and express its values. For this reason, the world listens to them (4:1-5). The values of the world remain a seductive attraction to believers, so that they must be warned against them (2:15 17). Nevertheless, the coming of the Son of God provides the assurance that the world and its values will pass away (2:17). The mission of the Son of God carries within it the means for overcoming the world and dealing with sins, and brings it knowledge of the one who is true as the ground of the confession of the faith. The overcoming of the world is manifest in "our faith," and the victor is "the one who believes" (5:4, 5). The overcoming of the world is also manifest in the mutual love for one another, which is grounded in the love of God. This love overcomes the hatred of the world.

Johannine Theology: Its Continuing Influence

Unlike the Gospels of Matthew, Mark, and Luke, which are featured successively in the three-year cycle of liturgical reading, there is no year of John. It is a slight consolation that at Christmas and Easter, readings from John are featured, and there are some readings from 1 John at Easter also. Featuring John at Christmas and Easter has given prominence to the prologue of the Gospel, with its proclamation of the incarnation of the Word. Because incarnation is also an important emphasis in 1 and 2 John, the Gospel and the Epistles have reinforced each other on this theme in the public consciousness. From the Johannine tradition, belief in the incarnation has become central to Christian faith.

In the Gospel prologue, the incarnation of the divine Word (λόγος) is affirmed. When, in the second century, Justin Martyr interpreted the λόγος in terms of the Platonic/Stoic doctrine, the divine rational mind expressed in nature and history was identified with the divine incarnation in Jesus Christ. In this perception, room was made for the recognition of God in the world at large, and the revelation in Jesus Christ became the key for understanding the world better than it understood itself. But this λόγος doctrine is not found in the Epistles.

It is frequently noted that the confession of the incarnation in 1 and 2 John is used to exclude those who fail to make the confession. While Justin's interpretation of the Johannine incarnation of the λόγος was inclusive, in the Johannine Epistles, the confession of the incarnation is the grounds for division and exclusion. What this means is that the human (Jesus) and the divine (Christ) are united in the flesh in one Jesus Christ. The opponents rejected the identification of the divine Christ with the human Jesus.

The importance of the Johannine confession for a constructive theology is the recognition that God is known, insofar as humans may know God, in the human life of Jesus. From this perspective, the incarnation is the "coming down of God" to be encompassed in human terms and apprehended by human minds. The insistence that *Jesus* is the Christ, the Son of God, locates the revelation and saving action of God in the life of a first-century Galilean Jew. The incarnation also affirms the value of the created world for God and is an expression of God's will to bring the world into a relationship of reciprocal love with himself. Thus the Johannine understanding of the incarnation is a basis for the development of theology and ethics.

The particularity of the christological confession is matched by the specific nature of the love command. It is the command to love one another or to love the brother. It is frequently noted that the more comprehensive commands known in the Synoptic Gospels, to love the neighbor and the enemy, are missing from the Johannine writings. Given the manifest acrimony expressed toward the opponent in the Epistles, a case can been made for arguing that the Epistles restrict love to the Johannine group while expressing hostility to those outside the group. There is an element of truth in this criticism. But the aim of the love command is to bring all into the sphere where the divine mutual love operates.

The Johannine tradition provides the clearest basis for the development of the classical Christology of Athanasius. It would be anachronistic, however, to read Athanasius back into John. Nevertheless, it is the Johannine tradition that most clearly stands in the way of any attempt to interpret Jesus in purely prophetic terms, laying the foundation for an incarnational Christology.

Liturgical reading from the Johannine Epistles is restricted to 1 John. This adds weight to Judith Lieu's complaint that 2 and 3 John have been unjustifiably ignored. Yet these two small letters throw a good deal of light on the situation addressed by the Epistles. Even 1 John is used sparingly in the season of Easter, when six readings are drawn from the Epistle in the three-year cycle of readings (1:1–2:5; 3:1-8, 14-24; 4:7-21; 5:1-9, 9-15). While the readings cover much of 1 John, they are concentrated in year B and are read in Easter weeks two to seven. Given this concentration and the selection of the readings, the focus is on Jesus' death in dealing with the problem of sin. Thus 1 John 2:1-2 speaks of Jesus Christ the righteous as the sinner's advocate with the Father, and as the expiation of our sins and the sins of the whole world.

At the same time, 1 John accentuates the role of the Father (God) in dealing with the problem of sin. It is God who sent the Son as the expiation for our sins (4:10). Indeed, the point of 4:7-21 is that the sending of the Son "that we might live through him" (4:9), "as the expiation for our sins" (4:10), "as the savior of the world" (4:14), happened because "God is love"(4:8, 16). In this way, 1 John establishes the principle that Jesus the Son reveals the Father. The loving action of the Son reveals the love of

God and reveals that God is love. Paul, like 1 John, interprets the death of Jesus "for us" as the revelation of God's love for us (Rom 5:8). In fact, John goes further in the passage bounded by the inclusion of 4:8 and 16. The sending of the Son as an expiation for sin involves the blood of Jesus Christ (1:7), that is, his death: "he gave his life for us" (3:16). It is this event that reveals the depth of God's love for the world. It is christologically significant that what happens in Jesus reveals God's love. It is also theologically significant that the fundamental understanding of the being of God is established in the giving of Jesus' life. But for the giving of Jesus' life to reveal that God is love, it is necessary to perceive that the giving of his life dealt with the problem of our sins—indeed, the sins of the whole world.

There is a second belief about the nature of God in 1:5 and it is affirmed as the message that we heard from him (Jesus): God is light. This is to affirm that God is self-revealing. But 1 John elaborates the message further by insisting that "in him is no darkness at all." In this way, it becomes clear that the revelation has specific content. The person who loves the brother walks in the light, but the one who hates the brother remains in the darkness. The light of God is the light of God's love, and to walk in the light is to walk in love. To say that God is light is to acknowledge the necessity of walking in the light. To acknowledge that God is love is to acknowledge the obligation to love one another. In 1 John, ethical obligation is theologically grounded. The theological grounding is not self-evident, but dependent on belief in Jesus Christ as the Son of the Father (3:23).

In 1 John, there is no danger of thinking of a Christology with its own independent significance. What Jesus is and does reveals what God is. What God is and does is the ground of the ethical obligation for believers living in God's world. While much of the Epistle's language operates at a level of generality, speaking of love and hate, 3:16-18 becomes quite specific. Love is known in the giving of Jesus' life for us; thus we ought to give our lives for our brothers. Such giving implies responding to the physical needs of the brother (fellow believer) and is incompatible with turning away from the obligation to the fellow believer.

The acknowledgment of obligation to the fellow believer, arising out of the love of God revealed in Jesus, raises the question of the broader obligation to the neighbor or even the enemy. First John does not explore, as Paul does in Romans 5, the idea that God's love reaches us while we are sinners and at enmity to God. From such a basis, 1 John might have been constrained to argue that the obligation is not restricted to the fellow believer. But this step is not taken. At the same time, there is no implied instruction to hate those who are not believers. The instruction (in 2 John) not to aid those whose teaching differs from the author's is not a call to hatred. There is no suggestion that such teachers are in a life-threatening situation. The call is not to assist a work that the author sees as destructive to the life of believers.

The Johannine Epistles reveal a pastoral context in which the understanding of the message provides the ethical basis for living together in a community of love for one another. The theological grounding of love has as its counterpart clear ethical obligations. There is a need to work out in detail what this might mean for the life of a believing community and for the mission of believers living in the world.

First John is concerned with the problem of sin. It was the work of Jesus to deal with sin, and believers need to confess their sins and be cleansed from all unrighteousness. Within the community, it seems that the problem of sin is to be understood in terms of the failure to love. Such a problem is made intelligible by the repeated emphasis on the obligation to love one another, to love the fellow believer. But if 1 John insists that the way to deal with sin is to confess and be cleansed, there are also the passages that insist that those born of God do not sin (3:9-10; 5:18), that those who abide in him do not sin (3:6).

Because of these passages, 1 John provides a basis for the development of teaching that affirms the possibility and necessity of sinless perfection for the believer. Indeed, from the nineteenth century on, there has been a Wesleyan holiness tradition that appeals to these texts. At the same time, it is necessary to notice the emphatic rejection of sinlessness in 1:6, 8. Just how to resolve these two perspectives is an issue to be dealt with in detailed commentary. Here, we note the way 1 John provides a basis for a holiness teaching that affirms sinless perfection. In that tradition, there is a danger that the individual will become so preoccupied with personal holiness that the ethical obligation of love for the other person will be overlooked. In 1 John, it is not possible to think of holiness in strictly personal terms. Rather, holiness is expressed in relation to God and one another. It is not an issue for the unrelated self. For John, holiness is not so much a separation from contamination as it is commitment to the other.

In dealing with the opponents, 1 and 2 John describe them as false prophets and the antichrist(s). This language has gripped the imagination of Christian groups through the ages. Many individuals and movements have been identified in this way. The danger of labeling those who differ from us is now widely recognized. Nevertheless, the Epistles bring into sharp relief the problem of those whose words and actions are destructive to the life of the believing community. The figure of the antichrist also alerts us to those destructive forces in the world at large. There are evil forces that need to be opposed, though to brand them as the antichrist(s) strips them of any grace and excludes any hope of reconciliation. Certainly there is no hint in 1 John that the opponents might be won over to the truth, and this constitutes a serious problem in the context of the understanding of God who is love, whose purpose is the salvation of the whole world. Also serious is the tendency inherent in this approach to demonize those who differ from us.

Appendix 1
The Catholic Epistles and Acts, Hebrews, and Revelation

While it might be argued that Acts, Hebrews, and Revelation could not be part of the CE collection because they are not epistles, it can also be argued that Hebrews is as much an epistle as 1 John, and Acts has something like an epistolary introduction, while Revelation is introduced by the letters to the seven churches of Asia Minor and has an epistolary closing greeting. Although the ancient collection of CE did not include Hebrews, Hebrews is now sometimes added to the number of the original seven Epistles referred to by Eusebius circa 320 CE (*Hist. eccl.* 2.23.23–25).[80] The addition of Hebrews to the CE is driven by the desire to place it in a traditional collection. But the strongest inclination in the early church was to link Hebrews to the Pauline corpus. To account for literary differences between Hebrews and Paul, Clement says that "the Epistle to the Hebrews is the work of Paul, and it was written to the Hebrews in the Hebrew language; but that Luke translated it carefully and published it for the Greeks, and hence the same style of expression is found in this epistle and in the Acts." He also explains that the Pauline ascription at the beginning of Hebrews is missing because the apostle to the Gentiles did not wish to scandalize his Hebrew (Jewish) readers (*Hist. eccl.* 6.14.2–4). But Hebrews is not translation Greek. Indeed, it is more polished and Attic in language, and quite different from Paul. Nevertheless, the placing of Hebrews immediately after the Pauline corpus reflects the tendency for it to be associated with Paul, if not actually its authorship by Paul. It lies outside the Pauline corpus, which is arranged from the longest to the shortest (Rom to Phlm).

Eusebius names James as the first of the seven CE that also include Jude. He does not name the other five; nor does he indicate the place of Jude in the order of the seven. The first extant list of the seven in order and by name is given by Athanasius in section 8 of his thirty-ninth Easter Festal Letter of 367 CE. Eusebius says that Clement (in the now-lost *Hypotyposeis*) gave brief accounts of the Scriptures, including "Jude and the other Catholic Epistles" (*Hist. eccl.* 6.14.1). What is unclear is whether

Clement referred to these as CE. More likely, it is Eusebius' category for writings discussed by name, like Jude. Later (ca. 375), Photius also mentions Clement's treatment of the CE. Here he is probably drawing his account from the passage already noted in Eusebius. It is unlikely that Clement knew the seven Epistles as a collection in the order outlined by Athanasius and named the CE. The CE were poorly attested early, but had come to be widely used by the time of Eusebius. For writings in this category (poorly attested early but widely used by the fourth century), Eusebius used the term *disputed* (Ἀντιλεγόμενα).[81]

Both Acts and Revelation were associated with other writings in the New Testament, and there is no tendency to place them in the CE. Only the priority of the Gospel collection separated Luke from Acts. Had the tradition that placed John fourth in that collection not been firm, Luke might have been placed fourth in order to maintain the connection with Acts. The connection between John and Revelation is strongly attested. But the negative attitude that developed toward Revelation might have led to the separation of the two writings. This was probably one factor leading to the separation of Revelation from both the Gospel and Epistles of John. Another, perhaps more important reason is that the end of Revelation (22:18-21) provides a solemn warning to readers of not only Revelation but the collected writings that we have come to know as the New Testament. The New Testament then closes expectantly awaiting the coming of the Lord, with a warning and characteristic closing blessing. Separation of the Johannine Epistles from Revelation is a consequence of the motivation to give priority to James, Peter, and John, in that order. This outweighed the reasons for keeping these four Johannine writings together in the canon. If this conclusion is correct, it means the canonical decision for the order James, Peter, John was based on the assumption that the John of the Epistles was the apostle (Gal 2:9). This is borne out by the additions to the title of 1 John naming the author as the Evangelist or the apostle.

Appendix 2
Historical Collections

In modern times, focus has fallen on the Johannine literature as an important collection within the New Testament, thus moving attention from the canonical collections of the Gospels and the CE. Ancient testimony going back at least as far as Irenaeus links the Gospel to the Letters of John and to Revelation by a common author, identified as the Beloved Disciple and named John the son of Zebedee. This view was not uncontested, but the major reason these books did not become a traditional collection within the New Testament was the drive to bring together the fourfold Gospel. This also led to the separation of Luke and Acts. The twentieth century has seen the restoration of both connections, so that Luke-Acts is viewed as one important strand of the traditions in the New Testament, along with the Johannine literature. In Luke-Acts, the unity is undergirded by common authorship, common address to Theophilus, and a connected and continuing story from Luke to Acts. The connection between the books in the Johannine corpus is neither as neat nor as obvious as that of Luke-Acts.

Appendix 3
A Comparative View of Johannine Vocabulary

	Matt	Mark	Luke	John	Ep John	1 John	2 John	3 John	Paul	NT
ἀγαπᾶν	8	5	13	36	31	28	2	1	33	141
ἀγάπη	1	1		7	21	18	2	1	75	116
αἰών	8	4	7	13	2	1	1		38	123
αἰώνιος	6	3	4	17	6	6			21	70
ἀλήθεια	1	3	3	25	20	9	5	6	47	109
ἀληθής	1	1		4	3	2		1	4	26
ἀληθινός			1	9	4	4			1	28
ἀληθινῶς	3	2	3	7	1	1			1	18
ἁμαρτάνειν	3		4	3	10	10			17	42
ἁμαρτία	7	6	11	17	17	17			64	173
ἀρχή	4	4	3	8	10	8	2		11	55
γεννᾶν	45	1	4	18	10	10			7	97
γινώσκειν	20	12	28	56	26	25	1		50	221
γράφειν	10	10	21	21	18	13	2	3	12	190
διάβολος	6		5	3	4	4			8	37
οἶδα	25	22	25	85	16	15		1	103	321

A Comparative View of Johannine Vocabulary (cont.)

	Matt	Mark	Luke	John	Ep John	1 John	2 John	3 John	Paul	NT
ἐντολή	6	6	4	11	18	14	4		14	68
ἐργάζεσθαι	4	1	1	8	2		1	1	18	41
ἔργον	6	2	2	27	5	3	1	1	68	169
ἔχειν	75	69	77	86	34	28	4	2	159	705
ζῆν	6	3	9	17	1	1			59	140
ζωή	7	4	5	36	13	13			37	135
θάνατος	7	6	7	8	6	6			47	120
θεός	51	48	122	83	67	62	2	3	548	1314
Ἰησοῦς	150	81	89	237	14	12	2		213	905
ἵνα	41	65	46	147	27	20	5	2	249	673
καθώς	3	8	17	31	13	9	2	2	84	178
κόσμος	8	3	3	78	24	23	1		47	185
λόγος	33	24	33	40	7	6		1	84	331
μαρτυρεῖν	1		1	33	10	6		4	8	76
μαρτυρία		3	1	14	7?	14			2	37
μένειν	3	2	7	40	27	24	3		17	118
μισεῖν	5	1	7	12	5	5			4	39

μονογενής	0	0	3	4	1	1				9
νικᾶν	4		1	1	6	6			3	28
νῦν	4	3	14	28	5	4	1		52	148
ὁμολογεῖν			2	4	6	5	1		4	26
ὄνομα	22	15	34	25	5	3		2	21	228
ὁρᾶν	13	7	14	31	8	7		1	10	114
ὅτι	141	101	173	271	78	75	2	1	282	1285
οὗτος	147	78	230	237	48				268	1388
παρρησία		1		9	4	4	4		8	31
πατήρ	64	18	56	137	18	14			63	415
περί	28	22	45	66	11	10		1	52	331
περιπατεῖν	7	9	5	17	10	5	3	2	32	95
πιστεύειν	11	14	9	98	9	9			54	241
πλανᾶν	8	4	1	2	3	3			6	39
πνεῦμα	19	23	36	24	12	12			146	379
ποιεῖν	84	47	88	110	16	13		3	82	565
πονηρός	26	2	13	3	8	6	1	1	13	78
σάρξ	5	4	2	13	3	2	1		91	147
σκοτία	2		1	8	6	6				17
σκότος	6	1	4	1	1	1			11	30

A Comparative View of Johannine Vocabulary (*cont.*)

	Matt	Mark	Luke	John	Ep John	1 John	2 John	3 John	Paul	NT
σωτήρ			2	1	1	1			12	24
τεκνίον				1	7	7				8
τέκνον	19	9	14	3	9	5	3	1	39	99
τέλειος	3				1	1			8	19
τελειοῦν			2	5	4	4			1	23
τηρεῖν	6	1		18	7	7			7	70
τυφλοῦν				1	1	1			1	3
ὕδωρ	7	5	6	21	4	4			1	76
φανεροῦν		3		9	9	9			22	49
φόβος	3	1	7	3	3	3			15	47
φυλάσσειν	1	1	6	3	1	1			8	31
φῶς	7	1	7	23	6	6			13	73
χαίρειν	6	2	12	9	4		3	1	29	74
χαρά	6	1	8	9	3	1	1	1	21	59
Χριστός	17	7	12	19	12	9	3		379	529
ψεῦδος				1	2	2			4	10
ψεύστης				2	5	5			3	10

Appendix 4
Johannine Parallels

1 John	*Gospel of John*
5:20. that we may know the one who is true	17:3. that they may know you the only true God

In each text, we have the use of ἵνα, followed by the use of γινώσκειν in the subjunctive. In each case, the object of knowledge is expressed using ἀληθινός. Thus we have a complex web of similarities at the levels of syntax, as well as shared vocabulary. The frequent use of ἵνα clauses is a Johannine characteristic (147 times in John and 27 times in the Johannine Epistles; see the list in Appendix 3).

1 John	*Gospel of John*
4:9. he has sent his only begotten Son	1:14. as the only begotten from the Father
	1:18. only begotten God (Son)
	3:16. he gave his only begotten Son
	3:18. of the only begotten Son of God

Five of the nine uses of μονογενής in the New Testament are found in the Gospel and 1 John. Interestingly, although the Gospel says God gave (ἔδωκεν) his only begotten son, 1 John expresses this motif using the characteristically Johannine verb ἀποστέλλειν, which, with πέμπειν, is used to express the Father's sending of the Son, but without using μονογενής. John 1:14 comes close when describing "the only begotten from the Father." Here, *sent* may be implied. This is another constellation of significant Johannine characteristics, one in which the author of 1 John has freely and appropriately brought together two important Johannine words that do not appear together in the Gospel. But note that the two parallel statements of the purpose of Jesus' mission from the Father bring τὸν υἱὸν τὸν μονογενῆ of the first statement into relation with ἀπέστειλεν in the second, so that ἔδωκεν in the first is clarified by ἀπέστειλεν in the second.

1 John	*Gospel of John*
4:6. the Spirit of truth	14:16-17. another Paraclete, the Spirit of truth
	cf. 15:26
	16:13. he, the Spirit of truth
1:6. we do not do the truth	3:21. but the one who does the truth

The phrase (in 1 John 1:6 and John 3:21) is intelligible as a Semitism meaning "to act faithfully." Use of it in the New Testament is a Johannine characteristic. The use of the participle with the definite article in John 3:21 is a characteristic of 1 John, and there is a concentration of this use in John 14–16. Here, as with other aspects of 1 John, similarities are stronger in relation to the Farewell Discourses of the Gospel than to the narrative sections.

1 John	*Gospel of John*
1:8. the truth is not in us	8:44. truth is not in him
2:21. he is not of (ἐκ) the truth	18:37. every one who is of (ὁ ὢν ἐκ) the truth
3:19. we are of the truth	
3:8. he is of the devil	8:44. you are of your father the devil
3:10. he is not of God (cf. 4:1-4, 6; 5:19)	8:47. the one who is of (ὁ ὢν ἐκ) God
2:16. it is of the world	8:23. you are of this world (cf. 18:36)
	15:19. if you were of the world (cf. 17:14, 16)
2:29. is begotten of him	1:13. those begotten of God
3:9. Everyone begotten of God (cf. 5.4, 18)	3:8. everyone begotten of the Spirit

In both 1 John 3:9 and John 3:8, the authors write πᾶς ὁ γεγεννημένος. Throughout the passages listed above, *of* translates the preposition ἐκ, which indicates the source or origin.

1 John	*Gospel of John*
3:1. that we should be called children of God	1:12. he gave them authority to be children of God (τέκνα θεοῦ; cf. 10:52)
3:2. Now we are children of God (cf. 3:10; 5:2)	
2:11. he walks in the darkness (cf. 1:6)	8:12. shall not walk in darkness (cf. 11:9, 10; 12:35)
4:20. he is not able to love God who he has not seen	6:46. not that anyone has seen the Father
	1:18. no one has seen God
3:16. he gave his life for (ὑπέρ) us	10:11. gives his life for (ὑπέρ) the sheep (cf. 10:15, 17, 18; 13:37, 38; 15:13)
1:8. we have no sin (guilt)	9:41. you would not have sin
5:13. that you may know that you have eternal life	3:15. that everyone who believes in him may have eternal life (cf. 3:16, 36; 5:24, 39; 6:40, 47, 54)
3:14. we have passed from death into life	5:24. he has passed from death into life
5:4. conquers the world; and this is the victory which conquers the world (cf. 5:5)	16:33. I have conquered the world
5:9. if we receive the witness of men	3:33. the one receiving his witness (cf. 3:11)
	5:34. but I do not receive the witness of man
3:5. he was revealed to take away sin	1:29. the one who takes away the sin of the world
5:6. the one who came through water and blood	19:34. immediately came out water and blood
2:28. abide in him	15:4, 7. remain in me (cf. 14:10; 6:56)
4:12. God abides in him (cf. 4:13, 15, 16)	

1 John	*Gospel of John*
3:4. everyone who does sin (cf. 3:8, 9)	8:34. everyone who does sin
4:16. and we have known and believed	6:69. and we have believed and known that
2:3. if we keep his commandments (cf. 2:4; 3:22, 24; 5:3)	14:15. you will keep my commandments
3:23. even as (καθώς) he gave (ἔδωκεν) commandment to us	14:31. even as the Father commanded me
	12:49. the Father who sent me has given (δέδωκεν) commandment to me
	13:34. a new commandment I give to you
2:17. the one doing the will of God abides for ever (μένει εἰς τὸν αἰῶνα)	8:35. the Son abides for ever
	12:34. the Christ abides for ever
3:3. he sanctifies himself	11:55. to sanctify themselves
2:6. even as he walked (καθώς ἐκεῖνος περιεπάτησεν)	
	2:21. but he (ἐκεῖνος) spoke concerning the temple of his body
cf. 3:3, 5, 7, 16; 4:17	3:30. he (ἐκεῖνος) must increase
	4:25. when he (ἐκεῖνος) comes the one speaking to you is he (ἐκεῖνος)

In the Johannine writings, ἐκεῖνος is not invariably used of Jesus, as John 1:8 shows. Nevertheless, there is a tendency to do so in both the Gospel and first Epistle.

Appendix 5
Prologue Parallels

The prologues of the Gospel (1:1-18) and 1 John (1:1-5) are by no means identical, but they stand together against anything else in the New Testament, sharing a large number of common features in a short space. Particularly striking are their openings and closings. R. E. Brown sets out the following similarities, including 1 John 1:5 as a relevant transitional verse (*Epistles*, 179). My view, close to Brown's, is that 1 John 1:5 summarizes the message of 1:1-4 in terms relevant to the opening claim of the opponents in 1:6-7.

	John 1:1-18		*1 John 1:1-4(5)*
1a	In the beginning was the Word	1a	What was from the beginning
1b	The Word was in God's presence	2d-e	Eternal life which was in the Father's presence
4a	In him (the Word) was life	1f	The word of life
4b	The life was the light of men	5d	God is light
5a-b	The light shines in the darkness, for the darkness did not overcome it	5e	and in Him there is no darkness at all
14a	The Word became flesh	2a	This life was revealed
14b	and made his dwelling among us	2f	and was revealed to us
14c	and we looked at his glory	1d	what we looked at
16a-b	Of his fullness have we all received	3d-e	The communion we have is with
17a	through Jesus Christ		the Father and with His Son,
18b	God the only Son		Jesus Christ

The parallels are quite marked and significant, though 1 John does not follow the Gospel in the same order. The rearrangement of order confirms a free working with the tradition. Thus, for example, the parallel with 17a and 18b in the Gospel is found in a reversal of order in the last two lines of 3d-e from 1 John.

PART VI

JUDE

CHAPTER 14

THE EPISTLE OF JUDE BETWEEN
JUDAISM AND HELLENISM

Jörg Frey

The issue of the historical context of the Epistle of Jude is a particular *crux interpretum*. In New Testament scholarship, this short text has received only marginal attention.[1] This is due to its brevity and obscurity, but also to its theological contents and uncertain origin. There are only a few hints that enable interpreters to specify the historical and theological location of the author and to render more precisely the profile of his adversaries. One of them is the *inscriptio* "Jude . . . brother of James" (Jude 1), but it provides numerous problems. Even though a majority of interpreters are convinced that the epistle was composed as a pseudepigraphon by a later author who used the name of Jude, the brother of the Lord, the question remains why this writer published his text under the name of a figure of rather marginal relevance.[2] What is the reason for the attribution to Jude, the brother of Jesus; what does such an attribution mean theologically; and how does the epistle fit into the early history of Christian tradition and theology? These questions are to be considered in view of both the Jewish and the Hellenistic elements of the text.

The Classification of Jude between Judaism and Hellenism in Scholarship

The point of departure of the present essay is the classification of Jude between Judaism and Hellenism. It adopts the observation that the short text strongly refers to biblical and early Jewish traditions, but is written in a profound, almost artistic rhetorical style. Thus, it seems to combine Jewish and Hellenistic elements. In New Testament scholarship, however, Jude is usually interpreted in close connection with 2 Peter, and in comparison with that epistle, which appears even more hellenized, Jude is often classified as more Jewish or Judeo-Christian than it actually is.

Judaism and Hellenism in Jude in the Mirror of Second Peter

This is observed by Anders Gerdmar in his Uppsala dissertation. Using Jude and 2 Peter as examples, the author critically reflects on the scholarly categories Judaism and Hellenism, which are often used as a dichotomy in New Testament scholarship.[3] According to his view, the classification of Jude as Jewish and the classification of 2 Peter as Hellenistic are chiefly the results of the heuristic key chosen to approach both texts.

Therefore, as an experiment, Gerdmar turns away from the common heuristic approach and seeks to demonstrate Jewish elements in 2 Peter and Hellenistic elements in Jude. The result, however, might be more challenging for the interpretation of 2 Peter than for Jude. While Gerdmar cannot provide evidence for a strong Hellenistic influence in Jude, 2 Peter becomes more Jewish in his analysis. Gerdmar points to the fact that 2 Peter independently adopts elements of Jewish exegetical tradition, such as in the references to Lot and Balaam, that are not used in Jude.[4] He also refers to the apocalyptic worldview in 2 Peter and the eschatological dimension of its soteriology, which is quite clearly oriented toward Jesus' Parousia.[5] In Gerdmar's view, even the quality of the language is remarkably lower in 2 Peter than in Jude. Generally, he concludes that Jude is more Hellenistic than 2 Peter.[6]

Many of these arguments, however, are questionable. One should ask whether it is possible, for example, to view anacolutha and anarthrous nouns as a general mark of bad style.[7] Most problematic in Gerdmar's study is his attempt to invert the literary relation of the two epistles and abandon the commonly accepted view that 2 Peter is based on Jude. Instead, he tries to understand 2 Peter as the literary model for the composition of Jude.[8] This creates numerous difficulties. If this sequence is presupposed, the composition of Jude can hardly be explained. Why would the author have written at all if 2 Peter had already existed as a testament of an apostle? Why would he have abandoned the "higher" attribution to Peter and chosen the rather unknown and unimportant figure of Jude? Why would he have left aside all the parts of 2 Peter 1 and 2 Peter 3, and only copied or modified the polemics of 2 Peter 2? How could we explain the fact that Jude is almost completely parallel to 2 Peter 2:1–3:3, but contains only very spurious parallels to the materials presented in 2 Peter 1:3-21 and 3:4-18? Moreover, can we assume that the author of Jude would have eliminated effective wordplays (as in 2 Pet 2:13) or expressive terms (as in 2 Pet 2:4, σειρά and ταρταρόω) due to the concern that his readers could probably not have understood them properly?[9] All these questions remain unsolved if the priority of 2 Peter is assumed, and they can be explained much better if we keep the *opinio communis* that 2 Peter knew and adopted Jude. This is confirmed by a synoptic comparison of the parallel passages of Jude 4-18 and 2 Peter 2:1–3:3,[10] even though we must admit that the author of 2 Peter never used his predecessor slavishly, but changed and modified the *Vorlage* according to his own argument. The scholarly consensus regarding the literary relation of the two writings is not shaken by Gerdmar's argument.[11]

To contextualize Jude, we should rather leave aside 2 Peter, which was composed considerably later, and interpret Jude in its own terms. There is no compelling reason to assume that the conflict that prompted the author of Jude to write was still the same for the author of 2 Peter. Nor is it textually plausible to link both epistles with the same group of opponents, or with the same milieu of early Christian tradition. Jude's polemics could also be used in a different situation to fight another type of heretic. The result is that Jude must be interpreted in its own terms, not in the light or shadow of the issues of 2 Peter. Similarly, 2 Peter is to be viewed as a rather unique composition that stresses its own ideas and puts them into a different literary framework. It is far from being a mere prolongation of the tradition of Jude.

Judeo-Christian Theology and Hellenistic Language

In New Testament scholarship, the classification of Jude between Judaism and Hellenism occurs with different emphases. Some interpreters point out the Jewish or Judeo-Christian traditions that determine the theological character of Jude, despite its Hellenistic linguistic shape.[12] Others highlight the literary art and the degree of hellenization in this writing, in spite of the Jewish matrix and the Palestine milieu in which the author is often located.[13] In his learned commentary, as well as in his other works on the Epistle of Jude and on the traditions of the relatives of Jesus, Richard Bauckham stresses the Jewish or Judeo-Christian aspect.[14] In recent scholarship, his works provide the most thorough attempt to prove the authenticity of the epistle—that is, its authorship by Jude, the brother of

Jesus—together with its localization within Palestinian Judeo-Christianity. Despite his explicit acknowledgment of the high level of Jude's language, Bauckham sees the intellectual background of the letter exclusively within Palestinian Jewish literature. To justify this, Bauckham points to the fact that Jude makes use of such apocryphal traditions as *1 Enoch* and the *Testament of Moses* and applies exempla from biblical tradition using the method of "midrash exegesis."[15] Furthermore, he points out that Jude does not always follow the Septuagint, but seems to presuppose the Hebrew text of the Bible in some of its scriptural allusions.[16] On the other hand, any influence of other early Christian texts (e.g., the Epistles of Paul) is denied. Bauckham strongly criticizes the characterization of Jude as an early catholic writing, which was current in Protestant scholarship since the Tübingen school of Baur and underwent a renewal with Ernst Käsemann's harsh critique of Jude. According to Bauckham, such a characterization is inadequate in view of Jude's lively expectation of the Parousia and its silence about the church and its offices. Moreover, the phrase ἅπαξ παραδο-θείση πίστις in verse 3 cannot be interpreted in the sense of a formal rule of belief or a *depositum fidei*. Bauckham stresses that the author, as well as his addressees, has an unbowed apocalyptic worldview,[17] which provides the basis of his polemics. The opponents are seen as representing the same libertine and antinomian teaching that Paul encountered in Corinth and the author of Revelation struggled against in Asia Minor. The widespread classification of Judas' adversaries as gnostics or early gnostics is rejected, because it interprets the text from circumstances of later times.[18]

Thus, the main arguments for dating Jude late are rejected, and Bauckham tries also to ease the remaining arguments. Unlike most interpreters, he suggests that the commemoration of "the words which were foretold by the apostles of our Lord Jesus Christ" (v. 17) does not refer to the apostolic time as having passed, but merely directs the addressees to the time in which the apostles founded their congregations. In addition, he interprets the phrase ἔλεγον ὑμῖν, which introduces the following quotation in verse 18, as indicating that most of the people who had been proselytized by the apostolic founders of the congregation were still alive when the epistle was written.[19] At least on this point, Bauckham's argument becomes forced. Yet it is from here that Bauckham derives his rather early dating of Jude.[20] The major argument for its authenticity is taken from the prescript: according to Bauckham, the enigmatic ascription of the epistle to "Jude, the brother of James" is comprehensible if one presumes the real authorship of Jude, the brother of Jesus. A pseudepigraphic author would have avoided such an indirect method of identifying Jude.[21] Even the elaborate Greek style is not necessarily an argument against the authorship of the brother of Jesus, since in the first century

CE, Palestine was interfused by the Hellenistic culture, and as a missionary, Jude might have come into contact with Greek language and culture quite early. Furthermore, the possible involvement of a secretary with even better language skills cannot be excluded.[22] By such questionable arguments, Bauckham views Jude as a relatively early testimony of Jewish Christian thought located in Palestine, not elsewhere.

The findings of J. Daryl Charles head in another direction,[23] although he also vehemently argues for a Palestinian location of the text and a date "roughly contemporary with the apostolic era."[24] But here the plea against the pseudepigraphic character of Jude seems to be strongly motivated by dogmatic reasons.[25] Charles' comprehensive account of stylistic elements rather points to different conclusions. Jude shows a regular use of the Greek language "with bits of artistic flare"[26] and a rich vocabulary that is utilized economically. The repetition of catchwords points to a deliberately chosen design, and the application of rhetorical figures such as parallelism, antithesis, and paronomasia demonstrates the stylistic ability of the author.[27] His affective style is utilized for the polemics against the heretical teachers. According to Charles, the author adopts not only exempla from the biblical and early Jewish tradition, but also mythological motifs from paganism, especially in verse 13.[28] How this can be brought into agreement with the assumed authorship of the brother of Jesus, as stated by Bauckham and also by Charles, remains unclear. One might consider the artistic literary virtuosity and the rhetorical skills unlikely for a Galilean missionary such as the brother of the Lord. But finally, Charles' argument for the authenticity of Jude is chiefly based on dogmatic reasoning. Admittedly, the traditions received in Jude suggest that the author wants to speak as representative of a Palestinian Jewish tradition—that is, as an exponent of a "Jewish matrix"[29] of theological thought. But at least in his language, the author is clearly affected by Hellenism, and a further influence of Hellenistic rhetoric and culture should not be excluded, even though the presence of pagan-mythological elements can hardly be proven convincingly. To explain this, Charles refers to Martin Hengel's works on the deep influence of Hellenistic language and culture on Palestinian Judaism,[30] which affected even conservative anti-Hellenistic circles.[31] With these seminal works, the dichotomic use of the categories Judaism and Hellenism and the influential differentiation between an earlier Palestinian and a later Hellenistic stratum of early Christianity were basically overcome. Nevertheless, the consequence is at best the possibility that a man from Galilee would have been able to gain the appropriate language skills. A Palestinian Jewish origin of Jude is not necessarily evidenced by the presence of Hellenistic culture in first-century Palestine. After all, it could be concluded that the author of Jude, like the Diaspora Jew Saul/Paul, was able to combine Jewish traditions and methods of exegesis with elements of Hellenistic rhetoric and style.

The Placement of Jude between Enoch and Paul

In his monograph on the theological placement of Jude, Roman Heiligenthal recommends studying Jude "between Enoch and Paul."[32] Heiligenthal does not see any need to defend the authenticity of the epistle. Similarily, it is not necessary for him to locate Jude in Palestine. Nevertheless, he seeks to elaborate the Jewish character of Jude. He sees the epistle as representing a kind of Jewish thought that is only lightly Christianized, as a "Christianized part of Enochic tradition"[33] that was handed down in Judeo-Christian or, more precisely, in Christian Pharisaic circles. On the other hand, Heiligenthal acknowledges the reception of a common Christian tradition, especially in the prescript and in the paraenesis, and he locates that tradition in Antioch. Accordingly, Jude would be "a Judeo-Christian representative of Antiochian theology,"[34] struggling against other Christians' tendencies to assimilate in the post-Pauline era.[35] The crucial feature of these adversaries, according to Heiligenthal, is neither a gnostic nor a mere libertine theology. In fact, the main feature lies in the denial of the angelic powers, which is criticized in verse 8. In the first place, this denial goes back to the Pauline devaluation of the "authorities and powers" (cf. 1 Cor 2:8; 15:24; Rom 8:39), but could also be influenced by a rationalistic-skeptical milieu.[36] In conclusion, Heiligenthal assumes that the position of the adversaries resembles the position of the author of Colossians, while the refusal to acknowledge angelic powers in Colossians is close to the position occupied by the author of Jude.[37] This reconstruction deserves serious consideration at various points. First, the adoption of Enochic tradition is evident not merely in the quotation from *1 Enoch* 1:9 in Jude 14-15, but also in other passages of Jude, especially in the mention of the fall of the angels in Jude 6 and in the concept of the "judgment written in advance" in Jude 3. According to *1 Enoch* 10:14, the fate of the Watchers provides a paradigm for the judgment of the godless in Jude. Thus, the Enoch tradition is actually of utmost importance for Jude's views. On the other hand, the references to the book of Enoch are connected to several other references to the Bible and, further, to early Jewish traditions.[38] Moreover, the Enoch tradition and the Watcher motif were so widespread in ancient Judaism that the references do not allow the assignment of Jude to any specific Enochic school.[39]

The more specific placement of Jude in Heiligenthal's monograph turns out to be more problematic. It is hardly possible to use the application of the metaphor of purity in verses 8 and 23 and (probably) in verse

12 as an argument for the adoption of Levitical or even Pharisaic concepts of purity.[40] And since belief in angels was not exclusively a Pharisaic idea, but was more widely spread in ancient Judaism, there is no sufficient evidence to place the background of Jude specifically within a group of Christian Pharisees.[41] Finally, the reference to Antioch or to a kind of Antiochian theology[42] remains totally speculative. Such a localization does no more than recognize the fact that Jude's argument is not necessarily of Palestinian origin.

However, Heiligenthal's view that the adversaries in Jude should be connected to the sphere of Pauline theology deserves serious consideration. The programmatic deprivation of the angels and the cosmic powers in Colossians and Ephesians is prefigured in Paul. It would be comprehensible if the author of Jude had noticed that such an attitude, which is led by an anti-mythological skepticism, challenges some crucial matters of faith, not least the position of the Lord himself. According to *1 Enoch* 1:9, quoted in Jude 14-15, the author attained the Parousia together with "myriads of saints"—that is, escorted by the angelic hosts. It is quite difficult to determine whether the denial of the power of the angels and the rejection of their adoration constituted the author's only real charge against his adversaries, or whether other elements should be linked with those, such as a programmatic antinomianism, a transgression of borders in the practice of meals (cf. v. 12), or in sexual behavior ("maculation of the flesh"; cf. vv. 8 and 23). The uncertainty is due to the fact that the behavior of the adversaries can be deduced only partly from the biblical exempla chosen by the author. Above all, the style of the writing is strongly shaped by the use of polemical topoi, which cannot provide a firm basis for reconstructing the position of the adversaries.

The placement of Jude between Enoch and Paul, and between the tradition of Enoch and the post-Pauline developments, offers a refinement of the localization of Jude between Judaism and Hellenism. On the other hand, it appears far too one-sided that Heiligenthal links the author of Jude mostly with Judaism, whereas the Hellenistic elements are almost totally linked with the adversaries.

Jewish and Hellenistic Traces in the Epistle of Jude

The challenge is to render more precisely what the Jewish and Hellenistic elements of Jude's position are. Is the text to be viewed as Jewish Christian merely because of its use of apocalyptic and other Jewish traditions? What are the features that may characterize a New Testament text as Jewish Christian or Judeo-Christian?

The Problem of Defining the Notion Judeo-Christian

As is well known, the features of Jewish Christianity or Judeo-Christianity are hard to define for both the earliest times and the later epochs in church history,[43] but a better consideration of those features would allow for greater clarity as to whether and how Jude can be viewed as Judeo-Christian. Which of the suggested features of Judeo-Christian identity are present? Is it sufficient to point to the reception of biblical and early Jewish traditions, or to the praxis of a (so-called midrashic) exegetical method that links the biblical history with the actual situation? Is the reference to apocalyptic traditions a distinctive feature of Judeo-Christian theology? And does the tendency toward demarcation against paganism and assimilation in Jude represent a type of Jewish thought, or is that merely a concern that was common in large parts of the early church and in distinctive currents of contemporary Judaism?

Most of the followers of Jesus in the first two or three decades were either born as Jews or came to the belief in Christ from the realm of the Godfearers, that is, the sympathizers of the synagogue. In this regard, one could label the whole epoch of early Christianity as Jewish Christian.[44] But the fact that such a classification would equally associate such distinctive figures as James, Peter, Paul, and Apollos with the category of Judeo-Christianity gives rise to some doubts. In the ancient sources, Judeo-Christians cannot be singled out as a separate group before the middle of the second century. Specific designations of the group are documented no earlier than the end of the second century, in Irenaeus and Tertullian.[45] This is not incidental but reflects the fact that the church was more determined by pagan Christian thought at the beginning of the second century. When the ancient sources describe Jewish Christian persons and groups, they partly refer to aspects of origin,[46] partly to characteristic features of the Jewish way of life,[47] and in some sources, mostly those of the heresiologists, to theological deviations from the so-called mainstream church. But none of those definitions succeed in comprehending the phenomenon as a whole. The ethnic definition is not useful because it is too vague. If one considers the different elements of the Jewish praxis to be the criteria for Judeo-Christian identity, the question emerges, what degree of Torah observance is required for a Christian to be called a Judeo-Christian? The third feature mentioned, the theological deviations, is also not very helpful, because Judeo-Christianity was far from being a uniform movement. Not all Jewish Christians were anti-Paulinists, and not all of them rejected proto-orthodox Christology. Theologically, there was a broad variety within Judeo-Christianity or between the so-called Judeo-Christian groups.[48]

The working definition of Jewish Christianity applied here depends on the following criteria: a basic holding of Jewish observance (which occurred as practice among Christians of Jewish origin as well as among those of pagan descent) and an ongoing relation to the synagogue.[49]

Evidence for a Jewish Christian Context of Jude

Can Jude be characterized as Judeo-Christian according to this definition? I do not think so. Only if it were considered to have been composed by the brother of the Lord or one of his disciples, or otherwise closely connected to the person and mission of James,[50] could Jude be located within a group that was more or less observing the Torah and in close contact with the synagogue. Since such a context has become implausible due to the insights into the pseudepigraphic composition of the epistle, the evidence for classifying the epistle as Judeo-Christian is far from persuasive.

The author addresses his potential recipients merely as Christians.[51] The belief in the κύριος (Jude 14-15) whose Parousia was expected is an early Christian concept, developed on the basis of Jewish traditions. Liturgical formulas such as the *salutatio* in verse 2 may originally come from Jewish tradition, but they could have been adopted by the author from earlier Christian tradition without any further dependence on actual Jewish usage. Similarly, the typological application of the history of Israel is not only a Judeo-Christian peculiarity; comparable admonitions can be found, for example, in 1 Corinthians 10:1-13 or Hebrews 3:7–4:13. In both cases, the typological reception of the Old Testament was probably developed in conversation with Gentile Christian groups. The *Epistle of Barnabas* shows that the typological reception of the Scriptures can even be turned completely against Israel.[52]

The actual features of Jewish Christian life, such as observing the Torah, circumcision, and the connections to non-Christian Jewish circles, are not mentioned in Jude at all. Such a lack of evidence is not only due to the brevity of the text. 3 John, which is even shorter, contains, for example, a hint that the wandering missionaries did not accept food from Gentiles (ἐθνικοί) (3 John 7).[53] This is an explicit element of Jewish behavior that was still alive in the Johannine circle. However, in the polemics of Jude, the problem of idolatry is not mentioned at all—not even the issue of sacrificing food to idols, which was of such great importance for the author of Revelation (Rev 2:14, 20; cf. 21:8; 22:15; cf. also 1 Cor 8–10). Other hints to a Jewish context of the author or addressees, as suggested by Heiligenthal, cannot be confirmed on closer inspection.

The phrase "defile the flesh" (Jude 8a: σάρκα μὲν μιαίνουσιν), which the author compares to the deeds of the Sodomites in verse 7 (ὁμοίως), does not necessarily point to the framework of Jewish halakah and ritual purity. The accusation might refer to sexual behavior,[54] or to the lack of respect regarding the difference between angels and human beings, which is suggested from the biblical examples of the Sodomites (v. 7) and the Watchers (v. 6).[55] The boundary between angels and humans was violated by the Watchers, who "left their own habitation" (v. 6), and also by the Sodomites, who went "after foreign flesh" (σὰρξ ἑτέρα), that is, wanted to have sexual intercourse with the angels who visited Lot (v. 7). In both instances, the sexual aspect is only of secondary relevance. More essential is the fact that the Watchers and the Sodomites did not keep the border between angels and humans, thereby neglecting the order of the creation. The accusation of "defil[ing] the flesh" in Jude 8 only occurs as a supplement to the more fundamental reproach of "blaspheming" the angels.[56] Here, we cannot see any connection to the Jewish halakah. The rather strange admonition to hate "even the garment spotted by the flesh" (v. 23) might be seen as strengthening the sexual connotations, or very generally as a prohibition of any contact with those who are caught up in heresy (cf. 2 John 10–11; Titus 3:10; etc.). Even in the enigmatic and elusive metaphor of σπιλάδες in verse 12a, the reference to the halakah is implausible. The reproach is targeted at cases where the adversaries eat with members of the community at the communal meals without making distinctions. The reason for the view that such a common participation is impossible is definitely not the fact that some regulations, such as the apostles' decree (Acts 15:29), were not observed properly. There is absolutely no hint in the text that this was the issue at stake. The argument is, rather, that in the view of the author, the adversaries did not belong to the true community; they participated in the communal meals as "godless" participants "without fear," but with the mere aims of "feeding themselves" (v. 12b) and deceiving others.[57] The normal meaning of the noun σπίλας is *rock* or *cliff*. Within the context of the metaphors of nature in verses 12-13, the noun denotes the danger of being shipwrecked,[58] which is implied in the presence of the heretics at the communal meals. If we understand the word, according to the dictionary of Hesychios, as μεμιασμένοι, that is, in the sense of *polluted, smudges* (which is rarely documented), then we are confronted with the same meaning as in verse 8. In none of these cases is there any allusion to the Jewish aspect of (ritual) purity.

Thus, it becomes apparent that the assumption of a Judeo-Christian or even Jewish character of Jude can only be advocated from the reception of biblical and early Jewish traditions. Of great interest are the reception of a series of admonitory exempla from the history of Israel,[59] the influence of the Enoch tradition, and the Moses haggadah.

The Reception of Jewish Traditions

Most prominent in Jude is the explicit quotation from *1 Enoch* 1:9 in Jude 14-15, where Enoch is introduced as "the seventh after Adam" (cf. *1 En.* 60:8) and a prophet whose word endures as a true prophecy about God's judgment of the godless.[60] In the quotation, however, the text from *1 Enoch* 1:9 is christologically modified by the insertion of the word κύριος.[61] Now the figure who appears for judgment is the κύριος, that is, the risen Christ.[62] This demonstrates that, according to the author's view, Enoch's prophecy will become fulfilled in Christ, in his Parousia for judgment. The quotation from *1 Enoch* 1:9 is the only explicitly marked citation from Scripture in Jude. Hence, Jude is the most obvious and the most explicit recipient of the Enoch tradition as Scripture in early Christianity.

In the light of the textual tradition, the question of the precise *Vorlage* is almost impossible to answer. The quotation matches in many details the Greek text of Codex Panopolitanus (6th cent. CE), but in certain elements, the phrase is more in accordance with the Ethiopian text. This becomes explicable if one assumes that the author of Jude (as well as the translator into Ethiopian) used a version of the Greek text that differed slightly from the only Greek codex handed down to us.[63] But there is no clear evidence for a direct translation from Aramaic, as conjectured by Richard Bauckham.[64] The insertion of κύριος may have been added to the text by the author of Jude himself.

Beside the prediction of judgment from *1 Enoch* 1:9, Jude presupposes the narrative of the fall of the angels with reference to the Watchers named Shemyaza and Asasel (*1 Enoch* 6–16; cf. Gen 6:1-4). The statement that "the angels who did not keep their estate, but left their own habitation, he had reserved in everlasting chains under darkness unto the judgment of the great day" (v. 6) can be interpreted as an exemplum of the impending judgment of the ungodly. It can be understood from the concept of a certain ἀρχή,[65] a heavenly or cosmic realm of authority and governance of the angels, handed over to them by God himself. In this realm, they act on behalf of God.[66] This means that when the "sons of the gods" (cf. Gen 6:1) leave this very sphere and thereby violate the given world order, they are liable to be punished. Similarly, when the adversaries of Jude deny the given world order by negating the honor of the angelic powers, this can be viewed as an outrageous trespass and act of godlessness.

The destiny of the Watchers is evaluated in *1 Enoch* 10:14 as a model for the fate of the godless in general. *First Enoch* 12:4 and 15:3 mention that they left the supreme heaven; *1 Enoch* 10:4–5 and 10:12 mention the "binding" of Asasel and Shemyaza. The phrase of the binding unto the "great day," which differs from *1 Enoch* 10:12 (but cf. *1 En.* 22:11 and 84:4), can now be explained by an exact parallel in 4QEn ar^b (4Q202) 1 iv 11.[67] The Greek version of *1 Enoch* 14:5 mentions bonds or chains,[68] as do also Origen, *Against Celsus* 5.22, and the Similitudes of Enoch (*1 En.* 54:3; 56:1).[69] The word *everlasting* (ἀΐδιος) might be added from *1 Enoch* 10:5 and 14:5. That the angels have been "reserved" unto the judgment is said in *2 Enoch* 7:2 and 18:4 and *Testament of Reuben* 5:5. On the other hand, the choice of the form τετήρηκεν in Jude 6 demonstrates the linguistic skills of the author, who uses the word τηρεῖν, thereby forming a link with the same word at the beginning of the verse (μὴ τηρήσαντας) as well as in verses 1, 13, and 21: the angels become reserved for judgment because they have not reserved (or kept) their proper sphere of power; thus, the punishment corresponds to the perpetration that necessitated it. Vice versa, there is a contrast to τηρεῖν in verses 1 and 21: while the addressees remain preserved in Christ as believers (v. 1) and may hope for mercy (v. 21), the godless—for whom the Watcher angels serve as prototype—have to expect darkness which is reserved for them (v. 13).[70] The reception of the episode of the Watcher angels in Jude 6 shows that the author autonomously adopted and designed scattered elements from the *Book of the Watchers* (and presumably also from other parts of the Enoch tradition). This demonstrates his familiarity with the Enoch tradition. However, such a familiarity could be gained entirely from Greek versions. An independent recourse to Aramaic texts cannot be demonstrated and is rather improbable.

The second reference to haggadic materials appears in Jude 9: "Michael, the archangel, when contending with the devil disputed about the body of Moses, and did not dare to bring a slanderous accusation against him, but said: 'The Lord rebuke you!'" Behind the statement is obviously the perception that the blasphemy, or rather the verbal attack on the position of celestial entities, is a perpetration that has to be punished because the celestial entities participate in the glory of God and accomplish a function with regard to the final judgment. Therefore, the author mentions that even the paramount among the created beings, the archangel Michael, did "not bring a slanderous accusation" (κρίσις βλασφημίας) against the devil; that is a sentence that would contain a βλασφημία. In fact, the archangel Michael did not judge by himself, but left the devil to the "rebuke," that is, the judicial action of the Lord.

The question about the original version of the text is hard to answer here. Clement of Alexandria, Origen, Didymus the Blind, and other church fathers saw in this passage of Jude a parallel to the *Assumption of Moses* (ἀνάληψις Μωσέως), a text related to the *Testament of Moses*. The version handed down to us in a Latin manuscript lacks the final section with the report about Moses' death. The complicated textual situation and tradition have been investigated comprehensively by Richard Bauckham.[71] He comes to the conclusion that the narrative probably existed in two different versions. The older version is the *Testament of Moses*, which deals with the topic of the struggle between Michael and the devil (Samael), who had accused Moses of murder and the related question of whether Moses could be buried by the angels. The later version is the distinctive text *Assumption of Moses*, in which the devil demands the material body of Moses. This version, originating from second-century Egypt, would have been available to the church fathers, while the *Testament of Moses* would have been a Palestinian Jewish source from the early first century CE.[72] Therefore, the testimonies of the church fathers are not reliable in terms of the source and the local background of Jude,[73] which draws on the older Palestinian *Testament of Moses*, not on the later Egyptian *Assumption of Moses*. The reference to a source that might have been known within the circles of the Palestinian Christianity serves Bauckham as another source of evidence for locating Jude within the Jewish Christian context of Palestine.[74]

However, the literary relationship between the two versions cannot be completely verified on the basis of the texts that have been preserved.[75] We can only guess which form of tradition the author of Jude was involved in and what kinds of traditions had influence on our first patristic witness, Clement of Alexandria. Considering the extended circulation of related traditions, it is hardly possible to state that the *Testament of Moses* tradition was known only in Palestine and not anywhere else. It is true that scholars mostly suppose that the *Testament of Moses* was originally composed in a Semitic language,[76] but there was also a Greek translation of the text, which was later translated into Latin. The facts that the different elements of the tradition were passed down in Greek, Latin, and Old Slavonic, and that Clement and Origen were familiar with a (probably edited) version of the tradition, weaken Bauckham's conclusions considerably. Therefore, a Palestinian origin of the author and the addressees cannot be concluded from the reception of the *Testament of Moses* in Jude 9.

The various and autonomous relations to postbiblical and haggadic traditions demonstrate the rootedness of the author in Jewish tradition. The fact that Jude 9 only briefly alludes to the tradition of the death of Moses could also be seen as a hint that the addressees were familiar with the related materials. Nevertheless, these findings do not allow an exact localization. A Semitic linguistic context is stipulated by neither the quotation from *1 Enoch* 1:9 nor the adoption of the tradition of Moses' death.

There is no compelling argument against the view that the transmission of both motifs could happen in Greek and outside of Palestine. At any rate, the language and style of Jude do not suggest an author whose mother tongue was Aramaic. On the contrary, Jude's language is the most pronounced feature of Hellenistic influence.

The Question of Hellenistic Elements in the Epistle of Jude

It was Origen who praised the style of the writing as "brief, but full of fluent words of heavenly grace."[77] Jude has a rich vocabulary,[78] a relatively large number of New Testament hapax legomena,[79] and a special density of rare words.[80] The author is skilled in variation, the use of synonyms and antonyms, but also in generating the coherence of his text by repeating catchwords and accentuating semantic lines in an effective rhetorical manner. He uses exalted expressions such as πᾶσαν σπουδὴν ποιεῖσθαι (v. 3), πρόκεινται δεῖγμα, δίκην ὑπέχειν (v. 7), κρίσιν ἐπενεγκεῖν (v. 8), and τὰ ἄλογα ζῷα (v. 10),[81] and effectively applies strong metaphors from nature (e.g., in v. 12, "waterless clouds"). The syntax avoids parataxis, but skillfully uses participles, particles (μέν—δέ, vv. 8, 10, 22-23, and conjunctions, which provide the logical structure of the text. Furthermore, the artistic usage of such rhetorical figures as paronomasia, alliteration, assonance, homoioteleuton, rhythm, and wordplay is remarkable. The π-alliteration in verse 3 has at best one parallel in the New Testament, in Hebrews 1:1, and demonstrates the artistic philological skills of the author. Despite his strong adoption of elements from Jewish tradition, he has a remarkable ability to use the Greek language.

However, does the command of language represent the only Hellenistic element in Jude? To what extent do further Hellenistic elements determine the text? J. P. Oleson suggests that the metaphors in Jude 12-13 adopt elements of pagan mythology[82]—namely the birth of Aphrodite as reported by Hesiod (*Theog.* 190–92), with an additional allusion to Euripides (*Herc. fur.* 850–52)—and J. D. Charles has adopted this idea.[83] The metaphoric mention of "raging waves of the sea, foaming out of their own shame" (Jude 13) does not allow the reference to the myth of Aphrodite; that is too far-fetched. The same is true for the word σπιλάδες in Jude 12, which is hard to translate. The fact that the narrative of Shemyaza (which is presumably the oldest core of the *Book of the Watchers*)[84] provides some parallels to the Greek myth of the titans[85] cannot support the assumption of an independent adoption of Greek mythology in Jude. The use of δεσμοῖς and ὑπὸ ζόφον (Hesiod, *Theog.* 718–29) is not a valid argument for the assumption that the author intended to allude to that myth, although educated recipients might have noticed the parallel.[86]

But at one point, the adoption of Hellenistic terminology is beyond dispute: namely, in Jude 19b, where the author accuses the adversaries of being ψυχικοί, πνεῦμα μὴ ἔχοντες. This is, in fact, one of the very few passages in Jude that cannot be explained within the context of early Jewish traditions.[87] The passage is of great importance primarily because with this opposition, the author possibly argues against the position of his opponents. If this is the case, then the challenge of the adversaries can be reconstructed. In their rejection of the belief in angels and the related positions, they might have expressed the claim to possess the pneuma or to be pneumatics themselves. From here, we can draw a connection to the Pauline tradition, both to the dialogue partners of Paul in Corinth and to the developments in post-Pauline times.

The dualistic use of the antithesis ψυχικός–πνευματικός occurs first in Paul in 1 Corinthians 2:14 and 15:44, 46.[88] Most likely, Paul adopted these terms or the antithesis from Corinthian groups.[89]

Earlier investigations tried to explain the usage as being derived from Gnosticism,[90] but all these attempts have failed because there is no clear evidence for a pre-Christian gnosis in ancient sources.[91] More plausible is the derivation from Hellenistic Jewish wisdom, where Genesis 2:7 is interpreted in a dualistic framework.[92] In fact, the human being as a whole is ψυχὴ ζῶσα, but without the inspiration of the life-giving πνεῦμα, it is earthly (1 Cor 2:15), corruptible, and therefore "merely" ψυχικός. From here, there is only a small step to the opposition between ψυχικός and πνευματικός.[93] There is some evidence to suggest that the group of "wisdom-oriented" Christians in Corinth intertwined their striving for wisdom and pneumatic claims (or the goal of completeness).[94] This certainly could have led to the vilification of other Christians as merely ψυχικοί.[95] In 1 Corinthians 2:14-15, Paul adopts the language of the Corinthians in order to verbalize his own understanding of the message of the cross. He confronts the representatives of wisdom thought with the contradiction between their claims and their behavior, and turns the speech to the infants and the carnal ones (σαρκικοί) into polemical rhetoric when addressing the so-called pneumatics (1 Cor 3:1).[96]

Except in 1 Corinthians, the word ψυχικός occurs in the New Testament only in James 3:15 and Jude 19. James 3:15 demonstrates the sapiential character of the terminology: true wisdom comes from above; that is, it is pneumatically inspired (cf. Wis 6–10); its opposite is earthly, psychic (that is, natural), and demonic. It is the simple dualism of Hellenistic Jewish wisdom.[97] One may assume that James 3:13-18 was polemically directed against the pneumatics, who were basing themselves on Paul or parts of the Pauline tradition.[98] There is no evidence for a direct dependence on 1 Corinthians because James 3:13-18 does not adopt the thematic accents set by Paul.[99] But it is possible that the dualistic understanding of wisdom provides the basis for rejecting "non-spiritual"[100] claims for wisdom.

Jude 19 seems to take up the use of ψυχικός in James 3:15.[101] The opposition ψυχικοί–πνεῦμα ἔχοντες is clearly meant to have a polemical effect on those people who stand for the pneumatic claim and therefore cause argument and breakups (v. 19a). Their possession of the pneuma is denied in view of their dangerous effect on the congregation. The author of Jude may have another argument of importance: those people do not acknowledge the celestial powers, and (in his view) this is to be read as a witness to their lack of cognitive faculty. Therefore, Jude polemicizes in verse 10: "these speak evil of those things which they know not." This characterizes their mundane and, as verse 10b climactically expresses, unreasoning, animal-like disposition.

In Jude 19 terminology appears that is not affiliated with Palestinian Judaism, but that might be rooted in Hellenistic Jewish wisdom theology. Although the antithesis first occurs in Paul, its occurrence in James 3:15 and Jude 19 imply familiarity with the Pauline Epistles.[102] With the same probability, it can be stated that the acquaintance with the antithesis was transmitted by the Epistle of James, which is not directly dependent on the Pauline Letters, even though it deals with Paul,[103] or with tendencies within Pauline communities.[104] Thus, we can conclude, Jude 19 adopts a broader terminological tradition influenced by Hellenistic Jewish circles.

The Epistle of James and the Second Epistle of Peter

A more precise localization of Jude is achievable on the basis of the textual references between Jude and other New Testament texts. As supposed by the majority of the exegetes, Jude was literarily adopted by 2 Peter, and even in the preface it alludes to the figure of James, the brother of the Lord, or to the epistle ascribed to James. In this respect, Jude provides the link between James and 2 Peter.[105] But here we have to consider only the connection to James, since 2 Peter is considerably later than Jude and cannot provide any useful information for positioning Jude. This was already suggested above in the discussion on Jude 19.

The Connection to the Epistle of James

Jude's connection to the figure of James, and respectively to the Epistle of James, is generated by the opening of the letter. The *superscriptio* Ἰούδας Ἰησοῦ Χριστοῦ δοῦλος, ἀδελφὸς δὲ Ἰακώβου exactly parallels the *superscriptio* of James in the word order Ἰησοῦ Χριστοῦ δοῦλος (Jas 1:1). From here it follows, in conjunction with the allusion to James, that the author of Jude was acquainted with the Epistle of James and knowingly hints at that letter.[106] This assumption would presume the notoriety of James among the addressees of the epistle. Thus, the author introduces himself as the brother of the very James who is known not only as a founding figure of early Christianity, but more precisely from the letter ascribed to him.

But the question is, why does the author introduce himself as "brother of James" and not "the brother of the Lord" if he is meant to be the Lord's brother Jude? Some have argued that a certain act of humility is expressed by the designation "brother of James."[107] This has often been taken as an argument for authenticity. Others assume that the true identity of the author needed to be concealed.[108] But both assumptions are incorrect. The text hints at James, a well-known person who does not have to be introduced, and this allows for explicit identification of the figure of Jude: throughout early Christianity, there was one single pair of brothers named James and Jude.[109] The twofold specification of Jude as "the servant of Jesus Christ, and brother of James" claims a particular authority: first, the authority of a Christian preacher,[110] and second, an authority that derives from contact with the leading figure of early Palestinian Christianity: James, the brother of the Lord. So the authority claimed by the author is a derivative one. But such a self-presentation is only plausible if this Jude was neither known personally to the addressees nor a figure of importance to them in general. His authority as a writer is mediated by the more famous figure of James. This legitimizes the author of Jude as a second James, another important figure of the beginning.[111] The choice of the pseudonym is therefore a sign of the effect of James and the epistle ascribed to him, as well as an indication that the author was aware of the postapostololic era in which he wrote the text, a fact that is also shown by verses 3, 20, and especially 17.

However, Jude's relations to the Epistle of James are not only confined to the *superscriptio*.[112] Both letters are universally addressed—that is, are catholic letters (Jas 1:1; Jude 1-2)—even though Jude's circle of addressees might be more specified. Both texts are characterized by a lack of a formal conclusion. Both are primarily directed by a paraenetic intention and make expanded use of exempla from the Scriptures. Both demonstrate familiarity with Jewish tradition and techniques of interpretation. At the same time, both are composed in an adequate or even elaborated Koine style that is remarkable in view of the adoption of Jewish tradition. James and Jude both apply various stylistic devices and are distinguished by a relatively rich vocabulary. Comparing the vocabulary of Jude and James, the considerable quantity of matches is striking. Of a total vocabulary of 227 words in Jude, J. D. Charles has counted 93 words matching the vocabulary of James—apart from the prepositions, pronouns, particles, and the word εἶναι. Twenty-seven words occur more than twice in both texts: "Aside from Jude-2 Peter and Colossians-Ephesians comparisons, the verbal correspondence in James and Jude, considering the brevity of the latter, is unmatched anywhere else in the NT."[113] A large portion of the analogies between the two letters can be understood as elements of a common Jewish or Jewish Christian matrix.[114] However, in connection with the personality and authority of James in the prescript and the verbal parallels in the *superscriptio*, the correspondences in the vocabulary are to be assessed as an evidence for intentional contact of Jude with both the Epistle of James and the value placed upon the tradition represented by the figure of James.

Since James extensively uses Hellenistic language patterns, and since the majority of exegetes do not support a Palestinian redaction of the letter ascribed to James,[115] neither the adoption of the Jewish matrix nor Jude's connection to the figure of James and the letter ascribed to him can provide evidence for localizing the author and addressees of Jude. On the contrary, the conjunction with James strengthens the impression that Jude does not stem from Palestinian Judeo-Christian circles.[116]

Why the author of Jude refers to the Epistle of James in this manner, and why he chose a widely unknown pseudonym that is linked with James but not with Jesus himself, can only be explained in terms of the author's theological concerns. It seems that the confrontation with the Pauline circle of influence plays an important role here. James deals in the most remarkable manner with antinomian tendencies that, from a certain per-spective, are already assumable in Paul and approvable in the post-Pauline tradition. By following James in this respect, Jude incorporates the critique of the antinomian and pneumatic tendencies of the post-Pauline era.

The Counterpart of the Epistle of Paul to the Colossians

At this point, we have to deal with the strongest reproach of the author against his adversaries, addressing their lack of respect regarding the angelic powers that are in charge of the world (v. 8).

All the other reproaches—as for instance those against the denial of Christ (v. 4), the immorality (v. 4) and defilement of the flesh (vv. 8, 23), the arrogance (v. 16), and the dishonesty (v. 16)—are polemic topoi and cannot be specified as featuring the adversaries. To the author, these atti-tudes might have appeared as a possible result of rejecting the celestial powers: if someone disrespects the κυριότηι, he will probably also deny the authority of the κύριος himself, his commandments, and his power to judge when he comes with the myriads of angels (vv. 14-15). Those who think and speak in that way presumptuously override all orders and exercise lawlessness. But it is hard to decide whether and to what extent the stated reproaches are in fact applicable to the adversaries.

The only reproach that is concrete enough is the accusation that the adversaries disobey the κυριότης and blaspheme the δόξαι (v. 8). Both notions may refer to the refusal to acknowledge the angelic powers, and therewith the transgression of the place that was given to humans.[117] For this reason, the doctrine of the angels becomes the key for understanding the epistle within the history of early Christian theology.[118] The author of Jude considered the angels to be of great importance, as can be proved by the adaptation of the Watcher episode (v. 6), the tradition of the argument between Michael and the devil (v. 9), and the passage from Enoch on the Parousia of the κύριος together with the myriads of angels (v. 14). According to the author, angelic beings have a central position in creation matters and eschatology. They take part in the earthly and celestial processes and function as guarantors of the world order. According to verse 9, not even the highest angel, the archangel Michael, had dared to pronounce a blasphemy against another angelic being. In the author's judgment, the lack of respect for such creatures or even the blasphemy against them not only shows a lack of cognitive faculty (v. 10), but is a severe deed of iniquity and a violation of the creational order, as it is "similarly" (v. 7) reported in the episode of the Sodomites.[119]

The terminology suggests a connection to the deuteropauline epistles, where κυριότης occurs as description for the angelic powers, beside other terms such as such as ἀρχή, ἐξουσία, and δύναμις (Col 1:16; Eph 1:21).[120] But on the basis of the traditional hymn in Colossians 1:15-20, Colossians assesses these angelic powers as a mere part of the creation ruled by Christ, not worthy to be worshipped (Col 2:18).[121] The author of Colossians even adopts the term στοιχεῖα τοῦ κόσμου from Galatians 4:3, 9, of which Paul made polemical use in order to reject the cosmic powers as objects of worship and obedience (Col 2:8, 20).[122] As is commonly known, the specification of the Colossian "heresy" or "philosophy" (Col 2:8) produces various difficulties. The possibility cannot be excluded that Jewish and pagan elements were intertwined within the doctrine of the opponents dealt with in the Colossians.[123] Therefore, the view of the author of Jude cannot be simply identified with the positions that Colossians fights against. A merely mirror-inverted positioning of Jude and Colossians, as suggested by Heiligenthal,[124] is inadequate. Rather, the view pronounced by Sellin may come closer to the historical truth.[125] According to him, the views of the Colossian philosophy have little in common with the orthodox author of Jude. Much more might be in common between the author of Colossians, who polemicizes against the worship of the angels, and the opponents addressed in Jude. Thus,

Colossians' christologically motivated criticism of worshipping angelic powers implies a real contradiction of the position taken in Jude, where the disrespect of angels is considered a blasphemy and a severe violation of the original type of faith.

At the same time, the position of Colossians corresponds to a series of authentic Pauline statements. Indeed, in 1 Thessalonians 3:13, Paul accepts the eschatological expectation as it is expressed in Jude 14-15, namely that with the coming of Christ, his whole heavenly host will appear. But in other contexts, the "powers and authorities" have a clear-cut negative connotation. In 1 Corinthians 2:8, they stand for inferior powers, which have a limited time and will be abolished in the end by the victorious Christ (1 Cor 15:24).[126] With soteriological intent, Romans 8:38 declares that these powers do not have the force to separate from Christ. This allows us to conclude that these powers are neither of negative (which is in the center here) nor positive importance for the life of the believers. The question of whether and how this soteriologically founded position in the Pauline circles can be linked with a kind of philosophical skepticism may remain unanswered.[127] It seems remarkable that the author of Colossians argues in a different way—that is, on a Christological and soteriological basis—against the θρησκεία τῶν ἀγγέλων (Col 2:18). He fights against the view that, besides Christ, the angelic powers may also influence the lives of the believers. As a consequence, any reverence of these angelic powers becomes dispensable.

The superiority of Christians over the angels is not merely a feature of a mystic or ecstatic piety. Even Paul himself speaks of such a superiority: "Do you not know that we shall judge angels?" (1 Cor 6:3). In Corinth, the gift of tongues was most likely understood as speaking the idiom of the angels (cf. 1 Cor 13:1). This implied a pneumatic consciousness of superiority over other believers as well. Such an attitude could lead to tensions within the congregation. Further paradigms of a certain rivalry between pneumatics and angelic beings can be shown in Hellenistic Jewish texts.[128] In fact, it is presumable that behind the contempt of the κυριότης and the sacrilege of the δόξαι stands a concept that is determined by a pneumatic claim and probably shaped by Pauline influences. Such a view can regard the world in Christ as disenchanted, and the belief in angels as represented by the author and the addressees of Jude as obsolete. Whether one may see in these adversaries wandering prophets, as Sellin states, and suggest relating the information about dirtiness (v. 12) to their unwashed appearance is a question to be left aside.[129] But it is possible that the pneumatic movement came with a certain antihierarchical and libertine feature that is reflected in the polemics of Jude.

Conclusion

The heretics of Jude most likely stand in relation to the position expressed in Colossians, and so are in line with Pauline theology or influence. The author of Jude counters their views with vehement polemics. His own views are deeply founded in Jewish apocalypticism, especially in the Enoch tradition, which shapes the author's image of the coming judgment. But by using the phrase ψυχικοί πνεῦμα μὴ ἔχοντες, Jude also adopts a figure of thought that is unmistakably of Hellenistic Jewish origin. This figure was already known to the Corinthian opponents of Paul, and was polemically redirected against their pneumatic claims. In James 3:14, the attribute ψυχικός shows the same negative connotation. The author of James also criticizes the seditious nature of pride and ostentatious wisdom. James 3:14 is probably also related to a position that was shaped by Paul himself, or by his later followers. We can assume that such a position inspired the author of Jude in his characterization of his opponents as ψυχικοί. It could even be that he intentionally absorbed these polemics and his borrowed identity as the "Second James" in order to argue against a doctrine that, in his view, challenged all traditional orders due to its pneumatic claims.[130] The connection to the statements in the Epistle of James and the traditions represented by James authorizes Jude's polemics against moral anarchy and the denegation of belief.

But Jude cannot be characterized as a Jewish Christian or Judeo-Christian document in the narrower sense of the category. Certainly the Jewish origin of the author is not at stake here, but this applies to almost every author of the New Testament. By choosing his pseudonym and linking himself to the Epistle of James, the author of Jude has borrowed his Jewish Christian identity. This is also confirmed by Jude's connection with a multiplicity of Jewish apocalyptic traditions. However, the author has to be placed within the dispute of the legacy and risks of the Pauline tradition. Therefore, the historical location should be presumed primarily in the ambit of the Pauline sphere, in Syria or rather in Asia Minor. Later on, the author of 2 Peter adopted and integrated most parts of Jude into another epistle designed as a testament of the apostle. He perpetuated the thread at a later date while referring explicitly to a collection of the Letters of Paul, which were "hard to understand" and all too easy to manipulate (2 Pet 3:15-16). Such a reference is not yet found in Jude itself. The historical place of Jude, therefore, is between James and 2 Peter. In the argument with opponents, whose position was probably close to that held in Colossians, Jude has absorbed not only (Palestinian) Jewish topics. Thus, Jude has to be understood as a specific product of the encounter between Judaism and Hellenism.

CHAPTER 15

SALVATION IN JUDE 5 AND
THE ARGUMENT OF 2 PETER 1:3-11

Scott J. Hafemann

An analysis of the rhetorical structure of Jude makes it clear that Jude 5 marks the transition from the body opening of the letter to the body proper. This corresponds to the fact that Jude 5 is also the lead scriptural support for the main point of the letter, the admonition of verse 3. As such, Jude 5 plays a pivotal role in the epistle's argument, as well as presenting Jude's view of the basis and motivation for God's judgment.[1] At the same time, however, Jude 5 poses a text-critical, exegetical, and ultimately theological conundrum for the interpreter. Although the focus of attention in recent literature has been on the christological question raised by the possibility of reading Ἰησοῦς for κύριος in this passage,[2] the history of the text raises another, even more important, though more nuanced problem. Does ἅπαξ modify the participle εἰδότας, thereby providing a parallel to verse 3 (τῇ ἅπαξ παραδοθείσῃ τοῖς ἁγίοις πίστει)? If so, then Jude's point is that, because they know all things ἅπαξ (taking εἰδότας causally), he wishes to remind them that, having saved the people from Egypt (leaving the logic of σώσας open for the moment), the Lord destroyed "the second time" (τὸ δεύτερον) those who were not believing. Or does ἅπαξ relate to σώσας, thereby providing the complement to τὸ δεύτερον (the second time)? If so, then Jude asserts that, because they know all things (again taking εἰδότας causally), he wishes to remind them

331

that, having saved the people from Egypt ἅπαξ, the Lord destroyed "the second time" (τὸ δεύτερον) those who were not believing.

Text-critically, the external evidence is almost equally divided, though the witness of ℵ, when combined with the strong minuscle tradition of 1241, 1243, and 1739, the Syriac and Coptic versional evidence, and the original hand of C, tips the scale slightly in favor of the reading πάντα ὅτι [ὁ] κύριος ἅπαξ, as reflected in the NA²⁷ textual variant (but note the "D" rating granted this decision in UBS⁴).[3] The weight of the decision therefore falls on internal considerations. Here, too, translations and students of the text are divided. The natural parallel to verse 3 created by taking ἅπαξ to modify εἰδότας, and the unusual grammar and apparently opaque meaning of verse 5b that results from taking ἅπαξ with σώσας, render the textual variant the more difficult, and hence the preferred reading. However, the textual variant naturally creates a theological problem: how can the Lord destroy those whom he has saved "once for all" without denying himself?[4] Faced with this dilemma, and in the shadow of verse 3, the tradition early on simplified the text by moving ἅπαξ forward to the previous clause.

Nevertheless, the overwhelming majority go against the most recent critical edition, often suggesting that reading ἅπαξ with σώσας is actually the easier reading because of the scribal desire to provide a complement to τὸ δεύτερον.[5] Rather than speaking against taking ἅπαξ to modify εἰδότας, the material parallel to verse 3 is often seen to provide confirmation for this decision. Two factors, however, render this majority judgment problematic. First is the difficulty of understanding τὸ δεύτερον (the second time) as a contrast to ἅπαξ, since πρῶτος, not ἅπαξ, usually signifies the idea of being first in contrast to being second.[6] This is matched by the uncertainty concerning a specific referent for such a ἅπαξ-salvation within the biblical narrative. As the most difficult reading, the question therefore is actually whether the textual variant is too difficult to be viable. The purpose of this essay is to suggest that the decision of the NA²⁷ is correct, and the view of the vast majority of scholars must be revisited. But if so, then the question concerning the meaning of Jude 5b must be addressed.

The Meaning of ἅπαξ in Jude 5

The adverb ἅπαξ represents a semantic field that includes the numerical meanings (1) *once*, designating an action that does not necessarily exclude or imply the existence of a subsequent action, and hence can be found in the idiom ἅπαξ καὶ δίς (repeatedly or more than once);[7] (2) *once only*, designating a singular action at that time, or at least an action not to be repeated as a matter of course, that is, a definitive but not necessarily ultimate occurrence, and hence an occurrence that can be modified temporally with a genitive such as ἅπαξ τοῦ ἐνιαυτοῦ (once a year)[8] or ἅπαξ διὰ τριῶν ἐτῶν (once every three years);[9] (3) *once for all*, implying a singular action that is considered to be both definitive and ultimate;[10] and (4) *once* in the nonnumerical, temporal sense of a previous action that precedes or qualifies a subsequent one (e.g., in the sense, "If at once you don't succeed, try, try again").[11]

Among the twelve occurrences of the word in the New Testament outside of Jude, we find examples of all three numerical meanings, and possibly the temporal sense: (1) In 2 Corinthians 11:25, Paul recounts that he was stoned "once" (ἅπαξ ἐλιθάσθην); in Philippians 4:16, Paul notes that the Philippians had sent aid to him "repeatedly" (ἅπαξ καὶ δίς); and in 1 Thessalonians 2:18, Paul had desired to visit the Thessalonians "more than once" (ἅπαξ καὶ δίς), but had been hindered by Satan from doing so. (2) In Hebrews 9:7, we read that the high priest enters the holy of holies "once a year" (ἅπαξ τοῦ ἐνιαυτοῦ), and in Hebrews 12:26-27, we find the expression ἔτι ἅπαξ used to refer to the heavens and earth being shaken "still once [more]," in the sense of the last and definitive time. (3) In Hebrews 6:4, "those who have been enlightened once for all" (ἅπαξ φωτισθέντας) cannot be brought again to repentance; in Hebrews 9:26 and 28, Christ is said to have been manifested "once for all" (ἅπαξ) at the consummation of the age and offered "once for all" (ἅπαξ) to bear the sins of many;[12] in Hebrews 10:1-2, the sacrifices offered "year after year" (κατ' ἐνιαυτόν) and "continually" (εἰς τὸ διηνεκές) are contrasted with "having been cleansed once for all" (ἅπαξ κεκαθαρισμένους); and in 1 Peter 3:18, we find ἅπαξ used to designate that Christ died for sins "once for all."[13] However, as the distinctions within the lexica illustrate, the intrinsically definitive nature of the work of Christ makes the distinction between categories two (the definitive act that is not to be repeated as a matter of course) and three (the definitive and ultimate act) within christological contexts in the New Testament very difficult to maintain.[14]

In turning our attention to the occurrences of ἅπαξ in Jude 3 and 5 against the backdrop of this data, two important observations emerge. First, in both verses it is used with a past participle, regardless of which reading we prefer for verse 5 (v. 3, ἅπαξ παραδοθείσῃ; v. 5, either εἰδότας ἅπαξ or ἅπαξ σώσας). This corresponds to the predominate, though not exclusive,[15] use found in the literature of ἅπαξ + past participle to indicate the definitive and ultimate meaning, "once for all." When used in this way, it can signal the basis for a further conclusion or action (cf. Heb 6:4; 9:28; 10:2, and the corresponding temporal use with ἐπεὶ + an indicative in *Herm. Mand.* 4:4:1; *Herm. Vis.* 3:3:4). Structurally, therefore, there is no semantic distinction between verses 3 and either reading of verse 5.

Second, in both possible readings the definitive and ultimate meaning "once for all" can be supported by their respective contexts. In Jude 3, the "faith" has been delivered definitively to the saints, so that Jude's readers are exhorted to contend for it against the "certain men" who have slipped into the church to deny the Lord by perverting God's grace into a justified immorality (v. 4). If ἅπαξ is taken with εἰδότας in verse 5, the same meaning for it emerges as for verse 3, since the πάντα in view would recall the "faith" and "grace" of verses 3-4, as well as pointing forward to the content of the ὅτι-clause: because they know all things *definitively once for all,* Jude wishes to remind them that, having saved the people from Egypt, the Lord destroyed those who were not believing "the second time" (τὸ δεύτερον). The emphasis thus falls on their past definitive reception of this knowledge (a point seen to be repeated twice) as the ground for the present warning concerning the current crisis—that is, that the false teachers who have slipped into the church, like Israel, will be destroyed for not believing a second time. Read in this way, Jude's point is not merely that they have received faith, grace, and knowledge once in the past. Rather, since their reception of these things was final and definitive, they should not waver in being convinced that judgment awaits those who pervert the grace of God into immorality.

But if ἅπαξ is taken with σώσας in verse 5, then the sense becomes, because they know all things, Jude wishes to remind them that, having saved the people from Egypt *definitively once for all,* the Lord destroyed those who were not believing "the second time" (τὸ δεύτερον). The point is not merely that Israel was saved once in the past. Rather, since Israel's salvation from Egypt was final and definitive (ἅπαξ), the Lord will destroy them when they do not believe a second time (τὸ δεύτερον). For although πρῶτος/πρότερος is commonly used with δεύτερος to indicate a sequence or enumerate a list,[16] ἅπαξ can be found with δεύτερος when the second element is intrinsically linked to or based upon the first (cf., e.g., its use in LXX Job 33:14; 40:5; 1 Kgs 26:8). The lexical argument against the use of ἅπαξ with σώσας as the complement to τὸ δεύτερον is therefore not conclusive. In fact, Metzger and Wikgren can even use the similarity between ἅπαξ and πρῶτον to argue that ἅπαξ was later moved into the ὅτι-clause in order to make the text somehow easier to understand.[17]

The Biblical Background to Jude 5: The "Second Time" in Numbers 14

The decision against taking ἅπαξ to be part of the ὅτι-clause thus ultimately rests on the apparent difficulty of ascertaining a suitable backdrop for Jude 5 when read in this way. Such a reading is usually considered contextually impossible because of the difficulty of ascertaining a "ἅπαξ-event" within the biblical narrative that can be associated with ἐκ γῆς Αἰγύπτου, while at the same time finding a suitable complement that can be described as τὸ δεύτερον, especially when it is kept in view that τὸ δεύτερον is not modifying the participle, τοὺς μὴ πιστεύσαντας, but the independent verb, ἀπώλεσεν. As Bauckham has observed, some suggest a second occasion of unbelief corresponding to a first occasion at the Red Sea (Exod 14:10-12; Ps 107:7), but there were many such incidents of unbelief (cf. Num 14:22; Ps 78:40-41). Bauckham therefore correctly concludes, "It is more likely that Jude intends to distinguish a first occasion on which God acted to save his people (at the Exodus) and a second occasion on which he acted to judge their disbelief."[18] But this merely shifts the problem to what incident of salvation is in view. The reference to Egypt is usually taken to be a direct reference to the Exodus event per se, while Numbers 14 is often rightly seen to be the backdrop for Israel's unbelief τὸ δεύτερον. But it is difficult to construe Numbers 14 as a corollary to the deliverance from Egypt, since there is no act of deliverance in Numbers 14 on the one hand (only its potential), and no act of unbelief directly associated with the Exodus on the other. Indeed, at that point, just the opposite is asserted (cf. Exod 14:31).

This difficulty is compounded by the attempt to see the Exodus event as the act of salvation from Egypt "definitively once for all," since Israel's departure and crossing of the sea is viewed within the Torah as the primary act within a series of acts of deliverance that stretches from Moses' first encounter with Pharaoh to the crossing of the Jordan into the promised land.[19] Moreover, although Deuteronomy 9:18 draws a comparison between Moses' petition a "second time" (δεύτερον) after Israel's sin with the golden calf and his first (τὸ πρότερον) experience when he went without food and drink for forty days and nights at the giving of the law, the attempt to read Jude 5 in this light is also problematic. The parallel passage in Deuteronomy 10:10 makes clear that the point of the comparison between the events of the Exodus and Israel's subsequent sin with the golden calf is that "the Lord did *not* desire to destroy Israel at this time" (καὶ οὐκ ἠθέλησεν κύριος ἐξολεθρεῦσαι ὑμᾶς), the exact opposite of the point made in Jude 5. This is confirmed by Exodus 32–34 itself, where the point is not the destruction of the people, but the restoration of the covenant. The use of πρότερος in Deuteronomy 9:18, rather than ἅπαξ, also speaks against the attempt to read Jude 5 as a reference to the Exodus event and the sin with the golden calf, respectively.[20] Faced with these difficulties, some commentators remain content with suggesting that the Lord's destruction of Israel the second time is a general reference to Israel's experience in the wilderness in a global but undefined manner.[21]

On the other hand, if we take Numbers 14 as our starting point for understanding τὸ δεύτερον in Jude 5, since it is the only place in the Exodus narrative where the Lord explicitly declares his intention to destroy those whom he has rescued from Egypt (καὶ ἀπολῶ αὐτούς; LXX Num 14:12) because they are not believing (οὐ πιστεύουσίν μοι; LXX Num 14:11; cf. 14:22-23, 27-28; 33-35),[22] the Torah itself suggests a very specific and different reading for the ἅπαξ-event than has been recognized. Although the terminology of a ἅπαξ/δεύτερον sequence is nowhere explicitly used within the Torah, the structural, theological, and linguistic parallels between Numbers 14 and Exodus 32–34 indicate that the corresponding ἅπαξ (i.e., the first, definitive act that is not to be repeated as a matter of course) to the τὸ δεύτερον in view in Jude 5 may not be limited to the initial Exodus event per se, as often suggested, but should include, in particular, the restoration of the covenant after Israel's sin with the golden calf.[23] Indeed, God's reestablishment of the covenant after the golden calf is set up with six references to Israel's deliverance "from (the land of) Egypt" as the backdrop of Israel's sin, as well as the issue at stake in Moses' prayer for her restoration, the heaviest concentration of such references in the Scriptures (cf. Exod 32:1, 4, 7, 8, 11, 23; cf. 33:1).

According to Numbers 14, the people's response to the report of the spies is the second time in which Israel's sin brings the nation to the point of destruction. As such, it provides the corresponding portrayal of the themes encountered for the first time in Exodus 32–34. Once again, the people wish to replace Moses, this time due not to his absence but their own desire to return to Egypt (cf. Num 14:4 with Exod 32:1). Like their first reaction in Exodus 32:1, the people's desire is again interpreted as a rebellion against God and a lack of faith in his presence and faithfulness (14:9; cf. Exod 32:4-9). In Numbers 14:11, the Lord therefore asks Moses rhetorically concerning the people, καὶ ἕως τίνος οὐ πιστεύουσίν μοι . . .; in response, God declares for the second time his intention to destroy the people (καὶ ἀπολῶ αὐτοὺς) and start over with Moses (14:12; cf. Exod 32:10).

Moreover, Moses' subsequent response to the divine decree is also the same as previously found in Exodus 32:11-13: he appeals for mercy for the people on the basis of God's concern for his own glory, since the report of the Egyptians concerning the Exodus will ensure that God's reputation will precede the people into the promised land (14:13). In fact, God's reputation is even more intimately tied to the fortunes of the Israelites than before, since his presence is now known to be in their midst in the pillar of cloud and fire (14:14). If God were to destroy them at this point, the Egyptians would therefore make a mockery of God's strength all the more, and the inhabitants of the promised land would conclude that "because the Lord could not bring this people into the land which He promised them by oath, therefore He slaughtered them in the wilderness" (14:16).[24] Even more importantly, God has already declared and demonstrated that he will display his power in mercy toward Israel (14:17-18; cf. Exod 34:6-7), so that God's own word is on the line. Moses thus appeals for forgiveness based on the same grounds as in Exodus 32, but now the tradition from Exodus 34:6f. and the display of divine grace after the incident with the golden calf (cf. Deut 9:18–10:10) can be added to the appeal, with God's promise from Exodus 34:6f. taking the place of his promise to the patriarchs quoted earlier in Exodus 32:13.

Moses' argument for God's mercy in Numbers 14 indicates that, from the perspective of the Torah, God's definitive act to save his people from the land of Egypt was the restoration of the covenant and the "second giving of the Law" after Israel's sin with the golden calf. For Numbers 14:16-19 indicates that it was this event, not the exodus from Egypt per se, that ultimately tied God's fate to that of his people.

Read from the perspective of Numbers 14, Exodus 32–34 provides the theological foundation for the turning point in the Exodus narrative. In response to Moses' intercession, God's response to Moses and the people's response to God in Numbers 14 once again parallel those found in Exodus 32–34. God again grants Moses' request not to destroy the people as such (14:20; cf. Exod 32:14), but at the same time declares that his glory must be vindicated (14:21; cf. Exod 32:33-35). Just as God's mercy reveals his sovereign glory, so too there comes a time when, in view of a continual disregard for God's kindness and provision, *not* to show mercy is the only way in which this same glory can be maintained. All those who have seen God's glory upheld in Egypt and the wilderness but have nevertheless refused to trust him "these ten times"[25] will therefore no longer be allowed to enter the promised land (cf. 14:22-23 with their unbelief in 14:11). Although God is still committed to preserve a remnant within the people, in faithfulness to his promises to Abraham, from Numbers 14 on it becomes clear that God has indeed destroyed those who did not believe the second time.

The Significance of Jude 5 for the Argument of the Letter and Its Theological Implications

Against the backdrop of Exodus 32–34 and Numbers 14, the force of Jude 5 within the argument of the letter as a whole becomes evident. Rather than merely restating that the readers have known all things "once for all," Jude 5 reminds them of the lesson to be learned from Israel's experience in the wilderness: the Lord destroyed those among Israel who did not believe because he had earlier saved them "once for all" by extending mercy to them in spite of their hardened condition. The use of ἅπαξ to modify σώσας indicates that the salvation in view is God's final and decisive act of patient mercy on behalf of those who have experienced God's provision and deliverance (Exod 34:6; Num 14:18-19), which we have seen refers to his earlier acts of covenant renewal after Israel's sin with the golden calf. Though they deserved to be judged because of their hard-hearted breaking of the covenant with their idolatry, God nevertheless acted mercifully to save them by instituting the tent of meeting (Exod 33:7-11) and providing Moses as their mediator (Exod 34:29-35), so that his presence might continue in their midst without destroying them (Exod 33:3, 5; 34:29-35). Hence, their eventual judgment in Numbers 14 is brought about because their subsequent unbelief τὸ δεύτερον (cf. Num 14:11) dishonors God's earlier definitive bestowal of mercy and grace on their behalf (cf. Exod 34:6-7; Num 14:18) by their failure to respond to God's sufficient provision and presence through Moses (Num 14:4, 8-10). The emphasis and application of the text thus falls not on the knowledge of Jude's readers, but on the nature and destiny of the false teachers, who provide the contemporary parallel to the unbelieving Israelites destroyed in the wilderness.[26]

Moreover, like the Numbers 14 narrative, Jude too is careful to distinguish between those who do and do not believe. Jude follows the Old Testament narrative by establishing a distinction between his readers, as the "saints" (v. 3), and the ungodly "scoffers" who have perverted the grace they have experienced into immorality (vv. 4, 8, 18). Like the unbelievers in Numbers 14:1-3 and Korah in Numbers 16:1-3, the false teachers of Jude's day are explicitly described in verse 19 as those who, "not having the Spirit" (πνεῦμα μὴ ἔχοντες), "create divisions" among the people of God by rising up against their leaders, now embodied in the apostolic witness (vv. 17-18). Hence, like those whom the Lord destroyed (cf. ἀπώλεσεν in v. 5 with καὶ ἀπολῶ αὐτοὺς in Num 14:12) because they did not believe (cf. τοὺς μὴ πιστεύσαντας in v. 5 with οὐ πιστεύουσίν μοι in Num 14:11), in Jude 11 the false teachers too will "perish [ἀπώλοντο] in Korah's rebellion."[27]

In stark contrast, Jude's readers, like Joshua and Caleb, who are said to have the Spirit and call the people to remain faithful (cf. Num 14:6-9, 24; 27:18; Deut 34:9), can be called to "pray in the Holy Spirit" (v. 20) and to "save" those who are doubting (vv. 22-23). Rather than being considered genuine believers who have lost their former faith, that is, "apostate Christians,"[28] for Jude the false teachers show themselves to be motivated by an evil nature (vv. 10, 18-19). In other words, they were never Christians to begin with. From the perspective of both Numbers 14 and Jude, those who have the Spirit persevere in faith, while those who do not have the Spirit eventually manifest their hardened unbelief. Though the false teachers, having slipped into the Church unnoticed (v. 4), may be temporarily mistaken for genuine members of the people of God (vv. 4, 12a), their behavior eventually betrays them (vv. 4, 8, 16, 19). To use the Pauline phrase, "not all those from Israel are Israel" (Rom 9:6).

Clearly, then, Jude's application of Israel's experience in the wilderness to the false teachers (cf. Jude 8) also carries with it an implicit warning for Jude's readers. The use of ἅπαξ to modify σώσας in verse 5 establishes a parallel between the salvation experienced by Israel in the wilderness and the faith delivered to the saints ἅπαξ in verse 3, thereby creating an explicit "second exodus" typology for understanding the current situation of Jude's readers. As such, verse 5 functions as part of Jude's overall "persuasive discourse" or "epistolary 'word of exhortation,'" in which he intends to influence the behavior of his audience;[29] only those who persevere in faithfulness to the faith can be considered to be among those who are genuinely "called" as a result of "having been loved by God the Father and kept by Jesus Christ" (v. 1). For, like Israel in the wilderness, they too have experienced God's salvation (cf. ἡ κοινὴ ἡμῶν σωτηρία in v. 3 with σώσας in v. 5). Having been kept (τετηρημένοις) by Jesus Christ (v. 1) means, therefore, that they must (and will; cf. the doxology) keep (τηρήσατε) themselves in the love of God (v. 21).

The indicative reality concerning God's judgment from verse 5 serves, along with the examples that follow in verses 6-16, to support the imperatives of both verses 3 and 17-23 that frame Jude's letter. Like Israel after the golden calf, Jude's readers have been saved "once, for all." Their response, unlike Israel's after the golden calf, is to contend for and build themselves up in the faith they have received ἅπαξ (vv. 3, 20).[30] Not to do so is to deny by virtue of their behavior the saving reality found in their "only Master and Lord, Jesus Christ" (v. 4). To do so, however, is to render by virtue of their perseverance in godliness the glory due to the only One who, as a result of their salvation (v. 3), is able to guard them from stumbling and to make them stand before him, blameless and with great joy (v. 24-25).

The Parallel between Jude 5 and 2 Peter 1:3-11

The emphasis in Jude 5 on the necessity of those who have been "saved once, for all" persevering in faithfulness to the faith, with its second-exodus typology, recalls 2 Peter 1:3-11, with its emphasis on the need to increase in the virtues listed in verses 5-7 in order to confirm one's election and thereby enter into the "eternal kingdom" (vv. 8-11). This common emphasis on the conditionality of the grace of God in regard to inheriting God's promises, which have been granted unconditionally, is not accidental. It reflects their common reliance on the structure of biblical covenants as the template for understanding God's relationship with his people. This becomes clear when we analyze the structure of 2 Peter 1:3-11.[31]

Although there is a long commentary tradition that considers verses 3-4 to be part of the opening greeting as the support for Peter's wish in verse 2 (cf., e.g., the commentaries of Calvin, Bigg, Windisch, Schrage, and Kelly), it seems more appropriate to take verses 3-4 to be the opening of the body of the letter, as reflected in the punctuation of the NA[27] text. Though not unattested in later Christian literature,[32] such a lengthy expansion of the greeting is rare in ancient letters and would be unique among the New Testament epistles. It would also be highly unusual, both theologically and rhetorically, to begin the body of a letter with the inference and imperatives of verses 5a-7b without the prior indicative to support them that verses 3-4 provide. To do so in this case would subvert the crucial theological structure of the text, in which, as in the rest of the New Testament, the imperatives necessitated by the gospel never exist apart from the indicative realities upon which they are based and from which they organically derive. Moreover, 1:3 is a genitive absolute construction, the regular placement of which is before the main clause that it modifies,[33] thereby also indicating its forward-looking relationship to verse 5a. As attested in the papyri, such genitive absolutes "may often be seen forming a string of statements, without a finite verb for several lines," just as we find here.[34] Finally, in a letter as carefully crafted as 2 Peter, it is easier to construe the instrumental reference διὰ τῆς ἐπιγνώσεως τοῦ καλέσαντος ἡμᾶς (through [by means of] the knowledge of the one who called us) as providing a transition from the greeting to the body of the letter than to see it as directly supporting verse 2, where it would be a redundancy in view of ἐν ἐπιγνώσει τοῦ θεοῦ (by means of the knowledge of God) in verse 2b. As Bauckham rightly observes, "The connection with v. 2 is largely stylistic, whereas the connection with vv. 5-7 is fundamental to the flow of argument."[35]

This decision is important because it both leads to and is confirmed by the threefold covenantal structure that emerges from the text once verses 3-4 are aligned with verses 5-11. Ever since the pioneering work of G. E. Mendenhall,[36] it has been widely recognized that the covenant structure found throughout the Old Testament, and the pattern of argumentation that derived from it, parallel key aspects of the suzerainty covenants attested in the ancient Near East, beginning with those found in the treaties between the Hittite kings and their vassals (ca. 1400–1200 BCE).[37] Despite their diversity of date, origin, content, and presentation, the structure of argumentation found in much of this covenant or treaty tradition presupposes three interrelated aspects also found intertwined throughout the Old Testament traditions:[38]

1. The historical prologue[39]
2. The covenant stipulations[40]
3. The covenant promises and curses[41]

As the foundation for the relationship between God and Israel through-out the Old Testament tradition, it is not surprising, then, that this same threefold structure is found in 2 Peter 1:3-11 and presupposed in Jude 5, since it has been shown that this covenant structure became the basis for a standard homiletic pattern in early Jewish and Christian literature.[42] The argument of 2 Peter, read against the backdrop of the covenant structure, outlines as follows:

1. The historical prologue (vv. 3-4)
2. The covenant stipulations (vv. 5-7, 10a)
3. The covenant promises and curses (vv. 8-9; 10bc-11)

This covenant structure explains how the promises that accompany an entrance into the eternal kingdom of God in verses 4 and 11 can be con-ditional, being based upon the commands of verses 5-7, while at the same time being expressions of grace, granted in accordance with one's calling and election as declared in verses 3 and 10. It also explains how, in Jude 5, God can destroy those whom he saves without dishonoring his own glory. On the one hand, both the stipulations and the promises of God are grounded in the prior act of God's calling and made possible by his power as described in verses 3-4; that is, the historical prologue precedes and supports the covenant stipulations and its promises. Hence, both the acts of divine deliverance and the fulfillment of the ensuing commands are expressions of God's sovereign grace and election. On the other hand, inasmuch as the focus of these stipulations is on the future, unfulfilled promises of God, the promises remain conditional. One must maintain the covenant relationship with God by keeping his stipulations in order to inherit the promises. Thus, as the covenantal structure of this pas-sage indicates, salvation is completely dependent upon the grace of God's calling and election as its necessary and sufficient condition, while at the same time being also completely dependent upon the response of those who have been called as its necessary condition.

Yet, inasmuch as the fulfillment of the covenant stipulations and the corresponding inheritance of the promises are both made possible by God's saving activity, the conditional nature of God's promises cannot be perverted into a covenant of partners, in which obedience to the covenant stipulations would be the sole or sufficient human basis for inheriting the promises. This would alleviate the determining character of the historical prologue by beginning effectively with the imperatives. Nor can the obedience described in verses 5-7 be viewed as contributions to the process;[43] this would eliminate the inextricable link between what God has done and continues to do, as outlined in the prologue, and what he stipulates as the corresponding response. The commands of verses 5-7 are neither the sufficient grounds for salvation nor a necessary human contribution to it. Rather, as Peter's argument will demonstrate, they are the inextricable expressions of the calling and election of God in the lives of his people. As verses 3-4 make clear, the historical prologue contains a surprising yet essential declaration of what it is that God has done to save his people under the new covenant established by Christ with the inauguration of the kingdom of God. The indicatives of the historical prologue (vv. 3-4) thus lead to the imperatives of the covenant stipulations (vv. 5-7), which in turn lead to the indicative promises of future blessing or curse (vv. 8-11).

In accordance with its covenant structure and rhetorical composition, the explicit purpose of this section is to codify and summarize the covenant relationship that exists in Christ between God and his people, in order that it might be continually remembered and repeated, even after Peter's death (cf. the inference in 1:12a). In the same way, Jude is calling on his readers to recall what they already know. This, too, is in keeping with the Old Testament admonitions concerning the necessity of preserving the covenant and its stipulations for future generations. It is this necessity that leads Peter to write his testament as an epistle to his churches, and it is this necessity that also dictates that the theological framework and content of his testament be that of the covenant relationship itself. Second Peter 1:3-11 and Jude 5 thus perform the same role within their respective letters. Structurally, the former declares, while the latter implies the content and call of the covenant relationship.

The implications of this parallel for the literary and canonical relationship between 2 Peter and Jude remain to be investigated.

Part VII

CONCLUSION

CHAPTER 16

A PROLEGOMENON TO A HISTORY OF THE "POSTAPOSTOLIC ERA" (EARLY CHRISTIANITY 70–150 CE)

Ernst Baasland

The seminar "Catholic Epistles and Apostolic Traditions" has concentrated on the Catholic Epistles as literature and their place within the canon of the New Testament. The references to historical events and to the apostolic and postapostolic periods have been part of our discussions. In the present paper, however, I will focus entirely on the postapostolic period as a challenge for current and future scholarship.

A seminar paper can hardly bring more than a prolegomenon to the big challenge: a reconstruction of the postapostolic period. A prolegomenon is, however, a starting point for a neglected debate.

The Challenge

The Definition

The term *early church* was and still is the most widely used category. The designation *postapostolic age* is relatively new in scholarship and is based on a relatively limited perspective. The Tübingen school introduced the term after 1835. An entirely new perception of early Christianity and the discovery of new Christian and pagan sources in the eighteenth century gave the Tübingen school great influence in the scholarly research.

F. C. Baur, the founder of the Tübingen school (and A. Ritschl, who increasingly became skeptical of Baur's theories) did not use the term *postapostolic period* in his own outline.[1] In the aftermath of Baur, it became widely used as a key term, based on Baur's reconstruction of the earliest Christianity.[2]

Baur dated most of the writings of the New Testament to the period after the apostolic age, with its history-shaping conflict between the Pauline and the Petrine/Jerusalem positions. Postapostolic implies both the thesis that most of the New Testament writings are pseudonymous and the concept that personalities (or ideas, *Ideenträger*) are most influential in historical development.

Postapostolic period can, however, be used in a more neutral sense, simply indicating the period after 70 CE. It implies that the apostles played an important role both before and after that date, through the memories and through their disciples.

The main problems with the term postapostolic are Baur's premises for using it, and that it leaves the terminus ad quem open: why should a postapostolic period end in 110 or 150 or 180?

The Period

The period 70–150 CE is indeed a distinctive period, for many reasons. The year 70 CE marks an important bracket, particularly through the following facts:

1. The fall of Jerusalem had a significant role.
2. Most of the original apostles died before this year.
3. Jewish Christianity separated itself more from Gentile Christianity.[3]
4. The Gospels were published.

Most scholars see the years 130–150 as the end of the postapostolic era,[4] based on the following observations:

1. The disciples of the apostles passed away before 150.
2. The writings of the New Testament were completed.
3. The writings of the Apostolic Fathers were also completed.
4. Marcion raised the question of canon.
5. Gnosticism became influential and parted from orthodox Christianity.
6. Extensive apologies and a Christian literature marked a new development,[5] starting with Justin's Apology in 150 CE.

Consequently, the period from 70 to 150 CE is indeed a specific historical period.[6] This fascinating period is a common ground for both New Testament and patristic scholars. Ideally, this should lead to a double effort, but on the contrary, the effort has been reduced and the study of this period is rather neglected, both in New Testament and in patristic scholarship.

One hundred years ago, positions existed at German universities with such names as professor of New Testament and patristics (e.g., A. Jülicher's position in Marburg). With a few exceptions at American universities, these positions have disappeared.

The Name

To give the period 70–130/150 CE a name is not easy. The alternatives are:

1. Postapostolic period
2. Early Catholicism[7]
3. "Time for combating heretical groups" ("Zeit der Ketzerbestreiter")[8]
4. Early Christianity,[9] specified by events outside Christianity or defined by the framework of the Roman empire,[10] mostly divided into two periods:
   a. The time of the early (Julian-Claudian-Flavian) emperors
   b. The time from Nerva to Marcus Aurelius/Commodus,[11] representing a climax in the history of the Roman Empire

As historians, we have to prefer the last alternative, early Christianity/ church (70–150 CE), as the first (or second) period of the early church.

The Sources

The most important category of sources is what historians call *primary sources*.[12] For the postapostolic age, a number of primary sources are available:

1. According to the most current dating of the New Testament writings, the majority of the canon (except the authentic Pauline letters and Q, or parts of Q) was written during this period. If that is correct, we have even in the New Testament much material for a reconstruction of the postapostolic era. On the other hand, the reconstruction of this period will highly depend on the assessment of the authenticity of (half of) the books of the New Testament.

2. In the period 70–150 CE, the writings of the Apostolic Fathers were completed. In recent scholarship, most scholars treat these writings as secondary, compared with the New Testament, and only a few scholars treat them as real parallels to the New Testament. An extensive comparison between the writings of the Apostolic Fathers and writings of the New Testament (after Paul) has so far not been accomplished. Most scholars state various influences from the New Testament on the Apostolic Fathers, while hardly any assume that parts of the New Testament know or refer to the writings of the Apostolic Fathers. The writings of the Apostolic Fathers, similar to those of the New Testament, consist of a variety of genres (eight letters; a church order; a sermon; epitreptic, apologetic, and apocalyptic tracts). As a whole, the Apostolic Fathers collection has a canon-like structure, in a certain analogy with the New Testament.

3. The period 70 to 150 CE also leaves us an overwhelming amount of sources, including papyri,[13] as well as Jewish (esp. Josephus, many Apocrypha and Pseudepigrapha), Greek (Plutarch, etc.), Roman (Plinius, Sueton, etc.), and gnostic literature, among others. Hardly any period of classical history has such a variety of available sources.

Due to the fact that so many sources are available, it might be seen as a challenge that a real history of the postapostolic era never has been written. The historical period from 70 to 150 remains in shadow. It is indeed surprising that New Testament (or patristic) scholars, as historians, have contributed little to the reconstruction of a very important historical period. This might have something to do with theological biases or anti-Catholic attitudes. In general, New Testament scholars are more exegetes than historians, and too often we lack a profound understanding of historical methodology and an interest in history-telling.

The Prospects

The history of Christianity before 70 CE (the apostolic age, *das Urchristentum*), or at least some perspectives on it, is told in the book of Acts. For the period from 70 to 150 CE (the postapostolic age), no history like the book of Acts is found. Acts gives the history of the apostolic age and in spite of extensive criticism of the book, Acts is the framework of nearly every history of the apostolic age.

We can use Hans Conzelmann's research as an example to illustrate this observation. Conzelmann's criticism of Acts does not leave many pieces of the book as reliable source. But in his *Geschichte des*

Urchristentums, the framework of Acts is the basis for his reconstruction of the history of the apostolic age.

The very lack of an Acts-like book makes the reconstruction of the history of 70–150 more difficult. It might be an open question why, between Acts and Eusebius, no history was written, or why such writings now are lost. Papias may have given such a history in one of his five lost books. If they were found, it would drastically change the source situation for recent scholarship.

In the apostolic age, Paul is the only historical figure who is reported in independent sources and who develops a theology that reflects his own self-understanding. In the postapostolic period, theologians and movements give us good possibilities for a reconstruction, not only in the province of Asia (Papias, 70–130 CE; Polycarp, d. 155 CE; Montanus and his movement; also Abercius/Bishop Avirkios Marcellos, Apollinarius, Melitos, etc.), but also in Syria (Ignatius, d. before 117 CE; Tatianus; Theophilus; and later Bardesanes, 154–222 CE) and Rome (Clemens, 70–110 CE; Hermas; Justin, d. 165 CE).

For this period, it is also possible to see the impact of Roman politics (laws, persecution, actions under Nero, Vespasian, Titus, Domitian, Nerva, Trajan, Hadrian) and to analyze the impact of the Jewish War/fall of Jerusalem (66–70 CE), the Diaspora revolt (116/117 CE), and the Bar Kokhba revolt (132–135 CE).[14]

These observations mean that the prospect for a real history of the postapostolic period should be better than the prospects for the history of the apostolic age. In spite of that, scholars have neglected the postapostolic period.

An Overview

Throughout the history of exegesis, there have been at least seven different patterns for understanding the postapostolic period. In this overview, I will particularly focus on what role the Catholic Epistles (CE) play in the reconstruction of the postapostolic era.

Evolutionistic Approaches

Baur (Tübingen) School

Baur's famous reconstruction is based on the theory that, from the very beginning, there was a conflict between Jewish Christianity and Pauline Hellenistic Christianity, and that through a dialectic development, the two forms of Christianity were harmonized in early Catholicism.[15]

All the writings in the New Testament (except the four genuine Pauline letters and Revelation) are postapostolic products and exhibit the various phases of a unifying movement, which resulted in the formation of the orthodox church of the second and third centuries. The Acts of the Apostles is a catholic irenicon that harmonizes Jewish and Gentile Christianity by liberalizing Peter and contracting or Judaizing Paul, and concealing the difference between them.

Ritschl School

A. Ritschl rejected many of Baur's basic assumptions (the role of Jesus, the importance of John, the authenticity of many of the New Testament writings, the evaluation of Revelation, etc.) and emphasized more the importance of individuals (*Persönlichkeiten*) like Jesus, Paul, and John. Ritschl's project was, however, to explain how early Catholicism had developed. For the postapostolic age, he came to conclusions similar to Baur's. Postapostolic early Catholicism had no important individuals and developed into the so-called *Durchschnittschristentum*.

Ritschl differentiated between the development of the teaching and the development of the Christian *Gemeinde- und Kirchenverfassung*.[16] The latter development took place in the postapostolic age and opened the way for an early Catholic church (*Durchschnittschristentum*).

Baur and Ritschl agreed on the evolutionistic approach and had a common interest in explaining why and how the Catholic Church was shaped. Despite criticism, there remained general agreement of this conception of the postapostolic period, following Baur and Ritschl.[17]

History of Religions School

Gunkel, Bousset,[18] Heitmüller, and Bultmann had the same evolutionistic perspective and came to similar conclusions concerning the postapostolic period. They emphasized the broader religious history perspective, showing that Judaism, Hellenistic culture, and gnosis fundamentally influenced Christianity. Accordingly, Christianity developed into a syncretistic religion. The conflict between Jews and Gentiles became less crucial, and the Hellenistic influence was part of the pre-Pauline communities.

The Tübingen, Ritschl, and history of religions schools mostly agreed on treating the CE as late products of early Catholicism or *Durchschnittschristentum*. Many scholars consider the Epistle of James to be the only exception, assuming that James represents a Jewish, Judaic/Judeo-Christianity.

The Notion of Early Catholicism

According to many Protestant scholars, Catholicism is a notion for Christianity in decline. Baur and Ritschl opened the way for this categorization, and Bousset and the history of religions school made only minor corrections to this concept. It is, however, hard to understand why this concept still played a key role for German Protestant scholars (mostly influenced by Bultmann's research) in the 1980s.[19] Even in a relatively recent ecumenical church history, E. Lohse uses this categorization in his approach to the postapostolic age.[20]

Today, scholars try to avoid the notion of early Catholicism as a concept for understanding the postapostolic age, not only because of Protestant prejudices or negative connotations, but mainly because this concept does not help our understanding of the phenomenon and the forces behind the postapostolic age.[21]

Approaches to Historical Explanation

We can often see very simple historical explanations behind the evolutionary approach, a model of man-movement-machinery-monument. It always starts with a person, who creates a movement, which eventually becomes increasingly monolithic. For many Protestant scholars, early Catholicism indicates a movement that has become a monument. Early Catholicism is a movement in decline, a very negative development.

One of Baur's students, Karl Marx, reacted against this and similar idealistic evolutionary approaches. He replaced them with materialistic explanations. He thus inspired many historians to go deeper into the question of forces, motives, *Kräfte*, which could explain the development of Christianity.

One hundred years ago, many Marxist authors and some popular books applied the Marxist approach to the growth of the early church. K. Kautsky's book on early Christianity,[22] in which he describes the proletarian character of the community with its communism, contempt for labor, and destruction of the family, became very influential. Not only class hatred, but Christianity declined until communism disappeared and Christians accepted proletarians and slaves and were led by an elite group of apostles and bishops. Only in monasticism did a sort of communism survive.

The Marxists had mostly a one-sided view. However, they put important questions on the agenda, and historical explanations became an element in many scholarly works. In the first decades of the twentieth century, important studies appeared both in the Chicago school (S. J. Case)[23] and in Germany.[24]

More recently, K. Aland's history of the church focuses less on Jewish heritage as a force, and more on the confrontation with the Roman culture.[25] In his explanation of the development of the postapostolic age, he differentiates between "die äussere und die innere Geschichte."[26] The more external forces include mission, social structure, feminism, and persecution. According to some scholars such as Aland, the decline of *Naherwartung* was the most important internal force. This force created the notion of apostolic writings/faith/ministry, and developed a hierarchy and the new Christian literature (*das Schrifttum der Frühzeit*).

In my opinion, Aland uses a methodologically important approach, but the forces he points out are highly disputable, both in the way he outlines them and in the way he excludes other, more important forces (e.g., Jewish heritage).

An influential Scandinavian church history (Christensen/Göransson)[27] tries to be more comprehensive, listing the following forces: Jewish heritage, tradition (and Scripture), liturgy, organization, concepts of holiness, and Imperium Romanum.

K. M. Fischer similarly lists four forces:[28] division from Judaism, struggle with gnosis, awareness of being a separate movement, and persecution.

More vague is the widely used church history edited by H. Jedin.[29] In the chapter "The Post-Apostolic Age,"[30] four perspectives are introduced: the conflict between Christianity and the Roman state power, the religious world as mirrored in its writings, the developments of the church's organization, and heterodox Jewish Christian currents.

In my opinion, even in the studies mentioned here, the understanding of the forces should be deeper and broader,[31] and in too many of the studies mentioned elsewhere in this paper, there is a lack of understanding of the nature of historical explanation[32] and contact with methods and studies in the science of history.

The Jewish Heritage Approach

For the evolutionistic approach, Jewish heritage disappears or develops into Jewish sects. The Jewishness of Christianity represents the classical conflict, but as a whole is more or less an episode. However, many scholars recognize Jewish heritage as more than an episode, and even as a fundamental part of Christianity. The Jewish heritage approach has the advantage of making the development of the church more easily understandable.

Jew and Gentile as Representing Two Different Cultures

The early church was part of a Jewish culture, living in a predominantly Hellenistic environment, with a variety of subcultures. The congregations had to adapt to a number of different cultures, and Roman rule presented legal and cultural challenges with which every social group had to struggle. After M. Hengel's seminal book *Judaism and Hellenism*,[33] the variety of groups within Judaism and the Hellenistic world has become a common area of scholarly work. One hundred years ago, Jew-Gentile relations were seen in terms of conflict, and not as a variety of forms or understood within the framework of contextualization

In R. Knopf's masterwork on the postapostolic period,[34] the perspective of Jewish versus Gentile structures most of the book. The first part pictures the Jewish communities after 70 CE, and the second—and of course largest—part reconstructs the Gentile church from 70 to 150 (mission, gnosis, rituals, church order, piety and ethics, theology in conflict with Judaism, *Griechentum* and gnosis).

The CE are not important sources, according to Knopf. He treats them more as sources for the reconstruction of the apostolic era. As sources for the postapostolic period, some of them (1–2–3 John, Jude, 2 Peter) illustrate the dispute with the upcoming gnosis.

The perspective of Jewish versus Gentile is fundamental also in D. G. Dix' book *Jew and Greek*.[35] According to Dix, James is an important source for Jewish Christianity, and the Epistle of James, 1 Peter, and Hebrews originate from Rome.[36] Jude is, for Dix, an interesting proof of the Nazareans' continued contact with Gentile Christendom. According to Dix, 2 Peter witnesses the continuing prestige of the Jerusalem church among Gentiles,[37] whereas the Epistles of John are expressions of the gospel for the Greeks.[38]

Leonard Goppelt's influential book on the postapostolic period combines different approaches.[39] He structures the period through two paragraphs:[40]

1. Die ausgehende apostolische Zeit (The apostolic time is fading out)
   a. Kirche und Welt: Das Verhältnis zum Imperium und die Mission
   b. Judentum und Christentum zwischen 70 und 135 (die Kirche in Palästina)
   c. Die Aufgliederung der Kirche und die Entwicklung der einzelnen Gebiete (Rom, Kleinasien, Syrien, Ägypten)

    d. Die gemeinsamen innerkirchlichen Probleme (der Weg
       zum Frühkatholizismus)
  2. Die Entwicklung der die Kirche gestaltenden Kräfte (The devel-
    opment of the forces that shaped the Church)
    a. Die Kirche, das Wort, die Tradition und der Kanon
    b. Die Reinheit und die Einheit der Kirche: Häresie und
       Christensünde
    c. Das kirchliche Amt
    d. Der Gottesdienst

The most important perspective, according to Goppelt, is the relation
between the Church and the Synagogue, but he does not analyse the CE
from that perspective. James, Jude, 2 Peter, and the Epistles of John deal
with questions that are typical in early Catholicism.

Jewish Christianity as the Mighty Minority

J. Jervell has taken a peculiar position in recent scholarship. He stresses
the importance of Jewish Christianity in the period 70–100 CE and the
significance of Jewish Christianity for the correct interpretation of Paul
and Luke-Acts.[41] Paul was accepted by earliest Jewish Christianity, and
only as time went on was it increasingly necessary for him to conform to
the conservatism of Jewish Christianity, a movement characterized as *the
mighty minority*. Jervell argues that Luke-Acts is not a Gentile Christian
but a Jewish Christian document.[42]

    Jervell has not received much support for his understanding of Luke-
Acts as a whole nor is it likely to in the future; but the emphasis on the
importance of Jewish Christianity in the late first century is a challenge
for scholarship in the years to come. The CE play no role at all in Jervell's
argumentation.

Jewish Heritage as Fundamental Heritage

There has been an important shift in the Jesus research: for a hundred
years, Jesus has seen seen as "un-Jewish," whereas recent research ("third
quest") underlines the Jewishness of Jesus. One can perhaps expect a
similar shift in regard to the understanding of the apostolic and postapostolic ages. The patristic scholar O. Skarsaune sees Jewish heritage as
fundamental in the first three centuries.[43] The Jewish influence is a sort
of common ground and framework of reference for the CE, the Apostolic
Fathers, and other sources from this early period.

The Geographical Approach

In the last decades, local history has been a trend in historical research. The first task of this approach is to analyze the development in a region; the second stage is to put the pieces together to form a national history. This kind of local history must also be important for historians who are reconstructing the postapostolic age.

J. Weiss

In his Urchristentum, J. Weiss proposes a basically geographical approach.[44] After the paragraphs on Urgemeinde, Gentile mission, and Paul, he traces the postapostolic period in two parts: the general development (Die Missionsgemeinden und die Anfänge der Kirche) and the church in the provinces (Judea, Syria, Asia Minor, Macedonia and Achaia, Rome). The last part is the most important (120 pages), and it is still an important contribution to this field of study.

W. Bauer

Bauer, who never achieved the building of a school like Baur's or that of Bauer's contemporary Bultmann, wrote a book on orthodoxy and heresy in earliest Christianity,[45] which influenced many American scholars and, for a period from 1960 to the 1980s, German scholarship as well.[46] A. Hilgenfeld's classical work on the history of heresy operated with strong borders between orthodoxy and heresy.[47] In contrast, Bauer assumes that the heresy in many provinces represented more the beginning stage than an opposition at a later stage. Bauer's famous thesis is that orthodoxy and heresy in earliest Christianity did not stand in relation to one another as primary to secondary. In many regions, heresy was the original manifestation of Christianity.

Bauer analyzes the situations of the churches in the different provinces. He provides the following outline: Edessa, Egypt, Asia Minor ("Ignatius of Antioch and Polycarp of Smyrna; Macedonia and Crete" and "Asia Minor prior to Ignatius"), and Rome and Christianity outside Rome.

In Edessa and even more in Egypt, the initial development of Christianity took forms that later appeared to be heretical. In Asia Minor (and further to the west), Paulinism was an important factor in the beginning. Paulinism was, however, open to various dogmatic expressions, and there existed in the same areas other forms of the religion of Christ—compatible with Paulinism, alienated from it, or wholly independent of it.

It was not until the postapostolic era that tensions increased and pressed for a solution. The explanation for this lies primarily in the decline of the eschatological expectation, which made the faithful increasingly unable and unwilling to tolerate disturbances and difficulties as incidental defects of a brief transitional period. If one has to prepare for a lengthy stay, one longs for orderliness and harmony in the house.

Köster's Comprehensive Geographical Approach

H. Köster and J. Robinson picked up Bauer's challenge and tried to provide a new map for the development of earliest Christianity.[48] In his *Introduction to the New Testament*, Köster gives a comprehensive view of the development in three church provinces: Palestine/Syria, Egypt, and Asia Minor/Greece/Rome.[49] One can dispute his categorization, and even more his reconstruction of the history of the provinces and how he situates the actual writings. However, the approach as such is very fruitful.

For Köster, Palestine/Syria was the place of origin for Jewish Christianity as well as Gnosticism. Though Gnosis was a key factor in Egypt, it was early Catholicism that originated there. In Asia Minor/Greece/Rome, apocalyptics developed alongside a more realistic attitude to the world (*Weltbewältigung*). The struggle against gnosis started in the West. Consequently, Köster places James and the Johannine tradition in Palestine/Syria, and Jude and the Petrine tradition in Asia Minor/Greece/Rome.

Writing-Oriented Approaches

Due to the lack of comprehensive books on the postapostolic age, we have to look for contributions on this period in introductions to the New Testament, theologies of the New Testament, and commentaries. In these studies, the different writings are treated as reflecting separate communities or as expressions of separate stages in the development of the postapostolic time.

Atomistic Approaches

The atomistic approach presupposes that every writing represents a community of its own. Consequently, we have about fifteen to twenty communities represented in the New Testament (Synoptics, Q, Acts?, 2 Thess, Col, Eph, Past, CE, John, Rev), and the Apostolic Fathers reflect at least ten different communities.

The problem with the atomistic approach is that these studies isolate the writings. Historians have to put the pieces together for a comprehensive picture of the postapostolic age, and the assumption that every book represents an independent theology/community makes it even more difficult to reconstruct a comprehensive picture.

H. Chadwick's Writing-Oriented Analysis

A writing-oriented analysis is more easily understood in patristic scholarship. The Apostolic Fathers are linguistically and theologically separate from one another, and thus H. Chadwick takes a basically writing-oriented approach in his study of the postapostolic era,[50] including such chapters as "'Barnabas,' Jewish Christianity, Trouble at Corinth," "Ignatius of Antioch," "Didache," "Marcion," and "Justin."[51]

Unfortunately, Chadwick does not include the New Testament writings in his approach, and he does not see the writings as parts of an analysis of Christianity in the various Roman provinces.

G. Theißen's Categorization

Many scholars see the problems with an atomistic view. Instead of isolating every piece of writing, they see several writings under the same category. In his most recent book, Theißen assumes that four groups dominated the period 70–110 CE:[52]

1. Jewish Christianity (*Gos. Heb.*, *Gos. Eb.*, and *Gos. Naz.*, and later James)
2. Synoptic Christianity (Q, Mark, and later Matt, Luke-Acts)
3. Pauline Christianity (2 Thess, Col, and later Past, Eph)
4. Johannine Christianity (John and later 1–2–3 John; dissidents)

In the period 110–180 CE, the four groups merged into an early Catholicism (represented by the Apostolic Fathers, the Apologists, 2 Peter, and particularly the canon), opposing two more radical movements: radical prophetic groups (Rev, Elchasai, Hermas, Montanists) and radical *Erlösungsreligion* (gnosis).[53]

Theißen is also providing an important and more comprehensive contribution to this field of study, even though his categorization is disputable and his writing-oriented approach has methodological problems.

Methological Problems Related to the Writing-Oriented Approach

Historians use traditions (symbolic sources) in two ways: as remains or relics, or as testimonies of witness of events.[54]

The theory of the Tübingen school starts from the assumption that all writings of the New Testament are writings with a tendency (*Tendenzschriften*). The New Testament represents a collection of polemical (or peacemaking) tracts of the apostolic and postapostolic age. Instead of contemporaneous, reliable history, the New Testament represents a series of intellectual movements and literary fictions.

Using the New Testament writings as relics has been very influential in New Testament scholarship, much more than among other historians, which may indicate that New Testament scholarship should raise this methodological question in a more profound manner.

The Social History Approach

As a reaction against the writing-oriented approach, and instead of an event- and person-oriented history, social history approaches also developed in New Testament scholarship. One hundred years ago, studies inspired by Marxism flourished, but E. Troeltsch[55] and S. J. Case[56] published influential social history books without the ideological premises of Marxism.

More recent studies on the social history of early Christianity concentrate on the first century, particularly on the apostolic times. In his influential book on *The First Urban Christians*,[57] W. A. Meeks analyzes the urban environment, the social level, formation of the *Ekklesia*, governance, rituals and patterns of belief, and patterns of life. The perspective is the Roman urban society, and the Pauline texts are most illuminating for Meeks.

Meeks has few references to the CE.[58] Similarly, the CE are hardly mentioned in P. E. Esler's collection of essays on *Modelling Early Christianity*.[59] Only in the first chapter ("Early Christian group formation and maintenance") are the CE frequently referred to.[60]

The most comprehensive social history approach is given by Ekkehard W. Stegemann and Wolfgang Stegemann.[61] The CE and particularly James are important in the chapter "The Social Composition of Urban Christian Communities after 70 C.E.,"[62] and 1 Peter in the paragraph "External Conflicts of Believers in Christ with Gentiles and Jews in the Diaspora."

In spite of the predominance of the theme *rich and poor* in the Epistle of James, no larger sociological/socio-anthropological study has so far been published. In 1 Peter, the theme *parepidemos/paroikos* is so crucial that studies from sociological perspectives were necessary. J. H. Elliott[63] and others[64] have contributed to this and other sociological/socio-anthropological themes.[65] These studies, however, are limited to separate writings and not part of comprehensive studies of early Christianity.

Theological (Transcendental) Approaches

Most New Testament scholars combine a history- or writing-oriented approach with a summary of some common theological themes (Christology, church order, sacraments, etc.). L. Goppelt's book is mentioned above, and E. W. Barnes may serve as an example of English scholarship.[66] N. Hyldahl combines a thematic and a writing-oriented approach, but orients his outline mostly on the literature.[67]

Traditional Thematic Theological Approaches

Patristic scholars and church historians tend to concentrate on a thematic approach, and it is indeed possible to illuminate how the main theological themes and many important terms were handled in many provinces. To a large extent, one can write a history of theology in the second century.[68]

C. Andresen limits himself to the task of "soziologische Typologie und ekklesiologische Typengeschichte."[69] He insists, however, that it is possible to give a comprehensive view of what he calls "Die Frühkatholische Kirche" (Kirchliches Selbstverständnis, Einheit der Christenheit, Verfassungsformen und Gemeindeleben, Gottesdienst und Frömmigkeit).

Bultmann's and Theißen's Transcendental Approaches

The third part of Bultmann's *Theology of the New Testament* is devoted to the development into the early Church. Similar to his *Urchristentum*, here he analyzes the answers given in the New Testament and the early Fathers to fundamental questions of man and time, man and world, salvation, cosmology, *das Verständnis des Imperativs*, and so on. Most characteristic is the way he orders the answers to the issue of "salvation as a present and a future event":[70] as *Shepherd of Hermas*, James, *Didache*, *Barnabas*, Hebrews, 2 Peter, *2 Clement*, Polycarp, Revelation, Colossians and Ephesians, 1 Peter, Pastoral Epistles, *1 Clement*, Ignatius. According to Bultmann, the chronological order is less important than the theological content.

G. Theißen speaks about religion instead of theology,[71] but the transcendental approach is even more predominant when he analyzes the cultural sign system of early Christianity and asks about their ethos and rituals. However, Theißen is not consistent when he comes to the postapostolic era, where he emphasizes the different crises rather than their ethos, rituals, and so forth.

A Reconstruction of the Postapostolic Time

So far we have seen a variety of approaches, which can indicate a creative scholarship, but more likely shows that scholarship has failed in its approach to Christianity in the years 70–150. The studies show entirely different methodologies and a lack of contact with the methodological debates in historiography.

In the following paragraph, I do not presume to solve all the open questions or give the correct methodology.[72] The article is a prolegomenon, and I have to limit myself to an outline of what I suggest might be a comprehensive approach to the so-called postapostolic age. Basically, I agree with, inter alios, J. Weiss, R. Knopf, and A. Harnack, assuming that we must have both a local history and a more general approach.

Local History

What exactly do we know about the different provinces? In the first two centuries CE, the Roman provinces became crucial for political, institutional, and sociological development. The structure of the provinces had huge implications for the shaping of the earliest Christianity. A. Harnack's important book on the earliest Christian mission[73] gave this approach a very solid foundation, and it is surprising that only a few scholars have followed his path.

The Roman provinces and the most important cities include Palestine/Jerusalem, Egypt/Alexandria,[74] Cyrenaica, Syria/Antioch, Asia Minor, Macedonia/Thessalonica, Achaia/Corinth and Athens, and Italy/Rome. In recent years, more extensive studies on Christianity in many of these provinces have been published, particularly on Syria/Antioch[75] and Rome.[76] It is interesting, however, how little these studies rely on hypotheses of the origin of pseudo-Pauline letters or the letters of the CE in their reconstruction of Christianity in these provinces.

In an approach to Christianity in the provinces, one should focus particularly on the cultural factors (the Old Testament and Jewish heritage, cultural conflicts between Judaism and Hellenism, contextualization, relations with the pagan society)[77] and the important sociological aspects (how people lived; communication/roads, i.e., where and how they traveled; work and stratification in the society; the influence of institutions in the Roman society on the church order).

We lack important information concerning persons, groups, events, and conflicts in many of these provinces. There is, however, enough information about most of them. The lack of information from some of the provinces has also to be explained.

Excursus: Available Sources according to Introductions to the New Testament

What is the role of the CE in the reconstruction of Christianity in these provinces? Are the writings relics or sources for a community?[78]

It is illuminating to compare the books on early Christianity mentioned in this paper and some of the most-used introductions to the New Testament (e.g., R. Knopf,[79] K. H. Schelkle,[80] W. G. Kümmel,[81] A. F. J. Klijn,[82] P. Vielhauer,[83] A. Wikenhauser and J. Schmid,[84] H. Conzelmann and A. Lindemann,[85] E. Lohse,[86] H.-M. Schenke and K. M. Fischer,[87] R. Brown,[88] U. Schnelle,[89] and articles in *RGG*,[90] *TRE*,[91] *ANRW*,[92] and AB[93]). Do they evaluate the writings of the CE differently?[94] One can expect that the books on introduction to the New Testament are accurate when it comes to location. The problem with the introductions, however, is their vagueness. They give mostly accurate datings, but when it comes to location and/or addressees, they often state that no certain answer can be given.

The Epistle of James

Many introductions state that a location is impossible to indicate,[95] while some suggest a more general location, like Hellenistic Jewish Diapora, as place of origin.[96] Most scholars, however, try to give a more precise location. According to many exegetes, the Epistle of James originated in Palestine[97] or Syria.[98] A few suggest Rome[99] or even Alexandria.[100]

The First Epistle of Peter

Scholars give a most accurate location for the First Epistle of Peter, compared with other CE. Most scholars seem to agree on two provinces as the possible location: Asia Minor, using 1 Peter 1:1-2 and the situation behind the text as indicators,[101] and Rome, taking 1 Peter 5:13 as a symbol for Rome.[102]

The Johannine Epistles

Scholars hesitate to give a more general location for the Johannine writings. Books with so many common characteristics, different from other New Testament writings, must be given a more specific location. Three possibilities are suggested. The first is a Johannine circle, inspired by a teacher, which could be located anywhere.[103] However, the Johannine circle is more important in the exegetical literature than in introductions to the New Testament; these books give a more precise location, and most scholars suggest Syria,[104] due to the widely suggested location of the

Gospel of John; or Asia Minor, particularly Ephesus,[105] where the traditions about John and/or the Presbyter are deeply rooted.

The Epistle of Jude

In contrast to 1 Peter and the Johannine letters, scholars argue strongly against a specific location for the Epistle of Jude.[106] Most scholars suggest an open or very general location.[107] If they explicitly mention locations, they indicate a number of possibilities.[108] A few scholars are very specific, and in this case, Palestine seems to be the best alternative.[109]

The Second Epistle of Peter

Many scholars see Jude and the Second Epistle of Peter together, and similarly, they often argue against a specific location for 2 Peter. Most scholars tend to give a more open or general location.[110] We see, however, that more than in the case of Jude, a more accurate location for 2 Peter is suggested: Asia Minor,[111] Syria,[112] and most frequently Rome,[113] emphasizing the relation to the Peter tradition.

Conclusions

The overview shows a variety of positions, which is a problem for the efforts to reconstruct earliest Christianity. According to introductions to the New Testament, the collection of CE hardly gives any reliable sources for this reconstruction. It might, however, indicate that the methods and tools for studying early Christianity in the period 70–140 CE have to be improved.

A more general location makes sense if one argues that early Catholicism was dominant, which would mean that a local history approach would hardly hold any interest. If we use the results in the books on introduction to the New Testament, the collection of CE mostly gives us material for illuminating the history of Syria. To a certain degree, the letters are also sources for the reconstruction of Christianity in Palestine, Asia Minor, and Rome. Macedonia, Achaia, and even Egypt are hardly mentioned as places of origin for the CE.

The General Development

In spite of the differences between theologies and provinces, a common pattern of Christianity and a similar development is visible. The common pattern and the various contextualized formations are two perspectives that can be held together in the analysis of at least six aspects.

Mission and Spread of Christianity

Christianity came very early to every province of the Roman Empire. Paul was the key figure, but he was only one of many missionaries in the first century. Paul's importance is also attested by the fact that Christianity became a strong factor in the provinces in which he founded churches. To follow the spread of Christianity in the different provinces is a task that recent scholarship needs to intensify, and it should include all the new insights we have gained since Harnack's groundbreaking book.[114] We have to analyze the general factors contributing to the spread of Christianity, such as the Roman roads and institutions as background for the arenas and methods of Christian mission.

Modern scholarship has been preoccupied with the theory of *Naherwartung*, that early Christianity expected the end of the world and the return of Jesus very soon. When this expectation faded, a new period began. For J. Weiss and A. Schweitzer, this theory was crucial, and in recent scholarship, J. G. Gager explains the development of Christianity through this understanding of time.[115] Gager uses K. Burridge[116] and H. Festinger,[117] assuming that a "cognitive dissonance" forced Christians to a new development.

Cultural Factors

After some general remarks on the common factors in Roman society, we have to go deeper into the main cultural factors:

1. The Old Testament and Jewish heritage turned out very different from one theology/province to the other. More recent "new" facts, like the fall of Jerusalem and the temple, have been differently interpreted.
2. The cultural conflicts between Judaism and Hellenism were important in the development of the Christian church(es).
3. The way theologians in the different provinces contextualized the gospel is an important issue in modern scholarship.
4. The memory of the apostles, the role of Christian teachers, and the factors contributing to an extended canon (New Testament) have to be analyzed.
5. The result must reflect the crucial question: what constituted a Christian identity in early Christianity during the period 70–150 CE?

Sociological and Socio-Anthropological Aspects

The institutions of Roman society provided an important basis for the development of leadership and church order. The norm system, internal power structure, external power structure (relation to state), educational tools, and so forth, have to be analyzed. In order to describe the mentality of earliest Christianity, we also have to analyze the concepts of honor and shame, clean and unclean, kinship, personality, and limited good, among others.[118]

Sociological and socio-anthropological methods are not much help in analyzing a historical movement. G. Geertz suggests an analysis in which myths, ethos, and worldview provide the pattern for interpretation.[119] Similarly, N. Smart describes the seven dimensions of religions.[120]

Accordingly, at least three dimensions of early Christianity in the period 17–150 CE should be analyzed: liturgy and devotion, ethos, and theology.

Liturgy and Devotion

Despite variations, the development of the liturgy followed the same pattern in the different provinces. The rituals as texts are conveyed only through relics in the writings from this period. They show, however, great similarity and common patterns.

The rituals were linked to buildings, holidays, and celebrations, which held the Christian communities together. However, the calendar of the Passover was highly disputed in this early period.

The rituals were also connected to experience, prayer, and other expressions of faith. The variety of expression between a more charismatic (e.g., the Montanists) and a more formal or mystical piety was very visible in this period, but for all groups, devotion had the same center: the Lord Jesus.[121]

The rituals were based on the sacraments of baptism and the Holy Communion. The understandings of the two (or other) sacraments may differ, but compared with other religions, the Christian rituals gave them a very clear identity.

The CE has some relics of this dimension of early Christianity, particularly 1 Peter. The liturgy of baptism is reflected in many parts of the letter.[122]

Ethos

Christian identity was even more formed through the ethos. Christians were perceived by many contemporaries as a Jewish sect, but their ethos gave them a different identity. They had their own interpretation of the

Old Testament, and they transformed the Old Testament in a Gentile setting in a way that made their difference from Jewish groups obvious.

On the other hand, Christians had to adopt or challenge the contemporary Hellenistic ethics, which they did. The Epistles of James and 1 Peter illuminate the dialogue with Hellenistic ethics and show how early a new Christian ethos was formed, and also that the ethos had a common pattern.[123]

Theology

Theology is often expressed in theological conflicts and in very personal expressions. Our interpretation of these statements can easily lead us to overstate the differences between persons and provinces. One should, however, evaluate these differences against the background of common narratives and patterns of thought.

The memories of Jesus,[124] the formation of the gospel tradition,[125] and the exclusion of apocrypha[126] were important in all the provinces, but developed differently in each, and in some of them, heretical groups played a greater role.

The formation of the Christian creed as a narrative also developed in the same direction in all the provinces, in spite of the disagreements on Christology.[127] Most of the narrative of the Apostolic Creed is referred to in the Epistles of Ignatius, and even the CE give many elements of this narrative.

Scholars tend to structure New Testament theology and religion very differently, and even more different is the shaping of New Testament theology and the theology of the Apostolic Fathers. It is, however, possible, and from a historian's point view preferable, to structure the theology of the two periods similarly. How to structure this theology of early Christianity exceeds the limits of this article.

Conclusions

The postapostolic age is a fascinating but neglected theme in both New Testament and patristic scholarship. An abundance of sources is available, but the pieces have only to a very limited extent been put together in a comprehensive picture. One should call the period early Christianity, 70–150 CE, and use the same methods historians use in their analysis of this period of the Roman Empire.

The CE play hardly any role in the reconstruction of this period, for two different reasons: either because scholars give the CE a relatively early dating, or simply because they are not recognized as important sources.

Since R. Knopf's book *Das nachapostolische Zeitalter* (1905), no comprehensive study has been published that deals exclusively with the period 70–150 CE. One can hope that New Testament and patristic scholars, in a joint venture with an improved methodology, will provide a comprehensive analysis. This article is but a prolegomenon to this important effort.

Appendix

SNTS Seminar, Catholic Epistles and Apostolic Traditions
Papers read from Montreal to Aberdeen (2001–2006)

Montreal, July 31–August 4, 2001

R. Feldmeier, "Wiedergeburt, Seelenheil und Unvergänglichkeit: Die Profilierung des Frühchristentums als Erlösungsreligion im 1 Petr"

M. Konradt, "Der Jakobusbrief als Brief des Jakobus: Erwägungen zum historischen Kontext des Jakobusbriefes im Lichte der traditionsgeschichtlichen Beziehungen zum 1 Petr und zum Hintergrund der Autorfiktion" (Respondent: D. Verseput)

P. Hartin, "James and the Jesus-Tradition: Some Theological Reflections and Implications" (Respondent: L. Doering)

Durham, August 6–10, 2002

J. Frey, "Der Judasbrief zwischen Judentum und Hellenismus" (Respondent: P. H. Davids)

R. W. Wall, "Acts and James: The Prospect of Intracanonical Readings" (Respondent: K.-W. Niebuhr)

J. Painter, "The Importance of the Johannine Epistles within the Catholic Epistles" (Respondent: J. C. Thomas)

Bonn, July 29–August 2, 2003

J. S. Kloppenborg, "The Reception of the Jesus Tradition in James" (joint session with the "Socio-Rhetorical Interpretation" seminar) (Respondent: K.-W. Niebuhr)

L. Doering, "Der 1. Petrusbrief als frühchristlicher Diasporabrief"

R. W. Wall, "A Unifying Theology of the Catholic Epistles: A Canonical Approach"

C. C. Newman, "The Theology of the Apostles: The Convictional World beneath the Catholic Epistles"

Barcelona, August 3–7, 2004

K.-W. Niebuhr, "A New Perspective on James" (Respondent: E. Baasland)

R. W. Wall, "The Priority of James" (Respondent: C. Newman)

R. Feldmeier, "Ethik und Heilszuspruch in den katholischen Briefen"

Halle, August 3–5, 2005

S. Hafemann, "God's Salvation 'Once and for All' in Jude 5 and the Covenant Argumentation of 2 Peter 1:3-11: Confirming One's Election in the CE"

E. Baasland, "The Post-Apostolic Era: Reflections on a Future Seminar Project"

R. W. Wall, "Catholic Epistles and Apostolic Traditions: Retrospective 2001–2004"

K.-W. Niebuhr, "Katholische Briefe und Aposteltraditionen: Ein Rückblick mit Ausblicken"

Aberdeen, July 25–29, 2006

D. R. Nienhuis, "Not by Paul Alone: James in the Early Christian Canon"

F. Prostmeier, "Die Endwicklung der Ämter in der frühchristlichen Literatur (Development of Offices in Early Christian Literature)"

R. Feldmeier, "Gottes Vorsehung in der frühchristlichen Literatur (God's Providence in Early Christian Literature)"

J. Painter, "James as the First Catholic Epistle"

NOTES

Chapter 1

1 The address was given at the last session of the SNTS Seminar on "Catholic Epistles and Apostolic Traditions" / "Katholische Briefe und Aposteltraditionen" at the General Meeting of the SNTS in Halle, August 5, 2005. The English version was translated by Grit Schorch and revised by the author.

2 Cf. Karl-Wilhelm Niebuhr, "A New Perspective on James?—Neuere Forschungen zum Jakobusbrief," *TLZ* 129 (2004): 1019–44.

Chapter 2

* This essay, "A Unifying Theology of the Catholic Epistles," was a contribution to the Colloquium Biblicum Lovaniense (July 2003), which met immediately prior to SNTS (Bonn) in 2003, and is included in *The Catholic Epistles and the Tradition* (BETL 176, ed. J. Schlosser; Leuven: Peeters, 2004), 43–71.

1 We should note in passing how different the status of this question is when compared to the scholar's scruples regarding the Pauline corpus of letters. Biblical theologians typically approach the Pauline collection, even inclusive of its disputed membership, with the presumption of its essential theological unity. Whoever their real authors or intended readers are and no matter in what literary shape they have arrived at our canonical doorstep, the Pauline collection extends the thought of a particular person, and the

369

theological conception of each Pauline letter is measured by the theological dispositions of that particular person.

2   H. Y. Gamble, "The New Testament Canon: Recent Research and the *Status Quaestionis*," in *The Canon Debate* (ed. L. McDonald and J. A. Sanders; Peabody, Mass.: Hendrickson, 2002), 288.

3   Eusebius clearly thinks the authority of these disputed CE, and especially James, was challenged not because of theological error but rather because of their lack of use. It may well be that his observation of their "catholicity" (if not canonicity) is a way of underwriting the theological and functional unity of the collection. Moreover, it should be said that the canonical redaction of the CE collection was contested through the Reformation and Luther's famous concerns about James, and the other four letters remain disputed by the Antiochene communion within the Orthodox Church to this day. Before Luther, however, were still others, such as Isho'dad of Merv, who in the ninth century considered only James, 1 Peter, and 1 John—the letters of the three pillars—as canonical. He claimed that other CE lacked religious authority because of their literary "style" (by which he surely means their subject matter—apocalyptical, mystical) and their lack of use in the teaching ministry of the ancient church, which is hardly different from Luther's criticisms of James. Only 1 Peter, and to a lesser extent 1 John, escaped the disputations of ancient Bible scholars.

4   For a record of these various canon lists, see B. M. Metzger, *The Canon of the New Testament* (Oxford: Clarendon, 1987), 299–300, 305–15. Indices of quotations and allusions are found in many sources as well; consider also the variety of data (and relevant indices) included in McDonald and Sanders, *The Canon Debate*.

5   What is clear from even a cursory reading of Eusebius' observations about "the traditional Scriptures" is this functional criterion of biblical authority, whether or not "any church writer made use of [a book's] testimony" (*Hist. eccl.* 3.3). Thus, for example, even though the authority of 2 Peter is rejected by some, Eusebius admits that "many have thought it valuable and have honored it with a place among the other Scriptures."

6   I acknowledge my debt to David Nienhuis for the observation, made in the context of a stimulating and ongoing private conversation, that the formation of the CE collection as a historical phenomenon has high purchase for understanding its ongoing canonical role in and theological contribution to NT theology. In particular, he suggests that the late addition (and composition) of the Letter of James in some sense "completes" and is constitutive for the CE collection qua collection. This is the central thematic of his University of Aberdeen dissertation, finished in 2005 under the direction of Professor Francis Watson.

7   For the idea that the biblical canon as a whole and each part within is judged as roughly analogous to an ecclesial (and ecumenical) *regula fidei*, see R. W. Wall, "Rule of Faith in Theological Hermeneutics," in *Between Two Horizons* (ed. J. Green and M. Turner; Grand Rapids: Eerdmans, 2000), 88–107.

8   James has 1,749 words/247 stichoi; 1 Peter has 1,678 words/237 stichoi; 1 John has 2,137 words/269 stichoi. Adding 2 John (245 words/32 stichoi) and 3 John (219/31 stichoi) to 1 John and 2 Peter (166 stichoi) to 1 Peter does not alter this arrangement, especially when throwing Jude (71 stichoi) into the mix.

9   Although dating biblical compositions is tricky business, the early use of both 1 Peter and 1 John would commend an early date of composition, probably some time during the first century in their final form. By the same token, 2 Peter and James are almost certainly much later pseudepigraphy—perhaps even concurrent with and intended for the completion of the CE collection. As an important element of his Aberdeen dissertation, D. Nienhuis promises a new thesis regarding the composition of James as it relates to the canonical redaction of the CE collection. It is my understanding that he is prepared to argue that James is pseudepigraphy motivated by canonical concerns—that is, by the constitutive role the letter would perform in completing a Pillars collection for use within an emergent NT canon.

10   Trobisch, for example, seems to posit a great deal of importance in the production of codices for the final redaction of the NT canon. See also E. J. Epp, "Issues in the Interrelation of New Testament Textual Criticism and Canon," in McDonald and Sanders, *The Canon Debate*, 503–5.

11   D. Trobisch, *Die Endredaktion des Neuen Testaments* (NTOA 31; Göttingen: Vandenhoeck & Ruprecht, 1996), 40–43.

12   For a fuller description of this project, and illustrations of it, see R. W. Wall and E. E. Lemcio, *The New Testament as Canon: A Reader in Canonical Criticism* (JSNTSup 76; Sheffield: JSOT Press, 1992).

13   R. W. Wall, "The Function of the Pastoral Epistles within the Pauline Canon of the New Testament: A Canonical Approach," in *The Pauline Canon* (ed. S. E. Porter; Leiden: Brill, 2004). I find no compelling objection to Trobisch's thesis that Paul himself may have placed a collection of his "major" letters into circulation, which were then added to and recognized as Scripture (if not also as canon) by important Pauline tradents shortly after his death; see his *Paul's Letter Collection* (Minneapolis: Fortress, 1994). Marcion did not create a Pauline canon, then, but simply valorized one already in circulation. What is more important than the fact of an early Pauline canon is the church's realization early on that Paul's teaching also supplied biblical warrants to heretical teaching, especially for various second-century gnostic movements, including the one founded by the teachings of Marcion. Given this internal threat to the church, the need for a second collection of letters to bring balance and constraint to the letters of the canonical Paul—perhaps a collection similar in emphasis to the concerns voiced by James to the Paul of Acts, according to Acts 21:20-21 (see below)—was readily apparent. In any case, I take it that Marcion is an important symbol of a canonical process that forms or edits collections of writings as necessary correctives, in order for them to function more effectively analogically to the church's *regula fidei*.

14   For this argument, see R. W. Wall, *Community of the Wise: The Letter of James* (NTC; Valley Forge, Pa.: Trinity, 1997), 148–52. Most of my exegetical comments about the meaning of James are found in expanded form in this book.

15   Even though, as many contemporary scholars have opined, James 2:14-26 does not carry the same hefty weight for its author that it has during its (esp. Protestant) *Wirkungsgeschichte*, it is probably this one text more than any other—precisely because of its "anti-Pauline" correction, not in spite of it—that attracted the canonizing community: James 2:14-26 captures well the intent of the canonical process, if not its authorial motive. Indeed, many understand Pauline tradition (rather than the traditions of a first- or second-century Judaism, which are rarely mentioned in any case) as the book's primary conversation partner. In any case, from a perspective within a NT setting, James now responds to what Paul might become or how Pauline traditions might be used if as a canon within the canon. It is from its profoundly Jewish ethos that canonical James corrects canonical Paul. But to focus attention on 2:22 (rather than 2:21) reminds the reader that the canonical motive is not adversarial but complementary of a closer analogy to the church's *regula fidei*.

16   See R. W. Wall, "The Canonical Function of 2 Peter," *BibInt* 9 (2001): 64–81.

17   I recognize that the nature of a pseudepigrapher's motive is an important feature of the critical discussion of the literary genre. My own view is that reducing the discussion of motive to a psychological level, whether or not in writing pseudepigraphy the author intends (or not) to commit a fraud, is misguided because such a motive is irrelevant to a letter's canonical status. Canonicity is a more functional consideration, having mostly to do with the religious utility of a book's performance. The canonical motive, which may also have occasioned its production (rather than more particular historical exigencies) and certainly determined whether to include 2 Peter in the CE collection, has to do with its theologically constructive relationship to 1 Peter—as indicated by 2 Peter 3:1-2.

18   For this point, see J. Painter, *1, 2, and 3 John* (SP; Collegeville, Minn.: Liturgical, 2002), 51–58, whose interpretive strategy is to read the three letters together; also C. C. Black, "The First, Second, And Third Letters of John," in *NIB* 12 (ed. L. E. Keck; Nashville: Abingdon, 1998), 365–78 (esp. 366).

19   R. Bauckham's study of members of Jesus' family, in particular James and Jude, makes a compelling case for their lasting influence within the Jewish church in Palestine: *Jude and the Relatives of Jesus in the Early Church* (Edinburgh: T&T Clark, 1990). In particular, they sought to preserve the Jewish legacy of the church, especially the importance of a Jewish way of salvation that elevated the church's moral obligations as conditional of life with God, against a Paulinism (but not necessarily Paul's idea) that "faith alone" liberated believers not only from sin's consequence but also from any moral responsibility to flee from sin. In my mind, the final redaction of the CE,

which is enclosed by James and Jude, reifies this point within the canon and in self-correcting conversation with the Pauline corpus.

20 See D. Moody Smith, "When Did the Gospels Become Scripture?" *JBL* 119 (2000): 3–20.

21 My deliberation presumes only a formal canon. We all recognize that informal "canons with the canon" delimit which books have "real" authority by their actual use—or lack of use—by their different readers. For this reason, it might be argued that the 1 Peter–1 John canon survives to this day, since other CE are typically neglected in worship and instruction.

22 This is a principal thematic developed in my seminar paper on "Acts and James," presented at the 2002 Durham meeting of the SNTS and included in this volume, although my interest is largely rhetorical (the role of a frontispiece within a canonical collection) rather than historical. Without doubt, the Fathers from Eusebius forward vested theological value in the proper ordering of the letters. The dissertation of D. Nienhuis promises to supply the historical justification project in making this same point; see n. 6 above.

23 I find, however, no hard evidence to prove B. M. Metzger's unsubstantiated assertion that "the Acts of the Apostles was added chiefly to prove Paul's apostolic character and to vindicate the right of his Epistles to stand alongside the Gospels" (*Canon*, 257–58). This more likely is an anachronistic construction of modern Protestant scholars to support a variety of claims about the canonical Paul, his Gentile mission, and his message. In any case, if this were true, such a move would have been grounded in a misreading of the book of Acts.

24 We should note the debates over the apostolicity of James and his "biological" relationship to Jesus, given the church's belief of Mary's perpetual virginity; the subtext of both debates was the ongoing authority of the Jacobian legacy within the broader church. In fact, the book of Acts would seem to legitimize the continuing importance of James on different grounds than his apostolicity or his relationship to Jesus: namely, his leadership of the Jerusalem church. In this regard, I note that in the preface to his early *Commentary on the Seven Catholic Epistles* (ca. 700), Bede the Venerable writes, "Although in the list of the apostles Peter and John are accustomed to be ranked as more important, the Letter of James is placed first among these for the reason that he received the government of the church of Jerusalem, from where the source and beginning of the preaching of the Gospel took place and spread throughout the entire world" (trans. D. Hurst, O.S.B.; CSS 82; Kalamazoo, Mich.: Cistercian Publications, 1985), 3.

25 Note, for example, the close linguistic and conceptual relationship between Acts 15:13-29; 21:17-26 and the Letter of James. I should mention that the addition of the dominical "do unto others" saying to the all-important 15:20, 29 (but strangely not to 21:25) in Codex Bezae may well have been intended to draw linguistically the close connection between the teachings of Jesus and of James, in order to underwrite James' religious authority for the future of the church. This is an important datum if the motive of this second version of Acts is primarily canonical, as I have suggested; cf. R. W.

Wall, "The Acts of the Apostles," in *NIB* 10 (ed. L. E. Keck; Nashville: Abingdon, 2002), 1–368, here 17–18.

26   Some scholars continue to argue that Clement of Alexandria, who wrote an interlinear commentary on 1 Peter and 1 John (*Adumbrations*), included James in this work as well. Since his commentary survives only in a much later and highly edited Latin "translation" from Cassiodorus, the inclusion of James may reasonably be doubted, given the silence of a Letter of James from this same period and region. The first important interpreter of the CE as a collection, including James, appears to be Didymus from the mid-fourth century, who is noteworthy as a pioneer of the commentary genre. It should be noted that Augustine mentions in passing a commentary on James (*Retract.* 58), but unfortunately we no longer possess a copy of it. In any case, the authority and importance of a Letter of James is almost certainly a fourth-century phenomenon.

27   Origen claims that James is Scripture, but evidently this is not then to claim that James is also canon. Recently, several scholars have demonstrated the differences between the two, from both historical and systematic perspectives.

28   Especially the *Ps.-Clem.*, *Gos. Heb.*, *Gos. Thom.*, *Ap. Jas.* and *1–2 Apoc. Jas.*, Eusebius' recollection of Hegesippus in *Hist. eccl.*, and Clement of Alexandria's *Hypotyposeis* portray James' personal piety, his reception of special revelation from God, his political importance in Jerusalem, and his martyrdom; however, whether or not fictitious, these personal characteristics do not carry over directly to the Letter of James, whose thematics are more practical and whose Jewish ethos and beliefs are not cast in overtly personal terms. I do find the repeated references to a priestly James—as the Aaron to Jesus' Moses—fascinating, given the letter's emphasis on purity; cf. S. McKnight, "A Parting within the Way: Jesus and James on Israel and Purity," in *James the Just and Christian Origins* (ed. B. Chilton and C. A. Evans; Leiden: Brill, 1999), 83–129. In this same collection, Chilton offers the suggestive hypothesis that the practice of Nazirite vow-keeping within primitive Christianity "has been underestimated, and that James' deep influence is perhaps best measured by the extent to which other prominent [Christian] teachers fell in with his program [of Nazirite purity]" (252).

29   I myself have argued, with others, that the Ebionites followed such a canon, which included Jesus traditions found in Matthew's gospel; see Wall and Lemcio, *New Testament as Canon*, 250–71. A more precise articulation of this same point would distinguish between the legacy of James the Christian leader and the Letter of James. In absence of a quotation or clear allusion to a textual tradition—a Letter of James—in their writings, one must assume that these various Jewish Christian groups were tradents of a Jacobian legacy rather than students of a Jacobian letter, even though the legacy is doubtless the principal source of the letter.

30   Most modern constructions of the authorship of James fail to distinguish a theory of its composition from its canonization in any case. But to argue that James is second-century pseudepigraphy simply avoids the vexing

silence of this letter into the third century, even among those groups who remembered James as the church's exemplary apostle. Given its apparent Palestinian sources, which seem to reflect a first-century *Sitz im Leben* and its literary genre as a Diaspora letter from the same period, if James is pseudepigraphy, then part of the motive for its composition must have been to preserve the memory of James, even if only to underwrite the letter's important role in the final redaction of the NT. These issues have recently been reconsidered in a highly suggestive essay by M. Konradt, "Der Jakobusbrief als Brief des Jakobus: Erwägungen zum historischen Kontext des Jakobusbriefes im Lichte der traditionsgeschichtlichen Beziehungen zum 1 Petr und zum Hintergrund der Autorfiktion," in *Der Jakobusbrief: Beiträge zur Aufwertung der "strohernen Epistel"* (ed. P. von Gemünden, M. Konradt, and G. Theißen; Münster: Lit, 2003), 16–53, in which he offers a traditio-historical theory of the letter's composition. His study compares the use of traditions James holds in common with 1 Peter, which form a discrete trajectory of earlier Pauline and Jesus traditions. His reconstruction of the "Antioch incident" in Galatians 2 (rather than Acts 15, which would have greater purchase for a canonical construction than Galatians 2) leads him to conjecture that the provenance of James is Antioch, where the pseudepigrapher would have edited the James legacy to produce a revised version of Christian existence, for a congregation in which trials occasioned a spiritual (rather than sociological) testing of the internal quality of its life with God. In a sense, the different handlings of common traditions about Christian existence reflect the different legacies of a missionary Peter (hence greater concern with the church's relations with pagan surrounding) and a pastor James (hence greater concern with believers' relations with other believers), which are already reflected in the book of Acts. Konradt's study, among its other accomplishments, links together James and 1 Peter in a way that may well have canonical implications of the sort that I am trying to cash out in this essay.

31 The Jewish background of James has been constructed by modern criticism; however, this background has more to do with maintaining a distinctively Jewish ethos than with the ongoing performance of particular elements of a Judaic religion, whether from the Second Temple or the Diaspora. In this sense, James' rejection of supersessionism is neither formalistic nor legalistic, but adheres in a principled way to a Jewish way of life—a way of life that James contends is threatened in part by the church's appropriation of the Pauline tradition. I would add that the addition of the Catholic collection to the NT canon serves this canonical function of delineating the boundary between Christianity and Judaism, not by doing so sharply, but rather by underwriting the continuity between them.

32 Ironically, Luther's negative appraisal of James—that it fails a Pauline test of orthodoxy—illustrates this same methodological interest in reading James and Paul together; yet Luther fails to engage the two according to the hermeneutics of the canonical process. To do so would have led him to recognize that the CE collection as a whole might actually render a Pauline

"justification by faith" gospel more faithful to the church's *regula fidei*, and for the very reasons he rejected James.

33 My formulation of the relationship between the Pauline and Catholic witnesses draws on an insight of James A. Sanders, who long ago commented that the Pauline witness concentrates upon the "mythos"—or unifying narrative—of God's salvation as articulated/promised in the Torah and fully articulated/fulfilled in Christ; cf. James A. Sanders, "Torah and Paul," in *God's Christ and His People: Studies in Honour of Nils Alstrup Dahl* (ed. Jacob Jervell and Wayne A. Meeks; Oslo: Universitets for laget, 1977). In my opinion, it is the ethos of the Torah—obedience as loving response to God's saving mercies—that the CE collection concentrates upon. The result of reading both corpora together, then, is a fuller presentation of God's gospel. See Wall and Lemcio, *New Testament as Canon*, 232–43.

34 While the logical relationship between Acts and the NT letters is reflected by the canonical process (see below), the narrator's own claim (Acts 1:1) is that Acts is better related to the preceding gospel, probably for christological rather than literary reasons.

35 As an exercise in a recent class on Acts, I had my students reflect upon the importance of studying a particular Pauline text (e.g., Ephesians, 2 Timothy) in light of their prior study of related pericopae in Acts (e.g., Acts 18:24–19:41, Acts 20:17-38). The purpose of their project was more than to identify common Pauline traditions; it was to explore the meanings of a Pauline text that were brought to clearer light by its intracanonical relationship with Acts.

36 For an argument that the church's title for this composition, Acts of the Apostles, reflects its interest in the religious authority of the church's apostles (including Paul and James), see R. W. Wall, "The Acts of the Apostles in the Context of the New Testament Canon," *BTB* 18 (1988): 15–23.

37 I am mindful of H. Räisänen's probing historicist response to his titular question, *Neutestamentliche Theologie?* (SB 186; Stuttgart: Verlag Katholisches Bibelwerk, 2000), which distinguishes more precisely between first and subsequent readers within faith and academic communities. The canonical approach presumes that biblical theology is a theological rather than historical enterprise, whose aims are determined by the church's (rather than the per se academy's) intentions and so are religiously formative more than intellectually informative.

38 Trobisch, *Endredaktion*.

39 Cf. O. Cullmann, *Peter: Apostle, Disciple, Martyr* (London: SCM Press, 1953), 63–69.

40 See Wall, "Canonical Function of 2 Peter," 77–79.

41 See P. N. Anderson, *The Christology of the Fourth Gospel* (Valley Forge, Pa.: Trinity, 1996), 274–77, who suggests that at the one point in Acts where Peter and John speak with one voice (4:19-20)—Peter alone speaks when they are teamed elsewhere in this narrative world—the narrator has composed a saying that combines Petrine (4:19) with Johannine (4:20) traditions.

Their pairing in Acts in both work and speech may well reflect an emerging consensus within the ancient church that their traditions, both personal and theological, are complement parts of an integral whole.

42   I think this critical conclusion is typically overstated, however, since there are fundamental differences between Scripture's Petrine witness and the Pauline kerygma.

43   The Jewish cast of Paul's story in Acts is a principal exegetical interest of my commentary on "Acts," in *NIB* 10; see 213–15 for an introduction to this narrative thematic.

44   Of course, the Pauline Letters would not disagree with this conclusion. I would argue, however, that for the Pauline tradition, these social, moral, and religious practices that mark out a people as Christian are the natural yield of "being in Christ," and that being in Christ is the result of profession that "Jesus is Lord." A Pauline redemptive calculus, whether understood politically or personally, is concentrated by the beliefs of the Pauline gospel rather than by the practices of the Pauline churches. It is this essential difference of logic that fashions—I think from the early church—a different spirituality, one centered by orthodox confession, from that found in the congregations of the CE traditions.

45   Tradition- or source-critical explanations of the linguistic similarities between James and 1 Peter, or even James and 1 John, typically presume roughly similar dates of composition. If James is a much later pseudepigraphy, as Nienhuis proposes, then the same linguistic or ideological similarities critics find that link James with other CE may well be rather the literary elements of a midrash-like composition that offers commentary on earlier, extant texts (namely 1 Peter, 1 John, perhaps Jude). In my opinion, this feature is consistent with the literary makeup of James; see my *Community of the Wise*, 20–21.

46   I take it that the community's ethos envisages what scholars have more recently termed *covenantal nomism*, according to which God chooses Israel to receive the Torah as both a symbol of God's faithfulness and a command to obey. In this sense, the Torah mediates and maintains God's faithful relationship with an obedient Israel, not as the result of human achievement, but by divine mercy; see E. P. Sanders' now-contested definition in *Paul and Palestinian Judaism* (Philadelphia: Fortress, 1977), 422–23.

47   In an earlier study, I argued that the theological center of the non-Pauline epistolary collection is suffering: "Introduction: New Testament Ethics," *HBT* 5 (1983): 49–94.

48   See J. H. Elliott, *1 Peter: A New Translation with Introduction and Commentary* (AB; New York: Doubleday, 2000), 97–103.

49   Painter, *1, 2, and 3 John*, 85.

50   R. Law, *The Tests of Life: A Study of the First Epistle of St. John* (Edinburgh: T&T Clark, 1909).

51   See Wall, "Canonical Function of 2 Peter," 72–74.

52   Wall, "Canonical Function of 2 Peter," 77–79.

Chapter 3

1 Niebuhr, "A New Perspective on James."

2 Karl-Wilhelm Niebuhr, "Der Jakobusbrief im Licht frühjüdischer Diaspo-rabriefe," *NTS* 44 (1998): 420–43.

3 For recent reviews of research regarding James, see P. H. Davids, "The Epistle of James in Modern Discussion," *ANRW* 2.25.5:3621–45; F. Hahn and P. Müller, "Der Jakobusbrief," *TRu* 63 (1998): 1–73; M. Konradt, "Theologie in der 'strohernen Epistel': Ein Literaturbericht zu neueren Ansätzen in der Exegese des Jakobusbriefes," *VF* 44 (1999): 54–78.

4 An important stimulus for the perception of a coherent structure came from studies that used linguistic methods: see W. H. Wuellner, "Der Jako-busbrief im Licht der Rhetorik und Textpragmatik," *LB* 43 (1978): 5–66; E. Baasland, "Literarische Form, Thematik und geschichtliche Einordnung des Jakobusbriefes," *ANRW* 2.25.5: 3646–84; H. Frankemölle, "Das seman-tische Netz des Jakobusbriefes: Zur Einheit eines umstrittenen Briefes," *BZ* 34 (1990): 161–97.

5 To reconstruct the situation of the addressees is one of the most important aims of the studies of W. Popkes. See his *Adressaten, Situation und Form des Jakobusbriefes* (SBS 125/126; Stuttgart: Verlag Katholisches Bibelwerk, 1986); idem, "James and Paraenesis, Reconsidered," in *Texts and Contexts: Biblical Texts in their Textual and Situational Contexts* (ed. T. Fornberg and D. Hellholm; Oslo: Scandinavian University Press, 1995), 535–61. Also see R. Hoppe, *Der theologische Hintergrund des Jakobusbriefes* (FB 28; Würzburg: Echter-Verlag, 1977).

6 M. Dibelius, *Der Brief des Jakobus: Mit Ergänzungen von H. Greeven, mit einem Literaturverzeichnis und Nachtrag hg. v. F. Hahn* (KEK 15; Göttingen: Vandenhoeck & Ruprecht, 1921; 12th ed., 1984).

7 The commendable series New Testament Theology (Cambridge University Press) also offers important contributions to studies of the Epistle of James; see A. Chester, "The Theology of James," in *The Theology of the Let-ters of James, Peter, and Jude* (ed. A. Chester and R. P. Martin; Cambridge: Cambridge University Press, 1994), 1–62.

8 In adopting some of B. S. Childs' proposals for a canonical approach—cf. for James *The New Testament as Canon: An Introduction* (London: SCM Press, 1984), 431–45; idem, *Grundstrukturen* (vol. 1 of *Die Theologie der einen Bibel*; Darmstadt: Wissenschaftliche Buchgesellschaft, 2003), 355–61—this line of thought is developed further by R. W. Wall: see his *Community of the Wise*; his "James and Paul in Pre-Canonical Context," in Wall and Lemcio, *New Testament as Canon*, 250–71; and his "Unifying Theology," in Schlosser, *Catholic Epistles and the Tradition*, as well as in this volume.

9 For this phrase and its context in recent research, see K.-W. Niebuhr, "Die paulinische Rechtfertigungslehre in der gegenwärtigen exegetischen Dis-kussion," in *Worum geht es in der Rechtfertigungslehre? Das biblische Funda-ment der "Gemeinsamen Erklärung" von katholischer Kirche und Lutherischem Weltbund* (ed. T. Söding; QD 180; Freiburg: Herder, 1999), 106–30.

10   This is illustrated impressively in the doctoral thesis of M. Konradt; see his *Christliche Existenz nach dem Jakobusbrief. Eine Studie zu seiner soteriologischen und ethischen Konzeption* (SUNT 22; Göttingen: Vandenhoeck & Ruprecht, 1998), and cf. my review in *TLZ* 125 (2000): 756–59.

11   In a recent study, F. Avemarie has interpreted the Epistle of James in connection with this new perspective on Paul; see his "Die Werke des Gesetzes im Spiegel des Jakobusbriefs: A Very Old Perspective on Paul," *ZTK* 98 (2001): 282–309. Cf. also M. Hengel, "Der Jakobusbrief als antipaulinische Polemik," in *Tradition and Interpretation in the New Testament* (ed. G. F. Hawthorne and O. Betz; Grand Rapids: Eerdmans, 1987), 248–78, enlarged considerably in his *Paulus und Jakobus: Kleine Schriften 3* (WUNT 141; Tübingen: Mohr Siebeck, 2002), 511–48.

12   Regarding the genre of early Jewish Diaspora letters, see I. Taatz, *Frühjüdische Briefe: Die paulinischen Briefe im Rahmen der offiziellen religiösen Briefe des Frühjudentums* (NTOA 16; Freiburg: Universitätsverlag, 1991). Also on these letters, with special regard to James, see M. Tsuji, *Glaube zwischen Vollkommenheit und Verweltlichung: Eine Untersuchung zur literarischen Gestalt und zur inhaltlichen Kohärenz des Jakobusbriefes* (WUNT 2.93; Tübingen: Mohr Siebeck, 1997), 5–50; K.-W. Niebuhr, "Jakobusbrief"; Donald J. Verseput, "Genre and Story: The Community Setting of the Epistle of James," *CBQ* 62 (2000): 96–110.

13   Cf. 1 Corinthians 15:7 and, for the martyrdom of James, Josephus, *Ant.* 20.197–203 (Eusebius, *Hist. eccl.* 2.23.20–25 as part of a collection of traditions about the death of the Lord's brother).

14   It is an open question where exactly the borders of the biblical Israel should be drawn during the early Jewish period in general and with regard to the time of origin of the Epistle of James in particular. See for this M. Bockmuehl, "Antioch and James the Just," in Chilton and Evans, *James the Just*, 155–98.

15   For further differentiation with regard to the genre of early Jewish Diaspora letters, see L. Doering, "Jeremia in Babylonien und Ägypten: Mündliche und schriftliche Toraparänese für Exil und Diaspora nach *4QApocryphon of Jeremiah C*," in *Frühjudentum und Neues Testament im Horizont Biblischer Theologie. Mit einem Anhang zum Corpus Judaeo-Hellenisticum Novi Testamenti* (ed. W. Kraus and K.-W. Niebuhr; WUNT 162; Tübingen: Mohr Siebeck, 2003), 50–79, here 68–71. See also Doering's contribution to the present volume.

16   For this and for the paraenesis in the New Testament, see W. Popkes, *Paränese und Neues Testament* (SBS 168; Stuttgart: Verlag Katholisches Bibelwerk, 1996), 107–11; K.-W. Niebuhr, "Art: Paränese 2: Neues Testament," *RGG⁴* 6: 930–31.

17   This principle is the starting point for several recent studies on James, see, e.g., T. B. Cargal, *Restoring the Diaspora: Discursive Structure and Purpose in the Epistle of James* (SBLDS 144; Atlanta: Scholars Press, 1993); M. Ludwig, *Wort als Gesetz: Eine Untersuchung zum Verständnis von "Wort" und "Gesetz" in israelitisch-frühjüdischen und neutestamentlichen Schriften: Gleichzeitig ein*

Beitrag zur Theologie des Jakobusbriefes (EHS 23, 502; Frankfurt: Lang, 1994); M. Klein, *"Ein vollkommenes Werk": Vollkommenheit, Gesetz und Gericht als theologische Themen des Jakobusbriefes* (BWANT 139; Stuttgart: Kohlhammer, 1995); T. C. Penner, *The Epistle of James and Eschatology: Re-reading an Ancient Christian Letter* (JSNTSup 121; Sheffield: Sheffield Academic, 1996).

18   For this, cf. my considerations on Jesus in K.-W. Niebuhr, "Jesus als Lehrer der Gottesherrschaft und die Weisheit: Eine Problemskizze," *ZPT* 53 (2001): 116–25; and on James, "Tora ohne Tempel: Paulus und der Jakobusbrief im Zusammenhang frühjüdischer Torarezeption für die Diaspora," in *Gemeinde ohne Tempel—Community without Temple: Zur Substituierung und Transformation des Jerusalemer Tempels und seines Kults im Alten Testament, antiken Judentum und frühen Christentum* (ed. B. Ego, A. Lange, and P. Pilhofer; WUNT 118; Tübingen: Mohr Siebeck, 1999), 427–60.

19   For the following, cf. K.-W. Niebuhr, "Exegese im kanonischen Zusammenhang: Überlegungen zur theologischen Relevanz der Gestalt des neutestamentlichen Kanons," in *The Biblical Canons* (ed. M. Auwers and H. J. de Jonge; BETL 163; Leuven: Leuven University Press and Peeters, 2003), 557–84.

20   Cf. Codex Bonifatius I.

Chapter 4

*   This paper was presented at the annual meeting of the Society for the Study of the New Testament (SNTS) held in Montreal, July 31–August 2, 2001. In writing my commentary (*James*), I incorporated material from this essay in the following sections: "Excursus 1: To the Twelve Tribes in the Dispersion" (pp. 53–55); "Excursus 2: James and the Heritage of Israel" (pp. 72–74); and "Excursus 4: James and the Heritage of Jesus" (pp. 83–85). I acknowledge with appreciation permission from Liturgical Press to publish this material in this present paper.

1   See McKnight, "Parting," 98: "James, the brother of Jesus, who carried on the vision of Jesus in its most consistent form and it is from the Jacobite tradition, as compared with the Pauline tradition, that we gain glimpses of the Jesus tradition in retrospect."

2   The use of the name "*James*" throughout this paper is simply a handy way of referring either to the letter itself or to the author of the letter. It is not meant to imply that the present writer accepts the view that James, the brother of the Lord, was the physical writer this letter.

3   See Todd C. Penner's excellent survey of the state of scholarship on the letter of James in "The Epistle of James in Current Research," *CurBS* 7 (1999): 257–308. Peter Davids, in his influential commentary (*Epistle of James: A Commentary*, 4), offers a very good chart of the positions of scholars prior to 1982. At a glance, one can see how evenly divided scholarship has been on the matter of assigning an early or a late date to the letter.

4   Richard Bauckham, "The Study of Gospel Traditions outside the Canonical Gospels: Problems and Prospects," in *The Jesus Tradition outside the*

Gospels (ed. David Wenham; vol. 5 of *Gospel Perspectives*; Sheffield: JSOT Press, 1985), 369–419, here 388.

5   See Patrick J. Hartin, *James and the Q Sayings*, 235–40; *A Spirituality of Perfection: Faith and Action in the Letter of James* (Collegeville, Minn.: Liturgical Press, 1999), 149–50.

6   Scholars such as Sophie Laws, for example, make the point that James reflects the general ethical teaching within the Christian community. See, e.g., her *Epistle of James*, 14: "The parallels which exist between Matthew and James are in sayings which could readily be absorbed into the general stock of Christian ethical teaching." See also, Penner, *Epistle of James and Eschatology*, 254. Other studies, however, have tried to be more precise in arguing for a dependence of James on the synoptic traditions of Jesus' sayings. See, for example, the different charts indicating the allusions in James to Q and other sources in Davids, Hartin, and Painter: Davids (*The Epistle of James: A Commentary*, 47–48) identifies thirty-six points of contact with the Synoptic Tradition (see also Peter Davids, "James and Jesus," in *Gospel Perspectives* [vol. 5, *The Jesus Tradition outside the Gospels*; ed. D. Wenham; Sheffield: JSOT Press, 1985], 63–84, here 66–67); Hartin (*James and the Q Sayings*, 141–42) identifies twenty-six points of contact with the synoptic tradition; John Painter (*Just James: The Brother of Jesus in History and Tradition* [Columbia: University of South Carolina Press, 1997; 2d ed., 2004], 261) lists thirty-three points of contact with the synoptic tradition.

7   The reluctance to endorse such a vision often stems from a different approach to the solution to the Synoptic Problem, in which the hypothetical Q source is seen as an unnecessary complication, and resort to a further source M is judged to complicate matters even more.

8   See, e.g., the studies of Vernon Robbins, such as his work, "Writing as a Rhetorical Act in Plutarch and the Gospels," in *Persuasive Artistry: Studies in New Testament Rhetoric in Honor of George A. Kennedy* (ed. D. F. Watson; Sheffield: JSOT Press, 1991), 142–68.

9   Davids, "James and Jesus," 68.

10   Robert Alter, *The Pleasures of Reading in an Ideological Age* (New York: Touchstone [Simon & Schuster], 1989), 112.

11   See the following: James 2:11, "For the one who said, 'You shall not commit adultery' also said, 'You shall not murder.'"; James 2:23, "Thus the scripture was fulfilled that says, 'Abraham believed God, and it was reckoned to him as righteousness.'"; James 4:6, "But he gives all the more grace, therefore it says, 'God opposes the proud, but gives grace to the humble.'" Wiard Popkes ("James and Scripture: An Exercise in Intertextuality," *NTS* 45 [1999]: 213–29) examined James' reference to these scriptural texts. He concluded that James' "knowledge of the Bible is second-hand" (228), namely that he had access to the scriptural references only through secondary sources, not through direct use of the Bible.

12   See Stephenson H. Brooks, *Matthew's Community: The Evidence of His Special Sayings Material* (JSNTSup 16; Sheffield: JSOT Press, 1987), 160.

13   See the charts identified previously in Davids, *Epistle of James: A Commentary*, 47–48; Hartin, *James and the Q Sayings*, 141–42; Painter, *Just James*, 261.

14   Davids, "James and Jesus," 70.

15   Luke Timothy Johnson (*The Letter of James* [AB; New York: Doubleday, 1995], 191) draws attention to the difficulty this verse poses for interpretation. He offers a number of possible interpretations, among them the following: it is "an implied exhortation to the brother who has wealth: he should 'exalt' in the humbling that inclusion within a community that does not honor him for the status wealth ordinarily brings with it and even condemns wealth altogether . . . the rich brother is reminded of the transitoriness of wealth in order to realize the better status he has among 'the lowly' who are blessed by God."

16   Martin Dibelius, *James: A Commentary on the Epistle of James* (trans. M. A. Williams; Philadelphia: Fortress, 1975), 85–86.

17   Wesley Hiram Wachob, *The Voice of Jesus in the Social Rhetoric of James* (Society for the New Testament Studies Monograph Series 106; Cambridge: Cambridge University Press, 2000), 116.

18   Vernon Robbins, "Writing," 148–49.

19   Vernon Robbins, "Writing," 167.

20   Robbins explains "recitation composition" in this way: "The dynamics and presuppositions surrounding recitation composition emerged as a teacher recited a traditional fable, anecdote, event, or saying in his own words to one or more students and the students wrote the brief unit in their own words, using as much or as little of the teacher's wording as worked well for them" ("Writing," 147).

21   Popkes, "James and Scripture," 227–28.

22   See Robbins, "Writing," 145.

23   Davids, *Epistle of James: A Commentary*, 107.

24   Wachob, *Voice of Jesus*, 120.

25   Luke Timothy Johnson, ("The Use of Leviticus 19 in the Letter of James," *JBL* 101 [1982]: 391–401) shows well how central Leviticus 19 is to the rhetoric of James.

26   As Wachob (*Voice of Jesus*, 201) says, "It appears that some of the earlier writings that make up the New Testament (the Epistle of James being one of them) were written by authors who were quite capable of, and had no hesitation in, performing Jesus' sayings in ways that justified their own views of how their communities should appropriate Jesus' interpretation of the Torah. James 2.1-13 is a very fine rhetorical elaboration that demonstrates this phenmenon [*sic*!]; and James 2.5 is an artful performance of the principal beatitude in the pre-Matthean Sermon on the Mount."

27   The English edition of Dibelius' commentary, *James*, was translated from H. Greeven's eleventh revised edition, produced in 1964. Martin Dibelius, *James: A Commentary on the Epistle of James* (ed. Helmut Koester; trans. M. A. Williams; Philadelphia: Fortress, 1976).

28   Dibelius, *James*, xii.

29   Dibelius, *James*, 3.

30   Dibelius, *James*, 6.

31   John H. Elliott, "The Epistle of James in Rhetorical and Social Scientific
     Perspective: Holiness-Wholeness and Patterns of Replication," *BTB* 23
     (1993): 71–81.

32   For example, my treatment of the importance of the concept of perfection
     in James was undertaken independently of Elliott's article that drew atten-
     tion to the importance of the same theme. (See Hartin, *A Spirituality of
     Perfection*).

33   The adjective τέλειος appears four times in chapter 1 (twice at 1:4, once at
     1:17, once at 1:25) and again at 3:2. The verb τελειόω, "to make perfect or
     complete," appears at 2:22, while the verb τελέω, "to fulfill, to accomplish,"
     occurs at 2:8. This clearly shows that it is an important concept that is of
     importance for this letter.

34   In this section, I summarize what can be found in a fuller treatment in my
     book, *A Spirituality of Perfection*, 17–39.

35   This can be seen in the following instances: Genesis 6:9, "Noah was a righ-
     teous man, blameless [τέλειος] in his generation"; Exodus 12:5, "Your lamb
     shall be without blemish [τέλειος], a year-old male"; Deuteronomy 18:13,
     "You must remain completely loyal [τέλειος] to the Lord your God."

36   Hartin, *A Spirituality of Perfection*, 26.

37   Dibelius, *James*, 74.

38   Hartin, *A Spirituality of Perfection*, 89.

39   Mary T. Douglas, *Purity and Danger: An Analysis of Concepts of Pollution and
     Taboo* (New York: Frederick A. Praeger, 1966); George W. Buchanan, "The
     Role of Purity in the Structure of the Essene Sect," *RQ* 4 (1963): 397–406;
     John H. Elliott, *The Elect and the Holy* (NovTSup 12; Leiden: Brill, 1966);
     idem, *A Home for the Homeless: A Sociological Exegesis of I Peter, its Situation
     and Strategy* (Philadelphia: Fortress, 1981); idem, "Epistle of James"; Jacob
     Neusner, *"The Idea of Purity in Ancient Judaism"* (Leiden: Brill, 1973); idem,
     "History and Purity in First-Century Judaism," *HR* 18 (1978): 1–17; Bruce
     Malina, *The New Testament World: Insights from Cultural Anthropology* (Lou-
     isville, Ky.: Westminster John Knox, 1993), 149–83.

40   Malina, *The New Testament World*, 174.

41   Elliott, "Epistle of James," 78.

42   Malina (*New Testament World*, 180–81) has said, "Much of the practical
     advice in Paul and the other New Testament letters is about making the
     margins of the group sharper and clearer. Emphasis is on firming up the
     focus of the group toward the center of the social body."

43   See McKnight, "Parting," 97.

44   See John H. Elliott, "Temple versus Household in Luke-Acts: A Contrast
     in Social Institutions," in *The Social World of Luke-Acts: Models for Interpreta-
     tion* (ed. Jerome H. Neyrey; Peabody, Mass.: Hendrickson, 1991), 211–40.

45   McKnight, "Parting," 112.

46   See, e.g., Dibelius, *James*, 66–68; Laws, *Epistle of James*, 47–49; Franz Muss-
     ner, *Der Jakobusbrief: Auslegung* (4th ed.; Freiburg: Herder, 1981), 11–12;

Davids, *Epistle of James: A Commentary*, 63–64; Johnson, *The Letter of James*, 167–69.

47   See Patrick J. Hartin, "'Who is Wise and Understanding among You?' (James 3:13): An Analysis of Wisdom, Eschatology and Apocalypticism in the Epistle of James," in *SBLSP* (Atlanta: Scholars Press, 1996), 490–92; and idem, *A Spirituality of Perfection*, 70–71.

48   M. Jackson-McCabe ("A Letter to the Twelve Tribes in the Diaspora: Wisdom and 'Apocalyptic' Eschatology in the Letter of James," in *SBLSP* [Atlanta: Scholars Press, 1996], 504–17) sees the roots of this hope for the twelve-tribe kingdom ultimately traceable back to the foundational documents of Judaism, the Pentateuch and the book of Joshua.

49   See the full text, Ezekiel 37:15-28; see also Ezekiel 47:13-23, and chapters 45 and 48. See also Jeremiah 3:18.

50   The *Psalms of Solomon* (written in the middle of the first century BCE) looks forward to the future restoration of the kingdom of Israel in this way:

> *"See, Lord, and raise up for them their king,*
> *the son of David, to rule over your servant Israel*
> *in the time known to you, O God.*
> *Undergird him with the strength to destroy the unrighteous rulers,*
> *to purge Jerusalem from gentiles*
>   *who trample her to destruction . . .*
> *He will gather a holy people*
>   *whom he will lead in righteousness;*
> *and he will judge the tribes of the people*
>   *that have been made holy by the Lord their God.*
> *He will not tolerate unrighteousness (even) to pause among them,*
>   *and any person who knows wickedness shall not live with them.*
> *For he shall know them*
>   *that they are all children of their God.*
> *He will distribute them upon the land*
>   *according to their tribes;*
>   *the alien and the foreigner will no longer live near them . . ."*

Text from R. B. Wright (trans., "Psalms of Solomon, 17:21-28," in *The Old Testament Pseudepigrapha* [vol. 2; ed. James H. Charlesworth; London: Darton, Longman & Todd, 1985], 639–70, here 667).

The Qumran community's eschatological expectation was centered around the reconstitution of God's twelve-tribe kingdom. They saw their exile in the desert as analogous to the forty years that Israel spent in the wilderness before they entered to take possession of the land. They saw the future unfolding in a parallel way to that of Joshua's entry into the promised land, where the land would be redivided once again among the twelve tribes. The Qumran community even imagined the order for the upcoming battle that would bring about this restoration of the fortunes of Israel, as bearing the structure of the twelve tribes in mind: "They shall arrange the chiefs of the priests behind the High Priest and of his second (in rank), twelve chiefs to serve in perpetuity before God. And the twenty-six chiefs of the divisions shall serve in their divisions and after them the chiefs of the levites to serve always, twelve, one per tribe." See Yigael Yadin, *The Scroll of the War of the Sons of Light against the Sons of Darkness* (trans. Batya and Chaim Rabin; Oxford: Oxford University Press, 1962), 38.

51   A comparison with the traditions on which the Gospel of Matthew relies (see Mark 6:6b-13 and Luke 9:1-6) shows that this saying is unique to Matthew and has been identified as coming from the M source, unique to the Gospel of Matthew. I agree with S. H. Brooks (*Matthew's Community*), who argues that the saying of Matthew 10:5b-6 predates Matthew because it contains phrases as well as ideas that are different from Matthew:

"A third phrase, *ta probata ta apololota oikou Israel*, is doubly rare. The phrase may echo the idea in Jeremiah 50.6 (27.6 LXX; see also Ezek 34.4). *Probata apololota* is present in Jeremiah 27.6 (LXX) but the text from Jeremiah does not refer to the 'house of Israel.' Although the term 'house of Israel' appears extensively in the LXX, it appears relatively infrequently in the NT. Matthew has *oikou Israel* only here and in 15.24. The combination of these three unique elements in one saying gives evidence for assigning vv. 5b-6 to the M sayings.

"Furthermore, the content of vv. 5b-6 is different from the interests of Matthew. Matthew develops his own understanding of the mission to the Gentiles by his redactional placement of 10.18 (par Mark 13.10). At 10.18, Jesus predicts a witness to Gentiles under conditions of persecution *within the mission of the disciples.*

"The occurrence of the 'lost sheep of the nation of Israel' at Matthew 15.24 ties the story of the Syro-Phoenician Woman together with the mission charge in 10.5-6. While the traditional relationship of the two verses is open to scholarly conjecture, the inclusion of 15.24 within a Markan pericope (Mark 7.24-30) is due to Matthew's composition. The statement of Jesus in 15.24, 'I was sent only to the lost sheep of the nation of Israel,' echoes 10.5-6; but the woman's daughter, a non-Israelite, is healed. Matthew indicates to his reader that even *within his ministry* Jesus was willing to go beyond his own limitation of mission to Israel." (S. H. Brooks, *Matthew's Community*, 49–50).

52   McKnight, "Parting," 129.

53   Johnson, *Letter of James*, 164.

54   Recent anthropological and sociological studies have shown that poverty is something that largely affects one's honor or status. See Bruce J. Malina, "Wealth and Poverty in the New Testament and its World," *Int* 41 (1987): 354–67. See also Patrick J. Hartin, "Poor," in *Dictionary of the Bible* (ed. David Noel Freedman; Grand Rapids: Eerdmans, 2000), 1070–71.

55   "Christians belong to a community of faith that embraces the same ways of acting with one another, with Jesus (through their faith in him), and with God (through their friendship with God [Jas 4:4]). Integrity demonstrates a consistency in faith and action, a consistency in relationships with others and with God. . . . An option for the poor that embraces every human

person regardless of their differences bears witness to what makes Christian existence authentic" (Hartin, *Spirituality*, 161).

56   David Rhoads ("The Letter of James: Friend of God," *CurTM* 25 [1998]: 473–86) observes, "Other elements of Jesus' teaching that may be reflected in the wisdom of James include healing, forgiveness, rescuing sinners, prohibiting oaths, a commitment to the poor, the encouragement that those who ask will receive, and the affirmation that God gives good gifts." (485).

57   The way the narrator describes this scene in the ministry of Jesus shows how overwhelming are the crowds of those who seek out Jesus for healing: "He told his disciples to have a boat ready for him because of the crowd, so that they would not crush him; for he had cured many, so that all who had diseases pressed upon him to touch him" (Mark 3:9-10).

58   Hartin, *A Spirituality of Perfection*, 124.

Chapter 5

*   I wish to express my gratitude to Trinity College and the Department for the Study of Religion (in the University of Toronto), and to the Social Sciences and Humanities Research Council of Canada for generous funding, which made research for the paper possible.

1   James 2:8 = Lev 19:18b (κατὰ τὴν γραφήν· Ἀγαπήσεις τὸν πλησίον σου ὡς σεαυτόν); 2:11a = Exod 20:13; Deut 5:17 (ὁ γὰρ εἰπόν· μὴ μοιχεύσῃς); 2:11b = Exod 20:15; Deut 5:18 (εἶπεν καί μὴ φονεύσῃς); 2:23 = Gen 15:6 (ἐπληρώθη ἡ γραφὴ ἡ λέγουσα· Ἐπίστευσεν δὲ Ἀβραὰμ τῷ θεῷ, καὶ ἐλογίσθη αὐτῷ εἰς δικαιοσύνην); 4:5 alludes to Genesis 6:1-7 (ἢ δοκεῖτε ὅτι κενῶς ἡ γραφὴ λέγει); 4:6 = Prov 3:34 (διὸ λέγει· Ὁ θεὸς ὑπερηφάνοις ἀντιτάσσεται, ταπεινοῖς δὲ δίδωσιν χάριν).

2   Although there is no manuscript support for the omission of Ἰησοῦ Χριστοῦ at 2:1, a significant number of scholars have suspected it as a secondary insertion. See Dale C. Allison ("The Fiction of James and its Sitz im Leben," *RB* 118 [2001]: 529–70, here 541–43) for the most recent discussion and documentation of arguments since Massebieau and Spitta.

3   Christoph Burchard, *Jakobusbrief*, 17: "Nur bleibt auch hier unsicher, ob für Jak der Name Jesu mit ihnen [die Themen der Jesusüberlieferung] verbunden war."

4   These four sayings marked with the formulae are γινώσκοντες ὅτι τὸ δοκίμιον ὑμῶν τῆς πίστεως κατεργάζεται ὑπομονήν (1:3); εἰδότες ὅτι μεῖζον κρίμα λημψόμεθα (3:1); οὐκ οἴδατε ὅτι ἡ φιλία τοῦ κόσμου ἔχθρα τοῦ θεοῦ ἐστιν; ὃς ἐὰν οὖν βουληθῇ φίλος εἶναι τοῦ κόσμου, ἐχθρὸς τοῦ θεοῦ καθίσταται (4:4); and γινωσκέτω ὅτι ὁ ἐπιστρέψας ἁμαρτωλὸν ἐκ πλάνης ὁδοῦ αὐτοῦ σώσει ψυχὴν αὐτοῦ ἐκ θανάτου καὶ καλύψει πλῆθος ἁμαρτιῶν (5:20).

5   Alan H. McNeile, *An Introduction to the Study of the New Testament* (Oxford: Clarendon, 1953), 208.

6   Mayor, *Epistle of St. James* (1892), 378–79 (65 parallels); Friedrich Spitta, *Der Brief des Jakobus* (vol. 2 of *Zur Geschichte und Litteratur des Urchristentums*; Göttingen: Vandenhoeck & Ruprecht, 1896), 158–77 (55 parallels);

Adolf Schlatter, *Der Brief des Jakobus* (Stuttgart: Calwer, 1932), 19–21 (45 parallels); Peter H. Davids, "James and Jesus" (47 parallels).

7   This claim is based on the work of Dean B. Deppe ("The Sayings of Jesus in the Epistle of James" [D.Th. diss., Free University of Amsterdam; Ann Arbor: Bookcrafters, 1989], 231–50), who surveyed sixty authors from Thiele (1833) to Davids (1985). Deppe's table (pp. 233–37) shows that almost every verse of James has been connected with the Jesus tradition by some interpreter. The twenty-five most commonly cited parallels are 1:2 (Q 6:22-23a), 4 (Matt 5:48), 5 (Q 11:9), 6 (Matt 21:21; Mark 11:23), 17 (Q 11:13), 19b-20 (Matt 5:22a), 22-25 (Q 6:47-49); 2:5 (Q 6:20b), 8 (Matt 22:39; Mark 12:31; Luke 10:27), 13 (Matt 5:7; Luke 6:36); 3:12 (Q 6:44), 18 (Matt 5:9; Luke 6:43); 4:2-3 (Q 11:9), 4a (Matt 12:39a; 16:4a; Mark 8:38), 4b (Q 16:13), 9 (Luke 6:21: 25b), 10 (Q 14:11; 18:14b), 11-12 (Q 6:37), 13-14 (Matt 6:34; Luke 12:16-21); 5:1 (Luke 6:24: 25b), 2 (Q 12:33b), 9b (Matt 24:33b), 10-11a (Q 6:22-23b), 12 (Matt 5:33-37), 17 (Luke 4:25).

8   See, e.g., Heinrich J. Holtzmann, *Lehrbuch der neutestamentlichen Theologie* (ed. A. Jülicher and W. Bauer; Sammlung theologischer Lehrbücher; Freiburg: Mohr Siebeck, 1897; 2d ed., 1911), 2:383: "Man behauptet augenfällige Uebereinstimmungen des Lehrgehaltes mit der einfachen Verkündigung Jesus, weil unter Brief verhältnismäßig mehr Anklänge an synopt. Herrnworte bietet, als irgend eine andere neutest. Schrift."

9   There is considerable debate over each of these statistics. In addition to 1 Corinthians 7:10-11 and 9:14, Dale C. Allison ("The Pauline Epistles and the Synoptic Gospels: The Pattern of the Parallels," *NTS* 28 [1982]: 1–32) lists 1 Corinthians 7:25; 11:23-26; 14:37; and 1 Thessalonians 4:15-17. Frans Neirynck ("Paul and the Sayings of Jesus," in *L'apôtre Paul: Personnalité, style et conception du ministère* [ed. A. Vanhoye; BETL 73; Leuven: Leuven University Press and Peeters, 1986], 265–321) treats only 1 Corinthians 7:10-11 and 9:14 as explicit references to commands of the Lord, the others being prophetic oracles or liturgical traditions cited by Paul. Estimates of the number of allusions to sayings of Jesus vary wildly, from Alfred Resch's estimate (*Der Paulinismus und die Logia Jesu in ihrem gegenseitigen Verhältnis untersucht* [TU 27; Leipzig: Hinrichs, 1904]), of 1,096 contacts, to the much more modest figures of Heinrich J. Holtzmann (*Lehrbuch*, 229–36), and W. D. Davies (*Paul and Rabbinic Judaism* [New York: Harper & Row, 1967; 3d ed.; Philadelphia: Fortress, 1980], 138–40), who includes, in addition to the six mentioned above, Rom 12:14, 17, 21; 13:7, 8-10; 14:10, 13, 14; 1 Thess 4:8, 9b; 5:2, 3, 6, 13, 15, 16; Col 3:5, 12, 13; 4:2, 3, 6a, 6b, 12; and Acts 20:35[!]; and Allison ("The Pauline Epistles and the Synoptic Gospels"), to the relatively skeptical views of V. P. Furnish (*Theology and Ethics in Paul* [New York and Nashville: Abingdon, 1968], 51–65), who admits only ten allusions.

10   Louis Massebieau, "L'Épître de Jacques est-elle l'oeuvre d'un chrétien?" *RHR* 31–32 (1895): 249–83, here 257.

11   Spitta, *"Brief des Jakobus,"* 2:158-77.

12 Deppe ("Sayings of Jesus," 237) indicates that all but one of the sixty authors surveyed by him identify this as a saying of Jesus.

13 Spitta, *"Brief des Jakobus,"* 2:178–83. Similarly, see A. Meyer, *Das Rätsel des Jacobusbriefes*, (BZNW 10; Giessen: Töpelmann, 1930), 85.

14 Spitta, *Brief des "Jakobus,"* 2:165. Similarly, Meyer, *Das Rätsel*, 85: "[Luke 6:20] wird ja auch die echte Form des Herrenwortes sein, wie es auch der Schätzung der Armen in den Psalmen entspricht."

15 Meyer, *Rätsel*, 176–77: "Das Ursprüngliche wäre etwa, daß in Analogie zu Gen 49 der Vater Jakob zu seinen Söhnen sprach; beidemal in der Diaspora. —Nach Analogie der Apokalypsen könnte man annehmen, daß er zu seinen Nachkommen redete, genauer ihnen einen Brief schriebe, natürlich an die jetzt lebenden Nachkommen, also über die Jahrhunderte hinweg."

16 Meyer, *Rätsel*, 86.

17 See V. Rose, "L'Épitre de saint Jacques est-elle un écrit chrétien?" *RB* 5 (1896): 519–34; E. Haupt, "F. Spitta, Der Brief des Jakobus," *TSK* 69 (1896): 747–68; Friedrich Hauck, *Der Brief des Jakobus* (Kommentar zum Neuen Testament 16; Leipzig: Deichert, 1926), 17; Mayor, *Epistle of St. James*, clxxvii–ccv; R. Patry, *L'Épitre de Jacques: dans ses rapports avec la prédication de Jésus* (Alençon: Guy, 1899); Martin Dibelius, *James*, 23.

18 Dibelius, *James*, 23. Earlier, James H. Ropes (*A Critical and Exegetical Commentary*, 32–33) wrote: "Note also the surely Christian reference to the 'elders of the church' (5:14). Again, if the discussion of faith and works in 2:14-26 implies a polemic against Paul or Paulinists, that is conclusive for the Christian origin of the epistle; and the position of recognized primary significance assumed for faith in 1:3 and 2:5 is both characteristic of Christian thinking and unlikely for a non-christian Jewish writer."

19 Dibelius, *James*, 29: "Whoever taught the paraenesis of the Christian communities passed on to these communities the sayings of Jesus whether he was aware of it or not" (on 5:12).

20 Dibelius, *James*, 29.

21 Dibelius, *James*, 17. Dibelius' comments are directed against those who appealed to the contacts with the Jesus tradition to support Jacobian authorship of the letter. But he adds, "[O]n the other hand, it is just as invalid to argue that James the brother of the Lord is not the author on the grounds that the writing lacks any of the detailed comments about Jesus which are to be expected from a brother. For a paraenesis is an impersonal writing, not a confession in which reminiscences would be expressed" (17). See also Hans Windisch, *Die katholischen Briefe* (HNT 4.2; Tübingen: Mohr Siebeck, 1911; 2d ed., 1930), 4: "Der Autor ist ein Sammler von schriftlich und mündlich überlieferter Paränese. . . . Auffallend ist, wie wenig er die Paränese christianisiert hat."

22 Dibelius, *James*, 28.

23 W. Brückner, "Kritik," 537: "So ist es auch leichter in allen stellen, an die hier gedacht werden kann, die unmittelbare Abhängigkeit vom Matthäusevangelium vorauszusetzen."

24 Massey Hamilton Shepherd, "The Epistle of James and the Gospel of

Matthew," *JBL* 75 (1956). See also C. N. Dillman, "A Study of Some Theological and Literary Comparisons of the Gospel of Matthew and the Epistle of James" (Ph.D. diss.; Edinburgh: University of Edinburgh, 1978).

25   Shepherd, "Epistle of James," 47.

26   F. Gryglewicz, "L'Épitre de St. Jacques et l'Évangile de St. Matthieu," *Roczniki Theologicano-Kanoniczne* 8.3 (1961): 33–55 (according to Deppe's summary, 156–58). Gryglewicz listed (1a) verbal similarities (κόσμος used pejoratively [1:27; 4:4 and Matt 18:7]; νεκρός used allegorically [2:26 and Matt 8:22]; ἐκκλησίας, "church," [5:14 and Matt 16:18]; διαλογισμοὶ πονηροί [2:4 and Matt 15:19]; appeal to the commandments against murder and adultery [2:11 and Matt 5:21-30]; δοκεῖν in 1:26; and redactional in Matthew; and the wording of James' sayings on prayer [1:6], titles [3:1], humiliation [4:10], and oaths [5:12]); and (2b) indications of direct dependence (the use of δοθήσεται αὐτῷ in 1:5 and Matt 7:7; the phrase ἐν πίστει in 1:6 and Matt 21:21-23; the similarity of ποιητὴς λόγου [1:22] to Matt 7:24; the use of στόμα and ἐχέρχεται in 3:10 and Matt 15:18-19; the use of rhetorical questions with illustrations drawn from nature; the theme of humility and exaltation [4:10 and Matt 23:12]; the use of θησαυρίζω, σής, and βρῶσις [5:2-3 and Matt 6:19-21]; the prohibitions of oaths [5:12 and Matt 5:33-36]; the expression ἀφεθήσεται αὐτῷ [5:15 and Matt 12:32]; and James's mitigation of Matthew's reference to amputation of hands [4:7; Matt 5:30]).

27   Deppe, "Sayings of Jesus," 151. Commenting on Gryglewicz' list of similarities between Matthew and James, Franz Mussner (*Der Jakobusbrief: Auslegung* [HTKNT 13.1; 3d ed.; Freiburg, Basel & Wien: Herder, 1975] 5n1) says: "Diese Wendungen und Begriffe erklären sich ohne weiteres durch die gemeinsame zugrunde liegende Tradition. Bei literarischer Abhängigkeit vom griechischen Mt hätte Jak den Text seiner Quelle in einem wenig wahrscheinlichen Maße abgewandelt."

28   It could be observed that the closest connections of James' critique of merchants are with the Jesus tradition in the *Gospel of Thomas*.

29   See Mayor, *Epistle of St. James*, 125, who cites as parallels not only Matthew 7:16; 12:33 but also Seneca, *Ep.* 87.25: *non nascitur ex malo bonum, non magis quam ficus ex olea* ("Good does not spring from evil any more than figs grow from olive trees"); Epictetus, *Diatrss.* 2.20.18: πῶς γὰρ δύναται ἄμπελος μὴ ἀμπελικῶς κινεῖσθαι, ἀλλ' ἐλαικῶς; ἢ ἐλαία πάλιν μὴ ἐλαικῶς ἀλλ' ἀ μπελικῶς ("For how is it possible for a vine to act not as a vine, but as an olive tree, or for an olive to act not as an olive but as a vine?"); Plutarch, *De Tranquillitate animi.* 472F: νῦν δὲ τὴν μὲν ἄμπελον σῦκα φέρειν οὐκ ἀξιοῦμεν οὐδὲ τὴν ἐλαίαν βότρυς ("We do not expect the vine to bear figs, nor the olive grapes"). Richard Bauckham (*James: Wisdom of James, Disciple of Jesus the Sage* [New Testament Readings; London: Routledge, 1999], 89) adds Seneca, *De ira* 2.10.6: *Quid enim, si mirari velit non in silvestribus dumis poma pendere? Quid, si miretur spineta sentesque non utili aliqua fruge compleri?* ("Do you think a sane person would marvel because apples do not hang from brambles in the woodland? Would he marvel because thorns and briars are

not covered with some useful fruit?") To this can be added Marcus Aurelius, *Meditations* 8.15: Μέμνησο ὅτι, ὥσπερ αἰσχρόν ἐστι ξενίζεσθαι, εἰ ἡ συκῆ σῦκα φέρει, οὕτως, εἰ ὁ κόσμος τάδε τινὰ φέρει ὧν ἐστι φορός· καὶ ἰατρῷ δὲ καὶ κυβερνήτῃ αἰσχρὸν ξενίζεσθαι, εἰ πεπύρεχεν οὗτος ἢ εἰ ἀντίπνοια γέγονεν ("Remember that, just as it is shameful to be surprised if the fig-tree produces figs, so it is to be surprised if the world produces the things of which it is the seed; and it is a shame for the physician and the navigator to be surprised, if a person has a fever, or if the wind is unfavorable").

30   The retrotranslation of the *Gospel of Thomas* is provided by the Berliner Arbeitskreis für koptisch-gnostische Schriften, under the direction of H. G. Bethge.

31   The International Q Project (IQP) reconstruction of Q 6:23 is χαίρετε καὶ ἀγαλλιᾶσθε, ὅτι ὁ μισθὸς ὑμῶν πολὺς ἐν τῷ οὐρανῷ· οὕτως γὰρ διώξωσιν τοὺς προφητὰς πρὸ ὑμῶν. James M. Robinson, Paul Hoffmann, and John S. Kloppenborg, eds., *The Critical Edition of Q: A Synopsis, Including the Gospels of Matthew and Luke, Mark and Thomas, with English, German and French Translations of Q and Thomas* (Hermeneia Supplements; Leuven: Peeters; Minneapolis: Fortress, 2000), 52.

32   See Robinson, Hoffmann, and Kloppenborg, *Critical Edition of Q*, 220.

33   Harold Riesenfeld (*The Gospel Tradition* [Philadelphia: Fortress, 1970], 15) argues that James shows dependence on M: "Of the eight Matthaean beatitudes, four are to be found in the Epistle of James and in the same order, a fact, by the way, which cannot be accidental. In any case the author of the epistle presupposes parts of the Sermon on the Mount as clearly well known to his readers. Indeed, we can establish that the verbal form of the sayings of Jesus which James presupposes is that of M and not of Luke." Riesenfeld here refers to the sequence 2:5 (Matt 5:3)–2:13 (Matt 5:7)–3:18 (Matt 5:9)–5:10-11a (Matt 5:11-12). Deppe ("Sayings of Jesus," 158–59), however, rightly observes that 2:13; 3:18; and 5:10-11 are not specific allusions, but only contain themes that appear in the Beatitudes. Riesenfeld omits from consideration 1:12 (Matt 5:11-12); 3:13 (Matt 5:5); 4:8 (Matt 5:8); 4:9 (Matt 5:4). Had he not done so, the sequential agreement he detected would vanish.

34   James 1:4 (ἡ δὲ ὑπομονὴ ἔργον τέλειον ἐχέτω, ἵνα ἦτε τέλειοι καὶ ὁλόκληροι, ἐν μηδενὶ λειπόμενοι) contains the lexeme τέλειος, which is redactional at Matt 5:48 (bis) and 19:21. But this word is even more frequent in James (1:4, 17, 25; 3:2). See Wolfgang Schenk, *Die Sprache des Matthäus* (Göttingen: Vandenhoeck & Ruprecht, 1987), 441.

35   Mayor, *Epistle of St. James*, lxii: "It is like the reminiscence of thoughts often uttered by the original speaker and sinking into the heart of the hearer, who reproduces them in his own manner"; lxiv: "[James] grew up under his Brother's influence, and . . . his mind was deeply imbued with his Brother's teaching."

36   Theodor Zahn, *Introduction to the New Testament* (3 vols.; Edinburgh: T&T Clark, 1909), 1:114.

37   See, e.g., Patry, *L'Épitre de Jacques*; James B. Adamson, *The Epistle of James*

(NICNT; Grand Rapids: Eerdmans, 1976), 21–22; idem, *James: The Man and His Message* (Grand Rapids: Eerdmans, 1989) 169–94, esp. 193; D. Guthrie, *New Testament Introduction* (Chicago: Intervarsity; London: Tyndale, 1970), 743.

38   J. E. Huther, *Kritisch exegetisches Handbuch über den Brief des Jacobus* (KEMeyerK 15; 3d ed.; Göttingen: Vandenhoeck & Ruprecht, 1870), 19; W. Beyschlag, "Der Jakobusbrief als urchristliches Geschichtsdenkmal," *TSK* 48 (1874): 105–66, here 143; Paul Feine, *Der Jakobusbrief nach Lehranschauungen und Entstehungsverhältnissen* (Eisenach: Wilckens, 1893), 134; G. H. Rendall, *The Epistle of St. James and Judaic Christianity* (Cambridge: Cambridge University Press, 1927), 172. According to Gerhard Kittel ("Der geschichtliche Ort des Jakobusbriefes," *ZNW* 41 [1942]: 71–105, here 93), James is the earliest Christian writing and represents the earliest stage of transmission of Jesus' sayings, when they were not directly attributed. "Es sich um eine Zeit handelt, in der die Jesustradition noch nicht »Buch«, sondern ganz unmittelbar lebendiges Besitztum der Jüngerschaft ist, in dem die Gemeinde lebt." Others holding that James' Jesus tradition was orally transmitted include L. E. Elliott-Binns, *Galilean Christianity* (SBT 16; London: SCM Press, 1956), 47; Eduard Lohse, "Glaube und Werke: Zur Theologie des Jakobusbriefes," *ZNW* 48 (1957): 1–22, here 11; W. D. Davies, *The Setting of the Sermon on the Mount* (Cambridge: Cambridge University Press, 1966), 403–4; B. R. Halson, "The Epistle of James: 'Christian Wisdom?'" *SE* 4 [TU 102] (1968): 308–14, here 314: "Could it be, then, that like the Synoptic writers . . . the compilers of our Epistle drew some of his basic material from orally preserved 'sayings of the Lord'—sayings preserved for the instruction of the churches, and that we have here traditions written down in literary independence of the synoptic Gospels?"; Sophie Laws, *Epistle of James*, 35; F. Hahn, "Die christologische Begründung urchristlicher Paränese," *ZNW* 78 (1981): 90–99; Davids, "James and Jesus," 68; idem, *The Epistle of James: A Commentary, on the Greek Text* (The New International Greek Testament Commentary; Grand Rapids: Eerdmans, 1982), 49; idem, "The Epistle of James in Modern Discussion," *ANRW* 2.25.5 (1988): 3621–45, here 3638; Deppe, "Sayings of Jesus," 224–25; Todd C. Penner, *The Epistle of James and Eschatology* (JSNTSup 121; Sheffield: JSOT, 1996), 119.

39   Laws (*Epistle of James*, 35) observes that there are parallels to Mark (2:8, 19), Q (1:5, 17; 2:5; 4:3), and Matthew (5:12), which "may serve to indicate that while the three may be regarded as distinct strata in the creation of the gospels, they did not necessarily exist in isolation from each other in oral tradition." Rufolf Hoppe (*Der theologische Hintergrund*, 119–48) stresses the similarities in theological outlook between James and the "Q material of the Matthaean community," which in Hoppe's view make the suggestion of James' dependence on Matthew superfluous (148). Davids, "James and Jesus," 68: "James is therefore using a pre-gospel form of what we might loosely term the Q tradition in a redaction (his own or someone else's) which differs from both of the two canonical gospels." By contrast, Davies

(*Setting*, 403) argues "that the parallels between James and Q are very few, being confined to the items marked by a dagger above [1:2, 5, 22; 4:10, 11-12; 5:2]." Oddly, Davies does not treat 2:5; 3:12; 4:1-3; 5:10 (all of which have Lukan as well as Matthaean parallels), as having Q parallels.

40   See, e.g., Bo I. Reicke, *The Epistles of James, Peter, and Jude* (AB 37; Garden City, N.Y.: Doubleday, 1964), 3; Davids, "Epistle of James," 36: "The vast majority of James' parallels are with the Q tradition, but only with those parts within the Sermon on the Mount/Plain (28 or 36 passages)." Though Davids argues that James uses "unwritten Jesus tradition," he asks, "Does this data indicate something about the early history of Q? It may be that Q is composite and that Luke records the more original form of the ethical paraenesis that later became the Sermon. Perhaps this was originally gathered for pre-baptismal instruction" (36). See also Rudolf Hoppe, *Jakobusbrief* (SKKNT 15; Stuttgart: Katholisches Bibelwerk, 1989), 56: "Die Mehrzahl der Parallelen des Jak stehen der matthäischen Bergpredigtüberlieferung nahe, die lukanisch Version der Feldrede ist eigentlich nur zur jakobeischen Verbindung von der Erwählung der Armen zu Teilhabern am Gottesreich . . . sowie zum Wehe über die Reichen . . . heranzuziehen." Wiard Popkes (*Adressaten*, 156–76, esp. 174–76) stresses the similarities between the "stream of the Sermon on the Mount tradition" (174), James, and the *Didache*, apparently imagining that James has selectively chosen from this fund of material in order to create an instruction for neophytes (175). Wesley H. Wachob, *The Voice of Jesus*, 142–43: "It is my opinion that the rhetoric of the pre-Matthean S[ermon on the] M[ount] or a collection of sayings very like it, is firmly set and functioning in the environment from which the letter of James originates."

41   Popkes, *Adressaten*, 159.

42   Hubert Frankemölle, *Brief des Jakobus*, 85: "Die Aufarbeitung der (gemeinsamen?) Vorgeschichte der Bergpredigt-Feldpredigt-Tradition und des Jakobusbriefes sowie der Didache fordern zu Recht Hoppe [*Der theologische Hintergrund*, 119–48] und Popkes [*Adressaten*, 56–76], ohne die Forderung schon einlösen zu können, letzterer verbindet sie sogar mit einer allen gemeinsam vorliegenden Tradition der 'Grundeinweisung für Neugetaufte' (155) und Neophyten-Unterweisung. . . ."

43   B. H. Streeter, *The Primitive Church: Studied with Special Reference to the Origins of Christian Ministry* (London: Macmillan, 1929), 193: "The contacts between Luke and James are of another character [than those between Luke and Hebrews]. 'There is the same fusion of Wisdom-ideas with the tradition and formation of the evangelic logia, and the same attitude towards wealth which has led many writers to ascribe a sort of Ebionistic sympathy to Luke'" (quoting J. Moffatt, *An Introduction to the Literature of the New Testament* [International Theological Library; 3d ed.; Edinburgh: Clark, 1918], 466).

44   Several earlier critics emphasized James' affinities with (pre-)Lukan material: K. F. Nösgen, "Der Ursprung und die Entstehung des dritten Evangeliums," *TSK* 53 (1880): 49–137, here 109; P. Feine, *Eine vorkanonische*

Überlieferung des Lukas in Evangelium und Apostelgeschichte: Eine Untersuchung (Gotha: Perthes, 1891), 70–72; idem, *Jakobusbrief*, 76–77. See more recently Adamson (*The Man and His Message: James*, 173–78), who has tabulated vocabularic similarities between Luke (esp. L material) and James.

45   Patrick J. Hartin, *James and the "Q" Sayings of Jesus* (JSNTSup 47; Sheffield, Sheffield Academic, 1991), chaps. 5–6; "James and the Q Sermon on the Mount/Plain," in *SBLSP* 28 (ed. David J. Lull; Atlanta: Scholars Press, 1989), 440–57.

46   Hartin (*James and the Q Sayings*, 152) notes that there is considerable debate as to whether Luke 6:24-26 derives from Q, and while remaining agnostic on this debate, he concludes that the woes "do have a close relationship with Q." Later, he argues that Luke 6:25 (cf. James 5:1-6) is "a familiar saying of Jesus belonging to the Q community which has developed in different ways in the Lucan formulation of Q and in the expression of James" (163–64).

47   Hartin (*James and the Q Sayings*, 148, 161) appears to treat the development of the Matthaean macarisms in three stages: (1a) the original four Q macarisms (Q 6:20b, 21a, 21b, 22-23), which were (2b) expanded into eight by the addition of Matthew 5:5, 7, 8, 9, which then (3c) Matthew edited under the influence of Isaiah 61:1-3, adding "in spirit" to "poor," reordering the second and third Q beatitudes to correspond with Isaiah's association of πτωχοί and παρακαλέσαι πάντας τοὺς πενθοῦντας (Isa 61:1-2 LXX), and emphasizing δικαιοσύνη, a word characteristic of Isa 61 (vv. 3, 8, 11). According to Hartin, James shows no signs of these final (redactional) developments.

48   Hartin, *James and the Q Sayings*, 164–69.

49   Hartin, *James and the Q Sayings*, 171.

50   Hartin adopts the division of Q proposed by A. Polag, *Fragmenta Q: Textheft zur Logienquelle* (Neukirchen-Vluyn: Neukirchener, 1979), 23–26. Alternate divisions of Q proposed by W. Schenk (*Synopse zur Redenquelle der Evangelien: Q-Synopse und Rekonstruktion in deutscher Übersetzung* [Düsseldorf: Patmos, 1981], 5–9) or J. S. Kloppenborg (*The Formation of Q: Trajectories in Ancient Wisdom Collections* [Studies in Antiquity and Christianity; Philadelphia: Fortress, 1987; repr. Harrisburg, Pa.: Trinity Press International, 2000], 92) would not alter the substance of Hartin's point.

51   Hartin, *James and the Q Sayings*, 186. Hartin employs the work of Richard J. Bauckham ("Study of Gospel Traditions," in *The Jesus Tradition Outside the Gospels* [ed. D. Wenham; Gospel Perspectives 5; Sheffield, JSOT, 1985] 369–419), who argues (1a) that Q was compiled from originally independent blocks and (2b) that in order to show any writer's dependence on Q, one would have to show that it contained "allusions to a wide range of Q material" (379).

52   That Q 6:23c is redactional has long been recognized. For a discussion, see John S. Kloppenborg, "Blessing and Marginality: The 'Persecution Beatitude' in Q, Thomas & Early Christianity," *Forum* 2.3 (1986): 35–56, esp. 44–49.

53 See Odil H. Steck, *Israel und das gewaltsame Geschick der Propheten: Unter-suchungen zur Überlieferung des deuteronomistischen Geschichtsbildes im Alten Testament, Spätjudentum und Urchristentum* (WMANT 23; Neukirchen-Vluyn: Neukirchener, 1967).

54 See above, n. 29.

55 See M. O'Rourke Boyle, "The Stoic Paradox of James 2:10," *NTS* 31 (1985): 611–17.

56 Deppe, "Sayings of Jesus," 97–98, citing *T. Zeb.* 5:3; 8:1-3: καὶ ὑμεῖς οὖ ν, τέκνα μου, ἔχετε εὐσπλαγχνίαν κατὰ παντὸς ἀνθρώπου ἐν ἐλέει, ἵνα καὶ ὁ Κύριος εἰς ὑμᾶς σπλαγχνισθεὶς ἐλεήσῃ ὑμᾶς· . . . 3 ὅσον γὰρ ἄνθρωπος σπλαγχνίζεται εἰς τὸν πλησίον, τοσοῦτον Κύριος εἰς αὐτόν; *b. Šab.* 151b; *Sifre* 93b; *Sib. Or.* 2.81: ῥύεται ἐκ θανάτου ἔλεος, κρίσις ὁπόταν ἔλθῃ. See also *1 Clem.* 13:2; Polycarp, *Phil.* 2:3.

57 After surveying many of the over 180 possible allusions to the Jesus tradition, Deppe ("Sayings of Jesus," 219–21) lists eight that he thinks are likely (1:5; 2:5; 4:2c-3, 9, 10; 5:1, 2-3a, 12); six that have parallels in both content and wording (1:6, 12, 17, 22-25; 3:12; 5:10-11a); nine that have parallels in termi-nology (1:21; 2:15; 4:4a, 8, 12, 17; 5:9a, 9b, 17); and twelve that have parallels in content (1:2, 4, 12, 19b-20; 2:10, 13, 14; 3:18; 4:4, 11-12; 5:6, 14).

58 Luke T. Johnson (*Letter of James*, 57) seems to agree: ". . . it is more likely [than dependence on Matthew] that [James] makes use of the traditions at a stage of development prior to the synoptic redaction, that is, at a stage roughly that of the gospel sayings source conventionally designated Q" (citing Hartin). But his view seems to have changed more recently: "James . . . does not appear to be dependent either upon Q or the written Gos-pels. Nevertheless, it is quite possible—perhaps probable—that James was familiar with a collection of sayings in which Jesus categorically prohibited oaths. In other words, James was familiar with a collection of Jesus logia similar to those in the pre-Matthean SM and/or Q-Matthew" (Wesley H. Wachob and L. T. Johnson, "The Sayings of Jesus in the Letter of James," in *Authenticating the Words of Jesus* [ed. Bruce Chilton and Craig A. Evans; NTTS 28; Leiden: Brill, 1999], 431–50, here 438).

59 Those who espouse the thesis of oral tradition tend not to inquire further into the dynamics of oral usage.

60 Zahn, *Introduction*, 1:114.

61 See above, n. 35.

62 Bauckham, *James: Wisdom*, 75, 81–83.

63 See Kloppenborg, *Formation*, 284–86, 302–6. See also Daniel J. Har-rington, "The Wisdom of the Scribe according to Ben Sira," in *Ideal Figures in Ancient Judaism* (ed. George W. E. Nickelsburg and John Collins; Chico, Calif.: Scholars Press, 1980), 181–88.

64 Bauckham, *James: Wisdom*, 82–83. Bauckham treats Sirach as a *novum* inso-far as he is "the first and almost the only Jewish sage in Antiquity to put his own wisdom in writing under his own name" (74–75) and concludes that "Ben Sira and James are the only two ancient Jewish sages who collected their own wisdom in written works attributed to themselves." Provided

that one stresses "Jewish," these statements might be correct. But once one sees sapiential literature in its broader context, the phenomenon to which Bauckham points is not unusual. It is true that the essentially conservative nature of sapiential works meant that attribution to ancient sages was often convenient. For example, the instruction of Amenote son of Hapu (Ptolemaic period) is attributed to a scribe of Amenophis III (U. Wilckens, "Zur ägyptisch-hellenistischen Litteratur," in *Aegyptiaca: Festschrift für Georg Ebers* [Leipzig: Engelmann, 1897], 142–52). But in the Hellenistic period, we also have several collections attributed to otherwise unknown persons, and no reason to doubt, for example, that the instruction of the Counsels of Piety of Sansnos (E. Bernand, *Inscriptions métriques de l'Egypte gréco-romaine: Recherches sur la poésie épigrammatique des Grecs en Egypte* [Annales littéraires de l'Université de Besançon; Centre de recherches anciennes 98; Paris: Les Belles Lettres, 1969], 165) or the instruction of *P3-wr-dl* (A. Volten, *Die moralischen Lehren des demotischen Pap. Louvre 2414* [vol. 2 of *Studi in memoria di Ippolito Rosellini nel primo centenario della morte (4 guigno 1843)*; Pisa: Lischi, 1955], 271–80) are not in the names of their actual authors.

65 Bauckham, *James: Wisdom*, 77.

66 Bauckham, *James: Wisdom*, 91.

67 P. W. van der Horst, *The Sentences of Pseudo-Phocylides: With Introduction and Commentary* (SVTP 4; Leiden: Brill, 1978), 81–83.

68 See Vernon K. Robbins, "Progymnastic Rhetorical Composition and Pre-Gospel Traditions: A New Approach," in *The Synoptic Gospels: Source Criticism and New Literary Criticism* (ed. C. Focant; BETL 110; Leuven: Leuven University Press and Peeters, 1993), 111–47.

69 T. Morgan, *Literate Education in the Hellenistic and Roman Worlds* (Cambridge Classical Studies; Cambridge: Cambridge University Press, 1999), chap. 4; R. Cribiore, *Writing, Teachers, and Students in Graeco-Roman Egypt* (American Studies in Papyrology 36; Atlanta: Scholars Press, 1996).

70 Theon, *Progymnasmata*. See Spengel 2:101; Walz 210; R. F. Hock and E. N. O'Neil, *The Progymnasmata* (vol. 1 of *The Chreia in Ancient Rhetoric*; SBLTT 27; Graeco-Roman Religion Series 9; Atlanta: Scholars Press, 1986), 94–95; George A. Kennedy, *Progymnasmata: Greek Textbooks of Prose Composition and Rhetoric* (Atlanta: Society of Biblical Literature, 2003), 19. Compare also Quintilian 1.9.2–3: students of rhetoric "should learn to paraphrase Aesop's fables . . . in simple and restrained language and subsequently to set down the paraphrase in writing with the same simplicity of style; they should begin by analyzing each verse, then give its meaning in different language, and finally proceed to a freer paraphrase in which they will be permitted now to abridge and now to embellish the original, so far as this may be done without losing the poet's meaning. . . . He should also set to write aphorisms [*sententiae*], chriae, and delineations of character [*ethologiae*], of which the teacher will first give the general scheme, since such themes will be drawn from their reading. In all of these exercises the general idea is the same, but the form differs." For a discussion of

paraphrase, see Heinrich Lausberg, *Handbook of Literary Rhetoric: A Foundation for Literary Study* (Leiden: Brill, 1998), §§1099–1121.

71 J. Debut ("Les documents scolaires," in *ZPE* 63 [1986]: 251–78) has compiled a list of school exercises on papyri and ostracka, supplemented and nuanced by Cribiore, *Writing, Teachers, and Students*, 173–287, and Morgan, *Literate Education*, 275–87.

72 Theon, *Progymnasmata* (ed. Spengel, 2:101–2). Actual examples of the declension of a chria can be seen in Bodleian Greek, Inscription 3019, P. J. Parsons, "A School-Book from the Sayce Collection," *ZPE* 6 (1970): 133–49, esp. 143–44; and E. G. L. Ziebarth, *Aus der antiken Schule: Sammlung griechischer Texte auf Papyrus, Holztafeln, Ostraka* (Kleine Texte für Vorlesungen und Ubungen 65; Bonn: Marcus & Weber, 1910), nos. 37, 47.320.

73 P. Jouguet and P. Perdrizet, eds., "Le Papyrus Bouriant n. 1: Un cahier d'écolier grec d'Egypte," in *Kolotes und Menedemos* (ed. Wilhelm Crönert; Studien zur Paläographie und Papyruskunde 6; Leipzig: Aveniarus, 1906; repr., Amsterdam: Hakkert, 1965), 153–54; R. F. Hock and E. N. O'Neil, *The Chreia in Ancient Rhetoric: The Classroom Exercises* (vol. 2 of *Writings from the Greco-Roman World*; Atlanta: Society of Biblical Literature; Leiden: Brill, 2002), 9–10.

74 Theon, *Progymnasmata* (Spengel, 2:97); Kennedy, *Progymnasmata*, 16.

75 E.g., *P.Mich.* inv. 25 (Hock and O'Neil, *Chreia in Ancient Rhetoric, Classroom Exercises*, 13–19); *P.Mich.* inv. 41 (Hock and O'Neil, *Chreia in Ancient Rhetoric, Classroom Exercises*, 20–23); *P.Vindob.G.* 19766 (Hock and O'Neil, *Chreia in Ancient Rhetoric, Classroom Exercises*, 38–40); *P.Sorb.* inv. 2150 (Hock and O'Neil, *Chreia in Ancient Rhetoric, Classroom Exercises*, 41–44); SB 1.5730 (Hock and O'Neil, *Chreia in Ancient Rhetoric, Classroom Exercises*, 45–49).

76 See n. 70 above. Theon supplies a typology of paraphrase ("variation in syntax, by addition, by subtraction, and by substitution") and paraphrases combining several of these techniques, plus combinations of these. "Syntactical paraphrase: we keep the same words but transpose the parts, which offers numerous possibilities. By addition: we keep the original words and add to them; for example, Thucydides (1.142.1) said, 'in war, opportunities are not abiding,' while Demosthenes (4.37) paraphrased this, 'opportunities for action do not await our sloth and evasions.' By subtraction: speaking in an incomplete way, we drop many of the elements of the original. By substitution: we replace the original word with another; for example, *pais* or *andrapodon* for *doulos*, or the proper word instead of a metaphor or a metaphor instead of the proper word, or several words instead of one or one instead of several" (Kennedy, *Progymnasmata*, 70). The translation is based on a restoration of lost Greek portions of Theon from Armenian fragments by Michel Patillon, ed., *Aelius Théon, Progymnasmata: Texte établi et traduit par Michel Patillon avec l'assistance, pour l'Arménien, de Giancarlo Bolognesi* (Collection des universités de France; Paris: Les Belles Lettres, 1997).

77 Parsons, "School-Book"; see also Morgan, *Literate Education*, 205–8.

78 Morgan, *Literate Education*, 207.

79 Morgan, *Literate Education*, 207.

80   See another elaboration (of a maxim from *Theognis*, 175) in Aphthonius, *Progymnasmata* (ed. Spengel 2.27); Kennedy, *Progymnasmata*, 100.

81   Hermogenes, *Progymnasmata* (ed. Rabe 10); Kennedy, *Progymnasmata*, 78.

82   The Homeric βουληφόρος and παννύχιον were evidently not common in the first and following centuries; they appear, respectively, in Apollonius Sophista' *Lexicon homericum* 52.30 [1st cent. CE] and Julius Pollux' *Onomasticon* 1.64 [2d cent. CE].

83   See Epictetus, *Diatr.* 3.22.90; Theon, *Progymnasmata* (ed. Spengel 2:98). The verse is also quoted in Cornutus, *De natura deorum* 37.9.

84   On recitation and transformation of chriae, see Hock and O'Neil, *Chreia in Ancient Rhetoric: Classroom Exercises*, 5–41; Lausberg, *Handbook*, §§1117–20; Vernon K. Robbins, *The Tapestry of Early Christian Discourse: Rhetoric, Society and Ideology* (London: Routledge, 1996), 104–6.

85   See in general, C. G. Kuechler, *De rhetorica epistolae Jacobi indole* (Leipzig: Glueck, 1818); E. Baasland, "Literarische Form, Thematik und geschichtliche Einordnung des Jakobusbriefes," *ANRW* 2.25.5 (1988): 3646–84, esp. 3655–59; Lauri Thurén, "Risky Rhetoric in James?" *NovT* 37 (1995): 262–84; idem, "The General New Testament Writings," in *A Handbook of Classical Rhetoric in the Hellenistic Period (330 B.C.–A.D. 400)* (ed. S. E. Porter; Leiden: Brill, 1997), 587–607, esp. 592–96. On James 2, see Duane F. Watson, "James 2 in Light of Greco-Roman Schemes of Argumentation," *NTS* 39 (1993): 94–121; Wachob, *Voice of Jesus*; J. S. Kloppenborg, "Patronage Avoidance in the Epistle of James," *Hervormde Teologiese Studies* 55.4 (1999): 755–94. On James 3, see Duane F. Watson, "The Rhetoric of James 3:1-12 and a Classical Pattern of Argumentation," *NovT* 33 (1993): 48–64.

86   See A. Wifstrand, "Stylistic Problems in the Epistles of James and Peter," *ST* 1 (1948): 170–82; J. N. Sevenster, *Do You Know Greek? How Much Greek Could the First Jewish Christians Have Known?* (NovTSup 19; Leiden: Brill, 1968), 3–21.

87   Similar sorites are found in Romans 5:3-5 (καυχώμεθα ἐν ταῖς θλίψεσιν, εἰδότες ὅτι ἡ θλῖψις ὑπομονὴν κατεργάζεται, 4 ἡ δὲ ὑπομονὴ δοκιμήν, ἡ δὲ δοκιμὴ ἐλπίδα· 5 ἡ δὲ ἐλπὶς οὐ καταισχύνει, ὅτι ἡ ἀγάπη τοῦ θεοῦ ἐκκέχυται ἐν ταῖς καρδίαις ἡμῶν) and 1 Pet 1:6-7 (. . . ἀγαλλιᾶσθε, ὀλίγον ἄρτι εἰ δέον [ἐστὶν] λυπηθέντες ἐν ποικίλοις πειρασμοῖς, 7 ἵνα τὸ δοκίμιον ὑμῶν τῆς πίστεως πολυτιμότερον χρυσίου τοῦ ἀπολλυμένου . . . εὑρεθῇ εἰς ἔπαινον καὶ δόξαν καὶ τιμὴν ἐν ἀποκαλύψει Ἰησοῦ Χριστοῦ).

88   Deppe ("Sayings of Jesus," 62–63) Mussner (*Jakobusbrief*, 67), Davids ("James and Jesus," 71), and Ralph P. Martin (*James* [WBC 48; Waco, Tex., Word, 1988], 17) take τέλειος in 1:4 to be eschatological (though Martin also argues that "it is primarily a statement about a person's character, not simply a record of his or her overt acts"). Laws, by contrast, stresses that "*teleios* is to be a complete person, having integrity, unlike the divided man of vv. 6-8" (*Epistle of James*, 54).

89   Dibelius (*James*, 71, 88–89) stresses that 1:12 is "an isolated saying which is connected neither with what follows nor with what precedes." Yet it seems more likely that 1:12 is structured deliberately to resume 1:2-4, echoing

its key terms (ὑπομένει/ὑπομονή, πειρασμός/περισμοί, δόκιμος γενόμενος/ τὸ δοκίμιον ὑμῶν) and structure.

90   Prov 3:11-12; Job 36:1-21; Sir 2:1-6; 4:17-19; Wis 3:4-6; *T. Jos.* 2:7: ἐν δέκα πειρασμοῖς δόκιμόν με ἀνέδειξε, καὶ ἐν πᾶσιν αὐτοῖς ἐμακροθύμησα· ὅτι μέγα φάρμακόν ἐστιν ἡ μακροθυμία; Seneca, *De providentia* 2.6: *patrium deus habet aduersus bonos uiros animum, et illos fortiter amat et "operibus" inquit "doloribus damnis exagitentur, ut uerum colligant robur."*

91   Judith 8:25-27: "Let us give thanks [εὐχαριστήσωμεν] to the Lord our God who is putting us to the test (πειράζει) as he did our ancestors. Remember what he did with Abraham and how he tested Isaac, and what happened to Jacob in Syrian Mesopotamia . . . for he has not tried us with fire as he did them, to search their hearts, nor has he taken vengeance on us; but the Lord scourges those who are close to him in order to admonish them"; 4 Macc 7:21-22: "What person who lives as a philosopher by the whole rule of philosophy and trusts in God and knows that it is blessed [μακάριόν ἐστιν] to endure any suffering for the sake of virtue, would not be able to overcome the emotions through godliness?"; 9:31-32: (during the torture of the second son) "I lighten my pain by the pleasures that come from virtue [ταῖς διὰ τὴν ἀρετὴν ἡδοναῖς], but you suffer torture by the threats that come from impiety"; 1QH 17.24-25: "Your rebuke has been changed into happiness and joy for me, my disease into everlasting healing and unending [bliss], the scoffing of my rival into a crown of glory for me, and my weakness into everlasting strength" (trans. García Martínez, 349); *2 Bar.* 52:5-7: "Rejoice in the suffering you now endure: why concern yourselves about the downfall of your enemies? Make yourself ready for what is reserved for you, and prepare yourself for the reward laid up for you."

The admonition to expect and even welcome suffering is found elsewhere too. Seneca (*Ep.* 71.7) places on Socrates' lips the admonition to follow a life of virtue in spite of criticism: *Quisquis volet tibi contumeliam faciat et iniuriam, tu tamen nihil patieris, si modo tecum erit virtus* ("Allow anyone who so desires to insult you and do you wrong; but if only virtue is in you, you will suffer nothing."). Epictetus says of the true Cynic: "For if God so advises you, be assured that he wishes you either to become great or to receive many stripes. For this too is a very pleasant strand woven into the Cynic's pattern of life: he must needs be flogged like an ass, and while he is being flogged he must love the men who flog him, as though he were the father and brother of them all" (*Diatr.* 3.22.54).

92   Q 6:22-23; 1 Thess 1:6; 2 Thess 1:4; 2 Cor 8:2; Rom 5:2-5; Heb 10:32-36; Acts 5:41; 1 Pet 1:6; 3:13; 4:13-14.

93   W. Nauck, "Freude im Leiden: Zum Problem einer urchristlichen Verfolgungstradition," *ZNW* 46 (1955): 68–80, here 73.

94   Thus E. G. Selwyn, *The First Epistle of St. Peter* (2d ed.; London: Macmillan, 1947; repr., Grand Rapids: Baker, 1981), 442–49, 450; H. Millauer, *Leiden,* 157; F. Schröger, *Gemeinde im 1. Petrusbrief: Untersuchungen zum Selbstverständnis einer christlichen Gemeinde an der Wende vom 1. zum 2. Jahrhundert*

(Schriften der Universitat Passau, Reihe Katholische Theologie 1; Passau: Universitätsverlag, 1981), 186; J. H. Elliott, *1 Peter*, 777.

95   Nauck's argument is built on the assumption that the tradition dates from the time of the Maccabean revolt, assuming apparently that Wisdom 3:4-6 dates from this period and that 4 Maccabees reflects the Maccabean revolt rather than the Caligula incident in 37 CE, as is not more commonly thought.

96   Compare 1 Peter 1:6: λυπηθέντες ἐν ποικίλοις πειρασμοῖς.

97   Aphthonius, *Progymnasmata* (ed. Spengel 2:26); Kennedy, *Progymnasmata*, 100.

98   Trials as persecution: Mayor, *Epistle of St. James*, 33–34; Dibelius, *James*, 71–72; Davids, *Epistle of James: A Commentary*, 67; R. P. Martin, *James*, 14–15; Deppe, "Sayings of Jesus," 62.

Trials as ordinary pressures: Laws, *Epistle of James*, 51–52; Ropes, (*Critical and Exegetical Commentary*, 133) argues that the "trials" are not religious persecution but more likely "grievous poverty"; Halson, "Epistle of James"; Hoppe, *Der theologische Hintergrund*, 22; Burchard, *Jakobusbrief*, 55: "Von amtlichen und Gewaltmaßnahmen gegen Christen verlautet aber nichts. . . . Konflikte mit Juden fehlen." W. H. Wachob, "The Apocalyptic Intertexture of the Epistle of James," in *The Intertexture of Apocalyptic Discourse in the New Testament* (ed. D. F. Watson; Symposium 14; Atlanta: Society of Biblical Literature; Leiden: Brill, 2002), 177: "the trials that concern James do not appear to be those of a particular persecution, as in 1 Peter, nor do they have the heightened 'connotations of eschatological tribulation' as in Paul. Instead, they are 'the personal experience of life in God's service,' similar to Ben Sira and other of the wisdom tradition'" (quoting Laws).

99   See n. 91 above.

100   A sorites is a chain-syllogism ('if *a* then *b*, if *b* then *c*, if *c* then *d*, therefore if *a* then *d*'). The syllogism in James is complete insofar as it calls on the audience to draw the conclusion that, "trials lead to completeness and maturity." The sorites employs the figure of κλῖμαχ (/ . . . *x* / *x* . . . *y* / *y* . . . *z*): ὑπομονήν / ὑπομονὴ . . . τέλειον ἐχέτω / τέλειοι. . . . On the figure, see Lausberg, *Handbook*, §§623–24.

101   Pss 1:1; 31:2; 33:8; 39:5; 83:6; 111:1; Prov 8:34; 28:14; Isa 56:2; Sir 14:1, 20; 26:1; *Pss. Sol.* 6:2; 10:2.

102   Lausberg, *Handbook*, §§1055–57, 1100; Plato, *Gorgias* 503E: εἰς τάξιν τινὰ ἕκαστος (δημιουγός) ἕκαστον τίθησιν ὃ ἂν τιθῇ, καὶ προσαναγκάζει τὸ ἕτερον τῷ ἑτέρῳ πρέπον τε εἶναι καὶ ἁρμόττειν, ἕως ἂν τὸ ἅπαν συστήσηται τεταγμένον τε καὶ κεκοσμημένον πρᾶγμα. ("The artist disposes all things in order, and compels the one part to harmonize and accord with the other part, until he has constructed a regular and systematic whole.")

103   E.g., Job 28:12-13 (σοφία), 20 (σοφία); 32:13 (σοφία); Prov 1:28 (σοφία); 2:4 (σοφία), 5 (ἐπίγνωσις θεοῦ); 3:3 (χάρις), 13 (σοφία); 8:9 (ἐπίγνωσις), 17 (σοφία); 12:3 (χάρις); 14:6 (σοφία); 21:21 (ζωή); Qoh 7:25 (σοφία); Sir 4:11 (σοφία); 6:18 (σοφία); 18:28 (σοφία); 25:9 (φρόνησις), 10 (σοφία); 28:16 (ἀνάπαυσις); 51:13, 16 (παιδεία), 20 (σοφία), 26 (σοφία); Wis 6:12 (σοφία).

104 Ronald A. Piper, "Matthew 7,7–11 par. Lk 11,9–13: Evidence of Design and Argument in the Collection of Jesus' Sayings," in *Logia: Les Paroles de Jésus—The Sayings of Jesus: Mémorial Joseph Coppens* (ed. J. Delobel; BETL 59; Leuven: Leuven University Press and Peeters, 1982), 412.

105 It is even possible that the binary pair of αἰτεῖν/δοθῆναι is also a secondary elaboration of the original ζητεῖν/εὑρίσκειν pair. Stephen J. Patterson, (*The Gospel of Thomas and Jesus* [Foundations & Facets: Reference Series; Sonoma, Calif.: Polebridge, 1993], 19) argues that the monostich of *Gos. Thom.* 2 and 92 "is no doubt primary over against the double-stich form of Thom 94 or the triple-stich form in Luke 11:9 ‖ Matt 7:7. . . . Thom 94, whose form is secondary in the sense that a second stich has been added to complement the first, no doubt preserves a primitive feature in presenting the couplet as an independent saying without the interpretive elements so in evidence in Thom 2 and 92. . . . [Q's version] adapts the older saying to serve as an introduction to the Q section on answer to prayer (Luke 11,10-13 ‖ Matt 7:8-11, Q) and creates for it a new point of reference not typical of the seeking-finding topos, whose natural referent is the wisdom quest, not the meeting of needs through prayer."

106 For a survey of redactional approaches to Q, see J. S. Kloppenborg, "The Sayings Gospel Q: Literary and Stratigraphic Problems," in *Symbols and Strata: Essays on the Sayings Gospel Q* (ed. Risto Uro; Suomen Eksegeettisen Seuran Julkaisuja, Publications of the Finnish Exegetical Society 65; Helsinki: Finnish Exegetical Society; Göttingen: Vandenhoeck & Ruprecht, 1996), appendix B. Of the eight approaches surveyed, only Migaku Sato (*Q und Prophetie* [WUNT 2.29; Tübingen: Mohr Siebeck, 1988]) includes Q 11:2-4, 9-13 among the "late unsystematic additions," and even Sato recognizes that 11:2-4, 9-13 is an earlier cluster of sayings incorporated into Q.

107 Cf. Sir 51:13-14: ἔτι ὢν νεώτερος πρὶν ἢ πλανηθῆναί με ἐζήτησα σοφίαν προφανῶς ἐν προσευχῇ μου. 14 ἔναντι ναοῦ ἠξίουν περὶ αὐτῆς καὶ ἕως ἐσχάτων ἐκζητήσω αὐτήν. ("While I was still young, before I went on my travels, I sought wisdom openly in my prayer; before the Temple I asked for her and I sought her out until the end.")

108 Hoppe, *Der theologische Hintergrund*, 32: "Dieser Anschluß [between 1:2-4 and 1:5-8] ist keinerwegs so zu verstehen, daß hier zwei unabhängige und beziehungslose Spruchreihen, die allein aus sich heraus zu erklären wären, durch den Stichwortanschluß formal miteinander verbunden werden, sondern der gegebene sachliche Zusammenhang wird durch den Anschluß εἰ . . . λείπεται auch formal hergestellt." The connection of perfection and wisdom is seen in Wis 9:6: "κἂν γὰρ τις ἦ τέλειος ἐν υἱοῖς ἀνθρώπων, τῆς ἀπὸ σοῦ σοφίας ἀπούσης εἰς οὐδὲν λογισθήσεται. ("For even if someone is perfect, if the wisdom that comes from you is wanting, that person is reckoned as nothing.")

109 Kloppenborg, "Patronage Avoidance," 768–70.

110 S. E. Porter, "Is Dipsuchos (James 1,8; 4,8) a 'Christian' Word?" *Bib* 71 (1991): 469–98.

111   According to Deppe ("Sayings of Jesus," 234, 237) forty-three of the fifty
      authors he surveyed saw an allusion to Matt 5:3 ‖ Luke 6:20b in James 2:5.

112   Deppe, "Sayings of Jesus," 91.

113   Spitta, *Brief des "Jakobus,"* 164–65.

114   Meyer, *Das Rätsel*, 85; Ps 36:11: οἱ δὲ πραεῖς κληρονομήσουσιν γῆν καὶ
      κατατρυφήσουσιν ἐπὶ πλήθει εἰρήνης; 36:22-23: ὅτι οἱ εὐλογοῦντες αὐτὸν
      κληρονομήσουσι γῆν, οἱ δὲ καταρώμενοι αὐτὸν ἐξολεθρευθήσονται. παρὰ
      κυρίου τὰ διαβήματα ἀνθρώπου κατευθύνεται, καὶ τὴν ὁδὸν αὐτοῦ θελήσει;
      1 Sam 2:8: ἀνιστᾷ ἀπὸ γῆς πένητα καὶ ἀπὸ κοπρίας ἐγείρει πτωχὸν καθίσαι
      μετὰ δυναστῶν λαῶν καὶ θρόνον δόξης κατακληρονομῶν αὐτοῖς; and *Pss.
      Sol.* 5:12: καὶ σὺ ἐπακούσῃ· ὅτι τίς χρηστὸς καὶ ἐπιεικὴς ἀλλ᾿ ἢ σὺ εὐφρᾶναι
      ψυχὴν ταπεινοῦ ἐν τῷ ἀνοῖξαι χεῖρά σου ἐν ἐλέει; 15:2: Ἐν τῷ θλίβεσθαί
      με ἐπεκαλεσάμην τὸ ὄνομα κυρίου, εἰς βοήθειαν ἤλπισα τοῦ θεοῦ Ιακωβ καὶ
      ἐσώθην· ὅτι ἐλπὶς καὶ καταφυγὴ τῶν πτωχῶν σύ, ὁ θεός.

115   So recently, Deppe, "Sayings of Jesus," 90; Wachob, *Voice of Jesus*, 138–40;
      and others.

116   Deppe ("Sayings of Jesus," 90) observes that "there are no references in
      the OT, intertestamental literature, or the Talmud specifically saying that
      God is giving the kingdom to the poor." The motif is apparently unat-
      tested in Greek and Roman literature. See G. Strecker and U. Schnelle,
      eds., *Neuer Wettstein: Texte zum Neuen Testament aus Griechentum und Hel-
      lenismus. Band 2: Texte zur Briefliteratur und zur Johannesapokalyse* (Berlin:
      de Gruyter, 1996), 1248–1342.

117   Wachob (*Voice of Jesus*, 120, 124, 125, 127, 129) develops the idea of 'reci-
      tation' first with regard to the use of Leviticus 19:15, 18 in James 2:8-9:
      "Technically speaking, then, James 2:8 is an 'abbreviation' (συστέλλειν) of
      Leviticus 19:18; and the Jamesian performance of the love-commandment
      is properly a rhetorical 'recitation' (ἀπαγγελία) of an ancient authority. . . .
      The identification of this allusion as a rhetorical 'recitation' is based on the
      fact that the letter of James emanates from a 'traditional rhetorical culture,'
      that is, a culture in which 'oral and written speech interact closely with one
      another'" (120, citing Vernon K. Robbins, "Writing," 160–62). Wachob
      (*Voice of Jesus*, 151) later argues that "James 2:5 is thoroughly explicable as
      a rhetorical recitation of a saying attributed to Jesus."

118   See R. E. Nadeau, "Hermogenes' *On Stases*: A Translation with an Intro-
      duction and Notes," *Speech Monographs* 31 (1964): 361–424.

119   Wachob, *Voice of Jesus*, 143–46; Vernon K. Robbins, "Pragmatic Relations
      as a Criterion for Authentic Sayings," *Forum* 1.3 (1985): 35–63, here 56:
      "The reasoning in the Lukan [= Q] version begins with the conviction that
      the people spoken to possess the kingdom of God. Since they are poor and
      hungry and weep now, 'Blessed are you who are poor and hunger and weep
      now.' This kind of 'direct' communication holds the potential for a strong
      response among Galilean Jews and for adaptation in the Matthean form by
      people who desire to belong to the kingdom but are not 'poor' according
      to the usual definition." See also G. A. Kennedy (*New Testament Interpreta-
      tion Through Rhetorical Criticism* [Chapel Hill: University of North Carolina

Press, 1984], 66), who observes that while Luke's (= Q's) speech is basically deliberative, "only verses 27-38 really contain advice for the future. The rest is predominantly praise and blame, that is to say, epideictic and nowhere does the sermon present the great promise of the kingdom of God as an incentive to action."

120 See Kennedy, *New Testament Interpretation*, 46–47.

121 Wachob, *Voice of Jesus*, 153.

122 Bauckham (*James: Wisdom*, 86–87) faults Wachob for this, though Bauckham's own account of the transformation merely describes rather than explains James' choices.

123 Wachob, *Voice of Jesus*, 63–113. Independently of Wachob, Watson ("James 2") arrived at the same conclusion. On the form, see [Ps.-Cicero], *Rhet. Ad Herennium* 2.18.28–2.31.50: "The most complete and perfect argument, then, is that which is comprised of five parts: the proposition (*propositio*), the reason (*ratio*), the proof of the reason (*confirmatio*), the embellishment (*exornatio*), and the résumé (*conplexio*). Through the proposition we set forth summarily what we intend to prove. The reason, by means of a brief example subjoined, sets forth the causal basis for the proposition, establishing the truth of what we are urging. The proof of the reason corroborates, by means of additional arguments, the briefly presented reason. Embellishment we use in order to adorn and enrich the argument, after the proof has been established. The résumé is a brief conclusion, drawing together the parts of the argument" (2.18.28). See also *Rhet. ad Herennium* 4.43.56–4.44.56 and the discussion by Burton L. Mack, "Elaboration of the Chreia in the Hellenistic School," in *Patterns of Persuasion in the Gospels* (ed. B. L. Mack and V. K. Robbins; Foundations & Facets: Literary Facets; Sonoma, Calif.: Polebridge, 1989), 53–57.

124 This is essentially the same pattern described by Hermogenes (*Progymnasmata*; ed. Rabe 10) and Aphthonius (*Progymnasmata*; ed. Spengel 2:26-27) within respect to the elaboration of a gnome.

125 Wachob (*Voice of Jesus*) divides these into an argument from example (v. 5), a statement of the opposite (v. 6a), and two arguments from social example (vv. 6b, 7).

126 On debt, default, and debt-recovery, see E. Neufeld, "Self-Help in Ancient Hebrew Law," *RIDA* 5, ser. 3 (1958): 291–98.

127 The IQP reconstructed 6:22 as μακάριοί ἐστε ὅταν ὀνειδίσωσιν ὑμᾶς καὶ ⟦(διώχ)⟧ωσιν καὶ ⟦(εἶπ)⟧ωσιν πᾶν πονηρὸν ⟦(καθ)⟧ ὑμῶν, with a dissent from Kloppenborg (Robinson, Hoffmann, and Kloppenborg, *Critical Edition of Q*, 50). For a justification, see Kloppenborg, "Blessing and Marginality," 38–44.

128 Commentators often wonder whether ἐπικληθὲν ἐφ' ὑμᾶς refers to baptism (Reicke, *Epistles of James, Peter, and Jude*, 29; R. P. Martin, *James*, 67). More basically, however, the phrase connotes the act of being given a surname (LSJ, 635b) and occurs several times in the LXX in reference to God adopting or taking possession of persons (or Israel): Gen 48:16; Deut 28:10; Isa

63:19; Amos 9:12; Bar 2:15; 5:4. In Dan 5:12; 10:1, the construction is used in giving a nickname or by-name.

Chapter 6

*   I thank Greta Konradt, Christine Rosin, Delia Richner, and Peter-Ben Smit for their assistance.

1   The main reasons for a pseudepigrahical authorship of James have been summarized succinctly by Christoph Burchard, *Der Jakobusbrief* (HNT 15.1; Tübingen: Mohr Siebeck, 2000), 4: "Gegen den Herrenbruder sprechen . . . die griechische Rhetorik . . ., die hellenistischen, wenn auch oft jüdisch vermittelten Züge seiner Theologie und Ethik, die sprachlichen und sachlichen Berührungen mit der nachpaulinischen frühchristlichen Literatur und was sich über die Adressaten ausmachen lässt." (See also: Matthias Konradt, *Christliche Existenz nach dem Jakobusbrief. Eine Studie zu seiner soteriologischen und ethischen Konzeption* [StUNT 22; Göttingen: Vandenhoeck & Ruprecht, 1998], 334n112.) The subsequent considerations will support this judgment traditio-historically. In the following, I will use *PsJames* in order to indicate the author of James and in order to distinguish him from the brother of the Lord. —I thank Greta Konradt, Christine Rosin, Delia Richner, and Peter-Ben Smit for their assistance.

2   Burchard, *Jakobusbrief*, 7.

3   See, e.g., Franz Mussner, *Der Jakobusbrief: Auslegung* (HThKNT 13.1; 5th ed.; Freiburg: Herder, 1987), 47–50; Patrick J. Hartin, *James and the Q Sayings of Jesus* (JSNTSup 47; Sheffield: Sheffield Academic, 1991).

4   It is well known that James 2:14-26 stands at the center of this question. Some authors, however, have recently postulated influence of Pauline traditions for various other parts of James as well, especially for the "law of freedom" (see Wiard Popkes, "The Law of Liberty [James 1:25; 2:12]," in *International Theological Studies: Contributions of Baptist Scholars* [vol. 1; ed. Faculty of Baptist Theological Seminary Rüschlikon; FS Günter Wagner; Bern et al.: Peter Lang, 1994], 131–42, here 136–38; Martin Klein, "Ein vollkommenes Werk," in *Vollkommenheit, Gesetz und Gericht als theologische Themen des Jakobusbriefes* [BWANT 139; Stuttgart: Kohlhammer, 1995], 143–44) and also for the theme of wisdom (Klein, 160–61).

5   See the overview in Konradt, *Christliche Existenz*, 330–32.

6   See the resemblances between both writings listed by Joseph B. Mayor, *The Epistle of St. James* (new ed. of the 1913; 3d ed. with a preface by C. J. Barber; Grand Rapids: Eerdmans, 1990), cii–cvii.

7   See Norbert Brox, *Der erste Petrusbrief* (EKK.NT 21; 3d ed.; Zürich: Benziger and Neukirchen-Vluyn: Neukirchener, 1989), 43–47; Reinhard Feldmeier, *Die Christen als Fremde: Die Metapher der Fremde in der antiken Welt, im Urchristentum und im 1. Petrusbrief* (WUNT 64; Tübingen: Mohr Siebeck, 1992), 193–98.

8   For priority of James, see, e.g., Mayor, *Epistle of St. James*, cii–cvii; Martin Hengel, "Der Jakobusbrief als antipaulinische Polemik," in *Tradition and Interpretation in the New Testament* (ed. Gerald F. Hawthorne and Otto

Betz; FS Earl E. Ellis; Grand Rapids: Eerdmans; Tübingen: Mohr Siebeck, 1987), 248–78, 251, and 269n26. The opposite position is argued by Wilhelm Brückner, "Zur Kritik des Jakobusbriefes," *ZWTh* 17 (1874): 530–41, here 533–37; T. E. S. Ferris, "The Epistle of James in Relation to I Peter," *CQR* 128 (1939): 303–8.

9   See James Hardy Ropes, *A Critical and Exegetical Commentary on the Epistle of St. James* (ICC; Edinburgh: T&T Clark, 1916; repr. 1991), 22; Martin Dibelius, *Der Brief des Jakobus. Mit Ergänzungen von H. Greeven, mit einem Literaturverzeichnis und Nachtrag hg. v. F. Hahn* (KEK 15; Göttingen: Vandenhoeck & Ruprecht, 1984), 48–49; Norbert Brox, "Der erste Petrusbrief in der literarischen Tradition des Urchristentums," *Kairos* NF 20 (1978): 182–92, here 186; Peter H. Davids, "The Epistle of James in Modern Discussion," *ANRW* 2.25.5 (Berlin: de Gruyter, 1988), 3621–45, 3634–35.

10 Martin Luther, *D. Martins Luthers Werke: Kritische Gesamtausgabe: Die Deutsche Bibel* (vol. 6; WA DB 6; Weimar, 1929), 10.

11 See, e.g., Philipp Vielhauer, *Geschichte der urchristlichen Literatur: Einleitung in das Neue Testament, die Apokryphen und die Apostolischen Väter* (4th ed.; Berlin: de Gruyter, 1985), 584; Helmut Köster, *Einführung in das Neue Testament im Rahmen der Religionsgeschichte und Kulturgeschichte der hellenistischen und römischen Zeit* (Berlin: de Gruyter, 1980), 731; Hans Hübner, *Die Theologie des Paulus und ihre neutestamentliche Wirkungsgeschichte* (vol. 2 of *Theologie des Neuen Testaments;* Göttingen: Vandenhoeck & Ruprecht, 1993), 387.

12 See, e.g., Roman Heiligenthal, *Werke als Zeichen: Untersuchungen zur Bedeutung der menschlichen Taten im Frühjudentum, Neuen Testament und Frühchristentum* (WUNT 2.9; Tübingen: Mohr Siebeck, 1983), 49–52; Klaus Berger, *Theologiegeschichte des Urchristentums: Theologie des Neuen Testaments* (2d ed.; Tübingen: Francke, 1995), 188–89; Todd C. Penner, *The Epistle of James and Eschatology. Re-reading an Ancient Christian Letter* (JSNTSup 121; Sheffield: Sheffield Academic, 1996), 47–74; and my own remarks in *Christliche Existenz*, 210–13, 241–46; as well as Burchard, *Jakobusbrief*, 125–26. The thesis of a reference by the author of James to Paul has recently been renewed by Friedrich Avemarie in "Die Werke des Gesetzes im Spiegel des Jakobusbriefes. A Very Old Perspective on Paul," *ZThK* 98 (2001): 282–309, here 289–94, which includes critical reference to my own argumentation. Avemarie reiterates my argumentation in a considerably shortened form, however. By maintaining that the differentiation between πίστις and ἔργα as it occurs in James 2 has no parallels in early Jewish literature, as many have done before him, he simply passes over the traditio-historically central reference to the fact that there was a separate early Christian development of the concept of faith, which was essentially grounded in the usage of πίστις in the context of early Christian missionary proclamation (see Egon Brandenburger, "Pistis und Soteria: Zum Verstehenshorizont von 'Glaube' im Urchristentum," *ZThK* 85 [1988]: 165–98). Apart from specific Pauline tradition, *saving* faith is spoken of here without connecting any antithesis to deeds with it. In light of this context, the genesis of the

problem of James 2:14-26 can easily be explained, especially if the pagan prerequisites for the reception of speaking about "faith" are considered. Furthermore, Avemarie repeats the argument that James 2:14-26 operates "mit dem Gegenbegriff vermeintlich nicht heilsrelevanter ἔργα." However, it cannot be inferred from James 2:14-26 that someone argued for an antithesis of faith and deeds, and PsJames himself does not bring up such an antithesis either. PsJames perceives Christians who have come to faith, but do not display corresponding behavior; with regard to this case, he merely inquires under what circumstances faith saves. Thereby, he makes use of "deeds" as a criterium of differentiation.

13   See esp. Berger, *Theologiegeschichte*, 419–30; Jens Herzer, *Petrus oder Paulus? Studien über das Verhältnis des Ersten Petrusbriefes zur paulinischen Tradition* (WUNT 103; Tübingen: Mohr Siebeck, 1998); Lothar Wehr, *Petrus und Paulus—Kontrahenten und Partner: Die beiden Apostel im Spiegel des Neuen Testaments, der Apostolischen Väter und früher Zeugnisse ihrer Verehrung* (NTAbh NF 30; Münster: Aschendorff, 1996), 181–215. Also cf. n. 119 below.

14   See Konradt, *Christliche Existenz*, 17–21.

15   But in different word order.

16   On the theme of joy, see below.

17   Ποικίλος is quite common (see, e.g., Philo and *Herm.*). With special regard to James 1:2 and 1 Peter 1:6, cf. 3 Macc 2:6; 4 Macc 17:7; 18:21.

18   See on this Konradt, *Christliche Existenz*, 102–5.

19   See Konradt, *Christliche Existenz*, 109–23.

20   On this topic, see Helmut Millauer, *Leiden als Gnade: Eine traditionsgeschichtliche Untersuchung zur Leidenstheologie des ersten Petrusbriefes* (EHS.T 56; Bern: Peter Lang, 1976); Angelika Reichert, *Eine urchristliche praeparatio ad martyrium:. Studien zur Komposition, Traditionsgeschichte und Theologie des 1. Petrusbriefes* (BBET 22; Bern: Peter Lang, 1989).

21   Cf. Ps 66:10; (Isa 48:10); Zech 13:9; Jdt 8:27; Mal 3:3; Wis 3:5-6; Sir 2:5; 1 QH 13:16; Philo, *Sacr.* 80; 1 Pet 1:7; 6 Ezra 16:74; further, Prov 17:3; 27:21; Sir 27:5; 1 QM 17:1; and, beyond the realm of biblical traditions, e.g. Plato, *Resp.* 3.413E; Seneca, *Prov.* 5:10.

22   Cf. below in section 3.

23   See also Millauer, *Leiden*, 183–84; Leonhard Goppelt, *Der erste Petrusbrief* (KEK 12.1; Göttingen: Vandenhoeck & Ruprecht, 1978), 98–99. Different: Brox, *Petrusbrief*, 63–64. Cf. 1 Peter 4:13b. By contrast, present joy *because of* suffering is the topic in 4:13a (cf. Millauer, *Leiden*, 184–85).

24   On this, see Wiard Popkes, *Adressaten, Situation und Form des Jakobusbriefes* (SBS 125/126; Stuttgart: Verlag Katholisches Bibelwerk, 1986), 134–36, 176; Peter H. Davids, *The Epistle of James: A Commentary on the Greek Text* (NIGTC; Grand Rapids: Eerdmans, 1982), 66.

25   Therefore, Proverbs 3:34 is not directly quoted from Scripture in either case, but has been adopted as a citation from early Christian tradition. The same divergence also occurs in *1 Clem.* 30:2 (without the article) and in Ignatius, *Eph.* 5:3. In the writings of the New Testament, there are no further citations of Prov 3:34 (but cf. Luke 1:51).

26	In 1 Peter 5:6, this is made explicit by the temporal indicator ἐν καιρῷ, which should be read as a continuation of the line of thought initiated by ἐν καιρῷ ἐσχάτῳ in 1 Peter 1:5 (cf. Goppelt, *Petrusbrief*, 337; Rainer Metzner, *Die Rezeption des Matthäusevangeliums im 1. Petrusbrief: Studien zum traditionsgeschichtlichen und theologischen Einfluß des 1. Evangeliums auf den 1. Petrusbrief* [WUNT 2.74; Tübingen: Mohr Siebeck, 1995], 96).

27	Cf. further Job 5:11; Ezra 17:24; 21:31; *Let. Arist.* 263; *1 Clem.* 59:3. With regard to the pattern of humiliation and exaltation, cf. also 2 Cor 11:7; Phil 2:8-9.

28	Here, however, the word order is different. On the comparison with the synoptic wisdom saying cf. Goppelt, *Petrusbrief*, 337n5; Metzner, *Rezeption*, 95–96.

29	Cf. Exod 3:19; 6:1; 13:3, 9, 14, 16; Deut 9:26, 26:8; etc.

30	Likewise Metzner, *Rezeption*, 96–97.

31	Verse 7, where Jesus-tradition may stand in the background (cf. Matt 6:25-34/Luke 12:22-32), underlines the idea that a Christian should and may surrender himself faithfully to God's hand by referring to God's care for him. After the call for soberness and watchfulness (cf. 1 Thess 5:6-8), which was also inserted into the underlying tradition by the author of 1 Peter, 1 Peter finally offers a redactional, vivid circumscription of the dangerous activities of the devil with the image of the lion (5:8; it is especially closely related to Ps 21:14 LXX; see further Ps 58:7; 1QH 13:9-11, 13-14; 2 Tim 4:17; etc.), before the call for resistance against the devil follows (v. 9a), whereby this call also refers to holding out in the midst of tribulations (v. 9b).

32	The flow of the argumentation presupposes that what is desired could also be an object of prayer. Secondly, it is possible that the object desired or prayed for can be wasted ἐν ταῖς ἡδοναῖς. Therefore, it must concern material goods. Cf., e.g., Wolfgang Schrage (*Ethik des Neuen Testaments* [GNT 4; 2d ed.; Göttingen: Vandenhoeck & Ruprecht, 1989], 300), who views James 4:1-2 as criticizing "die leidenschaftliche Gier nach Besitz und Lust." Hubert Frankemölle (*Der Brief des Jakobus* [ÖTK 17.2; Gütersloh: Gütersloher Verlagshaus; Würzburg: Echter Verlag, 1994], 590) considers every attempt to determine the object of οὐ δύνασθε ἐπιτυχεῖν to be as "fehl am Platze."

33	James 4:5 is a notorious crux. For a discussion of the various interpretative options, see the excursus in Burchard, *Jakobusbrief*, 171–74 (lit.!) and Konradt, *Christliche Existenz*, 81–84.

34	The promise attached to the call for resistance against the devil, καὶ φεύξεται ἀφ' ὑμῶν (cf. *Test. Iss.* 7:7; *Test. Dan.* 5:1; *Test. Naph.* 8:4; and also *Test. Sim.* 3:5; *Herm. Mand.* 12 2:4; 4:7; 5:2), may well derive from PsJames. Structurally parallel to this—i.e., also combined with a promise—PsJames first offers the positive counterpart to v. 7b in v. 8a within the admonition to move closer to God, hereby reinforcing the admonition of vv. 7a, 10 simultaneously. The latter admonition appears, because of the reduplication, as a frame.

35	It is *opinio communis* that 1 Peter 1:23 refers to conversion/baptism, and at least the majority of exegetes agree that the same is true for James 1:18. For the various interpretative options, see the discussion in Konradt, *Christliche Existenz*, 42–44.

36 John 3:3-8 calls being baptized γεννηθῆναι ἄνωθεν, resp. ἐξ ὕδατος καὶ πνεύματος; 1 John speaks of γεννηθῆναι ἐκ τοῦ θεοῦ (2:29; 3:9; 4:7; 5:1; etc.); Titus 3:5 speaks of a λουτρὸν παλιγγενεσίας. In post-NT literature, the compositum ἀναγεννᾶσθαι/ἀναγέννησις, which is used in 1 Peter 1:3, 23, has obviously become the standard expression (see Justin Martyr, *1 Apol.* 1.61.3-4, 10; 66.1; and *Dial.* 138.2; Tatian 5:3; *Acts. Thom.* 132; *Ps.-Clem. Contestatio* 1:2; *Ps.-Clem. Hom.* 11:26:1).

37 In 1 Peter 1:23, διὰ λόγου ζῶντος θεοῦ καὶ μένοντος is placed appositively next to οὐκ ἐκ σπορᾶς φθαρτῆς ἀλλὰ ἀφθάρτου and thus defines the preceding metaphors by identifying the seed with the word. (Cf. Goppelt, *Petrusbrief*, 132; different: Heinz Giesen, "Gemeinde als Liebesgemeinschaft dank göttlicher Neuzeugung: Zu 1 Pet. 1,22–2,3," *SNTSU.A* 24 [1999], 135–66, here 147.)

38 In early Jewish statements about conversion, the moment of one's "turning towards the truth" constitutes a fixed topos (cf. *Jos. Asen.* 8:9; 19:11; Philo, *Spec.* 4:178, *Virt.* 103, *Praem.* 27.58, etc.; Ps.-Philo, *De Jona* 119); cf. in early Christian writings, 1 Tim 2:4; Heb 10:26; *Herm. Vis.* 3:6:2, as well as the use of the expression λόγος ἀληθείας with regard to the missionary proclamation in 2 Cor 6:7; Col 1:5; Eph 1:13 (see on this Konradt, *Christliche Existenz*, 67n184).

39 See the texts referred to in n. 38. In 2 Timothy 2:15, the accentuation of the expression has been shifted because of the opposition against false teachers (cf. 2 Tim 2:18; cf. 1 Tim 6:3-5; 2 Tim 3:8; 4:4; Titus 1:14).

40 No Jewish roots can be traced for this. Also, apart from the bipartite scheme, there are only few usages of ἀποτίθεσθαι in this manner (*Let. Arist.* 122; Philo, *Post.* 48 [*Deus* 26; *Ebr.* 86]; *Spec.* 1:306; Josephus, *Ant.* 6.264).

41 In Colossians 3:10, however, ἐνδυσάμενοι corresponds (primarily) to ἀπεκδυσάμενοι (v. 9) and not to ἀπόθεσθε, and in Eph 4:22-24, τῷ πνεύματι τοῦ νοὸς ὑμῶν has been inserted between undressing and dressing. Ephesians 6:11, 14 echoes Romans 13:12, resp. 1 Thessalonians 5:8. Just as in 1 Thessalonians, however, the negative part of the bipartite scheme is missing. Finally, Colossians 3:12 takes up ἐνδυσάμενοι from v. 10, but only a catalogue of virtues can be found as its object (cf. further *Herm. Sim.* 6:1:4).

42 For Paul, the concept of clothing oneself with Christ is related to the idea that baptism as integration into the realm of Christ's salvation transcends separating differences between people, i.e., annuls them *coram Deo* (Gal 3:27-28), which has consequences for social interaction. In Ephesians 2:14; Colossians 3:11, this echoes in the discourse about the new human being that Christ has created in his person from both (i.e., from Jew and Gentile) by means of his sacrifice. In comparison, the salvation-historical difference between Jews and Gentiles bears no significance for the authors of James and 1 Peter; rather, honorary epithets of Israel are unpolemically adopted.

43 Cf. Philipp Carrington, *The Primitive Christian Catechism: A Study in the*

Epistles (Cambridge: Cambridge University Press, 1940), 35–36; further Sophie Laws, *The Epistle of James* (Black's New Testament Commentaries; Peabody, Mass.: Hendrickson, 1980), 84–85; Douglas J. Moo, *The Letter of James* (The Pillar New Testament Commentary; Grand Rapids: Eerdmans, 2000), 85.

44   At most, *1 Clem.* 13:1 may be compared with this: here, the call to discard vices is followed by the admonition to do τὸ γεγραμμένον.

45   Cf. Luke 8:13; Acts 8:14; 11:1; 17:11; 1 Thess 1:6; 2:13.

46   Not '*as*'! It is not about the instruction of neophytes (cf. Brox, *Petrusbrief,* 91–92).

47   For the reference of τὸ λογικὸν ἄδολον γάλα, see, e.g., Goppelt, *Petrusbrief,* 134–36; Brox, *Petrusbrief,* 91–92; Giesen, "Gemeinde," 157–60.

48   Contrary to a widespread position (cf. for many Franz Schnider, *Der Jakobusbrief* [RNT; Regensburg: Pustet, 1987], 46–48), the participle ἀποθέμενοι should probably not be interpreted as an imperative, but rather in terms of causality. On the causal understanding, cf. Giesen, "Gemeinde," 152–53. For a temporal interpretation, see Burchard, *Jakobusbrief,* 67, 82.

49   With this, PsJames designates not only a mere possibility, but rather the effective power of the word (see Konradt, *Christliche Existenz,* 80; Burchard, *Jakobusbrief,* 83–84). Compare also the use of the verb in 2:14; 3:8, 12; 4:2, 12 (see also 3:2).

50   However, different aspects of the citation are taken up. The author of 1 Peter refers to the positive characterization of the word, whereas James 1:10-11 takes up the transitory nature of mankind, focusing on the rich (on this focus, cf. Ps 37:1-2; 129:6; *2 Bar.* 82:7), as a contrast to the enduring character of the word.

51   Πᾶς occurs in this context also in *1 Clem.* 13:1, and further in Colossians 3:8; Hebrews 12:1—there, however, in a different syntactic position.

52   James 1:18 offers—especially through the introduction of the "word of truth" as an effective means of birth—the foundation for 1:21b-25. Simultaneously, the verse relates antithetically to the preceding statements (see the resumption of ἀποκυεῖν from 1:15): God does not tempt to evil, but much the opposite rather, and as Father of lights from whom only good things—in agreement with his being—proceed (1:17), he has led us to life through the word of truth.

53   See on this Konradt, *Christliche Existenz,* 41–74. On the structure of James, cf. Konradt, *Christliche Existenz,* 15–21, 311–15.

54   On the understanding of 1:18b, cf. Konradt, *Christliche Existenz,* 59–66.

55   See on this esp. William R. Baker, *Personal Speech-Ethics in the Epistle of James* (WUNT 2.68; Tübingen: Mohr Siebeck, 1995).

56   As in James 1:21(!), ψυχή does not denote a part of the human being, but the person itself (cf. Giesen, "Gemeinde," 139–40; Goppelt, *Petrusbrief,* 131).

57   On the instrumental use of ἐν, cf. Giesen, "Gemeinde," 140.

58   Likewise, e.g., Giesen, "Gemeinde," 140.

59   There are no other instances of ἀλήθεια in 1 Peter!

60 Cf. Martin Evang, "Ἐκ καρδίας ἀλλήλους ἀγαπήσατε ἐκτενῶς: Zum Verständnis der Aufforderung und ihrer Begründungen in 1 Petr 1,22f.," *ZNW* 80 (1989): 111–23, here 116.

61 Likewise Brox, *Petrusbrief*, 81; Eduard Schweizer, *Der erste Petrusbrief* (4th ed.; ZBK.NT 15; Zürich: Theologischer Verlag Zürich, 1998), 39; Evang, "Verständnis," 116–18; Giesen, "Gemeinde," 143–44. Different: Goppelt, *Petrusbrief*, 130.

62 Cf. Evang, "Verständnis," 114.

63 Correspondingly, the explicating sentence in 1:25b goes back to the author of 1 Peter. Cf. 1:10-12 and, on εἰς ὑμᾶς, esp. 1:10.

64 On the translation, cf. Schweizer, *Petrusbrief*, 42; Giesen, "Gemeinde," 159.

65 The quotation from Psalms, added in 2:3, also aims at encouraging to carry on: the call to yearn for "wordly milk" is substantiated by the reference to the positive initial experience.

66 The shape of the negative part of the pattern in 2:1, addressing mainly behavior causing severe disruptions in an intense community (cf. Schweizer, *Petrusbrief*, 41), also suits this orientation.

67 See on this, e.g., Hans-Peter Mathys, *Liebe deinen Nächsten wie Dich selbst: Untersuchungen zum alttestamentlichen Gebot der Nächstenliebe (Lev 19,18)* (OBO 71; Freiburg Schweiz: Universitätsverlag Fribourg; Göttingen: Vandenhoeck & Ruprecht, 1986), 132–34, on Leviticus 19:18; as well as Jürgen Becker, *Untersuchungen zur Entstehungsgeschichte der Testamente der zwölf Patriarchen* (AGJU 8; Leiden: Brill, 1970), 394–95; Matthias Konradt, "Menschen- oder Bruderliebe? Beobachtungen zum Liebesgebot in den Testamenten der Zwölf Patriarchen," *ZNW* 88 (1997): 296–310, here 308; and Thomas Söding, "Solidarität in der Diaspora: Das Liebesgebot nach den Testamenten der Zwölf Patriarchen im Vergleich mit dem Neuen Testament," *Kairos* 36/37 (1994/1995): 1–19, here 6, on the *T. 12 Patr.* 12.

68 It should be remarked, however, that this "quotation" occurs elsewhere as well (see n. 70).

69 In this context, the sins that have been covered are those of the apostate (cf. Konradt, *Christliche Existenz*, 57–58).

70 On its own, this connection is less significant, since this statement, which is based on Proverbs 10:12, occurs in a number of other instances in the early Christian tradition (see *1 Clem.* 49:5; *2 Clem.* 16:4; further, e.g., Clement of Alexandria, *Paed.* 3.91:3; *Strom.* 1.173.6; 2.65.3; 4.111.3, *Quis div. salv.* 38.2; SyrDid. 4 [p. 46 Vööbus]).

71 Καταλαλιά occurs in the New Testament otherwise only in 2 Corinthians 12:20; κατάλαλος occurs in Romans 1:30; the verb καταλαλεῖν occurs only in 1 Peter 2:12; 3:16, where it refers to the defamation of Christians by Gentiles.

72 Apart from James 3:13 and 1 Peter 1:15, 18; 2:12; 3:1, 2, 16, see Gal 1:13; Eph 4:22; 1 Tim 4:12; Heb 13:7; 2 Peter 2:7; 3:11.

73 Cf. 1 Peter 3:2 (ἀγνή); 3:16 (ἀγαθή).

74 For ἁγνίζειν as referring to ritual purification (locally, always connected with Jerusalem/the temple), cf. John 11:55; Acts 21:24, 26; 24:18.

75   In James 5:12 as well as in 1 Peter 4:8, πρὸ πάντων occurs as a transitional
     phrase. James as well as 1 Peter both use the (admittedly widespread) image
     of the wreath (στέφανος) in order to describe eschatological salvation (Jas
     1:12; 1 Pet 5:4). Ἐπιστρέφειν and πλανᾶσθαι are common verbs, but they
     occur in the NT only in James 5:19 and 1 Peter 2:25 in direct juxtaposition.
     Ἀπροσωπολήμπτως in 1 Peter 1:17 can be related to James 2:1, though
     the motif of God's impartiality, as well as the exhortation to impartiality
     on the part of humans, is widespread (see for evidence, Konradt, *Christliche
     Existenz*, 136nn228–29). The occurrence of ἐπιεικής in James 3:17 and
     1 Peter 2:18 is even less specific (cf., in the NT, Phil 4:5; 1 Tim 3:3; Titus
     3:2), as are the occurrences of πραΰτης in James 1:21; 3:13 and 1 Peter
     3:16 (cf. only Gal 5:23; 6:1; Eph 4:2; Col 3:12; 2 Tim 2:25; Titus 3:2). Also,
     the fact that both teach perceiving the present from the perspective of the
     τέλος (Jas 5:11; 1 Pet 1:9) is not of great significance. This also applies
     to the use of στηρίζειν in James 5:8 and 1 Peter 5:10, especially since the
     subject is "Christians" in one case, and "God" in the other. With respect to
     ἀνυπόκριτος (Jas 3:17; 1 Pet 1:22), the relatively frequent use of this word
     in early Christian writings, when compared with its use in the LXX and
     early Jewish writings (only in Wis 5:18; 18:16; never in the pseudepigrapha
     preserved in Greek, never in Philo nor in Josephus), is striking (cf., apart
     from James and 1 Peter, four further occurrences in the NT, all of them
     in the corpus Paulinum [Rom 12:9; 2 Cor 6:6; 1 Tim 1:5; 2 Tim 1:5]; cf.
     further *2 Clem.* 12:3), though in this particular case, Romans 12:9 and
     2 Corinthians 6:6 are closer in terms of content to the Petrine statement
     about "unfeigned brotherly love" than James 3:17. A formal analogy can
     be established between James 5:19-20 and 1 Peter 5:12: in both cases, the
     central concern of the writing is expressed in a concise manner at its end. In
     1 Peter 5:12, this is introduced as such *expressis verbis*. On the significance
     of James 5:19-20 within the context of the epistle, see Popkes, *Adressaten*,
     206; Lauri Thurén, "Risky Rhetoric in James?" *NT* 37 (1995): 262–84, esp.
     274; Konradt, *Christliche Existenz*, 314–15.

76   James, the brother of the Lord, and the traditions about him have been dis-
     cussed in a number of monographs in recent research. See M. I. Webber,
     " Ἰάκωβος ὁ Δίκαιος: Origins, Literary Expression and Development of
     Traditions about the Brother of the Lord in Early Christianity" (Ms. Diss.,
     Fuller Theological Seminary, 1985); Wilhelm Pratscher, *Der Herrenbruder
     Jakobus und die Jakobustradition* (FRLANT 139; Göttingen: Vandenhoeck
     & Ruprecht, 1987); and John Painter, *Just James*. See further the essays in
     Chilton and Evans, *James the Just*.

77   The fact that with James, the son of Zebedee, and Peter, only well-known
     apostles belonging to the Twelve were among the victims of the persecu-
     tion under Agrippa can be sufficiently explained by their public position (in
     Jerusalem). Conversely, this must not necessarily be linked to a more liberal
     attitude towards the Torah on the part of Peter. (For a different opinion,
     see, e.g., Martin Hengel, "Jakobus der Herrenbruder—der erste 'Papst'?"
     in *Glaube und Eschatologie* [ed. Erich Gräßer and Otto Merk; FS Werner

Georg Kümmel; Tübingen: Mohr Siebeck, 1985], 71–104, here 100; see also below on the incident in Antioch.)

78   Cf. for many Hengel, "Jakobus," 98–100; Markus Bockmuehl, "Antioch and James the Just," in Chilton and Evans, *James the Just*, 155–98, 186; Wolfgang Kraus, *Zwischen Jerusalem und Antiochia: Die "Hellenisten", Paulus und die Aufnahme der Heiden in das endzeitliche Gottesvolk* (SBS 179; Stuttgart: Verlag Katholisches Bibelwerk, 1999), 136.

79   Cf. Painter, *Just James*, 44 and elsewhere.

80   In general, one may well inquire whether a clearly defined hierarchy may be assumed for the congregational leadership. On the basis of Mark 3:20-21, 31-35; 6:1-6; John 7:5, it is commonly presumed that before Easter, James had reservations about his brother's work, and that the appearance of the risen Lord (1 Cor 15:7) provoked a turnaround; subsequently, James' importance increased steadily. In contrast, Roy Bowen Ward ("James of Jerusalem," *ANRW* 2.26.1:786–91) has questioned the value of the statements from the Gospels, and recently Painter (*Just James*, 12–44) has argued that James already belonged to the circle of his brother's followers before Easter. Often a change in leadership is inferred from Acts 12:17: James is first mentioned by name at the very moment of Peter's departure. This is, however, not an evident indication. The fact that, at the moment of his flight, Peter orders that James be informed could also be interpreted as an order to inform the leader of the congregation (cf. Painter, *Just James*, 44). Furthermore, the fact that James is not explicitly mentioned earlier in Acts may be explained by the assumption of a redactional tendency of Luke, whose primary focus is on Peter. Also Galatians 1:19 does not offer sufficient proof for Peter's exclusive leadership. The argument that Paul wished to meet the head of the Twelve during his first visit to Jerusalem may well be explained by the assumption that Peter had awakened Paul's interest in him as a missionary (cf. Roman Heiligenthal, "'Petrus und Jakobus, der Gerechte': Gedanken zur Rolle der beiden Säulenapostel in der Geschichte des frühen Christentums," *ZNT* 2 [1999], 32–40: "Paulus besuchte Petrus, weil dieser bereits durch Jesus an vorrangiger Stelle zur Mission unter den zwölf Stämmen Israels berufen war" [37]). William R. Farmer ("James the Lord's Brother, According to Paul," in Chilton and Evans, *James the Just*, 133–53) attempts to deduce Paul's interest in Peter from the assumption that Paul must have had contact with the Petrine mission during his time as a persecutor (143). Furthermore, it should be underlined that Paul mentions James as the only important head of the Jerusalem congregation besides Peter that he has met during his first visit in Jerusalem (Gal 1:19). Nothing is said about the content or the circumstances of the meeting. (Farmer ["James"] postulates, in view of Paul's first visit to Jerusalem, "that we have every reason to expect that at some point during the fifteen days, if not very early in the visit, the question of the Law and the circumstances of its binding force for Gentile converts would have come up" [138]). Was James' presence only accidental? Or—what seems more plausible to me— did Peter explicitly invite James to join them? In that case, James must

have already been a person of considerable importance in the Jerusalem congregation.

81   1 Corinthians 9:5 points to the traveling activities of the Lord's brothers as well. It seems likely that James is implied here. Paul, however, does not give any details about the context or the character of the journeys. Had James (together with his wife?) already visited existing congregations in Judea and its surroundings, or even in the Syriac area? Did he seize any opportunities to make the Christian message known in synagogal services? One may regard all of this as plausible, but one cannot know with certainty. There are no indications anywhere that he founded any congregations himself. In any case, Galatians 2:6-9 identifies Peter among the triad (James, Peter, John) as the head of the mission starting from Jerusalem.

82   If one follows the thesis of Gerd Theißen, presented in "Hellenisten und Hebräer (Apg 6,1-6): Gab es eine Spaltung der Urgemeinde?" in *Frühes Christentum* (ed. Hubert Cancik, Hermann Lichtenberger, and Peter Schäfer; vol. 3 of *Geschichte–Tradition–Reflexion*; Tübingen: Mohr Siebeck, 1996), 323–43, esp. 328, that the Hellenistic circle of the seven (Acts 6:1-6) constituted "einen ersten Versuch, neben den überregionalen Autoritäten der 'Zwölf' Ortsautoritäten für Jerusalem zu schaffen," (328) then one should rather say that the brother of the Lord (as a stationary leader of a congregation) followed in the footsteps of the circle of the seven, but did not replace Peter. In any case, no rivalry between Peter and the brother of the Lord can be construed from the sources. Interpreting 1 Corinthians 15:7 as a reference to rivalry (cf. most recently Pratscher, *Herrenbruder*, 35–46) is not justified by the text of 1 Corinthians 15 (cf. the apt remark of Heiligenthal, "Petrus und Jakobus," 36: "Diese These erscheint mir eher durch eine grundsätzliche Sicht des frühen Christentums als einer Konfliktgeschichte evoziert als durch den Textbefund"). The postulate of James' precedency is reflected, for example, in the vision scene in *Gos. Heb.* 7 (cf. Painter, *Just James*, 184–86), but this cannot be projected back into the earliest times without any qualifications.

83   Even before the persecution under Agrippa, Acts reports on Peter's travels around the country (Acts 9:32; on the missionary activities of Peter as well as the Twelve, cf. Theißen, "Hellenisten und Hebräer," 326–27, 338). Acts may also well convey a reliable picture by describing the central role Peter already played in the public proclamation in Jerusalem (2:14-41; 3:12–4:22; 5:15). Possibly, Peter also acted as a charismatic healer in this context (cf. Acts 3:1-10; 5:13-16), naturally with a corresponding external effect (cf., e.g., Heiligenthal, "Petrus und Jakobus," 37).

84   Cf. James D. G. Dunn, *A Commentary on the Epistle to the Galatians* (BNTC; London: Black, 1993), 109–10; Richard Bauckham, "James and the Jerusalem Church," in idem, *The Book of Acts in Its Palestinian Setting* (vol. 4 of *The Book of Acts in Its First Century Setting;* Grand Rapids: Eerdmans; Carlisle: Paternoster, 1995), 415–80, 442–50.

85   On this, see the remarks of Pratscher, *Herrenbruder*, 102–208, and Painter, *Just James*.

86   Cf. Hengel, "Jakobus," 88. The thesis that Jerusalem's claim to a leading
     position possessed juridical character (cf. Hengel, "Jakobus," 88, 102) intro-
     duces a category into the discussion that is hardly appropriate to it.

87   Often, the appearance of James in the first position of this trio is seen as
     an indication of his leading role (cf., e.g., Hengel, "Jakobus," 92; Farmer,
     "James," 143).

88   I assume that the sequence of events given in Galatians 2 correctly reflects
     the historical chronology. Likewise Gerhard Schneider, *Die Apostelgeschichte.
     2. Teil: Kommentar zu Kap. 9,1-28,31* (HThKNT 5.2; Freiburg: Herder,
     1982), 191; Traugott Holtz, "Der antiochenische Zwischenfall (Galater
     2.11-14)," *NTS* 32 (1986): 344–61, here 346–47; Craig C. Hill, *Hellenists
     and Hebrews: Reappraising Division within the Earliest Church* (Minneapolis:
     Fortress, 1992), 115–17; Andreas Wechsler, *Geschichtsbild und Apostelstreit:
     Eine forschungsgeschichtliche und exegetische Studie über den antiochenischen
     Zwischenfall (Gal 2,11-14)* (BZNW 62; Berlin: de Gruyter, 1991), 297–305,
     and many others. For a different opinion, see Gerd Lüdemann, *Studien zur
     Chronologie* (vol. 1 of *Paulus, der Heidenapostel*; FRLANT 123; Göttingen:
     Vandenhoeck & Ruprecht, 1980), 77–79, 101–5.

89   At first sight, εἰ σὺ Ἰουδαῖος ὑπάρχων ἐθνικῶς καὶ οὐχὶ Ἰουδαϊκῶς ζῇς
     (Gal 2:14) speaks in favor of the first possibility. However, maintaining
     that Peter lived "like a Gentile" is part of Paul's polemical account and
     certainly does not allow the conclusion that he would have regarded the
     Torah as obsolete (cf. Dunn, *Galatians Commentary*, 127–28). Even for the
     food regulations, this cannot be stated with sufficient certainty (cf. Holtz,
     "Der antiochenische Zwischenfall," 345). In any case, Acts 10:1–11:18 may
     well be attributed to Lukan redaction (cf. Christoph Heil, *Die Ablehnung
     der Speisegebote durch Paulus: Zur Frage nach der Stellung des Apostels zum
     Gesetz* [BBB 96; Weinheim: Beltz Athenäum, 1994], 153). In view of Gala-
     tians 2:7, it must be doubted that Peter had already practiced the openness
     toward the Gentiles in his own missionary activity before the Jerusa-
     lem council (cf. Rudolf Pesch, *Die Apostelgeschichte, 2. Teilbd.: Apg 13-28*
     [EKKNT 5.2; Zürich: Benzinger and Neukirchen-Vluyn: Neukirchener,
     1986], 86).

90   Cf. Heil, *Ablehnung*, 138.

91   Meat and also wine of the Gentiles were very closely associated with the
     pagan cult (cf. E. P. Sanders, "Jewish Association with Gentiles and Gala-
     tians 2:11-14," in *The Conversation Continues: Studies in Paul and John* [ed.
     Robert T. Fortna and Beverly R. Gaventa; FS J. L. Martyn; Nashville:
     Abingdon, 1990], 170–88, here 178–79). If the "apostolic decree" (Acts
     15:29) reflects the points of critique raised by the people of James (against
     Bockmuehl, "Antioch," 181), then searching for a solution in this direction
     obviously suggests itself (on the connection with the incident in Antioch,
     cf. below). The question of whether impurity of food is the issue (cf. decid-
     edly Sanders, "Jewish Association," 176–80, 185–86) or impurity of Gen-
     tiles as Gentiles (cf. Bockmuehl, "Antioch," 181), possibly leads toward a
     false alternative. The fact that the apostolic decree mentions idol meat,

blood, and things strangled points to food. πορνεία, however, cannot be placed into the same category, and points toward the impurity of a person (cf. 1 Cor 5:11!). The relevant early Jewish texts primarily refer to food as the problem (see Dan 1:5-16; 2 Macc 7:1-2; 3 Macc 4:4, 7; Esth 4:17 LXX; Tob. 1:10-11; and, positively, *Let. Arist.* 181: the participation of Jews at the royal banquet is possible without further ado, because it is guaranteed that the food is prepared according to the Jewish food laws). The command to separate from the Gentiles in *Jub.* 22:16 (cf. also Acts 10:28) is different in this respect. Taken by itself, *Jos. Asen.* 7:1 can be read in terms of an avoidance of meal fellowship with Gentiles on principle, but *Jos. Asen.* 20:8 gives a different impression.

92   According to Galatians 2:13, "the other Jews" have also withdrawn. But does this mean all of them? Or only those who had previously participated in meal fellowship with Gentiles?

93   Cf. the considerations of Ludger Schenke, *Die Urgemeinde: Geschichtliche und theologische Entwicklung* (Stuttgart: Kohlhammer, 1990), 320–23.

94   The suggestion of Paul Christoph Böttger, in "Paulus und Petrus in Antiochien: Zum Verständnis von Galater 2,11-21," *NTS* 37 (1991): 77–100, esp. 80–81, that the reference to Peter's ἐθνικῶς ζῆν has nothing to do with meal fellowship, but should rather be viewed as a criticism along the lines of 1 Thessalonians 4:5 and Ephesians 2:12 and parallelized with the reproach of Galatians 2:14a, does not suit the context of Galatians 2:11-14.

95   Paul's account does not clarify the question of whether these people from James were a delegation sent by the brother of the Lord, in order to intervene against the Antiochian praxis of which he had knowledge (ἀπὸ Ἰακώβου in Galatians 2:12 should be put with ἐλθεῖν in that case). It may also be possible that this refers to Christians from James' circle (putting ἀπὸ Ἰακώβου with τινας), who (within the framework of common visits?) had come to Antioch and first learned there of the practices that were unbearable for them. The idea of a delegation is preferred, e.g., by Pratscher, *Herrenbruder*, 79; L. Schenke, *Urgemeinde*, 323; Jürgen Wehnert, *Die Reinheit des "christlichen Gottesvolkes" aus Juden und Heiden: Studien zum historischen und theologischen Hintergrund des sogenannten Aposteldekrets* (FRLANT 173; Göttingen: Vandenhoeck & Ruprecht, 1997), 124; and Farmer ("James," 146–48), who additionally postulates as the context a planned "high-level meeting" about the Antiochian mission as the context, in which other delegations also participated. This, however, is hardly more than highly imaginative speculation.

96   Paul's reproach serves to parallelize the incident at Antioch with the Galatian crisis. In the latter context, "Judaizing adversaries" are accused of forcing the Galatians into circumcision to avoid persecution because of Christ's cross (6:12). The statement about "those of the circumcision" in 2:12 is evidently chosen as an anticipation of the problems of the Galatian crisis.

97   For this and the following, cf. Holtz, "Der antiochenische Zwischenfall," 348–49. On the other hand, the polemical character of Galatians 2:12 is not taken into account, e.g., by Wehnert, *Reinheit*, 124–25.

98   As a background for discussion, one must point out that the food laws in contemporary Judaism were emphasized differently, and diverging forms of observation and contact with Gentiles existed. For an overview on this, see, e.g., the elaborations of Bockmuehl, "Antioch," 164–68.

99   The people from James, for instance, could only prepare their own meals.

100 According to Acts 15, the brother of the Lord was not a member of the group of Christian Pharisees from which such an attitude would be primarily expected. Kenneth L. Carroll, in "The Place of James in the Early Church," *BJRL* 44 (1961): 49–67, 60, however, classifies James as a Christian Pharisee (60).

101 This is also reflected by the Lukan account of the council in Jerusalem. James' suggestion that the only obligations to be imposed on Gentile Christians bear the abstinence from idol meat, fornication, the meat of strangled animals, and blood (Acts 15:20) is followed by the argument that Moses had always had those who proclaimed him in every city, since he was read aloud in the synagogues on every Sabbath (15:21). If this explanation directly refers to v. 20, it must be understood as follows: the decree is necessary "weil die Juden seit Urzeiten an das im Synagogengottesdienst verlesene Gesetz gebunden sind und ihnen nicht ohne weiteres zugemutet werden kann, sich davon zu lösen," according to Jürgen Roloff (*Die Apostelgeschichte* [2d ed.; NTD 5; Göttingen: Vandenhoeck & Ruprecht, 1988], 233).

James' innocence (*Hellenists*, 187–88). On James' loyalty to the Torah, cf.
Josephus reports that the stoning of James (*A.J.* 20.200) provoked the protest of those who followed the law meticulously (201), probably to be understood as Pharisees (see on this Hengel, "Jakobus," 73; Ward, "James of Jerusalem," 785; and others; see, however, the differentiation by Hill, *Hellenists*, 190). Drawing any conclusions from this note of Josephus with respect to James' attitude toward the Torah, however, involves a number of difficulties, since it is possible, as Hengel assumes, that "die Protestierenden mehr das Machtstreben des ungestümen Hannas dämpfen [wollten], als die Jerusalemer Judenchristen verteidigen" ("Jakobus," 74). According to Hill, the protest concerned the legitimacy of Ananus' proceedings, not James' innocence (*Hellenists*, 187–88). On James' loyalty to the Torah, cf. Burchard, *Jakobusbrief*, 3; Hengel, "Jakobus," 80; Pratscher, *Herrenbruder*, 101, and many others.

102 See on this *Gos. Thom.* 12; *Gos. Heb.* 7; Hegesippus in Eusebius, *Hist. eccl.* 2.23.4, 7, 12, 15, 16; 4.22:4; *1 Apoc. Jas.* 32 (NTApo I, 6th ed.; 1990, 261), and elsewhere. Cf. Hengel, "Jakobus," 79–81; Painter, *Just James*, 125, 157, 162–63, 169, 185.

103 This aspect of the matter is formulated succinctly in *Let. Arist.* 139–42: ". . . To prevent our being perverted by contact with others or by mixing with bad influences, he hedged us in on all sides with strict observances connected with meat and drink and touch and hearing and sight, after the manner of the Law" (142).

104 Cf., e.g., Roloff, *Apostelgeschichte*, 227; Schneider, *Apostelgeschichte 2*, 189; Hengel, "Jakobus," 94–95; August Strobel, "Das Aposteldekret als Folge des antiochenischen Streites: Überlegungen zum Verhältnis von Wahrheit

und Einheit im Gespräch der Kirchen," in *Kontinuität und Einheit* (ed. Paul-Gerhard Müller and Werner Stenger; FS Franz Mußner; Freiburg: Herder, 1981), 81–104, here 86); Rudolf Pesch, "Das Jerusalemer Abkommen und die Lösung des Antiochenischen Konflikts: Ein Versuch über Gal 2, Apg 10,1-11,18, Apg 11,27-30; 12,25 und Apg 15,1-41," in Müller and Stenger, *Kontinuität*, 105–22, here 106–7; Alfons Weiser, "Das 'Apostelkonzil' (Apg 15,1-35): Ereignis, Überlieferung, lukanische Deutung," *BZ* NF 28 (1984): 143–67, here 152; Holtz, "Der antiochenische Zwischenfall," 354–55; Jürgen Becker, *Paulus: Der Apostel der Völker* (3d ed.; Tübingen: Mohr Siebeck, 1998), 103; Wehr, *Petrus und Paulus*, 69, 167–76; Heil, *Ablehnung*, 158. To the contrary, see David R. Catchpole ("Paul, James and the Apostolic Decree," *NTS* 23 [1977]: 428–44, here 442) and Wehnert (*Reinheit*, 129) for the view that the demands of the apostolic decree were the cause of the controversy in Antioch. They must have been "Teil der in Gal 2,12 erwähnten Jakobus-Botschaft" (Wehnert, *Reinheit*, 129). For a critique of this position, see W. Kraus, *Zwischen Jerusalem*, 151–52.

105   Whether this refers to incestuous relationships as in Lev 18 (vv. 6-18), or rather to fornication in general (see in Lev 18 [vv. 19-20, 22-23]), can remain open here. More important in terms of an interpretative background is that *"fornication"* occurs in early Jewish as well as in early Christian writings stereotypically as a characteristic of "paganism," and that the sexual ethos is held to be an important point of differentiation from the pagan world (see, e.g., Wis 14:24, 26; *Jub.* 25:1; *Let. Arist.* 152; *Sib. Or.* 3:594-600; 5:387-93; Ps.-Philo, *De Jona* 16, 105–6; Philo, *Jos.* 40–44; Col 3:5-7; Eph 4:17-19; 5:3-8; 1 Thess 4:3-5; Rev 14:8, 18:3). This whole complex is probably anchored in Leviticus 17–18, which is the primary point of reference for the "apostolic decree" (see Lev 18:24-30).

106   A third, possibly significant, reason for the people from James to intervene may have been a political motive. See on this Bockmuehl, "Antioch," 182–84.

107   Otherwise, Paul's charge against Peter, that he forced the Gentiles to ἰουδαΐζειν, would be incomprehensible (cf. Holtz, "Der antiochenische Zwischenfall," 349; W. Kraus, *Zwischen Jerusalem*, 160). ἰουδαΐζειν is thereby part of Paul's polemic (cf. on this question Holtz, "Der antiochenische Zwischenfall," 345–46, 354) and does not speak against the thesis that the demands assigned to the Gentile Christians were merely demands in line with the apostolic decree (cf. n. 91 above on the decree as reflecting the criticisms of the people from James). For Paul, however, these demands are connected with a fundamental decision.

108   Likewise Günter Bornkamm, *Paulus* (6th ed.; Stuttgart: Kohlhammer, 1987), 67–68; Catchpole, "Paul," 439–40; Holtz, "Der antiochenische Zwischenfall," 348; Roloff, *Apostelgeschichte*, 227; L. Schenke, *Urgemeinde*, 324; Becker, *Paulus*, 102; Hill, *Hellenists*, 126–27; Heil, *Ablehnung*, 162; Wehnert, *Reinheit*, 125, and many others.

109   On this, see Roloff, *Apostelgeschichte*, 227; Pesch, *Apostelgeschichte 2*, 81; Holtz, "Der antiochenische Zwischenfall," 355; Wechsler, *Geschichtsbild*,

361; Klaus Müller, *Thora für die Völker: Die noachidischen Gebote und Ansätze zu ihrer Rezeption im Christentum* (SKI 15; Berlin: Institut Kirche und Judentum, 1994), 157–63; Bauckham, "James and the Jerusalem Church," 459–60; Wehr, *Petrus und Paulus*, 168, 173; Heil, *Ablehnung*, 151–52; Wehnert, *Reinheit*, 209–45; W. Kraus, *Zwischen Jerusalem*, 146–49. Different, e.g., Alexander J. M. Wedderburn, "The 'Apostolic Decree': Tradition and Redaction," *NovT* 35 (1993): 362–89, here 363–70.

110 Cf. Holtz, "Der antiochenische Zwischenfall," 355. The Council of Jerusalem had given its affirmation to this as well, whereas for Paul, the acceptance of uncircumcised Gentiles meant that nothing was imposed on them in any other respect either.

111 See on this Wehnert, *Reinheit*, 239–57.

112 Cf. for many Bornkamm, *Paulus*, 67. This is easily explained by reference to the fact that, as a matter of course, meal fellowship in Jerusalem took place under the conditions of the Jerusalemites (cf. Hengel, "Jakobus," 94; Holtz, "Der antiochenische Zwischenfall," 352).

113 Holtz, "Der antiochenische Zwischenfall," 355. On the validity of the decree, cf. Marcel Simon, "The Apostolic Decree and its Setting in the Ancient Church," in idem, *Le Christianisme antique et son contexte religieux: Scripta Varia 2* (WUNT 23; Tübingen: Mohr Siebeck, 1981), 414–37, here 431–37; Bauckham, "James and the Jerusalem Church," 464–65.

114 In the same or a similar way, e.g., Roloff, *Apostelgeschichte*, 227; Hengel, "Jakobus," 94; Weiser, "Apostelkonzil," 152; Wehr, *Petrus und Paulus*, 174 ("Lukas hätte von sich aus zweifellos Petrus oder einem anderen der Zwölf die Rolle des Initiators überlassen"); Wehnert, *Reinheit*, 66–67, 68–70 ("Bei aller gebotenen Vorsicht darf . . . angenommen werden, daß in der von Lukas benutzten Überlieferung die Formulierung der Enthaltungsvorschriften mit der Person des Jakobus verknüpft war" [67]). See also Hill, *Hellenists*, 144–45.

115 Hengel, "Jakobus," 92 (emphasis in original), 96.

116 Cf. Hengel, "Jakobus," 95.

117 This would still be valid if the regulations of the apostolic decree were drawn up by Gentile Christians in Antioch as "eine Art freiwillige Selbstbeschränkung zum Zweck des Zusammenlebens mit den Judenchristen," as Pratscher has conjectured (*Herrenbruder*, 87). In any case, the regulations could hardly have been "decreed" without consulting the parties concerned, and the agreement of the Gentile Christians in Antioch must be assumed, to whatever extent they may have been involved in finding a solution to the problem.

118 On the high esteem for the Lord's brother in the Syriac area, see also the evidence in *Gos. Thom.* in logion 12 (cf. Pratscher, *Herrenbruder*, 151–54; Painter, *Just James*, 160–63). On the (later) positive reception of the Lord's brother in the "catholic" church, see Pratscher, *Herrenbruder*, 178–208.

119 See on this Berger, *Theologiegeschichte*, 418–30; cf. also Jürgen Becker, "Die Erwählung der Völker durch das Evangelium: Theologiegeschichtliche Erwägungen zum 1 Thess," in *Studien zum Text und zur Ethik des Neuen*

Testaments (ed. Wolfgang Schrage; BZNW 47; FS Heinrich Greeven; Berlin: de Gruyter, 1986), 82–101, here 100. This does not have to be a general solution, however. In any case, a discussion of this matter would have to take the aspect of the relationship between adherence to tradition and innovative, genuinely Pauline elements in Paul's arguments into consideration. To give only one example: is the use of χαρίσματα (Rom 12:6; 1 Cor 12:4, 9, 28; and more often, cf. 1 Pet 4:10) a specifically Pauline feature (the statistics of occurrences of the word in the New Testament clearly speak in favor of this), or is this a pre-Pauline tradition? Without being able to develop this extensively here, it seems to me that a solution has to be sought in the direction of an evaluation of 1 Peter as a witness of non-Pauline Christianity, which has, however, been influenced laterally by elements of the Pauline tradition. Thereby, it need not be assumed that these elements were known as distinctive Paulinisms (cf. Herzer, *Petrus*, passim). In the end, one can only speculate about the precise 'channels' of the traditions. However, if one considers, for example, that a "Peter party" existed in Corinth and that there seem to have been connections between Corinth and Antioch—as the fact that Paul assumes Barnabas is known in Corinth (1 Cor 9:6) suggests (likewise Helmut Merklein, *Der erste Brief an die Korinther: Kapitel 1-4* [ÖTBK 7.1; Gütersloh: Gütersloher Verlagshaus; Würzburg: Echter, 1992], 150), it becomes plausible that other groups could adopt Pauline traditions and incorporate them into non-Pauline channels of tradition.

120   In my opinion, James 2:14-26 is not dependent upon Pauline tradition; (cf. above, n. 12, and Matthias Konradt, "Der Jakobusbrief im frühchristlichen Kontext: Überlegungen zum traditionsgeschichtlichen Verhältnis des Jakobusbriefes zur Jesusüberlieferung, zur paulinischen Tradition und zum 1Petr," in *The Catholic Epistles and the Tradition* [ed. J. Schlosser; BETL 176; Leuven: Leuven University Press, 2004], 171–212, here 172–90). A connection, which may be well explained by referring to a common tradition, might be seen in the use of ψυχικός (Jas 3:15; 1 Cor 2:14) in the context of the reflection on wisdom in James 3:13-18 and 1 Corinthians 1–3, especially as the claim to possessing wisdom is disproved in both cases in a very similar way. While Paul charges the addressees with ζῆλος καὶ ἔρις (1 Cor 3:3), PsJames refers to ζῆλος πικρὸς καὶ ἐριθεία (Jas 3:14).

121   See Konradt, "Jakobusbrief im frühchristlichen Kontext," 190–207.

122   It cannot be taken for granted, however, that PsJames was familiar with all passages that have analogies in the Gospels as Jesus-tradition. In individual cases, the possibility has to be considered that ethical teaching has been turned into words of Jesus secondarily. The usage of James as a source for Jesus-traditions is therefore clearly limited, for methodological reasons.

123   See on this Gerhard Dautzenberg, "Ist das Schwurverbot Mt 5,33-37; Jak 5,12 ein Beispiel für die Thorakritik Jesu?," *BZ* NF 25 (1981): 47–66.

124   Various authors have argued for a close connection between James and Matthew. Hartin, *James and the Q Sayings*, 186–87, 195–96 (and elsewhere) considers James to be dependent on the sayings-source and familiar with its further development in the Matthean congregation (Q^Mt), but not with

its Matthean redaction. Agreements with Markan traditions were transmitted by the Matthean congregation. Other exegetes, however, postulate that the author of James must have had knowledge of Matthew's gospel itself, e.g., Brückner, "Kritik," 537; Shepherd, "Epistle of James," 40–51; Feliks Gryglewicz, "L'Épître de St. Jacques et l'Évangile de St. Matthieu," *RTK* 8 (1961): 33–55; Robert M. Cooper, "Prayer: A Study in Matthew and James," *Encounter* 29 (1968): 268–77.

125　Among other things, the understanding of the law, the theme of perfection, the absence of a pronounced pneumatological factor in the understanding of Christian existence, and the importance of the theme of judgment serving ethical motivation are common features. Cf. Konradt, *Christliche Existenz*, 324–27.

126　See, e.g., Ulrich Luz, *Das Evangelium nach Matthäus 1, Mt 1–7* (EKKNT 1.1; 2d ed.; Zürich: Benziger and Neukirchen-Vluyn: Neukirchener, 1989), 200, 220.

127　Recently, Metzner, *Rezeption*, has sought to prove the dependence of 1 Peter on Matthew. Luz (*Evangelium*, 76) considers this to be possible (more decidedly, on p. 220).

128　There is no passage, however, in which all three writings show close contacts with each other.

129　As is well known, this tendency culminates in Matthew 16:17-19.

130　See on this: David C. Sim, *The Gospel of Matthew and Christian Judaism: The History and Social Setting of the Matthean Community* (Studies of the New Testament and Its World; Edinburgh: T&T Clark, 1998), 188–92.

131　See Luz, *Evangelium*, 73–74.

132　Syria is also the majority opinion of the exegetes: see, e.g., Shepherd, "Epistle of James," 49–51; Klaus Kürzdörfer, "Der Charakter des Jakobusbriefes: Eine Auseinandersetzung mit den Thesen von A. Meyer und M. Dibelius" (Ms. diss., Tübingen, 1966), 128–30; Alfred F. Zimmermann, *Die urchristlichen Lehrer: Studien zum Tradentenkreis der* διδάσκαλοι *im frühen Urchristentum* (WUNT 2.2; 2d ed.; Tübingen: Mohr Siebeck, 1988), 194–96; Pratscher, *Herrenbruder*, 219n51; Burchard, *Jakobusbrief,* 7 (cf. there for alternatives).

133　Without being able to pursue this question any further here, in my opinion, a localization of 1 Peter in the Syriac area—instead of the common localization in Rome or Asia Minor—should be considered as a serious option on the basis of the traditio-historical findings presented earlier. The ascription of the letter to Peter, however, is as such also plausible for other locations; the existence of a "Peter-party" in Corinth (see 1 Cor 1:12) gives exemplary evidence that Peter's influence was widely spread.

134　Cf. Luz, *Evangelium*, 74, 75–76; Wolf-Dietrich Köhler, *Die Rezeption des Matthäusevangeliums in der Zeit vor Irenäus* (WUNT 2.24; Tübingen: Mohr Siebeck, 1987), 526, 534 (on Syria).

135　Peter H. Davids, "Palestinian Traditions in the Epistle of James," in Chilton and Evans, *James the Just*, 33–57, here 55. B. R. Halson ("The Epistle of James: 'Christian Wisdom?'" *StEv 4* [= TU 102; Berlin: de Gruyter, 1968],

308–14, here 312–13), views James as a collection of catechetical material, which originated in a catechetical school closely associated with James, the brother of the Lord.

136   R. P. Martin, *James*, lxxvi. Recently, this hypothesis has been taken up by Painter, *Just James*, 264.

137   This fact speaks against the possibility, considered most recently by Karl-Wilhelm Niebuhr in "Der Jakobusbrief im Licht frühjüdischer Diaspora-briefe," *NTS* 44 (1998): 420–43, here 431, "daß ein für die Gemeinden in der Diaspora bestimmtes Schreiben des Herrenbruders in Jerusalem *über-setzt* worden ist" (emphasis in original). Simultaneously, the Greek of the traditions taken up in James speaks against composition by the brother of the Lord at all, for the language could be explained much more logically if Greek were the vernacular. James may have had some knowledge of Greek, and it may have increased during the time in which he was responsible for the community in Jerusalem as its leader. This, however, does not neces-sarily mean that James reached the rhetorical level of James. And, above all, is it plausible that the community in Jerusalem (after the flight of the Hel-lenists) continued to cultivate traditions in Greek, especially to the extent demanded by the resemblances with 1 Peter?

138   In my opinion, James 1:18 does not fit well with the theology of the Lord's brother. According to this confessional statement, the conversion to Christian faith means a passing from death to life, whereby the Christians become a kind of ἀπαρχή of God's creatures. Philo uses the same meta-phor to describe the exceptional position of Israel as the special property of God (*Spec.* 4:180). If one (only) becomes God's property by converting to Christian faith according to James 1:18, then Israel's exceptional position is passed over de facto. (Taking the verse as a reference to Israel's election—in this sense, see Arnold Meyer, *Das Rätsel des Jacobusbriefes* [BZNW 10; Gießen: Töpelmann, 1930], 157–59, 269; and Martina Ludwig, *Wort als Gesetz: Eine Untersuchung zum Verständnis von 'Wort' und 'Gesetz' in israel-itisch-frühjüdischen und neutestamentlichen Schriften. Gleichzeitig ein Beitrag zur Theologie des Jakobusbriefes* [EHS.T 502; Bern: Peter Lang, 1994], 157–59—has no basis in the context of the letter, as the letter is neither a Jewish writing originally, nor a writing addressed to the Jewish people.) In my opinion, such a position can hardly be ascribed to the brother of the Lord.

139   Cf. Konradt, *Christliche Existenz*, 211–12 (with n. 32).

140   Finally, it would match perfectly that PsJames refers to Abraham and Rahab, both proselytes.

141   Thus the accurate characterization of Dibelius' view by Christoph Burchard, "Zu einigen christologischen Stellen des Jakobusbriefes," in *Anfänge der Christologie* (ed. Cilliers Breytenbach and Henning Paulsen; FS Ferdinand Hahn; Göttingen: Vandenhoeck & Ruprecht, 1991), 353–68, here 354.

142   Davids, "Palestinian Traditions," 34.

143   Davids, "Palestinian Traditions," 41.

144   Cf. the criticism of the dual-stage theories by Robert W. Wall, in *Commu-nity of the Wise*, 9–10, who argues that "editors" can hardly be regarded as

mere compilators, but rather, they rework and organize the material in the editorial process.

145 The existence of such circles can be regarded as certain on the basis of the tradition behind *Gos. Thom.* 12, of *Gos. Heb.* 7, and of a series of other early Christian witnesses (see Pratscher, *Herrenbruder*, 102–50; Painter, *Just James*, 105–223).

146 In addition to James 2:14-26, the confessional statement in James 1:18 makes good sense when assuming an ecclesial milieu containing Gentile Christians as well (cf. above, n. 138). The absence of circumcision, Sabbath, and purity regulations in James, all classical Jewish 'identity markers', does not necessarily mean much in this respect, since a striking concentration on the prescriptions of the Torah related to social life can also be observed in contemporary literature of the Jewish diaspora (see on this Karl-Wilhelm Niebuhr, "Tora ohne Tempel: Paulus und der Jakobusbrief im Zusammenhang frühjüdischer Torarezeption für die Diaspora," in *Gemeinde ohne Tempel—Community without Temple: Zur Substituierung und Transformation des Jerusalemer Tempels und seines Kults im Alten Testament, antiken Judentum und frühen Christentum* [ed. B. Ego, A. Lange, and P. Philhofer; WUNT 118; Tübingen: Mohr Siebeck, 1999], 427–60), and in any case, conclusions based on gaps in the letter lead one quickly onto thin ice because of the brevity of the letter. With this state of affairs, a positive indicator in favor of a decidedly Jewish-Christian context for the origin is lacking, at least. Burchard (*Jakobusbrief*, 5) is more decisive on this point: "Zur christlichen Existenz, wie Jak sie im Brief fordert, gehört nicht der Anschluß an das Judentum als Proselyt oder Gottesfürchtiger . . . samt entsprechender Bindung an die Thora . . . Da das auch für ihn selber gegolten haben dürfte, war er in diesem Sinn kein Judenchrist." The attribution of the epistle to a circle of Jerusalemite refugees does not fit the strong Hellenistic influence in the letter.

147 But see Pratscher, *Herrenbruder*, 221.

148 See on this above, n. 101.

149 See on this Konradt, *Christliche Existenz*, 317.

150 One may well argue about the extent of the hellenization, especially as it has been postulated by Martin Hengel in *Judentum und Hellenismus: Studien zu ihrer Begegnung unter besonderer Berücksichtigung Palästinas bis zur Mitte des 2. Jh.s v.Chr.* (3d ed.; WUNT 10; Tübingen: Mohr Siebeck, 1988). See, e.g., the critical voice of Louis H. Feldman, *Jew and Gentile in the Ancient World: Attitudes and Interactions from Alexander to Justinian* (Princeton: Princeton University Press, 1993), 3–44.

151 Burchard (*Jakobusbrief*, 4) rightly refers to "die hellenistischen, wenn auch oft jüdisch vermittelten Züge seiner Theologie und Ethik" as an important argument for the assumption of pseudepigraphy (cf. above, n. 1).

152 See on this Konradt, *Christliche Existenz*, 176–206; Niebuhr, "Tora ohne Tempel," esp. 452–55.

153 See on this interpretation Konradt, *Christliche Existenz*, 125–35, and above, n. 32.

154   On the interpretation of the love command in James, see Christoph Bur-
      chard, "Nächstenliebegebot, Dekalog und Gesetz in Jak 2,8-11," in *Die
      Hebräische Bibel und ihre zweifache Nachgeschichte* (ed. Erhard Blum, Chris-
      tian Macholz, and Ekkehard W. Stegemann; FS Rolf Rendtdorff; Neu-
      kirchen-Vluyn: Neukirchener, 1990), 517–33; Konradt, *Christliche Existenz*,
      184–94; as well as Gerd Theißen, "Nächstenliebe und Egalität: Jak 2,1-13
      als Höhepunkt urchristlicher Ethik," in *Der Jakobusbrief: Beiträge zur Reha-
      bilitierung der "strohernen Epistel"* (ed. Petra von Gemünden, Matthias Kon-
      radt, and Gerd Theißen; Beiträge zum Verstehen der Bibel 3; Münster: Lit,
      2003), 120–42.

155   Cf. Ekkehard W. Stegemann and Wolfgang Stegemann, *Urchristliche
      Sozialgeschichte: Die Anfänge im Judentum und die Christusgemeinden in der
      mediterranen Welt* (Stuttgart: Kohlhammer, 1995), 193–94; Painter, *Just
      James*, 249. It cannot be deduced from the Pauline texts mentioned above
      that *"poor"*—analogous to some Qumran texts (see 1QH 10:32, 34; 11:25;
      13:13-18, 22; 1QM 11:9; 1QpHab 12:3, 6, 10; 4QpPs37 2:9; 3:10)—served
      as a self-designation of the pious (see on this Leander E. Keck, "The Poor
      Among the Saints in the New Testament," *ZNW* 56 [1965]: 100–29, here
      117–19).

156   See on this Vincenzo Petracca, *Gott oder das Geld: Die Besitzethik des Lukas*
      (TANZ 39; Tübingen: Francke Verlag, 2003), 253–83, and Matthias Kon-
      radt, "Gott oder Mammon: Besitzethos und Diakonie im frühen Christen-
      tum," in *Diakonie und Ökonomie: Orientierungen im Europa des Wandels* (ed.
      Christoph Sigrist; Zürich: Theologischer Verlag Zürich, 2006), 107–54,
      esp. 126–30.

157   Gerd Theißen ("Urchristlicher Liebeskommunismus: Zum 'Sitz im Leben'
      des Topos ἅπαντα κοινά in Apg 2,44 und 4,32," in *Texts and Contexts* [Bibli-
      cal Texts in their Textual and Situational Contexts; ed. Tord Fornberg and
      David Hellholm; FS Lars Hartman; Oslo: Scandinavian University Press,
      1995], 689–712, here 696–700), demonstrates Luke's dependence on tradi-
      tion with regard to the Hellenistic topos of friendship as well, which stands
      sponsor in ἅπαντα κοινά in Acts 2:44; 4:32.

158   A general renunciation of personal property probably did not exist, since the
      references to the houses in Acts 2:46 and to the house of Mary in 12:2 pre-
      suppose that Christians continued to possess private property (see also 4:32).
      Cf. L. Schenke, *Urgemeinde*, 91: there were "nach wie vor 'Besitzende' in der
      Gemeinde, die aber die Nutzung ihres Eigentums allen ermöglichten. Sie
      pochten nicht auf Eigentum, sondern stellten es zur Verfügung, aber gerade
      nicht so, daß sie es verkauften und den Erlös in eine gemeinsame Kasse gaben,
      sondern so, daß sie andere partizipieren ließen." See also the summarizing
      conclusion of Schenke, *Urgemeinde*, 93: "daß es die in den beiden Summa-
      rien von Lukas beschriebene soziale Solidargemeinschaft in der Urgemeinde
      tatsächlich gegeben hat, auch wenn sie nach Form und Organisation nicht
      einfachhin dem idealen Typos folgte, den Lukas darstellt."

159   On the question of the precise historical core of Luke's account, see the
      proposal of Theißen ("Urchristlicher Liebeskommunismus," 706–10), who

considers the possibility that "urchristlicher Liebeskommunismus" is rooted in a reform idea of the Hellenists within the congregation in Jerusalem.

160 See Stegemann and Stegemann, *Urchristliche Sozialgeschichte*, 144.

161 Thus, e.g., R. P. Martin, *James*, lxii–lxvii; Painter, *Just James*, 140, 250–51. It is possible that this is reflected in James 5:6 (thus most recently Frankemölle, *Brief des Jakobus*, 663–65; Painter, *Just James*, 259), even if ὁ δίκαιος hardly refers to the brother of the Lord only, but rather, to persecuted Christians in general.

162 Davids ("Palestinian Traditions," 48) has postulated Palestinian local colouring for James 5:4, because the use of ἐργάται "reflects the situation in first-century Palestine, where absentee landlords (and also those who were not absentee) used hired workers to work their farms rather than slaves (as was common elsewhere in the Roman Empire and in the period when the Hebrew scriptures were being written)." However, PsJames' use of μισθὸς τῶν ἐργατῶν can be understood within the context of Diaspora Judaism without any problems. As is commonly known, PsJames takes up the commandment to pay day labourers on the same day here, which was widely taken up in early Jewish tradition (Lev 19:13; Deut 24:14-15; further Tob 4:14; Mal 3:5; Jer 22:13; Sir 34:22; *Test. Job* 12:3-4; Ps.-Phoc. 19; Philo, *Spec.* 4:195–96 and *Virt.* 88; Josephus, *A.J.* 4:288). *Test. Job*, a writing from the Jewish Diaspora, uses the term ἐργάτης in the same context as in James 5:4 (*Test. Job* 12:3).

163 Cf. Plutarch, *Mor.* 108A–B (καὶ γὰρ πολέμους καὶ στάσεις καὶ μάχας οὐδὲν ἄλλο παρέχει ἢ τὸ σῶμα καὶ αἱ τούτου ἐπιθυμίαι· διὰ γὰρ τὴν τῶν χρημάτων κτῆσιν πάντες οἱ πόλεμοι γίγνονται); Ps.-Lucian, *Cyn.* 15 (πάντα γὰρ τὰ κακὰ τοῖς ἀνθρώποις ἐκ τῆς τούτων ἐπιθυμίας φύονται, καὶ στάσεις καὶ πόλεμοι καὶ ἐπιβουλαὶ καὶ σφαγαί. ταυτὶ πάντα πηγὴν ἔχει τὴν ἐπιθυμίαν τοῦ πλείονος); Plato, *Phaed.* 66C; Philo, *Det.* 174; (*Jos.* 56); *Spec.* 4:85; Cicero, *De fin. bon.* 1.44.

164 On this, see Jürgen Roloff, *Die Kirche im Neuen Testament* (GNT 10; Göttingen: Vandenhoeck & Ruprecht, 1993), 83–85; W. Kraus, *Zwischen Jerusalem*, 33–38.

165 Roloff, *Kirche*, 83.

166 Cf. Roloff, *Kirche*, 275: "Weder wird dabei ein heilsgeschichtlicher Zusammenhang der Kirche mit Israel vorausgesetzt, noch wird das Recht dieser Übertragung reflektiert."

167 Thus most recently also Burchard, *Jakobusbrief*, 50. One can rule out that the *adscriptio* is directed to the Jewish people in general (against, e.g., James B. Adamson, *The Epistle of James* [NIC; 2d ed.; Grand Rapids: Eerdmans, 1993], 49–51), since James is oriented towards internal issues of the church throughout the letter. If Christians are the addressees, then it is impossible to limit the reference of the metaphorical expression of the "twelve tribes" to Jewish Christians a priori. Cf. Ropes, *Critical and Exegetical Commentary*, 127: "No kind of early, or of ingenious, dating can bring us to a time when a writer addressing Jewish *Christians* in distinction from unbelieving Jews would have addressed them as 'the twelve tribes,' if by the *term* he meant

'the Jews'; and if the term is here used for 'the People of God,' then the limitation to *Jewish* Christians is not contained in it" (emphasis in original).

168   Cf. Burchard, *Jakobusbrief*, 126–27.

169   Cf. likewise Burchard, "Nächstenliebegebot," 531; Klein, *"Ein vollkom-
       menes Werk,"* 206–7.

170   Burchard, *Jakobusbrief*, 49.

171   Cf. Sir 44:23; *2 Bar.* 78:4; *1 Clem.* 31:4.

172   On this, see Feldmeier, *Christen als Fremde*. See also Roloff, *Kirche*,
       268–73.

173   Burchard, *Jakobusbrief*, 50. See on this further Konradt, *Christliche Existenz*,
       64–66. In spite of the argumentation of Donald J. Verseput in "Wisdom,
       4 Q185, and the Epistle of James," *JBL* 117 (1998): 691–707, esp. 701–2,
       it seems irrefutable to me that there are at least some metaphorical over-
       tones in ἐν τῇ διασπορᾷ. A metaphorical reading remains still possible, by
       the way, when James, on the basis of its *adscriptio*, is placed in the tradi-
       tion of Jewish Diaspora letters (see on this, Tsuji, *Glaube*, 18–37; Niebuhr,
       "Jakobusbrief"; Davids, "Palestinian Traditions," 41–42; Verseput, "Genre
       and Story," 99–104). The thematic affinities that have been demonstrated,
       especially by Niebuhr, are an expression of the analogous problem constel-
       lations of Diaspora Judaism and Christianity, which were met with similar
       theological means. This is not surprising in view of the fact that Diaspora
       Judaism is the theological foundation of early Christian congregations.
       With ἐν τῇ διασπορᾷ (1:1b), an important signal for the reader is set (cf.
       Niebuhr, "Jakobusbrief," 423–24), which ties in with the horizon of social
       experiences of Diaspora Judaism as a minority (cf. Konradt, *Christliche Exis-
       tenz*, 65), continuously in danger of compromising its religious identity or
       of losing it completely in a Gentile context. In James, however, the contrast
       between the "twelve tribes" and the "nations" is missing (cf. e.g. 2 Macc
       1:27; *2 Bar.* 82:3; 83:5); instead of this, the addressees are called to keep
       themselves unstained by "the world" (1:27; cf. 4:4). And just as James does
       not indicate that the Diaspora situation is a punishment (cf. differently: Ep.
       Jer. 1; *2 Bar.* 78:5-6; 79:2-3; 84:2-4; *4 Bar.* 6:21), he also does not speak
       of the hope of God's mercy as oriented towards the collection and lead-
       ing back of the dispersed (see by contrast 2 Macc 1:27-29; *2 Bar.* 78:7; *4
       Bar.* 6:22). Furthermore, the endangering of the monotheistic confession
       as such by the cults of the Gentiles does not occur as a problem in James,
       as it does in Ep. Jer. (against Niebuhr, "Jakobusbrief," 434). The problem
       is, much rather, the lack of ethical consequences. Moreover, a significant
       formal difference should be taken into account: the Jewish Diaspora letters,
       when they are not addressed to individuals (*4 Bar.* 6:17 [2 Macc 1:10b]),
       are addressed to the "brothers" or simply to the "Jews in xy" (2 Macc 1:1
       [1:10b]; *2 Bar.* 78:2; cf. also Acts 15:23). The title *"Israel"* never occurs in
       the *adscriptio* (also not in *2 Bar.* 78:2); there is never a general reference
       to the diaspora (this, however, is a common characteristic of James and
       1 Peter). And finally, no letter is addressed to the entire Jewish Diaspora
       (*2 Bar.* comes closest to this, where the statement about the nine and a half

tribes emerges from the fictitious situation: now the tribes of the southern kingdom have been exiled as well; in this situation, one is assured of the fact that Israel, the nation with the twelve tribes, is still intact, and this supports the hope of the future salvation of God's people). In short: it seems plausible to me that PsJames makes use of the tradition of Jewish Diaspora letters, alluding to it and imitating it; but this reference is a broken one, which may be explained on the base of the early Christian context of the formation as well as of the addressees of James. If the letter is not "authentic," then reading the prescript on two levels is entirely unproblematic: it is part of the fictional authorship that the Lord's brother, as leader of the Jerusalemite congregation—in analogy to Jewish Diaspora letters—writes to fellow believers outside of Palestine. Hereby, ἐν τῇ διασπορᾷ is a designation for a location. Simultaneously, the phrase evokes a specific horizon of experience, as has been shown. The situation of Jewish Diaspora communities among the nations serves as a mirror for the challenge of the Christian communities in the "world" to persevere in their separation from the "world" in daily life. Therefore, addressing the letter to the "twelve tribes in the Diaspora" (on the relationship with James, see above) is an ingenious play on words by the author, and he, thereby, made use of tradition, as indicated by 1 Peter 1:1.

174   The only other occurrence is John 7:35.

175   Cf. Burchard, *Jakobusbrief*, 50, 127.

176   K.-W. Niebuhr, "New Perspective," has rejected this argument as "eine bemerkenswerte Pirouette" (1030). This, however, rests upon a misunderstanding of my argumentation, since—contrary to Niebuhr's assertion (see 1029, where he refers to the assumption of pseudepigraphy and then continues, "Die Adresse an 'die zwölf Stämme in der Diaspora' [1,1] muss *folglich* metaphorisch auf die ganze Christenheit gedeutet werden," [emphasis added])—the thesis that "twelve tribes in the diaspora" in the *adscriptio* refers to Christendom in the *adscriptio* is not a consequence of the assumption of pseudepigraphy, but is established otherwise (see n. 167 above). Thus, if the interpretation of James 1:1b as referring to Christendom is correct (and, additionally, this interpretation is clearly supported by the close traditio-historical connection of James 1:1 with 1 Peter, mentioned above), then one can well ask whether the ecclesiological model, which comes to the fore in James 1:1, fits with what was most likely the position of James.

177   The call for reversal in 4:8 is intended for those who got involved with the "world": καθαρίσατε χεῖρας, ἁμαρτωλοί, καὶ ἁγνίσατε καρδίας, δίψυχοι.

178   Cf. Popkes, *Adressaten*, 209.

Chapter 7

1   Here I follow the work of J. A. Sanders, whose interests in the canonical process, differently than for B. S. Childs, are both ideological—the importance of the history of the *idea* of a biblical canon within the ancient church—and hermeneutical—the recognition that the formation of the biblical canon is regulated by certain interpretive principles, which then

perform an interpretive role in regulating how the church continues to adapt these sacred texts to a faithful life

2   Different interpretive traditions appropriate this grammar differently; for example, in my own Anglican/Wesleyan tradition, whose *via salutis* emphasizes the progress of salvation (sanctification) toward the faithful believer's final justification, the theological agreements of the faith are inflected differently to underwrite the purchase of the faith community's moral conduct, supported by divine love. This spiritual calculus seems supported by the CE, which explains why the *Wirkungsgeschichte* of these texts within this faith communion is more "precious."

3   One may ask a couple of related questions in this regard: Why does the early church seem more interested in tensions between Petrine and Pauline traditions than between Pauline and Jacobian? Why is Bede (700 CE) among the first to write a commentary on the collection, and why, though he had access to a great library, does he mention very few prior interpreters of this literature? I look forward to the completion of David Nienhuis' Ph.D. research (Aberdeen) on these questions.

4   While the logical relationship between Acts and the NT letters is reflected by the canonical process (see below), the narrator's own claim (Acts 1:1) is that Acts is better related to the preceding gospel, probably for christological rather than literary reasons.

5   This same phenomenon may indicate that these seven individual compositions, when forming a whole collection, cohere around a common theological conception. While such a prospect is generally dismissed by critical scholarship, I think that it is entirely possible to construct a unifying theology of the CE—a project that I seek to begin in the appendix below.

6   As an exercise in a recent class on Acts, I had my students reflect upon the importance of studying a particular Pauline text (e.g., Eph, 2 Tim) in light of their prior study of related pericopae in Acts (e.g., Acts 18:24–19:41, Acts 20:17-38). The purpose of their project was more than to identify common Pauline traditions; it was to explore the meanings of a Pauline text that were brought to clearer light by its intracanonical relationship with Acts.

7   For an argument that the church's title for this composition, *Acts of the Apostles*, reflects its interest in the religious authority of the church's apostles (including Paul and James), see Wall, "Acts of the Apostles," in *BTB* 18, 15–23; also see the introductory comments to my "Acts," in *NIB* 10.

8   I am mindful of H. Räisänen's probing historicist response to his titular question, *Neutestamentliche Theologie?* which distinguishes more precisely between first and subsequent readers, within faith and academic communities. The canonical approach presumes that biblical theology is a theological rather than historical enterprise, whose aims are determined by the church's (rather than the per se academy's) intentions and so are religiously formative more than intellectually informative.

9   The various claims I make about Acts in what follows are more carefully developed in my commentary on "Acts," in *NIB* 10.

10   Trobisch, *Endredaktion*.

11   Cf. O. Cullmann, *Peter*, 63–69.

12   See Wall, "Canonical Function of 2 Peter," 77–79.

13   See P. N. Anderson, *Christology*, 274–77, who suggests that at the one point in Acts where Peter and John speak with one voice (4:19-20)—Peter alone speaks when they are teamed elsewhere in this narrative world—the narrator has composed a saying that combines Petrine (4:19) with Johannine (4:20) traditions. Their pairing in Acts in both work and speech may well reflect an emerging consensus within the ancient church that their traditions, both personal and theological, are complementary parts of an integral whole.

14   I think, however, that this critical conclusion is typically overstated, since there are fundamental differences between Scripture's Petrine witness and the Pauline kerygma.

15   The Jewish cast of Paul's story in Acts is a principal exegetical interest of my commentary on "Acts," in *NIB* 10.

16   Of course, the Pauline Letters would not disagree with this conclusion. I would argue, however, that for the Pauline tradition, these social, moral, and religious practices that mark out a people as Christian are the natural yield of "being in Christ" and that being in Christ is the result of profession that "Jesus is Lord." A Pauline redemptive calculus, whether understood politically or personally, is concentrated by the beliefs of the Pauline gospel rather than by the practices of the Pauline churches. It is this essential difference of logic that fashions—I think from the early church—a different spirituality, centered by orthodox confession, from that found in the congregations of the CE traditions.

17   For a defense of this interpretive strategy and illustrations of its usefulness for reading across the New Testament canon, see Wall and Lemcio, *New Testament as Canon*.

18   The Bede's early commentary on the CE is noteworthy for two reasons. First, his preface explains the importance of the arrangement of the CE, but presumes that its catholicity is also marked out by its integrity as a collection. Second, in this same preface, the Bede does not name any of the Christian Fathers or refer to antecedent works on the CE. In fact, the elemental nature of his preface might lead one to suppose that his work was an early effort to clarify the canonical importance of unused writings, since his primary interest lies with the authority of those who wrote the CE. One may also infer from the fact that the Bede did not also write commentaries on the Pauline Epistles, and simply cited in fragmentary fashion those who did, that he wrote about the CE in order to fill an evident gap in the ancient church; Bede the Venerable, *Commentary*.

19   Trobisch, *Endredaktion*, 40–43.

20   Bede, *Commentary*, 3.

21   Cf. R. Aus, "Three Pillars and Three Patriarchs: A Proposal Concerning Gal 2:9," *ZNW* 70 (1979): 252–61.

22   Writing a generation before Acts for readers struggling with a different theological concern, Paul's principal concern was with the Judaizing of his

Gentile mission, whose authorization was from the risen Christ, rather than from the Jerusalem pillars (Gal 1:11-15; 2:3-5), and confirmed by God's effective power (Gal 2:6-8)—a spiritual reality that these same pillars evidently (and not surprisingly) found difficult to embrace fully (Gal 2:11-14).

23   Of course, the unwritten assumption about this James is that he is the Lord's brother, and this relationship underwrites his authority in Jerusalem (see 1 Cor 15:7). As is well known, Acts does not refer to any second-generation leader of the church (e.g., James, Paul) as an apostle; this office is reserved only for the Twelve, to whom Luke gives "special" authority in his preface to Acts (1:1-26; cf. Luke 22:28-30).

24   Konradt, "Jakobusbrief als Brief des Jakobus."

25   These same tensions, mentioned directly in both Acts 15:1-2 and Galatians 2:11-14, are in the background of Matthew's gospel and certainly of the *Did.*, whose distinctive traditions are possibly of Antiochene origin.

26   See in particular the works of Esler, Cheung, and E. P. Sanders for tensions between Palestinian and Diaspora Jews over purity issues.

27   Wall, *Community of the Wise*; see appendix B below; cf. R. Bauckham, *James: Wisdom of James, Disciple of Jesus the Sage* (London: Routledge, 1999), 112–57.

28   See in particular S. Fowl and G. Jones, *Reading in Communion* (Grand Rapids: Eerdmans, 1991).

29   Cf. L. T. Johnson, *The Letter of James: A New Translation with Introduction and Commentary* (AB 37A; New York: Doubleday, 1995), 34–46.

30   R. Bauckham, "James and the Gentiles (Acts 15:13-21)," in *History, Literature, and Society in the Book of Acts* (ed. B. Witherington; Cambridge: Cambridge University Press, 1996), 154–84.

31   In fact, it is the importance of this Jewish legacy that convinces the Bede of the priority of James within the CE, and that it is responsible for the final form of the CE within the NT. The Petrine Epistles come next because of their concern to catechize proselyte Jewish converts to Christianity; the Johannine Epistles come last because they are addressed to Gentile converts, of whom the Bede says, "neither by race nor by belief had they been Jews" (from the preface to his *Commentary*). Curiously, he seems to retract this interpretation of the final form of the CE when trying to explain why Jude is placed last, whether then because it was of least importance or the last written.

32   See R. W. Wall, "Introduction to the Epistolary Literature of the New Testament," in *NIB* 10.

33   See Wall, "Canonical Function of 2 Peter."

34   For the occasion of 2 Peter as a response to false teachers, see T. S. Caulley, "The False Teachers in 2 Peter," *SBT 12* (1982): 27–42; for 2 Peter as an example of deliberative rhetoric that seeks to minimize the influence of false teachers, see D. Watson, *Invention, Arrangement and Style: Rhetorical Criticism of Jude and 2 Peter* (SBLDS 104; Atlanta: Scholars Press, 1988), 81–146.

35   This question is raised by C. C. Black in his commentary on the Johannine Epistles, *NIB* 12, 366–68.

Chapter 8

1   For an initial discussion of this interpretive strategy, see Wall and Lemcio, *New Testament as Canon*; Wall, "Acts and James," paper presented to SNTS, Durham, 2002; Wall, "A Theology of Staying Saved (Jas 2:22)," (paper presented at the annual meeting of the SBL, Atlanta 2003); and Wall, "Toward a Unifying Theology of the CE Collection," paper presented to CBL, Leuven, and to SNTS, Bonn, 2003.

2   Wall, "Acts and James," paper presented to SNTS, "Catholic Epistles Seminar," Durham, 2002.

3   Here again I want to alert this reader to the unpublished Ph.D. thesis of David Nienhuis (Aberdeen, 2005) on the formation of the CE collection, in which hewho argues that the composition of James (probably in the late second or early third century) wais motivated by its prospective role within an emergent "pillars" collection, precisely because it engages the Pauline canon and because its thematics "enable" a more coherent and "orthodox" use of the per se collection as a whole, which hitherto had included *Barnabas*, *1 Clement*, *Hermes*—writings that did not work well with 1 Peter and 1 John. My own work seeks to define more precisely what James' prospective role is and, especially, to demonstrate that the reception of the CE collection with Acts (and the James of Acts) provides the authorized justification for it.

4   In my unpublished SBL paper (Atlanta, 2003), "A Theology of Staying Saved," I argue that James 2:22, which is clearly redactional and supplies the hermeneutical key within a critical essay (1:22–2:26) that directly engages a received Pauline canon, clarifies in turn the intended role performed by James as frontispiece to the CE collection: to extend a Pauline pattern of salvation by specifying those faithful practices that "complete" professions of orthodox "faith" (which in James' use is a theological metaphor for the Pauline tradition).

5   Cf. D. Trobisch, *The First Editions of the New Testament* (Oxford: University Press, 2000), 80–85.

6   I should have noted in "Unifying Theology" (2003) that the relationship between the James of Acts and the epistolary James shifts the calculus by which a "priority of James" is calibrated. Within marginal Christianity loyal to the memory of James—as witnessed by apocryphal (mostly gnostic) writings such as *Gospel of Thomas*, *Apocryphon of James*, *First and Second Apocalypses of James*, and *Recognitions*—the "priority" of the person James was predicated on the priority of the risen Jesus' appearance to him, his renowned piety (leading to his martyrdom), his familial relationship with Jesus (rather than his membership in the apostolate), and perhaps later the "secrets" that the exalted Jesus revealed to him. The spiritual authority of the James of Acts is based upon none of these attributes. It is based upon

his leadership of the Jerusalem church, which is made effective by use of his prophetic gift for discerning the Spirit's will, interpreting Israel's Scriptures, and resolving intramural conflict to forge Christian unity. I would argue that these attributes are more "canonical," in that they supply readers with an orienting concern apropos for relating James to other canonical writings.

7   While some have claimed "occasional" uses of Acts in writings earlier than Irenaeus, he was the first to put Acts to a "canonical" use as the authorized narrative of Christian origins for the Catholic Church. That is, the manner in which a writing is used should determine the nature of a book's reception, whether as Scripture or as an occasional Christian writing. My point is that Irenaeus was the first to use Acts *as Scripture*.

8   The reception history of Acts during the patristic period is an obvious interest of H. J. Cadbury (*The Book of Acts in History* [London: Black, 1955]), given that his hypothesis of a unified Luke-Acts may be challenged by the history of their canonization, which suggests a disunified Luke and Acts (see my brief comment below). Cadbury does confirm the ancient observation of the strategic role that Acts subsequently performed in giving shape and structure to a Gospel-Letters canon as a literary bridge between them—an observation that is contextualized and expanded by D. Trobisch in his important study, *Endredaktion des Neuen Testaments* (see n. 5). In any case, their studies, along with others, have been evaluated (and on occasion corrected) by A. Gregory (*The Reception of Luke and Acts in the Period before Irenaeus* [WUNT 2.169; Tübingen: Mohr Siebeck, 2003], 299–351), who concludes (against Barrett's optimism) that Irenaeus was the first to show the "influence" of Acts—I would rather observe that Irenaeus was the first to use Acts as "Scripture"—in his *Against Heresies*, even though he was not alone in his knowledge of Acts (350–51). In this regard, I would only mention in passing—even though with keen interest—that several of the clearest allusions to traditions used in Acts are found in the writings of groups linked to James and other Jerusalem pillars. Again, this implicit use of Acts within the Jacobean community may well have anticipated the future role of Acts in the formation and canonization of a "pillars collection" with James as its frontispiece. In my opinion, two other monographs, by D. E. Smith (*The Canonical Function of Acts* [Collegeville, Minn.: Liturgical Press, 2002]) and, to a lesser degree, by C. Mount (*Pauline Christianity: Luke-Acts and the Legacy of Paul* [NovTSup104; Leiden: Brill, 2002]) are more useful for the purposes of this paper, since each seeks to understand Irenaeus' theological motive and hermeneutics in using Acts as a piece with the very idea of a biblical canon. In this sense, the use of Acts in Irenaeus' polemics defines its prospective canonical role—that is, the raison d'être for its admission into the biblical canon and its use by Scripture's faithful readers.

9   I do think these historical studies raise important questions of hermeneutical value. For example, given his use of an early recension of Luke's gospel or a "mutilated" version of its canonical form, why didn't Marcion use Acts? If he had not yet had a copy of Acts in hand, would his dependence on

the Pauline canon have been substantially qualified by its portrait of Paul, with conclusions not unlike Irenaeus'? Is "heresy," as Irenaeus defines it, a canonical issue more than it is a theological one?

10 See Mount's lucid commentary on book 3 of Irenaeus' *Against Heresies* in review of this point: *Pauline Christianity*, 11–58.

11 Mount, *Pauline Christianity*, 57.

12 Irenaeus does not seem alert to contemporary tensions among tradents of the Jerusalem apostles, evinced in the Nag Hammadi tractates, between those loyal to the memories (and secrets) of the "Beloved Disciple" and those communicants attached to the church catholic that idealized Peter, or between Pauline Christians and those who lionized the spiritual authority of James and considered Paul an opponent.

13 In my Durham paper, I noted in passing that Bede, with access to the body of patristic commentary, already seemed aware of this connection between Acts and the CE, using Acts to gloss parts of James and 1 Peter in particular (since the portraits of those apostles in Acts are more robust than that of John or Jude). Smith adds that the reverse is not the case, since there is no reference to the CE in Bede's commentary on Acts. In following patristic hermeneutical practice, Bede discerns that the appropriate use of Acts is to make meaning of the CE and especially of James; *Canonical Function of Acts*, 93.

14 While some have retrieved "occasional" uses of Acts in writings earlier than Irenaeus, he is the first to put Acts to a "canonical" use as the authorized narrative of Christian origins for the church catholic. That is, the manner in which a writing is put to use should determine the nature of a book's reception, whether canonical or incidental.

15 Whatever the narrator's "original" motive for portraying the central (human) characters of Acts, especially Paul, the reemergence and use of Acts at the end of the second century, especially by Irenaeus and especially in its "Western" version, almost certainly expanded the legacy and importance of the "canonical Paul" for the church catholic. In any case, as a methodological point, a serious distinction should be made between the authorial motive and canonical function of a biblical writing; see Robert W. Wall, "The Acts, of the Apostles" in *NIB* 10, 10, 26–32, 213–15.

16 For an example of this scholarly practice, see Gregory, *Reception*, 301–2.

17 Mount argues that Irenaeus' use of Acts "invents" a version of Christian unity for use in early catholic polemics that subverts both the intentions of the storytellers and the historical record of Christianity's origins. My point is rather that it is precisely this more poetic use of Acts that affords it canonical status and that defines its canonical role—not Luke's motive for writing Acts, whatever that was, and not the historical record of the church's beginnings, however that is reconstructed.

18 Similarly, the Pauline canon consisting only of nine or ten letters rather than thirteen, the Petrine tradition remembered by only 1 Peter without 2 Peter, 1 John without 2–3 John, or Jude without James (since Jude 1:1 mentions James), is incomplete of a robust apostolicity.

Chapter 9

*   This essay was first published in *Interpretation* 60.3 (2006). 245–59 and is reprintd here with the editor's permission.

1   G. Krodel, *The General Letters: Hebrews, James, 1–2 Peter, Jude, 1–2–3 John* (Minneapolis: Fortress, 1995).

2   See his *Hist. eccl.* 2.23.24–25. Eusebius quotes Dionysius of Alexandria (ca. 265 CE) in support of the authorship of the Gospel and "the Catholic Epistle" by the Apostle John, while attributing Revelation to another John (*Hist. eccl.* 7.25.7). Eusebius says that, in his *Hypotyposeis*, Clement of Alexandria gave concise commentary on "all Canonical Scriptures, not passing over even the disputed writings, I mean the Epistle of Jude and the remaining Catholic Epistles" (*Hist. eccl.* 6.14.1). This summary clarifies "the disputed writings," but it is unclear whether Clement mentioned "Catholic Epistles" or named epistles individually, such as Jude. For Clement, all of those epistles remained disputed. By Eusebius' time, he could say that 1 John and 1 Peter must be pronounced genuine (*Hist. eccl.* 3.25.2). By implication, the remainder (including James, see *Hist. eccl.* 2.23.24–25) remained disputed.

3   1 Peter's reference to the "*elect* exiles of the diaspora" seems to specify believing Jews. Further qualifications restrict the Diaspora reference geographically to Pontus, Galatia, Cappadocia, Asia, and Bithynia.

4   The term translated here as *exiles* is found only in Hebrews 11:13 and 1 Peter 1:1; 2:11 in the NT.

5   See P. H. Davids, *The Epistle of James: A Commentary on the Greek Text* (NIGTC; Grand Rapids: Eerdmans, 1982); R. P. Martin, *James* (WBC 48; Waco, Tex.: Word Books, 1988); Painter, *Just James*.

6   See n. 1 above and my *Just James*, 234–48, esp. 234–36.

7   This is broadly the argument used by Todd Penner in the SBL session devoted to my *Just James* in 2004.

8   See my *Just James*, 220–23.

9   See G. Currie Martin, "The Epistle of James as a Storehouse of the Sayings of Jesus," in *The Expositor* 7.3 (ed. Samuel Cox, William Robertson Nicoll, and James Moffatt; London: Hodder & Stoughton, 1907), 174–84. This reference is to p. 176. James has fifteen such uses of "brothers" (1:2, 16, 19; 2:1, 5, 14; 3:1, 10, 12; 4:11; 5:7, 9, 10, 12, 19). G. Currie Martin rightly sees James "as a Storehouse of the sayings of Jesus," especially in their Matthean form. Yet he does not argue for direct dependence of James on Matt or the reverse. Rather, he argues for the recognition of the independent use of Jesus tradition. For good reason, the NRSV avoids these references to brothers, but they are important rhetorical markers.

10   J. B. Adamson, *James: The Man and His Message* (Grand Rapids: Eerdmans, 1989), 188.

11   Adamson, *James*, 189–90.

12   Martin Dibelius, *James: A Commentary on the Epistle of James* (ed. H. Köster; rev. H. Greeven; trans. M. A. Williams; Hermeneia; Philadelphia: Fortress, 1976), 28–29.

13   J. H. Ropes, *A Critical and Exegetical Commentary on the Epistle of St. James* (ICC; Edinburgh: T&T Clark, 1916), 39.

14   The following table builds on the list given by R. P. Martin, *James*, lxxiv–lxxvi, and another from P. J. Hartin, *James and the Q Sayings of Jesus* (JSNTSup 47; Sheffield: JSOT Press, 1991), 141–42. Hartin notes twenty-six points of contact between James and the Synoptics, mainly Q^{Mt}.

15   Hartin, *James and the Q Sayings*, 214, 233, 240, 243.

16   R. E. Brown and J. P. Meier, *Antioch and Rome* (New York: Paulist, 1983), 55.

17   Hartin, *James and the Q Sayings*, 233.

18   I. Havener, *Q: The Sayings of Jesus: With a Reconstruction of Q by Athanasius Polag* (Wilmington, Del.: Michael Glazier, 1987), 103.

19   There is no comparable Jesus tradition about the tongue, but there is clear dependence on Jesus tradition in 5:12 (see Matt 5:33-37). Both texts deal with instruction not to swear by heaven or earth (or by any other oath), "but let your yes be yes and no be no." In Matthew, "anything in excess of this is of the evil one." For James, control of the tongue ensures "that you do not fall under judgement." Thus James' teaching about the tongue mediates wisdom tradition via the wisdom of Jesus.

20   In Paul, *epithymia* has the sense of sinful desire, the desire of the flesh, covetous desire. The use of the word in James is consistent with this.

21   James is the first known use of *dipsychos* (Jas 1:8; 4:8).

22   There is a wrong and unsuccessful asking (4:3). Such asking is motivated by lust (*hēdonē*, 4:1, 3) and covetousness (*epithymein*, 4:2). These overlapping terms are embodied in *epithymia* (1:14-15), which underlies the instability of the double-minded person (1:8; 4:8) and characterizes enmity toward God and friendship with the world (4:4-10). Friendship with God underlies true and pure religion, which is lived in the presence of God, the Father (1:26-27).

23   There is a significant thematic overlap between Jesus' comparative anecdote (parable?) with which Matt concludes the Sermon on the Mount (Q Matt 7:24-29) and the "mirror" image of James 1:22-25. Both are concerned with the problem of those who hear but fail to do what they hear.

24   S. Freyne, *Jesus, a Jewish Galilean* (London: T&T Clark, 2004). See especially chap. 2, "Jesus and the Ecology of Galilee."

25   See J. Painter, "The Power of Words: Rhetoric in James and Paul," in *The Missions of James, Peter, and Paul: Tensions in Early Christianity* (ed. Bruce Chilton and Craig Evans; NovTSup 115; Leiden: Brill, 2005), 235–73.

26   Editor's note: The following appendix and bibliography are not included in the *Interpretation* article.

Chapter 10

1   See K.-W. Niebuhr, "James in the Minds of the Recipients," included in this volume.

2   The most prominent advocates are Luke Timothy Johnson, *Letter of James* and *Brother of Jesus, Friend of God: Studies in the Letter of James* (Grand

Rapids: Eerdmans, 2004); Richard Bauckham, *James: Wisdom*; Douglas J. Moo, *The Letter of James* (PNTC; Grand Rapids: Eerdmans, 2000); and Patrick J. Hartin, *James* (SP 14; Collegeville, Minn.: Liturgical, 2003).

3   See, e.g., Davids, *Epistle of James: A Commentary*, 21; Penner, *Epistle of James and Eschatology*, 63–65; and Bauckham, *James: Wisdom*, 127–31.

4   See especially Richard Bauckham's "James and the Jerusalem Church," in *The Book of Acts in its First Century Setting* (ed. R. Bauckham; Grand Rapids: Eerdmans, 1995), 415–80, and Roy Ward's "James of Jerusalem in the First Two Centuries," *ANRW* 2.26.1:779–812, but also the relevant essays in Chilton and Evans, *James the Just*, and Bruce Chilton and Jacob Neusner, *The Brother of Jesus: James the Just and his Mission* (Louisville, Ky.: Westminster John Knox, 2001).

5   Exceptions to this include two scholars whose work also appears in this volume: Robert W. Wall, who has long approached the biblical text through this particular lens, and John Painter, who has come to it more recently.

6   This entire article is in fact a brief synopsis of the argument I make in my recent book: D. Nienhuis, *Not by Paul Alone: The Formation of the Catholic Epistle Collection and the Christian Canon* (Waco, Tex.: Baylor University Press, 2007).

7   Penner claims that "the writer of the epistle [of James] does not seem to indicate a familiarity with large sections of either Galatians or Romans, but only with isolated expressions" (*Epistle of James and Eschatology*, 71).

8   Section 3a–f has been pointed out by J. D. G. Dunn in *Romans 1–8* (WBC 38A; Waco, Tex.: Word Books, 1988), 197. I have adjusted his citations and added the parallels in sections 1 and 2.

9   A commonly held position, argued, e.g., by Ropes, *Critical and Exegetical Commentary*, 35; Dibelius, *James*; and Sophie Laws, *The Epistle of James* (BNTC; Peabody, Mass.: Hendrickson, 1980), 15–18.

10   Joseph B. Mayor, *The Epistle of St. James: The Greek Text with Introduction, Notes and Comments* (2d ed.; London: Macmillan, 1897; 3d ed., 1913; repr., Grand Rapids: Eerdmans, 1990).

11   See *Not by Paul Alone*, especially 113–17, 174–80, 187–97, 212–24, and 227–31.

12   Margaret M. Mitchell, "The Letter of James as a Document of Paulinism?" in *Reading James with New Eyes: Methodological Reassessments of the Letter of James* (ed. R. L. Webb and J. S. Kloppenborg; LNTS 342; London: T&T Clark, 2007), 75–98.

13   Mitchell, "Letter of James," 87–88.

14   See, e.g., John Reumann's *Righteousness in the New Testament* (Philadelphia: Fortress, 1982), 158, and Ralph Martin's *James*, 83–84.

15   See the first chapter of *Not by Paul Alone*, and especially the tables provided on pp. 91–97.

16   E.g., James Moffatt, *The General Epistles of James, Peter and Jude* (MNTC; London: Hodder & Stoughton, 1928), 1; Laws, *Epistle of James*, 42n3; and Johnson, who believes dependence on James is "virtually certain" (*Letter of James*, 79).

17   E.g., Dibelius, *James*, 32; Davids, *Epistle of James: A Commentary*, 8–9; and Penner, *Epistle of James and Eschatology*, 103.

18   James Drummond, *The New Testament in the Apostolic Fathers* (Oxford: Oxford University Press, 1905), 103–33; Ropes, *Critical and Exegetical Commentary*, 88–89; and James A. Brooks, "The Place of James in the New Testament Canon," *SJT* 12 (1969): 45–47.

19   Johnson provides an excellent survey (*Letter of James*, 75–79).

20   O. J. F. Seitz, "The Relationship of the Shepherd of Hermas to the Epistle of James," *JBL* 63 (1944): 131–40.

21   Ropes, *Critical and Exegetical Commentary*, 88–89; Dibelius, *James*, 32.

22   Consider the oft-cited strongest parallel in their shared use of the rare term δίψυχος: while James uses the word twice (1:8; 4:8), *Hermas* uses δίψυχος nineteen times, διψυχεῖν twenty times, and διψυχία sixteen times, repeating the word and its cognates so often it becomes a major subtheme of the text. When we compare the extensive knowledge and use of *Hermas* in the early centuries with the relative absence of James, is it more likely that Hermas developed this theme from its occurrence in James, or that the author of James appealed to what had become a well-known concept thanks to its use in the widely admired *Shepherd of Hermas*?

23   The one supposed allusion set forth for Irenaeus' knowledge of James comes from 4.16.2, where he calls Abraham a "friend of God," as James does in 2:23. The appellation is widely observable in Jewish literature before James, however, and elsewhere Irenaeus' appeals to Abraham are decidedly Pauline in their emphases (cf. 4.5.3-5 and 4.7.2).

24   *Marc.* 5.1.

25   *Marc.* 1.20.2; 4.3.3; 5.3.1–6.

26   He also says that Galatians 2 reveals that Paul, who was "yet inexperienced in grace, and anxious lest he had run or was running in vain, was then for the first time conferring with those who were apostles before him" (1.20.2). This conference was necessary; that is, "perchance he had not believed as they did, or was not preaching the gospel in their manner" (4.2.5).

27   *Marc.* 4.2.4.

28   *Marc.* 1.20.4; 4.2.5; 5.3.6.

29   *Praescr.* 23.9.

30   *Hyp.* 8 = Eusebius, *Hist. eccl.* 2.1.4.

31   Two examples: according to the *Gos. Heb.* (preserved in Jerome in *Vir. ill.* 211–13), James was a disciple present at the Last Supper, he was the first to meet the risen Lord, and the first Eucharist was a private celebration between the two. In the section of the *Ps.-Clem.* literature dated to the second century (*Recognitions* 1:27-71), James is the "Archbishop" of Jerusalem who leads the disciples in contest against the Jewish leadership and is attacked by a "hostile person" who bears close resemblance to Saul of Tarsus.

32   Three examples: in the semi-gnostic *Gos. Thom.*, the disciples ask Jesus whom they are to follow after he departs, and Jesus responds, "Wherever you are, you are to go to James the Just, for whose sake heaven and earth came into being" (12). In the *Apoc. Jas.*, the resurrected Jesus appears to

the disciples and James, and singles out James and Peter apart from the others to receive a revelatory discourse. Between the two, James is clearly depicted as the more authoritative. Finally, the two gnostic Apocalypses of James have the Lord appearing to James alone; the other disciples are cast in a negative light (*1 Apoc. Jas.* 42:20-24), and James basks in his revelatory power: "Now again I am rich in knowledge and I have a unique understanding, which was produced only from above. . . . That which was revealed to me was hidden from everyone" (*2 Apoc. Jas.* 47:7-19).

33   Bauckham, *Jude and the Relatives*, 45–57; Painter, *Just James*, 11–41; and Ward, "James of Jerusalem," *ANRW* 2.26.1, have offered historical arguments that challenge the apparent plain sense of these texts to argue that James was indeed a follower of the earthly Jesus. Whether or not their positions are accepted, in the end, we are still left with a biblical text that leaves readers with distinct impressions to the contrary.

34   See, e.g., *Comm. Jo.* 20.10.66 and *Comm. Rom.* 2.9.460–63; 4.1.63–73; 4.8.22–37.

35   Augustine, *Fid. op.* 27; in this essay, he asserts that the CE as a whole were written specifically against those who hold on Pauline grounds that "faith alone is sufficient for salvation."

36   *Hist. eccl.* 2.23.25.

37   For a detailed analysis of the emergence of the CE collection in the Eastern and Western churches, see the first chapter of *Not by Paul Alone*, and especially the tables on pages 91–97.

38   See Richard Bauckham's "2 Peter: An Account of Research," *ANRW* 2.25.5:3713–52.

39   The argument was made most recently by Trobisch, *First Edition*, 86–96, but others have argued similarly: see Denis M. Farkasfalvy, "The Ecclesial Setting of Pseudepigraphy in Second Peter and its Role in the Formation of the Canon," *SecCent* 5 (1985): 3–29; Marion Soards, "1 Peter, 2 Peter and Jude as Evidence for a Petrine School," *ANRW* 2.25.5:3827–49; and Wall, "Canonical Function of 2 Peter." My reading of 2 Peter here is heavily dependent on Trobisch's account.

40   Compare 1 Pet 1:2b with 2 Pet 1:2, and 1 Pet 5:11 with 2 Pet 3:18.

41   For a helpful list of links between James and Matt/Luke/Q, see Painter, *Just James* (2004), 260–62. The lack of complete verbal agreement between James and the canonical gospels has led many to argue that the letter was written before the advent of the canonical gospels. For a representative argument, see Hartin, *James and the Q Sayings*, and also the critique of Hartin in Penner, *Epistle of James and Eschatology*, 116–20.

42   See, e.g., the comments of Bauckham in *James: Wisdom*, 156, and Konradt in *Christliche Existenz*, 328–30.

43   See the third chapter of *Not by Paul Alone* for an extended analysis.

44   See Robert W. Wall, "Ecumenicity and Ecclesiology: The Promise of the Multiple Letter Canon of the New Testament," in Wall and Lemcio, *New Testament as Canon*, 184–207.

45   The notion that the closing of the canon was enabled by the aesthetic supe-
      riority of the final form over other available formats of the day is argued by
      Wall in "Function of the Pastoral Epistles," 35–36.

Chapter 11

*   This essay was originally a paper given in the seminar "Katholische Briefe
      und Aposteltraditionen" at the General Meeting of the SNTS in Montreal
      on August 1, 2001. The English version of this paper was first translated by
      Grit Schorch, then thoroughly revised by the author.
1   This tendency reaches from the commentaries of Goppelt, *Petrusbrief*,
      and Brox, *Petrusbrief* (2d ed., 1986), up to the newest commentary of J. H.
      Elliott (*1 Peter*, 344).
2   Gerhard Dautzenberg, "Σωτηρία ψυχῶν (1Pet 1:9)," *BZ* NF 8 (1964): 262–
      76, esp. 274.
3   Indeed, it cannot be shown that Philo was known to 1 Peter, but the famil-
      iarity of the letter with Hellenistic Jewish traditions—as primarily found
      in Philo—is obvious, as I have demonstrated concerning the metaphor of
      foreignness (Feldmeier, *Christen als Fremde*, 60–72). This familiarity shows
      itself again with regard to the themes of salvation of the soul and rebirth.
4   J. H. Elliott, *1 Peter*, 344. Similarily Goppelt, *Petrusbrief*, 104n63; and Brox,
      Petrusbrief, 67. If Brox argues, "Die Vorstellung von der im Gegensatz zum
      Leib unsterblichen Seele, die das Bessere im Menschen darstellt, ist dort
      [sc. in early Judaism and early Christendom] unbekannt," the assumption
      is definitely wrong concerning Hellenistic Judaism (cf. Philo) and remains
      also questionable concerning early Christendom. Here also the problem is
      comprehended in too minimalist a way. Of course the same Middle Pla-
      tonic concept of the soul may not be found in 1 Peter, but the following
      question remains of interest: Why does 1 Peter mention the soul so often
      in reference to the God-human relationship (see below)?
5   However, this is not merely true for Philo; cf. *T. Job* 3:5.
6   Accordingly, Christ—this is the summit of the anthem in chapter 2—is
      signified as shepherd and bishop of the souls, to whom the believers are
      returned from the aberration of their earlier lives (2:25). In 4:19, it is said
      that the persecuted Christians should confide their souls to the righteous
      Creator. The only exception seems to be the phrase in 3:20, which states
      that in Noah's ark, eight souls were saved from the flood. In the first sense,
      the souls are the lives of those who were saved from drowning by the ark.
      But here, consider that the allusion of the story of the flood was specifi-
      cally designed as *antitypos* to the salvation through baptism that is exempli-
      fied in the following verse. This indicates that the use of the notion ψυχή
      is probably due to careful consideration: if it is said that the eight ψυχαί
      "were saved by water" (διεσώθησαν δι᾽ ὕδατος—διά also means "by" in the
      sense of "by means of," while the alternative preposition ἐκ does not allow
      this wordplay), the very combination of ψυχή and σῴζειν resembles the
      σωτηρία ψυχῶν that happens via baptism.

7   Cf. the pseudo-Platonic treatise *Axiochus*. The theme with which the treatise is concerned is the justification of the immortality of the soul in confrontation with the human fear of death. There is spoken of the θεῖον πνεῦμα that is in the soul and constitutes its immortality (370C). In Plutarch, cf. *Sera* 560 BCE.

8   Cf. Folker Siegert, *Drei hellenistisch-jüdische Predigten* 2 (WUNT 61; Tübingen: Mohr Siebeck, 1992), 163–64, 166–67, 207.

9   *Metam.* 11.15; this seeing of the deity is the purposeful antithesis to *caecitas Fortunae*.

10   Cf. here Walter Burkert, *Antike Mysterien: Funktionen und Gehalt* (München: C. H. Beck, 1990), 84.

11   *De deis* 4.10. There, the reborn ἀναγεννώμενοι receive milk after the fasting. Cf. 1 Pet 2:2-3; also cf. Karl Wyss, *Die Milch im Kultus der Griechen und Römer* (RVV 15,2; Gießen: Töpelmann, 1914).

12   Cf. the explanations of Burkert, *Antike Mysterien*, mainly 83–86. According to Burkert, the testimonies of the ritual of rebirth are "teils zu vage, teils zu vielgestaltig, um einer einfachen und zugleich umfassenden Theorie Vorschub zu leisten" (84).

13   With a view to the correlations and dependencies between the texts of the New Testament, Burkert alerts, "Daß die Konzeption des Neuen Testaments von heidnischer Mysterienlehre direkt abhängig sei, ist philologisch-historisch bislang unbeweisbar" (*Antike Mysterien*, 86).

14   Cf. Hubert Frankemölle, *1. Petrusbrief. 2. Petrusbrief. Judasbrief* (NEchtB 18, 20; Würzburg: Echter, 1987), 33, 40; Brox, *Petrusbrief*, 62 et al.

15   So, for instance, Udo Schnelle, "Taufe II," *TRE* 32:663–74, esp. 671.

16   A good example is given by Goppelt, who in fact argues that the metaphor of rebirth stems from the Hellenistic world. Still, he does not go further into the matter, but declares instead that the speech of rebirth goes back "auf einen Motivzusammenhang aus dem Selbstverständnis der Qumrangemeinde," whereas the "den hellenistischen Menschen fremde Terminus der 'Neuschöpfung' . . . durch den allgemein verständlichen Begriff 'Wiedergeburt' ersetzt wurde" (Goppelt, *Petrusbrief*, 94). Cf. also the explanations of Johann Michl, *Die katholischen Briefe* (2d ed.; RNT 8.2; Regensburg: Pustet, 1968), 109–13.

17   In this regard, the judgment of Brox is significant when he says that the view on potential parallels in the history of religion does contribute "für das genaue Verständnis . . . nichts Unentbehrliches" because the metaphor of rebirth is "zu neutral und zu flexibel . . . um in jedem Fall eine religionsgeschichtliche Herkunft mitzuschleppen." One may see here not more than an image of an "einschneidenden (religiös-existentiellen) Neubeginn" (Brox, *Petrusbrief*, 61–62). Somewhat more careful is Karl Hermann Schelkle, *Die Petrusbriefe. Der Judasbrief* (HTKNT 13; Freiburg: Herder, 1980), 38, who nevertheless comes to a similar result.

18   There are some differences, which will not be explained here, since they can be clearly seen when comparing the conceptions of rebirth in 1 Peter with

the eleventh book of Apuleius, *Metam.* on the one hand and with Philo, *QE* 2:46 on the other.

19 In relation to the acting of God, the aorist participle ἀναγεννήσας is applied, stressing the ingressive aspect of the activity; it does not denote an ever-existing attribute of God; rather, the new procreation/rebirthing is based on a certain event in the past. This event can be the baptism, but this is not explicitly said.

20 Besides the Pauline Letters (here primarily Rom and 1 Thess) and Acts, the deuteropauline letters, Eph, Col, Titus, and Heb are to be mentioned as well.

21 Here, the background is the tradition of Israel's patrimony in the Old Testament, a concept originally related to the promised land. Already in early Judaism, this concept had become eschatologized as the earth being promised as heritage to the chosen (cf. esp. 1 Hen 5:6-8). *Pss. Sol.* 14:10 says that the pious men will inherit "life in happiness"; similarly, 1QS 11, 7-8 says that the chosen ones will take part in the inheritance of the saints. In the same sense, the NT speaks about the inheritance of eternal life (Mark 10:17 par.), the kingdom of God (Matt 25:34; 1 Cor 6:9-10; 15:50; Gal 5:21), and the salvation (Heb 1:14) as the (eternal) heritage, the granting of the eschatological salvation that is promised to the Christians (cf. Acts 20:32; Eph 1:14; 5:5; Col 3:24; Heb 9:15).

22 In Paul, the connection to the child-parent relationship is to be found again and again (cf. Rom 8:14-17; Gal 4:6-7).

23 In the context of the letter's introduction, the inheritance refers to the Dispersion and the earlier stressed foreignness of the Christians. In this world, the election has determined their social selection and stigmatization, their existence as foreigners. In contrast, the rebirth, which is depending here, leads to an eternal home; cf. also 2:25, where the homecoming "to the shepherd and bishop of your souls" is praised, which constitutes the point of the anthem of Christ.

24 There are found sequences of two and of three attributes in the pagan tradition (cf. Aristotle, *Cael.* 270A; 277B; 282A–B; Plutarch, *E Delph.* 19.392E; 20.393A et al.).

25 Especially to be found often in Philo of Alexandria, here in sequences of two and of three, with the attribute of imperishability (cf. *Leg.* 1:51 et passim).

26 For Aristotle, imperishability is the divine attribute that determines an unavoidable essential contradiction between God and our world of becoming and passing away. In Epicurus, the attribute *imperishable*, together with *beatific*, is the ultimate distinction for God and highlights the different nature of the gods as antitheses to the earthly world. This attribute was adopted by Middle Platonism, here also in respect to transcendence. Philo alone makes use of the word 150 times, and Plutarch uses it to signify the divine sphere in opposition to the growing and perishing world (cf. the concluding speech of Ammonios in *E Delph.*).

27 This attribute can denote purity in cult (cf. Plutarch, *Num.* 9.5, *Is. Os.* 79.383B, *Pyth. orac.* 3.395E; cf. further Philo, *Spec.* 1:113.250, *Fug.* 118),

but with a view to the essence of the divine, it can also apply to an onto-logical dimension insofar as the divine is not maculated per contact with the human being (cf. Plutarch, *E Delph*. 20fin, 393C; Apuleius, *De deo Socr.* 128). Also, the Jewish philosopher of religion Philo uses ἀμίαντος as an attribute for God; in Philo, *undefiled* is an attribute that characterizes the divine, from God's name to his wisdom unto the soul who communicates with him and the virtue (cf. *Leg.* 1:50; *Cher.* 50; *Det.* 169; *Migr.* 31; *Fug.* 50.114; *Somn.* 2:185; *Spec.* 4:40). Therefore, the notion ἀμίαντος gains an ethical meaning, even stronger than the notion ἄφθαρτος: in the Jewish tradition, ἀμίαντος denotes sexual inviolacy (so the purity of the cult is expressed in 2 Macc 14:24, 36, and the sexual inviolacy in Wis 3:13; 8:19-20; cf., in the NT, Heb 13:4), as, vice versa, sexual harassments (*T. Reu.* 1:6; *T. Levi* 7:3; 9:9; 14:6; 16:1; *T. Benj.* 8:2-3; cf. *T. Iss.* 4:4; Wis 14:26), idolatry (*Sib. Or.* 5:392; 4 Macc 5:36; 7:6; *Pss. Sol.* 2:3; 8:22), or passions at all (cf. Philo, *Cher.* 51) blemish the human and the soul.

28   Cf. Plutarch, *E Delph*. 19–21.392-93, where the transcendent divine perfec-tion is expressed through the same stylistic device as in 1 Peter 1:4, namely the triple repetition of a negative attribute. Here also, imperishability is especially important: 19.392E, ἀίδιον καὶ ἀγένητον καὶ ἄφθαρτον; 20.393A, ἀκίνητον καὶ ἄχρονον καὶ ἀνέκλιτον. For the combination of imperishability and purity as a feature of the divine, cf. further 20.393D, οὐκοῦν ἕν τ᾽ εἶναι καὶ ἄκρατον ἀεὶ τῷ ἀφθάρτῳ καὶ καθαρῷ προσήκει. Two generations later, the Middle Platonic thinker Apuleius, in *De deo Socr.* 4.128, conceives the sublimity of the gods therein "dass sie durch keinerlei Berührung mit uns befleckt werden."

29   Here also are to be found a variety of parallels, as in Philo, who uses the applied attributes ἀμάραντος and primarily ἄφθαρτος to characterize the celestial realm, as already mentioned above. Admittedly, from all the evi-dence, it cannot be concluded that 1 Peter depends directly on Philo. Too many testimonies of Diaspora Judaism have been lost for it to be possible to state this thesis. It could just as well be that only the identical milieu of the Diaspora synagogue had some influence on Philo and 1 Peter. Especially with regard to 1 Peter 1:4, the relation to Wis is outstanding. Here, all three notions are gathered as attributes of the celestial entities: ἄφθαρτος, in 12:1 from the divine spirit, 18:4 of the light of the divine law; ἀμίαντος in 4:2, in connection with the image of a competition as metaphor for a life in virtue (with the "unfading prize" for the victor); and ἀμάραντος in 6:12(13) for the wisdom.

30   This can be clarified by means of the attribute of God per se, imperish-ability. According to Wis, because humans are the image of God, they are disposed by God for imperishability (2:23), and this can be confirmed again by observance of the laws, despite the interim loss of imperishability due to the fall of mankind (6:18). For the martyr legends in 4 Macc 9:22, adher-ence to the Torah and to God in the middle of a corrupted world that is dominated by death points to the imperishable and eternal life, which already becomes imperishable through the process of dying. According to

the Hellenistic conversion novel *Joseph and Aseneth*, the Jew is the true wor-shipper of God and participates in the blessing and therefore in immortality and imperishability (8:5; 15:5; 16:16). Accordingly, the Gentile woman is granted imperishable youth and beauty after converting to Judaism (16:16; cf. also 18:9). In Philo, creation according to the image of God means that the human genus as an idea of God, as the image of God, is "imperish-able by nature" (φύσει ἄφθαρτος). Due to the turning to the realm of the flesh—Philo understands the fall of mankind in this way—the imperishabil-ity of the genus as configuration of the creation got lost (*Opif.* 152), even though imperishability remains in the form of the determination of the single human who shall "study to die to the life of the body, that a higher existence immortal and incorporal in the presence of Him who is Himself immortal and uncreated, may be their portion" (*Gig.* 14; cf. *Her.* 35; *Post.* 135; *Plant.* 44; *Ebr.* 136 et al.).

31   See above, nn. 27–30.

32   Cf. the contradictions of cornerstone and stumbling block (2:6-8), light and darkness (2:9), aberration and reversion (2:25), the inane outer and the imperishable inner (3:3-4), the exterior washing off of dirt and the interior purification of the conscience (3:21), and, last but not least, the admoni-tion against a backslide into the former way of life, which was dominated by desires (1:14; 2:11; 4:2-3). Cf. further the admonition against the devil who prowls like a hungry beast of prey (5:8) and the already mentioned contrast of present suffering with the coming glory, which is symptomatic of 1 Peter.

33   The commentary of Brox typically fades out this dimension. He is con-vinced that this explanation about the continuance of the word of God "etwas überflüssig anmutet, weil dieser Topos im Zusammenhang so wes-entlich nicht ist und er auch von niemand bestritten wurde." Otherwise, the author is not interested in the "Kurzlebigkeit des Menschen . . . im ganzen Brief sonst," which constitutes merely a "rhetorischen Kontrast zur Dauer-haftigkeit des Wortes" (Brox, *Petrusbrief*, 88).

34   Explained in detail by Feldmeier, *Christen als Fremde*, esp. 39–74.

35   In a variety of scripts, Philo signifies the "wise" as foreigners on the earth, where the context makes clear that he means almost those who observe the Jewish Torah, which educates them in the highest virtue (cf. esp. *Conf.* 75–82; further, *Her.* 267; *Agr.* 63–66; *Somn.* 1:45; *Congr.* 22-33 et al.). Espe-cially instructive for the context of the social exclusion is *QG* 4:39.

Chapter 12

1   Cf. E. Peterson, "Das Praescriptum des 1. Clemens-Briefes," in idem, *Frühkirche, Judentum und Gnosis* (Rome: Herder, 1959), 129–36: 129; C. Andresen, "Zum Formular frühchristlicher Gemeindebriefe," *ZNW* 56 (1965): 233–59, here 236n12, 243; K. Berger, *Formgeschichte des Neuen Tes-taments* (Heidelberg: Quelle & Mayer, 1984), 366; J. R. Michaels, *1 Peter* (WBC 49; Nashville: Thomas Nelson, 1988), xlvi–xlix; F. Schnider and W. Stenger, *Studien zum neutestamentlichen Briefformular* (NTTS 11; Leiden:

Brill, 1987), 33–41; Tsuji, *Glaube*, 29–32; U. Schnelle, *Einleitung in das Neue Testament* (4th ed.; UTB 1830; Göttingen: Vandenhoeck & Ruprecht, 2002), 452 (ET: *The History and Interpretation of the New Testament* [London: SCM Press, 1998], 406); J. H. Elliott, *1 Peter*, 12; more cautiously, L. Thurén, *The Rhetorical Strategy of 1 Peter: With Special Regard to Ambiguous Expressions* (Åbo: Åbo Akademis Förlag, 1990), 81–83 ("with certain reservations," 83); Verseput, "Wisdom," 702 ("perhaps even 1 Peter"), who, however, views James as Diaspora letter ("Wisdom," 702–4); idem, "Genre and Story."

2   P. Davids, *The First Epistle of Peter* (NICNT; Grand Rapids: Eerdmans, 1990), 13–14. He is followed by J. Prasad, *Foundations of the Christian Way of Life According to 1 Peter 1, 13–25* (AnBib 146; Rome: Ed. Pontificio Istituto Biblico, 2000), 59. More recently, however, Davids acknowledges the existence of the genre or text type; cf. Davids, "Palestinian Traditions," 41–42, 54. J. M. Lieu, originally rather skeptical regarding the genre ("'Grace to You and Peace': The Apostolic Greeting," *BJRL* 68 [1985/1986]: 161–78, here 173n43), states now, "A Jewish Diaspora letter tradition remains poorly attested, although not improbable, and further research is required here": Lieu, "Letters," in *The Oxford Handbook of Biblical Studies* (ed. J. W. Rogerson and J. M. Lieu; Oxford: Oxford University Press, 2006), 445–56, here: 451. One aim of the present contribution is to advance such research (below, "Early Jewish Diaspora Letters").

3   Thus recently for James, R. Hoppe, "Der Jakobusbrief als briefliches Zeugnis hellenistisch und hellenistisch-jüdisch geprägter Religiosität," in *Der neue Mensch in Christus* (ed. J. Beutler; QD 190; Freiburg: Herder, 2001), 164–89, here 173–75.

4   G. Strecker, *Literaturgeschichte des Neuen Testaments* (UTB 1682; Göttingen: Vandenhoeck & Ruprecht, 1992), 75n86 ("belegen die zahlreichen Parallelen zur hellenistischen Epistolographie, daß ein Rekurs auf die frühjüdische Briefschreibung wenig für das Verständnis der frühchristlichen Briefe austragen wird"), arguing explicitly against Peterson, "Praescriptum," 129, and Taatz, *Frühjüdische Briefe*.

5   Taatz, *Frühjüdische Briefe*. Some of the Jewish letters dealt with by Taatz are also discussed in Niebuhr, "Jakobusbrief"; M. F. Whitters, *The Epistle of Second Baruch: A Study in Form and Message* (JSPSup 42; London: Sheffield Academic Press, 2003), 86–101.

6   Thus, e.g., J. L. White, review of Taatz, *Frühjüdische Briefe*, *JBL* 112 (1993): 534–36, here 535–36.

7   The explicit author is an intratextual feature, a character in the text. For the model of author and reader (or addressee) adopted here, cf. H. Link, *Rezeptionsforschung: Eine Einführung in Methoden und Probleme* (2d ed.; Stuttgart: Kohlhammer, 1980), 25–29.

8   L. Doering, "Jeremiah and the 'Diaspora Letters' in Ancient Judaism: Epistolary Communication with the Golah as Medium for Dealing with the Present," in *Reading the Present in the Qumran Library: The Perception of the Contemporary by Means of Scriptural Interpretation* (ed. K. de Troyer and A. Lange; SBLSymS 30; Atlanta: Society of Biblical Literature, 2005), 43–72.

9 Cf. R. G. Kratz, "Der Brief des Jeremia," in O. H. Steck et al., *Das Buch Baruch, Der Brief des Jeremia, Zusätze zu Ester und Daniel* (ATD Apokryphen 5; Göttingen: Vandenhoeck & Ruprecht, 1998), 71–108, here 88; Doering, "Jeremiah and the 'Diaspora Letters,'" 49–53; I. Assan-Dhôte and J. Moatti-Fine, *Baruch, Lamentations, Lettre de Jérémie* (La Bible d'Alexandrie, 25, 2; Paris: Cerf, 2005), 292.

10 Cf., for suggestions for the calculation, which harmonizes data from Jeremiah 29 and elsewhere in Jeremiah, R. G. Kratz, "Die Rezeption von Jeremia 10 und 29 im pseudepigraphen Brief des Jeremia," *JSJ* 26 (1995): 2–31 (repr. in idem, *Das Judentum im Zeitalter des Zweiten Tempels* [FAT 42; Tübingen: Mohr Siebeck, 2004], 316–39), here 23–24 with n. 39 and the conclusion, 24: "Die Frist ist damit so offen formuliert, daß sie in die eigene Gegenwart des Verfassers (und Lesers) hinein und potentiell noch sehr viel weiter reicht." Cf. also Assan-Dhôte and Moatti-Fine, *Baruch*, 297–98.

11 Cf. Kratz, "Rezeption," passim.

12 Cf. S. Sherwin-White, "Seleucid Babylonia: A Case Study for the Installation and Development of Greek Rule," in *Hellenism in the East: Aspects of the Interaction of Greek and Non-Greek Civilizations from Syria to Central Asia* (ed. A. Kuhrt and S. Sherwin-White; London: Duckworth, 1987), 1–31; A. Kuhrt, "Alexander in Babylon," in *The Roots of the European Tradition: Proceedings of the 1987 Groningen Achaemenid History Workshop* (ed. H. Sancisi-Weerdenburg and J. W. Drijvers; Achaemenid History 5; Leiden: Nederlands Instituut for het Nabije Oosten, 1990), 121–30.

13 Cf. A. H. J. Gunneweg, "Das Buch Baruch. Der Brief Jeremias," *JSHRZ* 3.2 (1975): 167–92, here 185–86; Kratz, "Brief des Jeremia," 74.

14 For the date, cf. Gunneweg, "Buch Baruch," 186; G. W. E. Nickelsburg, *Jewish Literature between the Bible and the Mishnah: A Historical and Literary Introduction* (2d ed.; Minneapolis: Fortress, 2005), 35–37, 351–52; Kratz, "Brief des Jeremia," 82. Assan-Dhôte and Moatti-Fine, *Baruch*, 297–98, distinguish between a fourth-century date for the composition of the text and a second-century date for the Greek text.

15 Cf. Kratz, "Brief des Jeremia," 78–79, 84–85; C. A. Moore, *Daniel, Esther and Jeremiah: The Additions* (AB 44; New York: Doubleday, 1977), 325.

16 Text: A. Sperber, ed., *The Latter Prophets according to Targum Jonathan* (vol. 3 of *The Bible in Aramaic*; Leiden: Brill, 1962), 160–61; ET: R. Hayward, *The Targum of Jeremiah* (ArBib 12; Edinburgh: T&T Clark, 1987), 79.

17 . . . as Hayward, *Targum*, 79n8 seems to suggest.

18 Hayward, *Targum*, 38, views the origins of the Targum of Jeremiah "in the land of Israel during, or slightly before, the first century" CE and suggests that its "roots may be even older."

19 P. Churgin, *Targum Jonathan to the Prophets* (New Haven, Conn.: Yale University Press, 1927), 134–35. Churgin observes that in *Codex Reuchlianus*, both the MT and the letter are quoted, and concludes that in all other MSS, the letter has "forced out" the MT. But it is equally possible that the MT passage (itself, oddly, in Aramaic) was secondarily inserted into *Codex Reuchlianus*.

20   D. Dimant, *Qumran Cave 4. XXI. Parabiblical Texts*, part 4: *Pseudo-Prophetic Texts* (partially based on earlier transcriptions by J. Strugnell; DJD 30; Oxford: Oxford University Press, 2001), 91–260; L. Doering, "Jeremia in Babylonien und Ägypten."

21   [ויהי] | [בשל]שים ושש שנה לגלות ישראל קראו הדברים] האלה לפני| | כֹּל בני י[שראל על נהר סור במעמד ד]. I deviate here from Dimant, *Qumran Cave*, 220, by reconstructing the beginning of the passage as a temporal sentence; see Doering, "Jeremia in Babylonien und Ägypten," 65–67 (but restore ויהי at the end of line 5). It might also be worthwhile to consider the syntactically smoother restoration [ו]קראו, on account of a small hole to the right of the visible traces of the word.

22   See Doering, "Jeremia in Babylonien und Ägypten," 66 with n. 81; idem, "Jeremiah and the 'Diaspora Letters,'" 66 with n. 105.

23   J. A. Goldstein, "The Apocryphal Book of I Baruch," *PAAJR* 46/47 (1979/1980): 179–99; O. H. Steck, *Das apokryphe Baruchbuch: Studien zur Rezeption und Konzentration "kanonischer" Überlieferung* (FRLANT 160; Göttingen: Vandenhoeck & Ruprecht, 1993), 290–303 (both opting for 164–162 BCE); O. Kaiser, *Die alttestamentlichen Apokryphen: Eine Einleitung in Grundzügen* (Gütersloh: Gütersloher Verlagshaus, 2000), 56–57 (168– 139 BCE). The controversial issue of Baruch's literary unity (defended by Goldstein and Steck) cannot be further pursued here, and does not have to be for our purposes, in view of the recent tendency to date the final composition to the Maccabean period. However, a Pompeian date has been suggested by J. Schreiner in H. Groß, *Klagelieder*; J. Schreiner, *Baruch* (NEchtB 14; Würzburg: Echter, 1986), 46–47 (cf. also Gunneweg, "Buch Baruch," 168–69 for the final form).

24   For Bar 1:1–3:8, see E. Tov, *The Septuagint Tradition of Jeremiah and Baruch: A Discussion of an Early Revision of the LXX of Jeremiah 29–52 and Baruch 1:1–3:8* (HSM 8; Missoula, Mont.: Scholars Press, 1976), 111–33. For the whole book, see Steck, *Das apokryphe Baruchbuch*, 249–53; Assan-Dhôte and Moatti-Fine, *Baruch*, 69–71. Gunneweg, "Buch Baruch," 170, assumes a Hebrew original only for 1:15–2:35.

25   On reasons for the author fiction, see Steck, *Das apokryphe Baruchbuch*, 15–16, 303–5.

26   Syriac text: M. Kmosko, "Epistola Baruch filii Neriae," in *Patrologia Syriaca 1/2* (ed. R. Graffin; Paris: Firmin-Didot, 1904), 1208–37; ET: A. F. J. Klijn, "2 (Syriac Apocalypse of) Baruch," in *Old Testament Pseudepigrapha* 1 (ed. J. H. Charlesworth; ABRL; New York: Doubleday, 1983–1985), 615–52, here 647–52. For French and German translations, see the following note.

27   An early date is assumed by P. Bogaert, *Apocalypse de Baruch: Introduction, traduction du syriaque et commentaire* (2 vols.; SC 144, 145; Paris: Cerf, 1969), 1:294–95: ca. 95 CE; a late date by A. F. J. Klijn, "Die syrische Baruch-Apokalypse," *JSHRZ* 5.2 (1976): 103–91, here 114: between 100 and 130 CE. Taatz, *Frühjüdische Briefe*, 60, remains vague: between 70 and 130 CE. For the Letter of Baruch, cf. Whitters, *Epistle of Second Baruch*, passim (whose classification of it as "festal letter" [81–85], however, does not seem

substantiated). R. Nir, *The Destruction of Jerusalem and the Idea of Redemption in the Syriac Apocalypse of Baruch* (SBLEJL 20; Atlanta: Society of Biblical Literature, 2003), has argued that *2 Bar.* is a Christian text, but without sufficient reasons.

28   Cf. Bogaert, *Apocalypse de Baruch*, 1:67–78; Whitters, *Epistle of Second Baruch*, 1–23.

29   The complete text of *2 Bar.* is only proffered by the manuscript from the Bibliotheca Ambrosiana in Milan (= c) and an Arabic translation (= Mount Sinai Arabic 589). Thirty-eight MSS contain the letter only. Cf., for the textual quality of c, Bogaert, *Apocalypse de Baruch*, 1:72–73; Klijn, "Die syrische Baruch-Apokalypse," 118–19. Cf., for the Arabic MS, F. Leemhuis, A. F. J. Klijn, and G. J. H. van Gelder, *The Arabic Text of the Apocalypse of Baruch* (Leiden: Brill, 1986).

30   E.g., Klijn, "Die syrische Baruch-Apokalypse," 110–11, assumes a Hebrew original, while Bogaert, *Apocalypse de Baruch*, 1:353–380 thinks that an original in Koine Greek with Hebraisms is equally possible.

31   Thus Niebuhr, "Jakobusbrief," 428–29 with nn. 29–30, with details and references.

32   See in detail Doering, "Jeremiah and the 'Diaspora Letters,'" 60–62.

33   Text, numeration, and ET: J. Herzer, *4 Baruch (Paraleipomena Jeremiou)* (vol. 22 of *Writings from the Greco-Roman World*; Atlanta: Society of Biblical Literature, 2005). German translation in B. Schaller, "Paralipomena Jeremiou," *JSHRZ* 1.8 (1998): 661–777. Herzer bases his text on "a critical analysis" of the editions of Harris and Kraft & Purintun (*4 Baruch*, xxxvi). B. Heininger, Würzburg, has announced a new critical edition of the Greek text. A first result of his project group is a re-assessment of the longer text form; cf. A. Hentschel, "Beobachtungen zur Textüberlieferung der Paralipomena Jeremiou (Langversion)," *ZNW* 99 (2008): 149–66.

34   Herzer argues for a date (of the Jewish *Grundschrift*) between 125 and 132 CE; see Herzer, *Die Paralipomena Jeremiae* (TSAJ 43; Tübingen: Mohr Siebeck, 1994), 177–91 (in his *4 Baruch*, xxxiv, he gives 117–135 CE). More cautious is Schaller, "Paralipomena Jeremiou," 678–79 (first third of 2C CE). On the question of whether *4 Bar.* is dependent on *2 Bar.*, cf. Herzer, *4 Baruch*, xvi–xxiii, who affirms this and defends it against critics; one such recent critic is Schaller, "Paralipomena Jeremiou," 672–73 (both texts draw on the same or a similar source).

35   Cf. Schaller, "Paralipomena Jeremiou," 676–77, and Schaller, "Die griechische Fassung der Paralipomena Jeremiou: Originaltext oder Übersetzungstext?" in idem, *Fundamenta Judaica: Studien zum antiken Judentum und zum Neuen Testament* (ed. L. Doering and A. Steudel; SUNT 25; Göttingen: Vandenhoeck & Ruprecht, 2001), 67–103; ET: *JSP* 22 (2000): 51–89.

36   Contra M. Karrer, *Die Johannesoffenbarung als Brief* (FRLANT 140; Göttingen: Vandenhoeck & Ruprecht, 1986), 52: "ein eher privates Schreiben" (on *4 Bar.* 6:17-23); Taatz, *Frühjüdische Briefe*, 81: "persönliches Klageschreiben" (on *4 Bar.* 7:23-29).

37   The letter is not reproduced literally in Codex Barberini (= v) or in the

Slavonic version slav[a] (sigla according to Herzer, *4 Baruch*, xxxviii–xli); cf. Schaller, "Paralipomena Jeremiou," 734 (n. d on 6.16). The shorter text of MSS A and B, addressed to both Baruch and Abimelech, is given in the apparatus in Herzer, but the longer one (as per C [P] eth) is to be preferred (Herzer, *4 Baruch*, ad loc.).

38 B. Porten and A. Yardeni, *Letters, Appendix: Aramaic Letters from the Bible* (vol. 1 of *Textbook of Aramaic Documents from Ancient Egypt*; Jerusalem: Hebrew University, 1986), 54–55. I retain the translation "Jewish" here, with the qualification that some features of what later characterizes Jewishness have not yet developed at Elephantine.

39 Cf. the summary of the discussion in Taatz, *Frühjüdische Briefe*, 92.

40 Cf. Taatz, *Frühjüdische Briefe*, 99. However, AP 30 (with 31), equally discussed by Taatz (95–98), is a petition to the governor of Judah, Bagoas, not a Diaspora letter.

41 Cf. E. Bickermann, "Ein jüdischer Festbrief vom Jahre 124 v. Chr. (II Macc 1 1–9)," *ZNW* 32 (1933): 233–54, here 235–44; followed, inter multos alios, by C. Habicht, "2.Makkabäerbuch," *JSHRZ* 1.3 (1976): 167–285, here 199–200. But see on the date below, n. 47; on the letter as part of 2 Macc, see below, 2.4.

42 2 Macc 1:1: Τοῖς ἀδελφοῖς τοῖς κατ' Αἴγυπτον Ἰουδαίοις χαίρειν οἱ ἀδελφοὶ οἱ ἐν Ἱεροσολύμοις Ἰουδαῖοι καὶ οἱ ἐν τῇ χώρα τῆς Ἰουδαίας εἰρή νην ἀγαθήν. I use the edition by R. Hanhart, *Maccabaeorum liber 2* (Septuaginta: Vetus Testamentum Graecum auctoritate Societatis Scientiarum Gottingensis ed., 9, 2; Göttingen: Vandenhoeck & Ruprecht, 1959). On the prescript, cf. E. Bickermann, "Ein jüdischer Festbrief," 245: "Das Präskript ist also weder griechisch noch rein semitisch formuliert. Man wird es am besten als Versuch eines Übersetzers, den vollen Inhalt der jüdischen Segensformel in griechische [*sic*] Weise wiederzugeben, verstehen."

43 On these, cf. D. Schwiderski, *Handbuch des nordwestsemitischen Briefformulars: Ein Beitrag zur Echtheitsfrage der aramäischen Briefe des Esrabuches* (BZAW 295; Berlin: de Gruyter, 2000), 55–61, 155–64. Particularly the Aramaic phrases serve both to open and to structure the letter body.

44 For the former, cf. Schwiderski, *Handbuch*, 115–41; for the latter, cf. F. X. J. Exler, *The Form and Function of the Ancient Greek Letter: A Study in Greek Epistolography* (Washington, D.C.: Catholic University of America, 1923), 103–11.

45 Thus correctly Taatz, *Frühjüdische Briefe*, 25, pointing to a similar statement in Jonathan's letter to the Spartans (1 Macc 12:11).

46 Others make the reference to this period only start with "since Jason," etc., and relate the "distress," etc., to the time around 143 BCE.

47 D. R. Schwartz, *The Second Book of Maccabees: Introduction, Hebrew Translation, and Commentary* (Jerusalem: Yad Ben-Zvi, 2004), 16–19, 75–78, 289–95, has questioned this view of the letter. For v. 10a, Schwartz adopts the reading 148 (Sel., ca. 164 BCE), given by two MSS (55 and 62), and thinks this is not the date of the letter but a specification of the festival to be celebrated: "the days of the 'Tabernacles' in the month of Kislev of 148."

According to Schwartz, the real date of the letter is the one given in v. 7: 169 Sel., ca. 143 BCE; he takes the perfect γεγράφαμεν there as an epistolary tense ("we are writing"), implying that vv. 7-8 do not quote an earlier letter. Schwartz attempts to situate the letter (as well as the book) in the time following the end of Seleucid taxation in 170 Sel. (cf. 1 Macc 13:36-40), claiming that this is a better context than the rather insignificant year of 124 BCE; for the alleged insignificance, he relies on an early statement by A. Momigliano, who, however, later adopted 124 BCE as the date for both letter and book: "The Second Book of Maccabees," *CP* 70 (1975): 81–88, here 83–84. However, this proposal is not without its problems. Suffice it here to point out that (1) the transition between vv. 6 and 7 becomes syntactically rough (Schwartz' Hebrew translation glosses this over), (2) the mention of the year and Demetrius' reign in the middle of the body would be surprising, and (3) the request to celebrate, in 143 BCE, the Hanukkah of 164 BCE would seem somewhat odd. See now ET: *2 Maccabees* (CEJL; Berlin: de Gruyter, 2008), 11–12, 143–44, 519–29.

48 Cf. Taatz, *Frühjüdische Briefe*, 29: "verwaltungsrechtlich offiziell."

49 Cf. further on the proem H. Cancik, *Mythische und historische Wahrheit: Interpretationen zu Texten der hethitischen, biblischen und griechischen Historiographie* (SBS 48; Stuttgart: Kath. Bibelwerk, 1970), 108–26.

50 T. Nisula, "'Time has passed since you sent your letter': Letter Phraseology in 1 and 2 Maccabees," *JSP* 14 (2005): 201–22, here 211. Cf. R. Buzón, "Die Briefe der Ptolemäerzeit: Ihre Struktur und ihre Formeln" (Diss. phil., Heidelberg, 1984), 19–20, 59–65, 108–10, 167–68, 241–42. In the literary tradition, cf. also 1 Macc 12:18, 22; Add Esth E 17; Josephus, *B.J.* 1.643; *A.J.* 11.279; 12.49; 13.170.

51 Thus B. Z. Wacholder, "The Letter from Judah Maccabee to Aristobulus: Is 2 Maccabees 1:10b–2:18 Authentic?" *HUCA* 49 (1978): 89–133; followed by Taatz, *Frühjüdische Briefe*, 29–43. Cf. also D. Flusser, "The Dedication of the Temple by Judas Maccabaeus: Story and History," in *The Jews in the Hellenistic-Roman World: Studies in Memory of Menahem Stern* (ed. I. M. Gafni, A. Oppenheimer, and D. R. Schwartz; Jerusalem: Zalman Shazar Center & Historical Society of Israel, 1996), 55–78.

52 A case for the authenticity of 2 Macc 1:10b–18a and 2:16-18 has been made by J. G. Bunge, "Untersuchungen zum zweiten Makkabäerbuch: Quellenkritische, literarische, chronologische und historische Untersuchungen zum zweiten Makkabäerbuch als Quelle syrisch-palästinensischer Geschichte im 2. Jh. v. Chr." (Diss. phil., Bonn, 1971), 32–152. Schwartz more generally does not exclude the possibility that a nucleus is authentic: *Second Book*, 78 (ET: 144). Authenticity is denied by Habicht, "2.Makkabäerbuch," 202; H.-J. Klauck, *Ancient Letters and the New Testament: A Guide to Context and Exegesis* (with collaboration of D. P. Bailey; Waco, Tex.: Baylor University Press, 2006), 270. Also skeptical is Momigliano, "Second Book," 84. However, Bickermann's claim that the salutation χαίρειν καὶ ὑγιαίνειν (2 Macc 1:10b) would urge a date around 60 BCE ("Ein jüdischer Festbrief," 234, with reference to form parallels gathered by Exler, *Form and Function*,

32–33, 64) has been rightly rebutted: Exler gathered evidence merely from Egypt, not from other places like Greece or the Seleucid kingdom, and one early witness for the salutation is the letter on lead by Mnesiergos (4C BCE, Athens; *SIG³* 3:1259; text with translation and notes now in M. Trapp, ed., *Greek and Latin Letters: An Anthology with Translation* [Cambridge Greek and Latin Classics; Cambridge: Cambridge University Press, 2003], 50–51, 198–99). See Bunge, "Untersuchungen," 43–46. Bickermann's pupil J. A. Goldstein, in *II Maccabees* (AB 41A; New York: Doubleday, 1983), 157–66, has moved the date to 103/2 BCE and assumes an Egyptian origin. At any rate, the letter claims Jerusalem-Judean origin.

53   Thus convincingly Bunge, "Untersuchungen," 82–84.

54   Taatz, *Frühjüdische Briefe*, 29, claims that all agree that the letter was trans- lated from Aramaic. However, Bickermann viewed it as written in idiomatic Greek (see Goldstein, *II Maccabees*, 164), while Goldstein spots Hebraisms in 1:12, 18, 36 (164, 169–70, 171–72, 181), though hardly on sufficient grounds. More important is Hanhart's suggestion of possible translation Greek in 1:16 (μέλη ποιήσαντες, "chop off limbs"; cf. Dan 2:5, הִתְעֲבֵדוּן הַדָּמִין ... תֵּן וְתִנָּ) and 1:17 (ἔδωκεν, "deliver"; cf. Dan 11:6, וְתִנָּתֵן; παρέδωκεν is said to be Lucianic correction), but even Hanhart considers it possible that poor stylistic training rather than translation Greek proper is at stake: "Anwendung eines am Übersetzungsgriechisch entarteten Stiles." R. Hanhart, *Zum Text des 2. und 3. Makkabäerbuches: Probleme der Überlief- erung, der Auslegung und der Ausgabe* (NAWG 13; Göttingen: Vandenhoeck & Ruprecht, 1961), 18–19 (quotation, 19).

55   Taatz, *Frühjüdische Briefe*, 45.

56   For the view of 2 Macc as a festal book, cf. Bunge, "Untersuchungen," 184– 95; Momigliano, "Second Book," 87–88; also Schwartz, *Second Book*, 14–16 (ET: 8–10; assumes that the original emphasis was on Jerusalem and Nica- nor's day and that the final form, including the letters and 10:1-8, shifted the accent to promulgation of Hanukkah). R. Doran, *Temple Propaganda: The Purpose and Character of 2 Maccabees* (CBQMS 12; Washington, D.C.: Catholic Biblical Association, 1981), 105–7, criticizes some aspects of this theory.

57   Cf. for the whole issue Bunge, "Untersuchungen," 184–95. For the notion of 2 Macc as letter, cf. further the description in the Parisian Codex Regius 721 (*SS. patrum qui temporibus apostolicis floruerunt . . . opera* [ed. J. Clericus; Antwerp, 1698] 1:448): "ἡ δευτέρα [sc. 2 Macc] δὲ ἐν εἴδει ἐπιστολῆς οὖσα," as well as Rabanus Maurus' comment (*PL* 109, 1223): "Scriptis [*sic*—sc. 2 Macc] enim ab his videtur qui morati sunt in terra Juda, ad eos qui in exteris fugerunt regionibus." This view was later endorsed by G. Wernsdorf, *Commentatio historico-critica de fide historica libro- rum Maccabaicorum* (Breslau, 1747), 65–66. For the notion of the epitome as enclosure to the letters, cf. U. Kahrstedt, *Syrische Territorien in hellenis- tischer Zeit* (AGWG.PH NF 19.2; Berlin: Weidmannsche Buchhandlung, 1926), 133 ("das Geschichtswerk ist, modern gesprochen, eine Anlage zu dem Brief [here: the second letter], bezw. gibt sich als Anlage zu einem

gefälschten Brief"), following a suggestion by Ed. Meyer; now Klauck, *Ancient Letters*, 262 ("an addendum to the two festival letters").

58   For the history of the text(s) of Esther, cf. generally I. Kottsieper, "Zusätze zu Ester," in Steck et al., *Das Buch Baruch*, 109–207, here 117–36. For the relation between LXX and MT Esth cf. now E. Tov, "The LXX Translation of Esther: A Paraphrastic Translation of MT or a Free Translation of a Rewritten Version?" in Empsychoi Logoi—*Religious Innovations in Antiquity: FS P. W. van der Horst* (ed. A. Houtman et al.; Leiden: Brill, 2008) 507–26 (favoring the second alternative). For the possibility that epigraphic evidence for the name Μαρδοχαῖος in Alexandria early in the second century BCE testifies to the familiarity with the Mordecai-Esther tradition, cf. W. Horbury, "The Name Mardochaeus in a Ptolemaic Inscription," *VT* 41 (1991): 220–26. For the Greek texts, I follow R. Hanhart, ed., *Esther* (2d ed.; Septuaginta: Vetus Testamentum Graecum auctoritate Academiae Scientiarum Gottingensis ed., 8, 3; Göttingen: Vandenhoeck & Ruprecht, 1983).

59   Kottsieper, "Zusätze," 121–24, thinks of pro-Hasmonean Pharisaic circles during the final years of Alexander Jannai or the reign of Salome Alexandra, ca. 81–67 BCE, but this requires that the Ptolemy under whom the book is sent from Jerusalem to Egypt not be Ptolemy IX in the late second century BCE; see below, n. 61. Further, 2 Macc 15:36 may witness to familiarity with the term *Mordecai's day* already in second-century BCE Palestine, if this is indeed the place of the epitomist, as many hold, e.g., Momigliano, "Second Book," 82–83; Bunge, "Untersuchungen," 615–17 (and elsewhere).

60   For an explanation of why Esth is missing in Qumran that refers to the disapproval of Purim, see J. C. VanderKam, "Authoritative Literature in the Dead Sea Scrolls," *DSD* 5 (1998): 382–402, esp. 384–85 (14th Adar, the twelfth month in the 364-day calendar, would always fall on a Sabbath, which would be unacceptable in the framework of this calendar). Other reasons are added by I. Kalimi, "The Book of Esther and the Dead Sea Scrolls Community," *TZ* 60 (2004): 101–6. For traditions in 4QTales of the Persian Court relating, inter alia, to Esth, see recently S. White Crawford, "4QTales of the Persian Court (4Q550a–e) and its Relation to Biblical Royal Courtier Tales, Especially Esther, Daniel and Joseph," in *The Bible as Book: The Hebrew Bible and the Judaean Desert Discoveries* (ed. E. D. Herbert and E. Tov; London: The British Library, 2002), 121–38. Several scholars have argued that, despite the lack of a copy of Esther among the Qumran finds, (some text of) Esther was nevertheless known at Qumran; cf. S. Talmon, "Was the Book of Esther Known at Qumran?" *DSD* 2 (1995): 249–67; J. Ben-Dov, "A Presumed Citation of Esther 3:7 in 4QD^b," *DSD* 6 (1999): 282–84; K. de Troyer, "Once More, the So-called Esther Fragments of Cave 4," *RevQ* 19/75 (2000): 401–22.

61   Cf. the important article by E. J. Bickerman[n], "The Colophon of the Greek Book of Esther," *JBL* 63 (1944): 339–62, who argues that the dating refers to Ptolemy XII and Cleopatra V (p. 347), i.e., 78/77 BCE, although E. Schürer, *The History of the Jewish People in the Age of Jesus Christ (175*

B.C.–A.D. 135) (rev. and ed., G. Vermes, F. Millar et al.; 3 vols.; Edinburgh: T&T Clark, 1973–1987), 3:1, 505–6 (M. Goodman) considers also 114 BCE (Ptolemy IX, Cleopatra III) and 48 BCE (Ptolemy XIII, Cleopatra VII) to be possible dates, with some preference for the former.

62 *y. Hag.* 1:8, 76d; par. *y. Ned.* 10:10, 42b (R. Hiyya bar Abba requests a letter of recommendation from the *nāśî*); *y. Mo'ed Qat.* 3:1, 81c (Simeon bar Ba asks R. Haninah for such a letter). Cf. Acts 9:1-2 and warning letters in Acts 28:21.

63 *y. Hag.* 2:2, 77d; *y. Sanh.* 6:9, 23c; cf. *b. Sanh.* 107b; *b. Sotah* 47a (Simeon b. Shetah to Joshua b. Perahiah). Cf. D. Pardee, *Handbook of Ancient Hebrew Letters: A Study Edition* (with a chapter on Tannaitic letter fragments by S. D. Sperling, with the collaboration of J. D. Whitehead and P. E. Dion; SBLSBS 15; Chico, Calif.: Scholars Press, 1982), 204–7.

64 Taatz, *Frühjüdische Briefe*, 83 ("kann der Brief als Beleg dafür gelten, dass briefliche Kontakte offizieller Art, d.h. in Fragen der Gemeindeleitung und des Kults, zwischen Jerusalem und Diasporagemeinden bestanden").

65 *t. Sanh.* 2:6; *y. Sanh.* 1:2, 18d; *y. Ma'as. Sh.* 5:6, 56c; *b. Sanh.* 11b; cf. Pardee, *Handbook*, 189–96 (Sperling).

66 According to *y. Ma'as. Sh.* and *t. Sanh.* (MS Vienna), it is dictated by Gamaliel *and* the elders; according to *y. Sanh.* (ed. princ. Venice: רמא; MS Leiden: 'מא) and *t. Sanh.* in MS Erfurt ('מא), *only* by Gamaliel. Thus also *b. Sanh.*, where the elders are completely missing from the narrative framework. However, in the letter bodies, the addressors are in the plural. It is debated whether Gamaliel I or II is meant, an issue that cannot be pursued further here; cf. discussion, with a leaning toward Gamaliel II, in B. Salomonsen, *Die Tosefta, Seder IV: Nezikin, 3: Sanhedrin–Makkot* (Rabbinische Texte 1, 4.3; Stuttgart: Kohlhammer, 1976), 24–25n28.

67 *y. Sanh.* 1:2, 18d adds, "the inhabitants of the Diaspora of Greece." Note both the geographic distinction and the encompassing reference to the entire Diaspora here.

68 *MHG* Deut 26:13 (598 Fisch) = *Midr. Tanna'im* Deut 26:13 (176 Hoffmann): "To our brothers in the Upper and Lower South, to Shahlil and the seven southern areas" (letter no. 1); "To our brothers in Upper and Lower Galilee, to Simonia and Oved Beit Hillel" (no. 2). Both letters instruct about the beginning of the fourth year (in the shemittah cycle) and request swift tithing of sheaves (no. 1) and olives (no. 2); they mention also earlier correspondence from Jerusalem, from "our fathers" to "your fathers." Cf. Pardee, *Handbook*, 184–89 (Sperling).

69 I am informed here by work of the German linguist K. Ermert, *Briefsorten: Untersuchungen zu Theorie und Empirie der Textklassifikation* (Reihe Germanistische Linguistik 20; Tübingen: Niemeyer, 1979). He defines "letter types," *Briefsorten*, as "Textsorten [text types] im Rahmen der Kommunikationsform 'Brief,'" to be understood "als virtuelle Einheiten aus intentionalen, sozialen, situativen und thematischen Determinationsfaktoren und textinternstrukturellen und äußerlich formalen Folgemerkmalen" (1). However, there has been some debate whether the letter in general is a "form of

communication" and not rather a genre or text type of its own, as held by many New Testament scholars (cf. only Berger, *Formgeschichte*, 216–17; M. M. Mitchell, "Brief," *RGG4* 1:1757–62, here 1757–58). G. Diewald, *Deixis und Textsorten im Deutschen* (Reihe Germanistische Linguistik 118; Tübingen: Niemeyer, 1991), 278–81, 293–304, 330, helpfully suggests viewing the letter as one of five "basic text types" (*Grundtextsorten*), with the situation of communication being the dominant factor (for the letter: dialogical, not face-to-face, not oral); this allows for assigning individual text types to the basic text type letter, which we call letter types here.

70   For the following, cf. also Tsuji, *Glaube*, 22–37, from whom I deviate considerably at times.

71   Cf. Berger, *Formgeschichte*, 366; Klein, *"Ein vollkommenes Werk,"* 188–89; Davids, "Palestinian Traditions," 41–42; Tsuji, *Glaube*, 22–27; Niebuhr, "Jakobusbrief," passim; Bauckham, *James: Wisdom*, 11–28; Verseput, "Genre and Story," 96–110; cautiously, Burchard, *Jakobusbrief*, 9 ("wenn man Jak zur Untergattung Diasporabriefe rechnen darf").

72   Cf. W. Zimmerli and J. Jeremias, "παῖς θεοῦ," *TWNT* 5:653–713, here 662–64, 679–81; ET: *TDNT* 5:654–717, here 663–65, 680–81.

73   Rom 1:1; Gal 1:10; Phil 1:1; 2 Pet 1:1; Jude 1; Acts 4:29; 16:17. Cf. Tsuji, *Glaube*, 24–25.

74   Cf., e.g., the discussion in Burchard, *Jakobusbrief*, 3–4, 48.

75   Cf. Klein, *"Ein vollkommenes Werk,"* 185–90; Tsuji, *Glaube*, 22–25; Niebuhr, "Jakobusbrief," 422–23; Burchard, *Jakobusbrief*, 48–50, with differences in detail.

76   Cf. esp. Tsuji, *Glaube*, 25–26; Niebuhr, "Jakobusbrief," 423–24, 429–30.

77   Cf. Niebuhr, "Jakobusbrief," 432–42.

78   Cf. Bauckham, *James: Wisdom*, 20; Burchard, *Jakobusbrief*, 9; and particularly (but with simplifications) Tsuji, *Glaube*, 28–29. Cf. already Andresen, "Zum Formular," 233–36.

79   With, inter alios, A. Weiser, *Die Apostelgeschichte* (2 vols.; ÖTK 5; Gütersloh: Gütersloher Verlagshaus, 1981–1985), 2:371–75, 384–86; Wehnert, *Reinheit*, 44, 47–53, 57–58, 68–70; C. K. Barrett, *The Acts of the Apostles* (2 vols.; ICC; Edinburgh: T&T Clark, 1994–1998), 2:740–41; J. Jervell, *Die Apostelgeschichte* (KEK 3; Göttingen: Vandenhoeck & Ruprecht, 1998), 400n727, 405–6.

80   Cf., for the former, Andresen, "Zum Formular," 234–36; F. W. Danker, "Reciprocity in the Ancient World and in Acts 15:23-29," in *Political Issues in Luke-Acts* (ed. R. J. Cassidy and P. J. Scharper; Maryknoll, N.Y.: Orbis Books, 1983), 49–58, here 50; Wehnert, *Reinheit*, 48. For the latter, cf. Kennedy, *New Testament Interpretation*, 127; B. Witherington, *The Acts of the Apostles: A Socio-Rhetorical Commentary* (Grand Rapids: Eerdmans, 1998), 467–68.

81   Cf., in the *adscriptio* alone, *2 Bar.* 78:2 (and passim) (above, 1.4) and the rabbinic Diaspora letters attributed to Gamaliel, as well as to Simeon and Johanan (2.6).

82   For the textual problems, cf. B. M. Metzger, *A Textual Commentary on the Greek New Testament* (2d ed.; Stuttgart: Dt. Bibelgesellschaft, 1994),

379–83, arguing in favor of a fourfold decree as original: food offered to idols, eating blood, strangled meat, and unchastity. Whether this *modus vivendi* implies a "halakic" obligation of Gentile Christians in line with the regulations of Leviticus 17–18 (thus the dominant interpretation, e.g. Wehnert, *Reinheit*, 209–45) or rather requires Gentile Christians to respect taboos central to Jewish identity in the Diaspora (thus R. Deines, "Das Aposteldekret—Halacha für Heidenchristen oder christliche Rücksicht-nahme auf jüdische Tabus?," in *Jewish Identity in the Graeco-Roman World* [ed. J. Frey, D. R. Schwartz, and S. Gripentrog; AJAC (AGJU) 71; Leiden: Brill, 2007], 323–95) does not affect the main thrust of our argument here.

83 χάρις ὑμῖν καὶ εἰρήνη ἀπὸ παντοκράτορος θεοῦ διὰ Ἰησοῦ Χριστοῦ πληθυνθείη.

84 The *inscriptio* is considered the key to *1 Clem.* by T. Schmitt, *Paroikie und Oikumene: Sozial- und mentalitätsgeschichtliche Untersuchungen zum 1. Clemensbrief* (BZNW 110; Berlin: de Gruyter, 2002), 135–37.

85 Cf. the recurring address ἄνδρες ἀδελφοί: *1 Clem.* 14:1; 37:1; 43:4; 62:1; cf. Acts 1:16; 2:29, 37; 7:2; 13:15, 26, 38; 15:7, 13; 22:1; 23:1, 6; 28:17; cf. 4 Macc 8:19 (cf. LXX Ezek 11:15). Cf. also the common address ἀδελφοί: *1 Clem.* 4:7; 13:1; 33:1; 38:3; 41:1-2, 4; 45:1; 46:1; 52:1.

86 Cf. Eusebius, *Hist. eccl.* 4.23.10 (Hegesippus); cf. 3.16; Jerome, *Vir. ill.* 15. Cf. H. Löhr, *Studien zum frühchristlichen und frühjüdischen Gebet: Untersuchungen zu 1 Clem 59 bis 61 in seinem literarischen, historischen und theologischen Kontext* (WUNT 160; Tübingen: Mohr Siebeck, 2003), 115–19.

87 Cf. Peterson, "Praescriptum," 129–36; Andresen, "Zum Formular," 236–37, 241–43; Tsuji, *Glaube*, 35–36.

88 Cf. A. Stuiber, "Clemens Romanus I," in *RAC* 3 (1957), 188–97, here 194 ("Nachwirken des spätjüdischen Diasporabriefs"); Tsuji, *Glaube*, 35 ("möglichen Einfluss"); Löhr, *Studien*, 67n2 ("Anlehnung an den jüdischen Diaspora-Brief"), etc. An exception is Andresen, "Zum Formular," 241 ("ist es durchaus berechtigt, den 1. Klemensbrief in die Gattung christlicher Diasporaschreiben einzuordnen"). Since there is evidence of Jewish Diaspora letters to one community (above, 2.1; 2.5; cf. 1.5), the fact that *1 Clem.* is explicitly addressed to merely one community cannot be accepted as counterargument against its classification with Diaspora letters; contra H. E. Lona, *Der erste Clemensbrief* (KAV 2; Göttingen: Vandenhoeck & Ruprecht, 1998), 114 with n. 2.

89 Contested by K. Beyschlag, *Clemens Romanus und der Frühkatholizismus: Untersuchungen zu I Clemens 1–7* (BHT 35; Tübingen: Mohr, 1966), 23–24n3; Lona, *Clemensbrief*, 114.

90 Cf. Peterson, "Praescriptum," 131–32 with n. 7, 134; Tsuji, *Glaube*, 36. For *Mart. Pol.*, cf. also G. Buschmann, *Das Martyrium des Polykarp* (KAV 6; Göttingen: Vandenhoeck & Ruprecht, 1998), esp. 67–75. For the question of whether the Letter of Polycarp (= Pol., *Phil.*) knows *1 Clem.*, cf. Lona, *Clemensbrief*, 90–92.

91 Like *Mart. Pol.*, also the later (4C) *Martyrdom of Sabas the Goth* (= *Mart.*

Sab.); text: R. Knopf, ed., *Ausgewählte Märtyrerakten* (rev. G. Krüger; 4th ed. with *Nachtrag* by G. Ruhbach; Tübingen: Mohr Siebeck, 1965), no. 33.

92 Cf. Andresen, "Zum Formular," 252–55 ("Sprachrohr übergemeindlicher Zusammenkünfte," 252). The first specimen is the letter by Serapion of Antioch (190–211 CE) to Caricus and Pontius (Eusebius, *Hist. eccl.* 5.19.1–4).

93 For the model of author, cf. above, n. 7. For a circumspect discussion of the authorship of 1 Peter cf. R. Feldmeier, *Der erste brief des Petrus* (THKNT 15.1; Leipzig: EVA, 2005, 23–27; ET: *The First Letter of Peter* (Waco, Tex.: Baylor University Press, 2008, 32–40. Many scholars today date 1 Peter to the era of the Flavian Emperors. Within this period, different preferences are held. Many do not yet see actions by the Roman authorities as the source of Christian suffering and opt for the years up to ca. 92; cf. M. E. Boring, *1 Peter* (ANTC; Nashville: Abingdon, 1999), 33–34; J. H. Elliott, *1 Peter*, 134–38 ("sometime in the period between 73 and 92 CE," 138); Feldmeier, *Brief des Petrus*, 26–27(ET: 39–40). In contrast, J. Molthagen has argued that 1 Peter is evidence for governmental *cognitiones de Christianis*; he thus allows for the whole period of Domitian's reign (81–96; see Molthagen, "Die Lage der Christen im römischen Reich nach dem 1. Petrusbrief: Zum Problem einer domitianischen Verfolgung," *Hist* 44 [1995]: 422–58). The period before Domitian ("somewhere between 65 and 80") is favored by Goppelt, *Petrusbrief*, 65; ET: *A Commentary on I Peter* (Grand Rapids: Eerdmans, 1993), 45.

94 Cf. J. H. Elliott, *Home for the Homeless*, 38: "In each of its three New Testament occurrences (John 7:35; Jas. 1:1; 1 Pet. 1:1) the term *diaspora* circumscribes geographically and socially, as it did in its technical LXX usage, a body of people living beyond the limits of Eretz Israel (Palestine). . . . in Jas. 1:1 and 1 Pet. 1:1, contrary to conventional Jewish usage, *diaspora* is used for the first time as a designation for *Christians* (most probably an admixture of both Jewish and Gentile converts) who, like their former Jewish counterparts, now also live beyond the borders of Palestine." Cf. idem, *1 Peter*, 314. For Diaspora as a strictly Jewish term, cf. W. C. van Unnik, "'Diaspora' and 'Church' in the First Centuries of Christian History [1959]," in *Sparsa Collecta: The Collected Essays of W. C. van Unnik*, Part 3, *Patristica – Gnostica – Liturgica* (NovTSup 31; Leiden: Brill, 1983), 95–105.

95 Cf. Klein, "*Ein vollkommenes Werk*," 189; also Feldmeier, *Christen als Fremde*, 20. Cf. further Berger, *Formgeschichte*, 366: "Frühe christliche Gemeinden verstehen sich wie jüdische als 'Diaspora,' und vom Judentum wird das Mittel genommen, die räumlich voneinander Getrennten an einer einheitlichen Verkündigung teilhaben zu lassen."

96 Thus Burchard, *Jakobusbrief*, 50: "Auf die Christenheit angewandt . . . ist Diaspora dann insofern Metapher, als die Christen nicht durch historische Vorgänge an ihren Ort gekommen waren. Sie besagt in erster Linie nicht, daß sie auch zerstreut sind (so z.B. Klein), sondern daß sie in der Welt getrennt von der Welt leben müssen."

97 Thus D. Sänger, "διασπορά," in *EWNT* 1 (1980), 750–52; ET: *EDNT* 1 (1990), 311–12.

98   Goppelt, *Petrusbrief*, 80 (ET: 67, quoted here). Cf. Feldmeier, *Christen als Fremde*, 103–4: 1 Peter "verweist die Glaubenden nicht an einen himmlischen Ort bzw an ein himmlisches Staatswesen, sondern an eine irdische Gemeinschaft." This specific note needs to be observed vis-à-vis references like Phil 3:20; Heb 11:13; 13:14; *Herm. Sim.* 1:1-6; *2 Clem.* 5:1, 5-6; 6:3, 8; cf. Philo, *Cher.* 120–21.

99   Cf. Feldmeier, *Christen als Fremde*, 39–74. He points mainly to texts from Qumran (CD 4.2-3, 5-6; 6.4-6; 1QM 1.2-3) and Philo (e.g., *Conf.* 75–82; *QG* 4:39).

100   With Burchard, *Jakobusbrief*, 50 (here stated with reference to James).

101   Thus with Michaels, *1 Peter*, 6; Feldmeier, *Christen als Fremde*, 20 with n. 89, contra Sänger, "διασπορά."

102   See juxtaposition of election (partly phrased in terms of the covenant with the Fathers, God's preserving actions, etc.) and otherness (exhortation to keep the commandments, keep away from idolatry, etc.) in EpJer 3, 4-6, 7; 2 Macc 1:2, 3-5; 1:25; 2:2-3, 7-8, 17-18; *2 Bar.* 78:3-4, 7; 84:1-9; 85:1-3; *4 Bar.* 6:18-20, 21-23; 7:25-29.

103   A classic discourse is *Let. Aris.* 139–71; cf. also *Tob.* 13:1-5. On the ancient Jewish Diaspora, cf. the rather upbeat view by E. Gruen, *Diaspora: Jews amidst Greeks and Romans* (Cambridge, Mass.: Harvard University Press, 2002); different constructs are discussed by I. Gafni, *Land, Center and Diaspora: Jewish Constructs in Late Antiquity* (JSPSup 21; Sheffield: Sheffield Academic Press, 1997).

104   Cf. T. W. Martin, *Metaphor and Composition in 1 Peter* (SBLDS 131; Atlanta: Scholars Press, 1992), 160–61 (Martin considers 1 Peter 1:13 a "body opening," prefixed to the first thematic unit: 70–72). Martin tries to subsume these clusters under the "controlling metaphor" of Diaspora: 144–61, but see the criticism by Prasad, *Foundations*, 66–67.

105   Thus Feldmeier, *Christen als Fremde*, 148.

106   I hope to be able to address this in a further publication.

107   Cf. Feldmeier, *Christen als Fremde*, esp. 19–20, 177–79. It is to my mind merely a matter of accentuation whether one speaks of "parts two and three" of the letter body or, as Feldmeier (*Brief des Petrus*, 12–16; ET: 17-23) now proposes, of 2:11–5:11 forming a second part, with 2:11–4:11 and 4:12–5:11 as subparts.

108   Cf., with different accents, T. W. Martin, *Metaphor*, 85–134; L. Thurén, *Theology in 1 Peter: Argument and the Origins of Christian Paraenesis* (JSNTSup 141; Sheffield: Sheffield Academic Press, 1995), 11–29; J. H. Elliott, *1 Peter*, 11; J. Dryden, *Theology and Ethics in 1 Peter: Paraenetic Strategies for Christian Character Formation* (WUNT 2.209; Tübingen: Mohr Siebeck, 2006), 15–53.

109   For election and the exhortation to keep the commandments, flee the idols, etc., see above, n. 102. For *brother* references, see above, 1.6; 2.1; 2.2; 2.6. Cohesion of the people of God has emerged as one main feature of Jewish Diaspora letters.

110 This is sensed by Dryden, *Theology and Ethics*, 64–65n35, 118–19; however, he makes too little of Jewish epistolary paraenesis.

111 Cf. references to tribulations and suffering in *2 Bar.* (78:5-6; 79:3; 80:6-7; 81:3; 82:1; etc.), to those witnessed by Jeremiah in *4 Bar.* 7:23-29, and to the "time of evil" in 2 Macc 1:5.

112 Cf. Niebuhr, "Jakobusbrief," 440–42, who argues that this is also a major concern in James.

113 Gruen, *Diaspora*, 232–39, insists that most Diaspora texts do not exhibit such negative colors of Diaspora. While he offers salutary criticism of the prevalent "vale of tears" view, a complete denial of exilic perceptions of the Diaspora is unwarranted in view of some of the evidence discussed above; see further Doering, "Jeremiah and the 'Diaspora Letters,'" esp. 52–53.

114 Cf. Goppelt, *Petrusbrief*, 79 (ET: 66, quoted here): "And the ingathering is . . . described . . . as a future gathering around the Lord, when faith becomes vision (I Pet. 1:8)."

115 Michaels, *1 Peter*: "*Babylon* at the end of the epistle is . . . the counterpart to *Diaspora* at the beginning" (311). The term *the co-elect* is best taken as a personification of a church; cf. 2 John 1 (ἐκλεκτῇ κυρίᾳ). Alternatively, one could take it as an ellipsis; but note that ἐκκλησία is unattested in 1 Peter, and the proposals to tacitly complete διασπορά (T. W. Martin, *Metaphor*, 145–46) or ἀδελφότης (J. H. Elliott, *1 Peter*, 882) remain speculative. Why an unnamed woman should be referred to is hardly explicable, *pace* J. K. Applegate, "The Co-Elect Woman of 1 Peter," *NTS* 38 (1992): 587–604.

116 Cf., e.g., Schelkle, *Petrusbriefe*, 11; J. N. D. Kelly, *The Epistles of Peter and of Jude* (BNTC 17; London: A. C. Black, 1969), 33–34 (both of them cautiously); H. Balz and W. Schrage, *Die "Katholischen" Briefe: Die Briefe des Jakobus, Petrus, Johannes und Judas* (NTD 10; Göttingen: Vandenhoeck & Ruprecht, 1993), 63–64; Feldmeier, *Brief des Petrus*, 27–28 (ET: 40–42; combining the exilic reference with a Roman origin of the letter); and see the following note. For Thiede's theory of a possibly earlier date, see idem, "Babylon, der andere Ort: Anmerkungen zu 1Petr 5,13 und Apg 12,17," in *Das Petrusbild in der neueren Forschung* (ed. C. P. Thiede; Wuppertal: Brockhaus, 1987), 221–29. Already Eusebius, *Hist. eccl.* 2.15.2 takes "Babylon" in 1 Pet 5:13 as figurative reference to Rome, where "they say" the letter was written.

117 Cf. E. Best, *I Peter* (NCB; London: Oliphants, 1971; repr., 1977), 59–63 (Petrine school), 64–65 (Rome); Goppelt, *Petrusbrief*, 64–70 (ET: 48–53); J. H. Elliott, "Peter, Silvanus and Mark in I Peter and Acts: Sociological-Exegetical Perspectives on a Petrine Group in Rome," in *Wort in der Zeit: Festschrift K. H. Rengstorf* (ed. W. Haubeck and M. Bachmann; Leiden: Brill, 1980), 250–67; idem, *1 Peter*, 127–30; P. J. Achtemeier, *1 Peter: A Commentary on First Peter* (Hermeneia; Minneapolis: Fortress, 1996), 41–42. Arguments for a more developed Petrine school come from Soards, "1 Peter, 2 Peter and Jude," *ANRW* 2.25.5, and O. B. Knoch, "Gab es eine Petrusschule in Rom? Überlegungen zu einer bedeutsamen Frage," *SNTSU* 16 (1991): 105–26. Prasad (*Foundations*, 36–46) dismisses their arguments and

prefers to speak of a Petrine group instead. D. G. Horrell ("The Product of
a Petrine Circle? A Reassessment of the Origin and Character of 1 Peter,"
JSNT 24.86 [2002]: 29–60) is critical of all hypotheses of Petrine circles,
etc., but is nevertheless in favor of Rome as place of origin (31n8).

118   C.-H. Hunzinger, "Babylon als Deckname für Rom und die Datierung des
1. Petrusbriefes," in *Gottes Wort und Gottes Land: FS H.-W. Hertzberg* (ed.
H. Graf Reventlow; Göttingen: Vandenhoeck & Ruprecht, 1965), 67–77.

119   But not the passage in *Sib. Or.* 4 dealing with Nero's flight (4:114–19,
137–39).

120   Cf. U. Sals, *Die Biographie der "Hure Babylon": Studien zur Intertextualität
der Babylon-Texte in der Bibel* (FAT 2.6; Tübingen: Mohr Siebeck, 2004),
76–144, esp. 143–44.

121   Hunzinger, "Babylon," 73–74.

122   Cf. also Brox, *Petrusbrief*, 41–43; T. W. Martin, *Metaphor*, 146n44; Herzer,
Petrus, 264–65.

123   Hunzinger, "Babylon," 77: "im syrisch-kleinasiatischen Raum."

124   N. T. Wright, in a discussion of Mark 13, has argued that the "prophecies
of Isaiah and Jeremiah concerning the downfall of Babylon" have come
to "designate Jerusalem herself as Babylon": *Jesus and the Victory of God*
(London: SPCK, 1996), 354. However, without deciding on the validity of
Wright's claim, there is nothing to suggest a link with Jerusalem in 1 Peter
5:13. For a critique of the view that the Babylon of Rev refers to Jerusalem,
cf. G. Biguzzi, "Is the Babylon of Revelation Rome or Jerusalem?" *Bib* 87
(2006): 371–86, who counts 1 Peter, without further discussion, among the
texts calling "Rome with the epithet of 'Babylon'" (385).

125   And, on account of the merely indirect reference to Jerusalem, also of
James.

126   Thus Lieu, "Grace," 174.

127   Dan 3:98 (4:1) θ´; 6:25 (26) θ´; LXX Dan 4:34 (37) c: εἰρήνη ὑμῖν πληθυνθείη.
MT Dan 3:31; MT 6:26: שְׁלָמְכוֹן יִשְׂגֵּא.

128   Cf. Schwiderski, *Handbuch*, 329–32.

129   Where this contact lacked, ancient speakers of Greek would at least have
registered a salutation thus far from the Greek one-word greeting χαίρειν
as "oriental."

130   Cf. further 2 Pet 1:2; Pol., *Phil.* inscr.; *Mart. Pol.* inscr.; *Mart. Sab.* inscr.
(see above, n. 91); cf. also *Ep. Apos.* 1 (12) (Ge'ez); *Const. Ap.* 1.1.

131   In two contributions on James, Matthias Konradt has recently argued that
the well-known traditio-historical commonalities between James and 1
Peter (cf. Jas 1:2-3 with 1 Pet 1:6-7; Jas 1:18, 21 with 1 Pet 1:22–2:2; Jas 4:6-
10 with 1 Pet 5:5c–9; Jas 5:20 with 1 Pet 4:8) point, different realizations
in detail notwithstanding, to a common tradition, the historical context of
which is probably the Antiochene community, which, after the incident at
Antioch, sided with the position of the Jerusalem community, against Paul.
This suggestion is supported both by traditio-historical relations between
the Gospel of Matthew, whose origin is almost certainly Syria and probably Antioch, and 1 Peter, and by contacts with Pauline tradition, mainly

in 1 Peter but also in James, which along the lines of this argument are due to Paul's connection with Antioch before the incident. While this is not decisive for the question of where 1 Peter was written, Konradt's proposal helpfully correlates the development of early Christian tradition with the profile of James vis-à-vis both 1 Peter and the Pauline tradition. Cf. Konradt, "Jakobusbrief als Brief des Jakobus" (and the English version in the present volume); idem, "Der Jakobusbrief im frühchristlichen Kontext."

132   Despite the paucity of literary data before the second half of the second century, M. Goulder's denial of Peter's stay and death in Rome, in "Did Peter Ever Go to Rome?" *SJT* 57 (2004): 377–96, is unconvincing.

Chapter 13

1   The Catholic Epistles Seminar at SNTS, which began in 2001, may signal a renaissance of interest in these books as a collection.

2   See appendix 1 below.

3   The traditional title is used to refer to the group of Johannine Epistles, although it is recognized that 2 and 3 John are Hellenistic letters. But this is not true of 1 John. Reference to the individual writings is by their traditional titles of 1, 2, and 3 John. The traditional term Catholic Epistles is also retained for the same reason, and references to individual writings follow the same precedent as 1, 2, and 3 John.

4   *Epistles of John*, 12.

5   The removal of the pages containing the CE looks more like an ideological action than an accident. Were the pages removed as an objection to the inclusion of the CE or to the placing of them immediately after the Gospels, before Acts and the Epistles of Paul? While the latter suggestion has much to commend it, the action removed the CE from the collection altogether. On the place of the CE in the Eastern and Western canons, see "Canonical orders," below.

6   When Augustine began his *De consensu evangelistarum*, he adopted the view that the canonical order represented the order of writing. In the course of examining the evidence in writing *Cons.*, he came to the conclusion that if Mark used Matthew, he must also have used Luke—hence adopting the view first known to us in Clement of Alexandria, who, according to Eusebius (*Hist. eccl.* 6.14.5–7) taught in his now lost *Hypotyposeis* that the Gospels with genealogies (Matt and Luke) antedated those without genealogies (Mark and John). We may assume that his implied order was Matthew, Luke, Mark, John.

7   The place where the CE once stood is evidenced by sixty-seven missing pages after the Gospels. We may well think that the removal of the CE from this priority of place in Codex D was an intentional ideological act.

8   Earlier references to an individual catholic epistle do not refer to this canonical group of Epistles, even when one of them is the subject of the reference. Rather, the reference is to an encyclical letter of some sort.

9   While 2 Peter and Jude might also reflect a Jewish Christian context, the evidence suggests that the Johannine Epistles mark a move from the Jewish

context reflected in the shaping of the Gospel to a Gentile context that dominated the shaping of the Johannine Epistles. If this is correct, the ideological distance between the Pauline corpus and the CE is not as great as the gap between the two missions of Galatians 2:7-10. Bridging the gap, we find the Epistles attributed to John, one of the three pillars of the circumcision mission and the Jerusalem church. Though interpreting a gospel shaped by Jewish tradition and context, these epistles were written in the Roman Empire, facing problems and issues emerging from values and judgments characteristic of the Gentile world. None of the three epistles reflects a Jewish problem.

10   See appendix 1 below.

11   Jude may stand at the close of the CE so that James is first and Jude last, epistles by the brothers of Jesus forming the bookends of this collection. That would explain why Eusebius, when he names James as the first of the seven CE, also names Jude, and no other from the collection. To name the first and the last was to identify this collection. This might have been necessary, given that reference to a catholic epistle was used in a nonspecific way in earlier sources.

12   See appendix 2 below.

13   The references by Clement and Apollonius to a catholic epistle suggest that canonical status is not the specific point of a catholic epistle. The term, rather, is an indication of the scope of the address. It may be right to see pretension to authority in the scope of a wide address. This is apparently the ground of Apollonius' objection to the catholic epistle of Themiso (Eusebius, *Hist. eccl.* 5.18).

14   In the Elder's local community, the substance of 1 John could be presented orally/personally. Only when 1 John became a form of communication at a distance did it require a more personal introduction. It is for this reason that, from the beginning, 1 John had an independent life, but 2 John was at first known only as an attachment to 1 John.

15   The use of χαίρειν here, but not in the opening greeting of 2 John 3, draws attention to the distinction between the Christian greeting used by the Elder (2 John 3) and the secular greeting indicated by the use of the traditional term for a greeting in a Hellenistic letter (χαίρειν). The implication is that such people do not receive the welcome afforded to "brothers," not even the common greeting given to people at large.

16   Strecher, *Johannine Letters*, 3.

17   This represents a change in view based on my detailed work on the Johannine Epistles for the Sacra pagina commentary, *1, 2, and 3 John*. When I wrote the *NTS* article on "The Opponents" in 1984, I was inclined to think that the Epistles were written by two or three different authors, none of whom was the Evangelist. I now think the Epistles are the work of one author, not the Evangelist, though perhaps one of the final editors of the Gospel. Some of the reasons for this position appear in what follows.

18   It acknowledges the hospitality Gaius has provided for the supporters of the Elder (3 John 5-8), so that he and they become coworkers with the truth.

By contrast, those who provide hospitality for the deceivers come to share in their evil works (2 John 10-11).

19 See Rom 16:3, 9, 21; 1 Cor 3:9; 2 Cor 1:24; 8:23; Phil 2:25; 4:3; Col 4:11; 1 Thess 3:2; Phlm 1, 24.

20 With the substitution of ἐκκλησία for συναγωγή, the description of this practice is close to what the Gospel of John says the Jews/Pharisees did to the believers in Jesus, casting them out of the synagogue (9:22, 34; 12:42; 16:2). In the time of Jesus, συναγωγή and ἐκκλησία were used without distinction. Compare the use in Revelation 1:4, 11, 20; 2:1, 7, 8, 9, 11, 12, etc., and see also James 2:2. By the end of the first century, the former was used of a Jewish gathering, while the latter became the distinctive term to describe the gathering of believers in Jesus. Perhaps because of his mission to the nations in the 50s, Paul used the term ἐκκλησία distinctively of the Christian community. In John, the use of συναγωγή clearly indicates the Jewish institution, while the use of ἐκκλησία in 3 John is a Christian reference. What the Jews once did to the followers of Jesus, Diotrephes now does to the brothers.

21 Because 1 John was accompanied by 2 John, Diotrephes refused to receive both 1 and 2 John.

22 It is used in Rev 1:4, 11, 20; 2:1, 7, 8, 9, 11, 12, etc.

23 Although 1 and 2 John speak of the antichrist as a single eschatological figure, that figure is immediately identified with "many antichrists [who] have appeared" (2:18) and with those who reject the christological confession of 4:2 (and there are many false prophets, 4:1), who manifest the spirit of the antichrist. In 2 John 7, the many deceivers who have gone out into the world and refuse to confess Jesus Christ coming in the flesh are identified with "the Deceiver and the Antichrist." The refusal of the opponents to confess Jesus Christ coming in the flesh appears to have led the Elder to reinterpret the myth of the antichrist. There is no known use of the term antichrist before 1 and 2 John. Yet the treatment there implies an existing expectation of a singular eschatological figure. See 1 John 2:18; the expectation of the one encounters the appearance of many antichrists. The spirits need to be tested because many false prophets have gone out into the world (4:1), and they are identified by the refusal to confess Jesus Christ having come in the flesh (4:2). What they manifest is not the Spirit of God, but the spirit of the antichrist (4:3).

24 In 1 John 2:18-25, it is evident that to confess that Jesus is the Christ is to confess the Son. Here, the Son implies the Father-Son relationship, because to have the Son is to have the Father. It is the equivalent of the confession that Jesus is Son of God (4:15; 5:5). The name Jesus signifies the human, while Christ and Son of God are understood as references to the divine. The combined name (Jesus Christ) proclaims the unity of the divine and the human. That Jesus Christ has come in the flesh affirms that the divine has not absorbed the human, leaving no trace of it. Rather, the divine and the human are united in the flesh of Jesus Christ. So perhaps a better translation is, the Christ is Jesus; the Son of God is Jesus; Jesus Christ has come in the flesh.

25   See the excursus in G. Strecker, *The Johannine Letters: A Commentary on 1, 2, and 3 John* (trans. Linda M. Maloney; Hermeneia; Minneapolis: Fortress, 1996), 236–41.

26   Thus Strecker, *Johannine Letters*, 232–36.

27   In 1 John 2:15-17, the Elder exhorts his readers, "Do not love the world or the things of the world." In this attack on worldly values, the Elder names "the lust [ἐπιθυμία] of the flesh, the lust of the eyes and the boastful arrogance in reliance on the riches of life [ἀλαζονεία]." This corruption of love is found in the one who does not love his brother, who walks in the darkness rather than the light, and the darkness has blinded his eyes (1 John 2:9-11). Such love for the world expresses the will to possess the world, as is brought out by the double use of ἐπιθυμία, which bears the sense of covetousness. See the use of ἐπιθυμία with the cognate verb ἐπιθυμήσεις in Rom 7:7, where the meaning is "covetousness" and "you will [not] covet." This kind of love for the world is possessive and grasping, quite the opposite of the love of God for the world, which is characterized by giving (John 3:16; 1 John 3:16-17; 4:9-10).

28   See Paul's treatment in 1 Corinthians 8–10.

29   1 John 5:16-17 envisages a "mortal sin." The Elder does not commend prayer for one who has committed such sin. Compare Mark 3:28-30, but see more pointedly Hebrews 6:4-6. What is the mortal sin ("There is a sin that leads to death . . . and there is a sin that does not lead to death") according to 1 John 5:16-17? Probably it is the apostasy of falling in with the opponents who have separated from the Johannine community of the Elder. For Hebrews 6:4-6, too, there is no repentance for those who commit apostasy.

30   C. H. Dodd, *The First Epistle of John and the Fourth Gospel* (Manchester: Manchester University Press, 1937).

31   C. H. Dodd, *The Johannine Epistles* (MNTC; London: Hodder & Stoughton, 1946), xlvii–lvi.

32   A. E. Brooke, *A Critical and Exegetical Commentary on the Johannine Epistles* (Edinburgh: T&T Clark, 1912).

33   W. F. Howard, "The Common Authorship of the Johannine Gospel and Epistles," *JTS* 48 (1947): 12–25.

34   W. G. Wilson, "An Examination of the Linguistic Evidence Adduced against the Unity of Authorship of the First Epistle of John and the Fourth Gospel," *JTS* 49 (1948): 147–56.

35   A. P. Salom, "Some Aspects of the Grammatical Style of 1 John," *JBL* 72 (1955): 96–102.

36   For a brief discussion of these arguments, see J. Painter, *John: Witness and Theologian* (London: SPCK, 1975), 103–8.

37   See Birger Gerhardsson's important book, *Memory and Manuscript: Oral Tradition and Written Transmission in Rabbinic Judaism and Early Christianity* (Uppsala: Gleerup, 1961).

38   See Alan Culpepper, *The Johannine School* (SBLDS 26; Missoula, Mont.: Scholars Press, 1975), 258–59, and the discussion below.

39   See appendix 3 below.

40   A. E. Brooke, *Critical and Exegetical Commentary*, i–x.

41   See appendix 4 below.

42   See appendix 5 below.

43   Strecker, *Johannine Letters*, 9n8.

44   On this subject, see the celebrated article by Rudolf Bultmann, "γινώσκω, κτλ.," *TDNT* 1:689–719, and my summary treatment of it in *John: Witness*, 71–100.

45   Both 1 John 5:13 and John 20:31 use some form of πιστεύειν: either εἰς or ἐν, ζωὴν αἰώνιον or ζωήν, ἔχετε or ἔχητε, τὸ ὄνομα or τῷ ὀνόματι. In the light of the reading of 1 John 5:13, I am inclined to suggest that John 20:31b (καὶ ἵνα πιστεύοντες ζωὴν ἔχητε ἐν τῷ ὀνόματι αὐτοῦ) was read to mean "that believing in his name you may have life." Indeed, this seems to be the meaning of this unusual construction. How does πιστεύοντες function in this clause? The present participle is not normally used with ἵνα. Yet this is normally translated "and that believing you may have life." Here, the ἵνα is understood both as if it were ὅτι and as the first part of a purpose/consequence clause completed by the subjunctive ἔχητε. Perhaps a better reading is, "and believing that you may have life." However, just as ἵνα is separated from ἔχητε by πιστεύοντες, so πιστεύοντες is separated from the object of belief (ἐν τῷ ὀνόματι αὐτοῦ). I understand this phrase as the equivalent of εἰς τὸ ὄνομα αὐτοῦ in 1 John 5:13. There is evidence that εἰς and were sometimes used without distinction in this period. In John, the use of εἰς in 1:18 (εἰς τὸν κόλπον τοῦ πατρὸς) is indistinguishable from the use of ἐν in 13:23 (ἐν τῷ κόλπῳ τοῦ Ἰησοῦ). Thus, there is good reason for understanding 20:31b as "and believing in his name you may have life."

46   Lieu, *Theology*, 168, 212.

47   Culpepper, *Johannine School*, 258–59.

48   Wilhelm Bousset, *Jüdischer-Christlicher Schulbetrieb in Alexandria und Rom; Untersuchungen zu Philo und Clemens von Alexandria, Justin und Irenäus* (Göttingen: Vandenhoeck & Ruprecht, 1915), 267.

49   See my *John: Witness*, 4; and my *The Quest for the Messiah: The History, Literature and Theology of the Johannine Community* (Edinburgh: T&T Clark, 1991), 33n3. The distinction between school and community is also important for R. E. Brown, *The Community of the Beloved Disciple* (New York: Paulist, 1979), 101–2; *The Epistles of John* (AB 30; Garden City, N.Y.: Doubleday, 1982), 96n221.

50   R. B. Edwards, *The Johannine Epistles* (Sheffield: Sheffield Academic Press, 1996), 77.

51   J. Lieu, "What Was from the Beginning," *NTS* 39 (1993): 458–77.

52   Rudolf Schnackenburg, *Die Johannesbriefe* (HTKNT 13.3; Freiburg: Herder, 1953); ET: *The Johannine Epistles* (New York: Crossroad, 1992), 5, 13–15, especially point 2 on p. 14.

53   See my *John: Witness*, 112, 116, 124, 125.

54   H.-J. Klauck, "Zur rhetorischen Analyse der Johannesbriefe," *ZNW* 81 (1990): 205–24.

55   Duane F. Watson, "1 John 2:12-14 as *Distributio, Conduplicatio, and Expolitio*: A Rhetorical Understanding," *JSNT* 35 (1989): 97–110, and "Amplification Techniques in 1 John: The Interaction of Rhetorical Style and Invention," *JSNT* 51 (1993): 99–123.

56   Duane F. Watson, "A Rhetorical Analysis of 2 John According to Greco-Roman Conventions," *NTS* 35 (1989): 104–30, and "A Rhetorical Analysis of 3 John: A Study in Epistolary Rhetoric," *CBQ* 51 (1989): 479–501.

57   Law, *Tests of Life*, 25.

58   Thus Judith Lieu, *The Theology of the Johannine Epistles* (Cambridge: Cambridge University Press, 1991), 5–6, 13–16, 66; Ruth B. Edwards, *The Johannine Epistles* (Sheffield: Sheffield Academic Press, 1996), 37–38, 57–60, 64–65.

59   Lieu, *Theology*, 22.

60   Edwards, *Johannine Epistles*, 67.

61   Brown, *Epistles*, 47–48.

62   Pheme Perkins, *The Johannine Epistles* (New Testament Message 21; Wilmington, Del.: Michael Glazier, 1979), xxi–xxiii.

63   Brown, *Epistles*, 48–49.

64   Lieu, *Theology*, 13 and n. 17.

65   Lieu, *Theology*, 13; Edwards, *Johannine Epistles*, 64–65.

66   Lieu, *Theology*, 5, 13, 25.

67   Lieu, *Theology*, 13 and n. 17, 16. The same point is made by Edwards in *Johannine Epistles*, 64–65.

68   *Epistles*, 48–49.

69   Lieu, *Theology*, 13.

70   Lieu, *Theology*, 14–16; Edwards, *Johannine Epistles*, 65.

71   Schnackenburg, *Johannine Epistles*, 3n3, 77.

72   Edwards, *Johannine Epistles*, 58.

73   Lieu, *Theology*, 13.

74   References to τὸ χρῖσμα (1 John 2:27) and σπέρμα αὐτοῦ (3:9) may well draw on the language of the opponents. Those in whom τὸ χρῖσμα abides have no need that anyone teach them, and those born of God, in whom his σπέρμα abides, are not able to sin.

75   The verb used in 1:2, 3 is ἀπαγγέλλομεν; and in 1:5, ἀναγγέλλομεν. The meaning is indistinguishable, so that 1:5 takes up 1:1-3 and gives content to that message (ἀγγελία). In my commentary on *1, 2, and 3 John* (119–41), I treat 1:1-5 as the prologue. I now see 1:5 as the introduction of the first test at the beginning of the first major section of the Gospel (1:5–2:27). 1 John 1:5 is a resumptive explanatory summary of the message alluded to in 1:1-4. The language used to enunciate the message is guided both by the opponents' claim to be in the light (2:9) and the Johannine opposition of light and darkness (1 John 1:5-7; 2:8-11; and cf. John 1:4-5; 3:19-21). In 1 John, it becomes clear that to be in the light is manifest in love for one another. So light is a symbol for love and darkness a symbol for hatred. In Johannine terms, *God is light* overlaps *God is love* (1 John 4:8), but also draws attention to the revelatory nature of that love.

76 See my *Quest* (2d ed.; Nashville: Abingdon, 1993), 245–49.

77 In John 13:34-35; 15:12, 17, Jesus grounds the command to love one another (ἀλλήλους) in his love for them.

78 The choice of "brothers" in 3:14 is determined by the context of 3:11-18. Although 3:11 begins by referring to the original message, that we love one another (ἀλλήλους), what follows introduces the contrary example, "not as Cain who was of the evil one and slew his brother." The contrast between those who love their brother and those who do not separates those who have passed from death to life from those who abide in death. The meaning of love is exemplified here by appeal to Jesus, who gave his life for us, and this becomes the ground for the obligation, "and we ought [ὀφείλομεν] to give (our) lives for the brothers." Thus 1 John also affirms that the obligation to love is grounded in the self-giving of Jesus, though elsewhere this is taken to be evidence of God's love, and the theist statement is more central and dominant in 1 John than in the Gospel. But see John 3:16; 17:21, 23, 26.

79 See the discussion in the "Excursus: Sin and Sinlessness" in my *1, 2, and 3 John*, 160–64.

80 See Krodel, *General Letters*.

81 For the use of this category by Eusebius, see A. C. McGiffert, trans., "The Church History of Eusebius," in *The Nicene and Post-Nicene Fathers* 2.1 (ed. Philip Schaff; Edinburgh, 1890), 55n1, on *Hist. eccl.* 3.25.1.

Chapter 14

*   This paper was given in the seminar "Katholische Briefe und Aposteltraditionen" at the General Meeting of the SNTS in Durham on August 7, 2002. The German original is published in W. Kraus and K.-W. Niebuhr, eds. (in cooperation with L. Doering), *Frühjudentum und Neues Testament im Horizont Biblischer Theologie: Mit einem Anhang zum Corpus Judaeo-Hellenisticum Novi Testamenti* (WUNT 162; Tübingen: Mohr Siebeck, 2003), 180–210. The English version was first translated by Grit Schorch then thoroughly revised by the author. I am grateful to James A. Kelhoffer (St. Louis/Munich) and Ann-Sophie Wich (Munich) for reading and correcting the final version. On the interpretation of Jude, cf. J. Frey, *Der Judasbrief und der zweite Petrusbrief* (THK 15.2; Leipzig: Evangelische Verlagsanstalt, 2010).

1   According to a title of an article, Jude is "the most neglected book in the New Testament": cf. D. Rowston, "The Most Neglected Book in the New Testament," *NTS* 21 (1975): 554–63; C. A. Albin, *Judasbrevet* (Stockholm: Natur och kultur, 1962), 714: "die vielleicht am wenigsten bekannte und benutzte von den Schriften des NT"; R. J. Bauckham, "The Letter of Jude: An Account of Research," *ANRW* 2.25.5:3791–3826, here 3792, speaks of a "scholarly contempt," "scholarly neglect," and "ignorance of Jude." Cf. at last M. Ahrens, "Der Judasbrief—eine neutestamentliche Marginalie," *Texte und Kontexte* 22.3 (1999): 39–49.

2   Jude, the brother of the Lord, occurs in the NT only in the lists of the sisters of Jesus in Mark 6:3 and Matthew 13:55, where Jude is mentioned as one of the brothers of Jesus at the third and fourth place. In 1 Corinthians

9:5, Paul mentions a missionary activity of the brothers of Jesus without referring to Jude. The next mention of Jude is Hegesippus' notice about the grandnephew of Jesus (and grandchildren of Jude), who are accused in front of the emperor Domitian (in Eusebius, *Hist. eccl.* 3.20.1–6).The message shows that the "relatives of Jesus" played an important role in the Palestinian church until the end of the first century (cf. Bauckham, *Jude and the Relatives*, 45–133).

3   A. Gerdmar, *Rethinking the Judaism-Hellenism Dichotomy: A Historiographical Case Study of Second Peter and Jude* (ConBNT 36; Stockholm: Almquist & Wiksell, 2001); cf. my critical review in *TLZ* 128 (2003): 393–95. There is no need to discuss the objections raised by Gerdmar against the use of these categories in NT scholarship. He points to the fact that in NT scholarship, the traces of Hellenism have often been used for "anti-Jewish" purposes, since, e.g., Hellenism was seen as a way to overcome Jewish particularity by the universalistic Greek spirit. This may be true, for example, in the Hegelian concept of Ferdinand Christian Baur. Yet to forgo those categories cannot be a solution, since they are suggested especially in the Jewish sources, as, e.g., in 1 and 2 Macc, and not least applied by Jewish scholars (cf. L. I. Levine, *Judaism and Hellenism in Antiquity: Conflict or Confluence?* (Seattle: University of Washington, 1998).

4   Gerdmar, *Rethinking*, 135–50.

5   Gerdmar, *Rethinking*, 185–99. In this context, another suggestion deserves some consideration: namely, that the phrase θείας κοινωνοὶ φύσεως (2 Pet 1:4), often regarded as problematic, has to be read as a statement about the "angelomorphic" transfiguration of the believers, and not as an expression from Hellenistic metaphysics (Gerdmar, *Rethinking*, 232–42).

6   Cf. Gerdmar, *Rethinking*, 63: "If the quality of the language is a valid criterion of Hellenism, Jude is more Hellenistic than 2 Peter with its more correct Greek syntax and style and clearer relation to the Septuagint."

7   Strictly opposed to Gerdmar's views are the results of Thomas J. Kraus' comprehensive and careful investigation of style and language in 2 Peter. Kraus shows, e.g., that the author of 2 Peter integrates expressions generated by himself and even neologisms with great skills. His neologisms do not point to a lack of linguistic faculty, but rather to a remarkable stylistic ability. 2 Peter represents the highest level of stylistic ability in the NT. Cf. Th. J. Kraus, *Sprache, Stil und historischer Ort des zweiten Petrusbriefes* (WUNT 2.136; Tübingen: Mohr Siebeck, 2001), 367.

8   The distinctive point of reference is the literary comparison of the *salutatio* in Jude and 1 and 2 Peter. From this, Gerdmar concludes, "Jude's greeting is easiest to explain as an expansion of 1 and 2 Peter's or of an established formula" (*Rethinking*, 113). Gerdmar ignores, however, the question of whether this *salutatio* resembles liturgical usage. The closest parallels can be found in the *salutatio* of the Epistle of Polycarp and in the preface of the *Martyrdom of Polycarp*, where the triad mercy-peace-love occurs in the same form, but without literary dependence on Jude. In view of this connection, the *salutatio* cannot serve as an argument for Jude's dependence on 2 Peter.

9   Gerdmar, *Rethinking*, 118–23. Cf. the better argument of Th. J. Kraus, *Sprache*, 371, 373.

10   Cf. T. Fornberg, *An Early Church in Pluralistic Society: A Study of 2 Peter* (ConBNT 9; Lund: Gleerup, 1977); J. H. Neyrey, "The Form and Background of the Polemic in 2 Peter" (Ph. Diss., Yale University, 1977), 119–67; with less clarity, Watson, *Invention*, 160–88. Cf. the comprehensive account by Bauckham, "2 Peter," *ANRW* 2.25.5:3714–15; see also the commentaries: R. J. Bauckham, *Jude, 2 Peter* (WBC 50; Waco, Tex.: Word Books, 1983), 141; H. Frankemölle, *1. Petrusbrief. 2. Petrusbrief. Judasbrief* (2d ed., 1990), 82–84; H. Paulsen, *Der Zweite Petrusbrief und der Judasbrief* (KEK 17.2; Göttingen: Vandenhoeck & Ruprecht, 1992), 97–100; J. H. Neyrey, *2 Peter, Jude* (AB 37C; New York: Doubleday, 1993), 186–227. See also Th. J. Kraus, *Sprache*, 368–76, with additional arguments.

11   Similarly unconvincing is the thesis that both texts originate from the same Palestinian Jewish Christian milieu and are written against the same group of opponents. Based on the occurrence of "Balaam" (Jude 11; 2 Pet 2:15; cf. Rev 2:14), Gerdmar tries to connect those texts to the adversaries of the author in Asia Minor. But this argument is inconsistent with the view of Jude originating in Palestine (cf. Gerdmar, *Rethinking*, 278–97). Moreover, the topical character of the Balaam motif is disregarded.

12   Cf. Bauckham, *Jude, 2 Peter*, 7: "Despite his competence in Greek, the author's real intellectual background is in the literature of Palestinian Judaism."

13   Thus, e.g., J. D. Charles, *Literary Strategy in the Epistle of Jude* (Scranton: University of Scranton, 1993).

14   Bauckham, *Jude, 2 Peter*; idem, "Letter of Jude," *ANRW* 2.25.5; idem, *Jude and the Relatives*.

15   Bauckham, *Jude, 2 Peter*, 4, where he accepts the thesis by E. E. Ellis, *Prophecy and Hermeneutic* (WUNT 18; Tübingen: Mohr Siebeck, 1978), 221–26. Bauckham concedes the denotation *midrash* in a very general sense as a method of exegesis that relates biblical texts to the present-day experience of the readers. He also points to the thematic Pesharim from the Qumran community. But this is a rather far-fetched analogy.

16   Bauckham, *Jude, 2 Peter*, 7 and 87f., supposes to recognize this phenomenon in vv. 12 and 13. Here, Proverbs 25:14 or Isaiah 57:20 is possibly alluded to, but the meaning that the author seemingly takes from the scriptural allusions cannot be found in the LXX, only in the Hebrew text. However, the allusions to the Bible are not firmly assured. Therefore, the differences from the text of the LXX cannot be proof of the letter's adherence to the Hebrew text. The relation to *1 En.* 67:5-7 is recommended by C. D. Osburn, "1 Enoch 80:2-8 (67:2-5) and Jude 12-13," *CBQ* 47 (1985): 296–303.

17   Bauckham, *Jude, 2 Peter*, 9–11, concluding, "Jude's apocalyptic is not at all self-conscious. It is the world-view within which he naturally thinks and which he takes it for granted his readers accept" (11).

18   Bauckham, *Jude, 2 Peter*, 11–13.

19   Bauckham, *Jude, 2 Peter*, 13.

20 Bauckham, *Jude, 2 Peter*, 14. Bauckham concedes that Jude might have been alive until the year 90, so this is the latest possible date for the epistle. An even earlier dating of the script is postulated by J. A. T. Robinson, *Redating the New Testament* (London: SCM Press, 1976), 197 (before 62 CE); and E. E. Ellis, *Prophecy*, 226–36; idem, *The Making of the New Testament Documents* (BIS 39; Leiden: Brill, 1999), 292 (between 55 and 65 CE).

21 Bauckham, *Jude, 2 Peter*, 14.

22 Bauckham, "Letter of Jude," *ANRW* 2.25.5:3819. Later, Bauckham himself objects that a work within which content and form are so closely intertwined forbids stating the thesis of a secretary as the author (*Jude and the Relatives*, 177).

23 Charles, *Literary Strategy*; idem, "'Those' and 'These': The Use of the Old Testament in the Epistle of Jude," *JSNT* 38 (1990): 109–24; idem, "Jude's Use of Pseudepigraphic Source-Material as Part of a Literary Strategy," *NTS* 37 (1991): 130–45; idem, "Literary Artifice in the Epistle of Jude," *ZNW* 82 (1991): 106–24.

24 Charles, *Literary Strategy*, 63; cf. idem, "Jude's Use," 131n.4.

25 Cf. the excursus "Appendix: The Catholic Epistles and the Question of Pseudonymity" in Charles, *Literary Strategy*, 81–90, which interestingly does not refer to Jude specifically but to the CE generally. Charles points to the lack of external evidence for a pseudonymous redaction of early Christian texts (89), and, finally, to the "ethical question" (90). Furthermore, he states that in the case of pseudepigraphy, the script's claim of truth would be misleading, and therefore assigning canonicity and divine authority to such a text would be impossible: "NT injunctions to think, speak, and act the truth would render the practice of pseudonymity, at best, inconsistent with the standards of the OT, Jesus, and the apostles" (90). These overall judgments fall far short of the level of study that characterizes Charles' linguistic observations. Moreover, the argument in Charles' appendices is not organically compounded into the flow of the ruling argument. It rather seems to be a fig leaf obscuring the consequences of his findings in a seemingly orthodox manner, which casts a shadow on the author's scholarship.

26 Charles, *Literary Strategy*, 37.

27 Charles, *Literary Strategy*, 20ff.; cf. also idem, "Literary Artifice."

28 Charles, *Literary Strategy*, 162–63, with reference to J. P. Oleson, "An Echo of Hesiod's *Theogony* vv. 190-2 in Jude 13," *NTS* 25 (1979): 492–503.

29 Charles, *Literary Strategy*, 71–72.

30 Cf. Hengel, *Judentum und Hellenismus*, ET: *Judaism and Hellenism* (2 vols.; London: SCM Press, 1974); idem, *Juden, Griechen und Barbaren* (SBS 76; Stuttgart: Katholisches Bibelwerk, 1976), ET: *Jews, Greeks and Barbarians* (Philadelphia: Fortress, 1980); idem, "Jerusalem als jüdische und hellenistische Stadt," in *Judaica, Hellenistica und Christiana: Kleine Schriften 2* (WUNT 109; Tübingen: Mohr Siebeck, 1999), 115–56; idem and Ch. Markschies, *The Hellenization of Judaea in the First Century after Christ* (London: SCM Press, 1989).

31   Cf. M. Hengel, "Qumran und der Hellenismus," in *Judaica et Hellenistica: Kleine Schriften I* (WUNT 90; Tübingen: Mohr Siebeck, 1996), 258–94.

32   R. Heiligenthal, *Zwischen Henoch und Paulus: Studien zum theologiegeschichtlichen Ort des Judasbriefes* (TANZ 6; Tübingen: Francke, 1992).

33   Heiligenthal, *Zwischen Henoch und Paulus*, 63: "christianisierter Teil der Henochüberlieferung"; cf. on the whole 62–94.

34   Heiligenthal, *Zwischen Henoch und Paulus*, 158: "ein judenchristlicher Vertreter antiochenischer Theologie."

35   Heiligenthal, *Zwischen Henoch und Paulus*, 157.

36   Here, Heiligenthal (*Zwischen Henoch und Paulus*, 142–44) points to the euhemeristic explanation of myth that had entered Judaism and influenced, e.g., Philo; see *Conf.* 154. C. Bigg, *A Critical and Exegetical Commentary on the Epistles of St. Peter and Jude* (ICC 41; Edinburgh: T&T Clark, 1922), 240, had already assumed the skeptical background of the adversaries.

37   Heiligenthal, *Zwischen Henoch und Paulus*, 157, points to a mirror-inverted relationship: "Kol polemisiert gegen eine Anschauung wie sie in Jud vertreten ist; Jud gegen eine Theologie, die im Kol vertreten ist."

38   Several references cited by Heiligenthal (*Zwischen Henoch und Paulus*, 64–65), however, are too general to be convincing. Thus, the mention of the πίστις in Jude 3 cannot be explained from the perspective of the Enochic tradition. Also, the link between belief and spirit in Jude 20 and the phrase about blasphemy, or the "sins of the tongue," are not peculiarities of the Enoch tradition.

39   At least, the idea of a "Lehrhaus des Henoch" (Heiligenthal, *Zwischen Henoch und Paulus*, 63; cf. also 94) cannot be verified in the first century CE; cf. on this E. Rau, "Kosmologie, Eschatologie und die Lehrautorität Henochs" (Diss. theol., Hamburg University, 1974), 455–56. On the reception of the Enoch tradition in ancient Judaism and early Christianity, cf. the overview in G. W. E. Nickelsburg, *1 Enoch 1* (Hermeneia; Minneapolis: Fortress, 2001), 71–108; comprehensively, J. C. VanderKam, "1 Enoch, Enochic Motifs, and Enoch in Early Christian Literature," in *The Jewish Apocalyptic Heritage in Early Christianity* (ed. G. W. E. Nickelsburg and W. Adler; CRINT 2.4; Assen: van Gorcum, 1996), 33–101.

40   See pp. 317–18 below.

41   The problem of the idea of a certain group of Diaspora Pharisees is discussed in M. Hengel and R. Deines, *The Pre-Christian Paul* (London: SCM Press, 1991), 29–34. There are no clear sources for Pharisees living permanently in the Diaspora, let alone for Pharisaic schools outside of Palestine before 70 CE. For the time after 70 CE, Matthew 23:15 only demonstrates that scribes traveled to the Diaspora, where they did not live permanently. And from an earlier period, we know of Pharisees who had fled from Alexander Jannai and who tried to return to Eretz Israel as quickly as possible because of the dangers of impurity outside. From its beginnings, the Pharisaic movement was strongly linked with the land of Israel, and there is no reason to assume that it developed a firm institutional basis in the Diaspora.

42   Cf., similarly, K. Berger, *Theologiegeschichte* (1994), where the pan-Antiochenism leads itself ad absurdum.

43   On the problem of definition, see H. Lemke, *Judenchristentum zwischen Ausgrenzung und Integration: Zur Geschichte eines exegetischen Begriffes* (Hamburger Theologische Studien 25; Münster: Lit, 2001), 14–15. See also C. Colpe, "Das deutsche Wort 'Judenchristen' und ihm entsprechende historische Sachverhalte," in *Das Siegel der Propheten* (ed. C. Colpe; Arbeiten zur Neutestamentlichen Zeitgeschichte 3; Berlin: Institut Kirche und Judentum, 1990), 38–58; J. Carleton Paget, "Jewish Christianity," in *The Early Roman Period* (ed. W. Horbury, W. D. Davies, and J. Sturdy; vol. 3 of *The Cambridge History of Judaism*; Cambridge: Cambridge University Press, 1999), 731–75 (here 733–42, with reference to further bibliographical information).

44   Cf. the influential work of J. Daniélou, *Théologie du Judéo-christianisme* (Paris: Desclée, 1958), ET: *The Theology of Jewish Christianity* (London: Darton, Longman & Todd, 1964).

45   Cf. the collection of the most important testimonies in A. F. J. Klijn and G. J. Reinink, *Patristic Evidence for Jewish-Christian Sects* (NovTSup 36; Leiden: Brill, 1973).

46   For early examples, see Gal 2:12; Acts 10:45; 11:2: "οἱ ἐκ (τῆς) περιτομῆς"; later, Justin Martyr, *Dial.* 47.3; Origen, *Comm. Matt.* 16.12 and *Cels.* 2.1; Jerome, *Epist.*, 112.13: "credentes Iudaei"; Augustine, *Faust.* 19.17: "ex circumcisione credentibus."

47   See Ign. *Magn.* 8:1; 9:1 (Sabbath); 10:3; Ign. *Phld.* 6:1 (circumcision); Justin Martyr, *Dial.* 47.1.

48   Cf. generally Carleton Paget, "Jewish Christianity," 734–39.

49   As Carleton Paget ("Jewish Christianity," 739–41) suggests.

50   Cf. the conservative German commentary by G. Wohlenberg, *Der erste und zweite Petrusbrief und der Judasbrief* (KNT 15; Leipzig, 1915), 279, which starts with the presumption that the mission of Jude was an inter-Israelite phenomenon at the beginning. Thus, the reader of Jude must have been Jewish Christian too.

51   According to Wohlenberg (*Der erste und zweite Petrusbrief*, 279), the denomination of the addressees is after all so general that there seems to be no relation to their background, either in Jewish or in pagan Christianity.

52   *Barnabas* is an example of the difficulty that is at stake here. His world of thought stems from Judaism in several respects, but the position that he adopts toward the Jewish law is characterized by a strict rejection. This means that "its claim to being a Jewish Christian text in any meaningful way is surely lost" (Carleton Paget, "Jewish Christianity," 739). Cf. on *Barn.* also J. Carleton Paget, *The Epistle of Barnabas: Outlook and Background* (WUNT 2.64; Tübingen: Mohr Siebeck, 1994); R. Hvalvik, *The Struggle for Scripture and Covenant* (WUNT 2.82; Tübingen: Mohr Siebeck, 1996); J. N. Rhodes, *The Epistle of Barnabas and the Deuteronomic Tradition* (WUNT 2.188; Tübingen: Mohr Siebeck, 2004).

53   Cf. J. Frey, "Heiden–Griechen–Gotteskinder: Zu Gestalt und Funktion

der Rede von den Heiden im 4. Evangelium," in *Die Heiden: Juden, Christen und das Problem des Fremden* (ed. R. Feldmeier and U. Heckel; WUNT 70; Tübingen: Mohr Siebeck, 1994), 228–68, here 233. Cf. idem also on the warning against the εἴδωλα in 1 John 5:21

54 Thus the interpretation in 2 Peter 2:10, 18 adopting vv. 8, 10, and 18. Such an interpretation was suggested by H. Windisch, *Die katholischen Briefe* (1930), 41; W. Schrage, in Balz and idem, *Die "Katholischen" Briefe* (NTD 10; Göttingen: Vandenhoeck & Ruprecht, 1973), 232, among others; see also Paulsen, *Zweite Petrusbrief*, 65, who adds, however, that the topic of such a polemic, which provides difficulties for any clear identification, should not be underestimated. Even A. Vögtle, *Der Judasbrief. Der zweite Petrusbrief* (EKK 22; Solothurn: Benziger, 1994), 48–49, does not commit himself to the sexual interpretation, although he usually stresses that kind of reproach quite strongly.

55 Accordingly, the considerations in G. Sellin, "Die Häretiker des Judasbriefes," *ZNW* 77 (1986): 206–25, here 215–16; see on Jude 6f. also A. F. J. Klijn, "Jude 5 to 7," in *The New Testament Age: Essays in Honor of Bo Reicke* 1 (ed. W. C. Weinrich; Macon, Ga.: Mercer, 1984), 237–44.

56 A superfluous and hardly convincing construction is presented by Windisch, *Die katholischen Briefe*, 42, who states, "daß der Libertinismus den eignen Gelüsten der (dämonischen) Engel entgegenkommen wollte." Cf. the critique of Sellin, "Häretiker," 216.

57 Thus Vögtle, *Judasbrief*, 67.

58 See this metaphor also in 1 Tim 1:19; *Barn.* 3:6.

59 Cf. similar series of examples or paradigms in Sir 16:7-10; CD 2.17–3.12; 3 Macc 2:4-7; *T. Naph.* 3:4-5; *m. Sanh.* 10:3.

60 The discussions of whether or not the book of Enoch was considered as canonical by the author of Jude are based on anachronistic presumptions. In fact, the book of Enoch (or at least essential parts of it) is used here as a true prophecy and as a work to be quoted as the climax of scriptural examples. The number of manuscripts of the Enochic tradition from the library of Qumran demonstrates that this tradition was quite popular in certain Jewish circles. This could have been adopted by early Christians, especially in view of the mention of the Son of Man in the Similitudes of Enoch and the description of the judgment and the heavenly world. Cf. VanderKam, "1 Enoch." The argument stated by Charles in *Literary Strategy*, 156–59, that the work at most might have the character of a secondary inspiration, is too much determined by dogmatic reasoning. His thesis that the author would have utilized the book of Enoch primarily because of the importance that his addressees or even the opposed adversaries ascribed to it (so idem, "Jude's Use," 144; idem, "'Those' and 'These,'" 119n4) is not convincing. The author of Jude himself adopts arguments and concepts that were taken over from Enoch.

61 This word is missing from the Ethiopian manuscripts, and also from the Greek text of Enoch preserved in the Codex Panopolitanus (6C CE). In *1 En.* 1:9, it is God who comes for the judgment (cf. *1 En.* 1:1, 8); as in

passages in the Old Testament such as Jeremiah 25:30-31 and Isaiah 66:15-16, the name of God is cited (i.e., in the LXX, κύριος). In *1 En.* 52:5-9, the passage *1 En.* 1:3-7 is already related to the coming of the anointed and the chosen Messiah. Cf. here Nickelsburg, *1 Enoch 1*, 86, 149.

62   Cf. in the background the earlier Christian traditions referring to the coming of the κύριος "with all his saints" (1 Thess 3:13) or of the Son "with the holy angels" (Mark 8:38).

63   According to B. Dehandschutter, "Pseudo-Cyprian, Jude and Enoch: Some Notes on 1 Enoch 1:9," in *Tradition and Re-Interpretation in Jewish and Early Christian Literature* (ed. J. W. van Henten et al.; StPB 36; Leiden: Brill, 1986), 114–20, here 120.

64   Bauckham, in *Jude, 2 Peter*, 94–96, is aware of the weakness of the argument when conceding the additional knowledge of the Greek text (96). The single reason for supposing a translation from a Semitic source remains the aorist ἦλθεν, in which Bauckham wants to see a rendering of an Aramaic prophetical perfect. But the Aramaic text of the particular passage is unknown. Therefore, the difficulty could be solved by the assumption that the aorist was already in a Greek *Vorlage* of Jude. It is impossible to prove that the author himself translated from an Aramaic original, or that he possessed the linguistic capacity to do so.

65   Cf. here Rom 8:38; Col 1:16; 2:15; Eph 1:21; 3:10; 6:12. Cf. LXX Deut 32:8.

66   Cf. the basic statement in LXX Deut 32:8, where the angels of God are enthroned (ἀγγέλων θεοῦ; v. l. υἱῶν θεοῦ) as rulers over the nations. The original text seems to have spoken about the Sons of God or godly beings (בני אל); the version (בני אלוהים) in 4QDeut^j is a strong support of this assumption. In the Masoretic Text, this was changed to בני ישראל, probably for theological reasons (cf. E. Tov, *Der Text der Hebräischen Bibel* [Stuttgart: Kohlhammer, 1997], 223), whereas the LXX tradition kept the reference to angelic beings.

67   J. T. Milik, *The Books of Enoch: Aramaic Fragments of Qumran Cave 4* (Oxford: Clarendon, 1976), 175; cf. Nickelsburg, *1 Enoch 1*, 218.

68   Presumably, this element is dropped from the Ethiopian text; cf. Nickelsburg, *1 Enoch 1*, 251.

69   Cf. also *1 En.* 88:1; *Jub.* 5:6.

70   Cf. Bauckham, *Jude, 2 Peter*, 53. The principles of interpretation of the *lex talionis* are explicitly applied in the rewriting of the exodus and the plagues in the book of Wisdom; the punishment corresponds to the sin committed before, and the punishment of the idolatrous corresponds the blessing of Israel. Cf. Wis 11:5.

71   Cf. the excursus in Bauckham, *Jude, 2 Peter*, 65–76, and the more comprehensive presentation in idem, *Jude and the Relatives*, 235–80. Cf. also K. Berger, "Der Streit des guten und bösen Engels um die Seele. Beobachtungen zu 4QAmr^b und Judas 9," *JSS* 4 (1973): 1–18; his views are adopted in Heiligenthal, *Zwischen Henoch und Paulus*, 28–31.

72   See Bauckham, *Jude and the Relatives*, 244–45.

73 "We need no longer be mesmerized by the authority of the Alexandrian Fathers in identifying Jude's source" (Bauckham, *Jude and the Relatives*, 245).

74 According to Bauckham, *Jude and the Relatives*, 279–80.

75 Cf. J. F. Priest, "Moses, Testament of," *ABD* 4:920–22, here 920.

76 Cf. D. H. Wallace, "The Semitic Origin of the Assumption of Moses," *TZ* (1955): 321–28.

77 Origen, *Comm. Matt.* 10.17.

78 The vocabulary consists of 227 different words, compared with a total length of 457 words. According to O. Knoch (*Der erste und zweite Petrusbrief. Der Judasbrief* [RNT; Regensburg: Pustet, 1990], 153), this is the highest percentage of different words in the NT. In comparison, Paul's letter to Philemon uses only 141 different words, in relation to the total amount of 335 words; 1–3 John have a treasury of 302 words, in relation to the total amount of 2,601 words. Cf. R. Morgenthaler, *Statistik des neutestamentlichen Wortschatzes* (Zürich: Gotthelf, 1958), 164.

79 Fourteen words occur in the NT only in Jude (ἀποδιορίζειν, ἄπταιστος, γογγυστής δεῖγμα, ἐπαγωνίζεσθαι, ἐπαφρίζειν, μεμψίμοιρος παρεισδύνειν, σπιλάς, φθινοπωρινός, φυσικῶς, ἐπορνεύειν, πλανήτης, ὑπέχειν). Of these, only four (ἄπταιστος, ἐκπορνεύειν, πλανήτης, ὑπέχειν) are to be found in the LXX, i.e., the others are taken from outside the biblical tradition. Three further words (ἐμπαίκτης, συνευωχεῖσθαι, and ὑπέρογκος) cannot be counted as hapax legomena only because they are also adopted by the later 2 Peter, which uses Jude. Thus, they are also "new" words in Jude. Cf. Bauckham, *Jude, 2 Peter*, 6. Moreover, phraseological and syntactical Semitisms are relatively seldom in Jude, if one considers the strong influence of biblical tradition.

80 E. Fuchs and P. Reymond, *La deuxième épitre de Saint Pierre. L'Épitre de Saint Jude* (2d ed.; CNT 13b; Geneva: Labor et Fides, 1988), 138, count twenty-two words that occur only four times in the entire NT.

81 See Vögtle, *Judasbrief*, 9.

82 Oleson, "Echo."

83 Charles, *Literary Strategy*, 162–63. In my view, this is too uncritical, but gives additional evidence of the incoherence of the views held by Charles regarding the authorship and background of Jude.

84 Cf. Nickelsburg, *1 Enoch 1*, 165–66; idem, "Apocalyptic and Myth in 1 Enoch 6-11," *JBL* 96 (1977): 383–405; C. A. Newsom, "The Development of 1 Enoch 6-19: Cosmology and Judgment," *CBQ* 42 (1980): 310–29.

85 See, e.g., F. Dexinger, "Jüdisch-christliche Nachgeschichte von Genesis 6,1-4," in *Zur Aktualität des alten Testaments* (ed. S. Kreuzer and K. Lüthi; Frankfurt a. M.: Lang, 1992), 155–75, here 160f.; but cf. T. F. Glasson, *Greek Influence in Jewish Eschatology* (London: SPCK, 1961), 62–63.

86 Cf. the criticism by Bauckham, *Jude and the Relatives*, 149.

87 Thus Heiligenthal, *Zwischen Henoch und Paulus*, 56

88 G. Sellin, *Der Streit um die Auferstehung* (FRLANT 138; Göttingen: Vandenhoeck & Ruprecht, 1985), 185 with n. 266, points to the fact that in

Philo, ψυχικός has an entirely positive connotation. In 4 Macc 1:32, the term is not opposed to πνεῦμα.

89   U. Wilckens, *Weisheit und Torheit* (BHT 26; Tübingen: Mohr, 1959), 89ff.; M. Winter, *Pneumatiker und Psychiker in Korinth* (Marburger Theologische Studien 12; Marburg: Elwert, 1975), 230–31; Sellin, *Streit*, 183. The crucial point is that here, ψυχή does not have an entirely positive denotation, as would be expected from the Jewish tradition; cf. R. Jewett, *Paul's Anthropological Terms* (AGJU 10; Leiden: Brill, 1971), 340–54.

90   According to R. Reitzenstein, *Die hellenistischen Mysterienreligionen* (3d ed.; Leipzig: Teubner, 1927), 70–71; R. Bultmann, *Theologie des Neuen Testaments* (9th ed.; Tübingen: Mohr Siebeck, 1984), 177–78; and Wilckens, *Weisheit*, 89–90. The view is still alive in W. Schrage, *Der erste Brief an die Korinther* (vol. 1; EKK 6.1; Zürich: Benzinger, 1991), 263.

91   Cf. M. Hengel, "Die Ursprünge der Gnosis und das Urchristentum," in *Evangelium Schriftauslegung Kirche* (ed. J. Ådna, S. J. Hafemann, and O. Hofius; Göttingen: Vandenhoeck & Ruprecht, 1997), 190–223; C. Markschies, "Gnosis/Gnostizismus II/1," *RGG4* 3:1045–49; cf. the critical evaluation of Bultmann's view of a "Gnostic myth of the redeemer" in J. Frey, *Die johanneische Eschatologie I: Ihre Probleme im Spiegel der Forschung seit Reimarus* (WUNT 96; Tübingen: Mohr Siebeck, 1997), 133–40.

92   Philo, *Leg.* 1:32; in *Leg.* 3:247, ψυχή is related to the symbol of the cursed earth (Gen 3:17). Regarding the opposition of νοῦς over against ψυχή or over against the divine λόγος, see also *Somn.* 1:118–19 (with an explicitly negative use of ψυχή). Cf. E. Brandenburger, *Fleisch und Geist: Paulus und die dualistische Weisheit* (WMANT 29; Neukirchen-Vluyn: Neukirchener, 1968), 148–49; Sellin, *Streit*, 186–88.

93   Merklein, *Der erste Brief an die Korinther*, 123, points out that it is of minor importance where the opposition was actually formulated for the first time, either still within the Hellenistic Jewish wisdom speculation or only in its early Christian reception (but in any case before Paul).

94   Thus Sellin, *Streit*, 188n272.

95   On the structure of the parties or groups within the Corinthian community, cf. the most plausible explanation in Merklein, *Der erste Brief an die Korinther*, 134–52.

96   See Merklein, *Der erste Brief an die Korinther*, 251. Here, Paul replaces the expression ψυχικοί, which was probably used in a pejorative sense, with the expression σαρκικοί, which is more theologically specified. The Pauline idea of the σάρξ—as an orientation of life or even sphere of power that is opposed to God and connected with sin (cf. Gal 5:17; Rom 8:4ff.) cannot be derived from the theology of Hellenistic Judaism (as stated by Brandenburger, *Fleisch und Geist*), but is based on presumptions of the Palestinian wisdom tradition; cf. J. Frey, "Die paulinische Antithese von 'Fleisch' und 'Geist' und die palästinisch-jüdische Weisheitstradition," *ZNW* 90 (1999): 45–77; idem, "The Notion of 'Flesh' in 4QInstruction and the Background of Pauline Usage," in *Sapiential, Poetical and Liturgical Text:. Proceedings of*

the Third Meeting of the IOQS, Oslo, 1998 (ed. D. Falk, F. García Martínez, and E. Schuller; STDJ 35; Leiden: Brill, 2000), 197–226.

97 See Sellin, *Streit*, 188n272.

98 On the polemics, cf. H. Balz, "Der Brief des Jakobus," in Balz and Schrage, *Die "Katholischen" Briefe*, 1–59, here 42; and Hengel ("Jakobusbrief," 511–48), who considers the Epistle of James as an authentic polemical letter of James against Paul, and not as an answer to post-Pauline developments.

99 As suggested by B. Pearson, *The Pneumatikos-Psychikos Terminology in 1 Corinthians: A Study in the Theology of the Corinthian Opponents of Paul in Its Relation to Gnosticism* (SBLDS 12; Missoula, Mont.: Scholars Press, 1973), 14.

100 See W. Popkes, *Der Jakobusbrief* (THKNT 14; Leipzig: Evangelische Verlagsanstalt, 2001), 244, 250.

101 Cf. also Sellin, *Streit*, 188n272.

102 A direct relation to 1 Corinthians 2:14 is assumed by Sellin, *Streit*, 187n272; likewise Pearson, *Pneumatikos-Psychikos*, 13–14; Hoppe, *Der theologische Hintergrund*, 61.

103 Cf. Hengel, "Jakobusbrief." Even if one does not accept the assumption of James' authenticity, some of the observations regarding the polemical tendency of James are striking. The anti-Pauline direction of impact is challenged by Hahn and Müller, "Jakobusbrief," 41.

104 Cf. Popkes, *Jakobusbrief*, 37, assuming the reaction against a group of opponents using Pauline arguments.

105 Cf. Sellin, "Häretiker," 212, and F. Hahn, "Randbemerkungen zum Judasbrief," in *Studien zum Neuen Testament 2* (ed. F. Hahn, J. Frey, and J. Schlegel; WUNT 192; Tübingen: Mohr Siebeck, 2006), 642–52, here 652.

106 Thus Hahn, "Randbemerkungen," 650n36, and Rowston, "Most Neglected Book," 560–61.

107 Cf. Clement of Alexandria, *Adumbr. in Ep. Jud.* See, e.g., T. Zahn, *Einleitung in das Neue Testament* (2 vols.; 2d ed.; Leipzig: Deichert, 1900), 2:93; G. Wohlenberg, *Der erste und zweite Petrusbrief*, 279.

108 Cf. the relatively strange argument by H. Köster, "ΓΝΩΜΑΙ ΔΙΑΦΟΡΑΙ," *ZTK* 65 (1968): 160–203 (181).

109 The argument of Ellis in *Prophecy*, 127–28, that ἀδελφός does not stand for the real brother but for a missionary associate of James, is too artificial and cannot be based on the text.

110 The phrase goes eventually back to the Jewish honorary title "servant of God." The Christian use of it implies the idea of dedication or belonging to the Lord, Jesus Christ. Here, first of all, the phrase can indicate the Christian in general (1 Cor 7:22-23; Eph 6:6), but also those who provide a certain service (Col 4:12; 2 Tim 2:24). This second meaning has to be presumed here.

111 Thus Vögtle, *Judasbrief*, 17.

112 Charles, *Literary Strategy*, 74–77.

113 Charles, *Literary Strategy*, 77.

114 Charles, *Literary Strategy*, 74.

115 Cf. Popkes, *Jakobusbrief*, 69.

116 Thus also Hahn, "Randbemerkungen," 651n42.

117 Paulsen, *Zweite Petrusbrief*, 65: "Überschreitung des den Menschen zugemessenen Platzes." See there: κυριότης could denote (1) human authorities, (2) the "sovereign" of God (cf. *Did.* 4:1) or of Christ (cf. *Herm. Sim.* 5:6:1), or (3) angelic powers (cf. Col 1:16; Eph 1:21; cf. *1 En.* 61:10; *2 En.* 20:1 and the Greek fragment of the *Apoc. Zeph.* (Clement of Alexandria, *Strom.* 4.11.77). The first option has to be discarded. Also, the relation to Christ is not convincing, neither through the singular nor through the connection to the context of κύριος (contrary to Bauckham, *Jude, 2 Peter*, 56-57). The connection to δόξαι (cf. 1QH X, 8; *2 En.* 22:7; *Ascen. Isa.* 9:32) suggests also the obvious angelological interpretation of κυριότης.

118 See Heiligenthal, *Zwischen Henoch und Paulus*, 95: "Schlüssel zum theologiegeschichtlichen Verständnis des Briefes."

119 Thus Sellin, "Häretiker," 216.

120 On the background of those terms, see Ch. Stettler, *Der Kolosserhymnus* (WUNT 2.132; Tübingen: Mohr Siebeck, 2000), 182–83; R. Schwindt, *Das Weltbild des Epheserbriefes* (WUNT 148; Tübingen: Mohr Siebeck, 2002), 362–63. An adequate list of angelic powers can be found in *2 En.* 20:1; cf. on this Ch. Böttrich, "Das slavische Henochbuch," *JSHRZ* 5.7 (1995): 884 n. h–l. See also *T. Ab.* (B, long recension) 13:10; *T. Adam* 4; *1 En.* 61:10; on ἀρχαί, cf. also *T. Sol.* 20:15.

121 The expression θρησκεία τῶν ἀγγέλων is hard to interpret. It cannot alone mean the (divine) worship performed *by* the angels. Thus correctly M. Wolter, *Der Brief an die Kolosser. Der Brief an Philemon* (ÖTK 12; Gütersloh: Gütersloher Verlagshaus, 1993), 146. The view of Stettler (*Kolosserhymnus*, 67), who strives to invalidate the testimonies of the worship *of* angels, is not plausible. Embedding Colossians within the struggle against orthodox Jewish mystics alone, as Stettler (65) does, is hardly sufficient, even though the Jewish moment in the Colossian heresy is can not be disputed (cf. Col 2:11, 16).

122 στοιξεῖα τοῦ κόσμου is not only a simple catchword used by the adversaries; it is at the same time "ein Begriff aus der paulinischen Schule" (Stettler, *Kolosserhymnus*, 61). On the other hand, there is some evidence that the addressees associated this notion with aspects different from the relation to the Jewish law, which is in the center of Paul's adaptation of the notion in Gal 4:3, 9. Regarding Galatians 4, C. E. Arnold (*The Colossian Syncretism* [WUNT 2.77; Tübingen: Mohr Siebeck, 1995], 183–84) states "that the semantic range of *stoicheia* for first-century usage—for Paul as well as for his Gentile readers—includes the meanings 'spirits,' 'angels,' and 'demons.'" Therefore, the Pauline usage of the term cannot determine and restrain the extension of meaning transmitted in Col.

123 Cf. the comprehensive investigation of Arnold, *Colossian Syncretism*; further, Wolter, *Brief an die Kolosser*, 155–63.

124 Heiligenthal, *Zwischen Henoch und Paulus*, 120.

125 Sellin, "Häretiker," 221–22.

126 Cf. Stettler, *Kolosserhymnus*, 170–73.

127 On the skeptical point of view, cf. Heiligenthal, *Zwischen Henoch und Paulus*, 102–3, 144–45.

128 On the one hand, Sellin ("Häretiker," 219–20) mentions the *Prayer of Joseph* (in Origen, *Comm. Jo.* 2.31; see the text in A. Denis, *Fragmenta Pseudepigraphorum Graeca* [PVTG 3; Leiden: Brill, 1970], 61–62). Here, Jacob/Israel claims his superiority over against the archangel Uriel. On the other hand, we have the *Apoc. Ab.*, in which Abraham is placed at the same level as the worshipping beings around God's throne. Finally, Abraham even watches over the upper heavens and their angels from above (ch. 19). The rivalry between angels and humans as a topic is discussed in P. Schäfer, *Rivalität zwischen Engeln und Menschen* (SJ 8; Berlin: de Gruyter, 1975).

129 Cf. Sellin, "Häretiker," 224.

130 Whether this theological evaluation is rightly carried out or not is hard to decide, for we know the doctrine of the adversaries only indirectly, through the polemics of the author. Glancing at Col, it is not compelling that the rejection of the angelic powers endangers the belief in Christ.

Chapter 15

1 Following, e.g., Bauckham (*Jude, 2 Peter*, 44), who observes that vv. 5-16 are set off within Jude by the use of "the fuller disclosure formula" in v. 5, marking a major transition from the opening to the main body of the letter ("I wish to remind you that . . ."), and the similar marker in v. 17 ("remember the words of the apostles . . ."), both of which introduce the material to be used as the foundation of his argument; Watson (*Invention*, 47–49), who takes vv. 5-16 to be the *probatio*, in which the proofs to support the case are set out; and Charles (*Literary Strategy*, 28), who views vv. 5-16 to be the *pistis*, in which the paradigms used as persuasive evidence are laid out. But see Neyrey (*2 Peter, Jude*, 58), who sees v. 5 as a more general disclosure formula (as in Rom 1:13; 11:25; 1 Cor 10:1; 12:1; 1 Thess 4:13), with the body of the letter already beginning in v. 3.

2 To give just three recent examples, cf. Paulsen, *Zweite Petrusbrief*, 60–61; Neyrey, *2 Peter, Jude*, 61–62; and now Charles Landon, *A Text-Critical Study of the Epistle of Jude*, JSNTSup 135 (Sheffield: Sheffield Academic Press, 1996), 70–77. This attention is surprising in view of the fact that the external evidence for the reading [ὁ] κύριος is strong, and the only compelling internal trajectory is to suppose that the apparent ambiguity surrounding κύριος spawned the variants ὁ θεός, Ἰησοῦς, and θεός Χριστός, as well as the combinations of readings found in the tradition, rather than any other possibility.

3 Following the NA²⁷ apparatus, in favor of taking ἅπαξ as part of the εἰδότας-clause are (1) K (9C; Category V) and 𝔐 (including L.323.614), which read εἰδότας τοῦτο ἅπαξ ὁ κύριος and ἅπαξ τοῦτο respectively; (2) A (5C; Category I), B (4C; Category I), 33 (9C; Category II), 81 (1044; Category II), 2344 (11C; Category I), a few other minuscules, and the most important editions of the Vulgate (Vg.), which read εἰδότας ἅπαξ πάντα ὅτι Ἰησοῦς; (3) the corrector of P⁷², which reads εἰδότας ἅπαξ πάντα ὅτι θεὸς Χριστός (with the original reading πάντας); and (4) the second corrector of C (6C), 623

(1037; Category III), and a Vulgate MS, which read εἰδότας ἅπαξ πάντα ὅτι ὁ θεός. In favor of taking ἅπαξ as part of the ὅτι-clause with σώσας are (1) ℵ (4C; Category I) and Ψ (8C; Category II), which read πάντα ὅτι κύριος ἅπαξ, together with the variation of this reading with Ἰησοῦς found in 1241 (12C; Category I), 1739 (10C; Category I), 1881 (14C; Category II), a few other minuscles, all the extant Coptic versions, and Origen, as noted in the margin of MS 1739; and (2) the original hand of C (5C; Category II), 630 (14C; Category III), 1505 (1084; Category III), a few other minuscles, and the Harklensis Syriac version (515/516 CE), which support the textual variant, πάντα ὅτι ὁ κύριος ἅπαξ, together with the variation of this reading with ὁ θεός found in 1243 (11C; Category I), 1846 (11C; Category III), a few other minuscles, a few Vulgate MSS, the Philoxenian Syriac version (6C), and Clement of Alexandria (with a slight variation).

4   Cf. the observation of Jonathan Knight, *2 Peter and Jude* (NTG; Sheffield: Sheffield Academic Press, 1995), 42, concerning Jude 5: "Like the Old Testament writers he fails to comment on the moral capacities of a God who could act in this way (but this is an important question for interpreters today)." I would suggest that it was important for Jude as well.

5   The NASB, RSV, JB, KJV, and NIV all read ἅπαξ with εἰδότας, while the NRSV, NEB, and TEV take it with σώσας as part of the ὅτι-clause. Among modern commentators, Bigg, Bauckham, Neyrey, Kelly, Sidebottom, Green, Hillyer, Kistemaker, Plummer, Watson, Grundmann, Schlatter, Schrage, Reicke, Paulsen, and Schelke all take it with εἰδότας, while only Mayor, Charles, Craddock, and now Landon (*Text-Critical Study*, 145, 149) take it with σώσας.

6   Note, e.g., the contradictory comments of Kelly (*Epistles*, 255), who suggests that the motive for moving ἅπαξ to the ὅτι-clause was "in part to ease the awkward next time . . . but *hapax* means 'once only,' not 'once in a series,' and the balancing of 'faith once for all delivered' by 'you who know all things once for all' is unmistakable." But the difficulty of understanding ἅπαξ when read in the ὅτι-clause, and the "unmistakable" balance created with v. 3 when it is not so read, both lead one to the opposite textual conclusion than that reached by Kelly himself.

7   Cf., e.g., Deut 9:13; 1 Kgs 17:39; Neh 13:20; 1 Macc 3:20; *1 Clem.* 53:3.

8   Cf., e.g., Exod 30:10; Lev 16:34; 3 Macc 1:11; *T. Ab.* 8:4; 9:3; 15:7; *Jos. Asen.* 25:5; *Pss. Sol.* 2:8; 11:2; 12:6; *1 En.* (B) 16:1.

9   2 Chr 9:21.

10   Cf. Judg 6:39; 16:18, 28; 1 Chr 11:11; Ps 88(89):35; Isa 66:8; Hag 2:7; *1 En.* 16:1; *T. Ab.* 8:4; 9:3; *Apoc. Sedr.* 12:2.

11   Cf., e.g., *Herm. Mand.* 4:4:1; *Herm. Vis.* 3:3:4; and see the discussions in Liddell, Scott, and Jones, *A Greek-English Lexicon* (9th ed.; Oxford: Clarendon, 1968), 178; Bauer, Arndt, Gingrich, and Danker (BAGD), *A Greek-English Lexicon of the New Testament* (2d ed.; Chicago: University of Chicago Press, 1979), 80; Bauer, Aland, and Aland (BAA), *Griechisch-deutsches Wörterbuch* (6th ed.; Berlin: de Gruyter, 1988), 160–61; and G. Stählin, "ἅπαξ, ἐφάπαξ," in *ThWNT* 1 (1933), 380–83. Stählin, 381, suggests that Hebrews

6:4 and 10:2 may represent this fourth meaning, though its only sure attestation is in the variant to 1 Peter 3:20 found in K.69 and a few other MSS.

12   Stählin, "ἅπαξ," 381, views Hebrews 9:26-28 together with 12:26 as representing the less ultimate and strictly numerical nuance of "once." However, the contrast in 9:25-26 between ἅπαξ on the one hand and πολλάκις and κατ' ἐνιαυτόν (the same contrast found in 10:1-2) on the other, and the parallel in 9:28 between Christ's being offered as a sacrifice ἅπαξ and the fact in 9:27 that it is "appointed for a man to die once" (ἅπαξ), seem to indicate that the stress in this passage is on the ultimate singularity of Christ's act. For the corresponding emphasis on its definitive nature, see Hebrews 9:12, where we read that Jesus entered the holy place "once for all" (ἐφάπαξ). This is confirmed by the fact that Hebrews 9:28 goes on to assert that, based on this first coming, Christ will appear a second time (ἐκ δευτέρου). For the significance of this last point, see below.

13   In this sense, it corresponds to ἐφάπαξ as found in Rom 6:10; 1 Cor 15:6; Heb 7:27; 9:12; 10:10. For this categorization of Hebrews 6:4 and 10:2, see Stählin, "ἅπαξ," 381–82, and BAA, who also view Hebrews 6:4 and 10:2 as representing the idea of "once for all." But while BAGD, 80, accept this understanding of Hebrews 10:2, they place Hebrews 6:4 in the category of a mere numerical designation. In contrast to the position here, Stählin (381), BAA (160–61), and BAGD (80) all place 1 Peter 3:18 in the category of *once* as merely a numerical designation. But in support of the above understanding, see Goppelt, *Petrusbrief*, 242.

14   In Stählin's translation, "Einmaligkeit (Unwiederholbarkeit)," this can be seen to bring out the nuance associated with Christ's work in both Heb 9:26-28; 12:26; 1 Pet 3:18 and Heb 6:4; 10:2, even though he puts them in different semantic categories.

15   Stählin, "ἅπαξ," 381. Stählin, however, says that this is the exclusive pattern in the NT, since he does not consider Hebrews 9:26-27 and 1 Peter 3:18 as part of this category, where it occurs with infinitive (Heb 9:27) and indicative (Heb 9:26; 1 Pet 3:18).

16   Besides the profane literature, cf. *L.A.E.* 8:2; *1 En.* 89:4-48.; *T. Ab.* 13:6; *T. Reu.* 2:4; 3:3; *T. Levi* 2:7; 3:2; 8:5; *T. Dan* 3:4; Bar 7:2; *Sib. Or.* 3:202; *Jub.* 2:4; *Herm. Sim.* 9:1:5; 9:19:2; *Herm. Mand.* 10:3:2; Matt 21:28; 22:26; Mark 12:21; 14:72; Luke 12:38; 20:30; John 4:54; 21:16; 1 Cor 12:28; 15:47; Heb 8:7; 10:9; Rev 4:7; 8:8; 20:6; *Did.* 1:2; etc. This use of πρῶτος is also implied in the many texts where δεύτερος is found alone; cf., e.g., Gen 22:15; Exod 4:8; 40:7; Num 1:1; 9:1; 2 Sam 14:29; 1 Chr 29:22; 1 Esd 5:56-57; 2 Esd 3:8; 4:24; Hag 1:1, 5; Zech 1:1; Jonah 3:1; etc.

17   See the dissenting opinion to that of the committee by Bruce Metzger and Allen Wikgren, in Metzger, *Textual Commentary* (3d ed., corrected; London: United Bible Societies, 1975), 724, who argue that although, in their view, ἅπαξ originally modified the participle εἰδότας, it did not seem to fit well there, and since τὸ δεύτερον "appeared to call for *a word like* πρῶτον, ἅπαξ was moved within the ὅτι-clause so as to qualify σώσας" (emphasis added). Also see Paulsen, *Zweite Petrusbrief,* 60.

18   Bauckham, *Jude, 2 Peter*, 50, following Chaine, Schelkle, Kelly, Cantinat, and Grundmann.

19   See the approximately one hundred times that ἐκ γῆς Αἰγύπτου is used in the LXX.

20   Contra Neyrey (*2 Peter, Jude*, 62), who simply concludes concerning τὸ δεύτερον that "Jude alludes to no biblical incident, but inasmuch as Paul in his typology of the Exodus generation cites Exodus 32:4, 6 in 1 Corinthians 10:6-13, that is as good an allusion as any."

21   In addition to Neyrey, *2 Peter, Jude*, cf. also Paulsen, *Zweite Petrusbrief*, 61–62.

22   Hence, though he specifically quotes Numbers 14:11, 22-23, statements like that of Charles (*Literary Strategy*, 106), though accurate, are too general as an explanatory background for the specific point of Jude 5: "Accounts of Israel's unbelief in the wilderness, after the incredibility of miraculous deliverance from Egypt, are found in Numbers 11, 14, 26 and 32 (cf. 1 Cor 10:1-5 and Heb 3:7-4:10) . . . God delivered Israel once-for-all (*hapax*) in the OT; the second time (*to deuteron*) God did not deliver, rather He judged." It is striking that the arguments of both 1 Corinthians 10:1-5 and Hebrews 3:7–4:10 are also built specifically on Numbers 14, esp. vv. 22-23, 28-30, 35, with Hebrews viewing it through the lens of Psalms 95:7-11. For a similar use of the Numbers narrative as a whole, Bauckham (*Jude, 2 Peter*, 50) points to Deut 1:32; 9:23; Ps 106:24; Sir 16:10; CD 3.7-9; *L.A.B.* 15:6.

23   For a development of the meaning of Exodus 32–34 within the narrative of the Pentateuch and its later development in the LXX and prophetic tradition, see Scott J. Hafemann, *Paul, Moses, and the History of Israel, The Letter/ Spirit Contrast and the Argument from Scripture in 2 Corinthians 3* (WUNT 81; Tübingen: Mohr Siebeck, 1995), 189–254.

24   On the purpose of this argument from reputation being to "promulgate truth and inculcate faith and ensure right conduct," rather than as an act of vanity, see Meir Sternberg, *The Poetics of Biblical Narrative, Ideological Literature and the Drama of Reading* (Bloomington: Indiana University Press, 1985), 102.

25   Cf. Exod 5:21; 14:11; 15:24; 16:2; 17:2-3; 32:1-6; Num 11:1, 4ff.; 12:1; 14:2.

26   For the view that Jude's list in vv. 5-7 is part of a traditional Jewish schema, in which various examples of divine judgment against apostasy and hardheartedness are usually listed in order to warn the readers of the consequences of sin, together with a comparison of the evidence from Sir 16:7-10; CD 2.17–3.12; 3 Macc 2:4-7; *T. Naph.* 3:4-5; *m. Sanh.* 10:3; and 2 Pet 2:4-8, see Paulsen, *Zweite Petrusbrief*, 62; Bauckham, *Jude, 2 Peter*, 46–47; and Neyrey, *2 Peter, Jude*, 59 (all following the work of K. Berger, J. Schlosser). But as Bauckham points out, Jude's use of this schema is unique: rather than providing a warning to the readers in support of a general maxim or paraenetic application, Jude uses it as a prophetic type of the false teachers, treating "his version of the tradition practically as a scriptural citation" (*Jude, 2 Peter*, 47).

27   Korah's rebellion in Numbers 16 provides a paradigm within the wilder-
     ness narratives of a lack of faith manifesting itself in defiance against the
     authority of God's leader (cf. 16:1-3, 13-14, 41). It is instructive to note that
     here, too, Moses twice acts as intercessor to stop the total destruction of
     the people (cf. 16:22, 45). Again, therefore, we have the theme of a second
     time. For this same theme of defiance against Moses as a parallel to defiance
     against God, see Numbers 17:5, 10 (Heb 17:20, 25); 20:2-3, 10; 21:5.

28   This is the view of the vast majority of commentators. For the former des-
     ignation, see Bauckham, *Jude, 2 Peter*, 50; for the latter, Michael Green, *2
     Peter and Jude* (rev. ed.; TNTC 18; Leicester: InterVarsity, 1987), 177.

29   For this former designation of Jude's encoded speech acts and their purpose,
     see Stephan J. Joubert, "Persuasion in the Letter of Jude," *JSNT* 58 (1995):
     75–87, here 75–77; Joubert follows Perelman, Thurén, Stubbs, Van Dijk,
     and Austin in this matter. To accomplish this goal, he suggests that Jude
     employs "epideictic discourse" (the assignment of praise and blame in order
     to affect an audience) in accordance with a "'positive/negative presentation'
     strategy" (79–80). Obviously, the readers represent the positive pole of this
     approach, and the false teachers the negative. For the latter description,
     which rightly emphasizes the homiletic setting and style of Jude among
     Hellenistic Jewish and Christian works, see again the important work of
     Charles, *Literary Strategy*, 23ff. Charles follows Watson in arguing that Jude
     be viewed as predominantly deliberative rhetoric, with aspects of epedeictic
     and forensic speech as well (cf. 27–28), in which "there exists throughout
     the short epistle a fundamental tension between the ungodly and the faith-
     ful" (48; cf. 94). But regardless of the formal descriptive category chosen,
     the hortatory purpose of Jude is apparent from a direct reading of the text,
     which follows the common rhetorical pattern of, first, a narration of the
     purpose of the writing in vv. 3-4; next, the proof to support it; and finally, a
     restatement of it in the conclusion of vv. 17-23. For this, cf. Charles, *Liter-
     ary Strategy*, 28–29.

30   The argument of Jude in this regard is remarkably similar to that found in
     Hebrews 6:4-6, where we also find ἅπαξ used with an aorist participle to
     establish a definitive act that implies a necessary consequence, i.e., "those
     who have been enlightened once for all" (τοὺς ἅπαξ φωτισθέντας) and then
     fall away (παραπεσόντας, again with an implied ἅπαξ?) cannot be brought
     again to repentance. For, as Hebrews 6:9 indicates, falling away in view of
     the ἅπαξ-nature of the enlightenment is not to be classed with the "better
     things" that pertain to the nature of an original genuine salvation (cf. τὰ
     κρείσσονα καὶ ἐχόμενα σωτηρίας), but rather is indicative of a hardened
     rejection of Christ (6:6). Here, too, the OT backdrop for the argument is
     Numbers 14.

31   For the development of this point and its relationship to 2 Peter 1:3-11, see
     Scott J. Hafemann, "Covenant Relationship," in *Central Themes in Biblical
     Theology, Mapping Unity in Diversity* (ed. Scott J. Hafemann and Paul R.
     House; Grand Rapids: Baker, 2007), 20–65.

32   See Ign. *Eph.* 1:1; Ign. *Rom.* 1:1; Ign. *Smyrn.* 1:1.

33   So Nigel Turner, *Syntax* (vol. 3 of *A Grammar of New Testament Greek*;
     ed. J. H. Moulton; Edinburgh: T&T Clark, 1963), 322. A close structural
     parallel is found in the prologue to Sir 1:1-15, which also begins in 1:1 with
     a genitive absolute clause (πολλῶν καὶ μεγάλων . . . δεδομένων) that intro-
     duces a long string of dependent clauses and grounds an inferential impera-
     tive (cf. οὖν in Sir 1:15). Here, the many and great things in view are those
     things given through the law and the prophets in the scriptural deposit of
     Israel's faith. Frederick W. Danker ("2 Peter 1: A Solemn Decree," *CBQ* 40
     [1978]: 64–82, here 79–80) also points to the imperial decree from Seleucus
     II found in *OGIS* 227, 1–3, where this same genitive absolute construc-
     tion follows an epistolary greeting and declares "the benefactor's bounties."
     Such a grammatical style is thus by no means without precedent. How-
     ever, Danker's larger thesis that vv. 3–11 are a "conscious intent to create a
     decretal effect" (80) by use of the form and language typical of Hellenistic
     imperial and civic decrees seems difficult to sustain. By his own observa-
     tion, when compared to such decrees, 2 Peter lacks "purity," is the result
     of a "creative design," and evinces a "free adaptation of decretal language"
     (66). Indeed, in seventeen of Danker's twenty-seven alleged parallels, he
     himself admits that 2 Peter goes its own way. The remaining parallels are
     too general to be convincing. Most problematic is the fact that whereas the
     decrees use language related in part to what is found in vv. 5-7 to describe
     the benefactor, in 2 Peter this section is aimed at the recipients as a series of
     imperatives (cf. 72–73). The same is true of the "call" motif in v. 3 (76). It is
     highly questionable, therefore, that the apostles viewed themselves as bene-
     factors, or that 1:1 also casts the recipients of the letter in the role of bene-
     factors, so that the letter "establishes a dynamic reciprocity between three
     benefactor-entities: Peter, representative of apostolic tradition; the writer's
     community; and Jesus Christ" (80). As the covenant structure indicates,
     rather than possessing "a partnership in benefaction" or exercising a "reci-
     procity between Benefactor and Recipients" (81), the benefaction in view
     in vv. 1-11 is completely one-sided, with God's people in total dependence
     upon him as recipients only. There is no doubt that this section does evince
     a solemn tone also found in the decrees, but this merely reflects the subject
     matter common to both the covenant and the decree, i.e., a "solemn call to
     faithful allegiance to One whom the Christian community would recognize
     as the greatest Benefactor of the ages" (65). Bauckham's judgment in *Jude, 2
     Peter*, 174, concerning Danker's thesis is therefore appropriate: "The most
     that might be said is that the highly rhetorical style of vv. 3-11 echoes some
     of the kind of language used in official decrees. . . . It does not follow that
     the passage is intended to resemble a decree."

34   Quote from Moulton as found in A. T. Robertson, *A Grammar of the Greek
     New Testament in the Light of Historical Research* (Nashville: Broadman,
     1934), 513. Robertson himself points out that such strings of phrases are
     less common in the NT. This is evidence of the elevated style of 2 Peter.

35   Bauckham, *Jude, 2 Peter*, 173.

36   G. E. Mendenhall, "Covenant Forms in Israelite Tradition," *BA* 17 (1954):

50–76. For the significant advancement of this insight in terms of the development and interrelationship of the tribal concept of kinship with that of kingship, leading to the presentation of God as "God [king] and father," see F. M. Cross, "Kinship and Covenant in Ancient Israel," in *From Epic to Canon* (ed. F. M. Cross; Baltimore, Md.: Johns Hopkins University Press, 1998), 3–21.

37   The modern history of the study of the covenant structure of the OT is a complex one, in which no consensus exists concerning the origin or lines of dependence and development between the various treaty formulas found in the ancient Near East and the OT. For a helpful survey, see Ernest W. Nicholson, "Covenant in a Century of Study Since Wellhausen," in *God and His People: Covenant and Theology in the Old Testament* (ed. Ernest W. Nicholson; Oxford: Clarendon, 1986), 3–117. As this history shows, the parallels between the OT covenant structures and these treaties from the ancient Near East must not be taken to mean that the OT traditions are directly derived from or dependent upon any one or more of these parallels. Nevertheless, whatever its origin, by all accounts the OT covenant structure outlined here was well established canonically by the NT era as central to an understanding of the relationship between God and Israel.

38   Cf. Gen 17:1-21; Exod 19–24; 34:1-28; Deut 4:1-20; 6:1-25; 10:12–11:7; 28:69–30:20; Josh 23; 1 Sam 12; 2 Kgs 17; Pss 78; 89; Jer 11:1-11; 31:31-34; Ezek 16; 20; Hos 6; Neh 9; etc., as well as the general pattern of indicative-imperative-promise found throughout the OT.

39   The prologue recounts the saving acts of the king on behalf of his vassal that have led to and support the covenant relationship. Cf., e.g., Exod 19:1–20:2; Josh 24:1-13, 17-18. These past acts are the gracious, one-sided provisions on the part of the king that provided the foundation for the expected obedience on the part of the vassal. The historical prologue may also be preceded by a preamble identifying the king.

40   The stipulations outline the necessary responses of the vassal if the covenant relationship is to be maintained. Cf., e.g., Exod 20:3-17; 21–24; Josh 24:14-15. These are the conditions that must be kept by the vassal in order to inherit the promises that the king made upon entering into the covenant relationship.

41   This section states the promises themselves, often implied in the historical prologue (e.g., future deliverance for the vassal based on the past deliverance already experienced), which will be fulfilled if the covenant stipulations are kept, as well as the corresponding curses or judgment that will befall the vassal if the covenant is not maintained. Cf., e.g., Deut 28; Josh 24:20. These promises and curses are the focus of the covenant stipulations.

42   Cf. Bauckham (*Jude, 2 Peter*, 173), who recognizes that vv. 3-11 "appear to follow" this pattern; he points to the work of K. Baltzer (*The Covenant Formulary*, 1971) as support for its OT backdrop, and to that of K. P. Donfried (*The Setting of Second Clement in Early Christianity*, NovTSup 38, 1974) for its development in the early Church and application to the whole of 2 Peter. Bauckham himself does not develop this insight further, due to

his preference for the traditions of the early church fathers and Hellenistic moral philosophy as the key interpretive parallels to this section.

43   In commenting on v. 5, it is therefore important not to speak of the believer's diligence "as something brought in alongside of what God has already done (vv. 3-4)," or to conclude that "the Christian must engage in this sort of *cooperation* with God in the production of a Christian life which is a credit to Him," as often found (quotes from D. Edmond Hiebert, "The Necessary Growth in the Christian Life: An Exposition of 2 Peter 1:5-11," *BSac* 141 [1984]: 43–54, here 44; and Green, *2 Peter*, 67 as quoted by Hiebert, 45; emphasis added).

Chapter 16

1   Ferdinand Christian Baur, *Das Christenthum und die christliche Kirche der drei ersten Jahrhunderte* (Tübingen: L. F. Fues, 1853; 3d ed. 1868) and Albrecht Ritschl, *Die Entstehung der altkatholischen Kirche* (2d ed.; Bonn, 1857) To compare, see E. D. Pressensé, *Histoire des trois premiers siècles de l'église chrétienne* (Paris, 1858). The first volume contains the first century, under the title *Le siècle apostolique*.

2   Starting with the Baur student F. C. A. Schwegler, *Das nachapostolische Zeitalter in den Hauptmomenten seiner Entwicklung* (Tübingen, 1845/1846), but also used by G. V. Lechler (prof. in Leipzig), *Das apostolische und das nachapostolische Zeitalter* (2d ed.; Leipzig, 1857), and later by Johannes Weiss' student Rudolf Knopf, *Das nachapostolische Zeitalter* (Tübingen, 1905).

3   James D. G. Dunn, *The Parting of the Ways: Between Christianity and Judaism and Their Significance for the Character of Christianity* (London: SCM Press, 1991), 231ff.

4   Some scholars see 110 as a bracket, e.g., Gerd Theißen, *Die Religion der ersten Christen: Eine Theorie des Urchristentums* (Gütersloh: Gütersloher Verlag, 2000) and Per Bilde, *En religion bliver til: En undersøgelse af kristendommens forudsætninger og tilblivelse indtil år 110* (Fredriksberg: Anis, 2001).

5   Franz Overbeck, professor of NT and early Christianity in Basel from 1870, argued that the period before is the period of so-called *Christian Urliteratur*: Overbeck, *Schriften bis 1873* (vol. 1 of *Werke und Nachlaß*; Stuttgart: Metzler, 1994).

6   Many patristic scholars tend to see the shift about 200 CE, e.g., Carl Andresen, *Die Kirchen der alten Christenheit* (Stuttgart: Kohlhammer, 1971), in which the first period (to the end of second century) is "Die Frühkatholische Kirche" and the second part is "Die altkatholische Kirche," followed by "Die Reichskatholische Kirche."

7   Starting with A. Ritschl and increasingly popular in Protestant scholarship.

8   Hans Lietzmann, *Geschichte der Alten Kirche* (4 vols.; Berlin: de Gruyter, 1936–1944; repr. in one vol, 1999).

9   The most frequent name in English (B. H. Streeter, "The Rise of Christianity," in *The Imperial Peace* [vol. 11 of *The Cambridge Ancient History;* Cambridge: Cambridge University Press, 1936], 253–93; Philip Carrington: *The*

Early Christian Church [vol. 1; Cambridge: Cambridge University Press, 1957], 238–501), and also French and partly German scholarship (e.g., F. C. Baur).

10   Christoph Markschies, "Alte Kirche," *RGG4* 1:345.

11   Ernest Renan, *Histoire des origines du Christianisme* (Paris: Lévy, 1863). The first volume, *Vie de Jésus* (Paris, 1863), is well known. More interesting, however, are the last volumes: the sixth, *L'Église Chrétienne* (Paris, 1879), and the seventh, *Marc-Auréle* (Paris, 1882).

12   The older books (e.g., by Bernheim, Langlois, and Saignobos) on this topic are still some of the best. See also my analysis of this problem in Ernst Baasland, *Theologie und Methode* (Wuppertal: Brockhaus, 1992), 183–92, as well as Jean-Nicolas Corvisier, *Sources et méthodes en histoire ancienne* (Paris: Presses universitaires de France, 1997); W. Howell and W. Prevenier, *From Reliable Sources: An Introduction to Historical Methods* (Ithaca: Cornell University Press, 2001).

13   Adolf Deissmann opened the way for new insights through his study of the papyri, inter alia, in *Bibelstudien* (Marburg: N. G. Elwert, 1895). See also J. van Haelst, *Catalogue des papyrus littéraires juifs et chrétiens* (Paris: Publications de la Sorbonne, 1976).

14   J. M. G. Barclay, *Jews in the Mediterranean Diaspora: From Alexander to Trajan (323 BC–117 CE)* (Edinburgh: T&T Clark, 1996). He has a local history approach, dealing mostly with Egypt but also with other cities and provinces (231–319).

15   F. C. Baur, *Paulus, der Apostel Jesu Christi: Sein Leben und Wirken, seine Briefe und seine Lehre. Ein Beitrag zu einer kritischen Geschichte des Urchristentums* (Stuttgart: Becher & Müller, 1845); idem, *Christenthum*.

16   The first part deals with the development of theology (Die Entwicklung der christlichen Grundanschauung), the second part with church order (Die Entwicklung der christlichen Gemeinde- und Kirchenverfassung).

17   Adolf B. C. Hilgenfeld, *Die Ketzergeschichte des Urchristentums* (Leipzig, 1886); Otto Pfleiderer, *Das Urchristenthum, seine Schriften und Lehren, in geschichtlichem Zusammenhang beschrieben* (Berlin: Reimer, 1887); Carl (Karl) Heinrich von Weizsäcker, *Das apostolische Zeitalter der christlichen Kirche* (Freiburg: Mohr, 1886); Johannes Weiss, *Das Urchristentum* (Göttingen: Vandenhoeck & Ruprecht, 1917).

18   Wilhelm Bousset, *Kyrios Christos: Geschichte des Christusglaubens von den Anfängen des Christusglaubens bis auf Irenäus* (ed. Gustav Krüger and Rudolf Bultmann; Göttingen: Vandenhoeck & Ruprecht, 1913; 2d ed. 1921). His chapters on the postapostolic age are divided into two parts: "Der Christus-Kult im nachapostolischen Zeitalter," 216–74, and "Die Ausgestaltung des Christentums auf Grund des Christus-Kultus und seine verschiedenen Typen," 275–335.

19   For a more comprehensive criticism of this concept, see Baasland, *Theologie und Methode*, esp. 386–87.

20   E. Lohse, in *Alte Kirche und Ostkirche* (ed. V. R. Kottje and B. Moeller; vol. 1 of *Ökumenische Kirchengeschichte*; München: Kaiser, 1970; 5th ed., 1989),

53–72. Lohse differentiates between two periods: (1) Christianity about 100 CE (mission, the Gospels, persecutions) and (2) early Catholic Church (ethics, ecclesiology ["Gemeindeverfassung"], creed, Holy Scripture).

21 Siegfried Schulz, *Die Mitte der Schrift: Der Frühkatholizismus des Neuen Testaments als Herausforderung an den Protestantismus* (Berlin: Kreuz Verlag, 1976), made the following concept the key to understanding the New Testament: the Synoptics/Acts are expressions (131–226), the Johannine writings are reactions against (227–56), and every piece of Christian writing, from the Epistle to the Hebrews to Polycarp (257–382), are variations of early Catholicism. In my opinion, this book showed that the concept is a blind alley.

22 K. Kautsky, *Foundations of Christianity* (New York: S. A. Russell, 1953); trans. of *Ursprung des Christentums* (Stuttgart: J. H. W. Dietz, 1908), part 4: "The Beginnings of Christianity."

23 Shirley Jackson Case, *The Evolution of Early Christianity: A Genetic Study of First-Century Christianity in Relation to its Religious Environment* (Chicago: University of Chicago Press, 1914).

24 Ernst Lohmeyer, *Soziale Fragen im Urchristentum* (Wissenschaft und Bildung. Einzeldarstellungen aus allen Gebieten des Wissens 172; Leipzig, 1921) and *Vom Begriff der religiösen Gemeinschaft* (ed. Richard Hönigswald; Wissenschaftl. Grundfragen 3; Leipzig, 1925).

25 K. Aland, *Geschichte der Christenheit* (Gütersloh: Gütersloher Verlagshaus, 1980), the first three chapters, 11ff.

26 Aland, *Geschichte*, 51–90, 91ff. Similarly, W. Wischmeyer, "Alte Kirche," *EKL* 1:43–47, emphasizes inter alia the following forces: communication, persecutions, synagogue, ancient art, and theology (44). Also, Eckehart Stöve, "Kirchengeschichtsschreibung," *TRE* 18:535–60, differentiates between internal and external history (537).

27 T. Christensen and S. Göransson, *Kyrkohistoria* (vol 1; Stockholm, 1969), 26–59: "Den efterapostolske tid, ca. 64–ca. 140." They do not use the concept of force, but in my opinion, the will to provide historical explanations is stronger than in other church histories, leading to the given outline.

28 K. M. Fischer, *Das Urchristentum* 1 (ed. K. Meier and H. J. Rogge; Berlin: Evangelische Verlagsanstalt, 1985), 127–75 (the last chapter); overlapping K.-W. Tröger, *Das Christentum im zweiten Jahrhundert* (vol. 2 of *Das Urchristentum*; ed. Meier and Rogge; Berlin: Evangelische Verlagsanstalt, 1988). Tröger uses very vague categories in his book (Roman Empire, mission, Christian literature, theological concepts, ecclesiological structures, challenges).

29 H. Jedin, *From the Apostolic Community to Constantine* (vol. 1 of *The Early Church*; Freiburg: Herder, 1969).

30 Jedin, *From the Apostolic Community to Constantine*, 35–48.

31 Walter H. Wagner, *After the Apostles: Christianity in the Second Century* (Minneapolis: Fortress, 1994), sees the development as a response to five ideological challenges (creator and creation, human nature and destiny, identities of Jesus, the church's place, and Christians and society).

32   Paul Gardiner, *The Nature of Historical Explanation* (Oxford: Clarendon, 1962).

33   Hengel, *Judentum und Hellenismus* (*Judaism and Hellenism*). "Die Ausgestaltungen des Christentums auf Grund des Christus-Kultus und seine verschiedenen Typen," 275–333 (Ign.–Heb, parts from *1 Clem.*, Eph, Past–*1 Clem.*).

34   Knopf, *Das nachapostolische Zeitalter.*

35   D. G. Dix, *Jew and Greek: A Study in the Primitive Church* (London: Dacre, 1953).

36   Dix, *Jew and Greek*, 72.

37   Dix, *Jew and Greek*, 65.

38   Dix, *Jew and Greek*, 88ff.

39   Leonhard Goppelt, *Die apostolische und nachapostolische Zeit* (Die Kirche in ihrer Geschichte Band 1, Lieferung A; Göttingen: Vandenhoeck & Ruprecht, 1962; 2d ed. 1966); ET: *Apostolic and Post-Apostolic Times* (Grand Rapids: Baker, 1970; 2d ed. 1977).

40   Goppelt, *Die apostolische und nachapostolische Zeit*, part 4, 74–103 ("Die ausgehende apostolische Zeit: Die Festigung der Kirche und ihres Evangeliums gegenüber Verweltlichung") and part 5, 103–51 ("Die Entwicklung der die Kirche gestaltenden Kräfte").

41   J. Jervell, *Luke and the People of God: A New Look at Luke-Acts* (Minneapolis: Augsburg, 1972). The most important article by Jervell on the importance of Jewish Christianity is "A Mighty Minority," *ST* 34 (1980): 13–38; repr. in *The Unknown Paul: Essays on Luke-Acts and Early Christian History* (Minneapolis: Augsburg, 1984), esp. 26–51, 162–64.

42   This point is demonstrated by an exegesis of Luke 2:21, in which the circumcision of Jesus is an indication of Jesus' legitimacy to speak and act in the name of God. Jervell, "The Circumcised Messiah," in *The Unknown Paul*, 138–45.

43   O. Skarsaune, *In the Shadow of the Temple: Jewish Influences on Early Christianity* (Downers Grove, Ill.: InterVarsity, 2002). Similarly in his outline of the earliest church in idem, *Fra Jerusalem til Rom og Bysants* (Oslo: Tano, 1987), 26–86, ET: "We Have Found the Messiah: Jewish Believers in Jesus in Antiquity," *Mishkan* 45 (2005): 5–122.

44   Weiss, *Urchristentum.*

45   W. Bauer, *Rechtgläubigkeit und Ketzerei im ältesten Christentum* (ed. G. Strecker; Tübingen, 1934; repr., Tübingen: Mohr, 1964).

46   R. Grant, A. Ehrhard, and, later, H. Köster and J. Robinson. More recently, B. D. Ehrman has published collections of both orthodox and heterodox sources: *After the New Testament: A Reader in Early Christianity* (New York: Oxford University Press, 1999) and *Lost Christianities: The Battle for Scriptures and Faiths We Never Knew* (New York: Oxford University Press, 2003).

47   Hilgenfeld, *Ketzergeschichte.*

48   H. Köster and J. Robinson, *Trajectories through Early Christianity* (Philadelphia: Fortress, 1971); trans. of *Entwicklungslinien durch die Welt des frühen Christentums* (Tübingen: Mohr, 1971). The book deals mostly with the apostolic time.

49 H. Köster, *Introduction to the New Testament* (2 vols.; Philadelphia: Fortress, 1982); trans. of Köster, *Einführung*.

50 H. Chadwick, *The Church in Ancient Society: From Galilee to Gregory the Great* (Oxford: Oxford University Press, 2001), 1–64: the first followers of Jesus, the Jewish matrix, Jews and Christians survive Rome's crushing and revolt, etc.

51 Chadwick, *The Church in Ancient Society*, 65–99.

52 Theißen, *Religion*.

53 Theißen, *Religion*, in the Danish edition, 270–80.

54 Ernst Bernheim, *Lehrbuch der historischen Methode und der Geschichtsphilosophie* (Leipzig: Duncker & Humblot, 1903), 294ff., and my analysis in *Theologie und Methode*, 184ff.

55 E. Troeltsch, *Die Soziallehren der christlichen Kirchen und Gruppen* (Tübingen: Mohr, 1912).

56 Case, *Evolution*.

57 W. A. Meeks, *The First Urban Christians: The Social World of the Apostle Paul* (New York, 1983).

58 Only in the periphery are texts from the CE referred to, in the chapters on social level, ecclesia, and eschatology.

59 P. E. Esler, *Modelling Early Christianity* (New York: Routledge, 1995). Also, R. A. Horsley, ed., *Christian Origins: A People's History of Christianity.* (vol. 1; Minneapolis: Fortress, 2005), wishes to provide a sort of socio-historical approach; he ends up, however, with a mixture of different approaches, analyzing movements, cities, and social patterns and practices.

60 There are a few references in the chapters on family and honor, Paul, kinship and ideology, and oppression, war, and peace.

61 Stegemann and Stegemann, *Urchristliche Sozialgeschichte*; ET: *The Jesus Movement: A Social History of its First Century* (trans. O. C. Dean; Minneapolis: Fortress, 1999).

62 Stegemann and Stegemann, *Urchristliche Sozialgeschichte*, 302–16, 332ff.

63 J. H. Elliott, *Home for the Homeless*.

64 Applied in, e.g., Neyrey, *2 Peter, Jude*.

65 Possible approaches are, inter alia, classical themes in socio-anthropological research (clean/unclean, honor/shame, etc.), conflict as phenomenon, the interpretative model of cognitive dissonance (especially with reference to Leon Festinger and John Gager) for understanding the early church's responses to the shock of Jesus' crucifixion and the nonoccurrence of the Parousia, power and authority, etc.

66 E. W. Barnes, *The Rise of Christianity* (London: Longman's, Green, 1947). In his outline, he mixes general, theological, and more biographical perspectives (XIV: Early Christian writing outside the New Testament; XV: Baptism; XVI: Eucharist; and XVII: The Christian Movement and the Roman Empire; taxation, pacifism, genius of the emperor, Josephus, Tacitus, Pliny, Suetonius, Marcus Aurelius, and the early apologists).

67 Niels Hyldahl, *Den ældste kristendoms historie* (Copenhagen: Museum Tusculanum, 1982), 287–356. He uses the term *postapostolic time* and proposes

the following outline: Destruction of the Temple, Johannine Literature (Christology), Roman Empire and Christians (Persecutions), Ministry (*1 Clem.*, Pastorals, Ignatius), Marcion (Jewish roots), Hegesippus (Papias and the beginning of patristic literature).

68   Recently, Susanne Hausammann, *Alte Kirche: Zur Geschichte und Theologie in den ersten vier Jahrhunderten* (4 vols.; Neukirchen-Vluyn: Neukirchener Verlag, 2001–2004).

69   Andresen, *Kirchen*.

70   Bultmann, *Theologie*, 513–47.

71   Theißen, *Religion*.

72   My book, *Theologie und Methode*, 331–400, has a number of observations on the different methodological questions involved.

73   A. Harnack, *Die Mission und Ausbreitung des Christentums in den ersten drei Jahrhunderten* (Leipzig: Hinrichs, 1906), esp. vol. 2, 77–262.

74   Birger A. Pearson, *Gnosticism and Christianity in Roman and Coptic Egypt* (New York: T&T Clark, 2004).

75   Wayne A. Meeks and Robert L. Wilken, *Jews and Christians in Antioch in the First Four Centuries of the Common Era* (Missoula, Mont.: Scholars Press, 1978); Christine Kondoleon, *Antioch: The Lost Ancient City* (Princeton: Princeton University Press, 2000); Magnus Zetterholm, *The Formation of Christianity in Antioch* (London: Routledge, 2003).

76   Peter Lampe, *Die stadtrömischen Christen in den ersten beiden Jahrhunderten: Untersuchungen zur Sozialgeschichte* (WUNT 2.18; Tübingen: Mohr-Siebeck, 1987).

77   P. Lampe and Ulrich Luz, "Post-Pauline Christianity and Pagan Society," in *Christian Beginnings: Word and Community from Jesus to Post-Apostolic Times* (ed. J. Becker; Louisville, Ky.: Westminster John Knox, 1993).

78   R. G. Collingwood, *The Idea of History* (Oxford: Clarendon, 1993), 278ff., with polemical remarks against the scissors-and-paste historians.

79   R. Knopf, *Einführung in das Neue Testament* (ed. H. Lietzmann and H. Weinel; 4th ed.; Giessen: Töpelmann, 1934).

80   K. H. Schelkle, *Das Neue Testament* (Kevelaer: Butzon & Bercker, 1963).

81   W. G. Kümmel, *Einleitung in das Neue Testament* (Heidelberg: Quelle & Meyer, 1963).

82   A. F. J. Klijn, *An Introduction to the New Testament* (Leiden: Brill, 1967).

83   Vielhauer, *Geschichte*.

84   A. Wikenhauser and J. Schmid, *Einleitung in das Neue Testament* (Freiburg: Herder, 1973).

85   H. Conzelmann and A. Lindemann, *Arbeitsbuch zum Neuen Testament* (11th ed.; Tübingen: Mohr, 1995).

86   E. Lohse, *Einleitung in das Neue Testament* (Theologische Wissenschaft 4; Stuttgart, 1972).

87   H.-M. Schenke and K. M. Fischer, *Einleitung in die Schriften des Neuen Testaments* (vols. 1–2; Gütersloh: Gütersloher, 1978–1979).

88   R. E. Brown, *An Introduction to the New Testament* (ABRL; New York: Doubleday, 1997).

89 Schnelle, *Einleitung*.

90 In *RGG4*, see the articles on James (R. Hoppe, 4:361–63), 1 Peter and 2 Peter (R. Feldmeier, 6:1179–82), the Johannine Epistles (F. Vauga, 4:549–52), and Jude (R. Heiligenthal, 4:600–601).

91 In *TRE*, see the articles on James (H. Paulsen, 16:488–95), 1 Peter and 2 Peter (N. Brox, 26:308–14, 314–19), the Johannine Epistles (H. Thyen, 17:186–200), and Jude (H. Paulsen, 17:307–10).

92 In *ANRW* 2.25.5, see the articles on James (Baasland, "Literarische"), 1 Peter (E. Cothenet, 3685–3712), the Johannine Epistles (K. Wengst, 3753–72), and Jude (Bauckham, "Letter of Jude").

93 In AB, see the articles on James (S. Laws, 3:621–28), 1 Peter (J. H. Elliott, 5:269–78, 282–87), the Johannine Epistles (R. Kysar, 3:900–912), and Jude (3:1098–1103).

94 The studies on the CE, which have been debated in our seminar over the years, are not included in this overview. I also exclude from this overview the introductions (e.g., from Anglo-American scholars D. Guthrie, R. Gundry, J. M. Robinson, R. Martin), in which most of the CE are dated early.

95 Lohse, *Einleitung*, 131; Vielhauer, *Geschichte*, 580; Conzelmann and Lindemann, *Arbeitsbuch*, 410; Wikenhauser and Schmid, *Einleitung*, 579.

96 Hoppe, *RGG4* 4:362.

97 Laws, AB 3:622ff.; Brown, *Introduction*, 740–41; Schelkle, *Das Neue Testament*, 194 (or Syria).

98 Schenke and Fischer, *Einleitung*, 240; Kysar, AB 3:908–9 (or Asia Minor or Palestine); Kümmel, *Einleitung*, 365 (or Palestine); Paulsen, 442.

99 Knopf, *Einführung*, 94.

100 Schnelle, *Einleitung*, 443.

101 Vielhauer, *Geschichte*, 566; Brox, *TRE* 26:314; Conzelmann and Lindemann, *Arbeitsbuch*, 416 (with some reservations); Schnelle, *Einleitung*, 459.

102 Knopf, *Einführung*, 92; Kümmel, *Einleitung*, 374; Schelkle, *Das Neue Testament*, 205–6; Lohse, *Einleitung*, 134; J. H. Elliott, AB 5:277.

103 Thyen, *TRE* 17:195; Kysar, AB 3:912 (located in Ephesus, Palestine, or Syria).

104 Kümmel, *Einleitung*, 393 (1 John), 398; Vielhauer, *Geschichte*, 422; Schenke and Fischer, *Einleitung*, 196–97; Lohse, *Einleitung*, 114 (or in Asia Minor).

105 Knopf, *Einführung*, 96; Schelkle, *Das Neue Testament*, 199; Klijn, *Introduction*, 108 (or Syria); Conzelmann and Lindemann, *Arbeitsbuch*, 382, 384; Wengst, *ANRW* 2.25.5:3766–67; Vauga, *RGG4* 4:551; Schnelle, *Einleitung*, 522.

106 Kümmel, *Einleitung*, 378; Wikenhauser and Schmid, *Einleitung*, 584 (not Palestine).

107 Vielhauer, *Geschichte*, 544; Conzelmann and Lindemann, *Arbeitsbuch*, 421; Paulsen, *TRE* 17:309.

108 Knopf, *Einführung*, 97 (Egypt, Syria, or Asia Minor); Conzelmann and Lindemann, *Arbeitsbuch*, 421 (Alexandria, Palestine, Antioch, or Asia Minor); Heiligenthal, *RGG4* 4:601 (Syria, Palestine, Asia Minor, or even Alexandria).

109 Schelkle, *Das Neue Testament*, 197. Schnelle suggests Asia Minor (*Einleitung*, 476f.).

110 Vielhauer, *Geschichte*, 579; Conzelmann and Lindemann, *Arbeitsbuch*, 425 (or Alexandria, Palestine, Antioch, or even Rome); Feldmeier, *RGG4* 6:1179; Schnelle, *Einleitung*, 486 (Rome or Egypt).

111 Knopf, *Einführung*, 98 ("im Osten," Egypt, or perhaps Asia Minor).

112 Schenke and Fischer, *Einleitung*, 319.

113 Schelkle, *Das Neue Testament*, 210 (or Egypt); Klijn, *Introduction*, 162–63 (or Antioch); Kümmel, *Einleitung*, 383 (as a guess); Elliott, AB 5:287.

114 Harnack, *Mission*.

115 J. G. Gager, *Kingdom and Community* (Englewood Cliffs, N.J.: Prentice Hall, 1975).

116 K. Burridge, *New Heaven, New Earth: A Study of Millenarian Activities* (New York: Schocken Books, 1969).

117 H. Festinger, *A Theory of Cognitive Dissonance* (Stanford: Stanford University Press, 1957).

118 Malina, *New Testament World*.

119 G. Geertz, *The Interpretation of Cultures: Selected Essays* (New York: Basic Books, 1973). He understands culture as "a system of inherited conceptions expressed in symbolic forms by means of which people communicate, perpetuate, and develop their knowledge about and attitudes toward life" (89).

120 N. Smart, *In Search of Christianity* (New York: Harper & Row, 1979); *Worldviews: Crosscultural Explorations of Human Beliefs* (Englewood Cliffs, N.J.: Prentice Hall, 1982); *Dimensions of the Sacred: An Anatomy of the World's Beliefs* (Berkeley: University of California Press, 1996). He mentions the following dimensions: experience, social (fellowship), narrative, dogma, ethics, ritual, material.

121 L. W. Hurtado, *The Lord Jesus: Devotion to Jesus in the Earliest Church* (Grand Rapids: Eerdmans, 2003).

122 M.-È. Boismard, "Une liturgie baptismale dans la Prima Petri," *RB* 63 (1956): 182–208; *RB* 64 (1957): 161–83.

123 The earliest Christian catechism should be seen not only as an internal matter, but more as the formation of a Christian ethos in a Hellenistic context (see, e.g., Carrington, *Primitive Christian Catechism*, and Selwyn, *First Epistle*).

124 J. D. G. Dunn, *Jesus Remembered* (Grand Rapids: Eerdmanns, 2003).

125 R. Bauckham, ed., *The Gospel for All Christians: Rethinking the Gospel Audiences* (Edinburgh: T&T Clark, 1998).

126 E.g., J. K. Elliott, ed., *The Apocryphal New Testament* (Oxford: Clarendon, 1993) and *The Apocryphal Jesus: Legends of the Early Church* (Oxford: Oxford University Press, 1996).

127 Ferdinand Kattenbusch, *Das Apostolische Symbol, seine Entstehung, sein geschichtlicher Sinn, seine ursprüngliche Stellung im Kultus und in der Theologie der Kirche* (vols. 1–2; Leipzig: Hinrichs, 1894/1900; repr., Darmstadt: Wissenschaftliche Buchgesellschaft, 1962); Hans Lietzmann, *Symbolstudien I–XIV* (Darmstadt, 1966).

BIBLIOGRAPHY

Adamson, J. B. *The Epistle of James.* 2d ed. New International Commentary on the New Testament. Grand Rapids: Eerdmans, 1993.

———. *James: The Man and His Message.* Grand Rapids: Eerdmans, 1989.

Ahrens, M. "Der Judasbrief – eine neutestamentliche Marginalie." *Texte und Kontexte* 22.3 (1999): 39–49.

Aland, K. *Geschichte der Christenheit.* Gütersloh: Gütersloher Verlagshaus, 1980.

Albin, C. A. *Judasbrevet.* Stockholm: Natur och kultur, 1962.

Allison, Dale C. "The Fiction of James and its Sitz im Leben." *Revue biblique* 118 (2001): 529–70.

———. "The Pauline Epistles and the Synoptic Gospels: The Pattern of the Parallels." *New Testament Studies* 28 (1982): 1–32.

Alter, Robert. *The Pleasures of Reading in an Ideological Age.* New York: Simon & Schuster, Touchstone, 1989.

Anderson, P. N. *The Christology of the Fourth Gospel.* Valley Forge, Pa.: Trinity, 1996.

Andresen, C. *Die Kirchen der alten Christenheit.* Stuttgart: Kohlhammer, 1971.

———. "Zum Formular frühchristlicher Gemeindebriefe." *Zeitschrift für die neutestamentliche Wissenschaft und die Kunde der älteren Kirche* 56 (1965): 233–59.

Applegate, J. K. "The Co-Elect Woman of 1 Peter." *New Testament Studies* 38 (1992): 587–604.

Arnold, C. E. *The Colossian Syncretism.* Wissenschaftliche Untersuchungen zum Neuen Testament 2.77. Tübingen: Mohr Siebeck, 1995.

Assan-Dhôte, I., and J. Moatti-Fine. *Baruch, Lamentations, Lettre de Jérémie*. La Bible d'Alexandrie 25, 2. Paris: Cerf, 2005.

Aus, R. "Three Pillars and Three Patriarchs: A Proposal Concerning Gal 2:9." *Zeitschrift für die neutestamentliche Wissenschaft und die Kunde der älteren Kirche* 70 (1979): 252–61.

Avemarie, F. "Die Werke des Gesetzes im Spiegel des Jakobusbriefs: A Very Old Perspective on Paul." *Zeitschrift für Theologie und Kirche* 98 (2001): 282–309.

Baasland, E. "Literarische Form, Thematik und geschichtliche Einordnung des Jakobusbriefes." Pages 3646–84 in *Aufstieg und Niedergang der römischen Welt: Geschichte und Kultur Roms im Spiegel der neueren Forschung* 2.25.5. Edited by W. Haase and H. Temporini. Berlin: de Gruyter, 1988.

———. *Theologie und Methode*. Wuppertal: Brockhaus, 1992.

Baker, W. R. *Personal Speech-Ethics in the Epistle of James*. Wissenschaftliche Untersuchungen zum Neuen Testament 2.68. Tübingen: Mohr Siebeck, 1995.

Balz, H. "Der Brief des Jakobus." Pages 1–59 in Balz and Schrage, *Die "Katholischen" Briefe: Die Briefe des Jakobus, Petrus, Johannes und Judas*. Das Neue Testament Deutsch 10. Göttingen: Vandenhoeck & Ruprecht, 1993.

Balz, H., and W. Schrage. *Die "Katholischen" Briefe: Die Briefe des Jakobus, Petrus, Johannes und Judas*. Das Neue Testament Deutsch 10. Göttingen: Vandenhoeck & Ruprecht, 1973; 4th ed., 1993.

Barclay, J. M. G. *Jews in the Mediterranean Diaspora: From Alexander to Trajan (323 BCE–117 CE)*. Edinburgh: T&T Clark, 1996.

Barnes, E. W. *The Rise of Christianity*. London: Longman's, Green, 1947.

Barrett, C. K. *The Acts of the Apostles*. 2 vols. International Critical Commentary. Edinburgh: T&T Clark, 1994–1998.

Bauckham, R., ed. *The Gospel for All Christians: Rethinking the Gospel Audiences*. Edinburgh: T&T Clark, 1998.

———. "James and the Gentiles (Acts 15:13-21)." Pages 154–84 in *History, Literature, and Society in the Book of Acts*. Edited by B. Witherington. Cambridge: Cambridge University Press, 1996.

———. "James and the Jerusalem Church." Pages 415–80 in *The Book of Acts in its First Century Setting*. Edited by R. Bauckham. Grand Rapids: Eerdmans, 1995.

———. *James: Wisdom of James, Disciple of Jesus the Sage*. London: Routledge, 1999.

———. *Jude and the Relatives of Jesus in the Early Church*. Edinburgh: T&T Clark, 1990.

———. *Jude, 2 Peter*. Word Biblical Commentary 50. Waco, Tex.: Word Books, 1983.

———. "The Letter of Jude: An Account of Research." Pages 3791–3826 in *Aufstieg und Niedergang der römischen Welt: Geschichte und Kultur Roms im Spiegel der neueren Forschung* 2.25.5. Edited by W. Haase and H. Temporini. Berlin: de Gruyter, 1988.

———. "2 Peter: An Account of Research." Pages 3713–52 in *Aufstieg und Niedergang der römischen Welt: Geschichte und Kultur Roms im Spiegel der neueren*

Forschung 2.25.5. Edited by W. Haase and H. Temporini. Berlin: de Gruyter, 1988.

———. "The Study of Gospel Traditions outside the Canonical Gospels: Problems and Prospects." Pages 369–419 in *The Jesus Tradition outside the Gospels*. Edited by David Wenham. Vol. 5 of *Gospel Perspectives*. Sheffield: JSOT Press, 1985.

Bauer, W. *Rechtgläubigkeit und Ketzerei im ältesten Christentum*. Edited by G. Strecker. Tübingen: Mohr Siebeck, 1934. 2d ed., 1964.

Baur, F. C. *Das Christenthum und die christliche Kirche der drei ersten Jahrhunderte*. Tübingen: L. F. Fues, 1853. 3d ed., 1868.

———. *Paulus, der Apostel Jesu Christi: Sein Leben und Wirken, seine Briefe und seine Lehre. Ein Beitrag zu einer kritischen Geschichte des Urchristentums*. Stuttgart: Becher & Müller, 1845.

Becker, J. "Die Erwählung der Völker durch das Evangelium: Theologiegeschichtliche Erwägungen zum 1 Thess." Pages 82–101 in *Studien zum Text und zur Ethik des Neuen Testaments*. Edited by Wolfgang Schrage. Beihefte zur Zeitschrift für die neutestamentliche Wissenschaft 47. Berlin: de Gruyter, 1986.

———. *Paulus: Der Apostel der Völker*. 3d ed. Tübingen: Mohr Siebeck, 1998.

———. *Untersuchungen zur Entstehungsgeschichte der Testamente der zwölf Patriarchen*. Arbeiten zur Geschichte des antiken Judentums und des Urchristentums 8. Leiden: Brill, 1970.

Bede the Venerable. *Commentary on the Seven Catholic Epistles*. Translated by D. Hurst. Cistercian Studies 82. Kalamazoo, Mich.: Cistercian Publications, 1985.

Ben-Dov, J. "A Presumed Citation of Esther 3:7 in 4QD[b]." *Dead Sea Discoveries* 6 (1999): 282–84.

Berger, K. *Formgeschichte des Neuen Testaments*. Heidelberg: Quelle & Mayer, 1984.

———. "Der Streit des guten und bösen Engels um die Seele: Beobachtungen zu 4QAmrb und Judas 9." *Journal of Semitic Studies* 4 (1973): 1–18.

———. *Theologiegeschichte des Urchristentums: Theologie des Neuen Testaments*. Tübingen: Francke, 1994. 2d ed., 1995.

Berger, P. L., and T. Luckmann. *The Social Construction of Reality: A Treatise in the Sociology of Knowledge*. Garden City, N.Y.: Doubleday, 1966.

Bernand, E. *Inscriptions métriques de l'Egypte gréco-romaine: Recherches sur la poésie épigrammatique des Grecs en Egypte*. Annales littéraires de l'Université de Besançon. Centre de recherches anciennes 98. Paris: Belles Lettres, 1969.

Bernheim, E. *Lehrbuch der historischen Methode und der Geschichtsphilosophie*. Leipzig: Duncker & Humblot, 1903.

Best, E. *I Peter*. New Century Bible. London: Oliphants, 1971. Repr., 1977.

Beyschlag, K. *Clemens Romanus und der Frühkatholizismus: Untersuchungen zu I Clemens 1–7*. Beiträge zur historischen Theologie 35. Tübingen: Mohr Siebeck, 1966.

Beyschlag, W. "Der Jakobusbrief als urchristliches Geschichtsdenkmal." *Theologische Studien und Kritiken* 48 (1874): 105–66.

Bickermann, E. J. "The Colophon of the Greek Book of Esther." *Journal of Biblical Literature* 63 (1944): 339–62.

———. "Ein jüdischer Festbrief vom Jahre 124 v. Chr. (II Macc 1 1–9)." *Zeitschrift für die neutestamentliche Wissenschaft und die Kunde der älteren Kirche* 32 (1933): 233–54.

Bigg, C. *A Critical and Exegetical Commentary on the Epistles of St. Peter and Jude.* International Critical Commentary 41. Edinburgh: T&T Clark, 1922.

Biguzzi, G. "Is the Babylon of Revelation Rome or Jerusalem?" *Biblica* 87 (2006): 371–86.

Bilde, P. *En religion bliver til: En undersøgelse af kristendommens forudsætninger og tilblivelse indtil år 110.* Fredriksberg: Anis, 2001.

Black, C. C. "The First, Second, And Third Letters of John." Pages 365–78 in *The New Interpreter's Bible* 12. Edited by L. E. Keck. Nashville: Abingdon, 1998.

Bockmuehl, M. "Antioch and James the Just." Pages 155–98 in *James the Just and Christian Origins.* Edited by B. Chilton and C. A. Evans. Leiden: Brill, 1999.

Bogaert, P. *Apocalypse de Baruch: Introduction, traduction du syriaque et commentaire.* 2 vols. Sources chrétiennes 144, 145. Paris: Cerf, 1969.

Boismard, M.-É. "Une liturgie baptismale dans la Prima Petri." *Revue biblique* 63 (1956): 182–208; 64 (1957): 161–83.

Boring, M. E. *1 Peter.* Abingdon New Testament Commentaries. Nashville: Abingdon, 1999.

Bornkamm, G. *Paulus.* 6th ed. Stuttgart: Kohlhammer, 1987.

Böttger, P. C.. "Paulus und Petrus in Antiochien: Zum Verständnis von Galater 2,11-21." *New Testament Studies* 37 (1991): 77–100.

Böttrich, Ch. "Das slavische Henochbuch." *Jüdische Schriften aus hellenistischrömischer Zeit* 5.7 (1995): 781–1040.

Bousset, W. *Jüdischer-Christlicher Schulbetrieb in Alexandria und Rom; Untersuchungen zu Philo und Clemens von Alexandria, Justin und Irenäus.* Göttingen: Vandenhoeck & Ruprecht, 1915.

———. *Kyrios Christos: Geschichte des Christusglaubens von den Anfängen des Christusglaubens bis auf Irenäus.* Edited by Gustav Krüger and Rudolf Bultmann. Göttingen: Vandenhoeck & Ruprecht, 1913. 2d ed., 1921.

Boyle, M. O'Rourke. "The Stoic Paradox of James 2:10." *New Testament Studies* 31 (1985): 611–17.

Brandenburger, E. *Fleisch und Geist: Paulus und die dualistische Weisheit.* Wissenschaftliche Monographien zum Alten und Neuen Testament 29. Neukirchen-Vluyn: Neukirchener, 1968.

———. "Pistis und Soteria: Zum Verstehenshorizont von 'Glaube' im Urchristentum." *Zeitschrift für Theologie und Kirche* 85 (1988): 165–98.

Brooke, A. E. *A Critical and Exegetical Commentary on the Johannine Epistles.* Edinburgh: T&T Clark, 1912.

Brooks, J. A. "The Place of James in the New Testament Canon." *Scottish Journal of Theology* 12 (1969): 41–51.

Brooks, S. H. *Matthew's Community: The Evidence of His Special Sayings Material.*

Journal for the Study of the New Testament Supplement Series 16. Shef-field: JSOT Press, 1987.

Brown, R. E. *The Community of the Beloved Disciple.* New York: Paulist, 1979.

———. *The Epistles of John.* Anchor Bible 30. Garden City, N.Y.: Doubleday, 1982.

———. *An Introduction to the New Testament.* Anchor Bible Reference Library. New York: Doubleday, 1997.

Brown, R. E., and J. P. Meier. *Antioch and Rome.* New York: Paulist, 1983.

Brox, N. *Der erste Petrusbrief.* 2d ed. Evangelisch-katholischer Kommentar zum Neuen Testament 21. Zürich: Benzinger and Neukirchen-Vluyn: Neukirch-ener, 1986. 3d ed., 1989.

———. "Der erste Petrusbrief in der literarischen Tradition des Urchristen-tums." *Kairos* NF 20 (1978): 182–92.

Brückner, W. "Zur Kritik des Jakobusbriefes." *Zeitschrift für wissenschaftliche Theologie* 17 (1874): 530–41.

Buchanan, G. W. "The Role of Purity in the Structure of the Essene Sect." *Römische Quartalschrift für christliche Altertumskunde und Kirchengeschichte* 4 (1963): 397–406.

Bultmann, R. "γινώσκω, κτλ." Pages 689–719 in *Theological Dictionary of the New Testament* 1. Edited by G. Kittel and G. Friedrich. Translated by G. W. Bromiley. Grand Rapids: Eerdmans, 1964.

———. *Theologie des Neuen Testaments.* 9th ed. Tübingen: Mohr Siebeck, 1984.

Bunge, J. G. "Untersuchungen zum zweiten Makkabäerbuch: Quellenkritische, literarische, chronologische und historische Untersuchungen zum zweiten Makkabäerbuch als Quelle syrisch-palästinensischer Geschichte im 2. Jh. v. Chr." Diss. phil., Bonn, 1971.

Burchard, Ch. *Der Jakobusbrief.* Handbuch zum Neuen Testament 15.1. Tübin-gen: Mohr Siebeck, 2000.

———. "Nächstenliebegebot, Dekalog und Gesetz in Jak 2,8-11." Pages 517–33 in *Die Hebräische Bibel und ihre zweifache Nachgeschichte.* Edited by Erhard Blum, Christian Macholz, and Ekkehard W. Stegemann. Neukirchen-Vluyn: Neukirchener, 1990.

———. "Zu einigen christologischen Stellen des Jakobusbriefes." Pages 353–68 in *Anfänge der Christologie.* Edited by Cilliers Breytenbach and Henning Paulsen. Göttingen: Vandenhoeck & Ruprecht, 1991.

Burkert, W. *Antike Mysterien: Funktionen und Gehalt.* München: C. H. Beck, 1990.

Burridge, K. *New Heaven, New Earth: A Study of Millenarian Activities.* New York: Schocken Books, 1969.

Buschmann, G. *Das Martyrium des Polykarp.* Kommentar zu den Apostolischen Vätern 6. Göttingen: Vandenhoeck & Ruprecht, 1998.

Buzón, R. "Die Briefe der Ptolemäerzeit: Ihre Struktur und ihre Formeln." Diss. phil., Heidelberg, 1984.

Cadbury, H. J. *The Book of Acts in History.* London: Black, 1955.

Cancik, H. *Mythische und historische Wahrheit: Interpretationen zu Texten der heth-itischen, biblischen und griechischen Historiographie.* Stuttgarter Bibelstudien 48. Stuttgart: Kath. Bibelwerk, 1970.

Cargal, T. B. *Restoring the Diaspora: Discursive Structure and Purpose in the Epistle of James.* Society of Biblical Literature Dissertation Series 144. Atlanta: Scholars Press, 1993.

Carleton Paget, J. *The Epistle of Barnabas: Outlook and Background.* Wissenschaftliche Untersuchungen zum Neuen Testament 2.64. Tübingen: Mohr Siebeck, 1994.

———. "Jewish Christianity." Pages 731–55 in *The Early Roman Period.* Edited by W. Horbury, W. D. Davies, and J. Sturdy. Vol. 3 of *The Cambridge History of Judaism.* Cambridge: Cambridge University Press, 1999.

Carrington, P. *The Early Christian Church.* Vol. 1. Cambridge: Cambridge University Press, 1957.

———. *The Primitive Christian Catechism: A Study in the Epistles.* Cambridge: Cambridge University Press, 1940.

Carroll, K. L. "The Place of James in the Early Church." *Bulletin of the John Rylands University Library of Manchester* 44 (1961): 49–67.

Case, S. J. *The Evolution of Early Christianity: A Genetic Study of First-Century Christianity in Relation to its Religious Environment.* Chicago: University of Chicago Press, 1914.

Catchpole, D. R. "Paul, James and the Apostolic Decree." *New Testament Studies* 23 (1977): 428–44.

Caulley, T. S. "The False Teachers in 2 Peter." *Studia Biblica et Theologica* 12 (1982): 27–42.

Chadwick, H. *The Church in Ancient Society: From Galilee to Gregory the Great.* Oxford: Oxford University Press, 2001.

Charles, J. D. "Jude's Use of Pseudepigraphic Source-Material as Part of a Literary Strategy." *New Testament Studies* 37 (1991): 130–45.

———. "Literary Artifice in the Epistle of Jude." *Zeitschrift für die neutestamentliche Wissenschaft und die Kunde der älteren Kirche* 82 (1991): 106–24.

———. *Literary Strategy in the Epistle of Jude.* Scranton: University of Scranton, 1993.

———. "'Those' and 'These': The Use of the Old Testament in the Epistle of Jude." *Journal for the Study of the New Testament* 38 (1990): 109–24.

Chester, A. "The Theology of James." Pages 1–62 in *The Theology of the Letters of James, Peter, and Jude.* Edited by A. Chester and R. P. Martin. Cambridge: Cambridge University Press, 1994.

Childs, B. S. *The New Testament as Canon: An Introduction.* London: SCM Press, 1984.

———. *Die Theologie der einen Bibel.* Vol. 1 of *Grundstrukturen.* Darmstadt: Wissenschaftliche Buchgesellschaft, 2003.

Chilton, B., and C. Evans. *James the Just and Christian Origins.* Leiden: Brill, 1999.

Chilton, B., and J. Neusner. *The Brother of Jesus: James the Just and his Mission.* Louisville, Ky.: Westminster John Knox, 2001.

Christensen, T., and S. Göransson. *Kyrkohistoria.* Vol. 1. Stockholm, 1969.

Churgin, P. *Targum Jonathan to the Prophets.* New Haven: Yale University Press, 1927.

Collingwood, R. G. *The Idea of History*. Oxford: Clarendon, 1993.

Colpe, C. "Das deutsche Wort 'Judenchristen' und ihm entsprechende historische Sachverhalte." Pages 38–58 in *Das Siegel der Propheten*. Edited by C. Colpe. Arbeiten zur Neutestamentlichen Zeitgeschichte 3. Berlin: Institut Kirche und Judentum, 1990.

Conzelmann, H., and A. Lindemann. *Arbeitsbuch zum Neuen Testament*. 11th ed. Tübingen: Mohr Siebeck, 1995.

Cooper, R. M. "Prayer: A Study in Matthew and James." *Encounter* 29 (1968): 268–77.

Corvisier, J.-N. *Sources et méthodes en histoire ancienne*. Paris: Presses universitaires de France, 1997.

Cribiore, R. *Writing, Teachers, and Students in Graeco-Roman Egypt*. American Studies in Papyrology 36. Atlanta: Scholars Press, 1996.

Cross, F. M. "Kinship and Covenant in Ancient Israel." Pages 3–21 in *From Epic to Canon*. Edited by F. M. Cross. Baltimore: Johns Hopkins University Press, 1998.

Cullmann, O. *Peter: Apostle, Disciple, Martyr*. London: SCM Press, 1953.

Culpepper, A. *The Johannine School*. Society of Biblical Literature Dissertation Series 26. Missoula, Mont.: Scholars Press, 1975.

Daniélou, J. *Théologie du Judéo-christianisme*. Paris: Desclée, 1958. ET: *The Theology of Jewish Christianity*. London: Darton, Longman & Todd, 1964.

Danker, F. W. "Reciprocity in the Ancient World and in Acts 15:23-29." Pages 49–58 in *Political Issues in Luke-Acts*. Edited by R. J. Cassidy and P. J. Scharper. Maryknoll, N.Y.: Orbis Books, 1983.

———. "2 Peter 1: A Solemn Decree." *Catholic Biblical Quarterly* 40 (1978): 64–82.

Dautzenberg, G. "Ist das Schwurverbot Mt 5,33-37; Jak 5,12 ein Beispiel für die Thorakritik Jesu?" *Biblische Zeitschrift* NF 25 (1981): 47–66.

———. "Σωτηρία ψυχῶν (1Pet 1:9)." *Biblische Zeitschrift* NF 8 (1964): 262–76.

Davids, P. H. *The Epistle of James: A Commentary on the Greek Text*. New International Greek Testament Commentary. Grand Rapids: Eerdmans, 1982.

———. *The Epistle of James: A Commentary on the Greek Text*. Exeter: Paternoster, 1982.

———. "The Epistle of James in Modern Discussion." Pages 3621–45 in *Aufstieg und Niedergang der römischen Welt: Geschichte und Kultur Roms im Spiegel der neueren Forschung* 2.25.5. Edited by W. Haase and H. Temporini. Berlin: de Gruyter, 1988.

———. *The First Epistle of Peter*. New International Commentary on the New Testament. Grand Rapids: Eerdmans, 1990.

———. "James and Jesus." Pages 63–84 in *The Jesus Tradition outside the Gospels*. Edited by David Wenham. Vol. 5 of *Gospel Perspectives*. Sheffield: JSOT Press, 1985.

———. "Palestinian Traditions in the Epistle of James." Pages 33–57 in *James the Just and Christian Origins*. Edited by Bruce D. Chilton and Craig A. Evans. Leiden: Brill, 1999.

Davies, W. D. *Paul and Rabbinic Judaism.* New York: Harper & Row, 1967. 3d ed. Philadelphia: Fortress, 1980.

———. *The Setting of the Sermon on the Mount.* Cambridge: Cambridge University Press, 1966.

Debut, J. "Les documents scolaires." *Zeitschrift für Papyrologie und Epigraphik* 63 (1986): 251–78.

Dehandschutter, B. "Pseudo-Cyprian, Jude and Enoch: Some Notes on 1 Enoch 1:9." Pages 114–20 in *Tradition and Re-Interpretation in Jewish and Early Christian Literature.* Edited by J. W. van Henten et al. Studia post-biblica 36. Leiden: Brill, 1986.

Deissmann, A. *Bibelstudien.* Marburg: N. G. Elwert, 1895.

Denis, A. *Fragmenta Pseudepigraphorum Graeca.* Pseudepigrapha Veteris Testamenti Graece 3. Leiden: Brill, 1970.

Deppe, D. B. "The Sayings of Jesus in the Epistle of James." D.Th. diss., Free University of Amsterdam. Ann Arbor: Bookcrafters, 1989.

De Troyer, K. "Once More, the So-called Esther Fragments of Cave 4." *Revue de Qumran* 19/75 (2000): 401–22.

Dexinger, F. "Jüdisch-christliche Nachgeschichte von Genesis 6,1-4." Pages 155–75 in *Zur Aktualität des alten Testaments.* Edited by S. Kreuzer and K. Lüthi. Frankfurt am Main: Lang, 1992.

Dibelius, M. *Der Brief des Jakobus: Mit Ergänzungen von H. Greeven, mit einem Literaturverzeichnis und Nachtrag hg. v. F. Hahn.* Kritisch-exegetischer Kommentar über das Neue Testament 15. Göttingen: Vandenhoeck & Ruprecht, 1921. 12th ed., 1984.

———. *James: A Commentary on the Epistle of James.* Edited by H. Köster. Revised by H. Greeven. Translated by M. A. Williams. Hermeneia. Philadelphia: Fortress, 1976.

Diewald, G. *Deixis und Textsorten im Deutschen.* Reihe Germanistische Linguistik 118. Tübingen: Niemeyer, 1991.

Dillman, C. N. "A Study of Some Theological and Literary Comparisons of the Gospel of Matthew and the Epistle of James." Ph.D. diss., University of Edinburgh, 1978.

Dimant, D. *Qumran Cave 4. XXI. Parabiblical Texts,* Part 4, *Pseudo-Prophetic Texts.* Discoveries in the Judaean Desert 30. Oxford: Clarendon, 2001.

Dix, D. G. *Jew and Greek: A Study in the Primitive Church.* London: Dacre, 1953.

Dodd, C. H. *The First Epistle of John and the Fourth Gospel.* Manchester: Manchester University Press, 1937.

———. *The Johannine Epistles.* Moffatt New Testament Commentary. London: Hodder & Stoughton, 1946.

Doering, L. "Jeremiah and the 'Diaspora Letters' in Ancient Judaism: Epistolary Communication with the Golah as Medium for Dealing with the Present." Pages 43–72 in *Reading the Present in the Qumran Library: The Perception of the Contemporary by Means of Scriptural Interpretation.* Edited by K. de Troyer and A. Lange. Society of Biblical Literature Symposium Series 30. Atlanta: Society of Biblical Literature, 2005.

———. "Jeremia in Babylonien und Ägypten: Mündliche und schriftliche Tora-paränese für Exil und Diaspora nach *4QApocryphon of Jeremiah C*." Pages 50–79 in *Frühjudentum und Neues Testament im Horizont Biblischer Theologie: Mit einem Anhang zum Corpus Judaeo-Hellenisticum Novi Testamenti*. Edited by W. Kraus and K.-W. Niebuhr. Wissenschaftliche Untersuchungen zum Neuen Testament 162. Tübingen: Mohr Siebeck, 2003.

Donfried, K. P. *The Setting of Second Clement in Early Christianity*. Supplements to Novum Testamentum 38. Leiden: Brill, 1974.

Doran, R. *Temple Propaganda: The Purpose and Character of 2 Maccabees*. Catholic Biblical Quarterly Monograph Series 12. Washington, D.C.: Catholic Biblical Association, 1981.

Douglas, M. T. *Purity and Danger: An Analysis of Concepts of Pollution and Taboo*. New York: Frederick A. Praeger, 1966.

Drummond, J. *The New Testament in the Apostolic Fathers*. Oxford: Oxford University Press, 1905.

Dryden, J. *Theology and Ethics in 1 Peter: Paraenetic Strategies for Christian Character Formation*. Wissenschaftliche Untersuchungen zum Neuen Testament 2.209. Tübingen: Mohr Siebeck, 2006.

Dunn, J. D. G. *A Commentary on the Epistle to the Galatians*. Black's New Testament Commentaries . London: A. C. Black, 1993.

———. *Jesus Remembered*. Grand Rapids: Eerdmanns, 2003.

———. *The Parting of the Ways: Between Christianity and Judaism and Their Significance for the Character of Christianity*. London: SCM Press, 1991.

———. *Romans 1–8*. Word Biblical Commentary 38A. Waco, Tex.: Word Books, 1988.

Edwards, R. B. *The Johannine Epistles*. Sheffield: Sheffield Academic Press, 1996.

Ehrman, B. D. *After the New Testament: A Reader in Early Christianity*. New York: Oxford University Press, 1999.

———. *Lost Christianities: The Battle for Scriptures and Faiths We Never Knew*. New York: Oxford University Press, 2003.

Elliott, J. H. *The Elect and the Holy*. Supplements to Novum Testamentum 12. Leiden: Brill, 1966.

———. "The Epistle of James in Rhetorical and Social Scientific Perspective: Holiness-Wholeness and Patterns of Replication." *Biblical Theology Bulletin* 23 (1993): 71–81.

———. *1 Peter: A New Translation with Introduction and Commentary*. Anchor Bible 37B. New York: Doubleday, 2000.

———. *A Home for the Homeless: A Sociological Exegesis of I Peter, its Situation and Strategy*. Philadelphia: Fortress, 1981.

———. "Peter, Silvanus and Mark in I Peter and Acts: Sociological-Exegetical Perspectives on a Petrine Group in Rome." Pages 250–67 in *Wort in der Zeit: Festschrift K. H. Rengstorf*. Edited by W. Haubeck and M. Bachmann. Leiden: Brill, 1980.

———. "Temple versus Household in Luke-Acts: A Contrast in Social Institutions." Pages 211–40 in *The Social World of Luke-Acts: Models for Interpretation*. Edited by Jerome H. Neyrey. Peabody, Mass.: Hendrickson, 1991.

Elliott, J. K., ed. *The Apocryphal Jesus: Legends of the Early Church*. Oxford: Oxford University Press, 1996.

———, ed. *The Apocryphal New Testament: A Collection of Apocryphal Christian Literature in an English Translation*. Oxford: Clarendon, 1993.

Elliott-Binns, L. E. *Galilean Christianity*. Studies in Biblical Theology 16. London: SCM Press, 1956.

Ellis, E. E. *The Making of the New Testament Documents*. Biblical Interpretation Series 39. Leiden: Brill, 1999.

———. *Prophecy and Hermeneutic*. Wissenschaftliche Untersuchungen zum Neuen Testament 18. Tübingen: Mohr Siebeck, 1978.

Epp, E. J. "Issues in the Interrelation of New Testament Textual Criticism and Canon." Pages 503–5 in *The Canon Debate*. Edited by Lee Martin McDonald and James A. Sanders. Peabody, Mass.: Hendrickson, 2002.

Ermert, K. *Briefsorten: Untersuchungen zu Theorie und Empirie der Textklassifikation*. Reihe Germanistische Linguistik 20. Tübingen: Niemeyer, 1979.

Esler, P. F. *Modelling Early Christianity*. New York: Routledge, 1995.

Evang, M. "Ἐκ καρδίας ἀλλήλους ἀγαπήσατε ἐκτενῶς: Zum Verständnis der Aufforderung und ihrer Begründungen in 1 Petr 1,22f." *Zeitschrift für die neutestamentliche Wissenschaft und die Kunde der älteren Kirche* 80 (1989): 111–23.

Exler, F. X. J. *The Form and Function of the Ancient Greek Letter: A Study in Greek Epistolography*. Washington, D.C.: Catholic University of America, 1923.

Farkasfalvy, D. M. "The Ecclesial Setting of Pseudepigraphy in Second Peter and its Role in the Formation of the Canon." *Second Century* 5 (1985): 3–29.

Farmer, W. R. "James the Lord's Brother, According to Paul." Pages 133–53 in *James the Just and Christian Origins*. Edited by Bruce D. Chilton and Craig A. Evans. Leiden: Brill, 1999

Feine, P. *Der Jakobusbrief nach Lehranschauungen und Entstehungsverhältnissen*. Eisenach: Wilckens, 1893.

———. *Eine vorkanonische Überlieferung des Lukas in Evangelium und Apostelgeschichte: Eine Untersuchung*. Gotha: Perthes, 1891.

Feldman, L. H. *Jew and Gentile in the Ancient World: Attitudes and Interactions from Alexander to Justinian*. Princeton: Princeton University Press, 1993.

Feldmeier, R. *Die Christen als Fremde: Die Metapher der Fremde in der antiken Welt, im Urchristentum und im 1. Petrusbrief*. Wissenschaftliche Untersuchungen zum Neuen Testament 64. Tübingen: Mohr Siebeck, 1992.

———. *Der erste Brief des Petrus*. Theologischer Handkommentar zum Neuen Testament 15.1. Leipzig: EVA, 2005. ET: *The First Letter of Peter*. Waco, Tex.: Baylor University Press, 2008.

Ferris, T. E. S. "The Epistle of James in Relation to I Peter." *Church Quarterly Review* 128 (1939): 303–8.

Festinger, H. *A Theory of Cognitive Dissonance*. Stanford: Stanford University Press, 1957.

Fischer, K. M. *Das Urchristentum*. Vol. 1. Edited by K. Meier and H. J. Rogge. Berlin: Evangelische Verlagsanstalt, 1985.

Flusser, D. "The Dedication of the Temple by Judas Maccabaeus: Story and History." Pages 55–78 in *The Jews in the Hellenistic-Roman World: Studies in Memory of Menahem Stern.* Edited by I. M. Gafni, A. Oppenheimer, and D. R. Schwartz. Jerusalem: Zalman Shazar Center & Historical Society of Israel, 1996.

Fornberg, T. *An Early Church in a Pluralistic Society: A Study of 2 Peter.* Coniectanea biblica: New Testament Series 9. Lund: Gleerup, 1977.

Fowl, S., and G. Jones. *Reading in Communion.* Grand Rapids: Eerdmans, 1991.

Frankemölle, H. *Der Brief des Jakobus.* Ökumenischer Taschenbuch-Kommentar-ÖTK 17.2. Gütersloh: Gütersloher Verlagshaus, 1994.

———. *1. Petrusbrief. 2. Petrusbrief. Judasbrief.* Die Neue Echter Bibel 18 and 20. Würzburg: Echter, 1987. 2d ed., 1990.

———. "Das semantische Netz des Jakobusbriefes: Zur Einheit eines umstrittenen Briefes." *Biblische Zeitschrift* 34 (1990): 161–97.

Frey, J. "Heiden–Griechen–Gotteskinder: Zu Gestalt und Funktion der Rede von den Heiden im 4. Evangelium." Pages 228–68 in *Die Heiden: Juden, Christen und das Problem des Fremden.* Edited by R. Feldmeier and U. Heckel. Wissenschaftliche Untersuchungen zum Neuen Testament 70. Tübingen: Mohr Siebeck, 1994.

———. *Die johanneische Eschatologie I: Ihre Probleme im Spiegel der Forschung seit Reimarus.* Wissenschaftliche Untersuchungen zum Neuen Testament 96. Tübingen: Mohr Siebeck, 1997.

———. *Der Judasbrief und der zweite Petrusbrief.* Theologischer Handkommentar 15.2. Leipzig: Evangelische Verlagsanstalt, 2008.

———. "The Notion of 'Flesh' in 4QInstruction and the Background of Pauline Usage." Pages 197–226 in *Sapiential, Liturgical and Poetic Texts from Qumran: Proceedings of the Third Meeting of the International Organization for Qumran Studies, Oslo, 1998.* Edited by D. Falk, F. García Martínez, and E. Schuller. Studies on the Texts of the Desert of Judah 35. Leiden: Brill, 2000.

———. "Die paulinische Antithese von 'Fleisch' und 'Geist' und die palästinisch-jüdische Weisheitstradition." *Zeitschrift für die neutestamentliche Wissenschaft und die Kunde der älteren Kirche* 90 (1999): 45–77.

Freyne, S. *Jesus, a Jewish Galilean.* London: T&T Clark, 2004.

Fuchs, E., and P. Reymond. *La deuxième épitre de Saint Pierre. L'Épitre de Saint Jude.* 2d ed. Commentaire du Nouveau Testament 13b. Geneva: Labor et Fides, 1988.

Furnish, V. P. *Theology and Ethics in Paul.* New York: Abingdon, 1968.

Gafni, I. *Land, Center and Diaspora: Jewish Constructs in Late Antiquity.* Journal for the Study of the Pseudepigrapha: Supplement Series 21. Sheffield: Sheffield Academic Press, 1997.

Gager, J. G. *Kingdom and Community.* Englewood Cliffs, N.J.: Prentice-Hall, 1975.

Gamble, H. Y. "The New Testament Canon: Recent Research and the *Status Quaestionis*." Page 288 in *The Canon Debate.* Edited by Lee Martin McDonald and James A. Sanders. Peabody, Mass.: Hendrickson, 2002.

Gardiner, P. *The Nature of Historical Explanation.* Oxford: Clarendon, 1962.

Geertz, G. *The Interpretation of Cultures: Selected Essays.* New York: Basic Books, 1973.

Gerdmar, A. *Rethinking the Judaism-Hellenism Dichotomy: A Historiographical Case Study of Second Peter and Jude.* Coniectanea biblica: New Testament Series 36. Stockholm: Almquist & Wiksell, 2001. Reviewed by S. Hafemann, *Theologische Literaturzeitung* 128 (2003): 393–95.

Gerhardsson, B. *Memory and Manuscript: Oral Tradition and Written Transmission in Rabbinic Judaism and Early Christianity.* Uppsala: Gleerup, 1961.

Giesen, H. "Gemeinde als Liebesgemeinschaft dank göttlicher Neuzeugung: Zu 1 Pet. 1,22–2,3." *Studien zum Neuen Testament und seiner Umwelt* 24 (1999): 135–66.

Glasson, T. F. *Greek Influence in Jewish Eschatology.* London: SPCK, 1961.

Goldstein, J. A. "The Apocryphal Book of I Baruch." *Proceedings of the American Academy of Jewish Research* 46/47 (1979/1980): 179–99.

———. *II Maccabees.* Anchor Bible 41A. New York: Doubleday, 1983.

Goppelt, L. *Die apostolische und nachapostolische Zeit.* Die Kirche in ihrer Geschichte Band 1, Lieferung A. Göttingen: Vandenhoeck & Ruprecht, 1962. 2d ed., 1966. ET: *Apostolic and Post-Apostolic Times.* Grand Rapids: Baker, 1970. 2d ed. 1977.

———. *Der erste Petrusbrief.* Kritisch-exegetischer Kommentar über das Neue Testament 12.1. Göttingen: Vandenhoeck & Ruprecht, 1978. ET: *A Commentary on I Peter.* Grand Rapids: Eerdmans, 1993.

Goulder, M. "Did Peter Ever Go to Rome?" *Scottish Journal of Theology* 57 (2004): 377–96.

Gowan, D. E. "Wisdom and Endurance in James." *Horizons in Biblical Theology* 15 (1993): 145–53.

Green, M. *2 Peter and Jude.* Tyndale New Testament Commentaries 18. Rev. ed. Leicester: InterVarsity, 1987.

Gregory, A. *The Reception of Luke and Acts in the Period before Irenaeus.* Wissenschaftliche Untersuchungen zum Neuen Testament 2.169. Tübingen: Mohr Siebeck, 2003.

Gruen, E. *Diaspora: Jews amidst Greeks and Romans.* Cambridge, Mass.: Harvard University Press, 2002.

Gryglewicz, F. "L'Épître de St. Jacques et l'Évangile de St. Matthieu." *Roczniki Teologiczno-Kanoniczne* 8 (1961): 33–55.

Gunneweg, A. H. J. "Das Buch Baruch: Der Brief Jeremias." *Jüdische Schriften aus hellenistisch-römischer Zeit* 3.2 (1975): 167–92.

Guthrie, D. *New Testament Introduction.* London: Tyndale, 1970.

Habicht, C. "2. Makkabäerbuch." *Jüdische Schriften aus hellenistisch-römischer Zeit* 1.3 (1976): 167–285.

Haelst, J. van. *Catalogue des papyrus littéraires juifs et chrétiens.* Paris: Publications de la Sorbonne, 1976.

Hafemann, S. J. "Covenant Relationship." Pages 20–65 in *Central Themes in Biblical Theology, Mapping Unity in Diversity.* Edited by Scott J. Hafemann and Paul R. House. Nottingham: InterVarsity, 2007.

————. *Paul, Moses, and the History of Israel, The Letter/Spirit Contrast and the Argument from Scripture in 2 Corinthians 3*. Wissenschaftliche Untersuchungen zum Neuen Testament 81. Tübingen: Mohr Siebeck, 1995.

Hahn, F. "Die christologische Begründung urchristlicher Paränese." *Zeitschrift für die neutestamentliche Wissenschaft und die Kunde der älteren Kirche* 78 (1981): 90–99.

————. "Randbemerkungen zum Judasbrief." Pages 642–52 in *Studien zum Neuen Testament 2*. Wissenschaftliche Untersuchungen zum Neuen Testament 192. Edited by F. Hahn, J. Frey, and J. Schlegel. Tübingen: Mohr Siebeck, 2006.

Hahn, F., and P. Müller. "Der Jakobusbrief." *Theologische Rundschau* 63 (1998): 1–73.

Halson, B. R. "The Epistle of James: 'Christian Wisdom?'" *Studia evangelica 4*. Texte und Untersuchungen 102. Berlin: de Gruyter (1968): 308–14.

Hanhart, R., ed. *Esther*. 2d ed. Septuaginta: Vetus Testamentum Graecum auctoritate Academiae Scientiarum Gottingensis ed., 8, 3. Göttingen: Vandenhoeck & Ruprecht, 1983.

————. *Maccabaeorum liber II*. Septuaginta: Vetus Testamentum Graecum auctoritate Societatis Scientiarum Gottingensis ed., 9, 2. Göttingen: Vandenhoeck & Ruprecht, 1959.

————. *Zum Text des 2. und 3. Makkabäerbuches: Probleme der Überlieferung, der Auslegung und der Ausgabe*. Nachrichten der Akademie der Wissenschaften in Göttingen, no. 13. Göttingen: Vandenhoeck & Ruprecht, 1961.

Harnack, A. *Die Mission und Ausbreitung des Christentums in den ersten drei Jahrhunderten*. Leipzig: Hinrichs, 1906.

Harrington, D. J. "The Wisdom of the Scribe According to Ben Sira." Pages 181–88 in *Ideal Figures in Ancient Judaism*. Edited by George W. E. Nickelsburg and John Collins. Chico, Calif.: Scholars Press, 1980.

Hartin, P. J. *James*. Sacra pagina 14. Collegeville, Minn.: Liturgical, 2003.

————. *James and the Q Sayings of Jesus*. Journal for the Study of the New Testament: Supplement Series 47. Sheffield: Sheffield Academic Press, 1991.

————. "James and the Q Sermon on the Mount/Plain." Pages 440–57 in *Society of Biblical Literature 1989 Seminar Papers*. Edited by David J. Lull. Society of Biblical Literature Seminar Papers 28. Atlanta: Scholars Press, 1989.

————. "Poor." Pages 1070–71 in *Dictionary of the Bible*. Edited by David Noel Freedman. Grand Rapids: Eerdmans, 2000.

————. *A Spirituality of Perfection: Faith and Action in the Letter of James*. Collegeville, Minn.: Liturgical, 1999.

————. "Who is Wise and Understanding among You? (James 3:13): An Analysis of Wisdom, Eschatology and Apocalypticism in the Epistle of James." Pages 483–503 in *Society of Biblical Literature Seminar Papers*. Atlanta: Scholars Press, 1996.

Hauck, F. *Der Brief des Jakobus*. Kommentar zum Neuen Testament 16. Leipzig: Deichert, 1926.

Haupt, E. "F. Spitta, Der Brief des Jakobus." *Theologische Studien und Kritiken* 69 (1896): 747–68.

Hausammann, S. *Alte Kirche: Zur Geschichte und Theologie in den ersten vier Jahrhunderten*. 4 vols. Neukirchen-Vluyn: Neukirchener, 2001–2004.

Havener, I. *Q: The Sayings of Jesus: With a Reconstruction of Q by Athanasius Polag*. Wilmington, Del.: Michael Glazier, 1987.

Hayward, R. *The Targum of Jeremiah*. The Aramaic Bible 12. Edinburgh: T&T Clark, 1987.

Heil, Ch. *Die Ablehnung der Speisegebote durch Paulus: Zur Frage nach der Stellung des Apostels zum Gesetz*. Bonner biblische Beiträge 96. Weinheim: Beltz Athenäum, 1994.

Heiligenthal, R. "'Petrus und Jakobus, der Gerechte': Gedanken zur Rolle der beiden Säulenapostel in der Geschichte des frühen Christentums." *Zeitschrift für Neues Testament* 2 (1999): 32–40.

———. *Werke als Zeichen: Untersuchungen zur Bedeutung der menschlichen Taten im Frühjudentum, Neuen Testament und Frühchristentum*. Wissenschaftliche Untersuchungen zum Neuen Testament 2.9. Tübingen: Mohr Siebeck, 1983.

———. *Zwischen Henoch und Paulus: Studien zum theologiegeschichtlichen Ort des Judasbriefes*. Texte und Arbeiten zum neutestamentlichen Zeitalter 6. Tübingen: Francke, 1992.

Hengel, M. "Der Jakobusbrief als antipaulinische Polemik." Pages 248–78 in *Tradition and Interpretation in the New Testament*. Edited by G. F. Hawthorne and O. Betz. Grand Rapids: Eerdmans, 1987.

———. "Jakobus der Herrenbruder – der erste 'Papst'?" Pages 71–104 in *Glaube und Eschatologie*. Edited by Erich Gräßer and Otto Merk. Tübingen: Mohr Siebeck, 1985.

———. "Jerusalem als jüdische und hellenistische Stadt." Pages 115–56 in *Judaica, Hellenistica et Christiana: Kleine Schriften II*. Wissenschaftliche Untersuchungen zum Neuen Testament 109. Tübingen: Mohr Siebeck, 1999.

———. *Juden, Griechen und Barbaren*. Stuttgarter Bibelstudien 76. Stuttgart: Katholisches Bibelwerk, 1976. ET: *Jews, Greeks and Barbarians*. Philadelphia: Fortress, 1980.

———. *Judentum und Hellenismus: Studien zu ihrer Begegnung unter besonderer Berücksichtigung Palästinas bis zur Mitte des 2. Jh.s v.Chr.* 3d ed. Wissenschaftliche Untersuchungen zum Neuen Testament 10. Tübingen: Mohr Siebeck, 1988. ET: *Judaism and Hellenism*. 2 vols. London: SCM Press, 1974.

———. *Paulus und Jakobus: Kleine Schriften 3*. Wissenschaftliche Untersuchungen zum Neuen Testament 141. Tübingen: Mohr Siebeck, 2002.

———. "Qumran und der Hellenismus." Pages 258–94 in *Judaica et Hellenistica: Kleine Schriften I*. Wissenschaftliche Untersuchungen zum Neuen Testament 90. Tübingen: Mohr Siebeck, 1996.

———. "Die Ursprünge der Gnosis und das Urchristentum." Pages 190–223 in *Evangelium Schriftauslegung Kirche*. Edited by J. Ådna, S. J. Hafemann, and O. Hofius. Göttingen: Vandenhoeck & Ruprecht, 1997.

Hengel, M., and R. Deines. *The Pre-Christian Paul*. London: SCM Press, 1991.

Hengel, M., and Ch. Markschies. *The Hellenization of Judaea in the First Century after Christ*. London: SCM Press, 1989.

Herzer, J. *4 Baruch (Paraleipomena Jeremiou). Writings from the Greco-Roman World* 22. Atlanta: Society of Biblical Literature, 2005.

———. *Die Paralipomena Jeremiae.* Texte und Studien zum antiken Judentum 43. Tübingen: Mohr Siebeck, 1994.

———. *Petrus oder Paulus? Studien über das Verhältnis des Ersten Petrusbriefes zur paulinischen Tradition.* Wissenschaftliche Untersuchungen zum Neuen Testament 103. Tübingen: Mohr Siebeck, 1998.

Hiebert, D. E. "The Necessary Growth in the Christian Life: An Exposition of 2 Peter 1:5-11." *Bibliotheca sacra* 141 (1984): 43–54.

Hilgenfeld, A. B. C. *Die Ketzergeschichte des Urchristentums.* Leipzig, 1886.

Hill, C. C. *Hellenists and Hebrews: Reappraising Division within the Earliest Church.* Minneapolis: Fortress, 1992.

Hock, R. F., and E. N. O'Neil. *The Chreia in Ancient Rhetoric: The Classroom Exercises. Writings from the Greco-Roman World* 2. Atlanta: Society of Biblical Literature, 2002.

———. *The Progymnasmata.* Vol. 1 of *The Chreia in Ancient Rhetoric.* Society of Biblical Literature Texts and Translations 27; Graeco-Roman Religion Series 9. Atlanta: Scholars Press, 1986.

Holtz, T. "Der antiochenische Zwischenfall (Galater 2.11-14)." *New Testament Studies* 32 (1986): 344–61.

Holtzmann, H. J. "Das Problem des ersten johanneischen Briefes in seinem Verhältnis zum Evangelium," *Jahrbücher für protestantische Theologie* 8 (1882) 128–52.

———. *Lehrbuch der neutestamentlichen Theologie.* Edited by A. Jülicher and W. Bauer. Sammlung theologischer Lehrbücher. Freiburg: Mohr Siebeck, 1897. 2d. ed., 1911.

Hoppe, R. *Jakobusbrief.* Stuttgarter kleiner Kommentar, Neues Testament 15. Stuttgart: Katholisches Bibelwerk, 1989.

———. "Der Jakobusbrief als briefliches Zeugnis hellenistisch und hellenistisch-jüdisch geprägter Religiosität." Pages 164–89 in *Der neue Mensch in Christus.* Edited by J. Beutler. Quaestiones disputatae 190. Freiburg: Herder, 2001.

———. *Der theologische Hintergrund des Jakobusbriefes.* Forschung zur Bibel 28. Würzburg: Echter-Verlag, 1977.

Horbury, W. "The Name Mardochaeus in a Ptolemaic Inscription." *Vetus Testamentum* 41 (1991): 220–26.

Horrell, D. G. "The Product of a Petrine Circle? A Reassessment of the Origin and Character of 1 Peter." *Journal for the Study of the New Testament* 24/86 (2002): 29–60.

Horsley, R. A., ed. *Christian Origins: A People's History of Christianity.* Vol. 1. Minneapolis: Fortress, 2005.

Horst, P. W. van der. *The Sentences of Pseudo-Phocylides: With Introduction and Commentary.* Studia in Veteris Testamenti pseudepigraphica 4. Leiden: Brill, 1978.

Howard, W. F. "The Common Authorship of the Johannine Gospel and Epistles." *Journal of Theological Studies* 48 (1947): 12–25.

Howell, W., and W. Prevenier. *From Reliable Sources: An Introduction to Historical Methods*. Ithaca: Cornell University Press, 2001.

Hübner, H. *Die Theologie des Paulus und ihre neutestamentliche Wirkungsgeschichte*. Vol. 2 of *Theologie des Neuen Testaments*. Göttingen: Vandenhoeck & Ruprecht, 1993.

Hunzinger, C.-H. "Babylon als Deckname für Rom und die Datierung des 1. Petrusbriefes." Pages 67–77 in *Gottes Wort und Gottes Land: FS H.-W. Hertzberg*. Edited by H. Graf Reventlow. Göttingen: Vandenhoeck & Ruprecht, 1965.

Hurtado, L. W. *The Lord Jesus: Devotion to Jesus in the Earliest Church*. Grand Rapids: Eerdmans, 2003.

Huther, J. E. *Kritisch exegetisches Handbuch über den Brief des Jacobus*. Kritisch-exegetischer Kommentar über das Neue Testament 15. Göttingen: Vandenhoeck & Ruprecht, 3d ed., 1870.

Hvalvik, R. *The Struggle for Scripture and Covenant*. Wissenschaftliche Untersuchungen zum Neuen Testament 2.82. Tübingen: Mohr Siebeck, 1996.

Hyldahl, N. *Den ældste kristendoms historie*. Copenhagen: Museum Tusculanum, 1982.

Ilan, T. *Lexicon of Jewish Names in Late Antiquity*, Part I, *Palestine 330 BCE–200 CE*. Texte und Studien zum antiken Judentum 91. Tübingen: Mohr Siebeck, 2002.

Jackson-McCabe, M. A. "A Letter to the Twelve Tribes in the Diaspora: Wisdom and 'Apocalyptic' Eschatology in the Letter of James." Pages 504–17 in *Society of Biblical Literature Seminar Papers*. Atlanta: Scholars Press, 1996.

Jedin, H. *From the Apostolic Community to Constantine*. Vol. 1 of *The Early Church*. Freiburg: Herder, 1969.

Jervell, J. *Die Apostelgeschichte*. Kritisch-exegetischer Kommentar über das Neue Testament 3. Göttingen: Vandenhoeck & Ruprecht, 1998.

———. "The Circumcised Messiah." Pages 138–45 in *The Unknown Paul: Essays on Luke-Acts and Early Christian History*. Minneapolis: Augsburg, 1984.

———. *Luke and the People of God: A New Look at Luke-Acts*. Minneapolis: Augsburg, 1972.

———. "A Mighty Minority." *Studia Theologica* 34 (1980): 13–38. Repr. in *The Unknown Paul: Essays on Luke-Acts and Early Christian History*. Minneapolis: Augsburg, 1984.

Jewett, R. *Paul's Anthropological Terms*. Arbeiten zur Geschichte des antiken Judentums und des Urchristentums 10. Leiden: Brill, 1971.

Johnson, L. T. *Brother of Jesus, Friend of God: Studies in the Letter of James*. Grand Rapids: Eerdmans, 2004.

———. "The Letter of James." Pages 117–225 in *The New Interpreter's Bible* 12. Nashville: Abingdon, 1998.

———. *The Letter of James: A New Translation with Introduction and Commentary*. Anchor Bible 37A. New York: Doubleday, 1995.

———. "The Use of Leviticus 19 in the Letter of James." *Journal of Biblical Literature* 101 (1982): 391–401.

Joubert, S. J. "Persuasion in the Letter of Jude." *Journal for the Study of the New Testament* 58 (1995): 75–87.

Jouguet, P., and P. Perdrizet, eds. "Le Papyrus Bouriant n. 1: Un cahier d'écolier grec d'Egypte." Pages 153–54 in *Kolotes und Menedemos.* Edited by Wilhelm Crönert, 153–54. Studien zur Paläographie und Papyruskunde 6. Leipzig: Aveniarus, 1906. Repr., Amsterdam: Hakkert, 1965.

Kahrstedt, U. *Syrische Territorien in hellenistischer Zeit.* Abhandlungen der Gesellschaft der Wissenschaften zu Göttingen, Philologisch-historische Klasse, NF 19.2. Berlin: Weidmannsche Buchhandlung, 1926.

Kaiser, O. *Die alttestamentlichen Apokryphen: Eine Einleitung in Grundzügen.* Gütersloh: Gütersloher Verlagshaus, 2000.

Kalimi, I. "The Book of Esther and the Dead Sea Scrolls Community." *Theologische Zeitschrift* 60 (2004): 101–6.

Karrer, M. *Die Johannesoffenbarung als Brief.* Forschungen zur Religion und Literatur des Alten und Neuen Testaments 140. Göttingen: Vandenhoeck & Ruprecht, 1986.

Kattenbusch, F. *Das Apostolische Symbol, seine Entstehung, sein geschichtlicher Sinn, seine ursprüngliche Stellung im Kultus und in der Theologie der Kirche.* 2 vols. Leipzig: Hinrichs, 1894/1900. Repr., Darmstadt: Wissenschaftliche Buchgesellschaft, 1962.

Kautsky, K. *Foundations of Christianity.* New York: S. A. Russell, 1953. ET: *Ursprung des Christentums.* Stuttgart: J. H. W. Dietz, 1908.

Keck, L. E. "The Poor Among the Saints in the New Testament." *Zeitschrift für die neutestamentliche Wissenschaft und die Kunde der älteren Kirche* 56 (1965): 100–129.

Kelly, J. N. D. *The Epistles of Peter and of Jude.* Black's New Testament Commentaries 17. London: A. C. Black, 1969.

Kennedy, G. A. *New Testament Interpretation through Rhetorical Criticism.* Chapel Hill: University of North Carolina Press, 1984.

———. *Progymnasmata: Greek Textbooks of Prose Composition and Rhetoric.* Atlanta: Society of Biblical Literature, 2003.

Kittel, G. "Der geschichtliche Ort des Jakobusbriefes." *Zeitschrift für die neutestamentliche Wissenschaft und die Kunde der älteren Kirche* 41 (1942): 71–105.

Klauck, H.-J. *Die antike Briefliteratur und das Neue Testament.* Paderborn: Schöningh, 1998. ET: *Ancient Letters and the New Testament: A Guide to Context and Exegesis,* with collaboration of D. P. Bailey. Waco, Tex.: Baylor University Press, 2006.

———. "Zur rhetorischen Analyse der Johannesbriefe." *Zeitschrift für die neutestamentliche Wissenschaft und die Kunde der älteren Kirche* 81 (1990): 205–24.

Klein, M. *"Ein vollkommenes Werk": Vollkommenheit, Gesetz und Gericht als theologische Themen des Jakobusbriefes.* Beiträge zur Wissenschaft vom Alten und Neuen Testament 139. Stuttgart: Kohlhammer, 1995.

Klijn, A. F. J. *An Introduction to the New Testament.* Leiden: Brill, 1967.

———. "Jude 5 to 7." Pages 237–44 in *The New Testament Age: Essays in Honor of Bo Reicke.* Vol. 1. Edited by W. C. Weinrich. Macon, Ga.: Mercer, 1984.

———. "2 (Syriac Apocalypse of) Baruch." Pages 615–52 in *Old Testament Pseude-pigrapha* 1. Edited by J. H. Charlesworth. Anchor Bible Reference Library. New York: Doubleday, 1983–1985.

———. "Die syrische Baruch-Apokalypse." Pages 103–91 of *Jüdische Schriften aus hellenistisch-römischer Zeit* 5.2. Gütersloh: Gütersloher Verlagshaus, 1976.

Klijn, A. F. J., and G. J. Reinink. *Patristic Evidence for Jewish-Christian Sects.* Supplements to Novum Testamentum 36. Leiden: Brill, 1973.

Kloppenborg, J. S. "Blessing and Marginality: The 'Persecution Beatitude' in Q, Thomas & Early Christianity." *Forum* 2.3 (1986): 35–56.

———. *The Formation of Q: Trajectories in Ancient Wisdom Collections.* Studies in Antiquity and Christianity. Philadelphia: Fortress, 1987. Repr., Harrisburg, Pa.: Trinity, 2000.

———. "Patronage Avoidance in the Epistle of James." *Hervormde teologiese studies* 55.4 (1999): 755–94.

———. "The Sayings Gospel Q: Literary and Stratigraphic Problems." In *Symbols and Strata: Essays on the Sayings Gospel Q.* Edited by Risto Uro. Suomen Eksegeettisen Seuran Julkaisuja, Publications of the Finnish Exegetical Society 65. Helsinki: Finnish Exegetical Society, 1996.

Kmosko, M. "Epistola Baruch filii Neriae." Pages 1208–37 in *Patrologia Syriaca* 1/2. Edited by R. Graffin. Paris: Firmin-Didot, 1894–1926.

Knight, J. *2 Peter and Jude.* New Testament Guides. Sheffield: Sheffield Academic Press, 1995.

Knoch, O. B. *Der erste und zweite Petrusbrief. Der Judasbrief.* Regensburger Neues Testament. Regensburg: Pustet, 1990.

———. "Gab es eine Petrusschule in Rom? Überlegungen zu einer bedeutsamen Frage." *Studien zum Neuen Testament und seiner Umwelt* 16 (1991): 105–26.

Knopf, R., ed. *Ausgewählte Märtyrerakten.* Revised by G. Krüger. 4th ed. with *Nachtrag* by G. Ruhbach. Tübingen: Mohr Siebeck, 1965.

———. *Einführung in das Neue Testament.* Edited by H. Lietzmann and H. Weinel. 4th ed. Gießen: Töpelmann, 1934.

———. *Das nachapostolische Zeitalter.* Tübingen, 1905.

Köhler, W.-D. *Die Rezeption des Matthäusevangeliums in der Zeit vor Irenäus.* Wissenschaftliche Untersuchungen zum Neuen Testament 2.24. Tübingen: Mohr Siebeck, 1987.

Kondoleon, C. *Antioch: The Lost Ancient City.* Princeton: Princeton University Press, 2000.

Konradt, M. *Christliche Existenz nach dem Jakobusbrief: Eine Studie zu seiner soteriologischen und ethischen Konzeption.* Studien zur Umwelt des Neuen Testaments 22. Göttingen: Vandenhoeck & Ruprecht, 1998.

———. "Gott oder Mammon: Besitzethos und Diakonie im frühen Christentum." Pages 107–54 in *Diakonie und Ökonomie: Orientierungen im Europa des Wandels.* Edited by Christoph Sigrist. Zürich: Theologischer Verlag Zürich, 2006.

———. "Der Jakobusbrief als Brief des Jakobus: Erwägungen zum historischen Kontext des Jakobusbriefes im Lichte der traditionsgeschichtlichen Beziehungen zum 1 Petr und zum Hintergrund der Autorfiktion." Pages 16–53 in

Der Jakobusbrief: Beiträge zur Aufwertung der "strohernen Epistel." Edited by P. von Gemünden, M. Konradt, and G. Theißen. Münster: Lit, 2003.

———. "Der Jakobusbrief im frühchristlichen Kontext: Überlegungen zum traditionsgeschichtlichen Verhältnis des Jakobusbriefes zur Jesusüberlieferung, zur paulinischen Tradition und zum 1Petr." Pages 171–212 in *The Catholic Epistles and the Tradition*. Edited by J. Schlosser. Bibliotheca ephemeridum theologicarum lovaniensium 176. Leuven: Leuven University Press, 2004.

———. "Menschen- oder Bruderliebe? Beobachtungen zum Liebesgebot in den Testamenten der Zwölf Patriarchen." *Zeitschrift für die neutestamentliche Wissenschaft und die Kunde der älteren Kirche* 88 (1997): 296–310.

———. "Theologie in der 'strohernen Epistel': Ein Literaturbericht zu neueren Ansätzen in der Exegese des Jakobusbriefes." *Verkündigung und Forschung* 44 (1999): 54–78.

Köster, H. *Ancient Christian Gospels: Their History and Development*. Harrisburg: Trinity, 1990.

———. *Einführung in das Neue Testament im Rahmen der Religionsgeschichte und Kulturgeschichte der hellenistischen und römischen Zeit*. Berlin: de Gruyter, 1980.

———. "ΓΝΩΜΑΙ ΔΙΑΦΟΡΑΙ." *Zeitschrift für Theologie und Kirche* 65 (1968): 160–203.

Köster, H., and J. Robinson. *Trajectories through Early Christianity*. Philadelphia: Fortress, 1971. Translation of *Entwicklungslinien durch die Welt des frühen Christentums*. Tübingen: Mohr Siebeck, 1971.

Kottsieper, I. "Zusätze zu Ester." Pages 109–207 in O. H. Steck et al., *Das Buch Baruch, Der Brief des Jeremia, Zusätze zu Ester und Daniel*. Das Alte Testament Deutsch Apokryphen 5. Göttingen: Vandenhoeck & Ruprecht, 1998.

Kratz, R. G. "Der Brief des Jeremia." Pages 71–108 in O. H. Steck et al., *Das Buch Baruch, Der Brief des Jeremia, Zusätze zu Ester und Daniel*. Das Alte Testament Deutsch Apokryphen 5. Göttingen: Vandenhoeck & Ruprecht, 1998.

———. "Die Rezeption von Jeremia 10 und 29 im pseudepigraphen Brief des Jeremia." *Journal for the Study of Judaism in the Persian, Hellenistic, and Roman Periods* 26 (1995): 2–31. Repr. pages 316–39 in *Das Judentum im Zeitalter des Zweiten Tempels*. Forschungen zum Alten Testament 42. Edited by R. G. Kratz. Tübingen: Mohr Siebeck, 2004.

Kraus, Th. J. *Sprache, Stil und historischer Ort des zweiten Petrusbriefes*. Wissenschaftliche Untersuchungen zum Neuen Testament 2.136. Tübingen: Mohr Siebeck, 2001.

Kraus, W. *Zwischen Jerusalem und Antiochia: Die "Hellenisten", Paulus und die Aufnahme der Heiden in das endzeitliche Gottesvolk*. Stuttgarter Bibelstudien 179. Stuttgart: Verlag Katholisches Bibelwerk, 1999.

Krodel, G. *The General Letters: Hebrews, James, 1–2 Peter, Jude, 1–2–3 John*. Minneapolis: Fortress, 1995.

Kuechler, C. G. *De rhetorica epistolae Jacobi indole*. Leipzig: Glueck, 1818.

Kuhrt, A. "Alexander in Babylon." Pages 121–30 in *The Roots of the European Tradition: Proceedings of the 1987 Groningen Achaemenid History Workshop*. Edited by H. Sancisi-Weerdenburg and J. W. Drijvers. Achaemenid History 5. Leiden: Nederlands Instituut for het Nabije Oosten, 1990.

Kümmel, W. G. *Einleitung in das Neue Testament*. Heidelberg: Quelle & Meyer, 1963.

Kürzdörfer, K. "Der Charakter des Jakobusbriefes: Eine Auseinandersetzung mit den Thesen von A. Meyer und M. Dibelius." Ms. diss., Tübingen, 1966.

Lampe, P. *Die stadtrömischen Christen in den ersten beiden Jahrhunderten: Untersuchungen zur Sozialgeschichte*. Wissenschaftliche Untersuchungen zum Neuen Testament 2.18. Tübingen: Mohr-Siebeck, 1987.

Lampe, P, and U. Luz. "Post-Pauline Christianity and Pagan Society." In *Christian Beginnings: Word and Community from Jesus to Post-Apostolic Times*. Edited by J. Becker. Louisville, Ky.: Westminster John Knox, 1993.

Landon, Ch. *A Text-Critical Study of the Epistle of Jude*. Journal for the Study of the New Testament: Supplement Series 135. Sheffield: Sheffield Academic Press, 1996.

Lausberg, H. *Handbook of Literary Rhetoric: A Foundation for Literary Study*. Leiden: Brill, 1998.

Law, R. *The Tests of Life: A Study of the First Epistle of St. John*. Edinburgh: T&T Clark, 1909.

Laws, S. *The Epistle of James*. Black's New Testament Commentaries. Peabody, Mass.: Hendrickson, 1980.

Lechler, G. V. *Das apostolische und das nachapostolische Zeitalter*. 2d ed. Leipzig, 1857.

Leemhuis, F., A. F. J. Klijn, and G. J. H. van Gelder. *The Arabic Text of the Apocalypse of Baruch*. Leiden: Brill, 1986.

Lemke, H. *Judenchristentum zwischen Ausgrenzung und Integration: Zur Geschichte eines exegetischen Begriffes*. Hamburger Theologische Studien 25. Münster: Lit, 2001.

Levine, L. I. *Judaism and Hellenism in Antiquity: Conflict or Confluence?* Seattle: University of Washington, 1998.

Lietzmann, H. *Geschichte der Alten Kirche*. 4 vols. Berlin: de Gruyter, 1936–1944. Repr. in one vol., 1999.

———. *Symbolstudien I–XIV*. Darmstadt, 1966.

Lieu, J. M. " 'Grace to You and Peace': The Apostolic Greeting." *Bulletin of the John Rylands University Library of Manchester* 68 (1985/1986): 161–78.

———. "Letters." Pages 445–56 in *The Oxford Handbook of Biblical Studies*. Edited by J. W. Rogerson and J. M. Lieu. Oxford: Oxford University Press, 2006.

———. *The Theology of the Johannine Epistles*. Cambridge: Cambridge University Press, 1991.

———. "What Was from the Beginning." *New Testament Studies* 39 (1993): 458–77.

Link, H. *Rezeptionsforschung: Eine Einführung in Methoden und Probleme*. 2d ed. Stuttgart: Kohlhammer, 1980.

Lohmeyer, E. *Soziale Fragen im Urchristentum*. Wissenschaft und Bildung. Einzeldarstellungen aus allen Gebieten des Wissens 172. Leipzig, 1921.

———. *Vom Begriff der religiösen Gemeinschaft*. Edited by Richard Hönigswald. Wissenschaftl. Grundfragen 3. Leipzig, 1925.

Löhr, H. *Studien zum frühchristlichen und frühjüdischen Gebet: Untersuchungen zu*

1 Clem 59 bis 61 in seinem literarischen, historischen und theologischen Kontext. Wissenschaftliche Untersuchungen zum Neuen Testament 160. Tübingen: Mohr Siebeck, 2003.

Lohse, E. *Die Entstehung des Neue Testaments.* Theologische Wissenschaft 4. Stuttgart: Kohlhammer, 1972.

———. "Glaube und Werke: Zur Theologie des Jakobusbriefes." *Zeitschrift für die neutestamentliche Wissenschaft und die Kunde der älteren Kirche* 48 (1957): 1–22.

———. "Das Christentum um die Wende vom 1. zum 2. Jahrhundert. Die frühkatholische Kirche." Pages 53–72 in *Alte Kirche und Ostkirche.* Edited by V. R. Kottje and B. Moeller. Vol. 1 of *Ökumenische Kirchengeschichte.* München: Kaiser, 1970. 5th ed., 1989.

Lona, H. E. *Der erste Clemensbrief.* Kommentar zu den Apostolischen Vätern 2. Göttingen: Vandenhoeck & Ruprecht, 1998.

Lüdemann, G. *Paulus, der Heidenapostel, Bd. 1: Studien zur Chronologie.* Forschungen zur Religion und Literatur des Alten und Neuen Testaments 123. Göttingen: Vandenhoeck & Ruprecht, 1980.

Ludwig, M. *Wort als Gesetz: Eine Untersuchung zum Verständnis von "Wort" und "Gesetz" in israelitisch-frühjüdischen und neutestamentlichen Schriften: Gleichzeitig ein Beitrag zur Theologie des Jakobusbriefes.* Europäische Hochschulschriften 23, 502. Frankfurt am Main: Lang, 1994.

Luther, M. D. *Martin Luthers Werke: Kritische Gesamtausgabe.* Die Deutsche Bibel 6. Weimar, 1929.

Luz, U. *Das Evangelium nach Matthäus 1, Mt 1-7.* Evangelisch-katholischer Kommentar zum Neuen Testament 1.1. 2d ed. Zürich: Benziger and Neukirchen-Vluyn: Neukirchener, 1989.

Mack, B. L. "Elaboration of the Chreia in the Hellenistic School." Pages 53–57 in *Patterns of Persuasion in the Gospels.* Edited by B. L. Mack and V. K. Robbins. Foundations & Facets: Literary Facets. Sonoma, Calif.: Polebridge, 1989.

Malatesta, E. *Interiority and Covenant: A Study of [einai En] and [menein En] in the First Letter of Saint John.* AnBib 69. Rome: Biblical Institute Press, 1978.

Malina, B. *The New Testament World: Insights from Cultural Anthropology.* Louisville, Ky.: Westminster John Knox, 1993.

———. "Wealth and Poverty in the New Testament and its World," *Interpretation* 41 (1987): 354–67.

Markschies, C. "Alte Kirche." Page 345 in *Religion in Geschichte und Gegenwart: Handwörterbuch für Theologie und Religionswissenschaft* 1. Edited by Hans Dieter Betz, Don S. Browning, Bernd Janowski, and Eberhard Jüngel. 4th ed. Tübingen: Mohr Siebeck, 1998.

———. "Gnosis/Gnostizismus II/1." Pages 1045–49 in *Religion in Geschichte und Gegenwart: Handwörterbuch für Theologie und Religionswissenschaft* 3. Edited by Hans Dieter Betz, Don S. Browning, Bernd Janowski, and Eberhard Jüngel. 4th ed. Tübingen: Mohr Siebeck, 2001.

Martin, G. C. "The Epistle of James as a Storehouse of the Sayings of Jesus." Pages 174–84 in *The Expositor.* Edited by Samuel Cox, William Robertson Nicoll, and James Moffatt. Seventh Series 3. London: Hodder & Stoughton, 1907.

Martin, R. P. *James*. Word Biblical Commentary 48. Waco, Tex.: Word Books, 1988.

Martin, T. W. *Metaphor and Composition in 1 Peter*. Society of Biblical Literature Dissertation Series 131. Atlanta: Scholars Press, 1992.

Massebieau, L. "L'Épître de Jacques est-elle l'oeuvre d'un chrétien?" *Revue de l'histoire des religions* 31–32 (1895): 249–83.

Mathys, H.-P.. *Liebe deinen Nächsten wie Dich selbst: Untersuchungen zum alttestamentlichen Gebot der Nächstenliebe (Lev 19,18)*. Orbis biblicus et orientalis 71. Freiburg Schweiz: Universitätsverlag Fribourg, 1986.

Mayor, J. B. *The Epistle of St. James: The Greek Text with Introduction, Notes and Comments*. London: Macmillan, 1892. 2d ed., 1897. 3d ed., 1913. Repr., Grand Rapids: Eerdmans, 1990.

McDonald, L., and J. A. Sanders. *The Canon Debate*. Peabody, Mass.: Hendrickson, 2002.

McGiffert, A. C., trans. "The Church History of Eusebius." Pages 1–403 in *Nicene and Post-Nicene Fathers*. Edited by Philip Schaff. Second Series 1. Edinburgh, 1890.

McKnight, S. "A Parting within the Way: Jesus and James on Israel and Purity." Pages 83–129 in *James the Just and Christian Origins*. Edited by Bruce D. Chilton and Craig A. Evans. Leiden: Brill, 1999.

McNeile, A. H. *An Introduction to the Study of the New Testament*. Oxford: Clarendon, 1953.

Meeks, W. A. *The First Urban Christians: The Social World of the Apostle Paul*. New York, 1983.

Meeks, W. A., and R. L. Wilken. *Jews and Christians in Antioch in the First Four Centuries of the Common Era*. Missoula, Mont.: Scholars Press, 1978.

Mendenhall, G. E. "Covenant Forms in Israelite Tradition." *Biblical Archaeologist* 17 (1954): 50–76

Merklein, H. *Der erste Brief an die Korinther: Kapitel 1–4*. Ökumenischer Taschenbuch-Kommentar 7.1. Gütersloh: Gütersloher Verlagshaus, 1992.

Metzger, B. M. *The Canon of the New Testament*. Oxford: Clarendon, 1987.

———. *A Textual Commentary on the Greek New Testament*. 3d corrected ed. London: United Bible Societies, 1975. 2d ed., Stuttgart: Dt. Bibelgesellschaft, 1994.

Metzner, R. *Die Rezeption des Matthäusevangeliums im 1. Petrusbrief: Studien zum traditionsgeschichtlichen und theologischen Einfluß des 1. Evangeliums auf den 1. Petrusbrief*. Wissenschaftliche Untersuchungen zum Neuen Testament 2.74. Tübingen: Mohr Siebeck, 1995.

Meyer, A. *Das Rätsel des Jacobusbriefes*. Beihefte zur Zeitschrift für die neutestamentliche Wissenschaft 10. Gießen: Töpelmann, 1930.

Michaels, J. R. *1 Peter*. Word Bible Commentary 49. Nashville: Thomas Nelson, 1988.

Michl, J. *Die katholischen Briefe*. 2d ed. Regensburger Neues Testament 8.2. Regensburg: Pustet, 1968.

Milik, J. T. *The Books of Enoch: Aramaic Fragments of Qumran Cave 4*. Oxford: Clarendon, 1976.

Millauer, H. *Leiden als Gnade: Eine traditionsgeschichtliche Untersuchung zur Leiden-stheologie des ersten Petrusbriefes.* Europäische Hochschulschriften 23. Theologie 56. Bern: Peter Lang, 1976.

Mitchell, M. M. "Brief." Pages 1757–62 in *Religion in Geschichte und Gegenwart: Handwörterbuch für Theologie und Religionswissenschaft* 1. Edited by Hans Dieter Betz, Don S. Browning, Bernd Janowski, and Eberhard Jüngel. 4th ed. Tübingen: Mohr Siebeck, 1998.

———. "The Letter of James as a Document of Paulinism?" Pages 75–98 in *Reading James with New Eyes: Methodological Reassessments of the Letter of James.* Edited by R. L. Webb and J. S. Kloppenborg. Library of New Testament Studies 342. London: T&T Clark, 2007.

Moffatt, J. *The General Epistles of James, Peter and Jude.* Moffatt New Testament Commentary. London: Hodder & Stoughton, 1928.

———. *An Introduction to the Literature of the New Testament.* 3d ed. International Theological Library. Edinburgh: Clark, 1918.

Molthagen, J. "Die Lage der Christen im römischen Reich nach dem 1. Petrusbrief: Zum Problem einer domitianischen Verfolgung." *Historia* 44 (1995): 422–58.

Momigliano, A. "The Second Book of Maccabees." *Classical Philology* 70 (1975): 81–88.

Moo, D. J. *The Letter of James.* Pelican New Testament Commentaries. Grand Rapids: Eerdmans, 2000.

Moore, C. A. *Daniel, Esther and Jeremiah: The Additions.* Anchor Bible 44. New York: Doubleday, 1977.

Morgan, T. *Literate Education in the Hellenistic and Roman Worlds.* Cambridge Classical Studies. Cambridge: Cambridge University Press, 1999.

Morgenthaler, R. *Statistik des neutestamentlichen Wortschatzes.* Zürich: Gotthelf, 1958.

Mount, C. *Pauline Christianity: Luke-Acts and the Legacy of Paul.* Supplements to Novum Testamentum 104. Leiden: Brill, 2002.

Müller, K. *Thora für die Völker: Die noachidischen Gebote und Ansätze zu ihrer Rezeption im Christentum.* Studien zu Kirche und Israel 15. Berlin: Institut Kirche und Judentum, 1994.

Mussner, F. *Der Jakobusbrief: Auslegung.* 3d ed. Herders theologischer Kommentar zum Neuen Testament 13.1. Freiburg: Herder, 1975. 4th ed., 1981. 5th ed., 1987.

Nadeau, R. E. "Hermogenes' *On Stases*: A Translation with an Introduction and Notes." *Speech Monographs* 31 (1964): 361–424.

Nauck, W. "Freude im Leiden: Zum Problem einer urchristlichen Verfolgungstradition." *Zeitschrift für die neutestamentliche Wissenschaft und die Kunde der älteren Kirche* 46 (1955): 68–80.

Neirynck, F. "Paul and the Sayings of Jesus." Pages 265–321 in *L'apôtre Paul: Personnalité, style et conception du ministère.* Edited by A. Vanhoye. Bibliotheca ephemeridum theologicarum lovaniensium 73. Leuven: Leuven University Press and Peeters, 1986.

Neusner, J. "History and Purity in First-Century Judaism." *History of Religions* 18 (1978): 1–17.

———. *The Idea of Purity in Ancient Judaism.* Leiden: Brill, 1973.

Newsom, C. A. "The Development of 1 Enoch 6–19: Cosmology and Judgment." *Catholic Biblical Quarterly* 42 (1980): 310–29.

Neyrey, J. H. "The Form and Background of the Polemic in 2 Peter." Ph.D. Diss., Yale University, 1977.

———. *2 Peter, Jude.* Anchor Bible 37C. New York: Doubleday, 1993.

Nicholson, E. W. "Covenant in a Century of Study Since Wellhausen." Pages 3–117 in *God and His People: Covenant and Theology in the Old Testament.* Edited by Ernest W. Nicholson. Oxford: Clarendon, 1986.

Nickelsburg, G. W. E. "Apocalyptic and Myth in 1 Enoch 6–11." *Journal of Biblical Literature* 96 (1977): 383–405.

———. *1 Enoch 1.* Hermeneia. Minneapolis: Fortress, 2001.

———. *Jewish Literature between the Bible and the Mishnah: A Historical and Literary Introduction.* London: SCM Press, 1981. 2d ed. Minneapolis: Fortress, 2005.

Niebuhr, K.-W. "Art: Paränese 2: Neues Testament." Pages 930–31 in *Religion in Geschichte und Gegenwart: Handwörterbuch für Theologie und Religionswissenschaft* 6. Edited by Hans Dieter Betz, Don S. Browning, Bernd Janowski, and Eberhard Jüngel. 4th ed. Tübingen: Mohr Siebeck, 2003.

———. "Exegese im kanonischen Zusammenhang: Überlegungen zur theologischen Relevanz der Gestalt des neutestamentlichen Kanons." Pages 557–84 in *The Biblical Canons.* Edited by J.-M. Auwers and H. J. de Jonge. Bibliotheca ephemeridum theologicarum lovaniensium 163. Leuven: Leuven University Press and Peeters, 2003.

———. "Der Jakobusbrief im Licht frühjüdischer Diasporabriefe." *New Testament Studies* 44 (1998): 420–43.

———. "Jesus als Lehrer der Gottesherrschaft und die Weisheit: Eine Problemskizze." *Zeitschrift für Pädagogik und Theologie* 53 (2001): 116–25.

———. "A New Perspective on James? Neuere Forschungen zum Jakobusbrief." *Theologische Literaturzeitung* 129 (2004): 1019–1044.

———. "Die paulinische Rechtfertigungslehre in der gegenwärtigen exegetischen Diskussion." Pages 106–30 in *Worum geht es in der Rechtfertigungslehre? Das biblische Fundament der "Gemeinsamen Erklärung" von katholischer Kirche und Lutherischem Weltbund.* Edited by T. Söding. Quaestiones disputatae 180. Freiburg: Herder, 1999.

———. Review of M. Konrad, *Christliche Existenz nach dem Jakobusbrief. Theologische Literaturzeitung* 125 (2000): 756–59.

———. "Tora ohne Tempel: Paulus und der Jakobusbrief im Zusammenhang frühjüdischer Torarezeption für die Diaspora." Pages 427–60 in *Gemeinde ohne Tempel—Community without Temple: Zur Substituierung und Transformation des Jerusalemer Tempels und seines Kults im Alten Testament, antiken Judentum und frühen Christentum.* Edited by B. Ego, A. Lange, and P. Pilhofer. Wissenschaftliche Untersuchungen zum Neuen Testament 118. Tübingen: Mohr Siebeck, 1999.

Nienhuis, D. *Not by Paul Alone: The Formation of the Catholic Epistle Collection and the Christian Canon.* Waco, Tex.: Baylor University Press, 2007. (Revision of "The Letter of James in the Formation of the New Testament Catholic Epistle Collection." Ph.D. diss., University of Aberdeen.)

Nir, R. *The Destruction of Jerusalem and the Idea of Redemption in the Syriac Apocalypse of Baruch.* Society of Biblical Literature Early Judaism and Its Literature 20. Atlanta: Society of Biblical Literature, 2003.

Nisula, T. "'Time has passed since you sent your letter': Letter Phraseology in 1 and 2 Maccabees." *Journal for the Study of the Pseudepigrapha* 14 (2005): 201–22.

Nösgen, K. F. "Der Ursprung und die Entstehung des dritten Evangeliums." *Theologische Studien und Kritiken* 53 (1880): 49–137.

Oleson, J. P. "An Echo of Hesiod's *Theogony* vv. 190-2 in Jude 13." *New Testament Studies* 25 (1979): 492–503.

Osburn, C. D. "1 Enoch 80:2-8 (67:2-5) and Jude 12-13." *Catholic Biblical Quarterly* 47 (1985): 296–303.

Overbeck, F. *Schriften bis 1873.* Vol. 1 of *Werke und Nachlaß.* Stuttgart: Metzler, 1994.

Painter, J. *1, 2, and 3 John.* Sacra pagina. Collegeville, Minn.: Liturgical, 2002.

———. "James as the First Catholic Epistle." *Interpretation* 60.3 (2006): 245–59.

———. *Just James: The Brother of Jesus in History and Tradition.* Minneapolis: Fortress, 1999. 2d ed. Columbia: University of South Carolina Press, 2004.

———. *John: Witness and Theologian.* London: SPCK, 1975.

———. "The Power of Words: Rhetoric in James and Paul." Pages 235–73 in *The Missions of James, Peter, and Paul: Tensions in Early Christianity.* Edited by Bruce Chilton and Craig Evans. Supplements to Novum Testamentum 115. Leiden: Brill, 2005.

———. *The Quest for the Messiah: The History, Literature and Theology of the Johannine Community.* Edinburgh: T&T Clark, 1991. 2d ed. Nashville: Abingdon, 1993.

Pardee, D. *Handbook of Ancient Hebrew Letters: A Study Edition.* Society of Biblical Literature Sources for Biblical Study 15. Chico, Calif.: Scholars Press, 1982.

Parsons, P. J. "A School-Book from the Sayce Collection." *Zeitschrift für Papyrologie und Epigraphik* 6 (1970): 133–49.

Patillon, M., ed. *Aelius Théon, Progymnasmata: Texte établi et traduit par Michel Patillon avec l'assistance, pour l'Arménien, de Giancarlo Bolognesi.* Collection des universités de France. Paris: Belles Lettres, 1997.

Patry, R. *L'Épitre de Jacques: dans ses rapports avec la prédication de Jésus.* Alençon: Guy, 1899.

Patterson, S. J. *The Gospel of Thomas and Jesus.* Foundations & Facets: Reference Series. Sonoma, Calif.: Polebridge, 1993.

Paulsen, H. *Der Zweite Petrusbrief und der Judasbrief.* Kritisch-exegetischer Kommentar über das Neue Testament 17.2. Göttingen: Vandenhoeck & Ruprecht, 1992.

Pearson, B. *Gnosticism and Christianity in Roman and Coptic Egypt.* New York: T&T Clark, 2004.

———. *The Pneumatikos-Psychikos Terminology in 1 Corinthians: A Study in the Theology of the Corinthian Opponents of Paul in Its Relation to Gnosticism.* Society of Biblical Literature Dissertation Series 12. Missoula, Mont.: Scholars Press, 1973.

Penner, T. C. "The Epistle of James in Current Research." *Currents in Research: Biblical Studies* 7 (1999): 257–308.

———. *The Epistle of James and Eschatology: Re-reading an Ancient Christian Letter.* Journal for the Study of the New Testament: Supplement Series 121. Sheffield: Sheffield Academic Press, 1996.

Perkins, P. *The Johannine Epistles.* New Testament Message 21. Wilmington, Del.: Michael Glazier, 1979.

Pesch, R. *Die Apostelgeschichte, 2. Teilbd.: Apg 13-28.* Evangelisch-katholischer Kommentar zum Neuen Testament 5.2. Zürich: Benzinger, 1986.

———. "Das Jerusalemer Abkommen und die Lösung des Antiochenischen Konflikts: Ein Versuch über Gal 2, Apg 10,1-11,18, Apg 11,27-30; 12,25 und Apg 15,1-41." Pages 105–22 in *Kontinuität und Einheit: Für Franz Mussner.* Edited by Paul-Gerhard Müller and Werner Stenger. Freiburg: Herder 1981.

Peterson, E. "Das Praescriptum des 1. Clemens-Briefes." Pages 129–36 in idem *Frühkirche, Judentum und Gnosis.* Rome: Herder, 1959.

Petracca, V. *Gott oder das Geld: Die Besitzethik des Lukas.* Texte und Arbeiten zum neutestamentlichen Zeitalter 39. Tübingen: Francke Verlag, 2003.

Pfleiderer, O. *Das Urchristenthum, seine Schriften und Lehren, in geschichtlichem Zusammenhang beschrieben.* Berlin: Reimer, 1887.

Piper, R. A. "Matthew 7,7-11 par. Lk 11,9-13: Evidence of Design and Argument in the Collection of Jesus' Sayings." Page 412 in *Logia: Les Paroles de Jésus—The Sayings of Jesus: Mémorial Joseph Coppens.* Edited by J. Delobel. Bibliotheca ephemeridum theologicarum lovaniensium 59. Leuven: Leuven University Press and Peeters, 1982.

Polag, A. *Fragmenta Q: Textheft zur Logienquelle.* Neukirchen-Vluyn: Neukirchener, 1979.

Popkes, W. *Adressaten, Situation und Form des Jakobusbriefes.* Stuttgarter Bibelstudien 125/126. Stuttgart: Verlag Katholisches Bibelwerk, 1986.

———. *Der Jakobusbrief.* Theologischer Handkommentar zum Neuen Testament 14. Leipzig: Evangelische Verlagsanstalt, 2001.

———. "James and Paraenesis, Reconsidered." Pages 535–61 in *Texts and Contexts: Biblical Texts in their Textual and Situational Contexts.* Edited by T. Fornberg and D. Hellholm. Oslo: Scandinavian University Press, 1995.

———. "James and Scripture: An Exercise in Intertextuality." *New Testament Studies* 45 (1999): 213–29.

———. "The Law of Liberty (James 1:25; 2:12)." Pages 131–42 in *International Theological Studies: Contributions of Baptist Scholars* 1. Edited by the Faculty of Baptist Theological Seminary Rüschlikon. Bern: Peter Lang, 1994.

———. *Paränese und Neues Testament.* Stuttgarter Bibelstudien 168. Stuttgart: Verlag Katholisches Bibelwerk, 1996.

Porten, B., and A. Yardeni. *Letters, Appendix: Aramaic Letters from the Bible*. Vol. 1 of *Textbook of Aramaic Documents from Ancient Egypt*. Jerusalem: Hebrew University, 1986.

Porter, S. E. "Is δίψυχος (James 1,8; 4,8) a 'Christian' Word?" *Biblica* 71 (1991): 469–98.

Prasad, J. *Foundations of the Christian Way of Life According to 1 Peter 1,13–25*. Anchor Bible 146. Rome: Ed. Pontificio Istituto Biblico, 2000.

Pratscher, W. *Der Herrenbruder Jakobus und die Jakobustradition*. Forschungen zur Religion und Literatur des Alten und Neuen Testaments 139. Göttingen: Vandenhoeck & Ruprecht, 1987.

Pressensé, E. D. *Histoire des trois premiers siècles de l'église chrétienne*. Paris, 1858.

Priest, J. F. "Moses, Testament of." Pages 920–22 in *Anchor Bible Dictionary* 4. Edited by D. N. Freedman. New York: Doubleday, 1992.

Räisänen, H. *Neutestamentliche Theologie?* Sources bibliques 186. Stuttgart: Verlag Katholisches Bibelwerk, 2000.

Rau, E. "Kosmologie, Eschatologie und die Lehrautorität Henochs." Diss. theol., Hamburg University, 1974.

Reichert, A. *Eine urchristliche praeparatio ad martyrium: Studien zur Komposition, Traditionsgeschichte und Theologie des 1. Petrusbriefes*. Beiträge zur biblischen Exegese und Theologie 22. Bern: Peter Lang, 1989.

Reicke, B. I. *The Epistles of James, Peter, and Jude*. Anchor Bible 37. Garden City, N.Y.: Doubleday, 1964.

Reitzenstein, R. *Die hellenistischen Mysterienreligionen*. 3d ed. Leipzig: Teubner, 1927.

Renan, E. *Histoire des origines du Christianisme*. Paris: Lévy, 1863.

Rendall, G. H. *The Epistle of St. James and Judaic Christianity*. Cambridge: Cambridge University Press, 1927.

Resch, A. *Der Paulinismus und die Logia Jesu in ihrem gegenseitigen Verhältnis untersucht*. Texte und Untersuchungen 27. Leipzig: Hinrichs, 1904.

Reumann, J. *Righteousness in the New Testament*. Philadelphia: Fortress, 1982.

Rhoads, D. "The Letter of James: Friend of God." *Currents in Theology and Mission* 25 (1998): 473–86.

Rhodes, J. N. *The Epistle of Barnabas and the Deuteronomic Tradition*. Wissenschaftliche Untersuchungen zum Neuen Testament 2.188. Tübingen: Mohr Siebeck, 2004.

Riesenfeld, H. *The Gospel Tradition*. Philadelphia: Fortress, 1970.

Ritschl, A. *Die Entstehung der altkatholischen Kirche*. 2d ed. Bonn, 1857.

Robbins, V. K. "Pragmatic Relations as a Criterion for Authentic Sayings." *Forum* 1.3 (1985): 35–63.

———. "Progymnastic Rhetorical Composition and Pre-Gospel Traditions: A New Approach." Pages 111–47 in *The Synoptic Gospels: Source Criticism and New Literary Criticism*. Edited by C. Focant. Bibliotheca ephemeridum theologicarum lovaniensium 110. Leuven: Leuven University Press and Peeters, 1993.

———. *The Tapestry of Early Christian Discourse: Rhetoric, Society and Ideology*. London: Routledge, 1996.

———. "Writing as a Rhetorical Act in Plutarch and the Gospels." Pages 142–68 in *Persuasive Artistry: Studies in New Testament Rhetoric in Honor of George A. Kennedy*. Edited by D. F. Watson. Sheffield: JSOT Press, 1991.

Robertson, A. T. *A Grammar of the Greek New Testament in the Light of Historical Research*. Nashville: Broadman, 1934.

Robinson, J. A. T. *Redating the New Testament*. London: SCM Press, 1976.

Robinson, J. M., Paul Hoffmann, and J. S. Kloppenborg, eds. *The Critical Edition of Q: A Synopsis, Including the Gospels of Matthew and Luke, Mark and Thomas, with English, German and French Translations of Q and Thomas*. Hermeneia Supplements. Leuven: Peeters, 2000.

Roloff, J. *Die Apostelgeschichte*. Das Neue Testament Deutsch 5. Göttingen: Vandenhoeck & Ruprecht, 1988.

———. *Die Kirche im Neuen Testament*. Grundrisse zum Neuen Testament 10. Göttingen: Vandenhoeck & Ruprecht, 1993.

Ropes, J. H. *A Critical and Exegetical Commentary on the Epistle of St. James*. International Critical Commentary. Edinburgh: T&T Clark, 1916.

Rose, V. "L'Épitre de saint Jacques est-elle un écrit chrétien?" *Revue biblique* 5 (1896): 519–34.

Rowston, D. "The Most Neglected Book in the New Testament." *New Testament Studies* 21 (1975): 554–63.

Salom, A. P. "Some Aspects of the Grammatical Style of 1 John." *Journal of Biblical Literature* 72 (1955): 96–102.

Salomonsen, B. *Die Tosefta, Seder IV: Nezikin, 3: Sanhedrin–Makkot*. Rabbinische Texte. First Series 4.3. Stuttgart: Kohlhammer, 1976.

Sals, U. *Die Biographie der "Hure Babylon": Studien zur Intertextualität der Babylon-Texte in der Bibel*. Forschungen zum Alten Testament 2.6. Tübingen: Mohr Siebeck, 2004.

Sanders, E. P. "Jewish Association with Gentiles and Galatians 2:11-14." Pages 170–88 in *The Conversation Continues: Studies in Paul and John*. Edited by Robert T. Fortna and Beverly R. Gaventa. Nashville: Abingdon, 1990.

———. *Paul and Palestinian Judaism*. Philadelphia: Fortress, 1977.

Sanders, J. A. "Torah and Paul." In *God's Christ and His People: Studies in Honour of Nils Alstrup Dahl*. Edited by Jacob Jervell and Wayne A. Meeks. Oslo: Universitets for laget, 1977.

Sänger, D. "διασπορά." Pages 750–52 in *Exegetisches Wörterbuch zum Neuen Testament* 1. Edited by H. Balz and G. Schneider. Stuttgart: Kohlhammer, 1980. ET: Pages 311–12 in *Exegetical Dictionary of the New Testament* 1. Grand Rapids: Eerdmans, 1990.

Sato, M. *Q und Prophetie*. Wissenschaftliche Untersuchungen zum Neuen Testament 2.29. Tübingen: Mohr Siebeck, 1988.

Schäfer, P. *Rivalität zwischen Engeln und Menschen*. Studia judaica 8. Berlin: de Gruyter, 1975.

Schaller, B. "Die griechische Fassung der Paralipomena Jeremiou: Originaltext oder Übersetzungstext?" Pages 67–103 in *Fundamenta Judaica: Studien zum antiken Judentum und zum Neuen Testament*. Edited by L. Doering and A. Steudel. Studien zur Umwelt des Neuen Testaments 25. Göttingen:

Vandenhoeck & Ruprecht, 2001. ET: *Journal for the Study of the Pseudepigrapha* 22 (2000): 51–89.

———. "Paralipomena Jeremiou." *Jüdische Schriften aus hellenistisch-römischer Zeit*
1.8 (1998): 661–777.

Schelkle, K. H. *Das Neue Testament.* Kevelaer: Butzon & Bercker, 1963.

———. *Die Petrusbriefe. Der Judasbrief.* Herders theologischer Kommentar zum
Neuen Testament 13. Freiburg: Herder, 1980.

Schenk, W. *Die Sprache des Matthäus.* Göttingen: Vandenhoeck & Ruprecht,
1987.

———. *Synopse zur Redenquelle der Evangelien: Q-Synopse und Rekonstruktion in
deutscher Übersetzung.* Düsseldorf: Patmos, 1981.

Schenke, H.-M., and K. M. Fischer. *Einleitung in die Schriften des Neuen Testaments.* 2 vols. Gütersloh: Gütersloher, 1978–1979.

Schenke, L. *Die Urgemeinde: Geschichtliche und theologische Entwicklung.* Stuttgart:
Kohlhammer, 1990.

Schlatter, A. *Der Brief des Jakobus.* Stuttgart: Calwer, 1932.

Schmitt, T. *Paroikie und Oikumene: Sozial- und mentalitätsgeschichtliche Untersuchungen zum 1. Clemensbrief.* Beihefte zur Zeitschrift für die neutestamentliche Wissenschaft 110. Berlin: de Gruyter, 2002.

Schnackenburg, R. "Christian Perfection according to Matthew." Pages 158–89
in *Christian Existence in the New Testament* 1. Notre Dame, Ind.: University
of Notre Dame Press.

———. *Die Johannesbriefe.* Herders theologischer Kommentar zum Neuen Testament 13.3. Freiburg: Herder, 1953. ET: *The Johannine Epistles.* New York:
Crossroad, 1992.

Schneider, G. *Die Apostelgeschichte. 2. Teil: Kommentar zu Kap. 9,1-28,31.* Herders theologischer Kommentar zum Neuen Testament 5.2. Freiburg: Herder,
1982.

Schnelle, U. *Einleitung in das Neue Testament.* 4th ed. Uni-Taschenbücher 1830.
Göttingen: Vandenhoeck & Ruprecht, 2002. ET: *The History and Interpretation of the New Testament.* London: SCM Press, 1998.

———. "Taufe II." Pages 663–74 in *Theologische Realenzyklopädie* 32. Edited by G.
Krause and G. Müller. Berlin: de Gruyter, 2001.

Schnider, F. *Der Jakobusbrief.* Regensburger Neues Testament. Regensburg:
Pustet, 1987.

Schnider, F., and W. Stenger. *Studien zum neutestamentlichen Briefformular.* New
Testament Tools and Studies 11. Leiden: Brill, 1987.

Schrage, W. *Der erste Brief an die Korinther.* Vol. 1. Evangelisch-katholischer
Kommentar zum Neuen Testament 6.1. Zürich: Benzinger and Neukirchen-
Vluyn: Neukirchener, 1991.

———. *Ethik des Neuen Testaments.* Grundrisse zum Neuen Testament 4. Göttingen: Vandenhoeck & Ruprecht, 1989.

Schreiner, J. *Baruch.* Neue Echter Bibel 14. Würzburg: Echter, 1986.

Schröger, F. *Gemeinde im 1. Petrusbrief: Untersuchungen zum Selbstverständnis einer
christlichen Gemeinde an der Wende vom 1. zum 2. Jahrhundert,* Schriften der

Universitat Passau, Reihe Katholische Theologie 1. Passau: Universitätsverlag, 1981.

Schulz, S. *Die Mitte der Schrift: Der Frühkatholizismus des Neuen Testaments als Herausforderung an den Protestantismus.* Berlin: Kreuz Verlag, 1976.

Schürer, E. *The History of the Jewish People in the Age of Jesus Christ (175 B.C.–A.D. 135).* Revised and edited by G. Vermes, F. Millar et al. 3 vols. Edinburgh: T&T Clark, 1973–1987.

Schwartz, D. R. *The Second Book of Maccabees: Introduction, Hebrew Translation, and Commentary.* Jerusalem: Yad Ben-Zvi, 2004. ET: *2 Maccabees.* Commentaries on Early Jewish Literatrue. Berlin: de Gruyter, 2008.

Schwegler, F. C. A. *Das nachapostolische Zeitalter in den Hauptmomenten seiner Entwicklung.* Tübingen, 1845/1846.

Schweizer, E. *Der erste Petrusbrief.* 4th ed. Zürcher Bibelkommentare NT 15. Zürich: Theologischer Verlag, 1998.

Schwiderski, D. *Handbuch des nordwestsemitischen Briefformulars: Ein Beitrag zur Echtheitsfrage der aramäischen Briefe des Esrabuches.* Beihefte zur Zeitschrift für die alttestamentliche Wissenschaft 295. Berlin: de Gruyter, 2000.

Schwindt, R. *Das Weltbild des Epheserbriefes.* Wissenschaftliche Untersuchungen zum Neuen Testament 148. Tübingen: Mohr Siebeck, 2002.

Seitz, O. J. F. "The Relationship of the Shepherd of Hermas to the Epistle of James." *Journal of Biblical Literature* 63 (1944): 131–40.

Sellin, G. "Die Häretiker des Judasbriefes." *Zeitschrift für die neutestamentliche Wissenschaft und die Kunde der älteren Kirche* 77 (1986): 206-225.

———. *Der Streit um die Auferstehung.* Forschungen zur Religion und Literatur des Alten und Neuen Testaments 138. Göttingen: Vandenhoeck & Ruprecht, 1985.

Selwyn, E. G. *The First Epistle of St. Peter.* 2d ed. London: Macmillan, 1947. Repr. Grand Rapids: Baker, 1981.

Sevenster, J. N. *Do You Know Greek? How Much Greek Could the First Jewish Christians Have Known?* Supplements to Novum Testamentum 19. Leiden: Brill, 1968.

Shepherd, M. H. "The Epistle of James and the Gospel of Matthew." *Journal of Biblical Literature* 75 (1956): 40–51.

Sherwin-White, S. "Seleucid Babylonia: A Case Study for the Installation and Development of Greek Rule." Pages 1–31 in *Hellenism in the East: Aspects of the Interaction of Greek and Non-Greek Civilizations from Syria to Central Asia.* Edited by A. Kuhrt and S. Sherwin-White. London: Duckworth, 1987.

Siegert, F. *Drei hellenistisch-jüdische Predigten 2.* Wissenschaftliche Untersuchungen zum Neuen Testament 61. Tübingen: Mohr Siebeck, 1992.

Sim, D. C. *The Gospel of Matthew and Christian Judaism: The History and Social Setting of the Matthean Community.* Studies of the New Testament and Its World. Edinburgh: T&T Clark, 1998.

Simon, M. "The Apostolic Decree and its Setting in the ancient Church." Pages 414–37 in *Le Christianisme antique et son contexte religieux: Scripta Varia 2.* Edited by Marcel Simon. Wissenschaftliche Untersuchungen zum Neuen Testament 23. Tübingen: Mohr Siebeck, 1981.

Skarsaune, O. *Fra Jerusalem til Rom og Bysants.* Oslo: Tano, 1987.

———. *In the Shadow of the Temple: Jewish Influences on Early Christianity.* Downers Grove, Ill.: InterVarsity, 2002.

———. "We Have Found the Messiah: Jewish Believers in Jesus in Antiquity." *Mishkan* 45 (2005): 5–122.

Smart, N. *Dimensions of the Sacred: An Anatomy of the World's Beliefs.* Berkeley: University of California Press, 1996.

———. *In Search of Christianity.* New York: Harper & Row, 1979.

———. *Worldviews: Crosscultural Explorations of Human Beliefs.* Englewood Cliffs, N.J.: Prentice Hall, 1982.

Smith, D. E. *The Canonical Function of Acts.* Collegeville, Minn.: Liturgical, 2002.

Smith, D. M. "When Did the Gospels Become Scripture?" *Journal of Biblical Literature* 119 (2000): 3–20.

Soards, M. "1 Peter, 2 Peter and Jude as Evidence for a Petrine School." Pages 3287–49 in *Aufstieg und Niedergang der römischen Welt: Geschichte und Kultur Roms im Spiegel der neueren Forschung* 2.25.5. Edited by W. Haase and H. Temporini. Berlin: de Gruyter, 1988.

Söding, T. "Solidarität in der Diaspora. Das Liebesgebot nach den Testamenten der Zwölf Patriarchen im Vergleich mit dem Neuen Testament." *Kairos* 36/37 (1994/1995): 1–19.

Sperber, A., ed. *The Latter Prophets according to Targum Jonathan.* Vol. 3 of *The Bible in Aramaic.* Leiden: Brill, 1962.

Spitta, F. *Der Brief des Jakobus.* Vol. 2 of *Zur Geschichte und Litteratur des Urchristentums.* Göttingen: Vandenhoeck & Ruprecht, 1896.

Stählin, G. "ἅπαξ, ἐφάπαξ." Pages 380–83 in *Theologisches Wörterbuch zum Neuen Testament* 1. Edited by G. Kittel and G. Friedrich. Stuttgart: Kohlhammer, 1933.

Steck, O. H. *Das apokryphe Baruchbuch: Studien zur Rezeption und Konzentration "kanonischer" Überlieferung.* Forschungen zur Religion und Literatur des Alten und Neuen Testaments 160. Göttingen: Vandenhoeck & Ruprecht, 1993.

———. *Israel und das gewaltsame Geschick der Propheten: Untersuchungen zur Überlieferung des deuteronomistischen Geschichtsbildes im Alten Testament, Spätjudentum und Urchristentum.* Wissenschaftliche Monographien zum Alten und Neuen Testament 23. Neukirchen-Vluyn: Neukirchener, 1967.

Stegemann, E. W., and W. Stegemann. *Urchristliche Sozialgeschichte: Die Anfänge im Judentum und die Christusgemeinden in der mediterranen Welt.* Stuttgart: Kohlhammer, 1995.

Sternberg, M. *The Poetics of Biblical Narrative, Ideological Literature and the Drama of Reading.* Bloomington: Indiana University Press, 1985.

Stettler, Ch. *Der Kolosserhymnus.* Wissenschaftliche Untersuchungen zum Neuen Testament 2.132. Tübingen: Mohr Siebeck, 2000.

Stöve, E. "Kirchengeschichtsschreibung." Pages 535–60 in *Theologische Realenzyklopädie* 18. Edited by G. Krause and G. Müller. Berlin: de Gruyter, 1977–.

Strecker, G. *The Johannine Letters: A Commentary on 1, 2, and 3 John.* Translated by Linda M. Maloney. Hermeneia. Minneapolis: Fortress, 1996.

———. *Literaturgeschichte des Neuen Testaments*. Uni-Taschenbücher 1682. Göttingen: Vandenhoeck & Ruprecht, 1992.

Strecker, G., and U. Schnelle, eds. *Texte zur Briefliteratur und zur Johannesapokalypse*. Vol. 2 of *Neuer Wettstein: Texte zum Neuen Testament aus Griechentum und Hellenismus*. Berlin: de Gruyter, 1996.

Streeter, B. H. *The Primitive Church: Studied with Special Reference to the Origins of Christian Ministry*. London: Macmillan, 1929.

———. "The Rise of Christianity." Pages 253–93 in *The Imperial Peace*. Vol. 11 of *The Cambridge Ancient History*. Cambridge: Cambridge University Press, 1936.

Strobel, A. "Das Aposteldekret als Folge des antiochenischen Streites: Überlegungen zum Verhältnis von Wahrheit und Einheit im Gespräch der Kirchen." Pages 81–104 in *Kontinuität und Einheit*. Edited by Paul-Gerhard Müller and Werner Stenger. Freiburg: Herder, 1981.

Stuiber, A. "Clemens Romanus I." Pages 188–97 in *Reallexikon für Antike und Christentum 3*. Edited by T. Kluser et al. Stuttgart: Hiersemann, 1957.

Taatz, I. *Frühjüdische Briefe: Die paulinischen Briefe im Rahmen der offiziellen religiösen Briefe des Frühjudentums*. Novum Testamentum et Orbis Antiquus 16. Göttingen: Vandenhoeck & Ruprect and Freiburg: Universitätsverlag, 1991. Reviewed by J. L. White. *Journal of Biblical Literature* 112 (1993): 534–36.

Talmon, S. "Was the Book of Esther Known at Qumran?" *Dead Sea Discoveries* 2 (1995): 249–67.

Theißen, G. "Hellenisten und Hebräer (Apg 6,1-6): Gab es eine Spaltung der Urgemeinde?" Pages 323–43 in *Frühes Christentum*. Edited by Hubert Cancik, Hermann Lichtenberger, and Peter Schäfer. Vol. 3 of *Geschichte–Tradition–Reflexion*. Tübingen: Mohr Siebeck, 1996.

———. "Nächstenliebe und Egalität: Jak 2,1-13 als Höhepunkt urchristlicher Ethik." Pages 120–42 in *Der Jakobusbrief. Beiträge zur Rehabilitierung der "strohernen Epistel."* Edited by Petra von Gemünden, Matthias Konradt, and Gerd Theißen. Beiträge zum Verstehen der Bibel 3. Münster: Lit, 2003.

———. *Die Religion der ersten Christen: eine Theorie des Urchristentums*. Gütersloh: Güterloher Verlag, 2000.

———. "Urchristlicher Liebeskommunismus: Zum 'Sitz im Leben' des Topos ἅπαντα κοινά in Apg 2,44 und 4,32." Pages 689–712 in *Texts and Contexts: Biblical Texts in their Textual and Situational Contexts*. Edited by Tord Fornberg and David Hellholm. Oslo: Scandinavian University Press, 1995.

Thiede, C. P. "Babylon, der andere Ort: Anmerkungen zu 1Petr 5,13 und Apg 12,17." Pages 221–29 in *Das Petrusbild in der neueren Forschung*. Edited by C. P. Thiede. Wuppertal: Brockhaus, 1987.

Thurén, L. "The General New Testament Writings." Pages 587–607 in *A Handbook of Classical Rhetoric in the Hellenistic Period (330 B.C.–A.D. 400)*. Edited by S. E. Porter. Leiden: Brill, 1997.

———. *The Rhetorical Strategy of 1 Peter: With Special Regard to Ambiguous Expressions*. Åbo: Åbo Akademis Förlag, 1990.

———. "Risky Rhetoric in James?" *Novum Testamentum* 37 (1995): 262–84.

———. *Theology in 1 Peter: Argument and the Origins of Christian Paraenesis.* Journal for the Study of the New Testament: Supplement Series 141. Sheffield: Sheffield Academic Press, 1995.

Tov, E. *The Septuagint Tradition of Jeremiah and Baruch: A Discussion of an Early Revision of the LXX of Jeremiah 29–52 and Baruch 1:1–3:8.* Harvard Semitic Monographs 8. Missoula, Mont.: Scholars Press, 1976.

———. *Der Text der Hebräischen Bibel.* Stuttgart: Kohlhammer, 1997.

Trapp, M., ed. *Greek and Latin Letters: An Anthology with Translation.* Cambridge Greek and Latin Classics. Cambridge: Cambridge University Press, 2003.

Trobisch, D. *Die Endredaktion des Neuen Testaments.* Novum Testamentum et Orbis Antiquus 31. Göttingen: Vandenhoeck & Ruprecht, 1996.

———. *The First Edition of the New Testament.* Oxford: Oxford University Press, 2000.

———. *Paul's Letter Collection.* Minneapolis: Fortress, 1994.

Troeltsch, E. *Die Soziallehren der christlichen Kirchen und Gruppen.* Tübingen: Mohr, 1912.

Tröger, K.-W. *Das Christentum im zweiten Jahrhundert.* Vol. 2 of *Das Urchristentum.* Edited by K. Meier and H. J. Rogge. Berlin: Evangelische Verlagsanstalt, 1988.

Tsuji, M. *Glaube zwischen Vollkommenheit und Verweltlichung: Eine Untersuchung zur literarischen Gestalt und zur inhaltlichen Kohärenz des Jakobusbriefes.* Wissenschaftliche Untersuchungen zum Neuen Testament 2.93. Tübingen: Mohr Siebeck, 1997.

Turner, N. *Syntax.* Vol. 3 of *A Grammar of New Testament Greek.* Edited by J. H. Moulton. Edinburgh: T&T Clark, 1963.

Unnik, W. C. van. "'Diaspora' and 'Church' in the First Centuries of Christian History [1959]." Pages 95–105 in *Sparsa Collecta: The Collected Essays of W. C. van Unnik, Part 3, Patristica—Gnostica—Liturgica.* Supplements to Novum Testamentum 31. Leiden: Brill, 1983.

VanderKam, J. C. "Authoritative Literature in the Dead Sea Scrolls." *Dead Sea Discoveries* 5 (1998): 382–402.

———. "1 Enoch, Enochic Motifs, and Enoch in Early Christian Literature." Pages 33–101 in *The Jewish Apocalyptic Heritage in Early Christianity.* Compendia rerum iudaicarum ad Novum Testamentum 2,4. Edited by G. W. E. Nickelsburg and W. Adler. Assen: van Gorcum, 1996.

Verseput, D. J. "Genre and Story: The Community Setting of the Epistle of James." *Catholic Biblical Quarterly* 62 (2000): 96–110.

———. "Wisdom, 4 Q185, and the Epistle of James." *Journal of Biblical Literature* 117 (1998): 691–707.

Vielhauer, P. *Geschichte der urchristlichen Literatur: Einleitung in das Neue Testament, die Apokryphen und die Apostolischen Väter.* 4th ed. Berlin: de Gruyter, 1985.

Vögtle, A. *Der Judasbrief: Der zweite Petrusbrief.* Evangelisch-katholischer Kommentar zum Neuen Testament 22. Solothurn: Benziger and Neukirchen-Vluyn: Neukirchener, 1994.

Volten, A. *Die moralischen Lehren des demotischen Pap. Louvre 2414.* Vol. 2 of *Studi in memoria di Ippolito Rosellini nel primo centenario della morte (4 guigno 1843)*. Pisa: Lischi, 1955.

Wachob, W. H. "The Apocalyptic Intertexture of the Epistle of James." Page 177 in *The Intertexture of Apocalyptic Discourse in the New Testament*. Edited by D. F. Watson. Symposium 14. Atlanta: Society of Biblical Literature, 2002.

———. *The Voice of Jesus in the Social Rhetoric of James*. Society for New Testament Studies Monograph Series 106. Cambridge: Cambridge University Press, 2000.

Wachob, W. H., and L. T. Johnson. "The Sayings of Jesus in the Letter of James." Pages 431–50 in *Authenticating the Words of Jesus*. Edited by Bruce Chilton and Craig A. Evans. New Testament Tools and Studies 28. Leiden: Brill, 1999.

Wacholder, B. Z. "The Letter from Judah Maccabee to Aristobulus: Is 2 Maccabees 1:10b–2:18 Authentic?" *Hebrew Union College Annual* 49 (1978): 89–133.

Wagner, W. H. *After the Apostles: Christianity in the Second Century*. Minneapolis: Fortress, 1994.

Wall, R. W. "The Acts of the Apostles." Pages 1–368 in *The New Interpreter's Bible* 10. Edited by L. E. Keck. Nashville: Abingdon, 2002.

———. "The Acts of the Apostles in the Context of the New Testament Canon." *Biblical Theology Bulletin* 18 (1988): 15–23.

———. "The Canonical Function of 2 Peter." *Biblical Interpretation* 9.1 (2001): 64–81.

———. *Community of the Wise: The Letter of James*. The New Testament in Context. Valley Forge, Pa.: Trinity, 1997.

———. "Ecumenicity and Ecclesiology: The Promise of the Multiple Letter Canon of the New Testament." Pages 184–207 in *The New Testament as Canon: A Reader in Canonical Criticism*. Edited by E. E. Lemcio and R. W. Wall. Sheffield: JSOT Press, 1992.

———. "The Function of the Pastoral Letters within the Pauline Canon of the New Testament: A Canonical Approach." In *The Pauline Canon*. Edited by Stanley Porter. Leiden: Brill, 2004.

———. "Introduction: New Testament Ethics." *Horizons in Biblical Theology* 5 (1983): 49–94.

———. "Introduction to the Epistolary Literature of the NT." In *The New Interpreter's Bible* 10. Edited by L. E. Keck. Nashville: Abingdon, 2002.

———. "Rule of Faith in Theological Hermeneutics." Pages 88–107 in *Between Two Horizons*. Edited by J. Green and M. Turner. Grand Rapids: Eerdmans, 2000.

———. "A Theology of Staying Saved." Paper presented at the annual meeting of the Society for Biblical Literature. Atlanta, 2003.

———. "A Unifying Theology of the Catholic Epistles: a Canonical Approach." Pages 43–71 in *The Catholic Epistles and the Tradition*. Edited by J. Schlosser. Bibliotheca ephemeridum theologicarum lovaniensium 176. Leuven: Leuven University Press, 2004.

Wall, R. W., and E. E. Lemcio. *The New Testament as Canon: A Reader in Canonical Criticism.* Journal for the Study of the New Testament: Supplement Series 76. Sheffield: JSOT Press, 1992.

Wallace, D. H. "The Semitic Origin of the Assumption of Moses." *Theologische Zeitschrift* (1955): 321–28.

Ward, R. "James of Jerusalem in the First Two Centuries." Pages 779–812 in *Aufstieg und Niedergang der römischen Welt: Geschichte und Kultur Roms im Spiegel der neueren Forschung* 2.26.1. Edited by W. Haase and H. Temporini. Berlin: de Gruyter, 1992.

Watson, D. F. "Amplification Techniques in 1 John: The Interaction of Rhetorical Style and Invention." *Journal for the Study of the New Testament* 51 (1993): 99–123.

———. "1 John 2:12-14 as *Distributio, Conduplicatio,* and *Expolitio*: A Rhetorical Understanding." *Journal for the Study of the New Testament* 35 (1989): 97–110.

———. *Invention, Arrangement and Style: Rhetorical Criticism of Jude and 2 Peter.* Society of Biblical Literature Dissertation Series 104. Atlanta: Scholars Press, 1988.

———. "James 2 in Light of Greco-Roman Schemes of Argumentation." *New Testament Studies* 39 (1993): 94–121.

———. "The Rhetoric of James 3:1-12 and a Classical Pattern of Argumentation." *Novum Testamentum* 33 (1993): 48–64.

———. "A Rhetorical Analysis of 2 John According to Greco-Roman Conventions." *New Testament Studies* 35 (1989): 104–30.

———. "A Rhetorical Analysis of 3 John: A Study in Epistolary Rhetoric." *Catholic Biblical Quarterly* 51 (1989): 479–501.

Webber, M. I. "Ἰάκωβος ὁ Δίκαιος: Origins, Literary Expression and Development of Traditions About the Brother of the Lord in Early Christianity." Ms. diss., Fuller Theological Seminary, 1985.

Wechsler, A. *Geschichtsbild und Apostelstreit: Eine forschungsgeschichtliche und exegetische Studie über den antiochenischen Zwischenfall (Gal 2,11-14).* Beihefte zur Zeitschrift für die neutestamentliche Wissenschaft 62. Berlin: de Gruyter, 1991.

Wedderburn, A. J. M. "The 'Apostolic Decree': Tradition and Redaction." *Novum Testamentum* 35 (1993): 362–89.

Wehnert, J. *Die Reinheit des "christlichen Gottesvolkes" aus Juden und Heiden: Studien zum historischen und theologischen Hintergrund des sogenannten Aposteldekrets.* Forschungen zur Religion und Literatur des Alten und Neuen Testaments 173. Göttingen: Vandenhoeck & Ruprecht, 1997.

Wehr, L. *Petrus und Paulus – Kontrahenten und Partner: Die beiden Apostel im Spiegel des Neuen Testaments, der Apostolischen Väter und früher Zeugnisse ihrer Verehrung.* Neutestamentliche Abhandlungen NF 30. Münster: Aschendorff, 1996.

Weiser, A. *Die Apostelgeschichte.* 2 vols. Ökumenischer Taschenbuch-Kommentar 5. Gütersloh: Gütersloher Verlagshaus, 1981–1985.

————. "Das 'Apostelkonzil' (Apg 15,1-35): Ereignis, Überlieferung, lukanische Deutung." *Biblische Zeitschrift* NF 28 (1984): 143–67.

Weiss, J. *Das Urchristentum*. Göttingen: Vandenhoeck & Ruprecht, 1917.

Weizsäcker, C. H. *Das apostolische Zeitalter der christlichen Kirche*. Tübingen: Mohr Siebeck, 1886.

Wernsdorf, G. *Commentatio historico-critica de fide historica librorum Maccabaicorum*. Breslau, 1747.

White Crawford, S. "4QTales of the Persian Court (4Q550a–e) and its Relation to Biblical Royal Courtier Tales, Especially Esther, Daniel and Joseph." Pages 121–38 in *The Bible as Book: The Hebrew Bible and the Judaean Desert Discoveries*. Edited by E. D. Herbert and E. Tov. London: The British Library, 2002.

Whitters, M. F. *The Epistle of Second Baruch: A Study in Form and Message*. Journal for the Study of the Pseudepigrapha, Supplement Series 42. London: Sheffield Academic Press, 2003.

Wifstrand, A. "Stylistic Problems in the Epistles of James and Peter." *Studia theologica* 1 (1948): 170–82.

Wikenhauser, A., and J. Schmid. *Einleitung in das Neue Testament*. Freiburg: Herder, 1973.

Wilckens, U. *Weisheit und Torheit*. Beiträge zur historischen Theologie 26. Tübingen: Mohr Siebeck, 1959.

————. "Zur ägyptisch-hellenistischen Litteratur." Pages 142–52 in *Aegyptiaca: Festschrift für Georg Ebers*. Leipzig: Engelmann, 1897.

Wilson, W. G. "An Examination of the Linguistic Evidence Adduced against the Unity of Authorship of the First Epistle of John and the Fourth Gospel." *Journal of Theological Studies* 49 (1948): 147–56.

Windisch, H. *Die katholischen Briefe*. Handbuch zum Neuen Testament 4.2. Tübingen: Mohr Siebeck, 1911., 2d ed., 1930.

Winter, M. *Pneumatiker und Psychiker in Korinth*. Marburger Theologische Studien 12. Marburg: Elwert, 1975.

Wischmeyer, W. "Alte Kirche." Pages 43–47 in *Evangelisches Kirchenlexikon* 1. Edited by Erwin Fahlbusch et al. 3d ed. Göttingen: Vandenhoeck & Ruprecht, 1985.

Witherington, B. *The Acts of the Apostles: A Socio-Rhetorical Commentary*. Grand Rapids: Eerdmans, 1998.

Wohlenberg, G. *Der erste und zweite Petrusbrief und der Judasbrief*. Kommentar zum Neuen Testament 15. Leipzig, 1915.

Wolter, M. *Der Brief an die Kolosser. Der Brief an Philemon*. Ökumenischer Taschenbuch-Kommentar 12. Gütersloh: Gütersloher Verlagshaus & Würzburg: Echter, 1993.

Wright, N. T. *Jesus and the Victory of God*. London: SPCK, 1996.

Wright, R. B., trans. "Psalms of Solomon." Pages 639–70 in *The Old Testament Pseudepigrapha* 2. Edited by James H. Charlesworth. London: Darton, Longman & Todd, 1985.

Wuellner, W. H. "Der Jakobusbrief im Licht der Rhetorik und Textpragmatik." *Linguistica Biblica* 43 (1978): 5–66.

Wyss, K. *Die Milch im Kultus der Griechen und Römer.* Religionsgeschichtliche Versuche und Vorarbeiten 15.2. Gießen: Töpelmann, 1914.

Yadin, Y. *The Scroll of the War of the Sons of Light against the Sons of Darkness.* Translated by Batya and Chaim Rabin. Oxford: Oxford University Press, 1962.

Zahn, Th. *Einleitung in das Neue Testament.* 2 vols. 2d ed. Leipzig: Deichert, 1900. ET: *Introduction to the New Testament.* 3 vols. Edinburgh: T&T Clark, 1909.

Zetterholm, M. *The Formation of Christianity in Antioch.* London: Routledge, 2003.

Ziebarth, E. G. L. *Aus der antiken Schule: Sammlung griechischer Texte auf Papyrus, Holztafeln, Ostraka.* Kleine Texte für Vorlesungen und Übungen 65. Bonn: Marcus und Weber, 1910.

Zimmerli, W., and J. Jeremias. "παῖς θεοῦ." Pages 653–713 in *Theologisches Wörterbuch zum Neuen Testament 5.* Edited by G. Kittel and G. Friedrich. Stuttgart: Kohlhammer, 1954. ET: Pages 654–717 in *Theological Dictionary of the New Testament 5.* Edited by G. Kittel and G. Friedrich. Translated by G. W. Bromiley. Grand Rapids: Eerdmans, 1968.

Zimmermann, A. F. *Die urchristlichen Lehrer: Studien zum Tradentenkreis der* διδάσκαλοι *im frühen Urchristentum.* 2d ed. Wissenschaftliche Untersuchungen zum Neuen Testament 2.2. Tübingen: Mohr Siebeck, 1988.

AUTHOR INDEX